DATE DUE

OCT 2 2 1996			
GAYLORD			PRINTED IN U.S.A.

Physiology of Sports

Physiology of Sports

Edited by

T. REILLY
Professor of Sports Science,
Liverpool Polytechnic, UK

N. SECHER
Senior Registrar, Rigshospitalet,
Copenhagen, Denmark

P. SNELL
Assistant Instructor of Medicine,
Southern Western Medical School,
Dallas, USA

and

C. WILLIAMS
Professor and Head of Physical Education and Sports Science,
Loughborough University of Technology, UK

E. & F.N. SPON
An imprint of Chapman and Hall
London · New York · Tokyo · Melbourne · Madras

UK	Chapman and Hall, 11 New Fetter Lane, London EC4P 4EE
USA	Chapman and Hall, 29 West 35th Street, New York NY10001
JAPAN	Chapman and Hall Japan, Thomson Publishing Japan, Hirakawacho Nemoto Building, 7F, 1–7–11 Hirakawa-cho, Chiyoda-ku, Tokyo 102
AUSTRALIA	Chapman and Hall Australia, Thomas Nelson Australia, 480 La Trobe Street, PO Box 4725, Melbourne 3000
INDIA	Chapman and Hall India, R. Sheshadri, 32 Second Main Road, CIT East, Madras 600 035

First edition 1990

© 1990 E. & F.N. Spon

Typeset in 10/12 Palatino by Photoprint, Torquay, Devon
Printed in Great Britain by St Edmundsbury Press,
Bury St Edmunds, Suffolk

ISBN 0 419 13580 4 (HB)
   0 419 13590 1 (PB)

British Library Cataloguing in Publication Data

Physiology of sports.
   1. Sports & games. Physiological aspects
   I. Reilly, Thomas, *1941–*
   612'.044
   ISBN 0–419–13580–4

Library of Congress Cataloging in Publication Data

Physiology of sports/edited by T. Reilly ... (et al.).
      p. cm.
   Includes bibliographical references.
   ISBN 0–419–13580–4. – ISBN 0–419–13590–1 (pbk.)
   1. Sports–Physiological aspects. I. Reilly, Thomas,
   1941–
   RC1235.P49 1990
   612'.044–dc20

                                                      89–39251
                                                      CIP

Contents

Contributors   vii

Acknowledgements   ix

Preface   xi

Part One   Exercise

1   Metabolic aspects of exercise   3
Clyde Williams

2   Strength and weight-training   41
Klaus Klausen

Part Two   Locomotive Sports

3   Sprinting   71
P.F. Radford

4   Middle distance running   101
Peter Snell

5   Marathon running   121
R.J. Maughan

6   Race walking   153
R.O. Ruhling and J.A. Hopkins

7   Cycling   173
E.R. Burke, I.E. Faria and J.A. White

Part Three   Sport on Water and Ice

8   Swimming   217
Thomas Reilly

9   Rowing   259
Niels Secher

10   Sailing   287
Roy J. Shephard

11 Sport on ice   311
    H.A. Quinney

Part Four Games and Exercises
    12 The racquet sports   337
        Thomas Reilly

    13 Football   371
        Thomas Reilly

    14 Court games: volleyball and basketball   427
        Don MacLaren

    15 Physiology of sports: an overview   465
        Thomas Reilly and Neils Secher

        Index   487

Contributors

EDMUND R. BURKE Spenco Medical Corporation, Waco, Texas, USA

IRVINE E. FARIA Human Performance Laboratory, California State University, Sacramento, California, USA

J.A. HOPKINS Department of Science, New Heys Community Comprehensive School, Liverpool, UK

KLAUS KLAUSEN August Krogh Institute, University of Copenhagen, Copenhagen, Denmark

R.J. MAUGHAN Department of Environmental and Occupational Medicine, University of Aberdeen, Aberdeen, UK

DON MACLAREN Centre for Sport and Exercise Sciences, School of Health Sciences, Liverpool Polytechnic, Liverpool, UK

H.A. QUINNEY Department of Physical Education and Sports Studies, University of Alberta, Edmonton, Alberta, Canada

P.F. RADFORD Department of Physical Recreation and Sports Science, University of Glasgow, Glasgow, UK

THOMAS REILLY Centre for Sport and Exercise Sciences, School of Health Sciences, Liverpool Polytechnic, Liverpool, UK

R.O. RUHLING Department of Health, Sport and Leisure Studies, George Mason University, Fairfax, Virginia, USA

NEILS SECHER Department of Anaesthesia and Exercise Physiology Unit, Rigshospitalet, University of Copenhagen, Copenhagen, Denmark

ROY J. SHEPHARD School of Physical and Health Education and Department of Preventive Medicine and Biostatistics, Faculty of Medicine, University of Toronto, Toronto, Ontario, Canada

PETER SNELL Health Science Centre at Dallas, South Western Medical School, Dallas, Texas, USA

JOHN A. WHITE University of Ulster at Jordanstown, Newtownabbey, County Antrim, Northern Ireland

CLYDE WILLIAMS Department of Physical Education and Sports Science, Loughborough University of Technology, Loughborough, UK

Acknowledgements

The Editors are especially grateful for the comments of the following who helped to improve the first draft of manuscripts:

Jens Bangsbo

Jan P. Clarys

Claire Dickinson

Daniel B. Friedman

Adrian Lees

Bert Lyle

Kevin Robertson

Frank Sanderson

Rod Thorpe

Huub Toussaint

Preface

Recent decades have witnessed a remarkable expansion of the applications of scientific principles to sport and exercise. This has been associated with the emergence of sports science as a recognized academic discipline. Developments are such that most international teams now have a systematized scientific back-up as they prepare for major competitions. Applications of science to sport are especially evident in the field of physiology; indeed sports practitioners are quick to realize the importance of acquiring basic physiological knowledge that can be put to good effect.

Exercise physiology has for many years been a respected field in its own right. Exercise has conventionally been used as a medium for perturbing physiological systems to ascertain how they behaved under stress. Thus much information has been acquired in mainstream human physiology about acute physiological responses to exercise. Exercise physiologists have taken this further in establishing the ceilings in human physiological responses and in attempting to identify those factors that limit performance in various conditions. There has also been progress in understanding how the upper limits of physiological function can be pushed further by proper diet and nutritional manipulations. This information is continually being integrated and updated in textbooks of exercise physiology. These books have formed basic references not just for students of physiology and sports science but also for sports practitioners eager for literature about the physiological aspects of exercise and training.

The present text is unique in that it tries to spell out physiological implications for a number of sports, taken in turn. Thus, far from being another book on exercise physiology, it fits information about acute and chronic adaptations to exercise to the peculiarities of each sport. The individual requirements of each sport are first outlined before the demands of the sport, the fitness profiles of top performers and training regimens are considered.

Part One has two chapters that provide a general physiological background from which the physiology of particular sports may be approached. The principles outlined can be applied broadly to exercise and sports physiology. The opening chapter presents a detailed account of metabolic aspects of exercise. The other provides an analysis of muscular adaptations to strength training, a topic of importance to a wide range of sports.

Part Two considers locomotive sports, starting with short-term exercise – in the form of sprinting – and progressing to middle distance running, then to sustained endurance exercise. This is illustrated in the form of marathon running and competitive race-walking. Both short-term and endurance exercise apply to cycling and their considerations are integrated in the final chapter of the series of five.

In Part Three the physiology of sport on water and on ice is covered. The requirements of the various swimming events are compared in the opening chapter as is the specificity of exercise in the water. The sailor has entirely different demands (as has the rower) and hopefully with good craftsmanship stays clear of the water whilst propelling the vessel through it. The main sports conducted on ice are selected for treatment and discussed in full in the final chapter in this section.

Part Four is concerned with the physiology of games. An attempt is made to group games with features in common. Thus the various codes of football are examined together which serves to highlight differences between them as well as the similarities. The same applies to the racquet sports. The court games of basketball and volleyball are dealt with together in another chapter.

Physiology of Sports applies physiological knowledge to specific sports and represents these applications within a single text. Inevitably not all sports could be accommodated. Indeed a comprehensive text providing detailed coverage of say all the sports under the Olympic Games umbrella would itself be subject to criticism. Awesome in size, it would still omit major sports not included in the Olympic Games, some of which (for example, Rugby, squash) are in fact covered here. The final chapter is an attempt to present an overall perspective from which some sports not included in the core of the book might be viewed.

The contributors to this text are characterized not only for their scientific aptitudes but also for their practical insights into their specialist sports. This combination allows interpretations that go beyond those of the sports scientist operating in broad terms. In some chapters expertise is pooled so that the sport in question is treated in a comprehensive manner.

Physiology of Sports is designed for both the academic and the practitioner. Its content is of interest to lecturers and students of physiology, sports science, movement studies, physical education and coaching science. Additionally it will provide an educational resource for coaches and physical trainers as well as consultants in fitness and recreational centres that prescribe physical activities and sports for fitness purposes. It will also be of value to specialists in sports medicine and physical therapy in providing insights into sport-specific physiological stresses. For this range of readers it will help to interpret the significance of physiology for the sports that are analysed.

Part One
Exercise

1
Metabolic aspects of exercise

Clyde Williams

1.1 INTRODUCTION

In most sports the limitation to performance is the premature onset of fatigue. Training improves performance in a number of ways and not least, of course, through improvements in skill and greater experience. However, training delays the premature onset of fatigue and this in itself contributes to a significant improvement in performance. Fatigue is not a single phenomenon but the end result of a number of events within the closely coupled chain of reactions which follow the conscious decision to exercise. Inability to maintain a prescribed work task or level of exercise is a common expression of fatigue. The failure of metabolism to provide sufficient energy at the rate required by working muscles, to cover their energy demands, is the most common underlying mechanism for fatigue during dynamic physical activity. This 'energy crisis' in working muscles has different aetiologies as one might expect when one considers the range of physical activities which fall under the general heading of 'Sport'. In order to develop a broad picture of the metabolic support, and of course failure, underlying the performance of dynamic physical activity it is helpful to divide these activities into two general categories, namely the 'multiple sprint' sports and the 'endurance sports' (Williams, 1987). During participation in the multiple sprint sports, fatigue is associated with the accumulation of the end products of metabolism whereas during endurance sports, fatigue is associated with the depletion of the limited stores of carbohydrate in skeletal muscles. Of course many sports involve an unpredictable mixture of sprint and endurance activities and so localizing the cause of fatigue presents the sports scientist with a more complex set of problems. Therefore, the aim of this introductory chapter is to provide the reader with an overview of some of the metabolic responses to exercise, focusing, where appropriate, on mechanisms which attempt to explain the fatigue process and also on metabolic methods of assessing adaptations to training.

1.2 ENERGY BALANCE

The failure of metabolism to provide energy as rapidly as the working muscles require it is a very localized event and can be traced to individual motor units; however it is worthwhile setting these events against a much broader metabolic background. The energy balance equation summarizes, in a simple way, the relationship between food intake, energy expenditure and the fuel stores of the body as follows:

$$\text{Energy intake} = \text{Energy expenditure} \pm \text{Energy stored}$$

Energy intake is difficult to assess without the complete co-operation of the individual or group under study because it requires an accurate record of all the food and drink consumed over a minimum period of seven days. Useful as this information is, it only provides a snapshot of the energy intake and the composition of the diet over the period of observation. It does not give a comprehensive description of the habitual diet of the individual nor take into account, for example, seasonal variations. Nevertheless without this information it is virtually impossible to assess whether or not individuals involved in sport are matching their energy expenditures with adequate energy intakes. Energy intake and energy expenditure are expressed in terms of heat units, namely kilocalories or more correctly kilojoules (4.18 × kilocalories). These units reflect the way in which energy expenditure was, and to a certain extent still is, measured. The heat energy released as a result of metabolic processes can be measured in whole body calorimeters either directly or indirectly by determining the amount of oxygen consumed and carbon dioxide produced over a given period of time. The assessment of energy expenditure during free living is difficult even when using portable systems for measuring oxygen consumption. A compromise approach is one which uses heart rate monitoring or even small accelerometers to derive an estimate of the daily energy expenditure of the individual. Pre-calibration of the individual performing a range of normal activities, in the laboratory, while heart rate and oxygen consumption are measured is a necessary pre-requisite for any study using heart rate as a method of estimating energy expenditure during free living. Only when this preliminary biological calibration procedure is used do the results obtained begin to approach those found in whole body calorimetry studies. The recently developed doubly labelled water ($^2H_2^{18}O$) technique has the potential of providing a more accurate method of assessing energy expenditure during free living than the traditional methods (James, Haggarty and McGaw, 1988).

When considering the energy demands of exercise and the nutritional adequacy of the diet for active sportsmen and women it is worthwhile remembering that there is a significant amount of metabolic energy needed simply to fulfil the domestic requirements of the body. Maintenance energy expenditure can be assessed from the basal metabolic rate (BMR); however, in practice it is so difficult to fulfil the requirements necessary to obtain a truly basal condition that resting metabolic rate is measured as a close approximate (RMR). The RMR of someone sitting quietly at rest prior to the start of exercise can be assessed from a knowledge of the oxygen consumption and the respiratory exchange ratio (R) (i.e., the ratio of carbon dioxide production to oxygen consumption). The R value provides an estimate of the relative proportion of fat and carbohydrate being metabolized in order to provide the maintenance energy for normal bodily function. From the R value and the oxygen consumption the quantity of energy released per litre of oxygen consumed can be calculated (Consolazio and Johnson, 1963). It should be recognized, however, that the conversion of the metabolizable energy in food stuffs (which is about 95% of the absolute energy content of the food) captures only about 40% in the form of biochemically usable energy, namely ATP. The remaining 60% is lost as heat and it is this heat which maintains resting body temperature at 37°C. The resting or maintenance metabolic rate accounts for about two-thirds of the daily energy expenditure and can be estimated from equations based on the age and weight of the individual. For example, for the age range 18–30 years the BMR is estimated from the following equation (World Health Organization, 1985):

For men:–   BMR (kcal/24 h) $= 17.5\,W + 651$
For women:–   BMR (kcal/24 h) $= 14.7\,W + 496$

From these equations the BMR can be calculated per minute or per hour and then the contribution to energy expenditure of the daily round of activities can be estimated. For example, the energy expenditure during sleeping is calculated as $1.0 \times$ BMR whereas the waking resting energy expenditure is calculated as $1.4 \times$ BMR. Timing all activities throughout the day and then calculating their energy expenditure from tables of energy expenditure constants provides a useful first approximation of the overall energy expenditure of the individual (WHO, 1985; Durnin and Passmore; 1967). When considering the energy balance equation, factors which influence the resting metabolic rate are probably more important for weight loss, in sedentary individuals, than the increase in energy expenditure through physical activity. While an increase in habitual physical activity, through fitness training programmes, has been shown to decrease body fat in male subjects, the available evidence suggests that similar changes in body composition may not occur so readily in females unless accompanied by a reduced energy intake. It has been suggested that there is an increased efficiency with which food is metabolized in females on restricted dietary intakes, which may be a mechanism to protect limited, yet essential, fuel stores (for review see Brownell, Steen and Wilmore, 1987). It is also important to remember that a matching of energy intake and energy expenditure does not appear to occur on a day by day basis. Extensive studies completed in the late 1960s on military conscripts showed that an apparent energy balance only begins to appear, at least in arithmetical terms, when the period of observation is greater than seven days (Edholm *et al.*, 1970). Endurance runners appear to be able to maintain their energy balance on fairly modest intakes of approximately 2000–3500 kcal per day even though they cover considerable distances in training (Figure 1.1 and Figure 1.2). There is, of course, always the problem of the 'observer effect' when collecting information on energy intake when using even the 7 day weighed intake method (Marr, 1971). Nevertheless, it is surprising and encouraging that similar results for energy intake and food composition are obtained for similar groups even when the surveys are carried out by different observers (Short and Short, 1983). In very demanding endurance competitions, such as the Tour de France, energy balance appears to be maintained in spite of large energy expenditures of approximately 6000 kcal per day (25 MJ). The energy intakes required

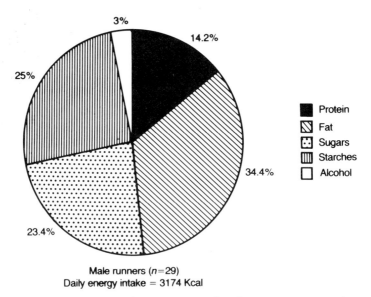

Male runners (*n*=29)
Daily energy intake = 3174 Kcal

Figure 1.1 Energy intake and composition of male runners.

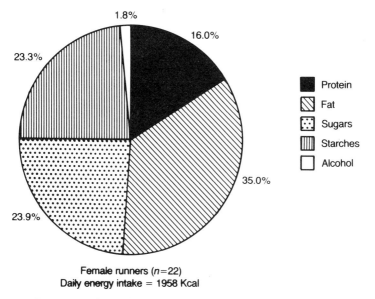

Figure 1.2 Energy intake and composition of female runners.

to match energy expenditure of the professional cyclists can only be achieved by daily supplementing their habitual diets with concentrated carbohydrate solutions (Saris, van Erp-Baart and Brouns, 1989). Should these cyclists be unable to consume high-energy diets on a daily basis then they may not be able to complete the 22 days of competition because of the lack of opportunity to make up the deficits incurred. While failure to maintain an energy balance, especially in terms of the carbohydrate intake, will inevitably lead to a reduction in physical performance, it is only on rare occasions that it is a life-threatening event. One such dramatic and tragic example was the loss of the famous Scott expedition in 1913 during its attempt to be the first to reach the South Pole. The daily energy expenditures of these explorers has recently been estimated to have been between 5000 kcal (21 MJ) and 7000 kcal (29 MJ)/day which was far in excess of their energy intakes of approximately 4300 kcal (18 MJ)/day. It has been suggested that this energy deficit was mainly responsible for the inability of Scott and his four companions to complete successfully the return journey from the South Pole rather than vitamin C deficiency (scurvy) (Stroud, 1987).

1.3 ENERGY STORES

The fuel for energy production is stored in the form of carbohydrate and

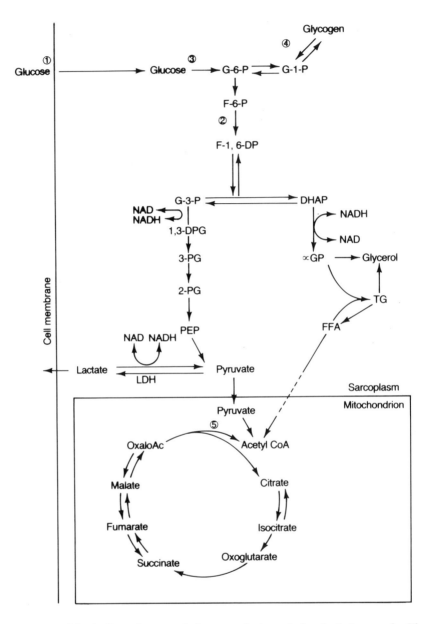

Figure 1.3 Metabolic pathways of glycogenolysis and glycolysis in muscle. The numbers indicate the various points at which the rates of glycogenolysis and glycolysis can be controlled. (1) Entry of blood glucose into the cell; (2) conversion of fructose-6-phosphate to fructose 1,6-diphosphate by the enzyme phosphofructokinase; (3) phosphorylation of glucose by the enzyme hexokinase; (4) glycogen degradation by the enzyme phosphorylase; (5) conversion of pyruvate to acetyl CoA by the enzyme pyruvate dehydrogenase.

fat whereas protein, which is the principal constituent of muscle, tends to be used as a fuel only when carbohydrate stores are particularly low (Lemon and Mullen, 1980; Callow, Morton and Guppy, 1986). Carbohydrate is stored in skeletal muscles and liver as a polymer of glucose called glycogen. Expressed in terms of glucose (glucosyl) units the glycogen concentration of human skeletal muscle is in the range 60–150 mmol kg^{-1} wet weight (w.w.) or 258–645 mmol kg^{-1} dry weight (d.w.). The metabolic intermediates in the stepwise degradation of glycogen are shown in Figure 1.3 together with the points in the pathway at which the rate of glycolysis can be controlled. The degradation of glycogen to form the phosphorylated glucose, glucose 6-phosphate, is controlled by the enzyme phosphorylase, namely phosphorylase a. The activation of phosphorylase, and hence glycogenolysis, occurs as a result of an increase in the sarcoplasmic concentration of Ca^{2+} and also as a result of an increase in circulating adrenaline. Once formed, glucose 6-phosphate is indistinguishable from the glucose 6-phosphate which is produced from the entry, into muscle, of blood glucose. The phosphorylation of glucose in this case is the result of the activity of the enzyme hexokinase, which is thought to be located on the inner membrane of the sarcolemma and to be involved in the control of glucose uptake by muscle. An increase in the glucose 6-phosphate concentration exerts an inhibitory influence over the activity of hexokinase. Thus, during the early part of exercise, when the glycogen and glucose 6-phosphate concentrations are high, the rate of phosphorylation of glucose is low, as is the uptake of glucose from the blood. However, during the later stages of prolonged exercise, when the glycogen concentration is low, the inhibition of hexokinase is lifted in the presence of a reduced concentration of glucose 6-phosphate producing intracellular conditions which are conducive to an increased influx of blood glucose (Wahren, 1973; Bonen et al., 1981).

The rate of stepwise degradation of glucose 6-phosphate, called glycolysis, can be changed by modifying the activity of the control enzyme phosphofructokinase (PFK). Thereafter the degradation process proceeds to the formation of pyruvate which has a number of potential fates. The main one, after entering the mitochondria, is aerobic metabolism which results in the production of carbon dioxide, water

Abbreviations: G-6-P, glucose-6-phosphate; G-1-P, glucose-1-phosphate; F-6-P, fructose 6-phosphate; F-1,6DP, Fructose 1,6 diphosphate; G-3-P, glyceraldehyde-3-phosphate; 2-PG, 2-phosphoglycerate; PEP, phosphoenolpyruvate; DHAP, dihydroxyacetone phosphate; alpha GP, alpha-glycerophosphate; NAD, nicotinamide–adenine dinucleotide; NADH, nicotinamide–adenine dinucleotide (reduced form); LDH, lactate dehydrogenase; TG, triglyceride.

and, of course, the oxidative phosphorylation of ADP to form ATP. When the rate of pyruvate formation exceeds the capacity of the available mitochondria to accept this glycolytic product it is converted into lactate or even alanine. The glycogen to pyruvate part of the pathway, or more correctly the Embden–Meyerhof pathway, normally has a greater capacity for pyruvate formation than has muscle to oxidize the pyruvate formed (Keul, Doll and Keppler, 1967). The fact that the Embden–Meyerhof pathway is a non-oxidative pathway or more commonly called an anaerobic pathway has sometimes caused confusion. The increased activity of this anaerobic pathway does not mean that it is proceeding in an anaerobic environment nor necessarily in a hypoxic environment. Notwithstanding this, however, a decrease in the available oxygen in the muscle cell will lead to an increase in the activity of this pathway (orginally known as the Pasteur effect). During glycolysis, glucose 6-phosphate, which is a six carbon molecule, is converted into two three carbon pyruvate molecules. Thus this increased glycolytic activity during exercise increases the number of molecules and as such would appear to change the osmotic balance within muscle cells. However, there are approximately 3–4 g of water stored with every gram of glycogen and so the degradation of glycogen may not, therefore, cause disruptive osmotic changes in muscle during exercise.

The size of the store of glycogen in the liver depends on the nutritional state of the individual. For example, in the fed state the adult liver weighing about 1.8 kg, contains approximately 90 g or 550 mmol of glucosyl units, whereas after an overnight fast the concentration of glycogen falls to about 200 mmol but after a number of days on a high carbohydrate diet it can increase to as much as 1000 mmol (Nilsson and Hultman, 1973). Interestingly, however, an overnight fast does not appear to lower muscle glycogen concentration as it does with liver glycogen (Maughan and Williams, 1981). Liver glycogen is the reservoir from which glucose is released in order to maintain blood glucose concentrations within a fairly narrow range of values and it is under the control of glucagon, a hormone which is released from the alpha cells of the Islets of Langerhans, in the pancreas, when blood glucose concentrations decrease (Newsholme, 1976). The central nervous system uses approximately 120 g of blood glucose a day as its main, but not exclusive, substrate for energy metabolism and so a reduction in blood glucose concentrations to low levels, i.e. hypoglycaemia, is frequently accompanied by dizziness and headaches. The passage of glucose into the liver, as a result of the digestion and absorption of carbohydrate foods, is not under hormonal control as is the entry of glucose into adipose tissue and muscle cells. Insulin, released from the beta cells of the Islets of Langerhans, regulates the uptake of glucose into muscle and fat cells but during exercise there is a decrease in insulin concentration which is inversely related to the circulating noradrenaline concentration (Pruett, 1970). The increase in noradrenaline concentration is the result of the outflow of this neurotransmitter from the sympathetic nerves, and also from the adrenal medulla. It is the increase in the concentration of this catecholamine during exercise which suppresses the release of insulin from the pancreas (Porte and Williamson, 1966). Carbohydrate metabolism in skeletal muscle during prolonged submaximal exercise, such as endurance running, can be sustained at a rate of 2.5–3.0 g min^{-1} (Williams, Brewer and Patton, 1984); therefore, if muscle had free access to blood glucose then there would be a rapid onset of severe hypoglycaemia. Thus the reduction in plasma insulin concentration during exercise does, in part, prevent the flow of blood glucose into working muscles.

Fat is stored in adipose tissue of which there are two types, namely white adipose tissue cells (WAT) and brown adipose tissue cells (BAT). Fat is stored as triacylglycerol (triglycerides) in these cells and also in skeletal muscles. White adipose tissue cells are the long-term storage sites for fat and it is from these cells that fatty acids are mobilized for use as a metabolic fuel for energy metabolism. Brown adipose tissue has a more specialist function in that it is apparently involved in the regulation of energy balance and also in cold-induced thermogenesis. Whereas WAT is innervated by relatively few sympathetic nerves and relies mainly on circulating catecholamines to stimulate the mobilization of fatty acids, BAT is richly supplied by sympathetic nerves and capillaries (Trayhurn and Ashwell, 1987). Unlike WAT, which has relatively few mitochondria, the mitochondrial density of BAT is very large and it is this characteristic which gives BAT its colour and more importantly, its capacity to increase its metabolic rate severalfold. Whereas in most cells the aerobic degradation of substrate is closely coupled to the formation of ATP by the process of oxidative phosphorylation, in BAT cells metabolism is able to proceed at a high rate in the presence of uncoupling of oxidative phosphorylation. The BAT cells are therefore, uneconomical in the conversion of fatty acids into ATP but, as a result of this energy-wasting activity, they are very good heat generators. Most of the studies on the physiological roles of BAT have been conducted on laboratory animals and little work has been carried out on human subjects. Therefore the contribution of BAT to the regulation of energy balance in response to overfeeding, and its contribution to increased heat production in response to cold exposure, in adult man has yet to be clearly established (Nicholls and Locke, 1984).

The average adult male has about 15% of his body weight as fat whereas lean females have about 20% of their body weight as fat. Even the very lean, almost emaciated-looking, male distance runners have a body fat content of approximately 5–10%; the very lean female distance runner has about 10% of her body weight as fat though lower values have been reported (Chapter 5). A relatively large proportion of this stored fat is available as a fuel during exercise and the more of the fatty acids used, the greater the sparing of the body's limited glycogen stores. Whereas glycogen is stored in association with water, fat is stored in the anhydrous form and so weight for weight it can provide more energy than carbohydrate. More importantly, however, the complete oxidative metabolism of one gram of fat yields approximately 39 kJ (9.3 kcal) whereas the oxidative metabolism of one gram of carbohydrate (glucose) yields only 16.7 kJ (3.75 kcal). Therefore, if a 70 kg man were required to store the glycogen equivalent of fat, instead of fat, then his body weight would increase by about 55 kg. This calculation, together with the knowledge that endurance training increases the capacity of working muscles for fat oxidation, helps explain why fat rather than carbohydrate is the ideal fuel for prolonged activity whether it be for the endurance runner or nature's remarkable endurance athletes, namely birds during their annual migration.

The triacylglycerol in adipose tissue and in muscle, is made up of free fatty acids and glycerol and in WAT it is stored almost entirely as a single droplet whereas in BAT it is stored as a number of droplets. Hydrolysis of triacylglycerol results in the release of free fatty acids (FFA) and glycerol in a ratio of approximately three to one. The FFA are released from the white adipose tissue cells located around the body and are transported in loose combination with plasma albumin in the systemic circulation. The amount of FFA taken up by working muscles is dictated by their plasma concentration and the blood flow (Gollnick, 1977). Therefore it is important to recognize that an increase in perfusion rate without an accompanying increase in plasma concentration will increase FFA uptake by working muscles. However, the metabolism of FFA is not directly proportional to their uptake by active muscles because their oxidation is determined by the number of mitochondria in muscle (Gollnick and Saltin, 1982). Those free fatty acids which are not immediately oxidized in the mitochondria are stored as intramuscular triglycerides which increase with training and decrease during prolonged exercise (Jansson and Kaijser, 1987). While there is a greater amount of energy released as a result of the aerobic metabolism of FFA than following the aerobic metabolism of an equal amount of carbohydrate, the rate of production is slower from fatty acids than from glycogen (McGilvery, 1975). The limiting factor is not the mobilization or transport of FFA to the working muscles, nor, during submaximal exercise the supply of oxygen, but the limited number of mitochondria available to take advantage of this high-energy substrate (Gollnick and Saltin, 1982).

Glycerol and those fatty acids not taken up by muscle pass into the

Table 1.1 ATP yield from aerobic and anaerobic metabolism

Reaction		ATP per mole of substrate	Respiratory exchange ratio R
Glycogen	. . . . lactate	3	—
Glycogen	. . . . CO_2, H_2O	37	1.00
Glucose	. . . . lactate	2	—
Glucose	. . . . CO_2, H_2O	36	1.00
Fatty acids	. . . . CO_2, H_2O	138	0.70
Acetoacetate	. . . . CO_2, H_2O	23	1.00
3-OH buterate.	. . . . . . CO_2, H_2O	26	0.80

(After McGilvery, 1975.)

liver where they are either converted back into triglycerides and then packaged in a protein coat, before being turned out into the general circulation as chylomicrons or the glycerol contributes to the regeneration of liver glycogen by the process known as gluconeogenesis. Fatty acids entering the liver are also oxidized as an energy source, however, when the liver glycogen concentration is low, such as during starvation or very prolonged submaximal exercise, only partial oxidation of fatty acids occurs resulting in the production of ketones. Ketones, namely acetoacetate and 3-hydroxybutyric acid can be used as a substrate for brain but, apparently, not for muscle metabolism (Robinson and Williamson, 1980). Thus the particular fates of glycerol and fatty acids in the liver depend on the nutritional status of the individual in general, and the concentration of liver glycogen in particular. In contrast to the mobilization of triglycerides into fatty acids and glycerol, which is almost entirely under the control of the catecholamines, the degradation of muscle glycogen is mainly initiated by the contractile activity of the muscle itself.

In addition to the two metabolic fuels, glycogen and fatty acids, the muscle has a small amount of ATP and a relatively small store of another high-energy compound called phosphocreatine (PCr) which is four to five times the size of the ATP store. The energy yield, in terms of ATP, from the main metabolic pathways are summarized in Table 1.1.

1.4 MUSCLE MORPHOLOGY

The aerobic metabolism of glycogen and fatty acids occurs in muscle fibres which are characterized by their high oxidative capacities, their apparently slow speeds of contraction and their high endurance quality. Fast contracting, fast fatiguing muscle fibres rely mainly on glycogenolysis for the resynthesis of ATP because of their lower oxidative capacities and the nature of their function (Barnard *et al.*, 1971; Burke *et al.*, 1971). These two populations of fibres are found in all muscles in different proportions and it is the presence of a greater amount of one or the other which dictates whether the muscle has predominantly fast or slow contractile speeds. The speed with which a muscle fibre contracts is related to the rate at which the energy-releasing conversion of ATP to ADP occurs. The splitting of the high energy phosphate, ATP, is catalysed by the enzyme myosin ATPase (myofibrillar adenosine triphosphatase) and muscles with high contractile speeds have been found to have high myosin ATPase activities (Barany, 1967).

The presence of the enzyme myosin ATPase can be located in muscle fibres by using histochemical techniques (Padykula and Herman, 1955), and so the proportion of fast and slow fibres in a muscle, can be estimated (Dubowitz and Brooke, 1973). Such techniques rely on a visual identification of reaction products from the catalytic activity of the enzyme. Factors such as temperature, pH and fixation need to be carefully controlled because they have an important influence on enzyme activity (Brooke and Kaiser, 1970).

In addition, these histochemical procedures also allow a qualitative assessment of the oxidative and glycolytic potential of the fast-contracting and the slow-contracting fibres (Essen *et al.*, 1975; Saltin *et al.*, 1977). The oxidative capacity of muscle is reflected by the activity of a number of enzymes, one of which is nicotinamide adenine dinucleotide–tetrazolium reductase (NADH-TR, also called NADH diaphorase); the enzyme used as an indicator of glycolytic potential in skeletal muscle, is α-glycerophosphate dehydrogenase (α-GPDH). By using these histochemical methods, each muscle fibre can be described not only in terms of its relative speed of contraction, e.g. fast twitch or slow twitch, but also in terms of its predominant means of producing energy, i.e., by oxidative or glycolytic metabolism. Three populations of muscle fibres are generally recognized when several sections of muscle are analysed by these procedures. They have been described as slow twitch oxidative (SO), fast twitch oxidative and glycolytic (FOG) and fast twitch glycolytic (FG) (Peter *et al.*, 1972). A more conservative nomenclature is favoured when describing human muscle, which is, Type I, Type IIa and Type IIb in place of SO, FOG and FG. The reason for the more conservative nomenclature is that whereas in animal studies both the histochemical profile and the contractile characteristics of muscle fibres can be determined directly, in studies using human subjects only the histochemical profiles of muscle fibres can be precisely described (Dubowitz and Brooke, 1973). Studies on the fibre composition of muscle from elite athletes have shown, as might be expected, that the endurance runners have a high proportion of Type I and Type IIa fibres whereas the elite sprinters have a high proportion of Type IIb fibres and only a small proportion of Type I fibres (Gollnick *et al.*, 1972; Costill *et al.*, 1976a,b).

The value of the histochemical characterization of human muscle fibres is extended by inclusion of a staining procedure for glycogen, because it allows the exercise-induced changes in glycogen concentration to be described for each population of fibres. Thus from changes in the intensity of the glycogen stain, the recruitment pattern of each of the muscle fibre populations can be described (Kugelberg and Edstrom, 1968). The results of studies using these techniques on both animal and human muscles have shown that the recruitment pattern during exercise of increasing intensity is as follows: Type I > Type IIa > Type IIb (Kugelberg and Edstrom, 1968; Gollnick *et al.*, 1973, 1974; Edgerton *et al.*, 1975). During prolonged high-intensity exercise, such as cross-country running, glycogen depletion occurs in the Type I fibres and the inability of these fibres to maintain the desired contractile rate is probably responsible for the onset of fatigue (Costill *et al.*, 1973). While glycogen depletion is not a limiting factor during a brief period of high intensity exercise, such as sprinting, it may be a contributory factor during brief intermittent high intensity exercise such as in the multiple sprint sports of Rugby, soccer and hockey (Saltin, 1973; MacDougall *et al.*, 1977). High intensity exercise requires the contribution of both the Type I and Type II fibres and there is some evidence to suggest that the Type II, i.e., fast twitch fibres, experience glycogen depletion more rapidly than the Type I fibres (Edgerton *et al.*, 1975; Essen, 1978a). This is not unexpected, of course, because the Type IIb fibres have a low aerobic capacity and derive their energy mainly from glycogenolysis.

In studies using laboratory animals the conversion of fibre populations has been shown to occur as a result of, for example, manipulating the thyroid status of the animals (Ianuzzo *et al.*, 1977), training and even prolonged electrical stimulation of selected skeletal muscles (Petite, 1986). The evidence for the conversion of fibre types in human subjects, following prolonged training, is not so convincing, but this is not in itself a denial of the plasticity of human skeletal muscle. There is a recent study, for example, which shows that very prolonged exercise, lasting several weeks, has profound influences on human muscle fibre composition which could be interpreted as an increase in the proportion of Type I fibres at the expense of the Type IIb fibres (Sjostrom, Friden and Ekblom, 1987).

1.5 SUBMAXIMAL EXERCISE

During low intensity exercise which can be sustained for more than

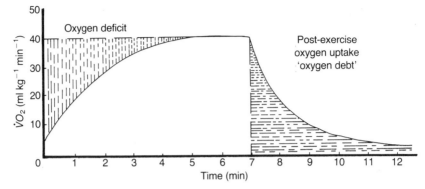

Figure 1.4 Schematic diagram of oxygen deficit/oxygen debt phenomena.

several minutes, such as walking, swimming or jogging, the energy needs of working muscles are provided by aerobic metabolism. This is easily demonstrated by measuring the oxygen uptake of an individual at different time intervals during exercise of constant intensity. At the start of exercise, however, the amount of oxygen used is less than that required and only after several minutes does the oxygen consumption reach a steady state where oxygen demand appears to be met by oxygen supply (Figure 1.4). The difference between the supply and demand for oxygen at the beginning of exercise is called the 'oxygen deficit' (Åstrand and Rodahl, 1970). The delay in achieving a steady state of oxygen consumption during submaximal exercise of constant intensity has been explained in terms of the sluggishness with which the cardiovascular system delivers oxygen at the onset of exercise (Margaria *et al.*, 1963). However, it must be appreciated that an increase in oxidative metabolism is stimulated by an increase in ADP concentration in the mitochondria. The contractile activity of muscle at the start of exercise increases the ADP concentration in the sarcoplasm and so it takes time for the translocation of the ADP from the sarcoplasm into mitochondria. Therefore, the delay in achieving a steady-state oxygen consumption is not simply the response of a sluggish cardiovascular system but is associated with the cellular events which are responsible for increasing metabolic rate. During the onset of exercise the deficit in the aerobic production of energy is covered by contributions from the following three non-oxidative or anaerobic reactions, namely,

$$PCr + ADP \rightarrow ATP + Cr$$
$$ADP + ADP \rightarrow ATP + AMP$$
$$Glycogen \rightarrow 3\ ATP + Lactate + H^+$$

Therefore, even during low intensity exercise there is an increase in muscle lactate concentration, and hence blood lactate concentrations, if only transiently, at the onset of exercise as shown over half a century ago by Bang (1936). However, as the duration of exercise progresses there is an ever-increasing contribution from aerobic metabolism to the energy requirements of the working muscles and a point will be reached where nearly all the oxygen demand is met by the oxygen supplied, i.e. an aerobic steady-state.

Training increases the capillary and mitochondrial density in skeletal muscles (Ingjer, 1979) and so these changes would be expected to contribute to a faster rate of oxygen consumption at the onset of exercise and hence a reduction in the oxygen deficit. There is some evidence to support this proposition from studies of the oxygen transport kinetics of trained and untrained individuals at the start of exercise (Weltman and Katch, 1976; Hagberg, Nagle and Carlson, 1978; 1980). However, the greater rate of oxygen transport is not simply the result of differences in the size of an individual's $\dot{V}O_{2max}$ as has been suggested in some studies (Hagberg, Nagle and Carlson, 1978; Powers, Dodd and Beadle, 1985), but more likely to be related to the training status of the individual (Hickson, Bomze and Holloszy, 1978). For example, in a study which examined the half-time of the oxygen uptake at the onset of submaximal exercise in male and female runners of similar training status but with different $\dot{V}O_{2max}$ values, there was no significant relationship with either the $\dot{V}O_{2max}$ values or the absolute running speeds (Lake *et al.*, 1986). However, the link between improvements in performance and oxygen uptake kinetics as a result of training in already well-trained athletes has, as yet, to be fully examined.

During prolonged exercise of submaximal intensity the motor units of Type I and IIa fibre are mainly responsible for locomotion (Vollestad, Vaage and Hermansen, 1984). When the glycogen concentration in these muscle fibres is reduced below a critical value they are then unable to continue their contribution to contractile activity, at the required rate, and so fatigue occurs. The limited glycogen stores in skeletal muscle can be increased in preparation for prolonged exercise by increasing the carbohydrate content of the diet during the three days prior to competition (Hultman, 1967; Costill, 1988). Carbohydrate loading, as the dietary and exercise preparation for endurance competition is popularly known, can even be achieved by simply supplementing, rather than radically changing, the normal diet with either simple or complex carbohydrates (Roberts *et al.*, 1988). Both types of carbohydrate supplementation have been shown to produce a significant improvement in endurance running capacity (Brewer, Williams and Patton, 1988). Supplementing the carbohydrate stores of the body in the hour before the start of exercise by consuming carbohydrate-containing solutions does not appear to be of benefit to the endurance capacity of the individual. One study has shown that ingesting a concentrated

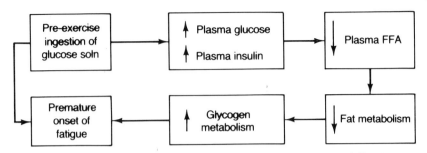

Figure 1.5 Diagram describing paradoxical onset of fatigue following pre-exercise ingestion of glucose solutions.

glucose solution 45 minutes before 30 minutes of treadmill running produces hypoglycaemia, a reduction in plasma free fatty acid concentrations and a greater glycogen utilization than occurs following the pre-exercise ingestion of water alone (Costill *et al.*, 1977). Furthermore, the supplementation of the body's carbohydrate stores in this way has been reported to reduce endurance capacity by 19% (Foster, Costill and Fink, 1979). This paradoxical early onset of fatigue is mediated through a glucose-stimulated increase in plasma insulin concentration as outlined in Figure 1.5. Reducing the availability of plasma-free fatty acids, for muscle metabolism, shifts the choice of fuel to carbohydrate and so there is an even greater demand on the limited glycogen stores. This increase in carbohydrate metabolism has also been clearly demonstrated in a series of exercise experiments in which the mobilization of fatty acids was depressed, by the pre-exercise administration of nicotinic acid (Bergstrom *et al.*, 1969; Pernow and Saltin, 1971).

Glucose solutions ingested immediately before exercise and during exercise, however, do not provoke the same degree of hyperinsulinaemia as occurs during rest. The explanation for this difference is that the rise in noradrenaline concentration, which accompanies the onset of exercise, inhibits the release of insulin (Porte and Williamson, 1966; Pruett, 1970). Fructose solutions have been used as a carbohydrate supplement immediately before and during exercise in an attempt to avoid the hyperinsulinaemia and to spare the limited glycogen stores, however, this has not yet proven to be as successful as initially predicted (Williams, 1989). The most notable study to demonstrate the benefits of ingesting concentrated carbohydrate-containing solutions immediately before and during exercise reported that trained cyclists extended their performance times by an hour beyond the time they were able to achieve while consuming only water. In this study there was no evidence, however, of a glycogen-sparing effect as a result of ingesting the carbohydrate solution. After three hours of cycling at 77% $\dot{V}O_{2max}$ the muscle glycogen concentrations were the same for both the water and the carbohydrate experiments. However, during the carbohydrate experiment the subjects continued cycling for a further hour suggesting that the exogenous carbohydrate was making a significant contribution to energy metabolism during the later stages of exercise (Coyle et al., 1986). An increased fat metabolism during exercise has been shown to exert a glycogen-sparing effect and produce an improvement in endurance capacity (Rennie, Winder and Holloszy, 1976). Caffeine in amounts equivalent to three cups of coffee has been reported to increase the mobilization of fatty acids and to increase the endurance capacity of trained cyclists when taken prior to exercise (Ivy et al., 1979). By way of contrast it is interesting to note that the carbohydrate loading procedure will reduce the fasting plasma FFA concentrations below normal and yet this procedure results in an improvement in endurance performance (Brewer, Williams and Patton, 1988). The decreased plasma FFA concentrations, following carbohydrate loading, are accompanied by an increased carbohydrate metabolism even at exercise intensities which would normally be covered by a greater amount of fat metabolism (Maughan et al., 1978). Whether this is a result of a decreased plasma FFA concentration per se or a change in the kinetics of glycogenolysis as a result of the increased glycogen concentrations remains to be established (Richter and Galbo, 1986). Nevertheless, carbohydrate loading combined with the pre-exercise ingestion of caffeine would appear to be the ideal nutritional preparation for prolonged exercise. However, the increased fatty acid mobilization and metabolism induced by the ingestion of caffeine does not appear to be effective in subjects who have undergone carbohydrate loading (Weir et al., 1987).

The most effective method of achieving glycogen sparing and an improvement in endurance capacity is, of course, training (Karlsson, Nordesjo and Saltin, 1974; Jansson and Kaijser, 1987). A clear illustration of glycogen sparing and thus improvement in endurance capacity are seen in a study in which subjects undertook six weeks of endurance training using one leg cycling (Hardman, Williams and Boobis, 1987). Endurance capacity in the trained leg improved by approximately 500% after training whereas $\dot{V}O_{2max}$ improved by only 22%. The glycogen utilization and lactate production of the quadriceps muscles after approximately 30 minutes of cycling were significantly less after training compared with the values obtained before training (Table 1.2). The reduction in glycogenolysis and the lower muscle lactate concentrations, in the trained leg during exercise, does not support the proposition that low blood lactate concentrations after training are mainly the result of a more rapid lactate clearance rather than a decreased lactate production (Donovan and Brooks, 1983). The restoration of muscle glycogen stores may take as long as two days, especially

Table 1.2 Changes in muscle metabolism during single-leg submaximal exercise following endurance training (mmol^{-1} kg^{-1}dw)

| | Trained Leg | |
	Pre-training	Post-training
Glycogen	−250.0	−91.7*
PCr	−27.1	−9.1
ATP	−2.0	−0.4
ADP	+0.46	+0.19
Glu-1-P	+1.02	+1.02
Fru-1-P	+0.11	−0.01
Fru-1,6-DP	−0.02	+0.20
Pyruvate	+0.59	+0.56
Lactate	+48.70	+11.10*

*Significantly different from pre-training values ($p < 0.05$).

in well-trained individuals who have high pre-exercise concentrations (Piehl, 1974). In the immediate post-exercise period, however, the permeability of skeletal muscle membranes to glucose appears to be greater than exists prior to exercise and so in conjunction with an increased activity of glycogen synthase the conditions appear to be conducive for rapid glycogen resynthesis (Holloszy and Narahara, 1965; Fell *et al.*, 1982). To take maximal advantage of these optimal conditions for glycogen resynthesis carbohydrate should be consumed immediately after exercise because to delay the provision of exogenous glucose appears to lead to an incomplete restoration of muscle glycogen (Ivy *et al.*, 1988).

1.6 ANAEROBIC THRESHOLD

During exercise of increasing intensity there is a rise in blood lactic acid concentration and this response was first reported over half a century ago (Owles, 1930; Bang, 1936). While the appearance of lactate in blood during exercise is the result of an increased glycogenolysis, it is important to recognize that its concentration is, at any time, the result of a balance between the rates of production and removal (Brooks, 1986). Nevertheless during exercise of increasing intensity, the rise in blood lactate concentration is an indication of increased glycogen metabolism (Saltin and Karlsson, 1971). This increase in blood lactate concentration has been interpreted as a reflection of the onset of hypoxia in skeletal muscles and the exercise intensity at which anaerobic metabolism complements the regeneration of ATP by aerobic metabolism has been called the 'anaerobic threshold' (Wasserman and McIlroy, 1964; Wasserman *et al.*, 1973; Davis, 1985; Katz and Sahlin, 1988). The identification of the anaerobic threshold from an examination of the non-linear increases in pulmonary ventilation rates is based on the simple premise that hypoxia in working skeletal muscles leads to the formation of lactic acid which leaves the muscle and stimulates respiration (Wasserman and McIlroy, 1964; Wasserman *et al.*, 1973). The translocation of the lactic acid from the skeletal muscle to the venous circulation probably occurs as lactate and hydrogen ions independently of each other (Mainwood and Renaud, 1985). The hydrogen ions are buffered by the plasma bicarbonate resulting in an increase in carbon dioxide production and an accompanying increase in pulmonary ventilation. This is known as respiratory compensation for metabolic acidosis and is one of the first lines of defence against the development of acidosis. More recently the terms 'ventilatory threshold' and 'lactate threshold' have been used when attempting to define the anaerobic threshold from changes in respiratory and blood lactate responses to exercise. However, the premise that an increase in blood lactate concentration during exercise of increasing intensity reflects hypoxia in working muscles is not a widely accepted one (Gollnick and Hermansen, 1973; Brooks, 1985). There is persuasive evidence from animal studies to suggest that lactate production can occur under aerobic conditions (Connett, Gaueski and Honig, 1984) and that mitochondrial function is only impaired at extremely low partial pressures of oxygen (Chance and Quistorff, 1978). Although there is apparently not the same evidence available from human studies, there are studies which show that blood lactate concentrations can be increased during submaximal exercise (Jansson, Hjemdahl and Kaijser, 1986) and during maximal exercise (Spriet, Ren and Hultman, 1988) by stimulating glycogenolysis through the infusion of adrenaline. This limited circumstantial evidence suggests that lactate formation during submaximal exercise may not be the result of hypoxia but there may be other reasons for an increase in lactate concentration. For example, the transient increase in blood lactate concentration at the start of low-intensity exercise may simply be the consequence of fibre recruitment because when muscle fibres begin to contract there is an increase in glycogenolysis and as a result the production of lactate. Therefore, it is not unreasonable to expect that at the onset of exercise newly recruited muscle fibres, or more correctly motor units, will contribute some lactate and hydrogen ions to the general circulation. At higher exercise intensities, however, blood lactate does not decrease but increases as exercise continues, suggesting that the rate of production exceeds the rate of removal. Another explanation for the increase in blood lactate concentration during exercise of increasing intensity could be the net effect of differential metabolic rates of the Embden–Meyerhof and mitochondrial oxidative pathways (Keul, Doll and Keppler, 1967).

Nevertheless the concept of an 'anaerobic threshold' is a very attractive one because it offers a method of identifying the exercise intensity at which anaerobic metabolism makes a significant contribution to the provision of ATP. In theory, the anaerobic threshold provides, in a non-invasive way, a picture of what may be happening in working muscles, albeit however, not in sharp focus. It is now well established that endurance training increases the exercise intensity at which there is a significant rise in blood lactic acid concentration (Williams *et al.*, 1967; Hurley *et al.*, 1984). This improvement in aerobic capacity is a consequence of a training-induced increase in the number of capillaries surrounding the Type I and Type IIa fibres along with an increase in the number of mitochondria within these populations of fibres (Ingjer, 1979; Gollnick and Saltin, 1982). These changes should be detectable as changes in the anaerobic threshold whether it is measured as the lactate or the ventilatory threshold.

Thus in theory, the anaerobic threshold concept offers a submaximal method of assessing responses to training and also a way of describing the 'aerobic capacity' of an individual in terms of the % $\dot{V}O_{2max}$ (Williams *et al.*, 1967; Lafontaine, Londeree and Spath, 1981; Williams, Brewer and Patton, 1984). This particular definition of aerobic fitness allows individuals with different $\dot{V}O_{2max}$ values to be compared because the anaerobic threshold responds to endurance training and is independent of $\dot{V}O_{2max}$ *per se*. For example, the aerobic fitness of males and females can be compared on a basis which reflects their training background rather than simply having separate scales for males and another for females, as presently exists when $\dot{V}O_{2max}$ alone is used as a measure of fitness (Ramsbottom *et al.*, 1989). Furthermore, the concept of an anaerobic threshold is also appealing because it may be more sensitive to training-induced adaptations than $\dot{V}O_{2max}$ alone. This is especially useful for assessing the adaptations to training of well-trained individuals who often show little additional improvements in $\dot{V}O_{2max}$ with further training, but significant improvements in endurance capacity (Daniels, Yarborough and Foster, 1978; Williams and Nute, 1986).

When it comes to the methods of assessing the anaerobic threshold, however, there is less than universal agreement about how it should or can be measured. There is considerable support for the idea that the anaerobic threshold can be determined from the ventilatory responses to exercise of increasing intensity. The exercise of choice is cycling and the protocol favoured is one which involves an increase in exercise intensity every minute (Wasserman, 1986). The respiratory changes used to detect the anaerobic threshold tend to be the $\dot{V}_E/\dot{V}O_2$ rather than $\dot{V}_E$ alone as originally suggested by Wasserman *et al.*, (1973) (Caizzo *et al.*,

1982; Yoshida *et al.*, 1981). However, it is common practice to use a number of respiratory responses to exercise in an attempt to confirm the inflection or break points used to identify the anaerobic threshold or more correctly the 'ventilatory threshold' (Yoshida *et al.*, 1981). Although the appearance of break points at different exercise intensities for different respiratory responses has been suggested as a means of identifying the anaerobic threshold, the lack of clarity surrounding the identification of the 'ventilatory threshold' is a cause for concern. For example, it is common practice for authors to report that the ventilatory threshold was identified by two or more independent observers in order to introduce objectivity into the process (Buchfuhrer *et al.*, 1983; Farrell and Ivy, 1987). Some authors report that a mathematical treatment of the appropriate respiratory variable should be used to locate the 'threshold' in an attempt to achieve objectivity and reliability (Orr *et al.*, 1982). Other authors, using this latter approach, question the existence of any real abrupt changes in the respiratory responses to exercise of increasing intensity (Shorten and Williams, 1982). To add to this debate only some (Caizzo *et al.*, 1982; Yoshida *et al.*, 1981; Ivy *et al.*, 1980) but not all investigators find a high correlation between the ventilatory and the lactate thresholds. There is also some evidence which suggests that these two thresholds can be manipulated independently of each other by using different exercise protocols (Hughson and Green, 1982), or lowering muscle glycogen concentrations prior to exercise (Hughes, Turner and Brooks, 1982) or even using subjects who are unable to produce lactic acid, namely patients with McArdle's disease (Hagberg *et al.*, 1982).

The lack of general agreement about how best to identify the elusive 'anaerobic threshold' may of course be an indication that the signals are too weak and too readily masked by metabolic and respiratory 'noise' to provide reproducible and precise indications of changes in muscle metabolism. It is then surprising that such good agreement has been found between changes in blood lactate concentrations and the ventilatory threshold during exercise of increasing intensity (Ivy *et al.*, 1980). Nevertheless while the physiological mechanism underlying the anaerobic threshold and even its existence has (Jones and Ehrsham, 1982; Davis, 1985; Brooks, 1985) and continues to be debated (McLellan, 1987), many authors continue to use it to describe the aerobic fitness of their subjects as an adjunct to $\dot{V}O_{2max}$ (Bunc *et al.*, 1987; Vago *et al.*, 1987).

Irrespective of how close the link is between the changes in blood lactate concentrations and the ventilatory threshold, blood lactate values during submaximal exercise have been shown to have good correlations with running performance and in some cases they are stronger than those obtained between $\dot{V}O_{2max}$ and performance (Jacobs, 1986;

Ramsbottom, Nute and Williams, 1987). Some authors have chosen to examine the relationship between lactate thresholds and performance (Farrell *et al.*, 1979; Tanaka and Matsuura, 1984) whereas others have used reference lactate concentrations (Kindermann, Simon and Keul, 1979; Lafontaine, Londeree and Spath, 1981; Kumagai *et al.*, 1982; Sjodin and Jacobs, 1981; Williams and Nute, 1983). The detection of the lactate threshold requires an excessive amount of blood sampling which is unacceptable for routine purposes and so a compromise is the use of reference concentrations; the most popular of which is 4 mmol l^{-1}, referred to as the 'onset of blood lactate accumulation' (OBLA). However, a running speed equivalent to a blood lactate concentration of 2 mmol l^{-1} is closer to the speeds freely chosen by endurance athletes during marathon running than the speeds equivalent to 4 mmol l^{-1} (Tanaka and Matsuura, 1984; Williams, Brewer and Patton, 1984). Therefore, in an assessment of aerobic fitness the use of a reference blood lactate concentration of 2 mmol l^{-1} rather than 4 mmol l^{-1} would appear to be more appropriate. Although the physiological and metabolic bases for OBLA have been proposed (Sjodin *et al.*, 1982), it is quite clear from a consideration of the relationship between blood lactate concentration and exercise intensity that significant accumulation occurs before a concentration of 4 mmol l^{-1} is reached. Therefore, 'OBLA' set at this particular concentration is something of a misnomer and really no more than a convenient reference lactate concentration. It should not be interpreted as 'the lactate or anaerobic threshold' because this confuses rather than clarifies the description of the metabolic responses to exercise. For example, a change in the carbohydrate content of the diet (Yoshida, 1986) or an exercise-induced decrease in muscle glycogen concentration (Sjodin and Jacobs, 1981; Farrell and Ivy, 1987; Fric *et al.*, 1988) will alter the concentration of blood lactate but this may not necessarily change the exercise intensity at which lactate begins to increase, i.e., the lactate threshold. Therefore while accepting these limitations, blood lactate concentrations of 2 mmol l^{-1} and 4 mmol l^{-1} are useful reference concentrations for following the responses to training, but they are not, as has been proposed, the equivalent of the aerobic and anaerobic thresholds respectively (Kindermann, Simon and Keul, 1979).

It has been suggested that training at an exercise intensity equivalent to a blood lactate concentration of 4 mmol l^{-1} produces optimum adaptations (Kindermann, Simon and Keul, 1979: Hollman *et al.*, 1981). Prescribing training intensities in relation to a fixed blood lactate concentration is based on the idea that an exercise intensity equivalent to a concentration of 4 mmol l^{-1} represents the highest lactate steady state an individual can sustain. At an exercise intensity above the lactate steady state it has been suggested that there is an abrupt increase in blood lactate concentration and an early onset of fatigue. An intensity equivalent to the lactate steady state allows the individual to exercise long enough at a sufficiently provocative work-load, to achieve both the necessary duration and intensity for optimum adaptations to occur. Recognizing that setting a fixed blood lactate concentration as a universal lactate steady state is a sweeping generalization, Stegman, Kindermann and Schnabel (1981) described a method by which the lactate threshold of the individual could be calculated and confirmed that this individual anaerobic threshold was closer to the lactate steady state than was the fixed lactate value of 4 mmol l^{-1} (Stegman and Kindermann, 1982). Exercise intensities equivalent to individually calculated lactate thresholds could be tolerated for approximately an hour whereas at exercise intensities corresponding to a blood lactate concentration of 4 mmol l^{-1} fatigue occurred in less than half this time (Stegman and Kindermann, 1982). The accessibility of portable automated blood lactate analysers has led to an increased interest, by coaches, in using this metabolic approach to the prescription of training intensities. Although some studies have reported the benefits of training at an exercise intensity equivalent to 4 mmol l^{-1} (Sjodin, Jacobs and Sveden-hag, 1982; Yoshida, Suda and Takeuchi, 1982) more training studies are required in order to obtain a clearer picture of the advantages of this method over traditional methods. The traditional approach to training is, of course, based on empirical information which has been gathered over many years and it is characterized, irrespective of the sport, by the application of a wide range of exercise intensities and durations. Therefore the prediction of a training intensity from laboratory measurements may only contribute to one aspect of what is, of necessity, a comprehensive programme of fitness training.

A further development has been the suggestion that the anaerobic threshold can be detected from measurements of heart rates during exercise of increasing intensity. The point at which the heart rate departs from its linear relationship with exercise intensity has been termed the 'deflection point' and reported to be coincident with the lactate threshold (Conconi *et al.*, 1982). However, in the studies designed to show the coincidence in the changes of these two physiological variables, the authors first established the exercise intensity at which the heart rate deflection point occurred and then, in a separate experiment, they measured blood lactate concentrations at exercise intensities around the previously determined heart rate deflection point for each of their subjects. The lactate measurements were made on blood samples obtained after exercise rather than during exercise, which is quite a different approach to the question of whether or not there is coincidence between the lactate and ventilatory thresholds! While the heart rate deflection point may, in itself, be of some value, the attempt to link it with the anaerobic threshold through the lactate threshold by this method appears somewhat contrived. Nevertheless the measurement of heart rate in this way may offer a very useful practical method of monitoring responses to exercise and training, however, it does not shed greater light on the enigma of the anaerobic threshold.

1.7 MAXIMAL EXERCISE

The numbers of participants in the multiple sprint sports which include, for example, football, hockey, the racquet sports, etc. far outweigh the numbers taking part in distance running, even when it was at its most popular. Brief periods of maximal exercise interspersed with periods of lower intensity activity are characteristic of the multiple sprint sports. The level of activity and the recovery between periods of high intensity exercise varies between sports and within the sport itself. While recognizing that brief periods of high intensity exercise are part of the common experience, irrespective of the arena in which they are performed, this aspect of human performance has not received as much attention as, for example, prolonged submaximal exercise. There has, however, been some confusion of terms which may have given rise to the impression that there is a large body of literature on the metabolic responses to maximal exercise. Exercise physiologists have used the term maximal exercise to describe the exercise intensity at which an individual reaches maximal oxygen uptake (Essen, 1978b). However, during brief maximal exercise of 5–6 s duration, the period of maximal continuous activity frequently observed during multiple sprint sports, the power outputs achieved are two to three times higher than those recorded as 'maximal' during a maximal oxygen uptake test (Lakomy, 1984, 1986).

In previous studies which have declared that 'maximal exercise' of 10 s duration can be repeated indefinitely as long as there is a recovery period of 25–30 s, the exercise intensity has only been that which is required to achieve maximal oxygen uptake. The absence of a significant increase in blood lactate concentration during exercise of this intensity led to it being described as 'alactic' (Margaria et al., 1969), suggesting that the resynthesis of ATP occurs only as a result of the phosphorylation of ADP by the phosphocreatine stores within the muscle. However, more recent studies have shown that during a brief period of high intensity exercise of just 6 s duration, muscle lactate concentration increases by approximately 200% (Table 1.3; Boobis, Williams and Wootton, 1982). During this brief period of high intensity exercise, phosphorylation of ADP by phosphocreatine contributes 50% to ATP resynthesis whereas glycolysis contributes the remaining 50% (Boobis,

Table 1.3 Muscle metabolites before and after 6 seconds of cycle ergometer exercise of maximal intensity (mmol kg^{-1} dw, mean ± SD)

	Pre-exercise		Post-exercise		% change
Glycogen	266.9	(± 28.1)	229.0	(± 42.5)	−14.2
PCr	84.3	(± 2.3)	54.8	(± 11.3)	−35.0
ATP	24.4	(± 0.9)	22.2	(± 1.1)	−8.3
ADP	3.7	(± 0.3)	4.0	(± 0.4)	+8.1
AMP	0.19	(± 0.04)	0.23	(± 0.05)	+21.1
Glucose	1.8	(± 0.7)	2.7	(± 0.9)	+50.0
Glu-1-P	0.08	(± 0.05)	0.54	(± 0.18)	+575
Glu-6-P	1.3	(± 0.5)	11.0	(± 4.4)	+746
Fru-6-P	0.13	(± 0.07)	1.98	(± 0.78)	+1423
Fru-1,6-DP	0.13	(± 0.15)	0.53	(± 0.22)	+308
Triose-P	0.34	(± 0.07)	0.38	(± 0.04)	+12
Pyruvate	0.17	(± 0.04)	0.46	(± 0.16)	+171
Lactate	9.29	(± 1.82)	28.40	(± 7.73)	+205

1987). Once the phosphocreatine concentrations have fallen to low values peak power output cannot be restored even though glycolysis continues to provide ATP (Wootton and Williams, 1983; Boobis, 1987; Spriet et al., 1987a).

Fatigue during maximal exercise of several seconds duration may be viewed as a simple mismatching between the rate of ATP utilization, by working muscles, and the rate at which it is replaced by the various phosphorylation processes. Although there is some support for this particular explanation for the fatigue process (Gollnick, 1986) an alternative explanation is that ATP utilization and not ATP resynthesis is inhibited, by the products of metabolism, namely hydrogen and or phosphate ions (Hultman, Spriet and Sodelund, 1987). The inhibition of mechanical activity in muscle and so a decreased ability to sustain a prescribed power output, has been attributed to a decreased availability of Ca^{2+} (Vollestad and Sejersted, 1988). Certainly an increased rate of ATP production by adrenaline-induced glycogenolysis does not appear to restore power output by human quadriceps muscles during the onset of fatigue (Spriet, Ren and Hultman, 1988). Furthermore, the decrease in muscle pH during high-intensity exercise or repeated periods of electrical stimulation does not completely inhibit glycolysis, suggesting that the muscle is still able to generate ATP even at very low pH values (Spriet et al., 1987b). Therefore this evidence contributes to the argument that fatigue is not simply the result of a mismatch between the rates of regeneration and utilization of ATP but that the inhibition of ATP utilization may be a significant contributory factor to the onset of fatigue.

The idea that an individual develops 'lactate tolerance' after training has been quoted so frequently in coaching circles that it has become accepted as a general truth. The ability to tolerate high intensity exercise for longer periods of time or to generate higher power outputs after training is usually accompanied by increased concentrations of muscle and blood lactate. However, when the post-training exercise intensity and duration are the same as the pre-training conditions then the lactate concentrations are unchanged or decreased. Fatigue occurs during dynamic exercise at muscle pH values which are higher in trained than in untrained subjects (Sahlin and Henriksson, 1984) and after training compared with values before training (Cheetham *et al.*, 1989); this strongly suggests that muscle becomes 'intolerant of lactic acid' after training. The mechanisms proposed for this 'intolerance' include an increase in intracellular buffering capacity (Parkhouse and MacKenzie, 1984) and possibly an improved removal rate of hydrogen ions out of muscle (Mainwood and Renaud, 1985). There is some evidence to suggest that training increases the buffering capacity of skeletal muscles and this is offered as an explanation for the improved work capacity during high intensity exercise (Sharp *et al.*, 1986; Cheetham *et al.*, 1989). How much of the apparent improvement in buffering capacity is the result of changes within the muscle itself and how much is the result of a more rapid efflux of hydrogen ions across the cell membrane is not entirely clear because of the difficulties of making these measurements on samples of human muscle. Furthermore, the current method involves the titration of homogenates of the whole muscle sample and so changes in intracellular buffering capacity have to be relatively large to overcome the 'dilution' effect of using a sample of muscle containing all fibre types (Sahlin, 1978).

The removal of hydrogen ions from the sarcoplasm of muscle as quickly as possible is, of course, an additional method of buffering. Support for the central role of hydrogen ions in the fatigue process comes from these studies which have shown improved exercise tolerance under conditions which favour an improved removal rate. When the blood perfusing an *in situ* preparation of canine gastrocnemius muscle was made alkalotic, with sodium bicarbonate, then the endurance capacity of the muscle in response to repeated electrical stimulation was significantly increased. When, however, the blood perfusing the working muscle was made acidotic, with ammonium chloride, then fatigue occurred earlier than under control conditions (Hirche *et al.*, 1975). In human studies the ingestion of bicarbonate solutions, up to three hours before exercise, has been shown to improve endurance capacity, during cycle ergometry (Jones *et al.*, 1977), as well as running times over 400 m (Goldfinch, McNaughton and Davies, 1988) and 1500 m (Wilkes, Gledhill and Smyth, 1983) and also improvements in swimming performance during interval training (Gao *et al.*, 1988). There is a transient rise in blood pH as a result of the ingestion of bicarbonate solutions as well, of course, as in plasma bicarbonate concentration. The clearance rate of the additional bicarbonate is relatively fast as reflected by the prompt rise in the pH of the individual's urine and this change in the normal pH is also a way of clearly detecting the use of the bicarbonate treatment as an aid to improved performance.

The quantification of high intensity exercise in physiological or metabolic terms has not been developed to the same extent as has the quantification of submaximal exercise. The gold standard or reference point for aerobic exercise is the maximal oxygen uptake of an individual. However, there is not, as yet, an equivalent gold standard for 'anaerobic exercise' which offers the same opportunities for standardization of exercise intensities. At present the anaerobic power of an individual is reported only in terms of the absolute values achieved during, for example, cycle ergometry or sprinting on a non-motorized treadmill (Lakomy, 1984, 1986; Cheetham *et al.*, 1986). Attempts have been made to describe the anaerobic capacity of an individual, based on the largest 'oxygen debt' which can be generated during dynamic exercise (Hermansen, 1969). More recently the concept of a maximal oxygen deficit has been proposed as a method of assessing the anaerobic capacity of an individual (Medbo *et al.*, 1988). Further studies are required to establish the usefulness of this particular concept before it is ready to take its place alongside maximal oxygen uptake as a cornerstone concept in exercise physiology.

Fitness for endurance sports can be best described in terms of the highest percentage of $\dot{V}O_{2max}$ an individual can sustain for prolonged periods of time irrespective of $\dot{V}O_{2max}$ *per se*. In the multiple sprint sports, fitness is reflected in the ability to repeat maximal sprints, separated by only short recovery periods, with only the minimum of fatigue. Therefore, fitness should be assessed in terms of the ability to reproduce maximal effort rather than only assessed in terms of the absolute power output or the maximal oxygen deficit achieved. Thus 'fatiguability' during repeated sprints may provide a more useful index of 'fitness' for participants in the multiple sprints sports than measurements of maximal power output (Wootton and Williams, 1983).

Unlike the adaptations to endurance training where there is clear evidence of an increase in the capacity for the aerobic production of ATP, sprint training has not been shown to produce such large changes in the key enzymes of the glycolytic pathway (Saltin and Gollnick, 1983). However, it has not been established whether or not training simply increases the number of motor units recruited during maximal exercise and therefore it is the additional 'muscle mass' which is responsible for the training-induced increase in power output (Cheetham *et al.*, 1989). An improvement in efficiency of contractile activity following high intensity training has also been suggested as an explanation for improved performance on the basis of studies on rodent muscles (Westra *et al.*, 1985). There is no reason to suggest, however, why this improvement in performance does not follow the same development as occurs during strength training, namely the neurogenic response preceding the myogenic adaptations of muscle (Chapter 2). Therefore, to search only for metabolic explanations for improved performances following sprint training of different durations, using subjects of varied levels of fitness, may at best be somewhat short sighted and at worse, misleading.

In summary, suffice to say that when individuals successfully meet the challenge of exercise during the preparation for and the participation in sport they do so as a result of an exquisitely orchestrated collection of physiological and metabolic events. While a knowledge of the metabolic events underlying the responses to exercise will not, on their own, explain successful performances nor the failure of performance we know as fatigue, they will provide invaluable pieces of the jigsaw from which a more complete picture of human performance can be built.

REFERENCES

Åstrand, P.O. and Rodahl, K. (1970) *Textbook of Work Physiology*. McGraw-Hill, London, pp. 284.

Bang, O. (1936) The lactate content of the blood during and after muscular exercise in man. *Scandinavian Archives of Physiology*, **74**, 51–82.

Barany, M. (1967) ATPase activity of myosin correlated with speed of muscle shortening. *Journal of General Physiology*, **50**, 197–218.

Barnard, R.J., Edgerton, V.R., Furkawa, T. and Peters, J.B. (1971) Histochemical, biochemical, and contractile properties of red, white and intermediate fibres. *American Journal of Physiology*, **220**, 410–414.

Bergstrom, J., Hultman, E., Jorfeldt, L., Pernow, B. and Wahren, J. (1969) Effect of nicotinic acid on physical working capacity and on metabolism of muscle glycogen in man. *Journal of Applied Physiology*, **26**, 170–176.

Bonen, A., Malcolm, S.A., Kilgour, R.D., MacIntyre, K.P. and Belcastro, A.N. (1981) Glucose ingestion before and during intense exercise. *Journal of Applied Physiology*, **50**, 766–771.

Boobis, L.H. (1987) Metabolic aspects of fatigue during sprinting, in *Exercise: Benefits, Limitations and Adaptations* (eds D. Macleod, R.J. Maughan, M. Nimmo, T. Reilly and C. Williams) E. & F.N. Spon, London, pp. 116–140.

Boobis, L.H., Williams, C. and Wootton, S.A. (1982) Human muscle metabolism during brief maximal exercise. *Journal of Physiology*, **338**, 21–22P.

Brewer, J., Williams, C. and Patton, A. (1988) The influence of high carbohydrate diets on endurance running performance. *European Journal of Applied Physiology*, **57**, 698–706.

Brooke, M.H. and Kaiser, K.K. (1970) Three 'myosin adenosine triphosphatase' systems: the nature of their pH lability and sulphydryl dependence. *Journal of Histochemistry and Cytochemistry*, **18**, 670–672.

Brooks, G.A. (1985) Anaerobic threshold: review of the concept and directions for future research. *Medicine and Science in Sports and Exercise*, **17**, 22–31.

Brooks, G.A. (1986) The 'lactate shuttle' during exercise: evidence and possible controls, in *Sports Science* (eds J. Watkins, T. Reilly and L. Burwitz). Proc. VIII Commonwealth and International Conference on Sport, Physical Education, Dance, Recreation and Health. E. & F.N. Spon Ltd, London, pp. 69–82.

Brownell, K.D., Steen, S.N. and Wilmore, J.H. (1987) Weight regulation practices in athletes: analysis of metabolic and health effects. *Medicine and Science in Sports and Exercise*, **19**, 546–556.

Buchfuhrer, M.J., Hansen, J.E., Robinson, T.E., Sue, D.Y., Wasserman, K. and Whipp, B.J. (1983) Optimising the exercise protocol for cardiopulmonary assessment. *Journal of Applied Physiology*, **55**, 1558–1564.

Bunc, V., Heller, J., Leso, J., Sprynarova, S. and Zdaanowicz, R. (1987) Ventilatory threshold in various groups of highly trained athletes. *International Journal of Sports Medicine*, **8**, 275–280.

Burke, R.E., Levine, D.N., Zajak, F.E., Tsairis, P. and Engel, W.K. (1971) Mammalian motor units: physiological–histochemical correlation in three types in cat gastrocnemius. *Science NY*, **174**, 709–712.

Caizzo V.J., Davis, J.A., Ellis, J.F., Azus, J.L., Vandagriff, R., Prietto, C.A. and McMaster, W. (1982) Comparison of gas exchange indices used to detect anaerobic threshold. *Journal of Applied Physiology*, **53**, 1184–1189.

Callow, M., Morton, A. and Guppy, M. (1986) Marathon fatigue: the role of plasma fatty acids, muscle glycogen and blood glucose. *European Journal of Applied Physiology*, **55**, 654–661.

Chance, B. and Quistorff, B. (1978) Study of tissue oxygen gradients by single and multiple indicators. *Advances in Experimental Medicine and Biology*, **94**, 331–338.

Cheetham, M.E., Boobis, L.H., Brooks, S. and Williams, C. (1986) Human muscle metabolism during sprinting. *Journal of Applied Physiology*, **61**, 54–60.

Cheetham, M.E., Boobis, L.H., Brooks, S. and Williams, C. (1989) Influence of sprint training on muscle metabolism in man. *Journal of Applied Physiology* (in press).

Conconi, F., Ferrari, M., Ziglio, P.G., Droghetti, P. and Codeca, L. (1982) Determination of the anaerobic threshold by a noninvasive field test in runners. *Journal of Applied Physiology*, **52**, 869–873.

Connett, R.J., Gaueski, T.E.J. and Honig, C.R. (1984) Lactate accumulation in fully aerobic, working dog gracilis muscle. *American Journal of Physiology*, **246**, H120–H128.

Consolazio, C.F. and Johnson, R.E. (1963) *The Physiological Measurements of Metabolic Functions in Man*. McGraw-Hill, London, pp. 439.

Costill, D.L. (1988) Carbohydrates for exercise: dietary demands for optimal performance. *International Journal of Sports Medicine*, **9**, 1–18.

Costill, D.L., Coyle, E.D., Dalsky, G., Evans, W., Fink, W. and Hoopes, D. (1977) Effects of elevated plasma FFA and insulin on muscle glycogen usage during exercise. *Journal of Applied Physiology*, **43**, 695–699.

Costill, D.L., Daniels, J., Evans, W., Fink, W., Krahenbuhl, G. and Saltin, B. (1976a) Skeletal muscle enzymes and fiber composition in male and female track athletes. *Journal of Applied Physiology*, **40**, 149–154.

Costill, D.L., Fink, W.J. and Pollock, M.L. (1976b) Muscle fiber composition and enzyme activities of elite distance runners. *Medicine and Science in Sports*, **8**, 96–100.

Costill, D.L., Gollnick, P.D., Jansson, E.D., Saltin, B. and Stein, E.M. (1973) Glycogen depletion pattern in human muscle fibres during distance running. *Acta Physiologica Scandinavica*, **89**, 374–383.

Coyle, E.D., Coggan, A.R., Hemmert, M.E. and Ivy, J.J. (1986) Muscle glycogen utilization during prolonged strenuous exercise when fed carbohydrate. *Journal of Applied Physiology*, **61**, 165–172.

Daniels, J., Yarborough, R.A. and Foster, C. (1978) Changes in $\dot{V}O_{2max}$ and running performance with training. *European Journal of Applied Physiology*, **39**, 249–254.

Davis, J.A. (1985) Anaerobic threshold: review of the concept and directions for future research. *Medicine and Science in Sports and Exercise*, **17**, 6–18.

Donovan, C.M. and Brooks, G.A. (1983) Endurance training affects lactate clearance, not lactate production. *American Journal of Physiology*, **244**, E83–E92.

Dubowitz, V. and Brooke, M.H. (1973) *Muscle Biopsy: A Modern Approach.* Saunders, London.

Durnin, J.V.G.A. and Passmore, R. (1967) *Energy, Work and Leisure*, Heinemann, London.

Edgerton, V.R., Essen, B., Saltin, B. and Simpson, D.R. (1975) Glycogen depletion in specific types of human skeletal muscle fibres in intermittent and continuous exercise, in *Metabolic Adaptation to Prolonged Physical Exercise* (eds H. Howald and J.R. Poortmans) Birkhauser Verlag, Basel, Switzerland, p. 402–415.

Edholm, O.G., Adam, J.M., Healy, M.J.R., Wolff, H.S., Goldsmith, R. and Best, T.W. (1970) Food intake and energy expenditure of army recruits. *British Journal of Nutrition*, **24**, 1091–1107.

Essen, B. (1978a) Glycogen depletion of different fibre types in human skeletal muscle during intermittent and continuous exercise. *Acta Physiologica Scandinavica*, **113**, 446–455.

Essen, B. (1978b) Studies on the regulation of metabolism in human skeletal muscle using intermittent exercise as an experimental model. *Acta Physiologica Scandinavica*, Suppl., **454**, 1–32.

Essen, B., Jansson, E., Henriksson, J., Taylor, A.W. and Saltin, B. (1975) Metabolic characteristics of fibre types in human skeletal muscle. *Acta Physiologica Scandinavica*, **95**, 153–165.

Farrell, P.A., Wilmore, J.H., Coyle, E.F., Billing, J.E. and Costill, D.L. (1979) Plasma lactate accumulation and distance running performance. *Medicine and Science in Sports*, **11**, 338–344.

Farrell, S.W. and Ivy, J.L. (1987) Lactate acidosis and the increase in $\dot{V}_E/\dot{V}_{O_2}$ during incremental exercise. *Journal of Applied Physiology*, **62**, 1551–1555.

Fell, R.D., Terblanche, S.E., Ivy, J.L., Young, J.C. and Holloszy, J.O. (1982) Effect of muscle glycogen content on glucose uptake following exercise. *Journal of Applied Physiology*, **52**, 434–437.

Foster, C., Costill, D.L. and Fink, W.J. (1979) Effect of pre-exercise feeding on endurance performance. *Medicine and Science in Sports*, **11**, 1–5.

Fric, J., Jr, Fric, J., Boldt, H., Stoboy, H., Meller, W., Feldt, F. and Drygas, W. (1988) Reproducibility of post-exercise lactate and anaerobic threshold. *International Journal of Sports Medicine*, **9**, 310–312.

Gao, J., Costill, D.L., Horswill, C.A. and Park, S.H. (1988) Sodium bicarbonate ingestion improves performance in interval swimming. *European Journal of Applied Physiology*, **58**, 171–174.

Goldfinch, J., McNaughton, L. and Davies, P. (1988) Induced metabolic alkalosis and its effects on 400 m racing time. *European Journal of Applied Physiology*, **57**, 45–48.

Gollnick, P.D. (1977) Free fatty acid turnover and the availability of substrates as a limiting factor in prolonged exercise. *Annals of the New York Academy of Science*, **301**, 64–71.

Gollnick, P.D. (1986) Metabolic regulation in skeletal muscle: influence of endurance training as exerted by mitochondrial protein concentration. *Acta Physiologica Scandinavica*, Suppl., **556**, 53–66.

Gollnick, P.D., Armstrong, R.B., Saltin, B., Saubert IV, C.W., Sembrowich, W.L. and Shepherd, R.E. (1973) Effect of training on enzyme activity and fiber composition of human skeletal muscle. *Journal of Applied Physiology*, **34**, 107–111.

Gollnick, P.D., Armstrong, R.B., Saubert IV, C.W., Piehl, K. and Saltin, B. (1972) Enzyme activity and fiber composition in skeletal muscle of untrained and trained men. *Journal of Applied Physiology*, **33**, 312–319.

Gollnick, P.D. and Hermansen, L. (1973) Biochemical adaptations to exercise: anaerobic metabolism. *Exercise and Sport Sciences Review*, **1**, 1–43.

Gollnick, P.D., Karlsson, J., Piehl, K. and Saltin, B. (1974) Selective glycogen depletion in skeletal muscle fibers of man following sustained contractions. *Journal of Physiology*, **214**, 59–67.

Gollnick, P.D. and Saltin, B. (1982) Significance of skeletal muscle oxidative enzyme enhancement with endurance training. *Clinical Physiology*, **2**, 1–12.

Hagberg, J.M., Coyle, E.M., Carroll, J.E., Miller, J.M., Martin, W.H. and Brooke, M.H. (1982) Exercise hyperventilation in patients with McArdle's disease. *Journal of Applied Physiology*, **52**, 991–994.

Hagberg, J.M., Hickson, R.C., Ehsani, A.A. and Holloszy, J.O. (1980) Faster adjustment to and recovery from a submaximal exercise in the trained state. *Journal of Applied Physiology*, **48**, 218–224.

Hagberg, J.M., Nagle, F.J. and Carlson, J.L. (1978) Transient O_2 uptake response at the onset of exercise. *Journal of Applied Physiology*, **44**, 90–92.

Hardman, A.E., Williams, C. and Boobis, L.H. (1987) Influence of single-leg training on muscle metabolism and endurance during exercise with trained limb and untrained limb. *Journal of Sports Sciences*, **5**, 105–116.

Hermansen, L. (1969) Anaerobic energy release. *Medicine and Science in Sports*, **1**, 32–38.

Hickson, R.C., Bomze, H.A. and Holloszy, J.O. (1978) Faster adjustment of O_2 uptake to energy requirement of exercise in the trained state, *Journal of Applied Physiology*, **44**, 877–881.

Hirche, H., Hombach, V., Langhor, H.D., Wacker, U. and Busse, J. (1975) Lactic acid permeation rate in working gastrocnemii of dogs during metabolic alkalosis and acidosis. *Pflugers Archiv*, **356**, 209–222.

Hollman, W., Rost, R., Liesen, H., Dufaux, B., Heck, H. and Mader, A. (1981) Assessment of different forms of physical activity with respect to preventive and rehabilitive cardiology. *International Journal of Sports Medicine*, **2**, 67–80.

Holloszy, J.O. and Narahara, H.T. (1965) Studies of tissue permeability. X. Changes in permeability to 3-methylglucose associated with contraction of isolated frog muscle. *Journal of Biological Chemistry*, **240**, 3493–3500.

Hughes, E.F., Turner, S.C. and Brooks, G.A. (1982) Effects of glycogen depletion and pedalling speed on 'anaerobic threshold'. *Journal of Applied Physiology*, **52**, 1598–1607.

Hughson, R.L. and Green, H.J. (1982) Blood acid–base relationships studied by ramp work tests. *Medicine and Science in Sport and Exercise*, **14**, 297–302.

Hultman, E. (1967) Studies on muscle metabolism of glycogen and active phosphate in man with special reference to exercise and diet. *Scandinavian Journal of Clinical and Laboratory Investigation*, **19**, Suppl. 94.

Hultman, E., Spriet, L.L. and Sodelund (1987) Energy metabolism and fatigue in working muscle, in *Exercise: Benefits, Limitations and Adaptations* (eds D. Macleod, R.J. Maughan, M. Nimmo, T. Reilly and C. Williams) E & F Spon, London, pp. 63–80.

Hurley, B.F., Hagberg, J.M., Allen W.K., Seals, D.R., Young, J.C., Cuddihee, R.W. and Holloszy, J.O. (1984) Effect of training on blood lactate levels during submaximal exercise. *Journal of Applied Physiology*, **56**, 1260–1264.

Ianuzzo, C.D., Patel, P., Chen, V., O'Brien, P. and Williams, C. (1977) Thyroidal trophic influence on skeletal muscle myosin. *Nature*, **270**, 74–76.

Ingjer, F. (1979) Effects of endurance training on muscle fibre ATP-ase activity, capillary supply and mitochondrial content in man. *Journal of Physiology*, **294**, 419–432.

Ivy, J.L., Costill, D.L., Fink, W.J. and Lower, R.W. (1979) Influence of caffeine and carbohydrate feedings on endurance performance. *Medicine and Science in Sports*, **11**, 6–11.

Ivy, J.L., Katz, A.L., Cutler, C.L., Sherman, W.M. and Coyle, E.F. (1988) Muscle glycogen synthesis after exercise: effect of time of carbohydrate ingestion. *Journal of Applied Physiology*, **64**, 1480–1485.

Ivy, J.L., Withers, R.T., Van Handel, P.J., Elger, D.H. and Costill, D.L. (1980) Muscle respiratory capacity and fibre types as determinants of the lactate threshold. *Journal of Applied Physiology*, **48**, 525–527.

Jacobs, I. (1986) Blood lactate: implications for training and research. *Sports Medicine*, **3**, 10–25.

James, W.P.T., Haggarty, P. and McGaw, B.A. (1988) Recent progress in studies on energy expenditure: are the new methods providing answers to the old questions? *Proceedings of the Nutrition Society*, **47**, 195–208.

Jansson, E., Hjemdahl, P. and Kaijser, L. (1986) Epinephrine induced changes in muscle carbohydrate metabolism during exercise in male subjects. *Journal of Applied Physiology*, **60**, 1466–1470.

Jansson, E. and Kaijser, L. (1987) Substrate utilization and enzymes in skeletal muscle of extremely endurance trained men. *Journal of Applied Physiology*, **62**, 999–1005.

Jones, N.L. and Ehrsham, R.E. (1982) The anaerobic threshold. *Exercise and Sports Science Reviews*, **10**, 49–83.

Jones, N.L., Sutton, J.R., Taylor, R. and Toews, C.J. (1977) Effects of pH on cardiospiratory and metabolic responses to exercise. *Journal of Applied Physiology*, **43**, 959–964.

Karlsson, J., Nordesjo, L-O. and Saltin, B. (1974) Muscle glycogen utilisation during exercise after physical training. *Acta Physiologica Scandinavica*, **90**, 210–217.

Katz, A. and Sahlin, K. (1988) Regulation of lactic acid production during exercise. *Journal of Applied Physiology*, **65**, 509–518.

Keul, J., Doll, E. and Keppler, D. (1967) The substrate supply of the human skeletal muscle at rest, during and after work. *Experientia*, **23**, 974–976.

Kindermann, W., Simon, G. and Keul, J. (1979) The significance of the aerobic–anaerobic transition for the dermination of work load intensities during endurance training. *European Journal of Applied Physiology*, **42**, 25–34.

Kugelberg, E. and Edstrom, L. (1968) Differential histochemical effects of muscle contractions on phosphorylase and glycogen in various types of fibres: relation to fatigue. *Journal of Neurology, Neurosurgery and Psychiatry*, **31**, 415–423.

Kumagai, S., Tanaka, K., Matsuura, Y., Matsuzaka, A., Hirakoba, K. and Asano, K. (1982) Relationship of the anaerobic threshold with 5 km, 10 km, and 10 mile races. *European Journal of Applied Physiology*, **49**, 13–23.

Lafontaine, T.P., Londeree, B.R. and Spath, W.K. (1981) The maximum steady state versus selected running events. *Medicine and Science in Sports and Exercise*, **13**, 190–193.

Lake, M., Nute, M.L.G., Kerwin, D.G. and Williams, C. (1986) Oxygen uptake during the onset of exercise in male and female runners, in *Sports Science* (eds J. Watkins, T. Reilly and L. Burwitz). Proc. VIII Commonwealth and Inter. Conf. Sport, Physical Education, Dance, Recreation and Health. Spon Ltd, London, pp. 92–97.

Lakomy, H.K.A. (1984) An ergometer for measuring the power generated during sprinting. *Journal of Physiology*, **354**, 33P.

Lakomy, H.K.A. (1986) Measurement of work and power using friction loaded cycle ergometers. *Ergonomics*, **29**, 509–514.

Lemon, P.W.R. and Mullen, J.P. (1980) Effect of initial glycogen levels on protein catabolism during exercise. *Journal of Applied Physiology*, **48**, 624–629.

MacDougall, J.D., Ward, G.R., Sale, D.G. and Sutton, J.R. (1977) Muscle glycogen repletion after high intensity intermittent exercise. *Journal of Applied Physiology*, **42**, 129–132.

Mainwood, R. and Renaud, D. (1985) The effect of acid–base balance on fatigue in skeletal muscle. *Canadian Journal of Physiology and Pharmacology*, **63**, 403–416.

Margaria, R., Cerretelli, P., Aghemo, P. and Sassi, G. (1963) Energy cost of running. *Journal of Applied Physiology*, **18**, 367–370.

Margaria, R., Olivia, R.D., DiPrampero, P.E. and Cerretelli, P. (1969) Energy utilization in intermittent exercise of supermaximal intensity. *Journal of Applied Physiology*, **26**, 752–756.

Marr, J.W. (1971) Individual dietary surveys: purpose and methods. *World Review of Nutrition and Dietetics*, **13**, 105–164.

Maughan, R.J. and Williams, C. (1981) Differential effects of fasting on skeletal muscle glycogen content in man and on skeletal muscle in the rat. *Proceedings of the Nutrition Society*, **40**, 45A.

Maughan, R.J., Williams, C., Campbell, D.M. and Hepburn, D. (1978) Fat and carbohydrate metabolism during low intensity exercise. *European Journal of Applied Physiology*, **39**, 7–16.

McGilvery, R.W. (1975) The use of fuels for muscular work, in *Metabolic Adaptation to Prolonged Physical Exercise* (eds H. Howald and J.R. Poortmans), Birkhauser Verlag, Basel, pp. 12–30.

McLellan, T.M. (1987) The anaerobic thresholds: concept and controversy. *Australian Journal of Science and Medicine in Sport*, **19**, 3–8.

Medbo, J.I., Mohn, A., Tabata, I., Bahr, R.M., Vaage, O. and Sejersted, O. (1988) Anaerobic capacity defined by maximum O_2 deficit. *Journal of Applied Physiology*, **64**, 50–60.

Newsholme, E.A. (1976) Carbohydrate metabolism *in vivo*: regulation of blood glucose level. *Clinics Endocrinology and Metabolism*, **5**, 543–578.

Nicholls, D.G. and Locke, R.M. (1984) Thermic mechanisms in brown fat. *Physiological Reviews*, **64**, 1–64.

Nilsson, L.H. and Hultman, E. (1973) Liver glycogen in man – the effect of total starvation or a carbohydrate-poor diet followed by carbohydrate refeeding. *Scandinavian Journal of Clinical and Laboratory Investigation*, **32**, 325–330.

Orr, G.W., Green, H.J., Hughson, R.L. and Bennett, G.W. (1982) Computer linear regression model to determine ventilatory anaerobic threshold. *Journal of Applied Physiology*, **52**, 1349–1352.

Owles, W.H. (1930) Alterations in the lactic acid content of the blood as a result of light exercise and associated changes in the CO_2-combining power of the blood and the alveolar CO_2 pressure. *Journal of Physiology*, **69**, 214–237.

Padykula, H.A. and Herman, E. (1955) The specificity of the histochemical method of adenosine triphosphatase. *Journal of Histochemistry and Cytochemistry*, **3**, 170–195.

Parkhouse, W.S. and MacKenzie, D.C. (1984) Possible contribution of skeletal muscle buffers to enhanced anaerobic performance: a brief review. *Medicine and Science in Sports and Exercise*, **16**, 328–338.

Pernow, B. and Saltin, B. (1971) Availability of substrates and capacity for prolonged heavy exercise in man. *Journal of Applied Physiology*, **31**, 416–422.

Peter, J.B., Barnard, R.J., Edgerton, V.R., Gillespie, C.A. and Stempel, K.E. (1972) Metabolic profiles of three fibres of skeletal muscle in guinea pigs and rabbits. *Biochemistry*, **11**, 2627–2633.

Petite, D. (1986) Regulation of phenotype expression in skeletal muscle fibres by increased contractile activity, in *Biochemistry of Exercise* (ed. B. Saltin) *International Series in Sports Science*, Vol. 16, Human Kinetics Publishers, Champaign, Illinois, USA, pp. 3–26.

Piehl, K. (1974) Glycogen storage and depletion in human skeletal muscle fibres. *Acta Physiologica Scandinavica*, Suppl., 402.

Porte, D. and Williamson, R.H. (1966) Inhibition of insulin release by norepinephrine in man. *Science*, **152**, 1248–1250.

Powers, S.K., Dodd, S. and Beadle, R.E. (1985) Oxygen kinetics in trained athletes different in $\dot{V}O_{2max}$. *European Journal of Applied Physiology*, **54**, 306–308.

Pruett, E.D.R. (1970) Glucose and insulin during prolonged work stress in men living on different diets. *Journal of Applied Physiology*, **28**, 199–208.

Ramsbottom, R., Nute, M.G.L. and Williams, C. (1987) Determinants of five kilometre running performance in active men and women. *British Journal of Sports Medicine*, **21**, 9–13.

Ramsbottom, R., Williams, C., Boobis, L.H. and Freeman, W. (1989) Aerobic fitness and running performance of male and female recreational runners. *Journal of Sports Science*, **7**, 9–20.

Rennie, M.J., Winder, W.W. and Holloszy, J.O. (1976) A sparing effect of increased plasma fatty acids on muscle and liver glycogen content in exercising rat. *Biochemical Journal*, **156**, 647–655.

Richter, E.A. and Galbo, H. (1986) High glycogen levels enhance glycogen breakdown in isolated contracting skeletal muscle. *Journal of Applied Physiology*, **61**, 827–831.

Roberts, K.M., Noble, E.G., Hayden, D.B. and Taylor, A.W. (1988) Simple and complex carbohydrate-rich diets and muscle glycogen content of marathon runners. *European Journal of Applied Physiology*, **57**, 70–74.

Robinson, A.M. and Williamson, D.H. (1980) Physiological roles of ketone bodies as substrates and signals in mammalian tissues. *Physiological Reviews*, **60**, 143–187.

Sahlin, K. (1978) Intracellular pH and energy metabolism in skeletal muscle of man. *Acta Physiologica Scandinavica*, Suppl., **455**, 35.

Sahlin, K. and Henriksson, J. (1984) Buffer capacity and lactate accumulation in skeletal muscle of trained and untrained men. *Acta Physiologica Scandinavica*, **122**, 331–339.

Saltin, B. (1973) Metabolic fundamentals in exercise. *Medicine and Science in Sports and Exercise*, **15**, 366–369.

Saltin, B. and Gollnick, P.D. (1983) Skeletal muscle adaptability: significance for metabolism and performance, in *Handbook of Physiology*. Section 10. *Skeletal muscle*. American Physiology Society, Bethesda, USA, pp. 555–631.

Saltin, B., Henriksson, J., Nygaard, E. and Andersen, P. (1977) Fiber types and metabolic potentials of skeletal muscles in sedentary man and endurance runners. *Annals of the New York Academy of Sciences*, **301**, 3–29.

Saltin, B. and Karlsson, J. (1971) Muscle glycogen utilization during work of different intensities, in *Muscle Metabolism During Exercise* (eds B. Pernow and B. Saltin), Plenum Press, New York, pp. 289–299.

Saris, W.H.M., Erp-Baart, van, M.A., Brouns, F., Westerterp, K.R. and ten Hoor, F. (1989) Study on food intake during extreme sustained exercise: Tour de France. *International Journal of Sports Medicine*, Suppl. 1, **10**, 562–3.

Sharp, R.L., Costill, D.L., Fink., W.J. and King, D.S. (1986) Effects of eight weeks of bicycle ergometer sprint training on human muscle buffer capacity. *International Journal of Sports Medicine*, **7**, 13–17.

Short, S.H. and Short, W.R. (1983) Four year study of University athletes' dietary intake. *American Dietary Association*, **82**, 632–645.

Shorten, M.J. and Williams, C. (1982) Respiratory responses to an incremental treadmill running test. *Journal of Physiology*, **332**, 38–39P.

Sjodin, B. and Jacobs, I. (1981) Onset of blood lactate accumulation and marathon running performance. *International Journal of Sports Medicine*, **2**, 23–26.

Sjodin, B. Jacobs, I. and Svedenhag, J. (1982) Changes in onset of blood lactate accumulation (OBLA) and muscle enzymes after training at OBLA. *European Journal of Applied Physiology*, **49**, 45–57.

Sjodin, B., Schele, R., Karlsson, J., Linnarsson, D. and Wallensten, R. (1982) The physiological background of the onset of blood lactate accumulation, in *Exercise and Sport Biology* (ed. P. Komi), Human Kinetics Publishers Champaign, Illinois, USA, pp. 43–56.

Sjostrom, M., Friden, J. and Ekblom, B. (1987) Endurance, what is it? Muscle morphology after an extremely long distance run. *Acta Physiologica Scandinavica*, **130**, 513–520.

Spriet, L.L., Ren, J.M. and Hultman, E. (1988) Epinephrine infusion enhances muscle glycogenolysis during prolonged electrical stimulation. *Journal of Applied Physiology*, **64**, 1439–1444.

Spriet, L.L., Soderlund, K., Bergstrom, M. and Hultman, E. (1987a) Anaerobic energy release in skeletal muscle during electrical stimulation in man. *Journal of Applied Physiology*, **62**, 611–615.

Spriet, L.L., Soderlund, K., Bergstrom, M. and Hultman, E. (1987b) Skeletal muscle glycogenolysis, glycolysis and pH during electrical stimulation in man. *Journal of Applied Physiology*, **62**, 616–621.

Stegmann, H. and Kindermann, W. (1982) Comparison of prolonged exercise tests at the individual anaerobic threshold and the fixed anaerobic threshold of 4 mmol l^{-1} lactate. *International Journal of Sports Medicine*, **3**, 105–110.

Stegman, H., Kindermann, W. and Schnabel, A. (1981) Lactate kinetics and individual anaerobic threshold. *International Journal of Sports Medicine*, **2**, 160–165.

Stroud, M.A. (1987) Nutrition and energy balance on the 'Footsteps of Scott Expedition' 1984–1986. *Human Nutrition. Applied Nutrition*, **41A**, 426–433.

Tanaka, K. and Matsuura, Y. (1984) Marathon performance, anaerobic threshold, and the onset of blood lactate accumulation. *Journal of Applied Physiology*, **57**, 640–643.

Trayhurn, P. and Ashwell, M. (1987) Control of white and brown adipose tissue by the autonomic nervous system. *Proceedings of the Nutrition Society*, **46**, 135–142.

Vago, P., Mercier, J., Ramonatxo, M. and Prefaut, Ch. (1987) Is ventilatory anaerobic threshold a good index of endurance capacity? *International Journal of Sports Medicine*, **8**, 190–195.

Vollestad, N.K. and Sejersted, O.M. (1988) Biochemical correlates of fatigue: a brief review. *European Journal of Applied Physiology* **57**, 336–347.

Vollestad, N.K., Vaage, O. and Hermansen, L. (1984) Muscle glycogen depletion patterns in Type I and subgroups of Type II fibres during prolonged severe exercise in man. *Acta Physiologica Scandinavica*, **122**, 433–441.

Wahren, J. (1973) Substrate utilization by exercising muscle in man. *Progress in Cardiology*, **2**, 255–280.

Wasserman, K. (1986) The anaerobic threshold: definition, physiological significance and identification. *Advances in Cardiology*, **35**, 1–23.

Wasserman, K. and McIlroy, M.B. (1964) Detecting the threshold of anaerobic metabolism in cardiac patients during exercise. *American Journal of Cardiology*, **14**, 844–852.

Wasserman, K., Whipp, B.J., Koyle, S.N. and Beaver, W.L. (1973) Anaerobic threshold and respiratory gas exchange during exercise. *Journal of Applied Physiology*, **35**, 236–243.

Weir, J., Noakes, T.D., Myburgh, K. and Adams, B. (1987) A high carbohydrate diet negates the metabolic effects of caffeine during exercise. *Medicine and Science in Sports and Exercise*, **19**, 100–105.

Weltman, A. and Katch, V. (1976) Minute by minute respiratory exchange and oxygen uptake kinetics during steady-state exercise in subjects of high and low max VO_2. *Research Quarterly*, **47**, 490–498.

Westra, H.G., De Haan, A., Van Doorn, J.E. and De Haan, E.J. (1985) The effect of intensive interval training on the anaerobic power of the rat quadriceps. *Journal of Sports Sciences*, **3**, 139–150.

WHO (1985) Energy and protein requirements, Technical report series 724, World Health Organization, Geneva.

Wilkes, D., Gledhill, N. and Smyth, R. (1983) Effect of acute induced metabolic alkalosis on 800 m racing time. *Medicine and Science in Sports and Exercise*, **75**, 277–280.

Williams, C. (1987) Short term activity, in *Exercise: Benefits, Limitations and Adaptations* (eds D. Macleod, R.J. Maughan, M. Nimmo, T. Reilly and C. Williams) E & F Spon, London, pp. 59–62.

Williams, C. (1989) Influences of starch and sugar intake on physical performance, in *Dietary Starch and Sugars in Man: A Comparison* (ed. J. Dobbing), Springer-Verlag, Basel, Switzerland, pp. 193–212.

Williams, C., Brewer, J. and Patton, J. (1984) The metabolic challenge of the marathon. *British Journal of Sports Medicine*, **18**, 245–252.

Williams, C. and Nute, M.L.G. (1983) Some physiological demands of a half-marathon race on recreational runners. *British Journal of Sports Medicine*, **17**, 152–161.

Williams, C. and Nute, M.L.G. (1986) Training induced changes in endurance capacity of female games players, in *Sports Science* (eds J. Watkins, T. Reilly and L. Burwitz), Proc. VIII Commonwealth and Inter. Conf. Sport, Physical Education, Dance, Recreation and Health. E. and F.N. Spon Ltd, London, pp. 11–17.

Williams, C.G., Wyndham, C.H., Kok, R. and Rahden von, M.J.E. (1967) Effect of training on maximum oxygen intake and on anaerobic metabolism in man. *Internationale Zeitschrift für angew Physiologie einschl Arbeitsphysiologie*, **24**, 18–23.

Wootton, S.A. and Williams, C. (1983) The influence of recovery duration on repeated maximal sprints, in *Biochemistry of Exercise* (eds H.G. Knuttgen, J.A. Vogel and J. Poortmans) International Series in Sports Science, Vol. 13, Human Kinetics Publishers, Champaign, Illinois, USA, pp. 269–273.

Yoshida, T. (1986) The effect of dietary modifications on anaerobic threshold. *Sports Medicine*, **3**, 4–9.

Yoshida, T., Nagata, A., Muro, M., Takeuchi, N. and Suda, Y. (1981) The validity of the anaerobic threshold determination by a Douglas bag method compared with arterial blood lactate concentration. *European Journal of Applied Physiology*, **46**, 423–430.

Yoshida, T., Suda, Y. and Takeuchi, N. (1982) Endurance training regimen based on arterial blood lactate: effects on anaerobic threshold. *European Journal of Applied Physiology*, **49**, 223–230.

2
Strength and weight-training

Klaus Klausen

2.1 INTRODUCTION

The maximal, external force which a muscle – or a group of muscles – can produce, depends on a number of factors as shown in Figure 2.1. The maximal contraction of the muscle implies a maximal activation of the spinal motor neurones involved (the 'motor pool'). This activation depends on a number of central nervous factors such as motivation, concentration and so on, and peripheral nervous factors such as reflex mechanisms mediated from different sensory organs (e.g. muscle spindles, tendon organs). The activation of the motor pool is probably also influenced by mutual inhibition of motor neurones supplying motor units of different fibre types. The development of maximal external force further implies a proper inhibition of antagonistic muscles.

The maximal force or tension produced by a muscle depends on the cross-sectional area of all the muscle fibres within the muscle – the physiological cross-sectional area. Thus, a muscle with a large cross-sectional area is able to produce greater maximal force than a muscle with a small cross-sectional area. However, the maximal, external force produced by two muscles with identical physiological cross-sectional areas may be different, either due to differences with regard to concentration and/or quality of the myofibrils etc., or due to differences between the muscles' biomechanical properties. The length–tension diagram of skeletal muscles (Figure 2.2) shows that the maximal, isometric force developed by a muscle depends on its length. As can be seen the maximal, active tension (curve II) is obtained when the muscle is pre-stretched about 10–20% above the equilibrium length (i.e. 100%). Less tension is obtained when the muscle is below equilibrium length, but when stretched above 120% the passive tension in the elastic components of the muscle will increase progressively (curve I), and

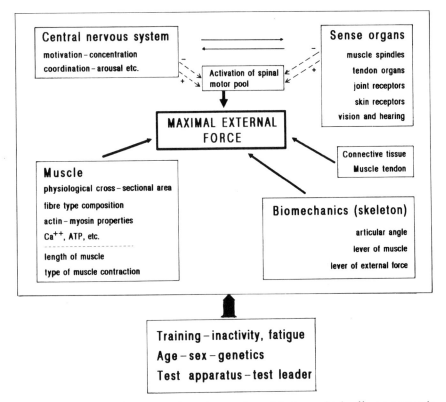

Figure 2.1 Schematic presentation of a number of factors which affect a person's ability to develop maximal, external force.

hence the total tension (passive and active (curve III) will remain almost constant from a length of 120% to about 155%, after which it will increase considerably, in spite of the fact that the active tension is now decreasing rapidly towards zero. In normal, easy standing the length of most muscles *in situ* will be about 110% and the range of shortening or lengthening about ±30% due to the limitations set by the joint movements.

Besides the variation in muscle tension (M in Figure 2.3) the external force (F in Figure 2.3) depends on the distance from the point of force application to the joint axis in question (a in Figure 2.3), and the lever arm of M (b in Figure 2.3). Due to the proportion between a and b the external force (F) will usually be much smaller than the force produced by the muscles (M). As can be seen from the equation in Figure 2.3 the external force (F) may be increased by a reduction of a. From a teleological point of view a short lever arm of the muscles is an

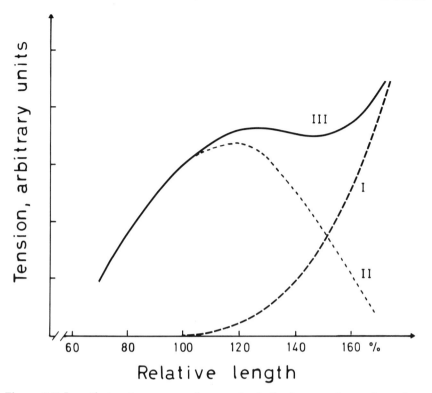

Figure 2.2 Length–tension curves of a muscle. I, the increase in tension when the inactive muscle is stretched. II, the maximal isometric tension produced by the muscle at different lengths of the muscle. III, the variation of the total, maximal, isometric tension of the muscle with length, i.e. the sum of the tension in curves I and II at any given length of the muscle. For further explanation see text.

advantage, because it allows large movements in the joints with relatively small changes in muscle length.

Experiments have shown (upper part of Figure 2.3) that the maximal isometric torque (F × a) of the knee-extensor muscles varies with the knee angle, and the highest values are obtained at an angle of about 110–120°, and not – as one should expect from the length–tension diagram in Figure 2.2 – at an angle of 90°, where the length of the extensor muscle is maximal, within the limits of the experiment. It has been shown that the main reason for the maximal torque at about 120° is that the lever arm of the extensor muscles increases from a knee angle of 90° to 120°. The decrease in torque seen during further extension towards 180° is explained by the gradual decrease in muscle tension due to the shortening of the extensor muscles (cf. Figure 2.2).

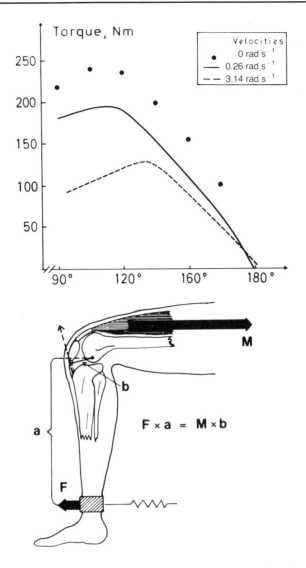

Figure 2.3 Lower half: The product of the tension produced by the muscles (M) and the lever arm of the muscles (b) in relation to the axis of the knee joint exert a torque on the knee joint, which can be measured as the external force (F) times the distance between the application of F to the joint axis (a). Note the proportion between M and F, and between b and a.

Upper half: F × a measured during maximal, isometric contraction at different knee angles, and during maximal knee-extension at two angular velocities (Redrawn after Thorstensson, Grimby and Karlsson (1976). For further explanation see text.

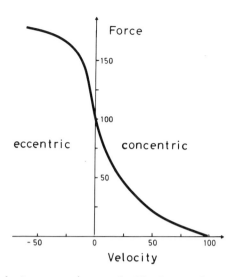

Figure 2.4 Force–velocity curve of a muscle. The force values at all velocities on the figure are given for the same muscle length.

The type of contraction is decisive for the muscle's ability to produce tension. Thus, the highest force values are obtained during eccentric (lenthening) muscle contraction. The maximal force obtained during isometric contraction is somewhat lower, and the lowest maximal values are obtained during concentric (shortening) contractions (Figure 2.4). During dynamic muscle contraction (concentric and eccentric) the maximal force developed further depends upon the speed of the contraction (Figure 2.4). Here it should be pointed out that the fibre type composition seems to influence very little the maximal, external force in human muscles, whereas the maximal velocity of muscle contraction in general increases with increasing percentage of fast twitch fibres.

The strength and stiffness of the connective tissue within the muscle and in the muscle tendons is of vital importance for the transfer of the tension, produced by the muscle fibres, to external force.

Muscular endurance is not easy to define, since it depends on the tension developed by the muscle. During isometric contraction the endurance of muscle – or a group of muscles – is defined as the time a given tension can be maintained. A maximal voluntary, isometric contraction (MVC) may be sustained for a few seconds whereas 50% MVC can be maintained by most muscles for about one minute and 10% MVC for more than 10 mins. Endurance during dynamic con-tractions (concentric or eccentric) is usually defined as the number of contractions against a given load which can be repeated at a given frequency (constant length of pauses between contractions). The dynamic endurance will increase with decreasing load and frequency. Training of muscular endurance will not be discussed in this chapter.

The qualities described above are influenced by several factors. For instance the development of the neuromuscular system, stature, etc. depends on genetic factors. The age of a person will influence most of the above-mentioned qualities and hence affect the maximal, external force that may be produced by a muscle. Thus in the growing child the physiological cross-sectional area of any muscle will increase with the increase in length to the second power, and the levers will increase with length to the first power. Qualitative changes ('maturation') take place during the growth of the child – especially in the nervous system (e.g. improved co-ordination and ability to concentrate). At pubescence a marked spurt in the growth of muscle strength is seen in boys, whereas it is absent in girls. This spurt in strength is usually ascribed to the male sex hormones. Thus the average adult male is higher and stronger than the average adult female. At old age the muscle strength decreases due to degenerative processes in muscle, tendons and bones, and in the nervous system. Fatigue caused by repeated or sustained muscle contractions will reduce the maximal, external force. It should be mentioned that obviously the measured maximal, external force is highly dependent on the test situation (test-apparatus, test-leader, etc.). Finally most of the above-mentioned organs and tissues are highly susceptible both to training and to inactivity.

2.2 TRAINING OF MUSCLE STRENGTH

During a period of strength training the typical sequence of improvement will be (1) an initial period where the maximal, external force is increasing rapidly week by week, followed by (2) a period with less increase towards an upper limit, set by the load used during training. If training is continued with the same load, no further improvement is seen in muscle strength, but endurance (e.g. number of contractions with the training load) will increase continuously. If further strength improvement is desired the training load should be increased, and as a result of this, muscle strength will increase towards a new upper limit (Figure 2.5). This procedure of increasing the training load each time a new limit is approached, is called progressive resistance exercise (PRE). The PRE is the basis of any type of modern strength training and is usually accredited to DeLorme (1945), although the principle was known in ancient Greece. As will be shown in the following, several other factors, besides the PRE, should be taken into account in order to obtain optimum increase in muscle strength.

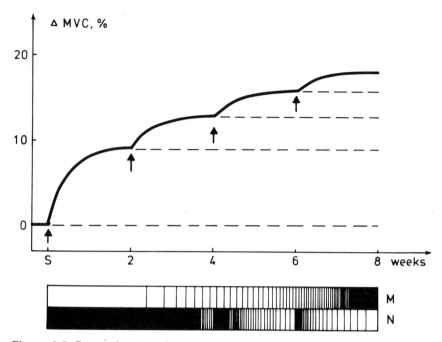

Figure 2.5 Curve showing the typical increase in muscle strength during 8 weeks of progressive resistance exercise (PRE). The increase in muscle strength is expressed as a percentage of initial strength (MVC, %). In this example the training load is adjusted (increased) every second week (arrows). Note the rapid increase in strength during the first two weeks towards a level of MVC = 9% followed by progressively smaller increases as training load is increased during the following weeks. An attempt has been made to illustrate the importance of neural factor (N) and muscle hypertrophy (M) for the strength increase during the 8 weeks of training. As can be seen neural factors dominate during the first weeks, whereas hypertrophy probably first begins to be of significance towards the end of the training period.

Isometric training is often preferred in laboratory experiments because isometric strength is fairly easy to measure under standardized conditions, either as the maximal, external force (Asmussen, Heebøll-Nielsen and Molbeck, 1959) or as the maximal, external torque exerted on a given joint (Darcus, 1953; Petersen, 1960) (cf. Figure 2.3). The term MVC is usually applied on both measures of maximal, voluntary, isometric force.

There has been some controversy in the past regarding the optimum load (tension), number of contractions, etc., which would give the most efficient improvement in MVC (Hettinger, 1961; Hettinger and Müller,

1953; Manz, Carnes and Carnes, 1983; Petersen, 1960). Now it is generally agreed that the most efficient isometric training is achieved when each contraction is near MVC and maintained for at least 3 s. Further, the number of contractions per training session should be rather high; or in other words, the duration of each contraction, times the number of contractions per day, should be large (McDonagh and Davies, 1984). However, it should be emphasized that neither the optimum number of contractions per training session nor per week is as yet conclusively established, and experiments have shown that training with contractions equal to 30–60% MVC may produce substantial increases in MVC in untrained subjects, provided the duration of each contraction is prolonged to about the time of exhaustion (e.g. Davies and Young, 1983; Hansen, 1963). The physiological explanation of these findings may be that an efficient recruitment of all motor units in the muscles is obtained either by a maximal but brief stimulation of the motor pool (Figure 2.1) or by a sustained stimulation, which will eventually result in an activation of the motor units with the highest thresholds, as the low threshold units become fatigued and are no longer able to maintain the desired tension in the muscle alone. Further, it should be pointed out, that at least in untrained subjects, training with submaximal loads will improve muscle strength during the first period of training simply because of 'motor learning', i.e. the subjects learn to co-ordinate the proper muscles involved in the training in question.

2.2.1 Weight-training

Training with weights is probably still the most common way of training in sports. Before training the maximal load which can be lifted once, the one repetition maximum (1 RM), is established by increasing the load gradually over a series of lifts with sufficient periods of rest in between lifts. Once established, the 1 RM is used as a measure of the maximal, concentric force of a muscle, or rather a group of muscles.

The training load is then expressed as the maximal number of times a given load can be lifted correctly without rest between lifts. The loads are characterized 2 RM, 6 RM, 12 RM etc. (Berger, 1962a, b). Another way of expressing the load is as a percentage of the 1RM (e.g. Hansen, 1967). The relationship between these two methods of describing the training load has been established empirically by McDonagh and Davies (1984) within the range of 1–12 RM. Thus 2, 4, 6, 8, 10 and 12 RM should correspond to about 95, 86, 78, 70, 61 and 53% of the 1 RM, respectively. The XRM method of describing the training load is the one which is mostly used in sports.

No single recipe can be given to obtain the most efficient gain in dynamic muscle strength, since the need of strength in different sports depends on, for example, the skills that characterize each sport. If the aim of training is restricted to obtain a fast gain in strength, it has been shown that 1–10 RM will give significant increases in strength when training is repeated 1–10 times per day (sets), and the optimum combination seems to be 6 RM for three sets performed at a frequency of three times per week (Berger, 1962a, b, 1963, 1967). Based on numerous investigations (Clarke, 1973) it is probably safe to conclude, that the most efficient effect of weight-training is obtained when principles similar to those used in isometric exercise (high loads – few repetitions) are applied. The optimum frequency of training may vary, depending on the number of muscle groups involved in the training. Thus elite weight-lifters may exercise as often as 5–7 times per week, whereas bodybuilders train less frequently, as it is thought that alternate days of rest are essential for the anabolism of new muscle tissue (MacQueen, 1954). Evidently untrained persons should train less frequently than well-trained persons in order to avoid too much muscle soreness and overtraining.

A variant of weight-training which is commonly used, both in sports and rehabilitation is pyramid training, which typically consists of training sets with increasing load, e.g. 10, 8, 6, 4, 2 and 1 RM (ascending pyramid). The physiological advantage of using the pyramid is stated to be that activation of all motor units is ensured. However, in the early weight-lifts in the pyramid all motor units may not be fully activated. This is more likely to be the case if a descending pyramid is applied, i.e. a pyramid where the above-mentioned loads are performed in the reversed order (McDonach and Davies, 1984).

Although very efficient, training with weights has some disadvantages. The risks involved, when handling the heavy weights, cannot be underestimated. It takes a certain amount of skill and experience to avoid accidents during training with loaded barbells. As a consequence of this, various types of apparatus and equipment have been developed on which the weights can be mounted for training of almost any muscle-group in the body. A detailed description of these apparatus will not be given here. Another disadvantage is that the load which can be lifted is limited by the 'weakest point' during the movement in question (cf. Figure 2.3). This means that during a maximal lift with constant velocity full activation of the muscles is only obtained at this point, while during the rest of the movement the activity of the muscles is sub-maximal. Therefore, in competitive weight-lifting speed of contraction during training is strongly emphasized. If the speed of contraction is kept as high as possible at any moment throughout a given lift, maximal activation of the muscles involved is to be expected, according to the force–velocity curve (Figure 2.4). However, this type of optimal speed adjustment during weight-lifting is very difficult to perform, and in most ordinary training programmes the duration of each lift is not specified. The problem about the 'weakest point' has led to the development of strength training apparatus which uses several new variants of dynamic strength training.

2.2.2 Isokinetic training

Isokinetic training started with the introduction of the Cybex-dynamometer, the use of which has been described and analysed by several authors (Perrine and Edgerton, 1978; Sapega *et al.*, 1982; Thistle, *et al.*, 1967; Thorstensson, Grimby and Karlsson, 1976; Yates and Kamon, 1983). By means of the Cybex it is possible to maintain a constant angular velocity with maximal activation of the muscles involved throughout the whole range of movement in the joint in question (e.g. knee-extension, elbow-flexion, etc.). Thus the maximal, external force or the maximal torque can be obtained and measured at any angle of the joint, and at any velocity within the limits of the dynamometer and the neuromuscular system. Isokinetic training is therefore also called 'accommodating resistance training'. Typical isokinetic, maximal torque curves from knee-extension at three velocities (0, 0.26 and 3.14 rad s^{-1}) are shown in Figure 2.3. Note that a maximum is obtained on each curve. This maximal value is called the 'peak torque', and is usually used as a measure of maximal isokinetic strength at a given velocity, although, as can be seen from the figure, the peak torque occurs at different angles, depending on the velocity of the movement. Peak torque increases, after a period of isokinetic training, resemble increases in, for example, 1 RM after a similar period of traditional weight-training (Lesmes *et al.*, 1978; MacDougall *et al.*, 1977; Pipes, 1978). Training velocity seems to be important for the improvement in peak torque, since significant increases in peak torque after training are only seen at angular velocities equal to or slower than the training velocity (Lesmes *et al.*, 1978) and it has been shown that training at a given velocity may increase strength selectively at that velocity (Ciaozzo, Perrine and Edgerton, 1980; Coyle and Feiring, 1980). However, in one experiment training at a velocity of 1.05 rad s^{-1} produced significant increases in peak torque at all velocities up to 3.14 rad s^{-1} (Krotkiewski *et al.*, 1979). It has been claimed that isokinetic training should be advantageous especially for competitive swimmers, because movements of the legs and arms in water are very much like isokinetic movements.

Recently, more advanced, computerized, motor-driven equipment has been developed for strength training and measurement of muscle strength. Thus the Kinetic Communicator (KINCOM), a hydraulic-driven device with microcomputer control allows measurement of both concentric and eccentric, isokinetic movements at velocities from zero to 3.7 rad s^{-1} (Farrell and Richards, 1986). Further, it is possible by means of this apparatus to adjust the speed of contraction in such a way that the force output of a muscle group is kept constant during the whole range of movement. So far the applicability of the KINCOM system for strength training has not been evidenced by scientific experiments.

SPARK is another, recently developed system (Thorstensson *et al.*, 1986). This apparatus allows both concentric and eccentric, isokinetic contractions at velocities from 0.017 to 6.981 rad s^{-1} and torque recordings up to 1200 Nm. Furthermore, the SPARK apparatus allows measurements of muscle strength during constant acceleration or deceleration. The apparatus seems promising for future investigations of the force–velocity relationships of various muscle groups during natural movements (Thorstensson *et al.*, 1986).

2.2.3 Variable resistance training

Variable resistance training is another variant of dynamic strength training. As mentioned before the maximal torque during, for example, a knee-extension, varies during the whole extension due to changes in muscle length and lever arms (Figure 2.3). The principle in variable resistance training is to vary the lever arm of the load to be lifted in such a way that there is accordance between the external and internal torque (about the joint in question). Or in other words, during a lift, the muscles involved should be activated equally at any position during the whole movement. Special, variable lever arms have been constructed for almost any muscle group in the body. Because of the optimal activation of the muscles over the whole range of movement, it has been postulated that variable resistance training should be superior to most other types of strength training. However, experiments do not support this assumption. Variable resistance training seems to be just as efficient as any of the above-described ways of training (Pipes, 1978). Because of sophisticated and attractive equipment the variable resistance principle has been used quite extensively during the past 10 years among non-competitive people who exercise regularly.

2.2.4 Omnikinetic training

Omnikinetic training is based on a series of hydraulic cylinders (Manz, Carnes and Carnes, 1983). The resistance of the cylinders is adjustable by means of a system of valves, and full range of movement in the joints is possible during training. At a given setting of the valves the resistance depends on the speed of contraction. The speed of contraction is set by the subject himself, and hence, during a training set the speed of contraction will decrease successively from the first to the last contraction. The tension developed will also decrease gradually as the muscles fatigue, but maximal activation of the muscles will ensure maximal performance during all contractions. The major new contribution from omnikinetics is that many of the cylinders allow concentric, dynamic training of both flexors and extensors about a joint during the movements back and forth. This is in contrast to other weight-training procedures, where the same muscle group is working concentrically during the lift, and eccentrically when the weight is moved back to the starting position. Omnikinetics is so called, because it is claimed to comprise all the advantages of the other training systems. So far this has to my knowledge not been confirmed by scientific experiment, but during the last few years the system has been adopted to some extent in competitive sports (e.g. ice-hockey, football, handball etc.).

2.2.5 Eccentric training

It is generally agreed that it is the development of high tensions which induces hypertrophy of muscles (Goldberg *et al.*, 1975; Goldspink, 1977). Hence, according to the force–velocity curve (Figure 2.4) it could be expected that eccentric training would be highly efficient for the development of strength. However, very few studies with eccentric strength training are reported in the literature, and the results are rather conflicting (Clarke, 1973; Johnson *et al.*, 1976), the main reason being that the efficiency of eccentric training is almost always evaluated from the improvement in concentric or isometric strength. One exception is a study by Laycoe and Marteniuk (1971), who found an increase in eccentric strength of 41.2% after 6 weeks of eccentric training (physical education students). The average increase in isometric strength of the group was only 17% and resembled the gain in strength found in another group of subjects who followed an isometric training programme over the same period of time. As mentioned above the concentric contraction of the muscles during a weight-lift is always followed by an eccentric contraction, when the weight is lowered again. This implies that part of the strength improvement during weight-lifting may be attributed to eccentric training. However, eccentric training as such is of limited interest in sports, since it involves either expensive equipment or help from another person.

Further, it should be pointed out that eccentric training is more harmful to the muscle and connective tissue than concentric training

(Armstrong, 1984; Hoppeler, 1986). So far no conclusive explanation has been given for this phenomenon. Structural and membrane damages may be essential (Armstrong, 1984). These damages are associated with an increased release of muscle enzymes, e.g. creatine kinase (CK). However, excess CK release is also seen following, for example, endurance running, and muscle soreness following eccentric exercise is not always associated with an increase in the CK release from the muscles (Newham, Jones and Edwards, 1983). Further, there is experimental evidence that the source of muscle soreness is not located in the muscle fibres, but rather in the connective tissue in the muscle (Newham *et al.*, 1983). All in all the whole problem of muscle soreness following strength training is as yet not well understood, but it is generally agreed that the soreness is related to repeated, high tension in the muscles (Hoppeler, 1986; Newham *et al.*, 1983).

2.2.6 Plyometric training

The word 'plyometric' is actually derived from the Greek work 'pleion' which means 'more'. Consequently 'pleiometric' means 'more length' and has, through phonetic transcription been changed to 'plyometric'. Plyometric training is almost exclusively applied to the extensor muscles of the legs, and consists of a vigorous lengthening of the active extensor muscles (eccentric contraction) immediately followed by a maximal, concentric contraction. This sequence of muscle activity is usually accomplished by having the person jump from, for example, a vaulting horse down on the floor in squatting position, and immediately from here jump up to standing position on another horse placed 1–2 m in front of the starting point. The aim is to jump as high as possible from the squatting position. Optimum heights for the initial jump down have been determined experimentally (Asmussen and Bonde-Petersen, 1974; Bosco *et al.*, 1982). Plyometric training 3–4 times a week over 6–8 weeks gives significant increases in jumping height, typically of the magnitude of 4–6 cm (Blattner and Noble, 1979). Jumping with additional weight is thought to improve the effect of plyometric training within certain limits of overload. The effect of plyometric training is highly specific, and its effect on isometric or concentric maximal strength is modest. Further it has been shown, for example, that isokinetic training is just as efficient as plyometric training for the improvement of jumping height (Blattner and Noble, 1979). The disadvantage of plyometric training is the risk of injuries during touch-down and take-off from the floor, where the tension in the muscles will reach very high ('supermaximal') values (cf. Figure 2.4).

2.2.7 Electrical stimulation

Electrical stimulation has been suggested as a mode of training for the development of muscle strength. One reason for this is that it has been shown that the force developed during optimal electrical stimulation of the adductor muscles of the thumb is about 30% greater than the MVC of the same muscle group (Ikai, Yabe and Ischii, 1967). Experiments seem to indicate that electrical stimulation is efficient for the restoration of MVC in atrophied muscles, whereas results from experiments with normal subjects are conflicting (McDonagh and Davies, 1984). The two main disadvantages in using electrical stimulation for the development of strength are (1) expensive equipment which should be handled by an expert, and (2) the stimulation is applied directly on the muscles, which means that no training of the 'motor pool' is involved (cf. Figure 2.1), and as is shown below, motor learning is essential for maximal or optimal activation of the muscles during any sport performance.

2.2.8 Subject's own body weight

The subject's own body weight is the load most easily at hand both for isometric and dynamic strength training. Push-ups, pull-ups, chin-ups, back-lifts, high-jumps, and so on have proved to be successful for the development of strength in almost all sports. For instance, in gymnastics with apparatus it is the only accepted way of strength training. The body weight can be used for strength development in an infinite number of ways. The effectiveness of training is mainly substantiated by progress in the sport in question, but also by scientific experiments (Berger, 1962c; Häkkinen and Komi, 1985b). The effect of using own body weight for strength training is enhanced by wearing vests with extra loads (Bosco *et al.*, 1984).

2.3 EFFECT OF STRENGTH TRAINING ON MUSCLE

The most conspicuous effect of strength training is the hypertrophy of muscle. This phenomenon has been extensively studied in animal experiments, and innumerable pieces of information regarding the events involved in the growth of muscle has been presented in the literature. In spite of all efforts the mechanisms behind work-induced hypertrophy of muscle are still obscure, but it is generally agreed that the critical event in initiating muscle hypertrophy is an increase in muscle tension, produced either by passive stretching or by active contraction (Goldberg *et al.*, 1975; Goldspink, 1977; Saltin and Gollnick, 1983).

2.3.1 Hypertrophy

Hypertrophy in human muscle due to strength training is usually evidenced by the excessive muscles seen in persons who perform in sports activities which imply engagement in heavy-resistance training (e.g. body-builders, weight-lifters, javelin- and discus throwers, shot-putters, etc.). However, it is still under dispute to what extent the large muscles of these persons are due to training on the one hand and to hereditary factors on the other.

The usual, quantitative measure of the size of human muscles is the cross-sectional area, which has been estimated from circumference measurements after proper correction for subcutaneous fat thickness. New techniques such as ultrasound scanning, X-ray tomography, etc. have made it possible to give a more direct and accurate estimate of the cross-sectional area.

The use of the cross-sectional area as a measure of the increase in muscle size lies in the fact that the strength of a muscle is closely related to its physiological cross-sectional area. However, it should be pointed out that these two areas are not necessarily identical, mainly because the longitudinal orientation of the fibres in the muscle is often different from the longitudinal orientation of the whole muscle. Thus, the estimation of, for example, the physiological cross-sectional area of the quadriceps muscle is almost impossible because of varying orientation of the fibres in the different parts of the muscle. A reasonable, perpendicular orientation of the scanning plane to the fibre orientation is only possible for part of the muscle (DeCarvalho *et al.*, 1985; DeLorme, 1945).

Muscle hypertrophy due to strength training has been demonstrated in many animal experiments (Goldberg, 1968; Gonyea, 1980; Gutmann, Schiaffino and Hanzlikova, 1971; Hall-Craggs, 1970; Ianuzzo, Gollnick and Armstrong, 1976; James, 1973; Morpurgo, 1897; Reitsma, 1969; Van Linge, 1962), but in humans hypertrophy is usually evidenced from cross-sectional studies, where muscles from so-called normal subjects are compared with muscles from groups of subjects engaged, one way or another, in strength training. Muscle hypertrophy has only been measured in a few longitudinal studies. Ikai and Fukunaga (1970) found a 23% increase in the cross-sectional area of the elbow flexors after 100 days of isometric training, and Fukunaga (1976), in a similar study, found an increase of 9% after 60 days of training. Lüthi *et al.* (1986) found an 8.4% increase of the cross-sectional area of the vastus lateralis muscle after 6 weeks of dynamic, concentric training. Another example is a study by Moritani and DeVries (1979), who found that 8 weeks of dynamic, concentric training of the elbow flexors resulted in an increase in the cross-sectional area of 7%, estimated from circumference measurements of the upper arm.

All in all it is safe to conclude from the above that any type of prolonged strength training will result in a certain degree of muscle hypertrophy, and the question is then, how this hypertrophy takes place.

Muscle fibre hypertrophy and/or hyperplasia are, from a theoretical point of view, the possible explanations of whole muscle hypertrophy. In animal studies both possibilities have been put forward, and detailed discussion of these experiments has been given by e.g. Saltin and Gollnick (1983). These authors favour the hypothesis that muscle hypertrophy is caused by fibre hypertrophy rather than by hyperplasia, because the formation of new cells within the muscle could disturb, for example, the existing architecture of the muscle and reduce the capacity for neuromuscular co-ordination.

Cross-sectional studies on humans have shown that hypertrophy of muscles is most pronounced in sport events such as weight-lifting and body-building. However, it seems as if this hypertrophy is brought about in different ways. Weight-lifters seem to have similar percentages of the main fibre types – fast twitch (FT) and slow twitch (ST) – as normal subjects, but show a preferential hypertrophy of FT fibres (Gardiner, 1963; Gollnick et al., 1972; Prince, Hikida and Hagerman, 1976). This has also been evidenced in longitudinal studies on normal subjects, who trained with heavy, near maximal loads (Dons et al., 1979; Houston et al., 1983; MacDougall et al., 1980). On the other hand, there is experimental evidence that body-builders show no selective FT-fibre hypertrophy (MacDougall et al., 1982; Tesch and Larsson, 1982). Further it seems that whole muscle hypertrophy in body-builders cannot be explained by fibre hypertrophy alone (Schantz et al., 1981; Tesch and Larsson, 1982), unless it is assumed that body-builders from birth are endowed with a larger number of fibres than normal persons. But in a more recent study (MacDougall et al., 1984) body-builders seemed to have the same number of muscle fibres in the biceps brachii muscle as normal subjects. Finally the number of capillaries per fibre in elite body-builders is double that in normal subjects (Schantz, 1982).

The above differences are probably related to the fact, that while the aim of training for the body-builder is only hypertrophy (or 'bulk'), the weight-lifter is interested in development of muscle strength and power. Hence the training programme is quite different in the two sport events. Without going into details, a hypertrophy-training programme consists of many sets with loads usually not exceeding 8 RM. Some muscle groups are trained with loads as small as 20–30 RM, but all muscles are exercised to complete exhaustion, and usually beyond the point of exhaustion. In contrast the weight-lifters exercise with heavier loads (2–6 RM) and fewer sets, and high speed of contraction is constantly emphasized. However, there is some overlap in the training methods used by the two groups (MacQueen, 1954; Sale and MacDougall, 1984). It should be emphasized that heavy resistance training does not seem to change the fibre type distribution in the trained muscles (Edström and Ekblom, 1972; Gollnick *et al.*, 1972; Lüthi *et al.*, 1986; Tesch and Karlsson, 1985; Thorstensson *et al.*, 1976). However, cross-sectional studies have shown, that subjects engaged in explosive sport events such as sprint running, shot-put, etc. have a higher percentage of FT-fibres than normal subjects (Costill *et al.*, 1976; Gregor *et al.*, 1979; Thorstensson *et al.*, 1977) and long-term endurance training (distance running, orienteering) seems to imply a higher percentage of ST-fibres than normal (Costill *et al.*, 1976; Costill, Fink and Pollock, 1976; Gollnick *et al.*, 1972; Gregor *et al.*, 1979; Jansson and Kaijser, 1977).

2.3.2 Force per unit cross-sectional area

As previously mentioned it is generally agreed that the maximal force which can be developed by a muscle is closely related to the physiological, cross-sectional area of the muscle. The reason for this relation being that the cross-section of a muscle fibre reflects the number of functional units (myofibrils) in the fibre. This point of view is supported by the experiments of Ikai and Fukunaga (1968), who showed that the maximal voluntary strength of the arm flexor muscles in adults and children (males and females) were not significantly different when expressed as force per unit cross-sectional area (46 N cm^{-1}) although the individual variation was considerable (34–65 N cm^{-2}). Similar values have been reported by others (Haxton, 1944; Nygaard, 1981) and much lower values have been found in some experiments (Maughan, Watson and Weir, 1983a, b; Moritani and DeVries, 1979).

The prerequisite that an increase in maximal, voluntary muscle strength may be explained by an increase in cross-sectional area alone is that there is a proportional increase of both variables during training. In longitudinal training studies on man the percentage increase in muscle strength is often much greater than the percentage increase in cross-sectional area (e.g. Dons *et al.*, 1979; Ikai and Fukunaga, 1970; Jansson, Sjödin and Tesch, 1978; Lüthi *et al.*, 1986) and in some cases considerable strength improvements have been observed without any significant increase in cross-sectional area (DeCarvalho *et al.*, 1985; Moritani and DeVries, 1979; Penman, 1970). Thus, variables other than the cross-sectional area must influence the development of muscle strength. In animal experiments increase in strength has been associated with an increased density of the myofilaments in the muscle cells (e.g. Helander, 1961). In some experiments on humans, strength training did not result in changes in volume density of myofibrils (Lüthi *et al.*, 1986;

MacDougall *et al.*, 1979), but in one experiment (Penman, 1970) a significant increase in myosin filament diameter and concentration was observed, along with a smaller distance between myosin filaments and a decreased number of actin filaments in orbit around the myosin filaments.

It is difficult to explain the different and sometimes conflicting results, concerning the effect of strength training on the muscle tissue. Much of the discrepancy must be attributed to differences with regard to the type, duration and intensity of the training programme. Further it should be borne in mind that anatomical differences, and probably also differences in fibre type distribution between subjects will influence the ratio between the strength and the cross-sectional area of the muscles. Finally the estimation of muscle strength per unit cross-sectional area is based on the assumption that all motor units in a given muscle are maximally activated during a maximal voluntary contraction, which as we shall see, is not always the case.

2.3.3 Effect of strength training on 'neural factors'

In sports, maybe with the exception of body-building, strength training is used as a tool to improve performance. However, it is well known that there is no unambiguous relation between performance and muscle strength. Empirical evidence points at the importance of selection of the proper strength training method for optimal improvement in the sport in question. For instance it is obvious that the need for strength in events such as archery, weight-lifting and basketball must be fundamentally different. In other words, qualities such as skill and co-ordination are equally decisive for good performance as muscle strength, and in many sport events these qualities are of major importance. Some experimental evidence is discussed below to show the importance of 'neural factors' in the development of maximal muscular performance.

In untrained subjects a maximal, voluntary effort (e.g MVC) will normally not imply a full activation of the stimulated muscles. This has been demonstrated by Ikai, Yabe and Ischii (1967), who measured the isometric strength of the adductor muscles of the thumb during MVC and during electrical stimulation (ES) of the ulnar nerve. It was shown that ES resulted in a 30% increase in muscle strength as compared to MVC. It was further shown that the decrease in muscle strength during 100 repeated contractions (5 MVC alternating with one ES) was much more pronounced during MVC than during ES. This indicates that central nervous fatigue is more important than peripheral fatigue in the muscles for the decrease in strength seen during repeated muscle contractions.

In another experiment (Ikai and Steinhaus, 1961) a similar response was shown during 30 min repeated MVC of the elbow flexor muscles. The subjects were unwarned exposed to a shot from a starter's gun a few seconds before some of the MVCs. This resulted in a 7–8% increase in the recorded maximal strength. A similar effect (12% increase) was observed when the subjects were asked to shout during the MVC performance. Further, it was possible by means of hypnosis to manipulate the MVC up and down with a value corresponding to about 20–30% of the subjects' normal MVC. These observations give strong evidence that normal untrained subjects are not able to activate their muscles maximally, probably due to inhibitory factors in the central nervous system (CNS). Although the exact nature of this CNS inhibition is not known, it is generally accepted that it may be more or less overcome when a person is in an excessive state of apprehension or anger, or if the person is exposed to a period of strength training.

The neuromotor effect of strength training is illustrated in the above hypnosis experiments, where an experienced weight-lifter was not able to further increase his MVC during hypnosis, probably because he was already able to produce a maximal activation of his muscles during normal condition, due to a year-long weight-training period. The importance of 'neural factors' for the development of strength is also substantiated by the finding that the percentage increase in MVC during a period of strength training may be 4 to 10 times greater than the percentage increase in muscle cross-sectional area (Fukunaga, 1967; Ikai and Fukunaga, 1970).

The integrated electrical activity registered by means of surface electrodes over the active muscles (IEMG) is frequently used as a measure of the number of active motor units and/or the firing frequency to the motor units. Several experiments have shown that the increase seen in MVC after various types of strength training is associated with an increase in maximal IEMG (Häkkinen and Komi, 1983, 1985a; Komi *et al.*, 1978; Moritani and DeVries, 1979) which implies that the increase in MVC during training to some extent is due to a more efficient activation of the motor pool (cf. Figure 2.1). This 'motor-learning' effect seems to be of major importance for the initial, rapid, strength increment seen during a training period (Häkkinen, Komi and Tesch, 1981; Moritani and DeVries, 1979) (see Figure 2.5).

The role of neural factors in the development of strength is also exemplified by the following findings

1. The improvement in MVC is much less when strength is tested in an 'unfamiliar' position, e.g. a joint angle or a body position which is different from the one which was used during training (Dons *et al.*, 1979; Lindh, 1979; Meyers, 1967; Rasch and Morehouse, 1957).

2. Training of only one limb results in an increase in strength in the untrained limb. This increase in strength in the contralateral limb is always less than the increase in the trained limb and is never associated with muscle hypertrophy (Coleman, 1969; Houston *et al.*, 1983; Ikai and Fukunaga, 1970; Meyers, 1967; Moritani and DeVries, 1979; Rasch and Morehouse, 1957).

3. In normal subjects the MVC during leg extension with both legs is less than the sum of the MVC of right and left leg (Asmussen, Heebøll-Nielsen and Molbeck, 1959; Secher, Rörsgaard and Secher, 1978; Vandervoort, Sale and Moroz, 1984). Probably, the same type of phenomenon has been observed during vertical jumping, where the sum of the jumping height with right and left leg was 17% higher than the jumping height reached in two-legged jumps (Van Soest *et al.*, 1985). Bilateral strength training will reverse this picture so that MVC during extension with both legs becomes greater than the sum of right and left leg extension MVC (Secher, 1975).

4. As mentioned earlier, the influence of strength training on the force–velocity curve is greatly dependent on the type of training. All types of training will shift the curve to the right (Figure 2.4), but isometric training will bring this shift about by an elevation of the MVC without a change in maximal velocity (zero load), while training with smaller loads at high velocities will increase maximal velocity without an increase in MVC (Duchateau and Hainaut, 1984; Kaneko *et al.*, 1983).

The above observations are usually allocated to changes in the CNS and phenomena such as impulse irradiation, selective fibre type recruitment, central inhibition, motor unit synchronization, and so on, have been used to explain the mechanisms behind the effect of strength training, although none of these factors are as yet completely understood. Other phenomena such as increased muscle excitability and shortening of contraction time (Schmidtbleicher and Haralambie, 1981), reflex potentiation (Sale *et al.*, 1982) and decreased reflex EMG/force ratio (Häkkinen and Komi, 1983) further point at various peripheral neuromuscular effects of strength training. A detailed discussion of all these phenomena has recently been given by Komi (1986) who emphasized that force development within a very short time is characteristic to most normal movements and is essential in most sport activities. A high rate of force development, obtained during strength training, implies a high degree of synchronization of impulses to the motor units and especially activation of all high-threshold units, combined with an improved reaction from the muscle spindles and the Golgi tendon organs.

It is a great concern to many coaches as to how they can use the information from strength training experiments carried out in laboratories all over the world. Here it should be pointed out that one of the most valuable conclusions, which can be drawn from the experimental evidence presented in this chapter, is the specificity of strength training. This means that strength training of the different muscle groups should be carried out in a way which resembles the activity and movements which are specific for the sport in question. Thus an archer should use isometric training to obtain improved stability of arms and shoulder; in high and long jumping unilateral, explosive, dynamic training is essential to improve the performance of the preferred leg for jumping, while bilateral training of the legs (and arms) are essential in rowing, etc. The PRE-principle should always be used (Figure 2.5), with few repetitions and high resistance. In young, healthy sportsmen and women the loads should never be less than 70% MVC, and high speed during each contraction should ensure maximal activation of most motor units in the muscles. The optimum frequency of training and rest is not well investigated in laboratory experiments. However, expirical evidence suggests that this optimum depends on the muscle mass involved in the training, and the individual state of training.

The principles described above are also valid in sport events where improvement of muscle strength is a goal in itself, such as in weight-lifting. However, in such events, where the whole muscle mass of the body is involved, a sufficient anabolism of bones, tendons and muscles becomes an essential and limiting factor. Further, the optimal balance between the amount of training given to the different muscle groups is essential for the optimum improvement in weight-lifting. Such differentiated strength training can only be effective after years of training, and the method used to obtain the right balance of strength between the muscle groups is different from one person to another. It must be concluded that, even though our knowledge about the physiological nature of strength increment due to training has improved considerably during the last decades, there are still a lot of questions to be solved. Unfortunately the exploration of the area has suffered because of the lack of a sufficient dialogue between scientists and people who are professionals in the practical field of strength training.

REFERENCES

Armstrong, R.B. (1984) Mechanisms of exercise-induced delayed onset muscular soreness: a brief review. *Medicine and Science in Sports and Exercise*, **16**, 529–538.

Asmussen, E. and Bonde-Petersen, F. (1974) Storage of elastic energy in skeletal muscle of man. *Acta Physiologica Scandinavica*, **91**, 385–392.

Asmussen, E., Heebøll-Nielsen, K. and Molbeck, S. (1959) Methods for evaluation of muscle strength. Communications No. **5**, 3–13.

Berger, R. (1962a) Effect of varied training programs on strength. *Research Quarterly*, **33**, 168–181.

Berger, R. (1962b) Optimum repetitions for the development of strength. *Research Quarterly*, **33**, 334–338.

Berger, R. (1962c) Comparison of static and dynamic strength increases. *Research Quarterly*, **33**, 329–333.

Berger, R. (1963) Comparative effects of three weight-training programs. *Research Quarterly*, **34**, 396–398.

Berger, R. (1967) Effect of maximum loads for each of ten repetitions on strength improvement. *Research Quarterly*, **38**, 715–718.

Blattner, S.E. and Noble, L. (1979) Relative effects of isokinetic and plyometric training on vertical jumping performance. *Research Quarterly*, **50**, 583–588.

Bosco, C., Viitasalo, J.T., Komi, P.V. and Luhtanen, P. (1982) Combined effect of elastic energy and myoelectrical potentiation during stretch–shortening cycle exercise. *Acta Physiologica Scandinavica*, **114**, 557–565.

Bosco, C., Zanon, S., Rusko, H., Dal Monte, A., Bellotti, P., Latteri, F., Candeloro, N., Locatelli, E., Azzaro, E., Pozzo, R. and Bonomi, S. (1984) The influence of extra load on the mechanical behavior of skeletal muscle. *European Journal of Applied Physiology*, **53**, 149–154.

Ciaozzo, V., Perrine, J. and Edgerton, R. (1980) Alterations in the *in vivo* force–velocity relationship. *Medicine and Science in Sports and Exercise*, **12**, 134.

Clarke, D.H. (1973) Adaptations in strength and muscular endurance resulting from exercise, in *Exercise and Sport Sciences Reviews*, (ed. J.H. Wilmore), Academic Press, New York, Vol 1, pp. 74–98.

Coleman, E.A. (1969) Effect of unilateral isometric and isotonic contractions on the strength of the contralateral limb. *Research Quarterly*, **40**, 490–495.

Costill, D.L., Daniels, J., Evans, W., Fink, W., Krahenbuhl, G. and Saltin, B. (1976) Skeletal muscle enzymes and fiber composition in male and female track athletes. *Journal of Applied Physiology*, **40**, 149–154.

Costill, D.L., Fink, W.J. and Pollock, M.L. (1976) Muscle fiber composition and enzyme activities of elite distance runners. *Medicine and Science in Sports and Exercise*, **8**, 96–100.

Coyle, E. and Feiring, D. (1980) Muscular power improvements: Specificity of training velocity. *Medicine and Science in Sports and Exercise*, **12**, 134.

Darcus, H.D. (1953) A strain-gauges dynamometer for measuring the strength of muscle contraction and for re-education muscle. *Annals of Physical Medicine* (London), **1**, 163–176.

Davies, C.T. and Young, K. (1983) Effect of training at 30 and at 100% maximal isometric force (MVC) on the contractile properties of the triceps surae in man. *Journal of Physiology*, **336**, 22–23P.

DeCarvalho, A., Jørgensen, J., Schibye, B., Klausen, K. and Holst Andersen, A. (1985) Controlled ultrasonographic measurements of cross-sectional areas of quadriceps muscle submitted to dynamic strength training. *Journal of Sports Medicine and Physical Fitness*, **25**, 251–254.

DeLorme, T.L. (1945) Restoration of muscle power by heavy-resistance exercises. *Journal of Bone and Joint Surgery*, **27**, 645–667.

Dons, B., Bollerup, K., Bonde-Petersen, F. and Hancke, S. (1979) The effect of weight-lifting exercise related to muscle fibre composition and muscle cross-sectional area in humans. *European Journal of Applied Physiology*, **40**, 95–106.

Duchateau, J. and Hainaut, J. (1984) Isometric or dynamic training: differential effect on mechanical properties of a human muscle. *Journal of Applied Physiology*, **56**, 296–301.

Edström, L. and Ekblom, B. (1972) Differences in sizes of red and white muscle fibres in vastus lateralis of musculus quadriceps femoris of normal individuals and athletes. Relation to physical performance. *Scandinavian Journal of Clinical and Laboratory Investigation*, **30**, 175–181.

Farrell, M. and Richards, J.G. (1986) Analysis of the reliability and validity of the kinetic communicator exercise device. *Medicine and Science in Sports and Exercise*, **18**, 44–49.

Fridén, J., Seger, J., Sjöström, M. and Ekblom, B. (1983) Adaptive response in human skeletal muscle subjected to prolonged eccentric training. *International Journal of Sports Medicine*, **4**, 177–183.

Fukunaga, T. (1976) Die absolute Muskelkraft und das Muskelkrafttraining. *Sportartz und Sportmedizin*, **11**, 255–265.

Gardiner, G. (1963) Specificity of strength changes of exercised and nonexercised limbs following isometric training. *Research Quarterly*, **34**, 98–101.

Goldberg, A.L. (1968) Protein synthesis during work-induced growth of skeletal muscle. *Journal of Cell Biology*, **36**, 653–658.

Goldberg, A.L., Etlinger, J.F., Goldspink, D.F. and Jablecki, C. (1975) Mechanism of work-induced hypertrophy of skeletal muscle. *Medicine and Science in Sports and Exercise*, **7**, 185–198.

Goldspink, D.F. (1977) The influence of activity on muscle size and protein turnover. *Journal of Physiology*, **264**, 283–296.

Gollnick, P.D., Armstrong, R.B., Saubert IV, C.W., Piehl, K. and Saltin, B. (1972) Enzyme activity and fiber composition in skeletal muscle of untrained and trained men. *Journal of Applied Physiology*, **33**, 312–319.

Gonyea, W.J. (1980) Role of exercise in inducing increases in skeletal muscle fiber number. *Journal of Applied Physiology*, **48**, 421–426.

Gregor, R.J., Edgerton, V.R., Perrine, J.J., Campion, D.S. and Debus, C. (1979) Torque velocity relationship and muscle fiber composition in elite female athletes. *Journal of Applied Physiology*, **47**, 388–392.

Gutmann, E., Schiaffino, S. and Hanzlikova, V. (1971) Mechanism of compensatory hypertrophy in skeletal muscle of the rat. *Experimental Neurology*, **31**, 451–464.

Häkkinen, K. and Komi, P.V. (1983) Changes in neuromuscular performance in voluntary and reflex contraction during strength training in man. *International Journal of Sports Medicine*, **4**, 282–288.

Häkkinen, K. and Komi, P.V. (1985a) Changes in electrical and mechanical behavior of leg extensor muscles during heavy resistance strength training. *Scandinavian Journal of Sports Science*, **7**, 55–64.

Häkkinen, K. and Komi, P.V. (1985b) Effect of explosive type strength training on electromyographic and force production characteristics of leg extensor muscles during concentric and various stretch-shortening cycle exercises. *Scandinavian Journal of Sports Science*, **7**, 65–76.

Häkkinen, K., Komi, P.V. and Tesch, P.A. (1981) Effect of combined concentric and eccentric strength training and detraining on force-time, muscle fiber and metabolic characteristics of leg extensor muscles. *Scandinavian Journal of Sports Science*, **3**, 50–58.

Hall-Craggs, E.C.B. (1970) The longitudinal division of fibres in overloaded rat skeletal muscle. *Journal of Anatomy*, **107**, 459–470.

Hansen, J.W. (1963) The effect of sustained isometric muscle contraction on various muscle functions. *Arbeitsphysiologie, Internationale Zeitschrift für Angew Physiologie*, **19**, 430–434.

Hansen, J.W. (1967) Effect of dynamic training on the isometric endurance of the elbow flexors. *Arbeitsphysiologie, Internationale Zeitschrift für Angew Physiologie*, **23**, 367–370.

Haxton, H.A. (1944) Absolute muscle force in the ankle flexors of man. *Journal of Physiology London*, **103**, 267–273.

Helander, E.A.S. (1961) Influence of exercise and restricted activity on the protein composition of skeletal muscle. *Biochemical Journal*, **78**, 478–482.

Hettinger, T. (1961) *Physiology of Strength*, Charles C. Thomas, Springfield, Illinois, USA.

Hettinger, T. and Müller, E.A. (1953) Muskelleistung und Muskeltraining. *Arbeitsphysiologie, Internationale Zeitschrift für Angew Physiologie*, **15**, 111–126.

Hoppeler, H. (1986) Exercise-induced ultrastructural changes in skeletal muscle. *International Journal of Sports Medicine*, **7**, 187–204.

Houston, M.E., Froese, E.A., Valeriote, St P., Green, H.J. and Ranney, D.A. (1983) Muscle performance, morphology and metabolic capacity during strength training and detraining: a one leg model. *European Journal of Applied Physiology*, **51**, 25–35.

Ianuzzo, C.D., Gollnick, P.D. and Armstrong, R.B. (1976) Compensatory adaptations of skeletal muscle fibre types to a long-term functional overload. *Life Science*, **19**, 1517–1524.

Ikai, M. and Steinhaus, A.H. (1961) Some factors modifying the expression of human strength. *Journal of Applied Physiology*, **16**, 157–163.

Ikai, M. and Fukunaga, T. (1968) Calculation of muscle strength per unit cross-sectional area of human muscle by means of ultrasonic measurement. *Internationale Zeitschrift für Angew Physiologie*, **26**, 26–32.

Ikai, M. and Fukunaga, T. (1970) A study of training effect on strength per unit cross-sectional area of muscle by means of ultrasonic measurement. *Internationale Zeitschrift für Angew Physiologie*, **28**, 173–180.

Ikai, M., Yabe, K. and Ischii, K. (1967) Muskelkraft und muskuläre Ermüdung bei willkürlicher Anspannung und electrischer Reizung des Muskels. *Sportartz und Sportmedizin*, **5**, 197–201.

James, N.I. (1973) Compensatory hypertrophy in the extensor digitorum longus muscle of the rat. *Journal of Anatomy*, **116**, 57–65.

Jansson, E. and Kaijser, L. (1977) Muscle adaptation to extreme endurance training in man. *Acta Physiologica Scandinavica*, **100**, 315–324.

Jansson, E., Sjödin, B. and Tesch, P. (1978) Changes in muscle fibre type distribution in man after physical training. *Acta Physiologica Scandinavica*, **104**, 235–237.

Johnson, B.L., Adamczyk, J.W., Tennøe, K.O. and Strømme, S.B. (1976) A comparison of concentric and eccentric muscle training. *Medicine and Science in Sports and Exercise*, **8**, 35–38.

Kaneko, M., Fuchimoto, T., Toji, H. and Suei, K. (1983) Training effect of different loads on the force–velocity relationship and mechanical power output in human muscle. *Scandinavian Journal of Sports Science*, **5**, 50–55.

Komi, P.V. (1986) Training of muscle strength and power: interaction of neuromotoric, hypertrophic and mechanical factors. *International Journal of Sports Medicine*, **7**, suppl., 10–15.

Komi, P.V., Viitasalo, J.I., Rauramaa, R. and Vihko, V. (1978) Effect of isometric strength training on mechanical, electrical and metabolic aspects of muscle function. *European Journal of Applied Physiology*, **40**, 45–55.

Krotkiewski, M., Anianson, A., Grimby, G., Björntorp, P. and Sjöström, L. (1979) The effect of unilateral isokinetic strength training on local adipose and muscle tissue morphology, thickness, and enzymes. *European Journal of Applied Physiology*, **42**, 271–281.

Laycoe, R.R. and Marteniuk, R.G. (1971) Learning and tension as factors in static strength gains produced by static and eccentric training. *Research Quarterly*, **42**, 299–306.

Lesmes, G.R., Costill, D.L., Coyle E.F. and Fink, W.Y. (1978) Muscle strength and power changes during maximal isokinetic training. *Medicine and Science in Sports and Exercise*, **10**, 266–269.

Lindh, M. (1979) Increase of muscle strength from isometric quadriceps exercises at different knee angles. *Scandinavian Journal of Rehabilitation Medicine*, **11**, 33–36.

Lüthi, J.M., Howald, H., Claassen, H., Rösler, K., Vock, P. and Hoppeler, H. (1986) Structural changes in skeletal muscle tissue with heavy-resistance exercise. *International Journal of Sports Medicine*, **7**, 123–127.

MacDougall, J.D., Elder, G.C.B., Sale, D.G., Moroz, J.R. and Sutton, J.R. (1980) Effects of strength training and immobilization of human muscle fibres. *European Journal of Applied Physiology*, **43**, 25–34.

MacDougall, J.D., Sale, D.G., Alway, S.E. and Sutton, J.R. (1984) Muscle fiber number in biceps brachii in body-builders and control subjects. *Journal of Applied Physiology*, **57**, 1399–1403.

MacDougall, J.D., Sale, D.G., Elder, G.C.B. and Sutton, J.R. (1982) Muscle ultrastructural characteristics of elite powerlifters and body-builders. *European Journal of Applied Physiology*, **48**, 117–126.

MacDougall, J.D., Sale, D.G., Moroz, J.R., Elder, G.C.B., Sutton, J.R. and Howald, H. (1979) Mitochondrial volume density in human skeletal muscle following heavy resistance training. *Medicine and Science in Sports and Exercise*, **11**, 164–166.

MacDougall, J.D., Ward, G.R., Sale, D.G. and Sutton, J.R. (1977) Biochemical adaptation of human skeletal muscle to heavy resistance training and immobilization. *Journal of Applied Physiology*, **43**, 700–703.

MacQueen, I.J. (1954) Recent advances in the technique of progressive resistance exercise. *British Medical Journal*, **2**, 1193–1198.

Manz, R.L., Carnes, R.L. and Carnes, V.B. (1983) *The Hydra-Fitness Manual for Omnikinetic Training*, Hydra-Fitness Industries Inc., Canada.

Maughan, R.J., Watson, J.S. and Weir, J. (1983a) Relationships between muscle strength and muscle cross-sectional area in male sprinters and endurance runners. *European Journal of Applied Physiology*, **50**, 309–318.

Maughan, R.J., Watson, J.S. and Weir, J. (1983b) Strength and cross-sectional area of human skeletal muscle. *Journal of Physiology, London*, **338**, 37–49.

McDonagh, M.J.N. and Davies, C.T.M. (1984) Adaptive response of mammalian skeletal muscle to exercise with high loads. *European Journal of Applied Physiology*, **52**, 139–155.

Meyers, C.R. (1967) Effects of two isometric routines on strength, size and endurance in exercised and nonexercised arms. *Research Quarterly*, 38, 430–440.

Moritani, T. and DeVries, H.A. (1979) Neural factors versus hypertrophy in the time course of muscle strength gain. *American Journal of Physical Medicine*, **58**, 115–130.

Morpurgo, B. (1897) Über Aktivitäts-Hypertrophie der willkürlichen Muskeln. *Virchows Archiv. Pathological Anatomy and Physiology*, **150**, 522–554.

Müller, E.A. and Rohmert, W. (1963) Die Geschwindigkeit der Muskelkraft-Zunahme bei isometrischem Training. *Internationale Zeitschrift für Angew Physiologie*, **19**, 403–419.

Newham, D.J., Jones, D.A. and Edwards, R.H.T. (1983) Large delayed plasma creatine kinase changes after stepping exercise. *Muscle and Nerve*, **6**, 380–385.

Newham, D.J., Mills, K.R., Quigley, B.M. and Edwards, R.H.T. (1983) Pain and fatigue after concentric and eccentric muscle contractions. *Clinical Science*, **64**, 55–62.

Nygaard, E. (1981) Morfologi og funktion i m.biceps brachii, Thesis, University of Copenhagen.

Penman, K.A. (1970) Human striated muscle ultrastructural changes accompanying increased strength without hypertrophy. *Research Quarterly*, **41**, 418–424.

Perrine, J.J. and Edgerton, V.R. (1978) Muscle force–velocity and power–velocity relationships under isokinetic loading. *Medicine and Science in Sports and Exercise*, **10**, 159–166.

Petersen, F.B. (1960) Muscle training by static, concentric and eccentric contractions. *Acta Physiologica Scandinavica*, **48**, 406–416.

Pipes, T.V. (1978) Variable resistance versus constant resistance strength training in adult males. *European Journal of Applied Physiology*, **39**, 27–35.

Prince, F.P., Hikida, R.S. and Hagerman, F.C. (1976) Human muscle fiber types in power lifters, distance runners and untrained subjects. *Pfligers Archiv.*, **363**, 19–26.

Rasch, P.J. and Morehouse, L.E. (1957) Effect of static and dynamic exercises on muscular strength and hypertrophy. *Journal of Applied Physiology*, **11**, 29–34.

Reitsma, W. (1969) Skeletal muscle hypertrophy after heavy exercise in rats with surgically reduced muscle function. *American Journal of Physical Medicine*, **48**, 237–258.

Sale, D.G. and MacDougall, J.D. (1984) Isokinetic strength in weight trainers. *European Journal of Applied Physiology*, **53**, 128–132.

Sale, D.G., McComas, J., MacDougall, J.D. and Upton, A.R.M. (1982) Neuromuscular adaptation in human thenar muscles following strength training and immobilization. *Journal of Applied Physiology*, **53**, 419–424.

Saltin, B. and Gollnick, P.D. (1983) Skeletal muscle adaptability: significance for metabolism and performance, in *Handbook of Physiology*, Section 10, *Skeletal Muscle* (eds. L.D. Peachy and R.H. Adrian), pp. 555–631.

Sapega, A.A., Nicholas, J.A., Sokolow, D. and Saraniti, A. (1982) The nature of torque 'overshoot' in Cybex isokinetic dynamometry. *Medicine and Science in Sports and Exercise*, **14**, 368–375.

Schantz, P. (1982) Capillary supply in hypertrophied human skeletal muscle. *Acta Physiologica Scandinavica*, **114**, 635–637.

Schantz, P., Randall Fox, E., Norgren, P. and Tyden, A. (1981) The relationship between the mean muscle fibre area and the muscle cross-sectional area of the thigh in subjects with large differences in thigh girth. *Acta Physiologica Scandinavica*, **113**, 537–539.

Schmidtbleicher, D. and Haralambie, G. (1981) Changes in contractile properties of muscle after strength training in man. *European Journal of Applied Physiology*, **46**, 221–228.

Secher, N.H. (1975) Isometric rowing strength of experienced and inexperienced oarsmen. *Medicine and Science in Sports and Exercise*, **7**, 280–283.

Secher, N.H., Rörsgaard, S. and Secher, O. (1978) Contralateral influence on recruitment of curarized muscle fibers during maximal voluntary extension of the legs. *Acta Physiologica Scandinavica*, **103**, 456–462.

Tesch, P.A. and Larsson, L. (1982) Muscle hypertrophy in body-builders. *European Journal of Applied Physiology*, **49**, 301–306.

Tesch, P.A. and Karlsson, J. (1985) Muscle fiber types and size in trained and untrained muscles of elite athletes. *Journal of Applied Physiology*, **59**, 1716–1720.

Thistle, H.G., Hislop, H.J., Moffroid, M. and Lohman, E.W. (1967) Isokinetic contraction: a new concept of resistive exercise. *Archives of Physical Medicine and Rehabilitation*, **48**, 279–282.

Thorstensson, A., Grimby, G. and Karlsson, J. (1976) Force–velocity relations and fiber composition in human knee extensor muscles. *Journal of Applied Physiology*, **40**, 12–16.

Thorstensson, A., Hulten, B., von Döbeln, W. and Karlsson, J. (1976) Effect of strength training on enzyme activities and fibre characteristics in human skeletal muscle. *Acta Physiologica Scandinavica*, **96**, 392–398.

Thorstensson, A., Larsson, L., Tesch, P. and Karlsson, J. (1977) Muscle strength and fiber composition in athletes and sedentary men. *Medicine and Science in Sports and Exercise*, **9**, 26–30.

Thorstensson, A., Oddsson, L., Karlsson, E. and Seger, J. (1986) Does acceleration influence the force–velocity relationship of concentric and eccentric contractions? *Medicine and Science in Sports and Exercise*, **18** (2 suppl.), S63.

Van Linge, B. (1962) The response of muscle to strenuous exercise. *Journal of Bone and Joint Surgery*, **44B**, 711–721.

Van Soest, A.J., Roebroeck, M.E., Bobbert, M.F., Huijing, P.A. and Van Ingen Schenau, G.J. (1985) A comparison of one-legged and two-legged counter-movement jumps. *Medicine and Science in Sports and Exercise*, **17**, 635–639.

Vandervoort, A.A., Sale, D.G. and Moroz, J. (1984) Comparison of motor unit activation during unilateral and bilateral leg extension. *Journal of Applied Physiology*, **56**, 46–51.

Yates, J.W. and Kamon, E. (1983) A comparison of peak and constant angle torque–velocity curves in fast- and slow-twitch populations. *European Journal of Applied Physiology*, **51**, 67–74.

Part Two
Locomotive Sports

3
Sprinting

P.F. Radford

3.1 INTRODUCTION

The word 'sprinting' is used in modern sport to describe behaviour as different as a runner racing flat-out over the last 150 m of a 10 000 m race, a tennis player running flat-out to return a drop-shot at the end of the fifth set of a tennis match, a schoolboy or girl running 100 m in the school sports, and a rugby forward running short bursts of 10–15 m as part of his or her training. Used in this way, the word 'sprinting' is a relative expression conveying the sense that someone is trying to run as fast as possible in the circumstances, even though the circumstances may not always be favourable to running at great speed, nor the performer particularly suited to the activity.

This use of the word 'sprinting' to convey the relative intensity of effort in running is unsatisfactory from the sports scientist's point of view. Many of the factors that tend to limit the performance of a 10 000 m runner who attempts to 'sprint' after nearly half an hour of continuous exercise, or a tennis player who attempts to 'sprint' after two to three hours of intermittent work, are quite different from the factors that operate when an elite sprinter comes fresh to the start of a 100 m race.

To make matters even more confusing, the word 'sprinting' is commonly used to describe fast and relatively short efforts in a whole range of other activities including swimming, skating, canoeing and cycling, in which the relative intensity and duration of the activity varies considerably.

For the purpose of this chapter it will be necessary to focus specifically on one particular form of sprinting and I have selected the widely known 'pure' version of sprinting – running a 100 m race in a track and field competition and the sprinters (male and female) who excel at it.

This should provide a useful model for other similar types of intensive short-duration activities in sport.

Anyone approaching this subject area for the first time should be cautious. Many studies over the past half-century have used as their subjects non-sprinters, or sprinters out of season, or sprinters in laboratory settings. Relatively few of the hundreds of published studies have examined elite men and women sprinters performing in genuine competitive situations. Those who live in the world of the elite sprinter know just how unwise it is to generalize from observations on the usual club or college runner, or even from the elite sprinters unless they are at their competitive best.

3.2 THE SPRINTERS

3.2.1 Anthropometry (males)

Sprinters come in a remarkable range of shapes and sizes. Elite male sprinters have ranged in height from 1.57 m to 1.90 m and in weight from 63.4 kg to 90 kg (Tanner, 1964; Hoffman, 1971; Khosla, 1978). They are on average the heaviest of all runners, but not the tallest, and the majority are significantly mesomorphic, and in relation to their skeletal dimensions they tend to be more heavily muscled than runners in other events. Tanner (1964) concluded that elite male sprinters were naturally endowed with large muscles, rather than having developed them by training. A large muscle mass may confer some advantages at the start of the race and in the early stages of acceleration, as the larger the cross-sectional area of a muscle the greater the forces it can develop (Ikai and Fukunaga, 1968). Before the body has developed any great forward velocity, absolute muscular strength can play its largest part. It is probably for this reason that the more heavily muscled sprinters do well at this stage: later in the race having the right type of muscles and the necessary skill and neuromuscular organization may be more important than muscle size.

In running 100 m the elite males take between 44 and 53 strides at a rate from 4.23 to 5.05 strides per second, with the sprinters having the longest legs producing the greatest stride lengths and the slowest striding rates compared with other elite male sprinters. In the Second World Athletics Championships in Rome in 1987, the eight finalists in the 100 m had a mean of 45.69 strides at a mean rate of 4.59 strides s^{-1} (Moravec et al., 1988). If a sprinter's legs are above an optimal length he will find it increasingly difficult to produce the rapid leg cadence that seems to be a prerequisite for good sprinting (Hoffman, 1971).

3.2.2 Anthropometry (females)

Female sprinters typically range in height from 1.57 m to 1.78 m, and in weight from 51.0 kg to 71.0 kg (Hoffman, 1972; Khosla and McBroom, 1984). They too, like the males, are the heaviest runners, but not the tallest.

In running 100 m, however, they use their physical resources quite differently from the males. Like the males, the females too take between 44 and 53 strides to run 100 m, and their typical rate of striding from 4.0 to nearly 5.0 strides s^{-1} is also very similar to their male counterparts. In the 1987 World Championships in Rome, the finalists averaged 49.35 strides which was 8% more than the males, but their mean rate of striding was 4.54 strides s^{-1} which was very similar to the males. As the leg length and standing height of elite female sprinters is less than their male counterparts, it is not surprising that their maximum stride length is shorter: 2.05–2.30 m compared with 2.17–2.40 m for the males. It is, however, sometimes misleading to talk of mean values for stride rate and stride length, for each sprinter runs the race with his or her own unique blend. There are, however, some interesting overall differences between males and females. In particular it should be noted that in comparison with males of the same leg length the female elite sprinters run with a markedly slower striding rate (Hoffman, 1972). Nevertheless the same general trend exists as for the males: the tallest sprinters run with the longest strides and the slowest rates, and the shortest run with shorter strides and the faster rates of striding.

Hoffman (1972) summarized the differences this way: 'The best female sprinters when compared with male sprinters of the same class, height, leg length and stride length, run about one second slower over 100 metres because of markedly lower frequencies of stride'.

Whether this relatively lower stride rate is because of overall lower levels of strength, or because of differences in muscle ultrastructure, fibre type distribution, or the series elastic component, between the females and males is not known, but the message to the coaches should be clear. Female elite sprinters do not run as their male counterparts do, and attention needs to be paid to their particular training needs.

3.2.3 Muscle

After even the most cursory examination of 100 m sprinters, it becomes clear that their special talents revolve around their ability to produce very large forces, very rapidly. Mero et al. (1981) examined the force production of sprinters in three different ability groups (100 m = 10.7, 11.1 and 11.5 s respectively). The fastest sprinters had 66.2% of fast-twitch fibres (FT or Type II), the intermediate group had 62.0% Type II and the slowest group 50.4% in their vastus lateralis muscles. In the average human vastus lateralis muscle, men have been found on average to be slightly below, and women slightly above, 50% Type II fibres (Komi and Karlsson, 1978).

Finding a large percentage of Type II fibres in sprinters' muscles should not come as a surprise for their presence confers both metabolic and mechanical advantages for running 100 metres. In the first 2–3 s of the sprint race, muscles increase their rate of fuel utilization one thousand fold (Newsholme and Start, 1973; Margaria, 1966) and power output and ATP turnover reaches its peak (Cheetham *et al.*, 1986; Boobis *et al.*, 1987). Metabolically, Type II fibres are well equipped for the rapid production of energy, possessing a high level of stored energy in the form of creatine phosphate, and the ability to rapidly convert muscle glycogen to lactic acid and so generate the ATP required for muscle contraction. Mechanically, these fibres can deliver very considerable forces in a very short period of time, possessing as they do much shorter contraction times than Type I fibres and the capability of producing much greater maximum tension. The main contractile difference between Type II and Type I fibres, however, is in the differences in the rates of hydrolysis of the myosin ATPase, but the maximum tension that a muscle fibre can achieve is a function of the number of actin and myosin filaments and the number of cross-bridges formed, regardless of the ATPase activity. There are, however, disadvantages: Type II fibres rapidly become fatigued and many of these fibres tend to remain unrecruited in all but the most intensive efforts. Type II fibres come in two main subtypes; and sprinters possess not only more of the Type IIb, which is the classic 'sprint' type, easily fatigued but capable of high tension and short contraction time, and which are recruited in rapid and powerful movements; they also possess an unusually large number of Type IIa fibres. These, although of the FT type, are reddish in colour and have better endurance capabilities than the other Type II fibres. Mero *et al.* (1981) found nearly 28% Type IIb fibres and nearly 40% IIa in their best sprinters.

The presence of Type II fibres is important at the start, during acceleration and at top speed. Mero, Luhtanen and Komi (1983) found a close relationship between acceleration velocity at the start and the presence of Type II fibres, and Mero *et al.* (1981) found that the percentage of Type II fibres correlated positively and significantly with maximum running velocity and stride rate, and negatively with the sprinters' best time over 100 m.

The role that the two subtypes of the Type II fibres play is perhaps hinted at in the findings of Mero *et al.* (1981), that the number of Type IIb fibres correlates negatively with muscle endurance ($r = - 0.60$; $P < 0.01$), and the number of Type IIa fibres correlated positively with stride rate

($r = 0.41$; $P <0.05$). Thus it seems that the presence of a high percentage of Type IIb together with other Type II fibres, may guarantee a fast start, but that Type IIa fibres may be needed to achieve very fast leg speed which tends to peak later in the race. The presence of a large number of Type IIa fibres would, however, be of particular importance to a 200 m or 400 m runner.

The principal metabolic differences between Type IIa and IIb are mainly in their enzyme concentrations. Type IIa have much higher concentrations of mitochondrial oxidative enzymes.

For the first few seconds of the race the intensity of the muscular work is so great that ATP is provided not only by the breakdown of the stored creatine phosphate, but also by the processes of glycolysis and glycogenolysis (Boobis, Williams and Wootton, 1983; Sjöholm et al., 1983; Jacobs, 1987). The relative contribution made by these processes during the first 2–3 s of a 100 m race is still not clear. It seems likely, however, that by about 5 s and before acceleration is over, it is by the process of glycolysis that energy is mainly supplied to complete the race, and although both Type IIa and IIb fibres have high concentrations of glycolytic enzymes, the higher resistance to fatigue of the Type IIa fibres may indicate that it is on these that the sprinters rely during the latter stages of the race.

It is now a familiar and predictable observation that elite male sprinters have a greater percentage of Type II fibres and that these fibres represent a greater cross-sectional area than for non-elite males. Further it is now usual to relate a sprinter's success to the presence of these fibres with their characteristics of high force generation and relatively rapid fatigability (Kotz and Koryak, 1984). It should be pointed out, however, that these observations are based on *male* sprinters; data demonstrating the same relationship between Type II fibres and the mechanical and metabolic characteristics of female sprinters are lacking. Gender differences are not well explored for sprinting, but evidence is growing for other populations that the interrelationships between fibre type, muscle elasticity, fatigue, muscular power and running speed are not the same for females as for males (Komi and Karlsson, 1978; Gregor et al., 1979; Miyashita and Kanehisa, 1979; Jacobs and Tesch, 1981; Karlsson and Jacobs, 1981; Komi, 1981; Morrow and Hosler, 1981; Cheetham et al., 1986).

3.2.4 Neuromuscular organization

For sprinters to be successful they must have the right sort of muscles, but they must also have the right sort of nervous system to drive them. Discussion of muscle fibre types of sprinters tends to draw attention away from the fact that muscle fibres are only part of an individual motor unit that consists of the motor nerve cell in the spinal cord, the motor nerve fibre to the muscle, the end-plate or junction between the nerve fibre and the muscle, and the colony of muscle fibres innervated by the motor nerve. The large forces produced by the sprinters are not merely the result of the mechanics or bioenergetics of contraction, they are also the result of the number, size, and speed of the motor units recruited, the synchrony of their firing and their excitability (Upton and Radford, 1976).

Upton and Radford (1976) conducted extensive neurophysiological investigations on elite sprinters; these failed to reveal any significant differences in nerve conduction velocities, or the number of motor units, between sprinters and controls. The potentiated 'late' responses of three selected muscles were, however, significantly better in sprinters than controls. Such a result could have arisen from increased motoneurone excitability or more synchronous firing of the units taking part in the late response, suggesting that the CNS as well as the muscle plays a major part in the sprinter's success. The difference in motoneurone excitability between elite sprinters and controls was significant ($P < 0.001$).

Elite sprinters seem to have central nervous systems that are particularly suited to making fast, alternating movements, even when insignificant forces are involved. There is ample evidence that they can run with faster striding rates than others (Radford and Upton, 1976), but they can also alternate their legs unusually rapidly even when running on the spot, and they can also alternate each of their hands and feet in simple tapping tasks faster than controls (Radford and Upton, 1976; Mero et al., 1981). These are all indications that elite sprinters are well 'organized' neurologically and that they possess better co-ordination than controls for rapid, alternating tasks. This of course makes them particularly suited to running races in which arms and legs are required to alternate 4.5–5.0 times per second.

The neural control, occurs at many levels, from the centrally stored motor programmes, to the relatively simple locomotor reflexes and muscle servo-mechanisms: all may be involved in elite sprinting in adjusting the arousal of the runner, maintaining the optimal movement patterns under pressure, preparing the muscles of the leg prior to ground contact, and selecting the best combination of motor units to produce the force required. There is, however, much to be done to finally understand the neural and co-ordination elements of elite sprinting.

3.3 THE EVENT

There can surely be few sporting events simpler in concept than a 100 m

Table 3.1 The five elements and their approximate times in a 100 m run for men and women

Element	Time (s)	
	Males (10.0)	Females (11.0)
Reaction-response	0.1–0.3	0.1–0.3
Initiation of locomotion	0.3–0.4	0.3–0.4
Running acceleration	5.5–7.0	5.0–6.0
Maximum velocity	1.5–3.0	1.5–2.5
Decreasing velocity	1.0–1.5	1.5–2.5

race. Nevertheless, the 100 m sprint has been slow to reveal its secrets to the sports scientist and even today there are many unanswered questions about the demands of the event itself, about the nature of the men and women who excel at it, and the degree to which performance in the various aspects of the race can be improved.

As with any other event, a detailed analysis of the physical demands of competition must be made before a training programme can be devised, the aim of which must be to prepare the athlete for such demands. To help analyse the demands made by the 100 m sprint, the race can be considered to have five elements (Doolittle and Tellez, 1984), although some writers use fewer divisions (Grosser, 1979; Woicik, 1983; Korchemny, 1985; Moravec et al., 1988). These elements and the approximate time that each phase might last in a 10.00 s, 100 m run for men or 11.00 s, 100 m run for women, are shown in Table 3.1.

There are many factors that will affect the duration of each of these phases, and from race to race individual sprinters will vary quite considerably in the relative contribution that each of these phases makes to their total time. Among these factors are such external ones as strength and direction of wind, air temperature, texture, hardness and resilience of the track surface; and such personal factors as motivation, technique, fitness and fatigue. The approximate time-duration of these elements is therefore only a guide. Each of the elements will be discussed separately, but it should be remembered that in competition, they become inseparably fused.

3.3.1 Reaction-response

For the present purposes, the reaction-response can be said to last from the firing of the starting gun to the moment when the sprinter commences the drive against the starting blocks. There has always been much discussion among coaches about how to ensure a fast reaction but a discussion of this would perhaps be out of place here. Nevertheless, reaction to the gun is an important part of a sprint race. Success here lies in finding how to combine the high arousal state of the sprinters, poised motionless but ready to unleash maximum muscular output, and the need to be physically and mentally disciplined, so that the focus of their attention enhances rather than hinders their response.

The sprinter's reaction and response in a crouch start are quite unlike the conditions in a normal laboratory-based reaction-time study. Sprinters are uniquely required to react to the gun:

1. very promptly,
2. in a disciplined way that sets off a series of movements in which arms and legs are skilfully integrated,
3. by generating the greatest forces they can as rapidly as they can.

The specific nature of a sprinter's reaction led Asami, Shibayama and Ikai (1966) to question the value of conventional reaction-time tests for sprinters, and they adapted a method devised by Cureton (1951) in which 'body reaction' was measured in the form of a vertical jump. They studied seven international sprinters and reported that their 'body reaction' time was not only better than other athletes such as throwers and distance runners, but that both of the component parts of this body reaction – 'nerve reaction time' and 'muscle contraction time' – were shorter for the sprinters. They also found that over a two-year period, both nerve reaction time and muscle contraction time improved for sprinters, which led them to conclude that proper training will result in 'improvement of the facilitation of synaptic activity and increase the speed of muscle contraction'.

The finding that sprinters have faster reactions than others, and that training will improve them even further, is supported by the work of Grosser (1979). His conclusions were based on a study of 20 good, but not outstanding, male German sprinters. When compared with 40 all-round athletes and 40 non-athletes, the sprinters were not only found to have the shortest reaction times, but over an eight month period of specific co-ordination, strength and endurance training, their reaction time became even shorter. Results from a battery of psychological tests administered at the same time also revealed that, when compared with the other groups, the sprinters had greater will-power, drive, readiness to achieve, ability to concentrate, and attention span.

In the starting blocks, all sprinters should be aware of their rivals but should not be adversely influenced by them, and their attention should be focused on whatever their training drills have prepared them for. Some will attempt to empty their minds, some will focus their attention on the awaited sound, and some will focus on the movement of the first body part to move which, for most sprinters using a conventional crouch start, is the left hand.

Atwater (1982) studied the conventional crouch start of eight male elite sprinters and found that of the 16 starts observed (two per athlete) the left hand was the first limb to move on 11 occasions and the mean time from gun to the first loss of hand contact was 0.21 s, with each athlete recording between 0.19 and 0.23 s on their better run and beween 0.19 and 0.34 s on their worse. These times are in general agreement with the data of Baumann (1976) who found that male sprinters in three different ability groups (100 m = 10.35, 11.11 and 11.85 s) had 'hands off' times of 0.214 s, 0.211 s and 0.211 s, respectively.

Under laboratory conditions the 28 'trained sprinters' studied by Bresnahan (1934) had faster times, and the sequence in which limbs broke contact with the ground were: (1) first hand off, 0.172 s; (2) rear foot off, 0.286 s; (3) front foot off, 0.443 s. This is the sequence of events that the crowd normally sees but it is by no means the whole story. Unseen by all but the most tutored eye, the sprinter has started to exert force on the blocks even before the hands move. Payne (1966) reported that the elite male sprinter in his study (the author of this chapter) had a reaction time of 0.12 s from the firing of the gun to the beginning of the first movement, a time very similar to the mean of 0.118 s for the 18 sprinters of varied ability in Henry's (1952) study. Baumann (1976), however, reported reaction by the rear foot on the blocks at 0.101 s for his best group and as quickly as 0.099 s for those with a mean 100 m time of 11.11 s. In Baumann's study the front foot lagged 0.02 s behind before applying forces, a result in conflict with that of Payne and Blader (1971), but these results will depend to a great extent on the distribution of body weight on the starting position, a detailed topic outside the limits of this chapter.

The observation that there is a time-delay between the firing of the starter's gun and the first application of a driving force on the starting blocks by sprinters, has been used by manufacturers to design and supply starting blocks which incorporate devices to record automatically the sprinter's reaction time and relay it to the starter. These devices are designed to help the starter decide when a false start has occurred, but there are no definitive data that would allow us to be certain that a sprinter has made a false-start, and so in the past, different manufacturers have used different time-intervals (e.g. 0.100 s and 0.120 s). The uncertainty that the modern starter experiences in deciding what a legitimate reaction-time interval might be will remain as long as there are variations in the time that it takes for the sound from the starter's gun to reach the sprinters, and variation in the sensitivity and mechanical delay in the starting blocks themselves.

In an analysis conducted by the International Athletic Foundation

Biomechanics Research Project (Moravec *et al.*, 1988), of reaction times at major international championships from 1978 to 1987 it was found that for male 100 m sprinters the mean reaction time ranged from as low as 0.147 s (S.D. = 0.019 s, *n* = 52) in the European Championships of 1982, to as high as 0.185 ± 0.031 s (*n* = 103) in the World Championships of 1987. The overall results from six major international championships from 1978 to 1987 was 0.164 ±0.023 s (*n* = 583).

Within these mean figures there is, of course, wide variation both between and within individuals. In the 1987 World Championships 100 m final for women, reaction times of individual sprinters ranged from 0.141 to 0.242 s, and the sprinter who recorded 0.141 s in the final, recorded 0.120 s in the semi-final but as slow as 0.193 s in a heat. In general, however, 100 m sprinters record better reaction times than 200 m sprinters, who record better reaction times than 400 m sprinters; and male sprinters record reaction times that are faster than their female counterparts in all the sprint events (Moravec *et al.*, 1988).

On the evidence of Atwater's (1982) and Baumann's (1976) data, the sprinters' reaction would seem to contribute relatively little to the overall performance, with their best reaction gaining only 1.5 m (in 100 m) over the very worst, and only a 40 cm difference between each member of the group's best trials; but in competition a poor reaction can lose the sprinter much more than this. If, after the gun, a sprinter can see the backs of his or her rivals, great discipline and composure is needed not to chase after them. In these circumstances tension levels tend to rise and it is hard to settle into the movement patterns and rhythm that are optimal to performance. Nevertheless, it has been reported that reaction time does not correlate significantly with overall performance level for 100 m sprinters (Henry and Trafton, 1951; Moravec *et al.*, 1988).

Thus the factors that limit performance in this phase of the event seem to be muscular, neurological, psychological and perceptual, involving attention, concentration and arousal. In making their preparations to improve this aspect of performance, coaches and sprinters should also be aware of the high arousal level in competition compared with training, and establish the desired focus of attention in the complex race environment.

3.3.2 Initiation of locomotion

This is the phase of the race when the athlete is on the starting blocks. It commences with the sprinter's reaction to the gun and finishes when the initial drive is completed and contact with the starting blocks is lost.

I have chosen this title rather than the alternative 'block clearance' because I think it helps convey more of an idea of what is happening at this time. I considered treating the start as a phase in its own right but eventully discarded the idea principally because the start is too large a unit to consider as a whole, for it includes the reaction, the initiation of locomotion and, if it is not to include the whole of the acceleration phase, an arbitrary decision has to be made about when it is completed.

This phase has two very important elements. The sprinter:

1. applies great forces into the blocks and/or ground which overcomes the inertia of the body and so commences the process of acceleration which continues for a large part of the race;
2. sets in action a precise sequence of movements and postural adjustments which act to initiate the locomotor patterns that follow.

Force production at the start

Mero, Luhtanen and Komi (1983), studied 25 male 100 m sprinters. Two groups were good but not outstanding ($n = 8$ and $n = 9$) and the third group consisted of sprinters only average in ability ($n = 8$). The two good groups spent 0.361 s and 0.360 s generating forces and the poorer group spent 0.368 s producing forces before contact with the blocks was lost and this phase concluded. These results are typical of elite and good male sprinters who, on average, usually spend between 0.320 and 0.370 s applying forces into the starting blocks (Henry, 1952; Payne, 1966; Springings and Elliott, 1972; Baumann, 1976).

Such uniformity among successful sprinters is partly the result of similarities in starting technique, weight distribution and foot-spacing, but in experimental situations these variables can be manipulated to increase significantly the time available to apply force. Henry (1952) was able to increase force-production time to a mean of 0.426 s by increasing the spacing between the feet to 26 in (66 cm) – a distance much greater than that usually used by elite sprinters. The initial gains were, however, lost before even 10 yards (9.14 m) had been covered.

A sprinter's technique, therefore, should be perfected to ensure the development of very high forces, or more precisely, high horizontal forces, and a high rate of force generation, rather than to increase the time available for applying forces. This is borne out by the sprinters in the study of Mero, Luhtanen and Komi (1983). All three groups took approximately the same time to develop forces, but in this time the better sprinters were able to generate significantly greater horizontal and vertical forces. Further insight into this principle is gained by the observation that the poorer sprinters took no longer to reach their peak horizontal force than did the good sprinters: for all the 25 sprinters in the study the mean time for the production of maximum horizontal force was 0.075 s. The difference was that in this time the better sprinters had produced significantly greater forces. Thus the better sprinters were characterized by the ability to generate greater forces per unit time, and this must be seen as one of the essential characteristics of a sprinter.

To achieve maximum acceleration of the body's centre of gravity the sprinters place themselves in the best mechanical position to exploit their muscular resources. Borzov (1979) reported that a group of elite male Soviet sprinters adopted 'set' positions in which the front knee angle ranged from 92° to 105° (mean 100°), and the rear knee angle ranged from 115° to 138° (mean 129°). This is similar to the sprinters in the study by Mero, Luhtanen and Komi (1983) who had a mean front knee angle of 108° and a mean rear knee angle of 134°: there were no differences between the groups in this study.

These positions place the quadriceps and gluteal muscles well within that mid-phase of their range of contraction where their greatest forces can be produced. Thus there would seem to be sound physiological reasons for sprinters placing themselves in starting positions such as these, for it is within this range of hip and knee angles that the hip and knee extensors can produce their greatest peak force.

Borzov (1979) went as far as to state that knee angles within this range are used by Soviet sprinters despite differences in the body size and proportions: he was reporting data on sprinters of 165–183 cm in height. This observation led Borzov to the surprising conclusion that there are 'optimum starting positions' and 'optimum starting angles' (i.e., 100° front knee, and 129° rear knee), which produce the fastest start out of the blocks. Borzov was, of course, an exceptional sprinter himself (and an exceptional starter) and his analysis of other elite sprinters is of unusual interest, and his conclusions do seem to be confirmed by independent Finnish research (Mero, Luhtanen and Komi, 1983). However, data on elite American sprinters seem to be at variance with Borzov's hypothesis. Seven of the eight sprinters in Atwater's (1982) study had front knee angles smaller than Borzov's 'optimal' angle, and one sprinter had the unusually acute angle of 56°: the group as a whole had a front knee angle of 89° in the 'set' position. The rear knee angle of Atwater's sprinters also failed to support the 'optimal' angle hypothesis of Borzov, with six of the eight sprinters failing even to fall within the range of Borzov's sprinters.

It is perhaps of interest to note that the mean front knee angle observed by Atwater was very similar to the advice given by coaches who, by and large, have been recommending front knee angles of approximately 90° for over 50 years.

The advantage conferred by the smaller angles of the sprinters in Atwater's study may be that this posture places the sprinter's centre of gravity in a lower position, making it easier to apply horizontal forces. Only very strong sprinters, however, would have any chance of converting such a low 'set' position into increased horizontal velocity out of the blocks. In Baumann's (1976) study the poorest sprinters left the blocks with a velocity of 2.9 m s^{-1}, whereas the sprinters in the best group had applied horizontal forces into the blocks so successfully that their centre of gravity had already been accelerated to 3.6 m s^{-1} before their front foot left the starting block.

Preferred limbs and movement patterns

It is not surprising perhaps, in the light of the above analysis, that modern coaches have placed so much emphasis on developing the strength of their sprinters, but muscle strength is not the only important factor. Henry (1952) in his discussion of the forces exerted in the sprint start wrote:

> . . . it would seem that something more than powerful leg muscles is required – it is also a matter of co-ordinating the available leg force in the most effective way; of exerting the force at the right instant and for the correct length of time.

Henry also reported that for the 18 male sprinters in his study (50 yards (45.7 m) = 5.75–6.76 s), their combined results were:

1. the duration of the front leg impulse was 0.344 s and had a peak horizontal force of 42.4 kg;
2. the duration of the rear leg impulse was 0.164 s and had a peak horizontal force of 56.8 kg;
3. the front leg was responsible for 66.1% of the sprinters' horizontal forward velocity at the start (66.6% for the six best sprinters).

Part of the skill in applying forces at the start must, therefore, involve the proper co-ordination of the contribution made by front and rear legs. One of the problems is to decide which leg the sprinter should have as the forward one. Not surprisingly, many coaches, after reading Henry's findings, have recommended that sprinters should use their stronger leg as the front leg at the start, but there is no evidence that sprinters naturally do this, nor that if they did, it would produce better results.

In virtually all cases, sprinters select and establish a forward foot for the 'set' position long before they become elite, and on the basis of what feels 'natural'. Radford (1977) reported that 93% of men who have competed in Olympic Games 100 m finals since 1896 employed starting positions in which the *left* foot was placed forward in readiness for the starting signal. This was hardly because they all believed the left leg was stronger. In one study at Glasgow University it was shown that of 836 Scottish and Canadian Physical Education students, 58% of the males and 54% of the females did not select the leg they believed to be the stronger for the front position at the start. The relationships between limb selection and strength is often puzzling – in the same study 50% of the men and 55% of the women did not select the leg they believed to be the stronger as their take-off leg even in the high jump! Limb preference at the start is, however, strongly associated with limb preferences for other bi-pedal tasks such as high-jumping and kicking, and with hand preference for such tasks as throwing and racquet games.

Barnes (1981) measured several physiological parameters of elite American male sprinters and hurdlers. Included in these measures was isokinetic knee extension at 5.23 rad s^{-1} (300° s^{-1}), a velocity very close to that used by the front leg in a sprint start. For knee extension at this velocity the four elite sprinters produced nearly 13% less torque with left leg than with right. Barnes did not analyse his data in terms of the sprint start, but it is known (author's data) that three of the elite group used left-foot forward starting positions (100 m = 10.16, 10.16, 10.27 s respectively). For these the inferiority of the front leg over the rear leg was about 17% for knee extension at 5.23 rad s^{-1}. Force production at the start is clearly not as straightforward an issue as many writers would have us believe.

From the evidence presently available it would seem that for us to understand limb selection at the start we must have as much knowledge of motor control and CNS motor programming as we do of strength and the characteristics of muscle. Successful starting, therefore, requires strong hip and knee extensors, a mechanically sound 'set' position that allows the great forces to be converted into horizontal velocity, a high level of skill that enables the sprinter to integrate fully the forces of front and rear legs so that their respective contributions are maximally co-ordinated, and a starting position which is consistent with other known and preferred motor patterns and limb preferences.

3.3.3 Running acceleration

For our purpose, running acceleration commences as soon as contact is lost with the starting blocks, and ceases when top speed is reached. The typical velocity curve of an elite sprinter shows a very steep rise at the start when the sprinter's overall horizontal velocity is at its lowest and acceleration is at its highest, and then as running speed increases, acceleration decreases until there is no further acceleration and top speed has been reached (Henry and Trafton, 1951; Ikai, 1968; Vaughan and Matravers, 1977; Morton, 1985) (Figure 3.1).

At the moment of leaving the blocks good male sprinters will already be moving at about 3.6 m s^{-1} (Baumann, 1976), and over the next three of four strides another 1.0 m s^{-1} will have been added to their speed (Korneljuk, 1982). This of course can only be done by the sprinter

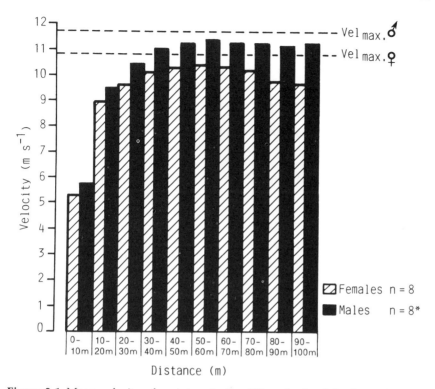

Figure 3.1 Mean velocity of sprinters in the 100 m finals of the Second World Athletic Championships, Rome 1987. Also shown is the fastest 10 m section time run in the race by a female (Vel_{Max} ♀) and male (Vel_{Max} ♂). *One sprinter did not finish, so his mean times from earlier rounds were substituted. (Data by kind permission of the International Athletic Foundation Biomechanics Research Project; see Moravec *et al.*, 1988.)

applying very great horizontal forces into the ground, but very considerable vertical forces are also produced, as the centre of mass is raised from its lowest position of about 0.65 m in the blocks to about 1.0 m after about 5 m have been run (Baumann, 1976).

Velocity increases very rapidly and by 30 m an elite male sprinter can be expected to be over 10 m s^{-1} or 90% of the maximum speed. It then takes up to 30 or 40 m to gradually increase sprinting speed to a maximum of approaching 12 m s^{-1} for men and 11 m s^{-1} for women, and maximum speed is not normally reached by elite male or female sprinters before 50 m.

Throughout this long acceleration phase striding rate remains fairly constant (Korchemny, 1985). In Atwater's study, stride rate was on average 4.20 strides per second over the first three strides, increasing to

4.48 strides per second at 50 yards (45.7 m). Although the overall striding rate may change only slightly during the first 5 s or so, the internal dynamics of the stride undergo very great change. In this time, stride length can increase by over 100% from 1.09 m to 2.44 m (author's data) and this is apparently due to increased overall velocity which enables the body to cover more ground in the air-borne phase of the stride (Schmolinsky, 1978). As a result, at 50 yards (45.7 m) the elite male sprinter may spend as much time in the air as he does on the ground. In Atwater's study the sprinters had a mean ground contact time of 0.111 s at 50 yards (49.6% of stride time), and 0.113 air-borne (50.4%): whereas in the first three strides, 76% of the time was spent in contact with the ground (Atwater, 1982; Armstrong, 1983).

The physical demands on the sprinter during the running acceleration phase are immense. The sprinter must develop very great forces very rapidly. At the early stages of the race the strong and well-conditioned extensors of the hip, knee and ankle carry much of the burden of accelerating the body maximally, but it is primarily the extensors of the hip that sprinters rely on (Baumann, 1976; Korneljuk, 1982).

Knowledge of the ways that sprinters use their strength at the start is still incomplete. Nevertheless, it is clear that over the first few strides the absolute muscle strength, and perhaps even muscle size (Radford, Nimmo and Roberts, 1980) of the sprinters is important. In this phase it seems to be the contractile component of the muscles that is primarily responsible for overcoming the inertia of the body and accelerating it to an overall running speed of about 6–7 m s^{-1}. After this, when the sprinter has reached about 20 m in the race, the series of elastic elements of muscle make an additional contribution, and this mechanical energy, which is stored in the muscles during stretching of the contracted muscle and then released immediately afterwards in the positive work phase, continues to aid the elite sprinter to the end of the race (Cavagna, Komarek and Mazzoleni, 1971).

No matter how strong or skilled the sprinter, new problems emerge as the running acceleration phase develops, which act to bring acceleration to an end. One is increasing air resistance, and another is the mechanical problem that arises when the descending foot contacts the ground at speed and produces a braking effect. These two factors work together to eventually stop any further acceleration, usually after 50 m, at which stage top running speed has been reached.

3.3.4 Maximum velocity

It does seem odd to many observers that an elite sprinter who may take 50–60 m or more to reach top speed, cannot maintain it for more than

20–30 m in the case of the males, and only 15–20 m in the case of the females. The reasons for this very short top-speed section seem to be both mechanical and physiological.

At top speed, elite male sprinters are characterized by a fast striding rate combined with a long stride, but striding rate is also related to leg length (Hoffman, 1971, 1972). In top speed running, only the very best sprinters have the required combination of strength and control to manipulate leg speed. Nevertheless it is through an improvement in striding rate (Mero *et al.*, 1981; Mann *et al.*, 1984; Mann, 1985) rather than stride length, that most sprinters produce new personal records (Ballreich, 1976).

To achieve this the sprinters require to be skilful as well as strong. They must produce as little vertical movement of the body as possible, but enough to allow alternation of the legs, and time for the recovering leg to be moved forward in preparation for an efficient foot-strike. This foot-strike is critical, for the foot must strike ahead of the body's centre of mass. To reduce the braking effect caused by the foot striking the ground, very good sprinters have the skill and control to 'recover' the foot before it is grounded so reducing its horizontal velocity (Mann *et al.*, 1984; Mann, 1985). There have been some great sprinters who have given the appearance of 'recovering' the foot so far as to appear to give it overall horizontal backward velocity at touchdown, but no data have ever been collected to show that any sprinter has achieved such an ideal (Hopper, 1969).

Rapid backward movement of the grounded leg is, of course, critically important (or rapid movement of the sprinter's mass over the grounded foot, depending on how you want to conceptualize it). For this the sprinters require very strong hip extensors (i.e. hamstring muscles and gluteals).

Mann *et al.* (1984) studied 15 American elite male sprinters and 20 elite female sprinters. They reported that at top speed the elite sprinters and good sprinters both produce the same impulse (FT) of about 22.7 kg s^{-1} (50 lb s^{-1}), but they achieve this in different ways. The average sprinter produces about 181.4 kg (400 lb) of force for about 0.125 s of ground contact, wheras the elite sprinter produces 226.8 kg (500 lb) of force for about 0.10 s. Thus the elite sprinters are characterized by higher force production and lower time for force generation (Mann *et al.*, 1984; Mann, 1985).

Everything happens very rapidly at this stage of the race and sprinters do not have time to think of developing 'strong' movements. Instead they should be thinking of 'leg speed' for it is only in trying to maintain a very fast foot action under the body that sprinters can hope to maintain their top speed.

Why even the best sprinters cannot maintain their top speed to the end of the race is still a matter of debate, but their attempts to do so seem always to be doomed except for a few men competing in the most favourable conditions. For this reason sprinters are taught to stress good running form so that at least it is not their technique that produces a braking effect, or wastes energy.

One factor they cannot overcome is air resistance which becomes a bigger factor the faster they run. Davies (1980) calculated that an elite sprinter running 10 m s^{-1} would run 0.25–0.5 s faster if it were not for the air resistance, and Pugh (1970) estimated that air resistance accounted for 16% of the total energy expended to run 100 m in 10.0 s. With 10–30 m of the race still left to run, all but the very best male sprinters lose the battle to maintain top speed as they enter the final phase of decreasing velocity.

3.3.5 Decreasing velocity

The reasons why sprinters begin to lose speed may be because of the accumulating effect of the grounding foot retarding forward speed, or because of the sprinter's increasing inability to keep the body in its critical position relative to foot strike (Mann and Sprague, 1983; Mann, 1985). It may be partly because of the effect of air resistance at high velocities, or problems in energy supply to the muscles and the inability to keep on exercising at such a high intensity and with such a high limb speed, both in recovery of the driving leg, and in the brief time for force generation.

Murase et al. (1976) concluded that the decreasing velocity was initially caused by:

1. deterioration of running form by failure of neuromuscular co-ordination; or
2. the decrease of phosphagen in the muscle.

Both of these mechanisms may be involved. Murase et al. (1976) found that the decrease in running speed was directly related to a decrease in anaerobic power during the sprint, which does suggest that strength is lost due to a reduction in the availability of the high-energy phosphates, although the work by Boobis et al. (1987) has shown that at the end of a 30 s all-out effort, subjects still have ample stores of phosphocreatine and glycogen. Substrate depletion is not a factor in a sprint race, but ATP levels will nevertheless have fallen considerably, due partly to the very high ATP turnover rates during the first 5 seconds of the race (Cheetham et al., 1986; Boobis et al., 1987) and partly due to inhibiting influences within the anaerobic system which tend to decrease the rate of ATP turnover as the race progresses.

It is the Type II fibres that would have been most subject to the reduction of ATP, and if reduction in ATP availability is severe enough it might result in fewer cross-bridge attachments being made and could cause a total failure of force production in some motor units (Cheetham *et al.*, 1986; Hultman, Spreit and Södelund, 1987). Mann and Sprague (1983) described the deterioration in movement pattern towards the end of the race and wrote: '. . . it is not simply the inability to produce the level of muscle effort, but the inability to produce the muscle force in the most efficient manner that hinders a sprinter as fatigue becomes a factor'.

In the study by Boobis *et al.* (1987), 8 weeks of training increased the sprinters' peak power by 7.5% and increased the total amount of work performed, but without a significant increase in ATP production, which strongly suggests that the trained muscle is more economical in its use of ATP (Cheetham *et al.*, 1986). In Grosser's (1979) study the sprinters were able to reduce the phase of deceleration from 11% to 8% after eight months of training biased towards specific sprinting co-ordination, suggesting that problems in neuromuscular co-ordination are as much to blame as is energy supply.

Figure 3.1 shows the velocity curve of the sprinters running in the World Championships in Rome 1987. One particularly interesting feature is the greater decrease in velocity for the female sprinters towards the end of the race. External factors may have had a modest influence on this. The men had an assisting wind of 0.95 m s^{-1}, and the women a very slight head-wind of 0.58 m s^{-1}: for record purposes the maximum permitted wind assistance is 2 m s^{-1}. Over the first 20 m the women ran at nearly 94% of the speed of the men, but over the last 20 m this had dropped to less than 87%. It must be remembered, however, that it takes the females 10% longer to complete their race and so their creatine phosphate and glycogen stores would be more depleted and their ATP turnover rates would have declined further in comparison with the males, with a corresponding reduction in power output. This may be further evidence that problems of energy supply are the main cause of the sprinters' loss of speed at the end of a 100 m race, rather than purely mechanical or co-ordination problems. In competition, sprinters are usually unaware of their decreasing velocity, and aim through maintenance of good technique and high leg speed to continue their top speed running to the finishing line.

3.4 TRAINING

Although sprinters over the course of their athletic lives improve by a smaller percentage than runners in most other events, the key elements in each of the five phases can all be improved with training. Reaction time, strength, power, leg speed, stride length, speed endurance and skill can all be improved, but the qualities that turn competent sprinters into elite ones are complex and elusive (Wood, 1985).

The simplest task is to improve the strength of sprinters, and a thorough analysis of the start and acceleration inevitably leads the coach to examine the role of the muscles surrounding the hip (Korneljuk, 1982; Mitreikin, 1985). The extensors in particular must be very strong. With strength training, muscle cross-sectional area may increase, particularly for males, which will greatly help in force production at the start (Ikai and Fukunaga, 1968, 1970). The range of strengthening work used by sprinters over the past 20 years is astonishing. Some of the best have devoted their time to heavy weights used in a somewhat old-fashioned antigravity way; others have employed isokinetic and accommodating resistance machines in the hope that by training against a resistance set at a similar velocity to that experienced in competition, it will prove easier to convert strength-gains into improved sprinting performance. Others have followed the principle of specificity and used training drills or uphill running as a form of strength-resistance. Surprisingly, some very good sprinters have included no recognized resistance work whatsoever in their training, other than the practising of sprint starts which in itself is a form of resistance training.

Although the propulsion of the body in sprinting is the direct result of the rapid and forceful concentric contractions of the hip, knee and ankle extensor muscles, coaches in recent years have become increasingly aware of the importance in sprinting of eccentric contractions. Eccentric contractions are those that occur when the active muscle is lengthened and which results in much greater force production than when the same muscle concentrically contracts (i.e shortens) (Bigland-Ritchie and Woods, 1976). Eccentric contractions occur on every stride as the sprinter's body weight is acted on by gravity during the airborne-phase and then is resisted by the grounded foot on re-contact. To prepare athletes for this eccentric element of their muscular work, coaches have turned to training systems using bounding, depth jumping or plyo-metrics, in which sprinters jump to the floor from a raised platform and, on landing, rebound into one or a series of either single or double-footed take-offs. These jumps from height and subsequent rebounding jumps have been used by coaches because they employ very short ground-contact time and require a very high rate of motor unit recruitment which helps prepare the athletes (jumpers as well as sprinters) for these elements of competition. The other perceived value of plyometrics has been that on landing from a height the quadriceps experience a brief but rapid eccentric load (i.e. they are lengthened while producing high forces) which enable them to produce a greater force than is possible in any conventional system of resistance training which employs concentric contractions of muscles to generate forces.

Another type of training in which muscles can be eccentrically loaded is running downhill, but this has never been popular with sprinters probably because in order to maintain control, running-technique has to be modified to check forward speed – a practice totally opposed to the objectives of all other running training and competition. The serious drawback to eccentric muscle training is that it causes muscle soreness which is not felt at the time but develops several hours later and which lasts at least 24 hours and sometimes much longer (Newham *et al.*, 1983; Goodyear *et al.*, 1985; Evans, 1987). Even more serious is the finding that this is the result of muscle cell damage caused by the high muscle tension generated by the relatively few muscle fibres that are recruited in this form of intensive exercise. Evidence of this damage can be seen in 33% of the muscle one hour after exercise, and 50% after 3 days, but can still be found in 10% after 6 days (Friden, Sjostrom and Ekblom, 1983). Byrnes *et al.* (1985) and Evans (1987) have found that in time this muscle damage is usually repaired, but how long the repair takes is uncertain as it must depend on the intensity and duration of the exercise that caused it, and how frequently this form of exercise is repeated. It may be that sprinters who regularly employ eccentric work in their training have chronic mild muscle damage (Evans, 1987). There is evidence, however, that infrequent eccentric exercise, or a less extreme form of eccentric muscle work, such as running itself, can help prevent this form of exercise-induced muscle soreness and damage (Byrnes *et al.*, 1985; Evans, 1987). Therefore, used sparingly, eccentric muscle work may have a prophylactic effect for the sprinter who will inevitably encounter some eccentric work every time he or she sprints in competition.

Strength training in all its forms has a part to play in injury prevention – an important topic for the pure sprinter. Coaches must design their resistance/conditioning programmes to ensure that their sprinters develop their strength in such a way that opposing and co-operating muscle groups retain their harmony. It is important for sprinters that the extensors of the hip and knee are strengthened, but to do so without also developing appropriate strength in the hip and knee flexors would be most unwise, as flexor–extensor imbalance is often cited as a major cause of injury. For example, developing quadriceps strength whilst ignoring the strength of hamstrings is a recipe for hamstring injury, the most common of all sprinters' injuries.

The ability to continue producing high forces after the first few seconds of the race is also trainable. *Speed-endurance* and *strength-endurance* training are themes in the training of most elite sprinters (Levchenko, 1984). It is possible that the effect produced by this form of training may be achieved by increasing the muscle's stores of creatine phosphate, although this is not likely to be a great increase (Gollnick and Hermansen, 1973; McCafferty and Horvath, 1977). Another possibility is that after appropriate anaerobic training, muscles are able to use ATP more effectively and maintain the same power output even if ATP turnover is decreasing (Cheetham *et al.*, 1986; Boobis *et al.*, 1987). The athletes in the study by Boobis *et al.* (1987) were involved in intensive interval training for 8 weeks, and increased their muscle glycogen by 36%, and their power output at all points in the sprint. This increase in muscle glycogen and possible increase in the efficient use of ATP could be very important outcomes of sprint training.

Recent evidence suggests that the role of muscle glycogen in sprinting has in the past been underestimated. There can now be little doubt that glycolysis and glycogenolysis are important sources of energy in a 100 m race, and that if, in addition to competition, a sprinter trains intensively, say 3–5 times per week, this could have a cumulative effect resulting in glycogen depletion which might reduce explosive power as much as 10–15% (Jacobs, 1987). Sprint coaches must now be aware of this possibility and adjust the training intensity accordingly, particularly prior to competition and also ensure that the sprinters' diets are kept rich in carbohydrates.

There is also evidence that with appropriate training some Type IIb fibres are modified into Type IIa which will give them better endurance qualities but still allow them to operate within the fast twitch range. This could prove to be an important training adaptation if it can be demonstrated that it occurs in sufficient magnitude to improve speed-endurance measurably (Edgerton, Gerchman and Carrow, 1969; Barnard, Edgerton and Peter, 1970; Jolesz and Sreter, 1981; Saltin and Gollnick, 1983; Åstrand and Rodahl, 1986).

Sprinters also have a task to perform in training that is quite unlike that facing athletes training for longer events, and that is to teach the body how to recruit all the muscular resources available without consideration of energy-cost or economy. All of us have motor units that are inhibited during normal activity, and which would only be recruited in 'fright and flight' situations. In competition, the sprinter experiences sufficient 'fright' to activate the stress hormones, adrenaline and noradrenaline. This may have two effects which might help explain why elite sprinters can produce far better performances in competition than they ever can in training. One effect is to alter the balance between the enzyme phosphofructokinase (PFK) and fructose bisphosphatase (FBPase) which may set up unusually high rates of glycolysis later in the race (Newsholme and Start, 1973). Another effect is to lower the threshold for the firing of some of the large Type II fibres that are normally inhibited except in stress situations. There is evidence that some of these normally inhibited motor units are recruited when force and speed demands are high enough, and their repeated recruitment in this way tends to reduce the level of inhibition and make such motor units more 'available' to the sprinter (Ikai and Steinhause, 1961; Burke, 1980; Coyle *et al.*, 1981). This effect is likely to be very specific, only working on those motor units in the motoneurone pool that are employed in a well-known and rehearsed motor programme. This process, has therefore been labelled 'disciplined disinhibition' and may well be one of the reasons why all sprinters include starting, and forms of very fast sprinting in their training, and why event rehearsal and running drills that mimic specific parts of the stride cycle, are also to be found in most contemporary elite sprinters' training (Radford, 1976; Schmolinsky, 1978; Grosser, 1979).

The inability of sprinters to run in training as quickly as they can in competition poses particular difficulties. Running at slower speeds rehearses a slightly different stride pattern, a different pattern of neuromuscular co-ordination and different pattern of recruitment of motor units. To overcome this, many types of speed drills have been devised (Schmolinsky, 1978) and many types of 'speed-assisted' training have been used. 'Speed-assisted' techniques have ranged from sprinting down slight gradients to running on high-speed treadmills, and to being towed behind cars or motorcycles (Dintiman, 1971; Wood, 1985). All have their problems, but their intention, that of giving sprinters the 'sensation of speed' and allowing them to rehearse the elements of top speed running without the pressures of competition, is very sound indeed (Ozolin, 1971). Some theorists have gone even further and claimed that speed-assisted training which forces sprinters to 'run' at velocities which they are otherwise incapable of achieving, helps to reorganize the firing and recruitment pattern of motor units and so helps sprinters eventually to run faster unaided. These claims are as yet no more than hypotheses, but electrical stimulation of muscle to provoke neuromuscular changes has undoubtedly been used by sprinters to help prepare their muscles for the very particular sort of tension development that they need (Shidlovsky, Kastrubin and Grigoriev, 1979).

Other drills to promote speed of movements of the hands/arms and feet/legs have also been used extensively in recent years, but I know of no clear evidence that these are on their own beneficial, and their apparent success may well be a secondary consequence of other training ingredients.

3.5 ABUSE OF DRUGS AND OTHER BANNED SUBSTANCES

It is regrettable that some of the world's top sprinters have achieved their results with assistance from anabolic steroids and related compounds, and other substances which are banned by the International Olympic Committee and the International Amateur Athletics Federation. The positive test on Canadian sprinter Ben Johnson at the 1988 Olympic Games brought such drug abuse to the notice of the public.

No reliable evidence exists about the number of sprinters involved but there can be little doubt that since at least the mid-1970s drug abuse by athletes has been a major problem internationally. Male and female sprinters of all standards have been involved. Sports scientists and coaches, therefore, must be cautious in their acceptance of the claims associated with certain training methods and programmes, or in using individual sprinters as a model or example. Many of the performances once believed to be the product of good coaching were undoubtedly built around the use of proscribed substances.

Of the different classes of pharmacological agents, anabolic steroids have been the most abused. This class also includes the administration of testosterone and the use of other manipulation techniques which result in an increase in the ratio in urine of testosterone to epitestosterone to above six. It also includes the administration of human choronionic gonadotrophin and other compounds which have related activity and which lead to an increased rate of production of androgenic steroids.

The effects of these compounds have been to increase the muscle mass of sprinters, particularly if the training included a lot of strength and power work used in conjunction with an increased food intake. Those who have used these substances have reported that they have increased their muscular power very noticeably. Primarily the effect has been to make it possible for them to include far more intensive, quality training sessions in their training than previously, thereby improving their speed-endurance as well.

The use of substances in this class also has an effect on the central nervous system by heightening competitiveness. It is likely that all phases of a sprint race are improved by using these substances. All responsible authorities concerned with the sport are now endeavouring to rid athletics of this abuse.

ACKNOWLEDGEMENTS

I am pleased to acknowledge the help given by the International Athletic Foundation Biomechanics Research Project who provided detailed analysis of the sprints in the Second World Championships in Rome, 1987, and details of some earlier championships.

REFERENCES

Armstrong, L.E. (1983) An evaluation of U.S. coaching literature following film analysis of sprint biomechanics. *Track and Field Quarterly Review*, **83**, 14–15.

Asami, T., Shibayama, H. and Ikai, M. (1966) The body reaction time in athletes, in *Proceedings of the International Congress of Sports Sciences, 1964*. Tokyo, Japanese Union of Sports Sciences, pp. 505–507.

Åstrand, P.-O. and Rodahl, K. (1986) *Textbook of Work Physiology*, 3rd ed. McGraw-Hill, New York, pp. 33–40.

Atwater, A.E. (1982) Kinematic analyses of sprinting. *Track and Field Quarterly Review*, **82**, 12–16.

Ballreich, R. (1976) Model for estimating the influence of stride length and stride frequency on the time in sprinting events, in *Biomechanics V-B* (ed. P.V. Komi), University Park Press, Baltimore, pp. 208–212.

Barnard, R.J., Edgerton, V.R. and Peter, J.B. (1970) Effects of exercise on skeletal muscle; I – biomechanical and histochemical properties. *Journal of Applied Physiology*, **28**, 762–766.

Barnes, W.S. (1981) Selected physiological characteristics of elite male sprint athletes. *Journal of Sports Medicine and Physical Fitness*, **21**, 49–54.

Baumann, W. (1976) Kinematic and dynamic characteristics of the sprint start, in *Biomechanics V-B* (ed. P.V. Komi), University Park Press, Baltimore, pp. 194–199.

Bigland-Ritchie, B. and Woods, J.J. (1976) Integrated EMG and O_2 during positive and negative work. *Journal of Physiology*, **260**, 267–277.

Boobis, L., Williams, C., Cheetham, M.E. and Wootton, S.A. (1987) Metabolic aspects of fatigue during sprinting, in *Exercise: Benefits, Limits and Adaptations* (eds D. Macleod, R. Maughan, M. Nimmo, T. Reilly and C. Williams), E. and F.N. Spon, London, pp. 116–140.

Boobis, L., Williams, C. and Wootton, S.A. (1983) Human muscle metabolism during brief maximal exercise. *Journal of Physiology*, **338**, 21P–22P.

Borzov, V. (1979) The optimal starting position in sprinting. *Yessis Review*, **14**, 4.

Bresnahan, G.T. (1934) A study of the movement pattern in starting the race from the crouch position. *Research Quarterly*, **1** (Suppl.), **5**, 5–11.

Burke, R.E. (1980) Motor unit types: functional specializations in motor control, in *Trends in Neurosciences*, Vol 3. Elsevier/North-Holland Biomedical Press, Amsterdam, pp. 255–258.

Byrnes, W.C., Clarkson, P.M., White, J.S., Hsieh, S.S., Frykman, A.N. and Maughan, R.J. (1985) Delayed onset muscle soreness following repeated bouts of downhill running. *Journal of Applied Physiology*, **59**, 710–715.

Cavagna, G.A., Komarek, L. and Mazzoleni, S. (1971) The mechanics of sprint running. *Journal of Physiology*, **217**, 709–721.

Cheetham, M.F., Boobis, L.H., Brooks, S. and Williams, C. (1986) Human muscle metabolism during sprint running. *Journal of Applied Physiology*, **61**, 54–60.

Coyle, E.F., Feiring, D.C., Rotkis, T.C., Cote III, R.W., Roby, F.B., Lee, W. and Wilmore, J.H. (1981) Specificity of power improvements through slow and fast isokinetic training. *Journal of Applied Physiology*, **51**, 1437–1442.

Cureton, T.K. (1951) *Physical Fitness of Champion Athletes*, University of Illinois Press, Urbana.

Davies, C.T.M. (1980) The effects of wind assistance and resistance on the forward motion of a runner. *Journal of Applied Physiology*, **48**, 702–709.

Dintiman, G.B. (1971) *Sprinting Speed: Its Improvement for Major Sports Competition.* Charles C. Thomas, Springfield.

Doolittle, D. and Tellez, T. (1984) Sprinting – from start to finish. *Track and Field Quarterly Review*, **84**, 5–8.

Edgerton, V.R.L., Gerchman, L. and Carrow, R. (1969) Histochemical changes in rat skeletal muscle after exercise. *Experimental Neurology*, **24**, 110–113.

Evans, W.J. (1987) Exercise-induced skeletal muscle damage, *The Physician and Sports Medicine*, **15**, 89–100.

Friden, J., Sjostrom, M. and Ekblom, B. (1983) Myofibrillar damage following intense eccentric exercise in man. *International Journal of Sports Medicine*, **4**, 170–176.

Gollnick, P.D. and Hermansen, L. (1973) Biochemical adaptations to exercise: anaerobic metabolism. *Exercise and Sport Sciences Reviews*, **1**, 1–43.

Goodyear, L.J., Byrnes, W., Clarkson, P., Howley, E., McCormick, K. and Trifletti, P. (1985) Serum creatine kinase and myoglobin responses following two different forms of exercise. *Medicine and Science in Sports and Exercise*, **17**, 277.

Gregor, R.J., Edgerton, V.R., Perrine, J.J., Campion, D.S. and DeBus, C. (1979) Torque–velocity relationships and muscle fibre composition in elite female athletes. *Journal of Applied Physiology*, **47**, 388–392.

Grosser, M. (1979) Determination of the fastest ten metre segment of the 100 meter sprint, in *Science In Athletics* (eds J. Terauds and G.D. Dales), Academic Publishers, California, pp. 71–83.

Henry, F.M. (1952) Force–time characteristics of the sprint start. *Research Quarterly*, **23**, 301–318.

Henry, F.M. and Trafton, I.R. (1951) The velocity curve of sprint running. *Research Quarterly*, **22**, 409–421.

Hoffman, K. (1971) Stature, leg length, and stride frequency. *Track Technique*, **46**, 1463–1469.

Hoffman, K. (1972) Stride length and frequency of female sprinters. *Track Technique*, **48**, 1522–1524.

Hopper, B.J. (1969) Characteristics of the running stride; 2 – speed of the driving foot. *Coaching Review*, **7**, 4–5.

Hultman, E., Spreit, L.L. and Södelund, K. (1987) Energy metabolism and fatigue in working muscle, in *Exercise: Benefits, Limits and Adaptations* (eds D. Macleod, R. Maughan, M. Nimmo, T. Reilly and C. Williams), E. and F.N. Spon, London, pp. 63–80.

Ikai, M. (1968) Biomechanics of sprint running with respect to the speed curve, in *Biomechanics I* (eds J. Wartenwailer, E. Jokl and M. Hebbelinck), Karger, New York.

Ikai, M. and Fukunaga, T. (1968) Calculation of muscle strength per unit cross-sectional area of human muscle by means of ultrasonic measurement. *Internationale Zeitschrift für Angewandte Physiologie*, **26**, 26–32.

Ikai, M. and Fukunaga, T. (1970) A study of training effect on strength per unit cross-sectional area of muscle by means of ultrasonic measurement. *Internationale Zeitschrift für Angewandte Physiologie*, **28**, 173–180.

Ikai, M. and Steinhause, A.H. (1961) Some factors modifying the expression of human strength. *Journal of Applied Physiology*, **16**, 157–163.

Jacobs, I. (1987) Influence of carbohydrate stores on maximal human power output, in *Exercise: Benefits, Limits and Adaptations* (eds D. Macleod, R. Maughan, M. Nimmo, T. Reilly and C. Williams), E. and F.N. Spon, London, pp. 104–114.

Jacobs, I. and Tesch, P. (1981) Short time, maximal muscular performance: relation to muscle lactate and fiber type in females. *Medicine Sport*, **14**, 125–132.

Jolesz, F. and Sreter, F.A. (1981) Development, innervation and activity-pattern induced changes in skeletal muscle. *Annual Review of Physiology*, **43**, 531.

Karlsson, J. and Jacobs, I. (1981) Is the significance of muscle fibre types to muscle metabolism different in females than in males? *Medicine in Sport*, **14**, 97–101.

Khosla, T. (1978) Standards on age, height and weight in Olympic running events for men. *British Journal of Sports Medicine*, **12**, 97–101.

Khosla, T. and McBroom, V.C. (1984) *Physique of Female Olympic Finalists*, Welsh National School of Medicine, Cardiff, pp. 1–23.

Komi, P.V. (1981) Fundamental performance characteristics in females and males. *Medicine Sport*, **14**, 102–108.

Komi, P.V. and Karlsson, J. (1978) Skeletal muscle fibre types, enzyme activities and physical performance in young males and females. *Acta Physiologica Scandinavica*, **103**, 210–218.

Korchemny, R. (1985) Evaluation of sprinters. *National Strength and Conditioning Journal*, **7**, 38–42.

Korneljuk, A.O. (1982) Scientific basis of sprinting speed development. *Track and Field Quarterly Review*, **82**, 6–9.

Kotz, Y.M. and Koryak, Y.A. (1984) Strength and speed strength of antagonist muscles in sprinters and distance runners. *Soviet Sports Review*, **19**, 109–112.

Levchenko, A. (1984) The sprint. *Legkaya Atletika*, **3**, 6–8.

Mann, R. (1985) Biomechanical analysis of the elite sprinter and hurdler, in *The Elite Athlete* (eds N.K. Butts, T.K. Gushiken and B. Zarins), Spectrum Publications, New York, pp. 43–80.

Mann, R., Kotmel, J., Herman, J., Johnson, B. and Schultz, C. (1984) Kinematic trends in elite sprinters. *Proceedings of International Symposium of Biomechanics in Sports*, Colorado Springs, pp. 17–33.

Mann, R. and Sprague, P. (1983) Kinetics of sprinting. *Track and Field Quarterly Review*, **83**, 4–9.

Margaria, R. (1966) Energy cost of sprint running, in *Proceedings of the International Congress of Sports Sciences, 1964*. Japanese Union of Sport Sciences, Tokyo, pp. 444–446.

McCafferty, W.B. and Horvath, S.M. (1977) Specificity of exercise and specificity of training: a subcellular review. *Research Quarterly for Exercise and Sport*, **48**, 358–371.

Mero, A., Luhtanen, P. and Komi, P.V. (1983) A biomechanical study of the sprint start. *Scandinavian Journal of Sports Sciences*, **5**, 20–28.

Mero, A., Luhtanen, P., Viitasalo, J.T. and Komi, P.V. (1981) Relationships between the maximal running velocity, muscle fiber characteristics, force production and force relaxation of sprinters. *Scandinavian Journal of Sports Sciences*, **3**, 16–22.

Mitreikin, V.G. (1985) The basis for using different weights in the preparation of sprinters. *Soviet Sports Review*, **20**, 26–27.

Miyashita, M. and Kanehisa, H. (1979) Dynamic peak torque related to age, sex and performance. *Research Quarterly*, **50**, 249–255.

Moravec, P., Růžička, J., Dostál, E., Sušanka, P., Kodejs, M. and Nosek, M. (1988) The 1987 International Athletics Foundation/I.A.A.F. Scientific Project Report: time analysis of the 100 m events at the Second World Championships in Athletics. *New Studies in Athletics* 3, No. 3 (September), 61–96.

Morrow Jr, J.R. and Hosler, W.W. (1981) Strength comparisons in untrained men and trained women athletes. *Medicine and Science in Sports and Exercise*, **13**, 194–198.

Morton, R.H. (1985) Mathematical representation of the velocity curve of sprint running. *Canadian Journal of Applied Sport Sciences*, **10**, 166–170.

Murase, Y., Hoshikawa, T., Yasuda, N., Ikegami, Y. and Matsui, H. (1976) Analysis of the changes in progressive speed during 100-metre dash, in *Biomechanics V-B* (ed. P.V. Komi), University Park Press, Baltimore, pp. 200–207.

Newham, D.J., McPhail, G., Mills, K.R. and Edwards, R.H.T. (1983) Ultrastructural changes after concentric and eccentric contractions of human muscle. *Journal of the Neurological Sciences*, **61**, 109–122.

Newsholme, E.A. and Start, C. (1973) *Regulation in Metabolism*. John Wiley, Chichester.

Ozolin, N. (1971) How to improve speed. *Track Technique*, **43**, 1373–1375.

Payne, A.H. (1966) The use of force platforms in the study of physical activities. Alta, **1**, 21–28.

Payne, A.H. and Blader, F.B. (1971) The mechanics of the sprint start, in *Biomechanics II* (eds J. Vredenbregt and J. Wartenweiler), S. Karger, Basel, pp. 225–231.

Pugh, L.G.C.E. (1970) Oxygen intake in track and treadmill running with observations on the effect of air resistance. *Journal of Physiology*, **207**, 823–835.

Radford, P.F. (1976) The scientific bases of sprint performances, Part 2 – skill and neuromuscular organisation. *Athletics Coach*, **10**, 2–5.

Radford, P.F. (1977) Movement patterns and the cerebral hemispheres – some observations on the preferred limb. *Scottish Journal of Physical Education*, **5**, 14–18.

Radford, P.F., Nimmo, M.A. and Roberts, J.A. (1980) Strength and speed of sprinters and distance runners. *Report of the Scottish Universities' Physical Education Association's Annual Conference*, pp. 26–32.

Radford, P.F. and Upton, A.R.M. (1976) Trends in speed of alternated movement during development and among elite sprinters, in *Biomechanics V-B* (ed. P.V. Komi), University Park Press, Baltimore, pp. 188–193.

Saltin, B. and Gollnick, P.D. (1983) Skeletal muscle adaptability: significance for metabolism and performance, in *Handbook of Physiology: Skeletal Muscle* (eds L.D. Peachey, R.H. Adrian and S.R. Geiger) Williams and Wilkins, Baltimore, p. 555.

Schmolinsky, G. (1978) *Track and Field: Athletics Training in the G.D.R.* Sportverlag, Berlin.

Shidlovsky, A.G., Kastrubin, E.M. and Grigoriev, Y.V. (1979) The use of central electroanalgesia to strengthen the adaptive processes in athletes. *Teoriya i Praktika Fizicheskoi Kultury*, **10**, 19–21.

Sjöholm, H., Sahlin, K., Edstrom, L. and Hultman, E. (1983) Quantitative estimation of anaerobic and oxidative energy metabolism and contraction characteristics in intact human skeletal muscle in response to electrical stimulation. *Clinical Physiology*, **3**, 226–239.

Springings, E.J. and Elliot, G.M. (1972) Cinematography and force-time recordings in sprint starting. *Track Technique*, **49**, 1561–1563.

Tanner, J.M. (1964) *The Physique of the Olympic Athlete*, George Allen and Unwin, London.

Upton, A.R.M. and Radford, P.F. (1976) Motorneurone excitability in elite sprinters, in *Biomechanics V-A* (ed. P.V. Komi), University Park Press, Baltimore, pp. 82–87.

Vaughan, C.L. and Matravers, D.R. (1977) A biomechanical model of the sprinter. *Journal of Human Movement Studies*, **3**, 207–213.

Woicik, M. (1983) Sprinting, *Track and Field Quarterly Review*, **83**, 16–17.

Wood, G.A. (1985) Optimal performance criteria and limiting factors in sprint running. Paper presented at the second International Amateur Athletic Federation medical congress, Canberra, Australia.

4
Middle distance running

Peter Snell

4.1 INTRODUCTION

The origins of competitive running extend well back into antiquity. Events were held in various ancient festivals throughout Greece, the best known of which began in Olympia in 776 BC and was held every four years until AD 493 when the Roman Emperor, Theodosius declared them a pagan festival and the games were discontinued. At the peak of their popularity in the 1100-year history of the Olympic Games, the running races included the stade (one length of the stadium or 192 metres), the diaulos (two stades, 384 metres) and a distance event of probably 24 stades or 4615 metres (Drees, 1968). The popularization of running in recent history was achieved by the revival of these Olympic Games through the vision of a French educator, Pierre De Coubertin. Under his guidance the first Games of the modern era was held appropriately in Athens, Greece in 1896. As with its ancient counterpart, the modern Olympic Games was restricted to males until the Amsterdam Games of 1928. Events were the same as those of today ranging from 100 metres to the marathon.

Traditionally, events involving primarily speed (100, 200, and 400 metres) were classed as 'sprints', those from 5000 metres and up were referred to as 'distance' races and events in between (800 and 1500 metres) were known as 'middle distance'. Thus the somewhat arbitrary classification distinguished events that required mainly speed, endurance or a combination of the two. The 800 metres is an event that is within the scope of a long sprinter (400 metres), whereas an endurance runner with some speed may be successful at 1500 metres. Unlike swimming, skating and canoeing where one individual is capable of success in a wide range of distances (e.g. Mark Spitz in swimming, Ian Ferguson in canoeing and Eric Heiden in skating), it is unknown for a runner to have achieved excellence in each of the three categories. Success in the combinations of 400–800 metres (Tom Courtenay, Alberto Juantorena), 800–1500 metres (Peter Snell, Sebastian Coe, Joachim Cruz) and 1500–5000 metres (Said Auoita, Kip Keino) is occasionally achieved but rarely spans three events. On the other hand the 5000/10 000 metres combination at the Olympic Games has been achieved by a relatively large number including Emil Zatopec, Vladimir Kuts, Lasse Viren and Miruts Yifter. These results suggest that the physiology of middle distance running has some aspects common to the physiology of shorter and longer events, but possesses its own unique features.

4.2 ENERGY DEMANDS OF MIDDLE DISTANCE RUNNING

A characteristic of middle distance running is that the energy demands for muscle contraction are considerably higher than the capacity of the athlete to provide using aerobic metabolism; thus there is a strong anaerobic component in particular in the 800 and 1500 metres events. The relative contribution of energy sources during maximal effort of various durations is shown in Figure 4.1. In events lasting up to about 30 s, adenosine triphosphate (ATP), the immediate fuel for muscle contraction, is provided anaerobically by high-energy stores of creatine phosphate (CP) present in muscle, and by the glycolytic breakdown of glycogen to lactic acid. From 50 s and longer, there is a rapid increase in the reliance on ATP production by aerobic metabolism. These energy sources have finite limits and accordingly govern the level of exertion possible for a particular time span.

The energy required for running speeds of up to about 75% of maximum oxygen uptake ($\dot{V}O_{2max}$) is produced primarily by the

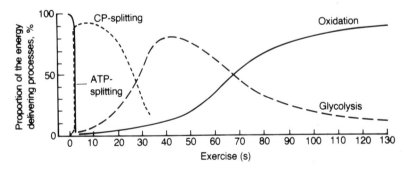

Figure 4.1 Schematic representation of the contribution of energy sources during maximal runs of different duration (from Keul, Doll and Keppler, 1972).

complete oxidation of glucose (from muscle and liver glycogen) and to a lesser extent fatty acids from both intramuscular stores and mobilized in the blood from extramuscular stores. Under these submaximal conditions an accurate estimate of energy expenditure may be obtained by measuring the athlete's oxygen consumption after about 5 minutes of running, when a 'steady state' has been achieved (i.e., a plateau of $\dot{V}O_2$). The energy cost of running per kg body weight is similar for men and women, although there is sufficient individual variability to convey an advantage for athletes with superior running economy. Conley and Krahenbuhl (1980) found that among highly trained and experienced runners, of similar $\dot{V}O_{2max}$, those with the lowest $\dot{V}O_2$ at 241 m min^{-1} performed better in a 10 km race. In a review of studies of energy cost of running, Leger and Mercier (1984) suggested the following relationship between running speed and oxygen cost:

$$\dot{V}O_2 = 0.19 \text{ (m min}^{-1}) + 2.2$$

At speeds above 70–75% $\dot{V}O_{2max}$, an increasing amount of energy is produced anaerobically, in which the glucose is not completely broken down to water and carbon dioxide possibly due to the lack of sufficient oxygen at the site of the reaction (see Williams, Chapter 1). The end product in this case is lactic acid, which diffuses into the blood stream or is taken up and used as a fuel by adjacent muscle fibres that are better adapted for aerobic activity. The use of this pathway is termed anaerobic metabolism and occurs in some muscle fibres well before a runner has reached $\dot{V}O_{2max}$. The running speed at which blood lactic acid levels increase rapidly is an important physiological marker, referred to as the 'lactate threshold' or in some literature, 'anaerobic threshold'. In highly conditioned marathon runners with a higher percentage of slow twitch muscle fibres, the lactate threshold may not be reached until a high fraction of the runners' $\dot{V}O_{2max}$ is being utilized. Beyond $\dot{V}O_{2max}$, all the additional energy must be supplied via anaerobic metabolism. For a runner with a $\dot{V}O_{2max}$ of 70 ml min^{-1} kg^{-1}, the speed at which this value is reached is about 360 m min^{-1} or 2 min 13 s 800 metre pace, with some variation due to individual differences in running economy.

Energy expenditure for the anaerobic component of running can only be crudely approximated. Two methods have been used:

1. Measurement of oxygen consumption above resting values for an extended period (20 min or more) during recovery. This assumes that the elevation of the $\dot{V}O_2$ represents the 'oxygen debt' resulting from the exercise, but other factors contribute to the post-exercise VO_2 and in addition values appear to be considerably overestimated (Sargent, 1926).

2. Estimation of the total lactate production from samples of venous blood. This approach requires assumptions concerning the distribution of lactate throughout the body fluids and the rate of lactate removal by oxidative metabolism.

The problems with these methods are accentuated at fast speeds, i.e., > 420 m min⁻¹ or 1 min 55 s for 800 metres and preclude an exact quantitative measure of energy expenditure. Estimates from data using the measurement of recovery oxygen (Sargent, 1926) suggest that at 85–90% of maximal speed the oxygen cost of running changes from a linear to an exponential function as shown in Figure 4.2. This figure has been constructed from Sargent's original data corrected for an over-estimation based on known values for running speeds of 300 m min⁻¹ among elite athletes. Thus the runner with 46 s 400 metre performance is able to 'cruise' at 52 s for 400 m pace compared to the athlete with a best time of 50 s for 400 m. The former is operating at 88.5% of his 400 m speed compared to 96% for the slower runner. Field experience coupled with laboratory data indicates that in order to run 800 m in 1 min 45 s, an athlete with a relatively slow personal best 200 m of 22.5, must possess exceptional aerobic capacity, i.e. a $\dot{V}O_{2max}$ in excess of 75 ml kg⁻¹ min⁻¹. On the other hand, the $\dot{V}O_{2max}$ of athletes with faster basic speed may be as low as 60 ml kg⁻¹ min⁻¹. A difference of 15 ml kg⁻¹ min⁻¹ amounts to about 5 m over the time span of the 800 m and indicates how superior aerobic capacity may effectively compensate for lower basic speed, which may translate to lower running economy and/

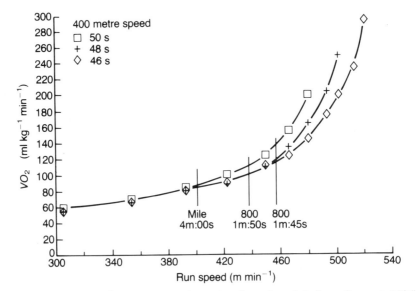

Figure 4.2 Estimated oxygen cost of running (based on data from Sargent, 1926).

or lower anaerobic capacity. Clearly, as the distance increases, the aerobic contribution assumes greater significance.

While most attention focuses on running technique when addressing economy, an often overlooked consideration is that of wind resistance. Kyle (1979) has shown that the advantage of running behind a competitor is significant, amounting to as much as 1.7 s per lap at world record mile pace. Thus the tactic of using other runners as a wind shield does have physiological consequences.

4.3 PHYSIOLOGICAL PROFILE OF THE ELITE RUNNER

4.3.1 Physical characteristics

Various anthropometric studies on Olympic athletes (Tanner, 1964); Carter, 1982) have shown that the combination of moderate height, light weight and low body fat is the predominant feature of middle distance runners. There is some variability in height, and in shorter events, particularly 400 m, there is a tendency towards greater mesomorphy. Runners in high intensity events are successful at the ages of 20–25 years, unlike athletes in longer distances, who maintain high-level performance into 35–40 years. Exceptions to this generalization are John Walker and Eamonn Coghan, who in their mid-30s were world-ranked in the mile/1500 m. Walker, in fact ran 3 min 52.5 s for the mile in 1988 at the age of 36.

4.3.2 Aerobic power and capacity

The term aerobic power is synonymous with $\dot{V}O_{2max}$ and defines the maximal amount of oxygen that the runner can utilize during a short (5–10 min) effort to exhaustion on a treadmill. Its value, which has a strong genetic component (Klissouras, 1971) appears to be determined by central circulatory capacity, in particular the pumping capacity of the heart (Saltin and Rowell, 1980). An athlete's $\dot{V}O_{2max}$ is important because theoretically it sets the upper limit of endurance performance. However, among those with values above 70 ml kg^{-1} min^{-1}, local muscle adaptations appear to be the key factor in performance (Snell and Mitchell, 1984). The range of $\dot{V}O_{2max}$ values among elite middle distance runners is shown in Table 4.1.

Aerobic capacity, often mistakenly used to describe aerobic power, is a measure of oxygen utilization for a given period of time. In events of 3000 m and upwards, this quality distinguishes the superior runner. The aerobic capacity is determined by the fraction of the individual's

Table 4.1 Personal best 1 mile times and $\dot{V}O_{2max}$ values measured on outstanding middle distance runners

Athlete	Best mile time	Year	$\dot{V}O_{2max}$ (ml kg^{-1} min^{-1})	Reference
Archie San Romani	4 min 7.2 s	1937	74.2	Dill, Robinson and Ross (1967)
Don Lash	4 min 7.2 s	1937	81.5	Dill, Robinson and Ross (1967)
John Landy	3 min 57.9 s	1954	76.6	Åstrand (1955)
Peter Snell	3 min 54.1 s	1962	72.3	Carter *et al.* (1966)
Kip Keino	3 min 53.4 s	1966	82.0	Saltin and Åstrand (1967)
Jim Ryan	3 min 51.3 s	1966	81.0	Daniels (1974)
John Walker	3 min 49.1 s	1977	82.0	(Snell, unpublished)
Steve Scott	3 min 47.7 s	1982	80·1	Conley *et al.* (1984)

aerobic power that may be sustained during prolonged running. Unlike $\dot{V}O_{2max}$, which depends on oxygen delivery, a high fractional utilization of aerobic power reflects adaptations in muscles specifically used in running. These adaptations include a well-developed capillary network and an increase in the metabolic potential of the muscle cells. It should be noted that the higher the athlete's aerobic power, the greater are the muscle adaptations in order to utilize a given percentage of that power during sustained effort such as in 5000 to 10 000 m races. The factor that appears to limit this submaximal or 'steady state' pace is the concentration of lactate in the contracting muscles (Farrell *et al.*, 1979). Much work has been done in laboratories to define this pace on the basis of deflection points of blood lactate, heart rate and ventilation (Conconi *et al.*, 1982; Reybrouck *et al.*, 1983; Farrell *et al.*, 1979).

4.3.3 Anaerobic power and capacity

The maximal rate of energy release for muscular work is known as anaerobic power and is governed by the ability to recruit a large number of muscle fibres rapidly. Biochemically it is dependent on the rate at which energy is produced via the glycolytic pathway (Newsholme, 1986). It is the quality that is required for speed of movement and is therefore well-developed in sprinters including 400 m runners and also in longer distance runners capable of rapid acceleration in a relatively slow-paced race. In terms of 400 and 800 m running, a high anaerobic power coupled with good running technique may allow an athlete to be more relaxed at race pace.

Anaerobic capacity refers to the amount of energy released that is not

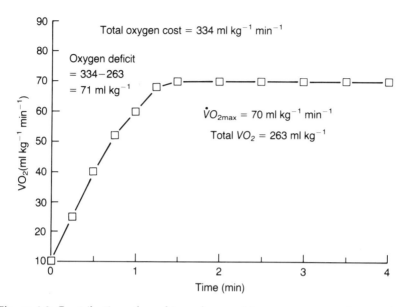

Figure 4.3 Contribution of aerobic and anaerobic energy sources for running a mile in four minutes by an athlete with a $\dot{V}O_{2max}$ of 70 ml kg^{-1} min^{-1} and an estimated total energy cost of 84 ml kg^{-1} min^{-1}.

accounted for by the uptake of oxygen. A high capacity is necessary for middle distance running, which involves energy expenditures well above that provided by $\dot{V}O_{2max}$. Figure 4.3 illustrates this point. The predicted oxygen cost of running a 4 minute mile is about 84 ml kg^{-1} min^{-1}, which translates into an absolute oxygen cost of 23.5 litres for a 70 kg runner. If such a runner has a $\dot{V}O_{2max}$ of 70 ml kg^{-1} min^{-1} and is able to utilize 75% of that aerobic power in the first minute and thereafter 100%, the oxygen utilization for the 4 minute mile is 18.4 litres leaving an 'oxygen deficit' of 4.9 litres (70 ml kg^{-1}). In the laboratory, anaerobic capacity may be estimated from the difference between oxygen cost of a short exhausting uphill run on the treadmill and the $\dot{V}O_2$ measured during the run. Values ranging from 70 to 80 ml kg^{-1} have been obtained for male middle distance runners (Medbo *et al.*, 1988). Attempts have been made to estimate the contribution of known components of anaerobic capacity (Medbo *et al.*, 1988). These components include, O_2 stored in blood and muscle (9%), high energy store in muscle (24%) intramuscular lactate (51%) and lactate transferred to the blood and extracellular fluid (16%). It is therefore not surprising that athletes with a high anaerobic capacity are able to reach levels of plasma lactate in the range 20–30 mM (Osnes and Hermansen, 1972).

The early work on fibre type (Costill *et al.*, 1976) indicates that middle distance runners have an even distribution of fast and slow twitch muscle fibres. The metabolic properties of these fibres as revealed by the activity of oxidative and glycolytic enzymes, reflect the emphasis placed by these runners on training intensity.

4.4 LIMITING FACTORS IN MIDDLE DISTANCE PERFORMANCE

Limitations to athletic performance may include a wide range of physiological, psychological and environmental factors. When the 1968 Olympic Games was held in Mexico City at an altitude of 2300 metres, those who were better adapted to high altitude performed better in events from 1500 to 10 000 metres. Likewise, adverse heat and humidity separates athletes who under more favourable conditions would have similar levels of performance. An understanding of human factors that limit performance is central to the design of effective training programmes. In conjunction with this analysis is the need for individual assessment of physiological abilities. The finishing time in an athletic event is made possible by a composite of physiological interactions that favour sustained production of energy, utilized at a high rate of efficiency. The dissecting of these components lends itself to laboratory testing where measurements may be made under controlled conditions. Typical measurements include $\dot{V}O_{2max}$, running economy, plasma lactate at a variety of submaximal speeds, percentage body fat and anaerobic capacity. In addition blood analysis is useful to determine iron status and indicators of overuse or overtraining such as plasma cortisol, testosterone and CPK.

4.4.1 Oxygen delivery and utilization

The primary organs, systems and steps involved in the transfer of O_2 from ambient air to the mitochondria of muscle cells are the lungs, the heart and central circulation, the blood and its O_2-carrying capacity and the local circulation, including the capillary network. Although not directly involved, the neural and endocrine systems have an important regulatory influence over the circulation.

Under normal conditions, blood flowing through the lungs during maximal exercise is fully saturated. However, highly trained individuals have been observed to exhibit reduced saturation of arterial blood. Research stimulated by the Mexico City Olympics has shown that lung function was an important factor in events requiring close to 100% $\dot{V}O_{2max}$. Individuals born at high altitude or who have had long-term acclimatization (2 years or more) were found to possess greater diffusing capacity than persons residing at sea-level. Dempsey (1986) has speculated that the arterial O_2 desaturation observed at maximal exercise in elite male athletes at sea-level, is due to the limitation of the lung diffusing capacity to match the very high blood flow.

The maximum capacity to circulate blood is dependent on the maximal stroke volume of the heart, which is in turn governed by the heart's filling capacity and its ability to eject blood during the contraction phase. The latter is in part, limited by the resistance offered by the circulatory system.

Oxygen-carrying capacity of the blood is determined by the total haemoglobin. The concentration of haemoglobin in women at 12–13 g dl^{-1} is significantly less than the 15–16 g dl^{-1} in men and accounts for a major part of the 'sex difference' in performance.

Saltin and Rowell (1980) emphasized the importance of capillary density in increasing the transit time of blood through capillary beds and allowing a more complete dissociation of O_2 from the oxyhaemoglobin complex. In addition, an increased number of capillaries per muscle fibre would decrease the O_2 diffusion distance from blood to mitochondria, as would an increase in the number of mitochondria. These factors may influence the pO_2 in the mitochondria and play a role in the regulation of substrate usage.

4.4.2 Lactic acid

The presence of a mild degree of lactic acidosis in the blood reduces the affinity of haemoglobin for oxygen and thus has a beneficial effect on oxygen transfer to the muscle cell. During short maximal efforts lactic acid accumulates rapidly in muscle cells and results in a lowering of muscle pH. When muscle pH drops from the normal resting value of 7.0 to 6.5 or lower, the function of acid-labile enzymes and contractile proteins in muscle is impaired (Sahlin, 1986). In addition, Sahlin (1986) has suggested that a high concentration of lactate ions in muscle could be harmful due to increased osmotic pressure, which would cause swelling of muscle and possibly local ischaemia.

Measurements of lactate in the blood do not necessarily serve as an index of muscle pH, as differences in intracellular buffers and lactate clearance rates make interpretation difficult. An interesting finding (Sharp et al., 1986) is that endurance-trained runners develop fatigue at a higher muscle pH than sprint-trained subjects. This concurs with observations in my laboratory on highly trained women distance runners, whose blood lactate levels following an anaerobic capacity test, are considerably lower than middle distance runners.

4.5 PHYSIOLOGICAL EFFECTS OF TRAINING

The goal of training is to improve performance within the limits of genetic endowment. As mentioned earlier, performance is ultimately dependent upon the amount of energy that the athlete is able to release using aerobic and anaerobic systems coupled to the efficiency with which this energy is used to produce movement across the ground.

In broad terms, running that is close to race pace may be expected to improve running economy. A large amount of race-related running, without the problems of rapid exhaustion, may be achieved through interval or repetition running at distances that are no more than half that of the racing distance. Economy measured at slow speeds (200–300 m min^{-1}) may not have any relevance at speeds that apply in middle distance races. An efficient running action is dependent on the practised, co-ordinated contraction and relaxation of muscle groups that are most favoured mechanically to perform the movement.

Aerobic conditioning involves development of both central circulatory capacity to improve oxygen delivery and local muscle capacity to extract and use oxygen. Training which improves the oxygen utilization by muscle is also appropriate for improving oxygen transport. Training studies have shown that improvement of the pumping capacity of the heart depends largely on its ability to stretch and fill during diastole (Martin et al., 1987). Some investigators have speculated that at typical maximal heart rates of 200 beats min^{-1}, the heart's output per beat (stroke volume) is limited by the short filling time during diastole. This is an interesting possibility as well-trained athletes have larger hearts and lower maximal heart rates than sedentary persons. The smaller hearts of dogs reach maximal rates of about 300; therefore it seems reasonable that geometric factors may limit heart rate in well-trained athletes.

Peripheral adaptations that enhance aerobic performance include improved oxygen availability to the muscle fibres through increased capillary and mitochondrial density (Saltin and Rowell, 1980). A further possibility is a greater capacity to increase muscle blood flow (Snell et al., 1987).

Training of anaerobic capacity involves primarily an increase in glycolytic enzymes, which may enhance the rate of energy release. It also involves an improved buffering capacity of both the muscle cell and its surrounding environment (Sharp et al., 1986; Parkhouse and McKenzie, 1984).

4.5.1 Continuous running

There has been much argument over the relative merits of interval running versus continuous running for development of endurance, especially as both methods have proven successful. Within each type, variations in intensity complicate analysis of the physiological effects. Recently, efforts have been made from large-scale field testing of runners, to define an optimum intensity level based on the heart rate response (Conconi *et al.*, 1982). These methods have the underlying assumption that the optimum training effect occurs when the exercise is performed at or just below the lactate or anaerobic threshold. Criticism of continuous training has been articulated on the basis that intensity is insufficient to ensure that all the muscle fibres required to support the speed of a middle distance event are being used. This concept is illustrated in Figure 4.4, which associates muscle fibre recruitment to muscular force, which in turn is closely related to running speed. Most continuous running at a heart rate of 140–160 beats min^{-1} is light to moderate and supported primarily by the slow twitch muscle fibre fraction of the musculature used in running. This being the case, why then is continuous running relevant for middle distance runners? Clues to this have come from the work in Sweden of Gollnick, Piehl and Saltin (1974) who analysed thigh muscle biopsies taken at timed intervals during cycling at an intensity of 75% $\dot{V}O_{2max}$. There was a progressive depletion of glycogen in ST fibres throughout the 2 hours of exercise. Glycogen stores in FT fibres were still full after the first hour indicating that they were not recruited. However, as the exercise continued and some of the ST fibres became totally depleted of glycogen, there was significant utilization of FT fibres. This study supports the belief that

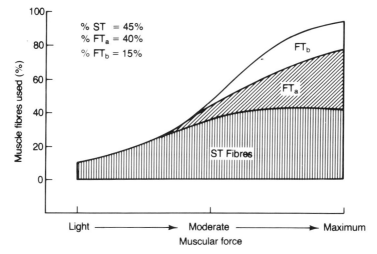

Figure 4.4 Percentage of muscle fibres recruited at increasing levels of effort. Note the recruitment order for the different fibre types (from Costill, Ball State University, 1982).

continuous training must be of sufficient duration and intensity to maximize its effect and further demonstrates that exercise of moderate intensity can be used to train FT fibres, provided the duration is sufficient to deplete glycogen in the ST fibres that are initially used.

4.5.2 Interval running

Interval running was popularized as a training method in the 1930s by the German 800 metre world record-holder Rudolf Harbig. The original method introduced by coach Gerschler and cardiologist Reindell, required periods of effort ranging from 30 to 70 seconds at an intensity that elevated the heart rate to about 180 beats per min. The effort phase was followed by sufficient recovery time to allow the heart rate to return to 120 beats min^{-1}. The method had instant appeal. It allowed the athlete to perform a large amount of work that was race-pace specific. In addition Reindell and Roskamm (1959) postulated a physiological basis for the beneficial effects of interval training on the central circulatory capacity. Their contention was that during the recovery phase, the heart rate declined at a proportionally greater rate than the return of blood to the heart. This resulted in a brief increase in the amount of blood that the heart pumped with each beat. In essence the idea was that the heart received a greater stretching stimulus during the initial phase of recovery than during the effort phase. In order to encourage the return of blood in the venous side of the circulation (normally facilitated by muscle contraction) athletes lay down during recovery. Unfortunately the critical blood flow measurements have not been made to confirm this hypothesis in man. It is likely that with the cessation of muscle action, the blood flow through the heart drops more rapidly than the decline of the heart rate.

Contemporary interval training encompasses a wider range of effort periods distinguished by the terms short- and long-intervals. It should not be confused with another form of training involving repeated effort, better described as high intensity training and referred to below.

Studies that attempt to evaluate the relative merits of continuous versus interval running generally find similar improvement in $\dot{V}O_{2max}$ (Pyke, Ewing and Roberts, 1978; Poole and Gaesser, 1985). In order to satisfy the constraints of a research design, the total work is usually kept constant. However, even the weekend athlete knows that it is possible to do a greater amount of training using slow continuous running rather than interval training. For the middle distance runner interval running is the most effective way to do a large amount or volume of event-specific work. The role of continuous running may be to allow a greater volume of this form of training before the onset of fatigue or overtraining.

4.5.3 High intensity running

The purpose of this form of running is to develop speed and anaerobic capacity. The experience of athletes is typical of the results from research by Houston and Thomson (1977). They used a 6 week programme of intense, intermittent hill running to determine performance and muscle metabolic changes in endurance-trained men. Impressive improvements were noted in an intensive treadmill run test (17%), peak blood lactate (14%) and high energy phosphates in muscle (15%). No change occurred in $\dot{V}O_{2max}$, anaerobic power or muscle fibre type. The ability of middle distance runners in peak form to reach high levels of plasma lactic acid is a consistent finding. Although it has been reasoned many years ago by Hill and Lupton (1923) that tissue buffers must play an important role in determining the highest level of lactate attainable, the actual documentation of the effect of training on the buffer capacity of human muscle has only recently been produced. Sharp *et al.* (1986) found that muscle lactate accumulation at exhaustion was increased 20% by sprint training without any change in muscle pH (6.65 and 6.69). The training also induced a 46% increase in the activity of the glycolytic marker enzyme PFK. (It should be acknowledged that performance in the post-training test was improved and this in itself could have led to a greater lactate production at the point of exhaustion.)

High intensity training should be approached with caution as there is some suggestion that aerobic capacity may be impaired. Ibara, Fisher and Conlee (1981) reported a decrease in the oxidative marker enzyme, SDH, after 6 weeks of anaerobic training. An elegant study from Gollnick's laboratory (Bertocci *et al.*, 1986) supports this position. They examined muscle homogenates from horses that had done repeated bouts of maximal exercise, which lowered muscle pH to 6.57. The respiratory rate of the muscle tissue was depressed and remained so for 8 hours after it was incubated in a buffer at a neutral pH. It is not clear if the horses were endurance trained. The study from Costill's laboratory discussed already (Sharp *et al.*, 1986) included a group of endurance-trained cyclists. After exercise to exhaustion on a cycle ergometer, their muscle pH was significantly higher than either the untrained or sprint-trained subjects even though they achieved a higher power output. This suggests that endurance training may offer some protection from the potentially damaging effects of low muscle pH.

4.5.4 Strength training

There is little doubt that some form of resistance training is beneficial to all runners, increasing in importance with the speed of the race. Runners are able to incorporate hill training in their workouts to provide resistance in a highly specific form. Theoretically strength training that induces hypertrophy should decrease aerobic capacity due to an increase in diffusion distance from capillary to muscle mitochondria. Weight-training is not likely to produce further increases in $\dot{V}O_{2max}$ in runners, but may improve muscle endurance as has been shown in cycling (Hickson, Rosenkoetter and Brown, 1980).

4.5.5 Overtraining

A simplified definition of training may well be, 'the maximal amount of event-specific training without overtraining'. Overtraining may be regarded as a state in which performance diminishes while the level of training is maintained or increased. Coaches have long been aware of the problem of overtraining but we are still not completely aware of its physiological basis. The term 'staleness' has been used in the past and was thought to refer to more of a psychological state related to a heavy schedule of races. Empirically, it has been found that when performance unexpectedly declines during the normal course of training and racing, a period of easy jogging often improves race times whereas an increase of training results in a continued decline in performance.

Studies in Finland (Kuoppasalmi *et al.*, 1980) have revealed that high intensity exercise increases the level of the catabolic hormone, cortisol, and decreases the level of the anabolic hormone testosterone for several hours. The same group (Adlercruetz *et al.*, 1986) has also demonstrated that when these changes persist, there is a strong association between these biochemical indicators of overtraining and decreased physical performance. These findings are consistent with the effects of steroid use (illegal in most sports) in various groups of athletes, who are able to recover more rapidly from intensive training, i.e., steroids appear to protect the body from overtraining. While the mechanism of this effect is not clear, biochemical studies in animals (Seene and Viru, 1982) have shown that androgens oppose the catabolic action of cortisol.

4.6 ERGOGENIC AIDS

Substances that improve the performance of the athlete above expected levels are referred to as ergogenic aids. The list of such substances is substantial and many are banned by the International Olympic Com-mittee and International Governing Bodies of various sports. Many athletes are continually looking for a 'competitive edge' and may be attracted by reports of an ergogenic effect of some substance. It is important to note that scientific studies are essential to distinguish between a true ergogenic effect and the well-known placebo effect in which performance is improved due to the athlete's faith in treatment. The following are substances or methods that are often used in an attempt to enhance performance.

4.6.1 Vitamins

When vitamins are used well in excess of demonstrated requirements they may be considered to be acting as a drug. While athletes probably have an increased need for water-soluble vitamins and minerals based purely on the high caloric expenditures in training, there has not been any research acceptable to the scientific community to demonstrate an ergogenic effect of any vitamin in the absence of a deficiency.

4.6.2 Blood doping

The process of blood doping, whereby an athlete receives a transfusion of his own previously withdrawn and stored blood, gives the athlete an overnight improvement in oxygen-carrying capacity. This results in an 8–10% increase in $\dot{V}O_{2max}$ and an improvement in lactate threshold, the latter indicating that the availability of oxygen at cellular level is enhanced during submaximal performance. Williams, Wesseldine and Schuster (1981) and Gledhill (1982) in a review, have discussed methodological problems, which may account for many of the conflicting results. Refrigerated blood cells are not protected from the ageing process as is the case with frozen cells and following phlebotomy, it is important that sufficient time is allowed for haemoglobin levels to recover to normal values before reinfusion.

A study by Brien and Simon (1988) has shown that red blood cell infusion has beneficial effects on performance in 1500 m runners. An infusion of 400 ml of previously frozen blood was found to increase haematocrit, haemoglobin and $\dot{V}O_{2max}$, each by about 10%. Although the improvement in performance was only 1.7% on average, this represented a mean decrease in race time of 4.5 s.

It should be emphasized that blood doping is illegal. Only recently has a test been developed that can positively confirm that an athlete has engaged in the practice.

4.6.3 Bicarbonate loading

Studies using placebos and a double-blind design have demonstrated a positive effect of a dose of 300–400 mg kg^{-1} of sodium bicarbonate taken orally 1–2 hours before a competitive effort over 800 metres (Wilkes, Gledhill and Smyth, 1983) and 400 metres (Goldfinch, McNaughton and Davies, 1988). Such a procedure substantially increases the plasma bicarbonate levels and therefore the buffering capacity of the blood. Times were improved 2% in the 800 metre and 3% in the 400 metre study. Plasma lactate and pH were elevated, suggesting that the raised extracellular bicarbonate facilitated the efflux of hydrogen ions (H$^+$) from the muscle cell.

4.6.4 Caffeine

The major pharmacological effect of caffeine is to potentiate the effects of adrenaline. In this regard, it should therefore promote the release of fatty acids from adipose stores and accelerate the breakdown of glycogen (glycogenolysis). Many athletes believe that caffeine increases endurance; however, the evidence from scientific studies is equivocal (Eichner, 1986). Studies demonstrating a positive effect have mainly used cycling as the exercise. Furthermore, Eichner (1986) has drawn attention to the negative effects of coffee and other caffeine-containing drinks, on cholesterol and blood pressure – two of the major risk factors for development of cardiovascular disease. From the standpoint of the metabolic needs of a middle distance runner, the use of caffeine cannot be recommended. Newsholme (1986) has emphasized that for a given production of ATP, fat requires 10% more oxygen than carbohydrate and for short events, efficient use of oxygen is more important than glycogen sparing.

4.7 TACTICAL CONSIDERATIONS

The primary tactical advice which emerges from the physiological discussion is to conserve as much energy as possible by running an even-paced race, by avoiding the extra distance involved when running at another athlete's shoulder in lane 2 and by allowing other runners to lead the race especially in windy conditions. Runners whose forte is endurance rather than speed, will need to ensure that the race is demanding enough so that the fast finishers are unable to utilize their sprinting speed. A common tactic, especially in races that tend to be slower than expected, is for someone to make a bid from 200–300 metres from the finish. It is critical that such an effort is made only when the athlete is sure of being able to 'last' to the finish line. Other tactics are in the psychological realm. The use of an explosive burst with 250 metres to go in an 800 metre race may cause an opponent unconsciously to concede the race at that point. In general a runner will expend the least energy for a given time under similar environmental conditions, when the race is run at a constant pace. In practice, however, the best times are usually achieved in 800 metre running when the first 400 metres is 1–2 s faster than the last. This is not the case in longer events in which the energy source is more heavily dependent on aerobic mechanisms. In these circumstances the ability to utilize maximally the full aerobic energy potential may be compromised by sporadic heavy use of anaerobic energy sources. Thus some runners who use mid-race spurts to 'break' the opposition, may only succeed in breaking themselves if the opposition chooses not to follow.

REFERENCES

Adlercreutz, H., Harkonen, M., Kuoppasalmi, K., Naveri, H., Huhtaniemi, I., Tikkanen, H., Remes, K., Dessypris, A. and Karvonen, J. (1986) Effect of training on plasma anabolic and catabolic steroid hormones and their response during physical exercise. *International Journal of Sports Medicine*, **7**, 27–28 Suppl.

Åstrand, P.O. (1955) New records in human power. *Nature*, **176**, 922–923.

Bertocci, L.A., Hodgson, D.R., Kelso, T.B., Grant, B.D. and Gollnick, P.D. (1986) Depressed mitochondrial respiration after intense exercise. *Medicine and Science in Sports and Exercise*, **12**, S78–S79.

Brien, A.J. and Simon, T.L. (1988) Effects of red blood cell infusion on 1500 m race time, in *Abstracts. New Horizons of Human Movement*, Vol. 13. SOSCOC, Seoul, p. 149.

Carter, J.E.L. (ed.) (1982) *Physical Structure of Olympic Athletes*. S. Karger, New York.

Carter, J.E.L., Kasch, F.W., Boyer, J.L., Phillips, W.H., Ross, W.D. and Susec, A. (1966) Structural and functional assessments on a champion runner – Peter Snell. *Research Quarterly*, **38**, 355–365.

Conconi, F., Ferrari, M., Ziglio, P.G., Droghetti, P. and Codeca L. (1982) Determination of the anaerobic threshold by a noninvasive field test in runners. *Journal of Applied Physiology*, **52**, 869–873.

Conley, D.L. and Krahenbuhl, G.S. (1980) Running economy and distance running performance of highly trained athletes. *Medicine and Science in Sports and Exercise*, **12**, 357–360.

Conley, D.L., Krahenbuhl, G.S., Burkett, L.N. and Millar, A.L. (1984) Following Steve Scott: physiological changes accompanying training. *The Physician and Sportsmedicine*, **12**, 103–106.

Costill, D.L., Daniels, J., Evans, W., Fink, W., Krahenbuhl, G. and Saltin, B. (1976) Skeletal muscle enzymes and fiber composition in male and female track athletes. *Journal of Applied Physiology*, **40**, 149–154.

Daniels, J.T. (1974) Running with Jim Ryun: a five year study. *The Physician and Sportsmedicine*, **2**, 62–67.

Dempsey, J.A. (1986) Is the lung built for exercise. *Medicine and Science in Sports and Exercise*, **18**, 143–155.

Dill, D.B., Robinson, S. and Ross, J.C. (1967) A longitudinal study of 16 champion runners. *Journal of Sports Medicine and Physical Fitness*, **7**, 4–27.

Drees L. (1968) *Olympia: Gods, Artists and Athletes*. Frederick A. Praeger, New York.

Eichner, E.R. (1986) The caffeine: effects on endurance and cholesterol. *The Physician and Sportsmedicine*, **14**, 124–132.

Farrell, P.A., Wilmore, J.H., Coyle, E.F., Billing J.E. and Costill, D.L. (1979) Plasma lactate accumulation and distance running performance. *Medicine and Science in Sports*, **11**, 338–344.

Gledhill, N. (1982) Blood doping and related issues: a brief review. *Medicine and Science in Sports and Exercise*, **14**, 183–189.

Goldfinch, J., McNaughton L. and Davies, P. (1988) Induced metabolic alkalosis and its effect on 400 m racing time. *European Journal of Applied Physiology*, **57**, 45–48.

Gollnick, P.D., Piehl, K. and Saltin, B. (1974) Selective glycogen depletion pattern in human muscle fibres after exercise of varying intensity and at varying pedal rates. *Journal of Physiology*, **241**, 45–57.

Hickson, R.C., Rosenkoetter, M.A. and Brown, M.M. (1980) Strength training effects on aerobic power and short-term endurance. *Medicine and Science in Sports and Exercise*, **12**, 336–339.

Hill, A.V. and Lupton, H. (1923) Muscular exercise, lactic acid and the supply and utilization of oxygen. *Quarterly Journal of Medicine*, **16**, 135–171.

Houston, M.E. and Thomson, J.A. (1977) The response of endurance-adapted adults to intense anaerobic training. *European Journal of Applied Physiology*, **36**, 207–213.

Ibara, G., Fisher, A.G. and Conlee, R.K. (1981) Effects of anaerobic training on selected aerobic factors in well-trained endurance runners. *Medicine and Science in Sports and Exercise*, **13**, 109 (abstract).

Jacobs, I. (1986) Blood lactate. Implications for training and performance. *Sports Medicine*, **3**, 10–25.

Keul, J., Doll, E. and Keppler, D. (1972) Energy metabolism of Human Muscle. University Park Press, Baltimore.

Klissouras, V. (1971) Heritability of adaptive variation. *Journal of Applied Physiology*, **31**, 338–344.

Kuoppasalmi, K., Naveri, H., Harkonen, M. and Adlercreutz, H. (1980) Plasma cortisol, androstenedione, testosterone and luteinizing hormone in running exercise of different intensities. *Scandinavian Journal of Clinical and Laboratory Investigation*, **40**, 403–409.

Kyle, C.R. (1979) Reduction of wind resistance and power output of racing cyclists and runners travelling in groups. *Ergonomics*, **22**, 387–397.

Leger, L. and Mercier, D. (1984) Gross energy cost of horizontal treadmill and track running. *Sports Medicine*, **1**, 270–277.

Lortie, G., Simoneau, J.A., Hamel, P., Boulay, M.R. and Bouchard, C. (1985) Relationships between skeletal muscle characteristics and aerobic performance in sedentary and active subjects. *European Journal of Applied Physiology*, **54**, 471–475.

Martin, W.H., Montgomery, J., Snell, P.G., Corbett, J.R., Sokolov, J.J., Buckey, J.C., Maloney, D.A. and Blomqvist, C.G. (1987) Cardiovascular adaptations to intense swim training in sedentary middle-aged men and women. *Circulation*, **75**, 3230–3330.

Medbo, J., Mohn, A-C., Tabata, I., Bahr, R., Vaage, O. and Sejersted, O. (1988) Anaerobic capacity determined by maximal accumulated O_2 deficit. *Journal of Applied Physiology*, **64**, 50–60.

Newsholme, E.A. (1986) Application of principles of metabolic control to the problem of metabolic limitations in sprinting, middle distance and marathon running. *International Journal of Sports Medicine*, **7**, 66–70, Suppl.

Osnes, J.B. and Hermansen, L. (1972) Acid-base balance after maximal exercise of short duration. *Journal of Applied Physiology*, **32**, 59–63.

Parkhouse, W.S. and McKenzie, D.C. (1984) Possible contribution of skeletal muscle buffers to enhanced anaerobic performance: a brief review. *Medicine and Science in Sports and Exercise*, **16**, 328–338.

Poole, D.C. and Gaesser, G.A. (1985) Response of ventilatory and lactate thresholds to continuous and interval training. *Journal of Applied Physiology*, **58**, 1115–1121.

Pyke, F.S., Ewing, A.S. and Roberts, A.D. (1978) Physiological adjustments to continuous and interval running training, in *Proceedings of the International Congress of Physical Activity Sciences*, Vol. 4 (eds F. Landry and W. Orban). Symposia Specialists, Miami, pp. 369–377.

Reindell, H. and Roskamm, H. (1959) A contribution to the physiological foundations of interval training under specific considerations of circulation. Cited by Down, M.G. (1966) Interval training: an appraisal of work rest cycle applications to training for endurance running. Loughborough University of Technology.

Reybrouck, T., Ghesquiere J., Cattaert, A., Fagard, R. and Amery, A. (1983) Ventilatory thresholds during short- and long-term exercise. *Journal of Applied Physiology*, **55**, 1694–1700.

Sahlin, K. (1986) Metabolic changes limiting muscle performance, in *Biochemistry of Exercise VI* (ed. B. Saltin). Human Kinetics, Champaign, Illinois, pp. 323–343.

Saltin, B. and Åstrand, P.-O. (1967) Maximal oxygen uptake in athletes. *Journal of Applied Physiology*, **23**, 353–358.

Saltin, B. and Rowell, L.B. (1980) Functional adaptations to physical activity and inactivity. *Federation Proceedings*, **39**, 1506–1513.

Sargent, R.M. (1926) The relation between oxygen requirement and speed in running. *Proceedings of the Royal Society*, Series B, **100**, 10–22.

Schnabel, A. and Kindermann, W. (1983) Assessment of anaerobic capacity in runners. *European Journal of Applied Physiology*, **52**, 42–46.

Seene, T. and Viru, A. (1982) The catabolic effect of glucocorticoids on different types of skeletal muscle fibres and its dependence upon muscle activity and interaction with anabolic steroids. *Journal of Steroid Biochemistry*, **16**, 349–352.

Sharp, R.L., Costill, D.L., Fink, W.J. and King, D.S. (1986) Effects of eight weeks of bicycle ergometer training on human muscle buffer capacity. *International Journal of Sports Medicine*, **7**, 13–17.

Snell, P.G., Martin, W.H. Buckey, J.C. and Blomqvist, C.G. (1987) Maximal vascular leg conductance in trained and untrained men. *Journal of Applied Physiology*, **62**, 606–610.

Snell, P.G. and Mitchell, J.H. (1984) The role of maximal oxygen consumption in exercise performance. *Clinics in Chest Medicine*, **5**, 51–62.

Tanner, J.M. (1964) *The Physique of the Olympic Athlete*. George Allen & Unwin, London.

Wilkes, D., Gledhill, N. and Smyth, R. (1983) Effect of acute induced metabolic acidosis on 800 m racing time. *Medicine and Science in Sports and Exercise*, **15**, 277–280.

Williams, M.H., Wesseldine, T.S. and Schuster, R. (1981) The effect of induced erythrocythemia upon 5-mile treadmill time. *Medicine and Science in Sports and Exercise*, **13**, 169–175.

5
Marathon running
R.J. Maughan

5.1 INTRODUCTION

As the 1970s gave way to the 1980s, marathon running changed from a minority sport engaged in by a small number of individuals to a mass-participation event attracting many thousands of runners to the major races. Training for and participating in endurance events suddenly became socially acceptable, for women as well as for men. These changes resulted in part from an increased awareness of the potential of exercise for improving health and fitness, but perhaps owed more to media exposure and advertising pressure from commercial interests. Although the marathon running boom lasted only a few years, the interest in endurance exercise which it stimulated seems set to last, and successful completion of a marathon remains a major goal for most joggers and runners. Indeed, most city marathons really contain more than one event: the front runners are highly trained and experienced athletes seeking to complete the distance in the fastest possible time; for the majority of the participants, however, the distance itself is sufficient challenge and the aim is simply to complete the race. Many of the latter group are poorly prepared in addition to being constitutionally unsuited to the event.

The increased interest in marathon running has provided a major stimulus to research, and marathon runners have been more intensively studied than any other sports participants in recent years. This interest, which was formerly restricted to the study of elite competitors as physiological curiosities, has been extended to include the slower runners.

5.2 ENERGY EXPENDITURE DURING MARATHON RUNNING

Marathon races are held on road courses over a distance which, for historical reasons, has been fixed as 42 195 m (26 miles 385 yards); there are at present no other constraints on the course. Consequently, the severity of races varies considerably in relation to their topography. Other environmental factors may also play a major role; races are not infrequently held at extremes of environmental temperature; wind and precipitation may pose additional problems for the runner. Altitude and air pollution are also factors affecting competitors in some events. In general, however, the problem is one of covering the distance in the shortest possible time.

Elite competitors complete the marathon in times of less than 2 h 10 min (2:10:00) whereas many of the slowest runners take more than 5 h to reach the finish. In events of this duration, energy requirements are met almost entirely by oxidative metabolism; the contribution of anaerobic metabolism is negligible as is evidenced by the low blood lactate concentrations observed at the end of races even in elite competitors (Costill, 1970). Energy expenditure can therefore be conveniently measured as oxygen consumption ($\dot{V}O_2$). For any given body weight, the energy expenditure during running is approximately linearly related to running speed over the range of speeds at which marathons are run: the total energy cost of covering a given distance is therefore relatively constant and independent of speed. Although there may be differences in efficiency related to running style, these are generally rather small, and the total energy expended by the elite runner in running a marathon is the same as that of the jogger, providing that body weight is the same. The major physiological requirement of marathon running can be summarized as the ability to sustain a high rate of oxygen consumption for prolonged periods. This can be achieved in two ways: by having a high maximum oxygen uptake ($\dot{V}O_{2max}$) or by the ability to exercise at a high proportion of $\dot{V}O_{2max}$ for the duration of the event. In practice, a combination of these two options is normally observed.

Many studies have confirmed the existence of a high $\dot{V}O_{2max}$ in successful marathon runners, and values between 70 and 80 ml kg^{-1} min^{-1} are generally observed in male runners able to complete the distance in less than 2:30 (Costill and Fox, 1969; Costill and Winrow, 1970; Pollock, 1977). There have been few published studies of elite female marathon runners, but Wilmore and Brown (1974) reported a $\dot{V}O_{2max}$ of 71 ml kg^{-1} min^{-1} in the then world record holder (2:49:40). Davies and Thompson (1979) found an average $\dot{V}O_{2max}$ of 58 ml kg^{-1} min^{-1} in nine female marathon runners with a rather slower average best time of 3:09. Since these studies, performances by women have improved dramatically, and in a more recent study involving nine elite long-distance runners, which included specialists at both 10 km and marathon distances, Pate et al. (1987) found a mean $\dot{V}O_{2max}$ of

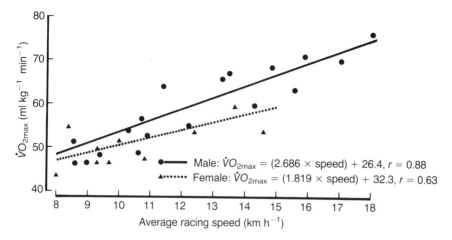

Figure 5.1 Relationship between $\dot{V}O_{2max}$ and marathon performance for 18 male and 10 female runners who all took part in the same race. The $\dot{V}O_{2max}$ was measured 2–3 weeks after the race. (Reproduced with permission from Maughan and Leiper, 1983.)

66.4 ml kg^{-1} min^{-1}; best performances of these runners at the marathon distance ranged from 2:28:54 to 2:39:21.

When comparisons are made between runners of widely different levels of performance, there is generally found to be a good relationship between running time and $\dot{V}O_{2max}$ (Figure 5.1). Foster, Daniels and Yarbrough (1977) reported a correlation coefficient of -0.86 between $\dot{V}O_{2max}$ and marathon time in 23 male runners with best times between 2:23 to 4:08; Maughan and Leiper (1983) observed a correlation coefficient of -0.88 between $\dot{V}O_{2max}$ and time in a single race in 18 male runners with a performance range from 2:19 to 4:53. Within a group of runners of comparable ability, however, there is not a significant relationship between $\dot{V}O_{2max}$ and performance (Costill, 1972). Even among elite competitors, some individuals do not have an outstandingly high aerobic power: a holder of the world's best performance of the time (2:08:33) was found to have a $\dot{V}O_{2max}$ of 70 ml kg^{-1} min^{-1} (Costill *et al.*, 1971a) and more recently a 2:10 performer could reach a value of only 67 ml kg^{-1} min^{-1} (Sjodin and Svedenhag, 1985). The energy costs of running are fairly constant, and are determined by speed and body weight, although there is some variability between individuals (see Section 5.3.6). Even so, however, it is clearly impossible for the individual with a $\dot{V}O_{2max}$ of 40 ml kg^{-1} min^{-1} to sustain for prolonged periods of time a running speed of 16 km h^{-1} (10 mph) which requires an oxygen consumption of about 50–55 ml kg^{-1} min^{-1}.

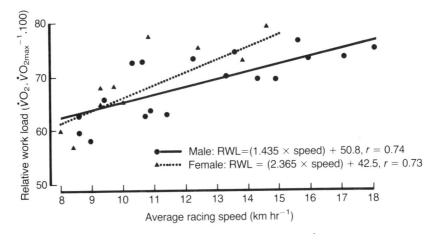

Figure 5.2 Relationship between fractional utilization of $\dot{V}O_{2max}$ and marathon performance for the same subjects as in Figure 5.1. The fractional utilization of aerobic capacity, or relative work load, is calculated as the oxygen consumption at average racing speed divided by the $\dot{V}O_{2max}$ achieved during uphill treadmill running. Since there is no wind resistance to overcome in treadmill running, the $\dot{V}O_2$ measured for the faster runners, but not for the slower runners, will be significantly less than would be measured during road running. (Reproduced with permission from Maughan and Leiper, 1983.)

The fraction of $\dot{V}O_{2max}$ which can be sustained for the duration of the race will have a major impact on performance. Elite performers generally utilize about 75% of $\dot{V}O_{2max}$ (Costill and Fox, 1969), but a wide range is apparent even among runners of comparable levels of performance. If runners with a wide range of performances are studied, the fastest runners use a higher proportion of their $\dot{V}O_{2max}$ than slower runners, and there is a significant correlation between race time and the fraction of $\dot{V}O_{2max}$ which runners utilize to run at their average pace (Figure 5.2). Maughan and Leiper (1983) found a correlation coefficient between the fraction of VO_{2max} utilized and the average running speed of 0.74 in 18 runners whose race times varied from 2:19 to 4:53 and Sjodin and Svedenhag (1985) found a correlation coefficient of 0.70 in 35 runners with performances of 2:12 to 3:52. In a smaller group, however, Farrell *et al.* (1979) found no such significant relationship ($r = 0.07$) in 13 runners with times from 2:17 to 3:49. For a group of runners, the fraction of $\dot{V}O_{2max}$ which can be sustained during a race is more closely related to the time taken rather than distance: in other words, the faster the runner, the higher the $\%\dot{V}O_{2max}$ which he is likely to be using. For any individual, the fraction of $\dot{V}O_{2max}$ which can be sustained decreases with the distance. Davies and Thompson (1979) found that a group of highly trained ultra-marathon runners employed 94% $\dot{V}O_{2max}$ over 5 km (15 min 49 s), 82% over 42.2 km (2:31) and 67% over 84.6 km (5:58). As with data relating to $\dot{V}O_{2max}$, however, there is no relationship between performance and fractional utilization of $\dot{V}O_{2max}$ within a group of runners of comparable ability. Those elite performers who cannot achieve outstandingly high values of $\dot{V}O_{2max}$ must compensate for this by employing a high fraction of their aerobic power. Results obtained from Derek Clayton in 1969 have been widely quoted. In that year he ran 2:08:33 for a marathon, but his $\dot{V}O_{2max}$ was found to be only 70 ml kg^{-1} min^{-1}; his exceptional performance was due in part to the ability to run for that distance at an average 86% of $\dot{V}O_{2max}$ (Costill et al., 1971a). Kjell-Erik Stahl who ran 2:10:38 for the distance in 1983, with a $\dot{V}O_{2max}$ of only 67 ml kg^{-1} min^{-1} (Sjodin and Svedenhag, 1985) was presumably able to work at a similarly high intensity.

Several points must be remembered when considering these figures. In many cases, laboratory measurements were not made close to the time of the marathon performance to which they have been compared (e g. Pollock, 1977). The laboratory measures of oxygen uptake at the average racing speed will inevitably underestimate $\dot{V}O_2$ in the race situation where the effect of air resistance has to be overcome. The exact effect of air resistance depends largely on running speed and wind conditions. For the fastest runners, oxygen consumption will be about 3–4 ml kg^{-1} min^{-1} higher in the race situation compared with treadmill running, and fractional utilization of $\dot{V}O_{2max}$ will be correspondingly increased by about 5·6%: for the slowest runners, the effect of overcoming air resistance is negligible (Maughan and Leiper, 1983). During a race, variations in running pace, gradient and wind resistance commonly occur, leading to fluctuations in the energy cost. Maron et al. (1976) measured the $\dot{V}O_2$ of two runners at intervals during a competitive event and found variations from 68% to 100% of $\dot{V}O_{2max}$.

The high rate of energy expenditure necessary for successful marathon running requires, in addition to a high rate of oxygen consumption, an adequate supply of substrate (fuel) and the ability to deal with the large amounts of heat produced. These factors will be dealt with elsewhere in this chapter.

5.3 PHYSIOLOGICAL CHARACTERISTICS OF ELITE MARATHON RUNNERS

5.3.1 Cardiorespiratory variables

The ability of elite marathon runners to achieve a high $\dot{V}O_{2max}$ and to run for prolonged periods at a high fraction of this $\dot{V}O_{2max}$ has already been described. The factors which contribute to this ability have been extensively studied. To achieve a high oxygen consumption, an effective system for the transfer of oxygen from the atmosphere to the site of utilization within the exercising muscles is essential. In the absence of any pulmonary insufficiency, the first stage of this process, the transfer of oxygen from the atmosphere to the blood passing through the lungs, is not a limiting factor, and lung function tests on elite endurance runners do not distinguish them from the general population (Martin and May, 1987).

Whole body oxygen consumption can be described by the following equation:

$$\dot{V}O_2 = \text{Heart Rate} \times \text{Stroke Volume} \times \text{a-v } O_2 \text{ difference}$$

Stroke volume is the volume of blood ejected by the heart with each beat, and the product of heart rate and stroke volume gives the cardiac output, the volume of blood pumped around the circulation each minute. The a-v O_2 difference is the difference in oxygen content between arterial and mixed venous blood, often referred to as the oxygen extraction.

The high cardiac output achieved by good marathon runners depends on a higher than normal stroke volume – at maximal work the heart rate is generally not different from that of untrained individuals and if anything is slightly less, but high stroke volumes are achieved as a consequence of increased heart size (Åstrand and Rodahl, 1986). Blomqvist and Saltin (1983) reviewed the cardiovascular adaptations to training and reported a cardiac output in Olympic athletes of 30 l min^{-1} at maximal exercise; this was achieved with a heart rate of 182 beats min^{-1} and a stroke volume of 167 ml. By comparison, untrained students achieved a maximum cardiac output of 20 l min^{-1}, with a heart rate of 192 beats min^{-1} and a stroke volume of 104 ml; in response to a period of endurance training, these individuals were able to increase maximum cardiac output to 23 l min^{-1}, with a heart rate of 190 beats min^{-1} and a stroke volume of 120 ml. The heart volumes of elite runners may not, however, be significantly larger than those of well-trained but non-elite athletes either in men (Pollock, 1977) or in women (Pollak et al., 1987). The increased stroke volume of the athlete is accompanied by a reduced heart rate at rest since resting cardiac output remains unchanged, and a low resting heart rate has long been recognized as an accompaniment of endurance fitness (Hoogerwerf, 1929). Well-trained endurance athletes also display an increased extraction of oxygen from the blood, in spite of the increased flow rate (Grimby and Saltin, 1971). This probably results from the increased capillarity of skeletal muscle in the endurance-trained individual which permits a greater mean transit time for the passage of red cells through the capillary bed (Saltin, 1986).

5.3.2 Haematological status

The oxygen-carrying capacity of the blood is determined largely by its haemoglobin content: each gram of haemoglobin can transport 1.36 ml oxygen. Artificial reduction of the haemoglobin content by withdrawal of blood reduces the oxygen-carrying capacity of the blood and leads to a reduction in $\dot{V}O_{2max}$ (Ekblom, Wilson and Åstrand, 1976; Woodson, 1984). Subsequent re-infusion of blood or red blood cells increases the circulating haemoglobin content and results in an increased $\dot{V}O_{2max}$ (Ekblom, Wilson and Åstrand, 1976; Robertson et al., 1984). Re-infusion of red blood cells has also been shown to improve times in a 5-mile (8 km) run, where a high aerobic capacity is known to be a major factor in determining performance (Williams et al., 1981). In recent years, the practice of 'blood doping', the removal of blood some weeks prior to competition and re-infusion of the red cells shortly before the race, has been followed by a number of top athletes in endurance events. In view of the apparent benefits of a high haemoglobin level, it seems surprising that highly trained marathon runners are generally observed to have a resting blood haemoglobin content somewhat lower than that of the general population. This phenomenon of athletic anaemia has been reviewed by Clement and Sawchuk (1984) and probably represents an adaption to training, but may also reflect a true iron deficiency resulting from inadequate dietary intake and an increased iron loss during strenuous exercise. In male athletes, there is probably an increased iron loss due to hard training but this loss should be balanced by an increased intake, as total nutrient intake must be increased to meet the high energy requirement. Women generally are more prone to anaemia and, in female athletes, a combination of pseudoanaemia and true iron deficiency is far more likely. The reduced haemoglobin concentration of endurance athletes is often considered to be an effect of the increased blood volume (Dill et al., 1974; Grimby and Saltin, 1971), and indeed the total blood haemoglobin content is increased in athletes (Brotherhood, Brozovic and Pugh, 1975; Remes, Vuopio and Harkonen, 1979). In spite of the evidence that blood re-infusion is effective in increasing both $\dot{V}O_{2max}$ and running performance, the low red cell count of the marathon runner may have some benefits. With a low red cell count, the viscosity of the blood – its resistance to flow through the blood vessels – is decreased; this may permit an increased muscle blood flow in hard exercise. A low resting red cell count may also be a useful adaptation in helping to off-set the haemoconcentration which occurs during exercise. The fall in haemoglobin concentration is thus partly offset, and is further compensated for by an increase in red cell 2,3-diphosphoglycerate (2,3-DPG) content (Brotherhood, Brozovic and Pugh, 1975; Remes, Vuopio and Harkonen, 1979). The ability of the blood to deliver oxygen to the muscles is enhanced by 2,3-DPG, and the increased concentration seen in the red blood cells of athletes may improve the oxygen supply to muscle although other factors such as temperature and pH should ensure that O_2 delivery is adequate. Adaptations occurring in response to training at altitude may produce similar benefits; the red cell mass is increased and 2,3-DPG concentrations are also increased. Before, and for a few years after the Olympic Games in Mexico City (altitude 2260 m), high altitude training was considered essential for endurance athletes, even if the competition was at sea level. After a few years, altitude training lost its popularity. This was probably a consequence of a failure to understand some of the requirements and limitations of the procedure; under appropriate conditions, considerable benefits can be gained from training at altitude.

5.3.3 Metabolic variables

There has been much argument as to whether $\dot{V}O_{2max}$ is limited by central (cardiorespiratory) factors or whether the limit is peripheral (muscular). This debate has arisen in part from the observation that trained endurance athletes not only have a highly developed cardio-vascular system, but also show marked changes in the oxidative capacity of their muscles. The balance of the available evidence now suggests that the capacity of the heart to pump blood around the circulation is probably the limiting factor to oxygen consumption in running (Saltin, 1986), but the metabolic changes which occur within the muscle in response to endurance training are of considerable importance to the marathon runner (for review, see Saltin and Gollnick, 1983). The activity of some of the enzymes involved in oxidative energy production is often used as a convenient measure of the total oxidative capacity of muscle; in particular, succinate dehydrogenase (SDH) is often used as a marker enzyme. Costill, Fink and Pollock (1976) showed that the SDH activity of samples obtained from the gastrocnemius muscle of elite distance runners was 3.4 times that of untrained men; values for good, non-elite runners were 2.8 times those of the untrained group. The activity of malate dehydrogenase, another enzyme involved in oxidative metab-olism was also found in that study to be twice as great in the trained men as in the untrained subjects, but there were no differences between the groups in the activity of enzymes involved in anaerobic energy production. The significance of these differences probably relates to their effect on the choice of fuel utilized during exercise rather than in determining the whole-body $\dot{V}O_{2max}$: this will be discussed in Section 5.4.2.

5.3.4 Muscle: fibre composition and capillary density

The refinement of the needle-biopsy technique for obtaining small muscle samples from healthy volunteers (Bergstrom, 1962) provided a major stimulus to the study of muscle characteristics in man. The properties of the major fibre types are discussed in Chapter 1. Muscle fibre composition of elite athletes was an obvious topic for study, and it has been clearly established that Type I fibres predominate in successful endurance athletes whereas top-class sprinters have muscles containing mostly Type II fibres (Saltin *et al.*, 1977). Costill, Fink and Pollock, (1976) found that 79% of the muscle fibres in the gastrocnemius muscle of elite distance runners could be classified as Type I fibres, with a range from 50 to 98%; non-elite middle distance runners had a mean of 62% Type I fibres and untrained men a mean of 58% Type I fibres. Not only were the elite runners' Type I fibres more numerous than Type II fibres, they were also 30% larger; this meant that 83% of the total muscle cross-sectional area was occupied by Type I fibres. Type I and Type II fibres were the same size in the other two groups of subjects. In contrast to these findings, however, Costill *et al.* (1987) have reported no difference in cross-sectional area of individual Type I and Type II muscle fibres in the gastrocnemius muscle of elite women distance runners, although Type I fibres were larger than Type II fibres in non-elite women distance runners. The finding of selective hypertrophy of the different muscle fibre types in response to specific types of training has been reported elsewhere (Saltin, 1973). Although training can clearly influence the size of individual muscle fibres, and can also dramatically alter their metabolic characteristics, there is no evidence to support the suggestion that changes in fibre composition can normally be induced as a result of training. In general terms then, at least part of the success of elite marathon runners can be attributed to genetic endowment. It is possible, however, to compensate to some degree by training: one of the subjects in the study of Costill, Fink and Pollock (1976) achieved a marathon time of 2:18 with equal proportions of Type I and Type II fibres. The oxidative capacity of both the major muscle fibre types can be greatly enhanced by training, so that in elite runners the capacity of Type II fibres to oxidize fuels, including fat, may exceed the oxidative capacity of the Type I fibres of untrained individuals (Saltin *et al.*, 1977).

Muscles of elite endurance athletes are also found to have a higher than average ratio of capillaries to muscle fibres (Hermansen and Wachtlova, 1971; Ingjer, 1979). The first of these studies found no difference between trained and untrained subjects in the number of capillaries per unit area of muscle, whereas Ingjer (1979) observed that the capillary density expressed per unit area was higher in elite athletes.

This may reflect differences in the level of performance of the two groups: Ingjer's subjects attained a mean $\dot{V}O_{2max}$ of 78 ml kg^{-1} min^{-1}, whereas those of Hermansen and Wachtlova achieved 71 ml kg^{-1} min^{-1}. In a separate report comparing trained and untrained individuals Ingjer (1978) observed a highly significant relationship between capillary density and $\dot{V}O_{2max}$. Some of these effects can be accounted for by differences in the fibre composition of the individuals studied, since it is generally recognized that Type I muscle fibres have a better capillary supply than that of Type II fibres (Saltin and Gollnick, 1983). In view of the crucial role of the capillary bed of muscle in providing a surface for exchange between muscle and blood, the highly developed capillarity of the elite marathon runner allows an improved transfer of oxygen, substrates and waste products at high perfusion rates.

5.3.5 Physical characteristics

Good marathon runners are generally short in stature and have a low body weight; a survey by Costill (1972) of all winners of the Boston Marathon from 1897 to 1965 showed an average height of 170 cm and an average weight of 61 kg. The low body weight of the elite runners is largely a consequence of low body fat content: skinfold estimates of body fat content among 114 runners in the 1968 US Olympic Trial race gave an average of 7.5% of body weight, less than half that of an age-matched, active, but not specially trained group (Costill, Bowers and Kammer, 1970). In their study of elite American long-distance and marathon runners, Pollock et al (1977) found an average height of 177 cm, body weight of 63.1 kg and body fat content, as determined by hydrostatic weighing, of 4.7%. This study also suggested that the use of equations derived from non-athletic populations to estimate the body fat content of elite athletes from anthropometric measurements might give erroneous results. Low values for body fat content (15%) among top-class women distance runners have also been reported (Wilmore and Brown, 1974) with some runners having less than 10% fat. Graves, Pollock and Sparling (1987) found low values for body fat content in elite (14.3% body fat) and non-elite (16.8%) female distance runners, with no significant difference between the two groups. Excess body fat serves no useful function for the runner and represents extra weight to be carried around the course, so the low body fat of elite runners confers a distinct advantage. The suggestion that extra fat stores may be useful in supplying fuel is ill-conceived, as the problem is one of mobilization and utilization; the total amount of fat oxidized during a marathon is small, amounting to no more than 150–200 g.

Before the popularization of marathon running with its consequent financial rewards, marathon runners were generally athletes who turned to distance running after a racing career over shorter distances on the track. Elite competitors were normally those who had competed at the highest level over distances up to 10 km. It is now more common for younger runners to attempt the marathon distance without experience over shorter distances. It is still true, however, that the most successful competitors seem to be older than those competing in shorter distance events. Performance falls off only slowly with increasing age, and many runners find that their best performances at the marathon distance are achieved in their late thirties and early forties.

5.3.6 Biomechanics and running economy

It requires no sophisticated laboratory analysis to distinguish the elite runner from the jogger – even the untrained eye can see that the fluent running action of the best marathon runners is generally quite different from that of the more modest performer. The exceptions to this rule – Alberto Salazar and John Treacy, for example – are few. Running style is partly an innate characteristic and partly a consequence of the modification of this style by prolonged training. Several studies have reported that elite runners are more economical in terms of the oxygen cost of running at a given speed. Cavanagh, Pollock and Landa (1977) found that the oxygen consumption of *elite* distance runners at a speed of 4.5 m s^{-1} (10 mph) was 53 ml kg^{-1} min^{-1} compared with a value of 56 ml kg^{-1} min^{-1} for good runners at the same running speed. In a comparison of 15 elite female distance runners with 13 good female distance runners, Pate *et al.* (1987) found that the mean $\dot{V}O_2$ of the elite runners at a treadmill speed of 3.8 m s^{-1} (8.6 mph) was 45.0 ml kg^{-1} min^{-1}, significantly lower than that of the good runners at the same speed (47.9 ml kg^{-1} min^{-1}); at the slightly faster speed of 4.1 m s^{-1} (9.2 mph), this difference persisted, with mean values for $\dot{V}O_2$ of 48.4 and 51.2 ml kg^{-1} min^{-1} for elite and good runners respectively. Based on a review of the literature, Costill (1972) concluded that, at a range of speeds, marathon runners used 5–10% less oxygen than middle distance runners: this represents an enormous advantage in events lasting in excess of 2 hours. The importance of an efficient running style is demonstrated by the existence of a significant relationship between the oxygen cost of running at a given speed and best marathon time (Farrell *et al.*, 1979), although Foster, Daniels and Yarbrough (1977) found no such significant relationship.

The biomechanical factors which might contribute to an efficient running style are not at present clear. Cavanagh, Pollock and Landa (1977) found that elite distance runners had a slightly shorter stride length, and correspondingly higher stride frequency, whèn running at the same speed as non-elite runners, but these differences were not statistically significant. There was no difference between the two groups of runners in their vertical oscillation during running, and yet, as mentioned above, the better runners had a superior economy of effort. In a biomechanical study of women marathon runners, Buckalew *et al.* (1985) found no differences in gait between the first 10 and last 10 finishers in the trial for the 1984 US Women's Olympic team.

5.3.7 Male and female marathon runners

In 1960, the best time ever recorded by a male marathon runner was 2:15:16. The best performance by a woman was 3:40:22, a record dating back to 1926. By 1970, the men's record had improved by 6 min 42 s; in the same time, the women's record improved by 37 min 29 s and the gap had narrowed to 54 min 19 s. A decade later, the men's record had not improved, but the women's record had been lowered to 2:25:42, and the gap between the sexes was only 17 min 8 s. At the time of writing, the men's record of 2:7:12 is only 13 min 54 s better than the women's record. This rapid improvement in women's marathon running standard at a time when men's performances are relatively stagnant has led to speculation that, in the not too distant future, the best women runners will be able to beat the best men. There is, however, little evidence to support this suggestion.

The values of $\dot{V}O_{2max}$ achieved by elite women athletes are generally lower than those of men in all sports even after correction for body weight (Wilmore, 1982). Part of this difference is a consequence of the higher body fat content of women compared with men, but even if body fat is taken into account, and $\dot{V}O_{2max}$ is expressed relative to lean body mass, most studies show that the values achieved by males are still higher, although the difference is considerably less. A number of factors other than body composition may contribute to the lower $\dot{V}O_{2max}$ of women. The maximum cardiac output that can be achieved is generally lower: this reflects a lower stroke volume as maximum heart rates are not different. Blood volume also tends to be lower in women than in men. Both these factors are of course related to body size, and both are strongly influenced by endurance training. In all the comprehensive studies to date, the elite male runners studied have been more highly trained than the women, and it is not clear whether a true sex-specific difference exists when both body size and training status are taken into account.

The haemoglobin concentration of the blood is generally lower in women than in men, and in view of the importance of haemoglobin for oxygen transport, this may be a significant factor in determining $\dot{V}O_{2max}$ (Woodson, 1984). Since hard endurance training tends to lower the resting haemoglobin content of blood, the problem of anaemia may be a serious one for many women marathon runners and should be monitored and corrected if necessary. The effects of the low haemoglobin content on women may be at least partly offset by a higher 2,3-DPG content relative to haemoglobin level seen in trained women (Pate, Barnes and Miller, 1985). In a comparison of performance-matched male and female competitors in a 24.2 km road race, Pate, Barnes and Miller (1985) found that the women runners did not differ from the men in terms of body fat content, $\dot{V}O_{2max}$ and maximum heart rate or in training status: this tends to confirm the suggestion that, once large numbers of women begin to train at levels close to those of elite men, the performance gap will become very small or may indeed disappear.

Muscle fibre composition shows a normal distribution in both males and females, with no sex difference in the relative proportions of Type I and Type II fibres present (Nygaard, 1981). Fibre cross-sectional areas are generally smaller in women than in men, but in both sexes hypertrophy occurs in response to training, making it difficult to compare subject groups of different training status. Studies on trained and untrained men and women have generally indicated a lower capillary to fibre ratio in females even after correction for fibre area, but again, this may reflect training status of the subjects studied (Ready and Alexander, 1982). There is some evidence that the glycolytic capacity of untrained male muscle is higher than that of muscle from women, although the muscle oxidative capacity is similar in both sexes (Nygaard, 1981; Green, Fraser and Ranney, 1984). This difference, if it persists in highly trained muscle, may have important consequences for the choice of metabolic fuel, favouring oxidative metabolism of fat as an energy source in female muscle during exercise. There have been some reports that women use more fat than men during submaximal exercise (Nygaard et al., 1984; Froberg and Pedersen, 1984), leading to a sparing of glycogen and a possible increase in endurance capacity. In other studies, however, there appeared to be no difference between men and women in the relative contributions of fat and carbohydrate to energy production during exercise (Costill et al., 1979; Pate, Barnes and Miller, 1985); both these latter studies involved well-trained, performance-matched subjects.

The training associated with preparation for marathon competition has been reported to have a significant impact on the hormonal status of women runners. It is well established that women engaged in strenuous training show an increased frequency of menstrual disorders including oligomenorrhoea (reduced frequency of menstruation) and secondary amenorrhoea (absence of menstruation after it has begun at puberty).

Until recently, this was seen primarily as a threat to reproduction, but these fears have largely been allayed by the fact that normal menstrual patterns are generally established if the training load is reduced. Conception is also possible even after prolonged periods of amenorrhoea, indicating that fertility may not be impaired. The reduced circulating oestrogen levels resulting from hard training, however, may cause problems, as oestrogen has an important role in maintaining the calcium content of bone. Women with amenorrhoea associated with training may be at an increased risk of both stress fractures and traumatic fractures as a result of a decreased bone mineral content (Lloyd *et al.*, 1986). The long-term effects of regular intense training on bone metabolism are not at present clear, but will emerge as distance running continues to grow in popularity among women.

5.4 ADAPTATION TO TRAINING

Many of the changes which occur in response to physical training have been described in the previous section on the physiological characteristics of the elite performer. At the highest level, these runners have all undergone an extensive training programme, and have also had the good fortune to have been endowed with inherited characteristics which predispose them to success in endurance events. In any consideration of the effects of training, the training response and the genetic potential must be considered separately.

  We have already seen that marathon running requires a high aerobic capacity and the ability to function for prolonged periods at a high fraction of this capacity. A primary aim of training must therefore be to develop these capabilities. Many studies have shown that endurance training results in an increase in $\dot{V}O_{2max}$, although the precise response depends on a number of different factors. The characteristics of a training programme can be summarized as the intensity, duration and frequency of the training sessions; other factors which must be considered include the period of time over which training is carried out and the initial level of fitness of the individual. There have been few long-term studies on healthy volunteers in which the relative importance of the different components of a training regimen have been investigated on a systematic basis, and in none of these studies has it been possible to examine the effects of training programmes comparable with those undertaken by marathon runners. The problems in mounting such a study stem largely from the difficulty of persuading healthy but untrained volunteers to train to run a marathon. We are forced therefore to rely on results obtained from three different models; first, the limited training studies which have been done in man; second, cross-sectional comparisons of runners who have followed different training programmes; third, studies of the effects of training on animals.

The relative effects of some of the different components of a training regimen on improvements in $\dot{V}O_{2max}$ have been summarized by Wenger and Bell (1986). This survey concluded that exercise intensity was the most important factor, with the greatest improvements in $\dot{V}O_{2max}$ occurring at training intensities of 90–100% of $\dot{V}O_{2max}$. There is obviously an interaction between training intensity and duration – if the intensity is very high, the effort cannot be sustained for prolonged periods, and there is some evidence that prolonged training sessions (in excess of 30–40 min) may be as effective as shorter sessions at a higher intensity. For improvements in $\dot{V}O_{2max}$ training should be carried out at least 3 times per week, although improvements are seen in very unfit subjects in response to only 2 training sessions per week. It is in trying to establish the optimum duration and frequency of training for marathon runners that the limitations of the available information become apparent. Many runners, and most good runners, expect to train on a daily basis, and often more than once per day, and will train for 1–3 hours per day. No controlled studies on the response to this type of training are available. Results of earlier studies on the training responses of rats, quoted by Saltin (1971), showed that the improvements (as measured by heart size) in response to 3 h running per day for 6 months were not greater than those resulting from 1 h running per day for 3 months if the running speed was the same. If, however, the speed was varied with the total distance kept constant, the greatest improvement resulted from the highest running speed. This again emphasizes the major role of intensity, as measured by running speed, as a determinant of the magnitude of the training response.

Cross-sectional studies of marathon runners of varying levels of performance have shown some significant relationships between indices of training load and performance. Foster (1983) found a significant relationship between training volume, measured as the average weekly mileage in the 8 weeks prior to competition, and marathon performance ($r = -0.61$), but no relationship between performance and an index of training intensity ($r = -0.20$); both these factors were rather poor predictors of performance compared with measured $\dot{V}O_{2max}$, which was closely ($r = 0.96$) related to running speed in the race. These results perhaps indicate some of the problems in assessment of training intensity – distance can readily be measured, but intensity is less easy to quantify. In an unpublished study involving a much larger ($n = 468$) sample of male marathon runners, all of whom competed in the same race, finishing time was related to a variety of indices of training carried out in the 6 months prior to the race: average weekly training distance ($r = -0.54$); highest weekly training distance ($r = -0.60$); longest single

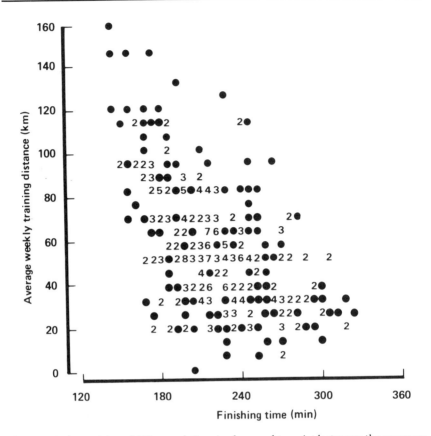

Figure 5.3 A good ($r = 0.54$) correlation is observed to exist between the average weekly training distance over the 6 months before a race and marathon finishing time. These results were obtained from 468 male runners who competed in the same race. Circles represent individual data points; where two or more data points coincide, the appropriate number is shown. In spite of the close correlation, a large variation between individuals is apparent at all levels.

training run ($r = -0.46$). All these correlations are highly significant, but there is nonetheless considerable variability between individuals. This is illustrated by the relationship between average weekly training distance and marathon finishing times (Figure 5.3). There is also a significant relationship between the period of time for which people had been training and race time ($r = -0.32$) but this was distorted to a degree by the advanced age of some of these runners. This type of information provides some evidence that training volume may be an important factor in marathon performance, but the results of these surveys must be interpreted with caution.

5.4.1 Central effects of training

The cardiovascular characteristics of the elite endurance athlete have been described earlier (Section 5.3.1). Successful competitors will invariably demonstrate an enlarged heart, which will permit a high cardiac output during strenuous exercise, a low resting heart rate and perhaps also a low maximum heart rate. The sedentary individual who embarks on an endurance training regimen will demonstrate some of these adaptations after only a few weeks. The increases in $\dot{V}O_{2max}$ which are observed in response to relatively short periods of endurance training may closely parallel the increases in the left ventricular end-diastolic volume (Åstrand and Rodahl, 1986). At rest, a low heart rate is characteristic of the endurance athlete although the mechanisms responsible for this adaptation are not fully understood. The average resting heart rate of 260 athletes who competed at the 1928 Olympic Games was 50 beats min^{-1}, with the lowest individual value being 30 beats min^{-1} (Hoogerwerf, 1929). Training does not increase the maximum heart rate which can be achieved during exercise as is sometimes supposed, but rather there is a tendency for the maximum heart rate to be reduced. Cardiac output, the product of the heart rate and stroke volume, is, however, increased at maximal exercise as the effect of an increased stroke volume outweighs any reduction in heart rate. At any given level of submaximal work, the cardiac output is very similar in the trained and untrained states; again reduced heart rate is balanced by an increased stroke volume at a given work load after training.

5.4.2 Peripheral effects of training

The debate regarding the primacy of central (cardiovascular) versus peripheral (muscular) factors as limitations to $\dot{V}O_{2max}$ seems to have been resolved in favour of the central circulation as the determinant of aerobic capacity (Saltin, 1986). There are, however, significant local changes within the muscles in response to endurance training (Saltin and Gollnick, 1983) and these have important consequences for marathon running ability. Muscle is an extremely plastic tissue, and although genetic factors are the major determinant of the quantity and quality of muscle present in the untrained individual, considerable changes in the functional characteristics can be induced. The major effects of endurance training on skeletal muscle are on its metabolic capacity and its capillary supply. Strength training on the other hand, mainly influences the size of a muscle and hence its force-generating capability.

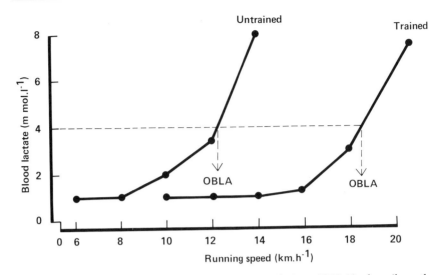

Figure 5.4 The onset of blood lactate accumulation (OBLA) describes the work load (running speed) corresponding to a blood lactate concentration of 4 mmol l^{-1}. In the trained state, a shift of the lactate–work load curve to the right is observed.

Many studies have shown that endurance training increases the mitochondrial content and oxidative capacity of the trained skeletal muscle, confirming the observation first made by Holloszy (1967) on rats trained by treadmill running. These trained animals (12 weeks progressive training) could run for 6 times as long on the treadmill as untrained rats, and this improved endurance capacity was attributed at least in part to the increased oxidative capacity of the muscles. Several studies have shown that training results in an increased activity of oxidative enzymes in the muscle, and the ability to oxidize both fat and carbohydrate, together with other fuels such as ketone bodies, is enhanced. The effects of endurance training on skeletal muscle and the significance of the changes which take place have been extensively reviewed (e.g. Saltin and Gollnick, 1983; Holloszy and Coyle, 1984; Matoba and Gollnick, 1984).

The major effect of the enzymatic changes which take place in muscle during training is to increase the contribution of fat, and correspondingly decrease the contribution of carbohydrate, to oxidative energy metabolism during submaximal exercise. This increased oxidation of fat is probably a consequence of an increase in the potential for oxidation of substrates relative to the glycolytic capacity, which shows little adaptive response to endurance training. The trained runner not only uses more fat and less carbohydrate at the same running speed, but also at the same relative exercise intensity expressed as a percentage of $\dot{V}O_{2max}$. Associated with the decreased rate of carbohydrate oxidation during exercise in the trained state is a decreased rate of conversion of glycogen and glucose to lactate. At any intensity within the normal range for endurance exercise, the trained individual has a lower blood lactate concentration than the untrained individual; again this is true whether the intensity is expressed in absolute or relative terms (Figure 5.4). These two effects, a decreased carbohydrate oxidation and decreased lactate production, result in a sparing of the body's limited carbohydrate stores. In view of the close links between the availability of glycogen as a fuel and endurance capacity (Section 5.6.2), this decreased glycogen utilization is a major factor in improving performance in marathon running.

The importance of a high capillary density in muscle for endurance performance and a description of the differences between trained and untrained muscle are reported elsewhere (Section 5.3.4). Studies of trained muscle show an increase in the capillary density, expressed as capillaries per fibre and as capillaries per unit area, providing an increased surface for exchange between blood and muscle. Several studies have shown parallel increases in $\dot{V}O_{2max}$ and in capillary density in response to training; significant increases in capillary density, resulting from growth of new capillaries, occur within the first few weeks of training (Andersen and Henriksson, 1977).

The central and peripheral adaptations which occur in response to training both contribute to improvements in endurance capacity. A well-developed oxygen transport system is essential for high rates of energy expenditure to be sustained, and a high capacity for fat oxidation within the muscle promotes endurance by sparing the body's limited glycogen stores. Together, these adaptations enable the trained runner to run at fast speeds without producing large amounts of lactic acid, and the maximum speed that can be achieved before large increases in the blood lactate concentration occur has been shown to be closely related to marathon running performance. The point at which an exponential increase in the blood lactate concentration begins to occur has been variously referred to as the anaerobic threshold or lactate threshold; these thresholds are commonly determined from measurements of the ventilatory response to exercise and are assumed to reflect metabolic acidosis resulting from anaerobic glycolysis. Perhaps a more useful concept is the onset of blood lactate accumulation (OBLA) which describes the exercise intensity at which a blood lactate concentration of 4 mmol l^{-1} is reached (Figure 5.4). Sjodin and Jacobs (1981) found a close relationship $(r = 0.96)$ between OBLA, expressed as the treadmill running speed, and marathon performance in a group of 18 runners with times ranging from 2:22 to 4:12. Several other studies have found similar high correlations between OBLA or anaerobic threshold and marathon performance (Sjodin and Svedenhag, 1985). This is not surprising, as OBLA depends on $\dot{V}O_{2max}$, the oxidative capacity of the muscle, and other factors including the oxygen cost of running.

5.5 TEMPERATURE REGULATION AND FLUID AND ELECTROLYTE BALANCE

Muscular activity is an inefficient process: only about 20–25% of the available chemical energy in the substrates used by muscle appears as useful work, with the remainder lost as heat. The resting rate of energy turnover is low, but running a marathon in a time of 2:30 requires an oxygen consumption of about 4 l min^{-1} for a 70 kg runner; this is equivalent to an energy expenditure of about 1.4 kW (20 kcal min^{-1}) throughout the race. If this increased rate of heat production is not balanced by a correspondingly high rate of heat loss, body temperature will rise above its normal level of 37–38°C. If none of the additional heat was lost, an increase in body temperature of about 5°C would occur within 15 min of running. The deep body temperature must be maintained within very narrow limits, and even before this point was reached, the runner would be forced to stop. Measurements made on marathon runners have shown that body temperature seldom rises by more than 2–3°C during the race. Pugh, Corbett and Johnson (1967) found that several marathon runners had a rectal temperature in excess of 40°C at the end of a race, with the highest individual value (41.1°C) being that of the winner of the race. Maughan (1985) measured post-race rectal temperature in 59 marathon runners and found values varying from 35.6 to 39.8°C with a mean of 38.3°C. Clearly, therefore, most of the additional heat produced during the race is lost from the body, and the rates of heat loss and heat production are closely matched. When body temperature is constant, the body's heat balance is described by the following equation:

$$R \pm C \pm K + M - E = 0$$

where R is radiant heat exchange, C = convective heat exchange, K = conductive heat exchange, M = metabolic heat production and E = evaporative heat loss. The first three variables may be positive or negative, depending on the relative temperatures of the skin and the environment; M is always positive and E always negative. At high rates of heat production, the physical processes of conduction, convection and radiation cannot achieve a sufficiently high rate of heat transfer from the body to the environment to prevent a rise in body temperature; if ambient temperature is high, heat may be gained by these mechanisms, further increasing the problem of thermoregulation. In this situation, the major avenue of heat loss is the evaporation of sweat secreted onto the skin surface. Evaporation is an effective method of heat loss; if 1 litre of water is evaporated from the skin surface, it removes approximately 2.4 MJ (580 kcal) of heat energy from the body. If a 2:30 marathon runner can produce sweat at a rate of 2 l h^{-1}, and if all of this is allowed to evaporate, the evaporative heat loss will precisely balance the rate of metabolic heat production, maintaining body temperature at a constant level if there are no other avenues of heat gain or heat loss.

5.5.1 Effect of variations in ambient temperature

Because of the intensity and duration of the effort involved, thermo-regulation during marathon running can be markedly influenced by environmental conditions. If the ambient temperature is high, heat will be gained by convection, radiation from hot objects in the environment and by conduction from the hot road surface. The only avenue of heat loss is then evaporation, and even this may be restricted if there is a following wind approximately equal to the runner's speed. The dangers of hyperthermia associated with marathon competition in the heat are well recognized (Fox, 1960; Wyndham and Strydom, 1969). The spectacular collapse of runners at the end of marathons (e.g. Pietri at the 1908 London Olympic Games, Peters at the 1954 Vancouver Empire Games and Andersen-Scheiss at the 1984 Los Angeles Olympic Games) has usually taken place on hot days. Even at moderate (23°C) environmental temperatures, however, Pugh, Corbett and Johnson (1967) found that some marathon runners had a post-race rectal temperature in excess of 40°C and Maron, Wagner and Horvath (1977) found that one runner, on a day when the temperature was 19°C recorded a peak temperature of 41.9°C during the latter stages of a race.

At low ambient temperatures, particularly if accompanied by wind and rain, hypothermia rather than hyperthermia may be a problem. The risk of hypothermia seems to be highest among runners who set off at a pace which they cannot sustain for the entire race (Maughan, Leiper and Thompson, 1985); body temperature is elevated and sweating is initiated to promote heat loss; if the runner is forced by fatigue or injury to slow down, the rate of heat production is decreased, but heat loss continues at a high rate and body temperature begins to fall. Body temperature will fall rapidly in lightly clad runners reduced to walking speed. In one marathon competitor who collapsed at the finish, rectal temperature was subsequently found to be 34.4°C (Ledingham et al., 1982). In another runner, who failed to complete the course, a rectal temperature of 33.4°C was recorded (Maughan, Leiper and Thompson, 1985).

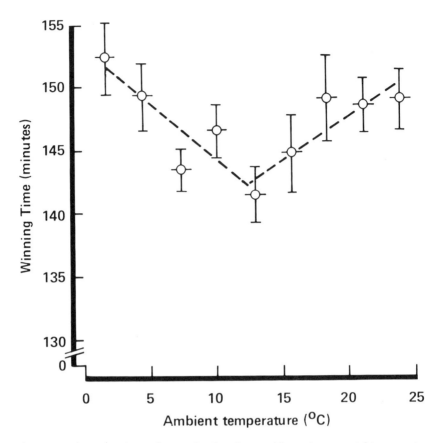

Figure 5.5 A comparison of race winning times with environmental temperature suggests that the optimum ambient temperature for marathon running is about 13°C for finishers taking about 2.5 hours. (Redrawn with permission from: Frederick, 1983.)

Marathon runners may thus encounter thermoregulatory problems at extremes of environmental conditions, but even in the same race, different competitors may respond quite differently (Maughan, 1985). The concept of an ideal environmental temperature for marathon running is supported by Frederick (1983), who related the winning times in 61 marathon races to climatic data (Figure 5.5). The races were held at average temperatures from 1°C to 24°C, and the data showed that the best times were generally recorded when ambient temperature was about 13°C. Frederick also suggested that the optimal temperature for slower runners might be rather higher on account of their lower rates of heat production.

5.5.2 Fluid and electrolyte balance

High rates of sweat secretion are necessary during hard exercise in order to limit the rise in body temperature which would otherwise occur. If the exercise is prolonged, this leads to progressive dehydration and loss of electrolytes. At very high sweat rates, much of the sweat secreted is not evaporated, but simply drips from the skin. This water loss is not effective in cooling the body, and increases the risk of dehydration without benefit to the runner. The rate of sweat secretion is proportional to the rate of heat production (i.e. running speed) and depends also on climatic factors. In a marathon race, the faster runners generally lose sweat at a higher rate than the slower runners, but they are active for a shorter period of time, so total sweat loss is unrelated to finishing time (Maughan, 1985). It is also apparent that rate of sweat secretion varies considerably between individuals, even when other factors such as running speed and ambient temperature are constant; the reasons for this inter-individual variability are not clearly understood. Marathon runners in the same race and with the same fluid intake may lose from as little as 1% to as much as 6% of body weight during a race (Whiting, Maughan and Miller, 1984). At high ambient temperatures, runners may lose 8% of body weight in a race, equivalent to about 5–6 l of water for a 70 kg individual (Costill, Kammer and Fisher, 1970). Fluid losses corresponding to as little as 2% of body weight can impair the ability to exercise (Saltin, 1964). The reduction in plasma volume may be particularly important, as there is a requirement for a high blood flow to the skin to promote heat loss, while blood flow to the working muscles must be maintained to provide an adequate supply of oxygen and substrates. Fatigue towards the end of a marathon may thus result as much from the effects of dehydration as from substrate depletion. The increased resting plasma volume of the highly trained runner may be an advantage in this situation.

Together with the water secreted as sweat are a variety of electrolytes and organic molecules. The electrolytes are present in varying concentrations, which bear some relationship to their concentration in plasma, but sweat composition varies widely between individuals and also varies at different times within the same individual. Table 5.1 gives an indication of the concentrations of the major electrolytes.

The total electrolyte content of sweat is less than that of plasma, so large sweat losses tend to concentrate the plasma. Although sweat potassium content may be high, large amounts of potassium are added to the plasma from liver, muscle and red cells during hard exercise, and plasma concentrations of most if not all the major electrolytes rise during prolonged exercise.

Table 5.1 Concentration (in meq l^{-1}) of the major electrolytes in plasma and in sweat (from Maughan, 1986a)

	Plasma	Sweat
Sodium	137–144	40–80
Potassium	3.5–4.9	4–8
Calcium	4.4–5.2	3–4
Magnesium	1.5–2.0	1–4
Chloride	100–108	30–70

5.5.3 Fluid replacement in exercise

Fluid intake during marathon running is aimed at replacing water losses and providing additional fuel for the muscles. Electrolyte replacement in exercise is not a priority, and the belief that a relationship exists between electrolyte loss and muscle cramp, although often advanced, has not been proved (Maughan, 1986b). Absorption of water from the gut, however, is promoted by the presence of small amounts of electrolytes. If the glucose content of drinks is high, more glucose will be absorbed, but the rate of water uptake will be decreased. As a compromise, therefore, drinks should generally contain relatively small amounts of glucose (about 40 g l^{-1}) together with small amounts of electrolytes, particularly sodium. Athletes should be well hydrated before exercise, and should begin drinking at the earliest possible opportunity. Fluid replacement may be more of a problem for the faster runners, as the time available for replacement is less, and the higher exercise intensity tends to reduce the availability of ingested fluids. A report by Noakes *et al.* (1985) suggests that it is possible for slow competitors in ultramarathon races to develop water intoxication as a result of excessive intake, but marathon runners should generally aim to drink as much as is possible during the race, particularly on hot days. The formulation of fluids for water and fuel replacement during exercise has been reviewed by Lamb and Brodowicz (1986).

5.6 NUTRITIONAL FACTORS

5.6.1 Nutrition for training

The most obvious effect of training for marathon competition on nutrition is the need for an increased energy intake to balance the additional energy expenditure. Other possible effects are on the requirement for specific nutrients, and have been the subject of considerable debate. The following suggestions have been made at various times:

1. There may be a need for a high protein intake as a consequence of an increased rate of protein oxidation during exercise;
2. Carbohydrate intake should be high to allow for resynthesis of muscle glycogen between training sessions;
3. Requirements for specific vitamins may be increased due to an increased rate of degradation or excretion;
4. Iron losses resulting from increased red cell destruction and losses in sweat may lead to anaemia in the absence of a high iron intake;
5. Requirements for electrolytes and trace elements may be increased by sweat losses;
6. Performance may be improved by nutritional ergogenic aids, including pollen, wheat germ and many others.

There is some justification for some, if not all of these suggestions, but there is at present a lack of experimental evidence on the dietary requirements of athletes engaged in strenuous training. Equally there is little published information on the dietary habits of these athletes.

In the early stages of an endurance training programme, it is a common observation that some loss of body weight occurs, the loss being primarily that of body fat. Once a steady body weight is attained, however, energy expenditure is balanced by intake; the question therefore is whether this increased total energy intake provides sufficient additional nutrients or whether there is a need for specific supplementation. There is little information available on the energy intake of marathon runners engaged in different levels of training, but if it is accepted that they are in energy balance, and use the figure of 4.2 kJ kg^{-1} km^{-1} (Margaria et al., 1963) as the energy cost of running on the level, then a 70 kg runner covering 160 km (100 miles) per week in training must consume at least 6.7 MJ day^{-1} in excess of the energy needed for his other activities. If a balanced diet is consumed, the additional intake will ensure an adequate supply of protein, minerals and vitamins as there is generally no justification for dietary supplements. Protein oxidation does not make a large contribution to energy supply during exercise, and marathon training will not significantly increase dietary protein requirements. The same is true of vitamins. This area has been the subject of a comprehensive review by Brotherhood (1984), who suggested that one possible exception to this generalization was iron. Iron deficiency has frequently been reported among endurance athletes, particularly runners, although it is not clear whether this reflects an inadequate uptake of dietary iron or an excessive loss (Clement and Sawchuck, 1984); in any case, where iron deficiency is identified, dietary modification or iron supplementation may be indicated (Section 5.3.2). The other specific requirement for the marathon runner who is training hard once or twice per day is for a high carbohydrate intake to replace the muscle and liver glycogen stores which are utilized during exercise. If adequate glycogen resynthesis does not take place after training, the capacity to perform another high intensity training session will be reduced. Costill, Bowers and Branam (1971) showed that a high carbohydrate diet (70% of energy intake as carbohydrate) enabled runners who were training for 2 h per day to maintain muscle glycogen levels, whereas if the carbohydrate content was only 40%, a progressive fall in muscle glycogen was observed. Sherman (1983) recommended a daily dietary carbohydrate intake of 500–600 g to ensure adequate glycogen resynthesis. This high carbohydrate intake should, of course, be accompanied by a large fluid intake to ensure replacement of water lost as sweat.

5.6.2 Nutrition for competition

There is no doubt that the performance of prolonged exercise such as marathon running can be substantially modified by dietary intake in the precompetition period. The pre-race period can be divided into two phases – the few days prior to the race, and race day itself.

Dietary manipulation to increase muscle glycogen content in the few days prior to exercise has been extensively recommended for marathon runners following observations that these procedures were effective in increasing endurance capacity in cycle ergometer exercise lasting about 2 h. The suggested procedure was to deplete muscle glycogen by prolonged exercise and to prevent resynthesis by consuming a low-carbohydrate diet for 2–3 days before changing to a high-carbohydrate diet for the last 3 days during which little or no exercise was performed. This procedure can double the muscle glycogen content and is effective in increasing cycling performance, measured as the time for which a given workload could be sustained (Ahlborg et al., 1967). In a race situation, however, the aim is to cover a given distance in the shortest possible time, and there have been no definitive studies showing that comparable improvements in marathon running performance can be achieved by the same means. Karlsson and Saltin (1971) showed that performance in a 30 km race was improved by 7.5 min when muscle glycogen stores were artificially elevated prior to competition: these runners were able to maintain their speed for longer and slowed down less in the closing stages of the race when glycogen levels were high.

Bebb *et al.* (1984) found that treadmill running time to exhaustion at 70% of $\dot{V}O_{2max}$ was improved by a high-carbohydrate diet fed in the 3-day period between two such exhausting runs. There seems little doubt that an increased dietary carbohydrate intake in the few days prior to a race is likely to lead to improved performance (Sherman and Costill, 1984) but some reservations have been expressed (Brotherhood, 1984) as many runners complain of fatigue and muscle discomfort associated with a high-carbohydrate intake.

On race day it is generally recommended that the last pre-race meal should be low in fat and high in carbohydrate and should be taken at least 3 hours before competition begins. Large intakes of carbohydrate taken about 30–60 min prior to exercise may have a detrimental effect on performance by causing an elevation of insulin and consequent inhibition of fatty acid mobilization (see Coyle and Coggan, 1984, for review). If less fat is available to the muscle, the limited glycogen stores will be used at a higher rate, thus hastening the onset of fatigue. During exercise, insulin secretion is inhibited, and carbohydrate feeding during, or perhaps immediately before, the race does not inhibit fat mobilization and may improve performance. The suggestion has been made that caffeine ingestion shortly before exercise may increase performance in endurance exercise by increasing fatty acid availability but its diuretic action may promote excessive fluid loss which is undesirable. Some long-distance runners prefer to take no food on the day of the race; fasting has been shown to increase endurance capacity in rats, by promoting fat utilization. In man, short-duration fasting does not significantly reduce the muscle glycogen content, although the liver glycogen stores are rapidly depleted. In theory, endurance performance could be improved by short-term fasting, but the evidence suggests that endurance capacity decreases with fasting of up to 36 hours (Dohm *et al.*, 1986; Loy *et al.*, 1986).

REFERENCES

Ahlborg, B., Bergstrom, J., Brohult, J., Ekelund, L.-G., Hultman, E. and Maschio, G. (1967) Human muscle glycogen content and capacity for prolonged exercise after different diets. *Forsvarsmedicin*, **3**, 85–99.

Andersen, P. and Henriksson, J. (1977) Capillary supply of the quadriceps femoris muscle of man: adaptive response to exercise. *Journal of Physiology*, **270**, 677–691.

Åstrand, P.-O. and Rodahl, K. (1986) *Textbook of Work Physiology*, 3rd edn, McGraw Hill, New York.

Bebb, J., Brewer, J., Patton, A. and Williams, C. (1984) Endurance running and the influence of diet on fluid intake. *Journal of Sports Sciences*, **3**, 198–199.

Bergstrom, J. (1962) Muscle electrolytes in man. *Scandinavian Journal of Clinical and Laboratory Investigation*, **14** Suppl. **68**, 1–62.

Blomqvist, C.G. and Saltin, B. (1983) Cardiovascular adaptations to physical training. *Annual Review of Physiology*, **45**, 169–189.

Brotherhood, J., Brozovic, B. and Pugh, L.G.C. (1975) Haematological status of middle and long-distance runners. *Clinical Science and Molecular Medicine*, **48**, 139–145.

Brotherhood, J.R. (1984) Nutrition and sports performance. *Sports Medicine*, **1**, 350–389.

Buckalew, D.P., Barlow, D.A., Fischer, J.W. and Richards, J.G. (1985) Biomechanical profile of elite women marathoners. *International Journal of Sport Biomechanics*, **1**, 330–347.

Cavanagh, P.R., Pollock, M.L. and Landa, J. (1977) A biomechanical comparison of elite and good distance runners. *Annals of the New York Academy of Sciences*, **301**, 328–345.

Clement, D.B. and Sawchuck, L.L. (1984) Iron status and sports performance. *Sports Medicine*, **1**, 65–74.

Costill, D.L. (1970) Metabolic responses during distance running. *Journal of Applied Physiology*, **28**, 251–255.

Costill, D.L. (1972) Physiology of marathon running. *Journal of the American Medical Association*, **221**, 1024–1029.

Costill, D.L., Bowers, R. and Branam, G. (1971) Muscle glycogen utilisation during prolonged exercise on successive days. *Journal of Applied Physiology*, **31**, 834–838.

Costill, D.L., Bowers, R. and Kammer, W.F. (1970) Skinfold estimates of body fat among marathon runners. *Medicine and Science in Sports*, **2**, 93–95.

Costill, D.L., Branam, G., Eddy, D. and Sparks, K. (1971) Determinants of marathon running success. *Internationale Zeitschrift für Angewandte Physiologie*, **29**, 249–254.

Costill, D.L., Fink, W.J., Getchell, L.H., Ivy, J.L. and Witzmann, F.A. (1979) Lipid metabolism in skeletal muscle of endurance trained males and females. *Journal of Applied Physiology*, **47**, 787–791.

Costill, D.L., Fink, W.J., Flynn, M. and Kirwan, J. (1987) Muscle fiber composition and enzyme activities in elite female distance runners. *International Journal of Sports Medicine*, **8**, 103–106, Suppl.

Costill, D.L., Fink, W.J. and Pollock, M.L. (1976) Muscle fiber composition and enzyme activities of elite distance runners. *Medicine and Science in Sports*, **8**, 96–100.

Costill, D.L. and Fox, E.L. (1969) Energetics of marathon running. *Medicine and Science in Sports*, **1**, 81–86.

Costill, D.L., Kammer, W.F. and Fisher, A. (1970) Fluid ingestion during distance running. *Archives of Environmental Health*, **21**, 520–525.

Costill, D.L. and Winrow, E. (1970) Maximal oxygen intake among marathon runners. *Archives of Physical Medicine*, **51**, 317–320.

Coyle, E.F. and Coggan, A.R. (1984) Effectiveness of carbohydrate feeding in delaying fatigue in prolonged exercise. *Sports Medicine*, **1**, 446–458.

Davies, C.T.M. and Thompson, M.W. (1979) Aerobic performance of female marathon and male ultramarathon athletes. *European Journal of Applied Physiology*, **41**, 233–245.

Dill, D.B., Braithwaite, K., Adams, W.C. and Bernauer, E.M. (1974) Blood volume of middle distance runners: effect of 2300 m altitude and comparison with non-athletes. *Medicine and Science in Sports*, **6**, 1–7.

Dohm, G.L., Becker, R.T., Israel, R.G. and Tapscott, E.B. (1986) Metabolic responses to exercise after fasting. *Journal of Applied Physiology*, **61**, 1363–1368.

Ekblom, B., Wilson, G. and Åstrand, P.-O. (1976) Central circulation during exercise after venesection and reinfusion of red blood cells. *Journal of Applied Physiology*, **40**, 370–383.

Farrell, P.A., Wilmore, J.H., Coyle, E.F., Billing, J.E. and Costill, D.L. (1979) Plasma lactate accumulation and distance running performance. *Medicine and Science in Sports*, **11**, 338–344.

Foster, C. (1983) $\dot{V}O_{2max}$ and training indices as determinants of competitive running performance. *Journal of Sports Sciences*, **1**, 13–22.

Foster, C., Daniels, J.T. and Yarbrough, R.A. (1977) Physiological and training correlates of marathon running performance. *Australian Journal of Sports Medicine*, **9**, 58–61.

Fox, R.H. (1960) Heat stress and athletics. *Ergonomics*, **3**, 307–313.

Frederick, E.C. (1983) Hot times. *Running (US)*, **9**, 51–53.

Froberg, K. and Pedersen, P.K. (1984) Sex differences in endurance capacity and metabolic response to prolonged heavy exercise. *European Journal of Applied Physiology*, **52**, 446–450.

Graves, J.E., Pollock, M.L. and Sparling, D.B. (1987) Body composition of elite female distance runners. *International Journal of Sports Medicine*, **8**, 96–102 Suppl.

Green, H.J., Fraser, I.G. and Ranney, D.A. (1984) Male and female differences in enzyme activities of energy metabolism in vastus lateralis muscle. *Journal of Neurological Science*, **65**, 323–331.

Grimby, G. and Saltin, B. (1971) Physiological effects of endurance training. *Scandinavian Journal of Rehabilitation and Medicine*, **3**, 6–14.

Hermansen, L. and Wachtlova, M. (1971) Capillary density of skeletal muscle in well-trained and untrained men. *Journal of Applied Physiology*, **30**, 860–863.

Holloszy, J.O. (1967) Biochemical adaptations in muscle. Effects of exercise on mitochondrial oxygen uptake and respiratory enzyme activity in skeletal muscle. *Journal of Biological Chemistry*, **242**, 2278–2282.

Holloszy, J.O. and Coyle, E.F. (1984) Adaptations of skeletal muscle to endurance exercise and their metabolic consequences. *Journal of Applied Physiology*, **56**, 831–838.

Hoogerwerf, S. (1929) Elektrokardiographische Untersuchungen der Amsterdamer Olympiakampfer. *Arbeitsphysiologie*, **2**, 61–75.

Ingjer, F. (1978) Maximal aerobic power related to the capillary supply of the quadriceps femoris muscle in man. *Acta Physiologica Scandinavica*, **104**, 238–240.

Ingjer, F. (1979) Capillary supply and mitochondrial content of different skeletal muscle fibre types in untrained and endurance trained men. A histochemical and ultrastructural study. *European Journal of Applied Physiology*, **40**, 197–209.

Karlsson, J. and Saltin, B. (1971) Diet, muscle glycogen and endurance performance. *Journal of Applied Physiology*, **31**, 203–206.

Lamb, D.R. and Brodowicz, G.R. (1986) Optimal use of fluids of various formulations to minimise exercise-induced disturbances in homeostasis. *Sports Medicine*, **3**, 247–274.

Ledingham, I., McA, MacVicar, S., Watt, I. and Weston, G.A. (1982) Early resuscitation after marathon collapse. *Lancet*, **2** (8207), 1096–1097.

Lloyd, T., Triantafyllou, S.J., Baker, E.R., Houts, P.S., Whiteside, J.A., Kalenak, A. and Stumpf, P.G. (1986) Women athletes with menstrual irregularity have increased musculoskeletal injuries. *Medicine and Science in Sports and Exercise*, **18**, 374–379.

Loy, S.F., Conlee, R.K., Winder, W.W., Nelson, A.G., Arnall, D.A. and Fisher, A.G. (1986) Effects of 24-hour fast on cycling endurance time at two different intensities. *Journal of Applied Physiology*, **61**, 654–9.

Margaria, R., Cerretelli, P., Aghemo, P. and Sassi, G. (1963) Energy cost of running. *Journal of Applied Physiology*, **18**, 367–370.

Maron, M.B., Horvath, S.M., Wilkerson, J.E. and Gliner, J.A. (1976) Oxygen uptake measurements during competitive marathon running. *Journal of Applied Physiology*, **40**, 836–838.

Maron, M.B., Wagner, J.A. and Horvath, S.M. (1977) Thermoregulatory responses during competitive marathon running. *Journal of Applied Physiology*, **42**, 909–914.

Martin, D.E. and May, D.F. (1987) Pulmonary function characteristics in elite women distance runners. *International Journal of Sports Medicine*, **8**, Suppl. 2, 84–90.

Matoba, H. and Gollnick, P.D. (1984) Response of skeletal muscle to training. *Sports Medicine*, **1**, 240–251.

Maughan, R.J. (1985) Thermoregulation in marathon competition at low ambient temperature. *International Journal of Sports Medicine*, **6**, 15–19.

Maughan, R.J. (1986a) Fluid and electrolyte balance during exercise, in *Nutrition in Sport* (eds D.H. Shrimpton and P.B. Ottaway), Shakiee, London, pp. 17–23.

Maughan, R.J. (1986b) Exercise-induced muscle cramp: a prospective biochemical study in marathon runners. *Journal of Sports Sciences*, **4**, 31–34.

Maughan, R.J. and Leiper, J.B. (1983) Aerobic capacity and fractional utilisation of aerobic capacity in elite and non-elite male and female marathon runners. *European Journal of Applied Physiology*, **52**, 80–87.

Maughan, R.J., Leiper, J.B. and Thompson, J. (1985) Rectal temperature after marathon running. *British Journal of Sports Medicine*, **19**, 192–196.

Noakes, T.D., Goodwin, N., Rayner, B.L., Branken, T. and Taylor, R.K.N. (1985) Water intoxication: a possible complication during endurance exercise. *Medicine and Science in Sports and Exercise*, **17**, 370–375.

Nygaard, E. (1981) Women and exercise – with special reference to muscle morphology and metabolism, in *Biochemistry of Exercise – IVB* (eds J. Poortmans and G. Niset), University Park Press, Baltimore, pp. 161–175.

Nygaard, E., Honnens, B., Tungelund, K., Chistensen, T. and Calbo, H. (1984) Fat as a fuel in energy-turnover of men and women. *Acta Physiologica Scandinavica*, **120**, 51A.

Pate, R.R., Barnes, C. and Miller, W. (1985) A physiological comparison of performance-matched female and male distance runners. *Research Quarterly in Exercise and Sport*, **56**, 245–250.

Pate, R.R., Sparling, P.B., Wilson, G.E., Cureton, K.J. and Miller, B.J. (1987) Cardiorespiratory and metabolic responses to submaximal and maximal exercise in elite women distance runners. *International Journal of Sports Medicine*, **8**, 91–95 Suppl.

Pollak, S.J., McMillan, S.T., Mumpower, E., Wharff, R., Knopf, W., Felner, J.M. and Yoganathan, A.P. (1987) Echocardiographic analysis of elite women distance runners. *International Journal of Sports Medicine*, **8**, 81–83 Suppl.

Pollock, M.L. (1977) Submaximal and maximal working capacity of elite distance runners. Part 1: Cardiorespiratory aspects. *Annals of the New York Academy of Sciences*, **301**, 310–322.

Pollock, M.L., Gettman, L.R., Jackson, A., Ayres, J., Ward, A. and Linnerud, A.C. (1977) Body composition of elite class distance runners. *Annals of the New York Academy of Sciences*, **301**, 361–370.

Pugh, L.G.C.E., Corbett, J.L. and Johnson, R.H. (1967) Rectal remperatures, weight losses and sweat rates in marathon running. *Journal of Applied Physiology*, **23**, 347–353.

Ready, A.E., and Alexander, M.J.L. (1982) A review of the comparison of skeletal muscle characteristics in males and females. *Australian Journal of Sport Science*, **2**, 10–15.

Remes, K., Vuopio, P. and Harkonen, M. (1979) Effect of long-term training and acute physical exercise on red cell 2,3-diphosphoglycerate. *European Journal of Applied Physiology*, **42**, 199–207.

Robertson, R.J., Gilcher, R., Metz, K.F., Caspersen, C.J., Allison, R.G., Abbot, R.A., Skrinar, G.S., Krause, J.R. and Nixon, P.A. (1984) Hemoglobin concentration and aerobic work capacity in women following induced erythrocythemia. *Journal of Applied Physiology*, **57**, 568–575.

Saltin, B. (1964) Circulatory response to submaximal and maximal exercise after thermal dehydration. *Journal of Applied Physiology*, **19**, 1125–1132.

Saltin, B. (1971) Guidelines for physical training. *Scandinavian Journal of Rehabilitation and Medicine*, **3**, 39–46.

Saltin, B. (1973) Metabolic fundamentals in exercise. *Medicine and Science in Sports*, **5**, 137–146.

Saltin, B. (1986) Physiological adaptation to physical conditioning. *Acta Medica Scandinavica*, Suppl., **711**, 11–24.

Saltin, B. and Gollnick, P.D. (1983) Skeletal muscle adaptability. Significance for metabolism and performance, in *Handbook of Physiology: Skeletal muscle.* (eds L.D. Peachey, R.H. Adrian and S.R. Geiger) American Physiological Society, Bethesda, pp. 555–631.

Saltin, B., Henriksson, J., Nygaard, E., Andersen, P. and Jansson, E. (1977) Fibre types and metabolic potentials of skeletal muscles in sedentary man and endurance runners. *Annals of the New York Academy of Sciences*, **301**, 3–29.

Sherman, W.M. (1983) Carbohydrate, muscle glycogen and muscle glycogen super-compensation, in *Ergogenic Aids in Sport* (ed. M.H. Williams), Human Kinetics, Champaign, Illinois.

Sherman, W.M. and Costill, D.L. (1984) The marathon: dietary manipulation to optimise performance. *American Journal of Sports Medicine*, **12**, 44–51.

Sjodin, B. and Jacobs, I. (1981) Onset of blood lactate accumulation and marathon running performance. *International Journal of Sports Medicine*, **2**, 23–26.

Sjodin, B. and Svedenhag, J. (1985) Applied physiology of marathon running. *Sports Medicine*, **2**, 83–99.

Wenger, H.A. and Bell, G.J. (1986) The interactions of intensity, frequency and duration of exercise training in altering cardiorespiratory fitness. *Sports Medicine*, **3**, 346–356.

Whiting, P.H., Maughan, R.J. and Miller, J.D.B. (1984) Dehydration and serum biochemical changes in marathon runners. *European Journal of Applied Physiology*, **52**, 183–187.

Williams, M.H., Wesseldine, S., Somma, T. and Schuster, R. (1981) The effect of induced erythrocythemia upon 5-mile treadmill run time. *Medicine and Science in Sports and Exercise*, **13**, 169–175.

Wilmore, J.H. (1982) The female athlete: physique, body composition and physiological profile. *Australian Journal of Sport Science*, **2**, 2–9.

Wilmore, J.H. and Brown, C.H. (1974) Physiological profiles of women distance runners. *Medicine and Science in Sports*, **6**, 178–181.

Woodson, R.D. (1984) Hemoglobin concentration and exercise capacity. *American Review of Respiratory Diseases*, **129**, Suppl, 572–575.

Wyndham, C.H. and Strydom, N.B. (1969) The danger of an inadequate water intake during marathon running. *South African Medical Journal*, **43**, 893–896.

6
Race walking

R.O. Ruhling and J.A. Hopkins

6.1 INTRODUCTION

Race walking is defined as a forward

> . . . progression by steps so taken that unbroken contact with the ground is maintained. At each step, the advancing foot of the walker must make contact with the ground before the rear foot leaves the ground. During the period of each step in which a foot is on the ground, the leg must be straightened (i.e not bent at the knee) at least for one moment, and in particular, the supporting leg must be straight in the vertically upright position. (International Amateur Athletic Federation Handbook, 1984).

As noted from these stipulations, race walking is neither walking nor running as normally encountered. In particular, the supporting leg is not straight in the vertically upright position in normal walking. The characteristic that distinguishes running from walking is that at some point in time, both feet are off the ground simultaneously, and therefore unbroken contact with the ground cannot be maintained.

6.2 HISTORY OF WALKING AND RACE WALKING

The physical anthropologists tell us that our evolution from quadrupedal to bipedal locomotion began in the Miocene times, some 15 to 25 million years ago (Sigmon, 1971; Prost, 1980; Rodman and McHenry, 1980), and was not completed until a little more than a million years ago in the form of *Homo habilis* (Napier, 1967). To move from quadrupedalism to bipedalism is significant because walking is probably the most important of the many evolved characteristics that separate men from the more primitive hominids. In particular, it is worthy to note that now most of the earth's environments could be met and conquered by man.

Napier (1967) has suggested that walking is a unique human activity that is closely associated with catastrophe: '. . . only the rhythmic forward movement of first one leg and then the other keeps him from falling on his face' (p. 56). Whenever one '. . . sets out in pursuit of his centre of gravity' a unique sequence of events occurs to ensure that balance is not lost, and that forward progress is maintained.

Since the fossil records can tell us that man has been walking for just about a million years, what kinds of data can tell us how long we've been race walking? Apparently, the only kind of record that is available for this type of activity is the written account of one's oral history. As reported by Lucas (1968, 1983), pedestrianism took its rightful place alongside other major sporting events as early as 1765 in England. By 1861, Edward Payson Weston, the 'apostle of walking' (Matthews, 1979) had a clear following, and was establishing many ultra-long distance walking records that are to this day unsurpassed: between 1861 and 1913, it has been proposed that he walked more than 100 000 miles (160 900 km), in competitive pedestrian tramps. Competition in his era

Table 6.1 Research on walking published since the 1930s

Decade	Authors	Associated topic	Year
1930	Bass	mechanics	1937
	Elftman	external forces	1938
	Elftman	energy changes	1939
1940	Erickson *et al.*	energy cost	1945–1946
1950	Henry	oxygen requirement	1953
	Sutton	physics	1955
	Booyens and Keatinge	energy expenditure	1957
	Cotes *et al.*	energy expenditure	1958
1960	Bobbert	energy expenditure	1960
	Cotes and Meade	energy expenditure	1960
	Ralston	energy expenditure	1960
	Cavagna *et al.*	external work	1963
	Workman and Armstrong	oxygen cost	1963
	Murray *et al.*	patterns	1964
	Dill	oxygen uptake	1965
	Cavagna and Margaria	mechanics	1966
	Perry	mechanics	1967
	Gray and Basmajian	electromyography	1968
	Menier and Pugh	oxygen uptake	1968
	Gersten *et al.*	external work	1969
	Johnston and Smidt	electrogoniometry	1969
	Ralston and Lukin	energy levels	1969

Table 6.1 *continued*

Decade	Authors	Associated topic	Year
1970	Morrison	mechanics	1970
	Paul	force and speed	1970
	Pollock *et al.*	body composition	1971
	Pugh	mechanical efficiency	1971
	Smidt	hip motion	1971
	Wyndham and Strydom	mechanical efficiency	1971
	Falls and Humphrey	oxygen uptake	1973
	Noble *et al.*	perceived exertion	1973
	van der Walt and Wyndham	energy expenditure	1973
	Waters *et al.*	translational motion	1973
	Zarrugh *et al.*	energy expenditure	1974
	Blessey *et al.*	metabolism	1976
	Cappozzo *et al.*	mechanics	1976
	Cavagna *et al.*	external work	1976
	Elliott and Blanksby	cinematography	1976
	Falls and Humphrey	energy cost	1976
	Andriacchi *et al.*	gait analysis	1977
	Cavagna and Kaneko	mechanics	1977
	Donovan and Brooks	muscular efficiency	1977
	Gehlsen and Dill	men and women	1977
	Pandolf *et al.*	energy expenditure	1977
	Fellingham *et al.*	caloric cost	1978
	Smit	exercise prescription	1978
1980	Mann and Hagy	biomechanics	1980
	Mochon and McMahon	ballistics	1980
	Robertson and Winter	mechanical energy	1980
	Shoenfeld *et al.*	physical fitness	1980
	Cavagna and Franzetti	mechanics	1981
	Wall and Charteris	kinematics	1981
	Zurrugh	mechanical efficiency	1981
	Alexander	mechanics	1984
	Hamill *et al.*	reaction forces	1984
	Bhambhani and Singh	cinematography	1985

involving frequent multi-day races bears little comparison with that undertaken by today's elite competitors over 20 km (12.4 miles) and 50 km (31 miles). Currently, speeds attained by Olympic-calibre race walkers range between 13 km h^{-1} (50 km event) and 15.0 km h^{-1} (20 km event), far in advance of those obtained by the early 'pedestrians'.

Anyone, in any era, who can walk for extended distances at speeds ranging from 10 km h^{-1} to 15 km h^{-1} has been repeatedly shown to be in exceptional aerobic endurance condition (Cotes and Meade, 1960;

Ralston, 1960; Dill, 1965; Menier and Pugh, 1968; Wyndham *et al.*, 1971; Blessey *et al.*, 1976; Fellingham *et al.*, 1978; Shoenfeld *et al.*, 1980; Franklin *et al.*, 1981; Hagberg and Coyle, 1983; Bhambhani and Singh, 1985).

What do these observations suggest concerning the physiology of either walking or race walking? Is one dealing with fitness as a function of speed, exclusively? Or must one also examine the specific technique, i.e. the biomechanics involved in each? Inasmuch as walking, *per se*, has been treated extensively elsewhere, as early as the 1930s and as recently as the 1980s (Table 6.1), the focus of this chapter will be on race walking, with an attempt being made to convey to the reader the particular physiological attributes which may lead to championship performances. Prior to a discussion of the physiological factors involved, however, a brief review of the biomechanics of race walking will be presented.

6.3 BIOMECHANICS OF RACE WALKING

Briefly, one must examine whether or not race walking is, in fact, different from walking and running as suggested earlier (Alexander, 1984). In comparison with conventional walking technique, the technique of race walking has the following special features.

1. There is no flexion of the supporting leg, until just prior to toe-off. This is required by the definition of walking and is the most obvious special feature of race walking.
2. Pelvic tilt is greatly increased, minimizing the rise of the body's centre of gravity (CG).
3. Pelvic rotation is greatly increased, enabling much longer steps to be taken, e.g. 125 cm compared to 80 cm in a normal walk.
4. A more powerful plantar flexion of the supporting ankle provides a greater horizontal component of forward drive.
5. The tracks of the feet approach a single line, reducing the lateral shift of the CG every step.
6. The arms are flexed to about a right angle throughout their swing, reducing their moment of inertia.

Those who have investigated the efficiency of race walking versus either conventional walking or running have reported the following. Marchetti *et al.* (1983) indicated the energy expenditure data which they collected on four national level race walkers compared favourably with results previously published by Zarrugh, Todd and Ralston (1974) regarding ambulation and race walking and by Menier and Pugh (1968) regarding running. Once the body segment data were analysed through their stereophotogrammetric technique, however, it was observed that race walking represented a less-efficient form of locomotion than running

(p. 674). They suggested that the recovery of energy by the elastic components in stretched muscles which is observed in running, apparently does not act in the same manner and/or to the same extent in race walking.

However, Cavagna and Franzetti (1981) noted a rise in the efficiency of race walking with increasing speed. This, together with an efficiency of more than 45% suggested to them that elastic recovery does have an important part to play at high speeds.

Formerly nationally competitive race walkers ($n = 10$) were studied in an attempt to examine both kinetic and kinematic characteristics of the lower extremeties during the phases of the race walking gait as defined by the rules (Cairns *et al.*, 1986). These data were compared to other locomotor activities performed by the same subjects: a normal self-selected velocity walk (6.59 km h^{-1}); a self-selected training race walk pace (10.40 km h^{-1}); a self-selected competitive race walk pace (13.07 km h^{-1}); and a jog at a velocity similar to that of the competitive race walk pace (13.00 km h^{-1}). When comparing the 'stance' versus the 'swing' phase among the four patterns of movement, Cairns *et al.* (1986) reported that the stance phase decreased from 62% to 54% to 50% to 41% while the swing phase increased from 38% to 46% to 50% to 59% among the conventional walk, the training race walk, the competitive race walk, and jog, respectively. Inasmuch as the competitive race walk pace was the fastest, the shortest time was spent in those two phases (0.68 ± 0.08 s). They also noted that the race walkers exhibited significantly increased maximal ankle dorsiflexion, maximal knee extension, angular displacements of the pelvis, medial ground–foot reaction forces, peak plantar flexion moment, and external peak knee hyperextension moment compared to when walking conventionally or running. These other differences which they observed seemed to reflect necessary angular configurations in the motion of the lower extremities so that higher velocities could be attained and the rules of correct race walking could still be observed.

Most other researchers who have attempted to investigate the biomechanics of race walking have arrived at similar conclusions, namely that race walking is '. . . a sport that demands a high degree of skill, mobility and stamina because the straight-leg-through-the-vertical rule calls for difficult posture changes for maximum speeds' (Payne, 1978, p. 301). Others have also come to essentially the same conclusion and the interested reader is encouraged to consult the following: Cotes, Meade and Wise, 1958; Blackburn, 1971c; Smidt, 1971; Cavagna, Thys and Zamboni, 1976; Cavagna and Kaneko, 1977; Mann and Hagy, 1980; van Ingen Schenau, 1980; Cavagna and Franzetti, 1981; Murray *et al.*, 1983; Douglass and Garrett, 1984; Fenton 1984; Hamill, Bates and Knutzen, 1984; Phillips and Jensen, 1984; Bhambhani and Singh, 1985; Dillman, 1985; White and Winter, 1985.

6.4 PHYSIOLOGICAL PROFILE OF THE RACE WALKER

Although several investigators have examined the physiological responses to walking (e.g. Henry, 1953; Cotes, Meade and Wise, 1958; Bobbert, 1960; Cotes and Meade, 1960; Ralston, 1960; Dill, 1965; Wyndham *et al.*, 1971; Pollock, 1973; Zarrugh, Todd and Ralston, 1974; Blessey *et al.*, 1976; Donovan and Brooks, 1977), few have devoted their investigations to the physiological characteristics of race walkers (Menier and Pugh, 1968; Blackburn, 1971a; Wyndham and Strydom, 1971; Thorstensson *et al.*, 1977; Reilly, Hopkins and Howlett, 1979; Kaimal *et al.* 1980; Franklin *et al.*, 1981; Hagberg and Coyle, 1983; Cairns, 1985).

Generally speaking, elite race walkers often exceed 800 km of training per month. This investment in training involves 60–70 hours at speeds ranging from 12 to 15 km h^{-1}. These speeds allow the race walker to maintain contact with the ground at a rate between 180 and 210 steps per minute. Their arduous training loads are reflected in the specific characteristics of elite calibre race walkers which are contained in Tables 6.2 and 6.3.

Table 6.2 Physical characteristics of elite calibre race walkers

Reference	n	Age (yr)	Height (cm)	Weight (kg)	BSA (m^2)	Fat (%)
Wyndham and Strydom (1971)	1	28.0	177.8	65.7	1.82	—
Thorstensson et al. (1977)	7	27.0	178.0	64.5	1.81	—
Reilly et al. (1979)	25	21.1	180.4	66.2	1.80	11.6
Kaimal et al. (1980)	10	29.6	—	—	—	8.0
Franklin et al. (1981)	9	26.7	178.7	68.5	1.86	7.8
Hagberg and Coyle (1983)	8	29.0	180.0	69.6	1.88	—
Marchetti et al. (1983)	4	22.8	173.3	59.8	1.72	—
Murray et al. (1983)	2	23.5	188.5	68.0	1.93	—
White and Winter (1985)	1	21.0	166.0	62.6	1.70	—
Mean	67	24.9	179.3	66.4	1.82	10.0
± SD		3.5	3.1	2.5	0.05	1.8

Table 6.3 Cardiorespiratory characteristics of elite calibre race walkers

Reference	n	HRmax (beats min^{-1})	$\dot{V}O_{2max}$ (ml kg^{-1} min^{-1}) STPD	$\dot{V}E_{max}$ (l min^{-1}) BTPS
Wyndham and Strydom (1971)	1	—	61.6	—
Reilly et al. (1979)	9	194	70.0	—
Kaimal et al. (1980)	10	—	60.6	—
Franklin et al. (1981)	9	191	62.9	156.0
Åstrand and Rodahl (1986)	1	—	77.3	—
Åstrand and Rodahl (1986)	*	—	72.0	—
Mean		193	64.9	156.0
± SD		2	4.7	—

*Indicates number in sample was not specified.

Although the data are varied and scattered, a physiological profile of the elite calibre race walker does emerge. From data reported elsewhere, it is apparent that the elite calibre race walker is younger on average than Grand National stock car drivers (Dawson, 1979), professional basketball players (centres, Parr et al., 1978), professional baseball players (Coleman, 1982), elite body builders (Pipes, 1979a), and ultramarathoners (Thompson et al., 1982). This profile of the elite calibre race walker shows, however, that he is older than a number of other types of athletes investigated, namely: cyclists (Burke, 1980), downhill skiers (Thorstensson et al., 1977), fencers (Vander et al., 1984), professional football players (Wilmore et al., 1976), Indian hockey players (Malhotra, Joseph and Sen Gupta, 1974) and swimmers (Holmer, Lundin and Eriksson, 1974). It may be that talented individuals in these sports come to the fore more quickly than do their counterparts in race walking. Alternatively race walkers may begin to specialize in their sport at a relatively late age.

The elite race walker is on average approximately the same age (24.9 years) as professional basketball forwards (25.3 years) and guards (25.2 years, Parr et al., 1978), elite (25.4 years, Pollock, 1977) and highly trained runners (24.6 years, Conley and Kranhenbuhl, 1980), professional racquetball players (25.0 years, Pipes, 1979b), professional soccer players (24.0 years, Gettman and Pollock, 1977), sprinters and jumpers (24.0 years, Thorstensson *et al.*, 1977), and volleyball players (25.3 years, Conlee *et al.*, 1982). The data on orienteers, cross-country skiers, and rowers appear to be equivocal. One study reported that the orienteers are older than race walkers (Knowlton *et al.*, 1980) while the other study suggested that race walkers are older then orienteers (Thorstensson *et al.*, 1977). Differences are probably due to sampling error and also reflect variability in age among top level competitors in these sports. More importantly, Thorstensson *et al.* (1977) classified both race walkers and orienteers as 'endurance trained athletes'. Hanson's (1973) cross-country skiers were older (26.3 years) while Ruhling and Storer's (1979) skiers were younger (23.0 years) than the average age of the elite calibre race walker. Furthermore, a similar pattern was noted amongst the elite rowers examined by Secher (1983) (25.6 and 25.1 years) and those tested by Hagerman, Hagerman and Mickelson (1979) (23.0 years): however the age distribution of the samples did overlap.

Another indication of the age for peak performance of elite race walkers is provided by the ages at which individuals have won medals in major championships or set world records. These data suggest that success is possible at a wide variety of ages. One may cite the success of 20-year-old Mercenerios in the 1987 World Cup 20 km and the bronze medal won over 50 km by 42-year-old Ivchenko (USSR) in the 1980 Olympiad. Race walkers are renowned for their long careers and a number have competed in three or four Olympiads. Golubnichiy (USSR) set a World 20 km record at 19 years of age and went on to compete in five Olympiads winning 2 gold, 1 silver and 1 bronze medal.

With regard to size, as evaluated by body surface area, the elite calibre race walker is similar to cyclists (Burke, 1980), downhill skiers (Thorstensson *et al.*, 1977), fencers (Vander *et al.*, 1984), elite (Pollock, 1977) and highly trained runners (Conley and Krahenbuhl, 1980) and ultra-marathoners (Thompson *et al.*, 1982), Indian hockey players (Malhotra, Joseph and Sen Gupta, 1974) and orienteers (Thorstensson *et al.*, 1977). However, the race walker is on average significantly smaller than professional baseball players (Coleman, 1982), professional basketball players (Parr *et al.*, 1978), elite body builders (Pipes, 1979a), cross-country skiers (Hanson, 1973; Ruhling and Storer, 1979), professional American football players (Wilmore *et al.*, 1976), elite rowers (Hagerman, Hagerman and Mickelson, 1979; Secher, 1983), professional soccer players (Gettman and Pollock, 1977), sprinters and jumpers (Thorstensson *et al.*, 1977), Grand National stock car drivers (Dawson, 1979), swimmers (Holmer, Lundin and Eriksson, 1974), and volleyball players (Conlee *et al.*, 1982), and only marginally larger (1.82 m^2 *vs* 1.67 m^2) than male figure skaters (Niinimaa, 1982). Being small serves as an advantage to the race walker competing in hot conditions as a large surface area relative to mass is favourable in losing heat to the environment.

The sparse information that is available concerning body fat (%) suggests that these race walkers are as lean or leaner (10.0% on the average) than all the other athletic groups previously reported, except for professional basketball centres (7.1%, $n = 1$; Parr et al., 1978), rowers (6.5%; Secher, 1983) and elite runners (4.7%; Pollock et al., 1977). Race walkers do not have repeatedly to lift the body weight during locomotion as high as do distance runners and so are not unduly penalized by having greater fat deposits than their running counterparts.

A search through the data on world-class walkers indicates many with weights in excess of runners of the same height. For example, one could examine the following Olympic champions – Bautista (20 km 1976), 1.70 m^2 and 65 kg; Damilano (20 km 1980), 1.83 m^2 and 70 kg; Pribilinec (20 km 1988), 1.68 m^2 and 66 kg; Gonzalez (50 km 1984), 1.75 m^2 and 64 kg; Gander (50 km 1980), 1.86 m^2 and 70 kg; Ivanenko (50 km 1988), 1.64 m^2 and 58 kg.

Interestingly, age (older), body size (smaller) and body fat (less) have all been shown to correlate highly with aerobic or endurance capabilities. The race walker, as profiled herein, appears to take on the physical characteristics of the elite endurance-trained athlete. Do these characteristics hold true once we examine the cardiorespiratory data? A number of researchers have suggested that to be considered an elite endurance athlete, one must have a maximum oxygen uptake ($\dot{V}O_{2max}$) in excess of 75 ml kg^{-1} min^{-1} (Franklin et al., 1981). Closer examination of Table 6.3 shows that although data from apparently six studies are reported, there are only four groups of researchers, namely: Åstrand and Rodahl from Sweden and Norway, Franklin et al. and Kaimal et al. from the United States, Reilly et al. from England and Wyndham and Strydom from South Africa. Only Franklin et al. (1981) have reported data for maximum minute ventilation. Once the six reports of $\dot{V}O_{2max}$ are evaluated with a weighted average, it is seen that a $\dot{V}O_{2max}$ of 65 ml kg^{-1} min^{-1} does not qualify one for the category of elite endurance athletes. (The Swedish and English race walkers were international representatives and their values on average exceeded 70 ml kg^{-1} min^{-1}.) Care must be taken here in interpreting these data as they were not collected from the world elite. Such data are not available in the scientific literature but it is known that walking at a speed of 15 km h^{-1} (which can be maintained for 20 km by the World's best) does require in excess of 65 ml kg^{-1} min^{-1} (see Menier and Pugh, 1968; Forsberg and Lundin, 1975, p. 44). This would suggest that the elite walkers may have $\dot{V}O_{2max}$ values in excess of 75 ml kg^{-1} min^{-1}.

It has also been demonstrated that it is not necessarily a large $\dot{V}O_{2max}$ that determines success in running or walking competitions, but rather the percentage of maximum that an athlete can maintain for that competition (Costill, Thomason and Roberts, 1973). This is partly dependent on the 'anaerobic threshold' (lactate inflection point) which Hagberg and Coyle (1983) showed was more important than $\dot{V}O_{2max}$ in determining 20 km race walk pace.

Inasmuch as Franklin et al. (1981) and Reilly, Hopkins and Howlett (1979) have conducted by far the most extensive physiological analyses of elite calibre race walkers, it should be noted that maximal values for the race walkers were obtained whilst running on a treadmill, a procedure that would not accommodate the specificity of race walking. Nevertheless, time to exhaustion on an incremental treadmill run test which should be a function of $\dot{V}O_{2max}$, has been found to be highly correlated ($r = 0.94$) with race walking performance over 20 km (Reilly, Hopkins and Howlett, 1979). A few more interesting items of information emerge from their reports to characterize these unique athletes. A resting bradycardia (< 54 and 63 beats min^{-1}, respectively), coupled with an average resting blood pressure of 123/68 and 130/82 mm Hg, respectively, suggests that top race walkers have a highly trained cardiovascular system. These attributes are obviously necessary since they spend a great deal of time in training for their event, either the 20 km or 50 km walk (Blackburn, 1971a,b,c; Hagberg and Coyle, 1983). They are then capable of completing their 150–250 km (600–1000 km per month) race walked each week during training.

Their pulmonary function parameters (Franklin et al., 1981; Reilly, Hopkins and Howlett, 1977) compare favourably with those reported by Raven (1977) on elite marathon runners (FVC of 5.1 l and 5.4 l vs 5.4 l, respectively; and FEV_1/FVC of 84.4% and 85.2% vs 80.4%, respectively). Taking the aforementioned data into consideration, the results may be juxtaposed alongside the following additional observations. Firstly, race walkers have been shown to possess a significantly lower percentage of fast twitch skeletal muscle fibres (41%) than either sprinters, jumpers, downhill skiers, or sedentary men (Thorstensson et al., 1977). This suggests that they have a greater predominance of slow twitch skeletal muscle fibres than those same athletic groups. Secondly, race walkers were intermediate in height and weight between distance runners on the one hand and middle distance and sprint men on the other. Their somatotype was close to that occupied by distance runners (Reilly, Hopkins and Howlett, 1979). Tanner (1964) in his study 'The Physique of the Olympic Athlete' found a somatotype of 2.5:4.5:4 for a group of 50 km walkers at the 1960 Olympiad. 'The 50 km walkers in general resemble the 1500 km runners, though they have shorter legs, like the 5000 m men, wider hips in relation to their trunk and rather larger calf muscles for their tibia size' (p. 104). He later speculated whether walking technique eventually pushes out the iliac crests or whether wider hips lead to a more efficient technique.

These observations suggest that race walkers are indeed aerobically trained endurance athletes. This is reinforced by a consideration of the training regimens of top race walkers.

6.5 PHYSIOLOGICAL DEMANDS OF RACE WALKING

It is apparent from the profiles previously presented that the elite race walker is close to par with the elite distance runner. Therefore, the demands of the sport are likely to be comparable to the demands of distance running. Åstrand and Rodahl (1986) referred to measurements made on the gold medal winner over 10 km at the 1948 Olympic Games. His $\dot{V}O_{2max}$ whilst race walking on the treadmill at a speed of 13.3 km h^{-1}, which corresponded to his average speed during the race, was 58 ml kg^{-1} min^{-1}. Assuming his $\dot{V}O_{2max}$ was 72 ml kg^{-1} min^{-1} this intensity would correspond to 80% $\dot{V}O_{2max}$. This level is close to the upper limit that marathon runners can maintain.

Inasmuch as the distances covered by the competitive race walker are similar to distances covered by runners, it is reasonable to expect that the training regimens designed for race walkers are broadly similar to the training regimens of runners. Due to the differences in speed between the two modes of locomotion, the regimen of the race walker will be greater in duration but lower in intensity than that of his running counterpart. Reilly, Hopkins and Howlett (1979) reported data from one subject during two typical workouts – a track training session and a road training session. The track session was conducted on a 400 m oval (tartan surface) while the road session was conducted 'over country roads and varying terrain' for a period of 2 h 6 min. Work on the track fluctuated between 800 m, 1000 m, 1200 m, and 1600 m while recovery time between distances averaged approximately 2 min in duration.

Prior to the track workout, the race walker warmed up for 11 min with a mean heart rate of 123 beats min^{-1}. This corresponded to 54% of maximum heart rate reserve (MHRR), resting and maximal heart rates being 48 and 186 beats min^{-1} respectively. The average heart rate during pooled work efforts was 167 beats min^{-1} (86% MHRR) achieved while averaging a pace of 13.0 km h^{-1}.

The effort on the road presented some interesting results, in terms of intensity. Although he walked at an average pace of 10.3 km h^{-1} (26.2% slower than on the track), his average heart rate of 134 beats min^{-1} (62% MHRR) was also significantly slower (24.6%) than his track workout. In fact his walking heart rate on the road (134 beats min^{-1}) was 5 beats per min less than his recovery heart rate during his track intervals (3.7% less)! Furthermore, his average heart rate for walking uphill was significantly higher (144 beats min^{-1}, 70% MHRR) than when walking either on the level (132 beats min^{-1}, 60.9% MHRR) or on a downhill (131 beats min^{-1}, 60.1% MHRR). These figures are lower than the 160 beats min^{-1} reported for continuous race walking at a speed of 12 km h^{-1} (Forsberg and Lundin, 1975). Walking at such a speed for 2–4 h would be typical of the type of session frequently carried out by elite race walkers today.

Reilly, Hopkins and Howlett (1979) summarized their findings by stating:

> Road training routes could be strategically selected to include frequent uphill sections to accentuate the physiological strain during long walks. An alternative method of enhancing the training stress would be to increase the velocity of walking to approximate competitive walking pace. This type of regimen when included in the training schedule would be performed for a reduced duration, though some long duration walks should still be retained. (p. 74).

Elite race walkers are generally competent at distance running. The inclusion of some running in their regimens would provide physiological stimuli associated with high intensity training. Race walking practices for prolonged periods would provide local muscular adaptations associated with long duration training. They would also entail specific effects: for example, the tibialis anterior muscle is active for a much greater period in the walking cycle than in the running cycle and would not be stimulated sufficiently for race walking by a regimen of running training.

There are several books on walking on the market (Sussman and Goode, 1967; Hopkins, 1976; Fletcher, 1978; Jacobson, 1980; Stutman, 1980; Inman, 1981; Yanker, 1983). Nevertheless there is a dearth of scientific information available on race walking. Consequently, more research should be conducted to more accurately and carefully elucidate that which truly characterizes the champion race walker.

6.6 CONCLUSION

From the available data, the elite calibre race walker appears similar to a variety of known aerobic endurance types of athletes. These include cyclists, elite and highly trained runners, orienteers, and ultra-marathoners. These race walkers are relatively small in stature and carry less than 10.0% body fat, on the average. Although their $\dot{V}O_{2max}$

values are a little lower than those of elite 10 000 m and marathon runners, race walkers do have a well-developed cardiopulmonary system capable of transporting them extreme distances for extended time periods at relatively fast speeds. Furthermore, it has been shown that the ability to maintain a 20 km race walk pace at the anaerobic threshold (lactate inflection point) is more important to success than an extremely high $\dot{V}O_{2max}$ *per se*.

Finally, success in international competition has been shown to be related to technical skills in race walking as well as a high level of fitness. The rules of the competition dictate the manner in which the race walker can move biomechanically and this has been shown to be less efficient than running.

REFERENCES

Alexander, R. McN. (1984) Walking and running. *American Scientist*, **72**, 348–354.

Andriacchi, T.P., Ogle, J.A. and Galante, J.O. (1977) Walking speed as a basis for normal and abnormal gait measurements. *Journal of Biomechanics*, **10**, 261–268.

Åstrand, P.-O. and Rodahl, K. (1986) *Textbook of Work Physiology*, McGraw-Hill, New York, pp. 650–651.

Bass, R. (1937) A study of the mechanics of graceful walking. *Research Quarterly*, **8**, 173–180.

Bhambhani, Y. and Singh, M. (1985) Metabolic and cinematographic analysis of walking and running in men and women. *Medicine and Science in Sports and Exercise*, **17**, 131–137.

Blackburn, J.H. (1971a) II(A)69 Race walking (20,000, 50,000 meters), in *Encyclopedia of Sport Sciences and Medicine* (ed. L.A. Larson), MacMillan, New York, p. 381.

Blackburn, J.H. (1971b) II(C)69 Race walking (20,000, 50,000 meters), in *Encyclopedia of Sport Science and Medicine* (ed. L.A. Larson), MacMillan, New York, p. 559.

Blackburn, J.H. (1971c) II(E)69 Race walking (20,000, 50,000 meters), in *Encyclopedia of Sport Sciences and Medicine* (ed. L.A. Larson), MacMillan, New York, pp. 704–705.

Blessey, R.L., Hislop, H.J., Waters, R.L. and Antonelli, D. (1976) Metabolic energy cost of unrestrained walking. *Physical Therapy*, **56**, 1019–1024.

Bobbert, A.C. (1960) Energy expenditure in level and grade walking. *Journal of Applied Physiology*, **15**, 1015–1021.

Booyens, J. and Keatinge, W.R. (1957) The expenditure of energy by men and women walking. *Journal of Physiology (London)*, **138**, 165–171.

Burke, E.R. (1980) Physiological characteristics of competitive cyclists. *The Physician and Sportsmedicine*, **8**, 79–84.

Cairns, M.A. (1985) Racewalking – a fitness alternative. *Journal of Physical Education, Recreation and Dance*, **56**, 50–51.

Cairns, M.A., Burdett, R.G., Pisciotta, J.C. and Simon, S.R. (1986) A biomechanical analysis of racewalking gait. *Medicine and Science in Sports and Exercise*, **18**, 446–453.

Cappozzo, A., Figura, F. and Marchetti, M. (1976) The interplay of muscular and external forces in human ambulation. *Journal of Biomechanics*, **9**, 35–43.

Cavagna, G.A and Franzetti, P. (1981) Mechanics of competition walking. *Journal of Physiology (London)*, **315**, 243–251.

Cavagna, G.A. and Kaneko, M. (1977) Mechanical work and efficiency in level walking and running. *Journal of Physiology (London)*, **268**, 467–481.

Cavagna, G.A. and Margaria, R. (1966) Mechanics of walking. *Journal of Applied Physiology*, **21**, 271–278.

Cavagna, G.A., Saibene, F.P. and Margaria, R. (1963) External work in walking. *Journal of Applied Physiology*, **18**, 1–9.

Cavagna, G.A., Thys, H. and Zamboni, A. (1976) The sources of external work in level walking and running. *Journal of Physiology (London)*, **262**, 639–657.

Coleman, A.E. (1982) Physiological characteristics of major league baseball players. *The Physician and Sportsmedicine*, **10**, 51–57.

Conlee, R.K., McGown, C.M., Fisher, A.G., Dalsky, G.P. and Robinson, K.C. (1982) Physiological effects of power volleyball. *The Physician and Sportsmedicine*, **10**, 93–97.

Conley, D.L. and Krahenbuhl, G.S. (1980) Running economy and distance running performance of highly trained athletes. *Medicine and Science in Sports and Exercise*, **12**, 357–360.

Costill, D.L., Thomason, H. and Roberts, E. (1973) Fractional utilization of the aerobic capacity during distance running. *Medicine and Science in Sports*, **5**, 248–252.

Cotes, J.E. and Meade, F. (1960) The energy expenditure and mechanical energy demand in walking. *Ergonomics*, **3**, 97–119.

Cotes, J.E., Meade, F. and Wise, M.E. (1958) Variations, in the vertical work done against gravity and in the energy expenditure of walking, between men and women and in relation to training. *Journal of Physiology (London)*, **141**, 28P.

Dawson, G.A. (1979) A fitness profile of Grant National stock car drivers. *The Physician and Sportsmedicine*, **7**, 60–66.

Dill, D.B. (1965) Oxygen used in horizontal and grade walking and running on the treadmill. *Journal of Applied Physiology*, **20**, 19–22.

Dillman, C.J. (1985) The need for interdisciplinary research in sports science, in *The Elite Athlete* (eds N.K. Butts, T.T. Gushiken and B. Zairns), Spectrum Publications, New York, pp. 110–113.

Donovan, C.M. and Brooks, G.A. (1977) Muscular efficiency during steady-rate exercise, II. Effects of walking speed and work rate. *Journal of Applied Physiology: Respiratory, Environmental and Exercise Physiology*, **43**, 431–439.

Douglass, B.L. and Garrett, G.E. (1984) Biomechanics of elite junior race walkers, in *Sports Biomechanics* (eds J. Terauds, K. Barthels, E. Kreighbaum, R. Mann and J. Crakes), Academic Publishers, Del Mar, CA, pp. 91–96.

Elftman, H. (1938) The measurement of the external force in walking. *Science*, **88** (2276), 152–153.

Elftman, H. (1939) Forces and energy changes in the leg during walking. *American Journal of Physiology*, **125**, 339–356.

Elliott, B.C. and Blanksby, B.A. (1976) A cinematographic analysis of overground and treadmill running by males and females. *Medicine and Science in Sports*, **8**, 84–87.

Erickson, L., Simonson, E., Taylor, H.L., Alexander, H. and Keys, A. (1945–1946) The energy cost of horizontal and grade walking on the motor-driven treadmill. *American Journal of Physiology*, **145**, 391–401.

Falls, H.B. and Humphrey, L.D. (1973) A comparison of methods for eliciting maximum oxygen uptake from college women during treadmill walking. *Medicine and Science in Sports*, **5**, 239–241.

Falls, H.B. and Humphrey, L.D. (1976) Energy cost of running and walking in young women. *Medicine and Science in Sports*, **8**, 9–13.

Fellingham, G.W., Roundy, E.S., Fisher, A.G. and Bryce, G.R. (1978) Caloric cost of walking and running. *Medicine and Science in Sports*, **10**, 132–136.

Fenton, R.M. (1984) Race walking ground reaction forces, in *Sports Biomechanics* (eds J. Terauds, K. Barthels, E. Kreighbaum, R. Mann and J. Crakes), Academic Publishers, Del Mar, CA, pp. 61–70.

Fletcher, C. (1978) *The New Complete Walker.* Knopf, New York.

Forsberg, A. and Lundin, A. (1975) Idrottsfysiologi: Rapport Nr. 15, Trygg Hansa, Stockholm.

Franklin, B.A., Kaimal, K.P., Moir, T.W. and Hellerstein, H.K. (1981) Characteristics of national-class race walkers. *The Physician and Sportsmedicine*, **9**, 101–110.

Gehlsen, G.M. and Dill, D.B. (1977) Comparative performance of men and women in grade walking. *Human Biology*, **49**, 381–388.

Gersten, J.W., Orr, W., Sexton, A.W. and Okin, D. (1969) External work in level walking. *Journal of Applied Physiology*, **26**, 286–289.

Gettman, L.R. and Pollock, M.L. (1977) What makes a superstar? A physiological profile. *The Physician and Sportsmedicine*, **5**, 64–68.

Gray, E.G. and Basmajian, J.V. (1968) Electromyography and cinematography of leg and foot ('normal' and flat) during walking. *Anatomical Record*, **161**, 1–15.

Hagberg, J.M. and Coyle, E.F. (1983) Physiological determinants of endurance performance as studied in competitive racewalkers. *Medicine and Science in Sports and Exercise*, **15**, 287–289.

Hagerman, F.C., Hagerman, G.R. and Mickelson, T.C. (1979) Physiological profiles of elite rowers. *The Physician and Sportsmedicine*, **7**, 74–83.

Hamill, J., Bates, B.T. and Knutzen, K.M. (1984) Ground reaction force symmetry during walking and running. *Research Quarterly for Exercise and Sport*, **55**, 289–293.

Hanson, J.S. (1973) Maximal exercise performance in members of the U.S. Nordic Ski Team. *Journal of Applied Physiology*, **35**, 592–595.

Henry, F.M. (1953) The oxygen requirement of walking and running. *Research Quarterly*, **24**, 169–175.

Holmer, I., Lundin, A. and Eriksson, B.O. (1974) Maximum oxygen uptake during swimming and running by elite swimmers. *Journal of Applied Physiology*, **36**, 711–714.

Hopkins, J.A. (1976) *Race Walking.* BAAB London.

Inman, V.T. (1981) *Human Walking.* Williams and Wilkins, Baltimore.

International Amateur Athletic Federation Handbook. (1984) Marshall Arts Print Service, West Sussex, England, p. 162.

Jacobson, H. (1980) *Racewalk to Fitness.* Simon and Schuster, New York.

Johnston, R.C. and Smidt, G.L. (1969) Measurement of hip-joint motion during walking. Evaluation of an electrogoniometric method. *Journal of Bone and Joint Surgery,* **51–A**, 1083–1094.

Kaimal, K.P., Franklin, B.A., Moir, T.W. and Hellerstein, H.K. (1980) Echocardiographic assessment of left ventricular dimensions in race walkers. (Abstract). *Medicine and Science in Sports and Exercise,* **12**, 136.

Knowlton, R.G., Ackerman, K.J., Fitzgerald, P.I., Wilde, S.W. and Tahamont, M.V. (1980) Physiological and performance characteristics of United States championship class orienteers. *Medicine and Science in Sports and Exercise,* **12**, 164–169.

Lucas, J. (1968) Pedestrianism and the struggle for the Sir John Astley belt, 1878–1879. *Research Quarterly,* **39**, 587–594.

Lucas, J. (1983) 'Three specially selected athletes' and a recapitulation of the Pennsylvania Walking Purchase of 1737. *Research Quarterly for Exercise and Sport,* **54**, 41–47.

Malhotra, M.S., Joseph, N.T. and Sen Gupta, J. (1974) Body composition and endurance capacity of Indian hockey players. *Journal of Sports Medicine and Physical Fitness,* **14**, 272–277.

Mann, R.A. and Hagy, J. (1980) Biomechanics of walking, running, and sprinting. *The American Journal of Sports Medicine,* **8**, 345–350.

Marchetti, M.A., Cappozzo, A., Figura, F. and Felici, F. (1983) Race walking versus ambulation and running, in *Biomechanics VIII-B* (eds H. Matsui and K. Kobayashi), Human Kinetics, Champaign, IL, pp. 669–75.

Matthews, G.R. (1979) The apostle of walking. *Journal of Physical Education, Recreation,* **50**, 29–30.

Menier, D.R. and Pugh, L.G.C.E. (1968) The relation of oxygen intake and velocity of walking and running, in competition walkers. *Journal of Physiology (London),* **197,** 717–721.

Mochon, S. and McMahon, T.A. (1980) Ballistic walking. *Journal of Biomechanics,* **13**, 49–57.

Morrison, J.B. (1970) The mechanics of the knee joint in relation to normal walking. *Journal of Biomechanics,* **3**, 51–61.

Murray, M.P., Drought, A.B. and Kory, R.C. (1964) Walking patterns of normal men. *Journal of Bone and Joint Surgery,* **46-A**, 335–360.

Murray, M.P., Guten, G.N., Mollinger, L.A. and Gardner, G.M. (1983) Kinematic and electromyographic patterns of Olympic race walkers. *The American Journal of Sports Medicine,* **11**, 68–74.

Napier, J. (1967) The antiquity of human walking. *Scientific American,* **216** (4), 56–66.

Niinimaa, V. (1982) Figure skating: what do we know about it? *The Physician and Sportsmedicine,* **10**, 51–56.

Noble, B.J., Metz, K.F., Pandolf, K.B., Bell, C.W., Cafarelli, E. and Sime, W.E. (1973) Perceived exertion during walking and running – II. *Medicine and Science in Sports,* **5**, 116–120.

Pandolf, K.B., Givoni, B. and Goldman, R.F. (1977) Predicting energy expenditure with loads while standing or walking very slowly. *Journal of Applied Physiology: Respiratory, Environmental and Exercise Physiology*, **43**, 577–581.

Parr, R.B., Wilmore, J.H., Hoover, R., Bachman, D. and Kerlan, R.K. (1978) Professional basketball players: athletic profiles. *The Physician and Sportsmedicine*, **6**, 77–84.

Paul, J.P. (1970) The effects of walking speed on the force actions transmitted at the hip and knee joints. *Proceedings of the Royal Society of Medicine*, **63**, 200–202.

Payne, A.H. (1978) A comparison of the ground forces in race walking with those in normal walking and running, in *Biomechanics VI-A* (eds E. Asmussen and K. Jorgensen), University Park Press, Baltimore, MD, pp. 293–302.

Perry, J. (1967) The mechanics of walking. A clinical interpretation. *Physical Therapy*, **47**, 778–801.

Phillips, S.J. and Jensen, J.L. (1984) Kinematics of race walking, in *Sports Biomechanics* (eds J. Terauds, K. Barthels, E. Kreighbaum, R. Mann and J. Crakes), Academic Publishers, Del Mar, CA, pp. 71–80.

Pipes, T.V. (1979a) Physiologic characteristics of elite body builders. *The Physician and Sportsmedicine*, **7**, 116–122.

Pipes, T.V. (1979b) The racquetball pro: a physiological profile. *The Physician and Sportsmedicine*, **7**, 91–94.

Pollock, M.L. (1973) The quantification of endurance training programs, in *Exercise and Sport Sciences Reviews* 1 (ed. J.H. Wilmore), Academic Press, New York, pp. 155–188.

Pollock, M.L. (1977) Submaximal and maximal working capacity of elite distance runners. Part I. Cardiorespiratory aspects, in *Annals of The New York Academy of Sciences 31 The Marathon: Physiological, Medical, Epidemiological and Psychological Studies* (ed. P. Milvy), The New York Academy of Sciences, New York, pp. 310–322.

Pollock, M.L., Gettman, L.R., Jackson, A., Ayres, J., Ward, A. and Linnerud, A.C. (1977) Body composition of elite class distance runners, in *Annals of The New York Academy of Sciences 31 The Marathon: Physiological, Medical, Epidemiological and Psychological Studies* (ed. P. Milvy), The New York Academy of Sciences, New York, pp. 361–370.

Pollock, M.L., Miller, H.S., Jr, Janeway, R., Linnerud, A.C., Robertson, B. and Valentino, R. (1971) Effects of walking on body composition of cardiovascular function of middle-aged men. *Journal of Applied Physiology*, **30**, 126–130.

Prost, J.H. (1980) Origin of bipedalism. *American Journal of Physical Anthropology*, **52**, 175–189.

Pugh, L.G.C.E. (1971) The influence of wind resistance in running and walking and the mechanical efficiency of work against horizontal or vertical forces. *Journal of Physiology (London)*, **213**, 255–276.

Ralston, H.J. (1960) Comparison of energy expenditure during treadmill walking and floor walking. *Journal of Applied Physiology*, **15**, 1156.

Ralston, H.J. and Lukin, L. (1969) Energy levels of human body segments during level walking. *Ergonomics*, **12**, 39–46.

Raven, P.B. (1977) Pulmonary function of elite distance runners, in *Annals of the New York Academy of Sciences 31 The Marathon: Physiological, Medical, Epidemiological and Psychological Studies* (ed. P. Milvy), The New York Academy of Sciences, New York, pp. 371–381.

Reilly, T., Hopkins, J. and Howlett, N. (1979) Fitness test profiles and training intensities in skilled race walkers. *British Journal of Sports Medicine*, **13**, 70–76.

Robertson, D.G.E. and Winter, D.A. (1980) Mechanical energy generation, absorption and transfer amongst segments during walking. *Journal of Biomechanics*, **13**, 845–854.

Rodman, P.S. and McHenry, H.M. (1980) Bioenergetics and the origin of hominid bipedalism. *American Journal of Physical Anthropology*, **52**, 103–106.

Ruhling, R.O. and Storer, T.W. (1979) Physiological responses to on-snow cross-country ski training, in *Science in Skiing, Skating and Hockey* (eds J. Terauds and H.J. Gros), Academic Publishers, Del Mar CA, pp. 55–61.

Secher, N.H. (1983) The physiology of rowing. *Journal of Sports Sciences*, **1**, 23–53.

Shoenfeld, Y., Keren, G., Shimoni, T., Birnfield, C. and Sohar, E. (1980) Walking: a method for rapid improvement of physical fitness. *Journal of the American Medical Association*, **243**, 2062–2063.

Sigmon, B.A. (1971) Bipedal behavior and the emergence of erect posture in man. *American Journal of Physical Anthropology*, **34**, 55–60.

Smidt, G.L. (1971) Hip motion and related factors in walking. *Physical Therapy*, **51**, 9–21.

Smit, P.J. (1978) Prescribing exercise – walking and jogging. *South African Medical Journal*, **54**, 1024–1026.

Stutman, F.A. (1980) *The Doctor's Walking Book*. Ballantine Books, New York.

Sussman, A. and Goode, R. (1967) *The Magic of Walking*. Simon and Schuster, New York.

Sutton, R.M. (1955) Two notes on the physics of walking. *American Journal of Physics*, **23**, 490–491.

Tanner, J.M. (1964) *The Physique of the Olympic Athlete*. Allen and Unwin, London.

Thompson, W.R., Nequin, N.D., Lesmes, G.R. and Garfield, D.S. (1982) Physiological and training profiles of ultra-marathoners. *The Physician and Sportsmedicine*, **10**, 61–65.

Thorstensson, A., Larsson, L., Tesch, P. and Karlsson, J. (1977) Muscle strength and fiber composition in athletes and sedentary men. *Medicine and Science in Sports*, **9**, 26–30.

van der Walt, W.H. and Wyndham, C.H. (1973) An equation for prediction of energy expenditure of walking and running. *Journal of Applied Physiology*, **34**, 559–563.

van Ingen Schenau, G.J. (1980) Some fundamental aspects of the biomechanics of overground versus treadmill locomotion. *Medicine and Science in Sports and Exercise*, **12**, 257–261.

Vander, L.B., Franklin, B.A., Wrisley, D., Scherf, J., Kogler, A.A. and Rubenfire, M. (1984) Physiological profile of national-class National Collegiate Athletic Association fencers. *Journal of the American Medical Association*, **252**, 500–503.

Wall, J.C. and Charteris, J. (1981) A kinematic study of long-term habituation to treadmill walking. *Ergonomics*, **24**, 531–542.

Waters, R.L., Morris, J. and Perry, J. (1973) Translational motion of the head and trunk during normal walking. *Journal of Biomechanics*, **6**, 167–172.

White, S.C. and Winter, D. (1985) Mechanical power analysis of the lower limb musculature in race walking. *International Journal of Sport Biomechanics*, **1**, 15–24.

Wilmore, J.H., Parr, R.B., Haskell, W.L., Costill, D.L., Milburn, L.J. and Kerlan, R.K. (1976) Football pros' strengths – and CV weakness – charted. *The Physician and Sportsmedicine*, **4**, 44–54.

Workman, J.M. and Armstrong, B.W. (1963) Oxygen cost of treadmill walking. *Journal of Applied Physiology*, **18**, 798–803.

Wyndham, C.H. and Strydom, N.B. (1971) Mechanical efficiency of a champion walker. *South African Medical Journal*, **45**, 551–553.

Wyndham, C.H., Strydom, N.B. van Graan, C.H., van Rensburg, A.J., Rogers G.G., Greyson, J.S. and van der Walt, W.H. (1971) Walk or jog for health: I. The energy costs of walking or running at different speeds. *South African Medical Journal*, **45**, 50–53.

Yanker, G.D. (1983) *Rockport's Complete Book of Exercise Walking*. Contemporary Books, Chicago, IL.

Zarrugh, M.Y. (1981) Power requirements and mechanical efficiency of treadmill walking. *Journal of Biomechanics*, **14**, 157–165.

Zarrugh, M.Y., Todd, F.N. and Ralston, H.J. (1974) Optimization of energy expenditure during level walking. *European Journal of Applied Physiology*, **33**, 293–306.

7
Cycling

Edmund R. Burke, Irvine E. Faria and John A. White

'The bipedal physique of the hominids is admirably designed for the efficient performance of long-sustained muscular activity, as well as for short bursts of intense exertion'. J.S. Weiner.

7.1 INTRODUCTION

The central concerns of this chapter are the physiological determinants of cycling. Through a review of current scientific knowledge and the application of that knowledge to the sport of cycling, one might optimize the achievement of human potential within the sport. As our knowledge of cycling physiology grows it is essential that there is continued open communication between the scientist and practitioner. This chapter represents an attempt to transcend the traditional boundaries between the exercise scientist, the coach and his cyclist. Each section represents an inquiry unique to the sport of cycling. The aim is to present the reader with a valid perspective within which to study the sport of cycling.

7.1.1 Characteristics of cycling and the cyclist

Competitive cycling, whether track or road, is physiologically demanding. Typically, races range from a 200 m sprint lasting approximately 10 s to the Tour de France of 23 days, covering approximately 5000 km. Between these extremes a whole range of individual, paired and team events exists. This vast range of competitive distances has resulted in cyclists specializing in specific events which have similar metabolic energy demands. The racing cyclist is typically low in body fat, possesses a high maximum oxygen uptake, exhibits a good anaerobic capacity and has strong lower limb musculature.

Road racing requires of the cyclist an aerobic capacity for prolonged exertion and an anaerobic potential to be called upon in breakaways, hill climbing, and 'all-out' sprints. Track racing requires a range of capabilities from sprint power through to endurance speed. Both road and track cycling demand a specific knowledge of tactics and strategies, mastery of skills and considerable courage.

The training procedures adopted by cyclists are those which, as closely as possible, simulate competitive conditions and attempts are often made to copy the training practices of champion cyclists. Emulation of champions, however, may be misguided since each individual possesses unique physical and physiological potentials.

During competition the cyclist's oxygen transport and energy conversion systems are often taxed to their limit. Therefore, a major portion of training is aimed toward the improvement of the oxygen transport, oxygen extraction and specific energy conversion systems. At the same time, tempo training is incorporated in order to enhance anaerobic capacity. Both road racing and track cyclists aim to raise their exercise tolerance so as to work at high percentages of maximum oxygen consumption.

Sprint events call upon the utilization of the high energy compounds adenosine triphosphate (ATP) and phosphocreatine (PC). Match sprints, which last approximately 10 s, rely heavily on the combined ATP-CP energy sources. Pursuit and kilometre races place high demands upon both the ATP and CP energy resources as well as the glycolytic energy systems. Long-distance road racing relies heavily on the oxidative breakdown of carbohydrates and fats for energy, with the capacity for exploiting a large portion of aerobic capacity over long time periods, while minimizing excess lactate production.

7.2 METHODS OF EVALUATION

7.2.1 Parameters considered

Regularly performed endurance exercise, such as long-distance cycling, can induce major physiological and biochemical adaptations in a variety of metabolic systems at cellular and organ levels. It is well recognized that specific training techniques bring about skeletal muscle enzymatic modifications that result in increased oxidative potential and contribute to improved work capacity. The most important adaptive response of skeletal muscle to endurance training is an augmentation of the muscle cell's respiratory capacity with increases in the ability to oxidize glycogen and fatty acids. Other cellular metabolic adaptations to endurance training include alterations in glycolytic capacity and acto-myosin ATPase activity.

By measuring the oxygen uptake, the onset time of blood lactate accumulation and the level of blood lactate concentrations in elite and highly trained cyclists during various cycling formats, it is possible to determine the physiological demands of cycling. These metabolic para-meters also shed light on the training state of the cyclist. Determinations resulting in an individual work-performance profile may be formulated for the cyclist, which together with anthropometric measurements allow recommendations to be made concerning the potential for success in specific cycling disciplines.

The validity of this profile is dependent upon several factors, including the accuracy of the measurements, methodology employed, data collection technique as well as the functional characteristics of the cyclists. The value of the findings lie in how they are applied during training and competition. By measuring metabolic responses during different cycling demands it becomes possible to review and evaluate those variables affecting performance. It is then possible to reveal those factors contributing to the relative strengths and weaknesses of the cyclist's performance. The multiple factors involved in the physiology of cycling require close and constant examination if optimum performance is to be achieved.

The tools used to study the physiology of cycling include the bicycle ergometer, rollers, cycling simulators, and the treadmill. Most often the cyclist is brought into the laboratory to pedal an ergometer of some design or ride a bicycle on a motor-driven treadmill. Researchers are more conscious today of the value of allowing cyclists to ride their own bicycles during performance tests. This practice by the researcher helps to ensure that the cyclist will not alter the cycling style, whereby much of the natural cycling technique may be preserved.

7.2.2 Motion study

The high-speed camera and computer graphics have provided valuable methods for analysis of body segment motion during cycling. Move-ments typically lasting only a few milliseconds can be precisely plotted and analysed, leading to accurate and extremely valuable information relating to the motion of body segments, limbs and joints while cycling. The graphical form allows easy interpretation and understanding of patterns of joint, limb and body segment motion, in relation to forces applied during cycling (Soden and Adeyefa, 1979).

7.2.3 Force determinations

A definitive and helpful method of measuring the external force that muscular action creates is the use of 'strain gauges'. These devices are fixed to structures of the bicyle, such as the crank or pedals. When these structures deform under pressure or force, the gauges also deform. Dedicated hardware and software interfaced with these gauges, provide the researcher with a continuous output of force or torque. Through this use of scientific instrumentation it becomes possible to determine the exact force, at a particular moment during pedalling, that the cyclist is applying (Brooke *et al.*, 1981; Hull and Jorge, 1985). This information may then be used to help discern the components of pedalling efficiency.

7.2.4 Electromyography

The visual systems employed for motion analysis of cycling, even though scientific and accurate, can only indicate the apparent movements. It is often necessary to know how the movements are actually performed against a resistive load. For this reason electromyographic techniques are employed in conjunction with biomechanical analyses (Hull and Jorge, 1985). Electromyography is generally used to indicate which muscle groups are active during a given segment of the pedal revolution. Surface electrodes are usually attached to the muscle groups to be studied. The action potentials generated are recorded during the pedalling action, thereby allowing the researcher to gain a more complete insight into the muscles employed and the extent of their involvement while pedalling.

7.2.5 Resistant forces

One of the principal inhibitors of the cyclist is drag. The forces of aerodynamic drag build to the square of gains in velocity and contribute 80–90% of the metabolic cost of cycling (Kyle, 1979). Although experiments in which varying body positions as well as the use of windshields and frames that completely enclose the bicycle have been conducted outdoors, the most controlled method of studying the effects of drag is in the wind tunnel (Nonweiler, 1956). Such studies are based on the concept that the effects on an object are identical whether it is moving in air at a set speed or if the object is held stationary while air is moved past at an equivalent speed. The technique used is to mount a bicycle and rider inside a large tunnel and blow air toward them at speeds comparable to a range of riding speeds. If the bicycle and rider are maintained in position against the wind force by attaching a force measuring device, the effect of different riding postures, cycling clothing, frame and wheel configuration, and other components can be determined.

7.2.6 Body fat and composition

A factor which influences cycling performance is body fat content or body composition. Two methods generally used to estimate body fat and composition include skinfold measures and underwater weighing. The accuracy of skinfold methods has recently been criticized by Clarys et al. (1987).

Excess body weight, such as superficial adipose tissue, which does not contribute to work output, places the cyclist at a disadvantage. High muscle-to-weight ratio is essential for hill climbing efficiency and the lean, strong cyclist has the advantage. For example, the estimated amount of body fat of elite cyclists ranges from 6–9% for senior men to 12–15% for senior women (Burke, 1980).

7.2.7 Muscle fibre types

One important characteristic which can influence a cyclist's performance potential is muscle fibre composition. Considerable attention has been devoted to the genetic as well as training influences on fibre type characteristics. The recruitment of different categories of muscle fibre can be related to the speed or intensity of cycling. In general, during slow, low intensity cycling, most of the muscle force is generated by the slow oxidative (SO) fibres, but as muscle tension increases with increasing speed using larger gears or in hill climbing, the fast oxidative glycolytic (FOG) fibres contribute to the work. The FOG fibres develop considerably greater forces than SO fibres, though they fatigue more easily. At sprinting speeds, where optimal cycling speed or strength is required, the fast glycolytic (FG) fibres develop the greatest force of contraction although they are most easily fatigued.

During long-distance cycling events initiated at submaximal or medium pace, the nervous system principally recruits the SO and some FOG fibres, i.e. those best adapted to endurance activity. Gradually, as these fibres become fatigued or effort increases, the nervous system solicits additional contributions from FOG and FG fibres, especially where breakaways occur and sprints for points or for the finish are required. Therefore, differential fibre fatigue may explain the onset of general fatigue at various stages in racing and the increased effort required to maintain pace until completion of the event.

Studies on the muscle fibre type distribution in male and female cyclists indicate a range of compositions according to event speciality. Elite road race (endurance) cyclists show higher percentages of SO fibres than sprint cyclists who are characterized by higher percentages of FOG and FG fibres (Sjøgaard *et al.*, 1985). While muscle fibre composition alone is not a reliable predictor of success in cycling, an understanding of fibre types and related metabolic activities is useful in the design of training regimens.

7.3 FACTORS INFLUENCING CYCLING PERFORMANCE

7.3.1 Bicycle ergometer vs treadmill

Maximal oxygen uptake ($\dot{V}O_{2max}$) is an important determinant of physical working capacity of the individual. Nevertheless it is recognized that during sustained optimal physical performance, anaerobic resources of energy are also utilized.

Standardized protocols for the establishment of $\dot{V}O_{2max}$ rely on incremental work loads produced on a bicycle ergometer or treadmill. The latter instrument produces between 7% (Hermansen, Hultman and Saltin, 1969) and 10% (McArdle, Katch and Pechar, 1973) greater values in non-specifically trained subjects. This is due primarily to the differences in relative muscle mass involved in running compared with cycling.

Since the adaptive responses to exercise are in part, a function of the specific movement patterns utilized in training, exercise assessment techniques should be specific to the sport in question. Withers *et al.* (1981) have demonstrated that endurance-trained cyclists registered higher $\dot{V}O_{2max}$ and 'anaerobic threshold' levels when tested during cycling compared with treadmill running. Similarly, Hagberg, Giese and Schneider, (1978) have demonstrated slightly higher $\dot{V}O_{2max}$ values in cyclists when performing (hazardous) treadmill cycling or standard bicycle ergometer tests compared with treadmill running.

This tendency for higher $\dot{V}O_2$ values when assessed in an activity which is sport or training specific suggests that cyclists should be tested utilizing a specific cycling protocol (Ricci and Leger, 1983). Moreover, attempts have been made to adapt or modify traditional bicycle ergometers to the specific needs of competitive cyclists, or incorporate the cyclist's own racing cycle into an ergometry system and so preserve the unique characteristics of the individual's cycling position (Brooke and Firth, 1974; Firth, 1981).

7.3.2 Maximal oxygen uptake

The average values for maximal oxygen uptake of elite cyclists are among the highest recorded (Burke, 1982). Table 7.1 documents the values recorded for various international representatives during the last 20 years. For comparison, Swedish elite male cross-country skiers seldom show $\dot{V}O_{2max}$ below 80 ml kg^{-1} min^{-1} and range between 80 and 94 ml kg^{-1} min^{-1} whereas female counterparts range from 70 to 75 ml kg^{-1} min^{-1} (Bergh, 1982). These data for elite cyclists suggest that

Table 7.1 Mean maximal oxygen uptake of elite cyclists

Reference source	No. of subjects	$\dot{V}O_{2max}$ ml kg^{-1} min^{-1}	Cyclist group (males)
Saltin and Åstrand (1967)	6	74.0	Swedish National Team
Israel and Weber (1972)	5	75.5	E. German National Team
Hermansen (1973)	16	73.0	Norwegian National Team
Stromme et al. (1977)	5	69.1	Swedish National Team
Stromme et al. (1977)	1	77.0	E. Merckx (5 times winner Tour de France)
Bonjer (1979)	12	67.6	Elite Dutch National Team
Hagberg et al. (1979)	9	70.3	US National Road Squad
Burke (1982)	23	74.0	US National Team
Faria et al. (1982)	4	68.0	Danish National Road Team
White et al. (1982a)	5	77.4	GB Olympic Road Team
Hahn et al. (1986)	11	70.0	Australian National Road Team

high oxygen uptake values are required for successful competition at the national and international level. The importance of maintaining high oxygen consumption levels relative to $\dot{V}O_{2max}$ may have more relevance to success during endurance cycling events than the absolute $\dot{V}O_{2max}$.

Krebs, Zinkgraf and Virgilio, (1983) investigated the predictability of bicycle performance in a 25 mile (40 km) time trial. Data from 35 competitive cyclists were used. Competitive experience was found to be the single best predictor of bicycling performance. Physiological parameters examined did not contribute to performance prediction. The data from this study suggest that the role of $\dot{V}O_{2max}$ is less important than experience in competitive cycling.

White *et al.* (1982a) examined seasonal variations in $\dot{V}O_{2max}$ and found increases of about 5% during the pre-season to peak-season period, although differences in absolute $\dot{V}O_{2max}$ values were observed between Olympic 'select' and 'non-select' cyclists. The results confirm those of Fagard *et al.* (1983) who found peak oxygen uptake increased 6% during the competitive season.

Complementary changes have been observed in oxygen delivery capacity as determined by cardiovascular adaptations. Fagard *et al.* (1983) also reported seasonal changes in cardiac structure and function and reported increased left ventricular total diameter and end-diastole, due primarily to greater septal and posterior wall thickness, whereas internal heart diameter remained unchanged. These results confirm the findings of Fananapazir *et al.* (1982) in young and mature cyclists who displayed increased left ventricular mass as well as mass:volume ratio changes during a competitive season.

Body size has an effect on the energy cost ($\dot{V}O_2$) while cycling. Swain *et al.* (1986) found that the absolute oxygen consumption while cycling on a level road increases with body weight for any given speed. The increased oxygen cost was large enough for the authors to conclude that body size is an important factor in competitive cycling. Furthermore, it has been estimated that the difference in frontal area between large and small cyclists may account for up to 20% of the resistive aerodynamic drag forces experienced in racing (Merrill, 1980).

7.3.3 Pedalling rate

There are a myriad of potential kinetic and kinematic parameters which may influence the efficiency of cycling performance. Such factors as pedal speed and crank length, changes in body position, various linear and angular displacements, velocities and accelerations of body segments and forces in joints and muscles serve as confounding factors in the determination of efficiency. In most studies of cycling efficiency the energy cost of the limb movement as related to joint forces with angular modifications, has not been taken into account.

The speed of limb movement has a marked effect on the gross efficiency of work output. Efficiencies of 19.6–28.8% have been reported in the literature (Dickinson, 1929; Garry and Wishart, 1931; Asmussen, 1953; Banister and Jackson, 1967; Asmussen and Bonde-Petersen, 1974; Hagberg, Giese and Mullin, 1974; Jordan and Merrill, 1974; Gaesser and Brooks, 1975; Seabury, Adams and Ramey, 1976; Faria, Sjøgaard and Bonde-Petersen, 1982; Merrill and White, 1984).

Faria, Sjøgaard and Bonde-Petersen (1982) found that with high power output a decrease in efficiency was not evident when pedal rate was increased while holding power output constant. Suzuki (1979) observed the highest cycling efficiency with the lowest pedalling rate and suggested that a decrease in work efficiency at high pedal rates is due to the longer cross-bridge engagement time of slow-twitch muscle fibres, causing them to shorten more slowly. The thought that the higher pedal frequency is associated with a substantial increase in energy expenditure due to recruitment of less economical fast-twitch fibres is open to question. It is not known whether the same form of fibre recruitment takes place at a high pedal frequency with lower power output as at a high pedal frequency with high power output.

Gaesser and Brooks (1975) found that efficiency decreased with increments in speed. This decrease of efficiency at the higher pedalling speeds may have been due to the use of unskilled riders in the study. Unskilled cyclists are often observed, especially at high pedal speeds, to employ excessive body movements. Their lack of 'spinning' technique accounts for mechanical inefficiency which may contribute to a greater energy cost. In contrast, the skilled cyclist pedals smoothly at high cadence (rev min^{-1}) without engaging muscle groups which do not contribute to pedalling speed.

Faria, Sjøgaard and Bonde-Petersen (1982) have demonstrated that the effect of changing pedal rate on efficiency, while the load is held constant, is negligible at high power outputs. There appears to be a significant advantage in employing a high pedalling rate at high power output. The faster pedal rate yielded a smaller oxygen cost for the racing cyclist. A pedalling frequency of 130 rev min^{-1} yielded a gross efficiency of 22%. This efficiency is close to the 21.3% found for cross-country skiing (Niinimaa, Dyon and Shephard, 1978), and 23% for rowing (Di Prampero et al., 1971). Hagberg et al. (1981) studying well-trained competitive cyclists found the most economical pedal rate to be 91 rev min^{-1}. The preferred rate, however, for each cyclist ranged from 70 to 102 rev min^{-1}.

Merrill and White (1984) studying highly trained cyclists who performed constant power output (75% $\dot{V}O_{2max}$) at varying pedal rates (approximately 70, 95 and 126 rev min⁻¹) reported relatively higher physiological responses at the highest pedal rate. Furthermore, gross and net muscular efficiency were significantly lower at the high pedal rate. It was concluded that equivalent power output, and hence road speed in experienced cyclists, is compromised by additional physiological costs of high pedal rates which adversely affect muscular efficiency.

7.3.4 Muscle recruitment

Henriksson and Bonde-Petersen (1974) designed a study to investigate the variation in electromyography (EMG) during a wide range of intensities of external work in cycling. It was found that during cycling the quadriceps muscle group is recruited proportionally to the changes in the body's oxygen uptake. The recruitment of muscle mass was found to be proportional to the external exercise up to an exercise intensity

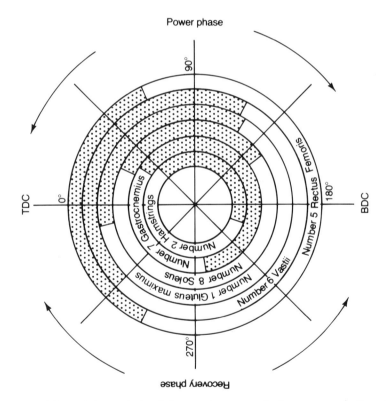

Figure 7.1 The activity periods of six muscle groups during one revolution of the pedals (from Faria and Cavanagh, 1978).

corresponding to 120% of the $\dot{V}O_{2max}$ for both m. rectus and m. vastus lateralis. Over a wider range of pedalling intensities the work of the quadriceps muscle is proportional to the total work of the cyclist.

The effect of saddle height and load on the pattern of surface muscle interaction was investigated by Desipres (1977) who found that the height of the saddle influenced plantar flexion of the foot significantly, but did not influence knee extension critically. Varying the height of the saddle did not significantly influence muscle activity. There were, however, several differences in muscle involvement. The rectus femoris was more active at the lower saddle height of 95% of the leg length than at 105%. Activity of the sartorius was quantitatively larger at 105% of saddle height. At the lower saddle height greater activity was evident in the quadriceps femoris.

Electromyographic studies have been used to identify the specific muscle involvement during the power and recovery phase of pedalling (Faria and Cavanagh, 1978). Figure 7.1 details the muscle recruitment sequence. Hip extension is a major movement executed during pedalling with the gluteus maximus (and part of the hamstring group) active during the first 45 degrees of the power phase and then is silent for the remainder of the revolution of the pedals. The hamstrings are active during the last 45 degrees of the power phase. The major knee extensors, including the vastii group and rectus femoris which compose the quadriceps, form a unique pattern of activity during pedalling. The vasti muscles are active at the same time as the hamstrings, over a 70 degree sector of the crank revolution, up to the point 15 degrees past the horizontal of the power phase. During the recovery phase the hip flexor muscle group, the iliopsoas and rectus femoris, are active. The rectus femoris begins its activity during the last 90 degrees of the recovery phase. It is also a generator of force during the first 60 degrees of the power phase. At the ankle, the gastrocnemius and soleus begin their involvement following both hip and knee extensors.

7.3.5 Fibre types

Burke *et al.* (1977) examined the characteristics of skeletal muscles in competitive cyclists. Compared with non-elite cyclists, elite competitive cyclists had significantly higher values of $\dot{V}O_{2max}$ and levels of the enzymes malate dehydrogenase (MDH) and phosphorylase (PA). No differences were evident between the groups for percentage of slow-oxidative (SO) and fast-oxidative glycolytic (FOG) and fast-glycolytic (FG) fibres or in the area of FOG plus FG or of SO fibres. While the activities of succinate dehydrogenase (SDH) and lactate dehydrogenase (LDH) did not differ significantly between the levels of cycling

Table 7.2 Muscle fibre composition of various cyclists

Study	Slow oxidative	Fast oxidative glycolytic	Fast glycolytic
Sjøgaard (1984)			
Competitive road cyclists	45%	35%	20%
Elite road cyclists	71%	20%	9%
Controls (untrained)	57%	31%	12%
Burke et al. (1977)			
Competitive road cyclists	53%	47%*	
Elite road cyclists	57%	43%*	

* Not analysed for subtypes FOG and FG.

proficiency, significant correlations were found between $\dot{V}O_{2max}$ and SDH ($r = 0.75$), $\dot{V}O_{2max}$ and MDH ($r = 0.73$) and between SDH and MDH ($r > 0.70$). These findings suggest that extremely high percentages of FG or SO fibres may not be a prerequisite for success in competitive cycling.

The variability of muscle fibre types in male and female cyclists is presented in Table 7.2. Studies (Burke et al, 1977; Sjøgaard, 1984; Sjøgaard et al., 1985) showed that successful distance (road) cyclists have relatively more slow-oxidative (SO) than fast-oxidative glycolytic (FOG) and fast glycolytic (FG) fibres. Sjøgaard (1984) demonstrated that in some elite road cyclists leg muscles may be composed of more than 70% SO fibres. In contrast, World-class sprint cyclists may have leg muscles composed predominantly of FOG and FG fibres (Burke et al., 1977, Sjøgaard et al., 1985).

Whereas previous research has shown that training may increase the endurance capacity of muscle, there is little evidence to support the contention that training changes the percentages of slow and fast fibres (Gollnick et al., 1973). The percentage composition of muscle fibres appears relatively constant and unaffected by training, suggesting that this characteristic of the champion cyclist may be largely inherited.

However, exceptions to this are the subtypes of fast fibres (FOG and FG) which show some modification with training. Following endurance training FG fibres take on the metabolic characteristics of FOG fibres. This modification suggests that these are used more often during racing and training and gain greater endurance ability. Although the mechanisms of these changes are not fully understood, this modification may explain why few FG fibres are found in the leg muscles of endurance cyclists (Sjøgaard, 1984).

The size of muscle fibres also varies markedly among elite cyclists as demonstrated by Sjøgaard (1984), although the study showed that in half the subjects studied slow fibres were larger than fast fibres. It was concluded that the heavy involvement of slow fibres during endurance training may cause these changes.

It must be recognized that while a high percentage of a particular fibre type may indicate potential for a specific cycling discipline, data collected from muscle biopsy studies do not necessarily reveal the determinants of success in cycling.

7.3.6 Ventilation

A high absolute maximum oxygen uptake is accompanied generally by a high ventilatory gas exchange ($\dot{V}_E$). Folinsbee et al. (1983) examined the respiratory pattern in elite cyclists. The mean $\dot{V}_{Emax}$ of the cyclists exceeded that of untrained subjects by 34.6% (183 l min^{-1} vs 138 l min^{-1}). Although the cyclists achieved greater maximum ventilation, many of the characteristics of the ventilatory response to cycling were similar to those of the untrained subjects. The cyclists were found to ultilize a much higher respiratory frequency to achieve their higher level of ventilation by a reduction of both inspiratory and expiratory time. The reduction in expiratory time made a significantly greater contribution to the rise in respiratory frequency than reduced inspiratory time. The results of this study showed no indication that the higher respiratory frequency confers any physiological advantage, but is a result of the increased ventilatory requirement of maximal exercise in highly trained individuals.

7.3.7 Anaerobic tolerance

There has been an ongoing debate about the value of physiological indicators of anaerobic energy production, in particular the concept of the so-called 'anaerobic threshold' (AT) as defined by Wasserman et al. (1973), its prediction from ventilatory parameters (Davis, 1985), the questionable assumptions underlying its interpretation (Brooks, 1985) as well as recent attempts to clarify the issues (Mader and Heck, 1986). The concept of exercise anaerobiosis may be viewed in terms of the onset of blood lactate accumulation (OBLA) as outlined by Karlsson and Jacobs (1982), and justified by Heck et al. (1985). The physiological parameters used to identify blood lactate dynamics have been regarded as sensitive markers for the evaluation of lactate tolerance/utilization and possibly relate to the underlying lactate 'shuttle' mechanism (Brooks, 1986).

Continuous bicycle ergometer training has been shown to be more effective than interval training at low power output and interval training at high power output in raising the 'AT'. Overend, Patterson and Cunningham (1986) found that when the average intensity of training was equated, continuous training, low power output and high power output interval training were equally effective in increasing $\dot{V}O_{2max}$ but only continuous training was effective in raising anaerobic 'threshold' as indicated by the so-called ventilatory inflection point.

When the local oxygen consumption is adequate to meet the demands of the cycling work rate, the energy needed may be supplied by ATP generated through aerobic mechanisms. However, if the energy needs of the muscle fibres exceed the capacity of the muscle cells to deliver energy aerobically, a greater proportion of ATP will be provided anaerobically. The consquence is increased anaerobic glycolysis needed to sustain the availability of ATP.

Miller, Lindholm and Manredi (1985) found that trained cyclists operate at a similar percentage (70–80%) of their $\dot{V}O_{2max}$ as trained runners prior to ventilatory adjustments associated with the 'anaerobic threshold'. Employing trained cyclists the authors found that the 'anaerobic threshold' (Tlac) was a better predictor of a 15-km time trial performance than $\dot{V}O_{2max}$. Burke, Fleck and Dickson (1981) observed low correlations between blood lactate levels and total ride time during the kilometre ($r = 0.51$) and individual pursuit ($r = 0.41$) competitions. However, no significant differences were found in blood lactates between kilometre, individual and team pursuit, as well as match sprint events, with blood lactate levels somewhat lower than those reported in various non-cycling exercise modes of similar durations. It was suggested that these differences were attributable to decreased blood flow resulting from the relatively prolonged muscle contraction–relaxation phase involved in the cycling action, compared with other activities.

The rates of enzymatic reactions are sensitive to temperature and an increase in muscle temperature will increase the rate of an enzymatic reaction. As a consequence the onset of metabolic acidosis may be delayed if warm-up precedes the exercise task. Protti, Meltzer and Sucec (1986) found that a warm-up at an intensity of 120% of the individual's work rate at the onset of metabolic acidosis was optimal for increasing $\dot{V}O_{2max}$ and the percentage of $\dot{V}O_{2max}$ prior to the onset of metabolic acidosis.

Notwithstanding the current debate on the mechanisms underlying 'anaerobic' energy production, Conconi et al. (1982) described a method for the determination of 'anaerobic threshold' by non-invasive techniques using non-linear changes in heart rate response to increments in work load. Furthermore, Droghetti et al. (1985) have extended the application for use in various sports, including cycling, in which the non-linear heart rate deflection point (Vd) at a velocity (intensity) related level can be used to identify OBLA. The use of this measure allows the simple estimation of training and/or competition levels of performance in relation to the relative aerobic/anaerobic demands of the activity.

7.3.8 Blood buffering

Bicarbonate, phosphate, and protein chemical buffers serve to maintain a consistency in the acid–base (pH) levels of the body fluids. The buffering system's responsibility for sequestering potentially harmful positively charged protons during high intensity cycling must be adequately sustained if work intensity is to be maintained. Physical training *per se* appears to enhance the body's buffering capacity, but interest has turned also to the speculation that a supplemented increase in the body's chemical buffer reserve prior to exercise might enhance short-term anaerobic work by delaying the fall in intracellular pH consequent to such effort (see Chapter 1).

Weatherwax *et al.* (1986) investigated the effect of sodium phosphate loading on an 8 km bicycle time trial performance. Although the cyclists covered the course slightly faster and incurred a higher lactate concentration following the phosphate loading, the change was not significant. Likewise, Ahlberg *et al.* (1986) found that phosphate supplementation on cycle ergometer performance was of limited value. Despite minor changes in peak lactate efflux and 'anaerobic threshold', the data indicated that phosphate supplementation did little to alter metabolic buffering efficiency.

MacLaren and Morgan (1985) reported that ingestion of sodium bicarbonate (0.25 g kg^{-1} body weight) two hours prior to exercise increased the time to exhaustion by 12% in the performance of a cycle ergometer ride at 100% $\dot{V}O_{2max}$. The improvement was considered a result of enhanced buffering capacity of the body which allowed the accumulation of higher lactate levels without a concomitant decrease in acidity (pH) levels than during control conditions using a placebo. This supported the notion that exogenous buffer supplementation can enhance maximal work performance.

7.3.9 Body position

The ability to sustain prolonged work is dependent upon an adequate supply of oxygen to the active muscles. It is well known that the mechanisms of high oxygen transport are affected by body position during work (Craig, 1960; Wang, Marshall and Shephford, 1960; McGregor, Adin and Sekeli, 1961; Bevegard, Holmgren and Johnsson,

1963). The racing cyclist generally assumes a semi-upright or deep forward-lean posture while pedalling, in order to optimize the aero-dynamic profile.

Faria, Dix and Frazer (1978) found the dropbar posture during cycling resulted in significantly higher oxygen uptake, work output, and pulmonary ventilation although no difference was found in heart rate. These data suggest that the body posture assumed during cycling is crucial for optimum performance, and a compromise is achieved between aerodynamic resistive forces and increased physiological demands.

7.3.10 Exercise intensity

Since the publication of two classical studies (Karvonen, Kentala and Mustala, 1957; Hollman and Venrath, 1962), heart rate has been used as an accepted means of quantifying physical training programmes. Sharkey and Holleman (1967) and Faria (1969) in similar experiments found a direct relationship between improvement in cardiovascular efficiency and the intensity of training. From these data it has become evident that to achieve an overload of the oxygen-uptake system, exercise at 70–85% of the heart rate reserve (HRR) is essential, where HRR = resting HR + X% (max HR-resting HR), the value for X being 70–85.

7.3.11 Mechanical parameters

Soden and Adeyefa (1979) investigated the forces applied to the pedals, saddle and handlebars in two young cyclists during speeding, hill climbing and starting. The forces were estimated from cine film records and the results were compared with force measurements obtained from an 'instrumented' pedal. Pedal forces of up to three times body weight were recorded during starting movements with significant handlebar loads. Climbing and speeding movements showed characteristic weight-distribution changes as well as force transfer across the handlebars.

Force application and movement patterns of the top six male 4000 m pursuit riders in the USA and the female 3000 m world champion were studied during simulated all-out competitive rides of 4 min 45 s. The cyclists rode a racing bicycle mounted on a road emulator. Data were collected on-line from both the legs during four periods of the ride. The average power output ranged from 331 to 449 W with cadences between 103 and 126 rev min^{-1}. LaFortune *et al.* (1983) found that during the first 180 degrees of the pedal revolution the riders were between 69 and 79% effective in their force application. Right and left asymmetries were found in total force applied, work done and pedal angle. The mean work asymmetry was found to be 4.3%. These results suggest that improvements in the style of even the elite cyclist may be in order.

Ribisl *et al.* (1982) examined the influence of toe clips during cycling upon ratings of perceived exertion. The use of toe clips by competitive cyclists resulted in a significant decrease in their perception of exertion and a concomitant increase in $\dot{V}O_{2max}$ over the condition without toe clips. In a somewhat similar study Brodowicz *et al.* (1982) examined the effect of toe clip use during cycle ergometry on the 'anaerobic threshold' of competitive and trained non-competitive cyclists. Competitive cyclists exhibited a significant increase in $\dot{V}O_2$-related 'anaerobic threshold' when using toe clips, while the non-competitive cyclist did not. These findings suggest that the competitive cyclists derived benefit from the use of toe clips, while the trained non-competitive cyclist may not gain such benefit.

The trained cyclist can benefit from the use and proper application of cleated shoes. Davis and Hull (1981) found that use of cleated shoes retards fatigue of the quadriceps muscle group. By allowing more flexor muscle utilization during the backstroke, cleated shoes distribute the workload and alleviate the peak load demand on the quadriceps group. Thus proper use and application of cleated shoes may increase pedalling efficiency.

The length of the crank arm and its influence on cycling efficiency was investigated by Conrad and Thomas (1983). Crank lengths of 165–180 mm at 2.5 mm increments, were used during a constant work load which averaged 79% of the cyclist's $\dot{V}O_{2max}$. During steady-state exercise there were no significant differences among any of the seven crank lengths in respect to $\dot{V}O_2$. It was concluded that for trained cyclists during work of approximately 80% of $\dot{V}O_{2max}$ different crank arm lengths within the range tested do not influence cycling efficiency. From this research it appears that the prediction of optimal crank arm length cannot be determined from the length of a leg segment.

These findings do not, however, agree with those of Carmichael, Loomis and Hodgson (1982) who found pedalling efficiency to vary with upper leg length at a fixed crank length. The effects of varied crank length on $\dot{V}O_2$ and heart rate were examined in nine competitive cyclists who exercised at a constant power output and pedal speed. The relationships were also examined among optimal crank length and leg segment lengths. Cycling bouts were 6 min in duration at approximately 75% $\dot{V}O_{2max}$, employing each of six crank lengths (150, 160, 170, 180, 190, 200 mm). Optimal crank length was considered that which resulted in the lowest $\dot{V}O_2$ and correlated significantly with upper leg length. Conclusions drawn from this study suggest that the crank length on most commercially available bicycles and ergometers is probably too long for the majority of cyclists.

Sanderson and Cavanagh (1985) examined the effect of pedal rate on the application of effective force in experienced recreational cyclists riding a racing bicycle mounted on a road emulator. The cyclists pedalled at 45 and 90 rev min^{-1} at a workload of 400 W. Increasing the pedal rate had the effect of increasing the effective force during the first 70 degrees of propulsion after the top dead centre (TDC). The effective force was nearly identical for both speeds between 70 and 180 degrees after the TDC. At the higher pedalling rate the effective force was lower during the recovery phase.

The energetics of riding a bicycle at constant power output while saddle height varied was examined by Hamley and Thomas (1967) and Nordeen-Snyder (1977). As saddle height was varied there existed a height at which submaximal $\dot{V}O_2$ was minimized and power output maximized: this occurred at approximately 109% of the height of the pubic symphysis. This finding points to the importance of individualizing saddle height.

7.3.12 The human-machine interface

During recent years attempts have been made to enhance cycling performance by improving the design of the bicycle. Most attention has been directed towards minimizing those factors which inhibit speed including wind resistance, rolling resistance, mechanical efficiency and weight (Whitt and Wilson, 1974) within the regulations laid down by the Union Cycliste Internationale (UCI). While much has been made of technical modifications by manufacturers, cycle design is still more of a 'black art' than an applied science (Burrows, 1985a). While aerodynamic drag accounts for 85–90% of the total resistance at 30 mph (48.3 kmh^{-1}) most of this is due to the cyclist's profile with only about 25% attributable to the bicycle itself. Hence, attempts to improve performance by use of 'low profile' machines with improved aerodynamics and materials design features may have produced no more than 1–2% improvement in sustained cycling performance (Burrows, 1985b). It would appear that since there are few real gains left in machine design and construction, then most room for performance improvement must come from the cyclist's physiognomy, rather than the bicycle's topology.

7.3.13 Nutritional considerations

Carbohydrates

Lipids and carbohydrates are major contributors to energy metabolism during prolonged exercise. Glycogen is the primary fuel called upon during hard muscular work (Bergström and Hultman, 1972). During supramaximal dynamic exercise, sprints, hill climbs and breakaways, muscle glycogen reduction begins in the FG fibres followed by FOG fibres and SO fibres (Secher and Nygaard, 1976; Thomson, Green and Houston, 1978). The reduction pattern is reversed when the dynamic work is submaximal. Saltin and Karlsson (1971) have shown that the rate of muscle glycogen utilization is exponentially related to exercise intensity. Glycogen reduction is accelerated during work in the heat and spared by endurance-trained muscle. The endurance-trained muscle has greater capacity to oxidize fats and thereby spare the use of glycogen.

It is well known that endurance cycling lowers blood glucose and that improvements in performance can be made when cyclists are fed carbohydrate during events lasting one to four hours (Coyle *et al.*, 1983, 1986). Although none of these studies noticed any difference in performance during the early stage of exercise when carbohydrates were given, the subjects were able to perform better over the final stages of the experiments. Carbohydrate feeding during cycling prevents premature exhaustion of muscle glycogen stores. Taking in carbohydrate during the event enables the muscles to obtain more energy from blood glucose, thereby lowering the demand placed upon the muscle glycogen stores (Ahlborg and Felig, 1977). The cyclist can perform better in competition before muscle glycogen stores are exhausted.

During submaximal cycling at 60–80% $\dot{V}O_{2max}$, muscle glycogen declines progressively until total depletion at exhaustion. The time until exhaustion is closely related to the amount of glycogen stored in muscle at the onset of exercise. Normally the muscle glycogen store is approximately 85–90 mmol kg^{-1} (wet muscle) and plays a key role during prolonged cycling; therefore resynthesis of muscle glycogen is an important component of the recovery process. Following prolonged work, muscle glycogen stores must be refilled using a diet rich in carbohydrate (over 60%) to ensure muscle glycogen replacement between hard training bouts and stages of a race. The question raised is whether different carbohydrates (glucose, fructose or sucrose) affect muscle glycogen resynthesis.

Blom *et al.* (1982) found that the rate of muscle glycogen resynthesis after prolonged exercise is the same for glucose and sucrose. The experimental load used to promote glycogen resynthesis was 0.7 g kg^{-1} body weight of glucose, fructose and sucrose (in water) every second hour of recovery. These findings may reflect the fact that insulin response to fructose is less pronounced, and suggest that for rapid glycogen repletion in the muscle after exercise, glucose ingestion is preferred to fructose. The work of Conlee, Lawler and Ross (1982) indicates the same is true for glycogen repletion in the liver.

White and Ford (1984) compared the effects of feeding a citrus-based carbohydrate drink with a glucose polymer drink in seven highly trained cyclists who exercised for two hours on a cycle ergometer at approximately 65% $\dot{V}O_{2max}$. Equal quantities of carbohydrate were supplied at 15 min intervals with a total energy delivery of approximately 28% of the estimated energy cost of the exercise. No differences were noted in plasma glucose concentrations between the two drinks, although the time course of plasma glucose concentration during and after exercise indicated a more rapid uptake and assimilation of carbohydrate from the citrus-based drink.

The effects of carbohydrate (CHO) feeding on exercise performance was investigated by Hargreaves et al (1984). Ten male subjects cycled intermittently on an electrically braked ergometer for a total of 4 hours. For each 30 min the cycling involved 20 min of steady-state work at 50% $\dot{V}O_{2max}$ and 10 min of intermittent (30 s cycling, 2 min rest) cycling at 100% $\dot{V}O_{2max}$. A final sprint ride to exhaustion was performed. In one trial the subjects ingested 43 g CHO in solid form and 400 ml of water at 0, 60, 120 and 180 min of exercise. The second trial consisted of giving each subject 400 ml of an artificially sweetened drink without solid CHO. No significant differences between trials were observed for $\dot{V}O_2$, heart rate and total energy expenditure. It was found, however, that ingestion of CHO in solid form resulted in a higher respiratory exchange ratio than with the control. Also, 20 min after each feeding, blood glucose values were significantly higher with solid CHO ingestion. Muscle glycogen utilization was lower and the sprint ride time to exhaustion was longer with the solid CHO feeding. The findings suggest that solid CHO ingestion maintains blood glucose levels during prolonged exercise, and enhances sprint performance at the end of such work.

Ingestion of a glucose polymer drink before and during prolonged cycling has resulted in significantly improved performance times. Seifert et al. (1986) found that ingestion of a glucose polymer plus 2% fructose at doses of 0.25 g kg^{-1} body weight at 10 mile (16 km) intervals, during an 80 mile (128 km) bicycle time trial, significantly improved finishing times. The polymer drink caused serum glucose levels to rise sharply after 40 miles (64 km). Fatty acid levels were found to be significantly lower and the cyclists were able to sustain a higher percentage of their $\dot{V}O_{2max}$ with polymer ingestion.

Caffeine

The effect of caffeine on physical performance has recently drawn interest among many different sport competitors. It has been reported that ingestion of caffeine prior to a prolonged bout of exercise results in a shift in the substrate oxidation mix. The result is increased utilization of fat and decreased utilization of carbohydrate during exercise. Ben-Ezra and Vaccaro (1982) examined the effect of caffeine on the 'anaerobic threshold' during a bicycle ergometer test to exhaustion. Competitively trained cyclists were administered caffeine at a dosage of 5 mg kg^{-1} body weight prior to the test. Compared to the control subjects, caffeine did not change the AT, $\dot{V}O_{2max}$ or total work time. These results suggest that a single dose of caffeine at the level used in this study does not influence work performance. In a similar study by Powers et al. (1982) using the same dosage, cycling time to exhaustion was not enhanced by caffeine ingestion. Caffeine did enhance the rate of lipid metabolism, but did not change the rate of plasma lactate accumulation. Similar results have been recorded by Casal and Leon (1982).

Ivy et al. (1979) found that 500 mg of caffeine, administered before and during a 2 h ride on an isokinetic bicycle ergometer, resulted in a 7.4% increase in work production. Costill, Dalsky and Fink (1978) found that ingestion of 330 mg caffeine prior to an exhausting bicycle ergometer ride at 80% $\dot{V}O_{2max}$ reduced the respiratory exchange ratio of trained cyclists. These trained cyclists were able to work 15 min longer after caffeine ingestion than during the control cycling bouts. More recent studies (Casal and Leon, 1982; Knapik et al., 1983; William, 1986) have failed to confirm the glycogen sparing effect of caffeine during long-term exercise. The conflicting evidence to date seriously questions the use of caffeine as an ergogenic aid during prolonged cycling.

Fluids

Studies have shown that even highly trained endurance athletes are quite intolerant to dehydration and heat stress (Claremont et al., 1976). Along with carbohydrate feedings, fluid replacement is crucial when training and competition continues beyond one hour. A successful approach is to combine fluid replacement with carbohydrate intake. Recent advances in the manufacture of carbohydrate formulations allow sophisticated liquid carbohydrate delivery systems involving complex carbohydrates rather than simple sugars. Using these approaches, the cyclist may avoid the negative effect of large increases in osmolarity and fluid shift associated with simple sugar intake, and can not only replace fluid but also provide important carbohydrate energy during endurance performance.

Costill and Saltin (1974) have outlined the prerequisites for fluid maintenance and replacement strategies for the optimization of endurance performance in which drinks should be: (1) hypotonic; (2) low in sugar concentration (< 2.5 g per 100 ml of water); (3) cold (8°–13°C); (4) consumed in volumes of 100–400 ml; and (5) palatable. Feedings should be initiated prior to and during competition, and body weight losses made up by fluid ingestion between training sessions and competition.

White and Ford (1983) compared the effects of a fluid maintenance/ replacement strategy using water and an isotonic citrus drink in seven highly trained cyclists who performed two hours of continuous bicycle ergometer exercise at approximately 67% $\dot{V}O_{2max}$. This resulted in approximately 3.5% body weight reduction via dehydration when fluids were not supplied (the control condition). Subsequently fluid volumes were supplied at 15 min intervals at 16°C during exercise and recovery in amounts based upon the subject's previously determined weight loss through exercise dehydration in the control condition. Both water and the citrus-based drink were equally effective in minimizing plasma volume decrements during exercise with restoration to pre-exercise levels during a 3 h recovery period, as well as preventing plasma osmolality disturbances. However, minimal electrolyte changes were associated with the isotonic drink.

These laboratory results confirmed findings during a competitive road race – also reported in the above study – in which large dehydration losses were observed under relatively favourable climatic conditions. It was concluded that fluid replacement during and after prolonged moderately severe exercise is essential for minimizing the physiological disturbance resulting from thermoregulatory imbalance. Finally, White, Ward and Nelson (1984) have outlined the importance of nutritional provision during ultra-distance cycling events which involve high total energy output at intensities of above 55% $\dot{V}O_{2max}$ over 24 hour periods. In such events over 50% of the total energy required may be supplied by repeated feedings of fluids, semi-solid and solid nutrients in order to sustain the performance required.

7.4 MEASURING THE CYCLIST'S POTENTIAL

The superior performances of contemporary cyclists are the result of a complex blend of many physiological, biomechanical, and psychological factors. An ongoing programme of specially selected and administered tests can benefit both the coach and athlete. Through the process of interpreting laboratory test findings, the coach and athlete both gain a better understanding of the physiological components of cycling. Test data serve to indicate the cyclist's strengths and weaknesses and provide a basis for planning the individual's training programme. Test results provide feedback for evaluating the effectiveness of a given training protocol. The coach may find that a training programme which is effective for one cyclist may be less effective for another.

Special testing, however, is not a magical means of selecting future winners. Excellence in athletic performance is a composite of many different factors. An attempt to predict cycling performance from a single physiological test, especially when technical, tactical and psychological components may influence the outcome, is not prudent.

7.4.1 Testing anaerobic power

The theoretical background to, and procedures for testing anaerobic power and capacity are still being developed. An assessment of these energy systems requires a distinction between their capacity and their power. The total amount of energy available to perform work using a given energy system is considered to be its energetic capacity. The maximum amount of energy that can be transformed during exercise, per unit of time, is referred to as the energetic power of that system.

The limiting factors for energy production and utilization for anaerobic work include: (1) the initial levels of ATP in the muscle fibre, (2) the initial levels of muscle glycogen; (3) the ability to tolerate a high level of lactate; (4) the ability to tolerate low intracellular pH; (5) the training level of the athlete, and (6) the distribution of skeletal muscle fibre types.

When testing the cyclist, every effort should be made to modify the commercially available bicycle ergometer to resemble the structural configuration of the racing bicycle or utilize the cyclist's own racing machine. If this is not possible the bicycle ergometer should be adjustable to meet the structural characteristics of the cyclist.

The Wingate Anaerobic Power Test (Bar-Or, 1981) may be used as a pre-training and post-training measure of the cyclist's anaerobic power. As anaerobic power increases, so will the ability to sustain a high intensity sprint on the bicycle. This test demands maximal cycling for 30 s on a bicycle ergometer, or alternatively repeated intervals of 6 s duration with limited recovery in order to determine a performance-related fatigue curve. The 30 s work output is said to reflect the rate of glycolysis and is called 'total anaerobic power output'. The tests, therefore, are described as a measure of both the ATP-CP and glycolytic systems.

A procedure for the assessment of the anaerobic power performance characteristics of racing cyclists using the performer's own racing machine attached to an 'ergowheel' ergometer has been described by White and Al-Dawalibi (1986). The test is a modification of the Wingate Anaerobic Power Test and involves five trials of 30 s 'all-out' sprints at a standardized power output of 15 W kg^{-1} body weight at 130 rev min^{-1}. The acceleratory and sustained power output times are used to determine performance capacity. The procedure has discriminated sprint performance ability within groups of elite cyclists, and changes in the anaerobic performance capacities of track sprint specialists during the pre-season to peak racing season period have been documented using this procedure (White et $al.$, 1982b).

Anaerobic power may also be measured using a Cybex 11 isokinetic dynamometer. Manning and Dooly-Manning (1986) found that anaerobic test results from the Wingate Anaerobic Power Test correlated with those taken on a Cybex machine using a knee extension at 3.14 and 4.20 rad s^{-1}.

7.4.2 Testing aerobic power

The direct measurement of oxygen consumption ($\dot{V}O_{2max}$) employing a continuous progressively loaded bicycle ergometer is the preferred aerobic test. Usually a test duration of 6–12 min is sufficient to elicit a maximal aerobic effort. The pedalling speed should be that which is natural to the cyclist. Experience has shown that load increments of 0.5 kp or 25 W every 2 min provides sufficient metabolic loading following initial warm-up at 3 kp or 150 W for females and 4 kp or 200 W for males. When the cyclist begins to reduce the pedal rate he or she should be encouraged to cycle off the saddle. Upon standing, the resistance should be increased 0.5 to 1.0 kp (25–50 W) and returned to the pre-standing load if the cyclist wishes to return to the saddle. Toward the end of the test this procedure may be repeated several times until volitional fatigue. Care must be taken not to cause intense local leg discomfort, which would prevent a maximal aerobic effort. During the test several physiological criteria should be attained to assure that the cyclist reached the maximum aerobic power (British Association of Sports Sciences, 1986).

Hahn et $al.$ (1986) investigated the effect of test duration on $\dot{V}O_{2max}$ in competitive road-race cyclists and concluded that 1 min, 25 W increments produced significantly higher $\dot{V}O_{2max}$ values than 3 min stage intervals, without the adverse thermoregulatory effects of an excessively long test. Similarly White and Al-Dawalibi (1987) reported that a 1 min, 25 W incremental exercise protocol produced significantly higher $\dot{V}O_{2max}$ values in racing cyclists than a 2 min, 50 W incremental procedure. Both studies concluded that a test duration of 10–12 min, following standardized warm-up, produced optimal aerobic power measures.

Direct determination, by expired gas analysis, of oxygen consumption is not always possible. Predictive equations have been developed to estimate oxygen consumption during a maximal cycling effort to serve as an alternative. However, in order to improve accuracy of a prediction equation in bicycle ergometry, the nature of the test protocol requires a continued progressive resistance test to volitional fatigue. The American

College of Sports Medicine (1986) published the following equation for use with the bicycle ergometer test for prediction of maximal oxygen uptake ($\dot{V}O_{2max}$);

Oxygen consumption (ml min^{-1}) = load (kgm min^{-1}) × 2
                                    + 3.5 (ml kg^{-1} min^{-1}) × body
                                    weight (kg^{-1})

7.4.3 Measurement of the 'anaerobic threshold'

One method of evaluating the effectiveness of a training programme or the maximum aerobic level (% $\dot{V}O_{2max}$) a cyclist can maintain without incurring excess blood lactate, is to determine the so-called 'anaerobic threshold' (AT). While the measurement of the onset of blood lactate accumulation (OBLA) level provides a criterion for assessing the AT (see Chapter 1), it necessitates invasive serial sampling of blood during the progressive bicycle ergometer test. During and following the exercise test blood lactate level is determined from venous samples or from a finger or ear lobe capillary sample.

A non-invasive method of measuring the 'anaerobic threshold' may be used in an incremental test of relative short duration in which the lactate threshold is estimated from the changes in ventilation. This method estimates the AT from alterations in specific respiratory gas exchange parameters. Wasserman et $al.$ (1973) demonstrated that the point of non-linear increases in ventilation ($\dot{V}_E$) and carbon dioxide

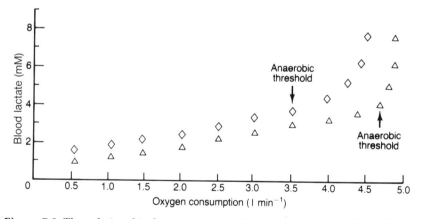

Figure 7.2 The relationship between maximal oxygen uptake and blood lactate accumulation during a continuous, progressive graded cycle ergometer test prior to ($\Diamond$) and following ($\triangle$) a training programme. While maximal oxygen consumption increased from 4.5 to 4.8 l min^{-1} (7%), the 'anaerobic threshold' relative to maximum oxygen uptake, increased from 3.5 to 4.6 l min^{-1} (31%).

production ($\dot{V}CO_2$), in combination with a decline in expired CO_2 tension (F_ECO_2) and an elevation of expired O_2 (F_EO_2), correspond with an increase in venous blood lactate. The AT or ventilatory inflection point has been used to reflect an imbalance between lactate entry into and exit from the plasma and represent a measure of anaerobic work tolerance.

Repeated tests, following training, reveal the effect of an elevated 'anaerobic threshold' and an increased oxygen consumption capacity (Figure 7.2). According to Wasselman *et al.* (1973) the point on the ventilation curve, when the cyclist exhibits respiratory compensation, as indicated by a sudden rise in ventilation, signals metabolic acidosis. In order to obtain linear data the test must begin with low power outputs with each stage lasting 2–3 min. From the results of the graded exercise tests the ventilatory threshold or AT may be plotted, as outlined in Figure 7.2.

Conconi *et al.* (1984, 1988) have further suggested the use of a non-linear increase in heart rate response to speed increments in cycling in determining the 'anaerobic threshold'. The associated blood lactate changes at the point of change in slope of heart rate increases plotted against speed (known as HR deflection velocity) allow the interpretation of the anaerobic tolerance capacity from relatively simple non-invasive field measures of performance in cycling.

7.4.4 Measuring power

Power is the product of torque and velocity. Isokinetic testing has become a common method of measuring leg power which is important to the cyclist. Conventional testing is done at the lower and upper limits of the velocity range of the dynamometer used. For the Cybex machine this range is 0–5.24 rad s^{-1}, 0–300 deg s^{-1} or 0–50 rev min^{-1}. The velocity considered for testing should be specific to the cyclist's competitive events.

Knee extension fatigue tests also provide useful information concerning the cyclist's leg power and the effect of a training protocol. The Thorstensson and Karlsson (1976) test which consists of 50 consecutive knee extensions at 3.14 rad s^{-1} (180 deg s^{-1}) may be used as a fatigue index. The test may also be used to determine the average leg power and total work output achieved by the cyclist.

7.4.5 Body composition assessment

Hydrostatic or underwater weighing is considered the most accurate indirect means of estimating body composition. The technique has served as a standard for other indirect techniques such as skinfolds. If the cyclist does not have access to a hydrostatic weighing facility then skinfolds may be used to express the amount of superficial adipose tissue distribution. However, generalized skinfold equations previously developed, e.g. Pollock, Schmidt and Jackson (1980), for the estimation of body density (BD) together with the Siri (1961) formula for the estimation of body fat, are no longer considered to yield accurate body composition estimates (Clarys *et al.*, 1987). Alternatively, the use of skinfold measures alone represent reliable indices for the assessment of external adipose tissue sites (Jackson, Pollock and McNabb, 1986).

7.5 IMPLICATIONS FOR TRAINING

Physical training and subsequent conditioning does not alter the energy expenditure required to perform a given level of work. Nevertheless, it does reduce the extent of cardiorespiratory changes necessary to achieve the required rate of oxygen consumption. The effects of training result in several broad metabolic and physical changes. At one extreme are the muscle fibre and metabolic changes which result from high intensity exercise of short duration, e.g. anaerobic work including strength training. At the opposite end of the continuum are the long-term effects of prolonged exercise repeated many times at a submaximal level, which enhances central and peripheral aerobic functional capacity.

7.5.1 Specificity

Success in bicycle racing involves physical preparation in a long-term training programme. Careful planning, keeping in mind the specificity of the sport and the varied distances is essential, so that the elements of the training programme should emulate competitive conditions as closely as possible.

Most cyclists use essentially three types of training intensities: (1) 'over distance' training (involving long hours in the saddle) designed to improve aerobic or oxidative capacity; (2) 'race pace' training designed to improve the body's lactate tolerance and utilization capacity, and (3) sprint training designed to improve efficiency and power of the ATP-CP energy system. Whilst it is impossible to cover all forms of training here, it is possible to outline some recent developments, e.g. 'anaerobic threshold' or OBLA training.

Early season training should be aimed towards building the stamina needed to endure the training and competition of the competitive season. A good aerobic foundation is essential for it is the pivotal element of both performance of and recovery from hard exercise. Such training should be designed to stimulate optimal development of the oxygen delivery system and of the oxygen extraction processes at the cellular level.

7.5.2 Oxygen delivery training

Elite cyclists are known to possess a high oxygen uptake capability. During competition the cyclist's oxygen-transport (cardiac output) and uptake (cell enzymes) systems are often loaded maximally or almost maximally (80–85% $\dot{V}O_{2max}$). Therefore, a major portion of the training programme should aim to improve the determinants of oxygen-transport and uptake.

Traditionally it was considered that all endurance training should be designed to improve the ability to consume oxygen, since cycling was considered primarily an event which lasted several hours on the road with some track events lasting over 4.5 min. Why cyclists spend so much time 'getting in miles' and neglecting training for time trial speed, 'breakaway' speed, pursuiting, hill climbing and so on, remains obscure. More recently a new concept of endurance training has been developed recognizing that $\dot{V}O_{2max}$ may not be the best predictor of endurance performance, and that the percentage of $\dot{V}O_{2max}$ that can be maintained over periods of prolonged exercise is more important. Of greatest significance perhaps is the pace a cyclist can maintain without accumulating large amounts of lactate in the muscles and blood.

If the oxygen-transport and oxygen-utilization systems are to be trained, they must be overloaded. To achieve an overload the training tempo has to be high. When the tempo is high for prolonged periods of time, the muscle and blood lactate levels are likely to increase. Reduction in tempo is dictated by build up of lactate. Reduced tempo relaxes the load on the heart, lungs and energy-conversion systems. Alternating between hard and easy tempo will, to a certain extent, counteract blood lactate increases while overloading the oxygen delivery and energy conversion systems. Various forms of interval and continuous training may be employed to this end.

Two basic training formats may be employed. The first format attempts to load the metabolic systems at or just above the 'anaerobic threshold'. The training stimulus should be at 80–90% of $\dot{V}O_{2max}$. Short recovery periods between bouts of exercise should be included. For example, high intensity cycling for periods lasting between 30 s and 2 min should prove to be an effective training stimulus. The training heart rate, in this example, should be close to the age-related maximal heart rate (220-age in years), with a recovery rate of approximately 120 beats min^{-1} before beginning the next cycling bout. As progress is made, the number and length of exercise periods should be increased while the recovery interval is shortened. The training volume and intensity should increase in a progressive manner. This type of interval training not only loads the whole of the aerobic system but also stresses the muscle cell's glycolytic system and results in significant lactate accumulation. Although the presence of excess lactate is distressing, a tolerance to it is built through repeated exposure. At the same time the pathways of lactate removal are enhanced. This relatively high-intensity training has a secondary benefit of raising the red blood cell's 2,3-DPG (diphosphoglycerate) level (Taunton, Taunton and Banister, 1974). Because this compound binds loosely with subunits of the haemoglobin molecule, it reduces its affinity for oxygen. The presence of 2,3-DPG increases the availability of oxygen to the working tissues.

The objective of the second form of training is the enhancement of cardiac output and oxidative capacity of muscle fibres. The expected outcome is an increased size, number and density of muscle cells' mitochondria, enhanced aerobic enzyme activity, enhanced glycogen metabolism and improved oxygen delivery. This form of training builds that essential foundation upon which future endeavours rely. Training sessions may last 60–90 min, including the warm-up and warm-down. Effective recruitment of muscle fibres may be achieved through sustained pedalling at 90–110 rev min^{-1}. The intensity of effort may be measured using heart rate reserve (HRR) (Karvonen, Kentala and Mustala, 1957) in which 70–85% of HRR is equivalent to about 57–78% of $\dot{V}O_{2max}$. Thus training intensity can effectively be monitored using the heart rate as an indicator of % $\dot{V}O_{2max}$ during road cycling. Clifford et al. (1986) found that there was no significant difference between the heart rate and oxygen consumption relationship in the laboratory and on the road.

By employing these two training formats both the 'anaerobic threshold' level and oxygen consumption capacity should be enhanced. Changes in the 'anaerobic threshold' as a result of endurance training are much larger than the concurrent changes in $\dot{V}O_{2max}$. Thus the 'anaerobic threshold' is a more sensitive measure of training effects. The level of 'anaerobic threshold' or percentage $\dot{V}O_{2max}$ which the cyclist is able to sustain without disturbing the balance between lactate entry into and exit from the plasma is a critical factor in the capacity for prolonged cycling. Benefits which result from physiological adaptations to anaerobic training include decreases in the oxygen cost of ventilation, lower accumulation of lactate and less reduction in glycogen at a given power output. The end result is a rise in the intensity of effort that can be sustained aerobically.

The importance of the so called 'OBLA training' to cycling has been illustrated by Conconi *et al.* (1982, 1984) who used 'anaerobic threshold' training in the preparation of Francesco Moser for the 1 h world record achievement. Therefore, it appears that this index of endurance capacity is important in most cycling events. In general, the type of training that improves 'anaerobic threshold' seems to require reasonably long distance sets with short recovery periods. While this may not be new to cycling, the pace at which the cyclist rides may be; consequently it is important to establish this pace, which can be done in several ways.

On a cycle ergometer the cyclist performs an incremental exercise test beginning at low intensity and increases the workload every 2–3 min until maximal work output is reached. The incremental workloads need to be ridden at a 'steady state' during which time heart rate, $\dot{V}O_2$ and blood lactate sampled from finger tip or ear lobe, are taken at the end of each increment. Road training speed and effort can then be determined for the cyclist, based on the heart rate equivalent of the 'anaerobic threshold' and monitoring of training intensity can be undertaken using a portable heart rate meter.

Recently, the non-invasive method developed by Conconi *et al.* (1984, 1988) in which a cycling test is used for the indirect evaluation of the 'anaerobic threshold' allows the deflection velocity relating cycling speed and heart rate to be calculated. A similar procedure has been described by Firth *et al.* (1987) which utilizes the cyclist's own machine mounted on high resistance training rollers under simulated conditions. Whatever the procedure adopted the cyclist needs to be re-evaluated periodically in order to adjust the intensity of the training programme in accordance with improvements made.

In summary, the goal of these forms of training is to raise the level of exercise at which aerobic energy production is supplemented by anaerobic mechanisms, that is to cycle at a higher steady-state level without an increase in lactate and lactate/pyruvate ratio in muscle or arterial blood. For example, a cyclist with a maximal oxygen consumption of 72 ml kg^{-1} min^{-1} and an AT of 70% $\dot{V}O_{2max}$ could cycle at steady-state oxygen uptake of 50 ml kg^{-1} min^{-1}; a rise of the AT to 80% steady-state oxygen uptake would raise the exercise intensity to a level corresponding to 57.6 ml kg^{-1} min^{-1}.

7.5.3 Anaerobic training

Successful bicycle racing requires of the cyclist both speed and power. These performance factors are limited by the metabolic energy available from the high-energy compound ATP. If the cyclist intends to ride fast for any distance, the anaerobic energy conversion systems must be highly trained. High anaerobic power represents the ability of the anaerobic systems (ATP-CP and lactate) to convert energy at a very high rate. The speed by which energy can be provided depends on the availability of ATP and its phosphate donor, creatine phosphate (CP) and the related enzymes. The cyclist needs a high anaerobic capacity for starts, acceleration, hill climbing, breakaways, sprints and finishes. Therefore, some portion of the training schedule must address the short-term high intensity cycling effort.

The purpose of such training is to recruit FOG and FG muscle fibres. These fibres contract rapidly and fatigue somewhat faster than SO fibres. The maximum involvement of these FOG and FG fibres requires a training intensity above 90% $\dot{V}O_{2max}$. Since this intensity is difficult to sustain, interval training is the method recommended. High intensity cycling periods of 8–30 s, interspersed with 20–30 s periods of active recovery, are advised. Results may be achieved with 8–12 repetitions and an active recovery interval that is twice the duration of the work period. Not more than two or three training sessions per week of this type of training is recommended. Level sprints and short uphill sprints with an easy return ride downhill are effective overload techniques. The intensity of the overload may be increased by reducing the duration of the recovery interval.

7.5.4 Blending the systems

Long distance or natural interval training serves to balance a well-planned training programme. This type of training, lasting 1–4 h is a blending of all the types of interval training previously discussed. Speed is kept high with increased tempo on uphill stretches. Energy must be delivered both aerobically and anaerobically. The object is to exploit a large portion of aerobic capacity over longer time periods. This type of training promotes technique, muscle fibre function, the muscles' capability to utilize fatty acids, and the ability to reprocess and use lactate, both of which result in the sparing of liver and muscle glycogen stores.

7.5.5 Strength training

The inclusion of progressive resistance strength training in the conditioning of the cyclist serves as an adjunct to the total training programme. Strength training is specific to the joint angle at which the training is performed. The training effect is related to the exact movement and type of strength which is trained. For cycling, dynamic strength is essential. When used, muscular strength training must be designed specifically to match the movements performed during cycling. If the cyclist is engaged in a weight-training programme to improve hip extensor strength, the resistance should be between 30 and 80 degrees of the hip angle.

It is evident that both knee flexion and extension are important in the production of force at different times in the pedal cycle. This means that a weight-training programme should include exercises which involve the knee flexors as well as the extensors.

Strength improves when a muscle is placed at an overload of two-thirds of its maximal strength. Maximal strength gain is best achieved using four to six repetitions and three to four sets for each muscle group. Training should occur three times per week until a point is reached when increases in strength no longer improve performance. At that point a maintenance programme should be sufficient. One set of six to eight repetitions for each muscle group is required for maintenance. Most competitive cyclists practise strength training during their off-season, and include a range of upper body exercises in order to promote arm-specific strength gains to supplement force application to the pedals in climbing, acceleration, sprinting and so on.

7.5.6 What to expect

During a training programme the initial changes in the physiological responses to repeated exercise have been shown to be due to readjustments in the central circulatory control. The redistribution of cardiac output is in favour of the working muscles. The initial effects of a training programme are reflected by two responses. The first is a marked change in the cardiovascular response to exercise and an increase in the 'anaerobic threshold' without a concomitant change in maximal aerobic power ($\dot{V}O_{2max}$). A second-order response is a slow decline in cardiac frequency for a given oxygen uptake. Where relatively large muscle groups are used, as in cycling, the limiting factor in exercise is the ability of the cardiovascular system to transport the required volume of blood rather than the capacity of the muscles to utilize oxygen.

7.5.7 Overtraining

Constant, severe training does not provide adequate time for recovery. Without sufficient recovery the training stimulus cannot be maximized. High intensity training extended for too long can lead to a failure to progress. Too much training over too long a period leads to decreased performance and possible 'burnout'. The cyclist must watch out for the appearance of signs of overtraining. The following serve as warning signals which, when present, suggest a reduction in training in terms of intensity, duration and frequency: (1) morning pulse five or more beats min⁻¹ above average; (2) rapid or persistent weight loss; (3) persistent drop in quality or quantity of sleep; (4) persistent fatigue; (5) dark, concentrated or cloudy urine, and (6) persistent pain or weakness in the joints.

The cyclist should learn to monitor the demands made upon the body. Some days inner feelings suggest an easy training session, while others may call for complete rest. If steady progress in training is expected, listen to the subjective suggestion. 'Train, don't strain'.

7.5.8 It's still individual

At this time it is still not possible to state specifically which exact form of training is best for individual elite cyclists. Most racers use distance training, interval training, sprint and hill climb training. The ideal ratio of interval to distance training has not yet been defined. Each individual with his or her natural endowment differs to the extent that training programmes must be individually prescribed to meet specific goals. However, exercise science is making rapid progress in understanding and explaining the underlying variables which affect optimal cycling performance.

7.6 OVERVIEW

The core of fundamental research which has been devoted to the sport of cycling is scattered in a variety of sources. This chapter has attempted to synthesize, integrate and apply the scientific knowledge pertaining to the physiology of cycling.

The physiological determinants of success in cycling are as varied as the range of cycling disciplines covered by the sport. Only by special attention to the principle of specificity of training can the coach and competitor hope to attain realistic goals. A variety of sophisticated scientific techniques have been utilized in order to define a work–performance profile of the cyclist, and so plan for training and competition. The evidence points to a range of physiological, biomechanical and nutritional factors which need to be utilized in the preparation of the competitive cyclist.

By using the techniques and protocols outlined, it is possible to evaluate the relative strengths and weaknesses of the cyclist, determine improvements in the individual's performance, and by use of training which simulates competitive conditions, help the individual to realize his or her potential. Finally, a note of caution; 'Practicing cyclists are very conservative about accepting anything that the boffins (sports scientists) tell them about cycling'. Vaughan Thomas.

ACKNOWLEDGEMENT

The authors wish to express their gratitude and appreciation to those fellow researchers whose works are discussed and cited in this chapter.

REFERENCES

Ahlberg, A., Weatherwax, R.S., Deady, M., Perez, H.R., Otto, R.M., Copperstein, D., Smith, T.K. and Wygard, J.W. (1986) Effect of phosphate loading on cycle ergometer performance. *Medicine and Science in Sports and Exercise*, **18**, S11.

Ahlborg, G. and Felig, P. (1977) Substrate utilisation during prolonged exercise preceded by ingestion of glucose. *American Journal of Physiology*, **230**, E188–E194.

American College of Sports Medicine (1986) *Guidelines for Exercise Testing and Prescription*. Lea & Febiger, Philadelphia.

Asmussen, E. (1953) Positive and negative muscle work. *Acta Physiologica Scandinavica*, **28**, 364–382.

Asmussen, E. and Bonde-Petersen, F. (1974) Apparent efficiency and storage of elastic energy in human muscle during exercise. *Acta Physiologica Scandinavica*, **92**, 537–545.

Banister, E.W. and Jackson, R.C. (1967) Effect of speed and load changes on oxygen intake for equivalent power outputs during bicycle ergometry. *International Journal of Work Physiology*, **24**, 284–290.

Bar-Or, O. (1981) The Wingate Anaerobic Power Test; characteristics and applications, *Symbioses*, **III**, 157–172.

Ben-Ezra, V. and Vaccaro, P. (1982) The influence of caffeine on the anaerobic threshold of competitively trained cyclists. *Medicine and Science in Sports and Exercise*, **14**, 176 (Abstract).

Bergh, U. (1982) *Physiology of Cross Country Skiing*. Human Kinetics Publishers, Champaign, Illinois.

Bergstrom, J. and Hultman, E. (1972) Nutrition for maximal sports performance. *Journal of the American Medical Association*, **221**, 999–1006.

Bevegard, S., Holmgren, A. and Johnsson, B. (1963) Circulatory studies in well trained athletes at rest and during heavy exercise, with special reference to the stroke volume and the influence of body position. *Acta Physiologica Scandinavica*, **57**, 26–59.

Blom, P., Vaage, O., Kardel, K. and Maehlum, S. (1982) Effect of different carbohydrates on the rate of muscle glycogen resynthesis after prolonged exercise. *Medicine and Science in Sports and Exercise*, **14**, 136 (Abstract).

Bonjer, J. (1979) Comparability of the results of the same exercise test carried out in different centres, in *Final Report 1966–1971*, Netherlands Contribution to the International Biological Programme, Amsterdam, North Holland Press, Amsterdam.

British Association of Sports Sciences (1986) Position statement on the physiological assessment of the elite athlete. (eds T. Hale, A. Hardman, P. Jakeman, C. Sharp and E. Winter).

Brodowicz, G.R., King, D.S., Ribisl, P.M., Boone, W.T. and Miller, H.S. (1982) Anaerobic threshold during cycle ergometry with and without toeclips. *Medicine and Science in Sports and Exercise*, **14**, 161 (Abstract).

Brooke, J.D. and Firth, M.S. (1974) Calibration of a simple eddy current ergometer. *British Journal of Sports Medicine*, **8**, 120–125.

Brooke, J.D., Hoare, J., Rosentrot, P. and Triggs, R. (1981) Computerised system for measurement of force exerted within each pedal revolution during cycling. *Physiology and Behaviour*, **26**, 139–143.

Brooks, G.A. (1985) Anaerobic threshold: review of the concept and directions for future research. *Medicine and Science in Sports and Exercise*, **17**, 22–31.

Brooks, G.A. (1986) The 'lactate shuttle' during exercise: evidence and possible controls, in *Sports Science* (eds J. Watkins, T. Reilly, and L. Burwitz) E. and F.N. Spon, London, pp. 69–82.

Burke, E. (1982) In case you're curious – mean $\dot{V}O_2$ scores of elite cyclists. *Bicycling*, **XXIII**, 29.

Burke, E.R. (1980) Physiological characteristics of competitive cyclists. *The Physician and Sportsmedicine*, **8**, 78–84.

Burke, E.R., Cerny, F., Costill, D. and Fink, W. (1977) Characteristics of skeletal muscle in competitive cyclists. *Medicine and Science in Sports*, **9**, 109–112.

Burke, E.R., Fleck, S. and Dickson, T. (1981) Post-competition blood lactate concentrations in competitive track cyclists. *British Journal of Sports Medicine*, **15**, 242–245.

Burrows, M. (1985a) Myths: all in the head angle? *Bicycle Action*, June, 50–52.

Burrows, M. (1985b) Myths II: high tech or tech hypes? *Bicycle Action*, July, 69.

Carmichael, J.K.S., Loomis, J.L. and Hodgson, L. (1982) The effect of crank length on oxygen consumption and heart rate when cycling at a constant power output. *Medicine and Science in Sports and Exercise*, **14**, 162 (Abstract).

Casal, D.C. and Leon, A.S. (1982) Metabolic effects of caffeine on submaximal exercise performance in marathoners. *Medicine and Science in Sports and Exercise*, **14**, 176 (Abstract).

Claremont, A., Costill, D., Fink W. and VanHandle, P. (1976) Heat tolerance following diuretic induced dehydration. *Medicine and Science in Sports*, **8**, 239–243.

Clarys, J.P., Martin, A.D., Drinkwater, D.T. and Marfell-Jones, M.J. (1987) The skinfold: myth and reality. *Journal of Sports Sciences*, **5**, 3–33.

Clifford, P.S., Coast, J.R., Swain, D.P., Milliden, M.C. and Stray-Gundersen, J. (1986) Heart rate/oxygen consumption relationship during cycling. *Medicine and Science in Sports and Exercise*, **18**, S36 (Abstract).

Conconi, F., Borsetto, C., Casoni, I. and Farrari, M. (1988) Noninvasive determination of anaerobic threshold in cyclists. *Medical and Scientific Aspects of Cycling* (eds E.R. Burke and M.M. Newson). Human Kinetics Publishers, Champaign, Illinois, pp. 79–91.

Conconi, F., Ferrari, M., Ziglio, P., Droghetti, P., Borsetto, C., Casoni, L., Cellini M. and Paolini, A. (1984) Determination of anaerobic threshold by a noninvasive field test in running and other sports activities, in *Current Topics in Sports Medicine* (eds N. Bachi, L. Prokop and R. Suchert), Urban and Schwarzenberg, Baltimore.

Conconi, F., Ferrari, M., Ziglio, P., Droghetti, P. and Codeca, L. (1982) Determination of anaerobic threshold by a noninvasive field test in runners. *Journal of Applied Physiology*, **52**, 869–873.

Conlee, R.K., Lawler, R. and Ross, P. (1982) Effect of fructose or glucose ingestion on glycogen repletion in muscle and liver after exercise or fasting. *Medicine and Science in Sports and Exercise*, **14**, 137 (Abstract).

Conrad, D.P. and Thomas, T.R. (1983) Bicycle crank arm length and oxygen consumption in trained cyclists. *Medicine and Science in Sports and Exercise*, **15**, 111 (Abstract).

Costill, D. and Saltin, B. (1974) Factors limiting gastric emptying during rest and exercise. *Journal of Applied Physiology*, **37**, 679–683.

Costill, D.L., Dalsky, G.P. and Fink, W.J. (1978) Effects of caffeine ingestion on metabolism and exercise performance. *Medicine and Science in Sports*, **10**, 155–158.

Coyle, E., Coggan, A., Hemmert, M. and Ivy, J. (1986) Muscle glycogen utilisation during strenuous exercise when feeding carbohydrate. *Journal of Applied Physiology*, **61**, 165–172.

Coyle, E., Hagberg, J., Hurley, B., Martin, W., Ehsani, A. and Holloszy, J. (1983) Carbohydrate feeding during prolonged strenuous exercise can delay fatigue. *Journal of Applied Physiology*, **55**, 230–235.

Craig, A.B., Jr (1960) Effect of position on expiratory reserve volume of the lungs. *Journal of Applied Physiology*, **15**, 59–61.

Davis, J.A. (1985) Anaerobic threshold: review of the concept and directions for future research. *Medicine and Science in Sports and Exercise*, **17**, 6–18.

Davis, R.R. and Hull, M.L. (1981) Measurement of pedal loading in bicycling. *Journal of Biomechanics*, **14**, 857–872.

Desipres, M. (1977) An electromyographic study of competitive road cycling conditions simulated on a treadmill. (University of the Orange Free State, Bloemfontein, RSA) (Unpublished report).

Di Prampero, P.E., Cortili, G., Celentano, F. and Cerretelli, P. (1971) Physical aspects of rowing. *Journal of Applied Physiology*, **31**, 853–857.

Dickinson, S. (1929) The efficiency of bicycle-pedalling, as affected by speed and load. *Journal of Physiology*, **67**, 242–255.

Droghetti, P., Borsetto, C., Casoni, I., Cellini, M., Ferrari, M., Paolini, A.R., Ziglio, P.G. and Conconi, F. (1985) Non-invasive determination of the anaerobic threshold in canoeing, cross-country skiing, cycling, roller and ice skating, rowing and walking. *European Journal of Applied Physiology*, **53**, 299–303.

Fagard, R., Aubert, A., Lysens, R. Staessen, J., Vanhees, L. and Amery, A. (1983) Noninvasive assessment of seasonal variations in cardiac structure and function in cyclists. *Circulation*, **67**, 896–901.

Fananapazir, L., Ryan-Woolley, B., Ward, C. and White, J.A. (1982) Echocardiographic left ventricular dimensions in two groups of road race cyclists during a training season. *British Journal of Sports Medicine*, **16**, 113–114 (Abstract).

Faria, I. (1969) Cardiovascular response to exercise as influenced by training of various intensities. *Research Quarterly*, **40**, 44–49.

Faria, I. (1984) Applied physiology of cycling. *Sports Medicine*, **1**, 187–204.

Faria, I., Dix, C. and Frazer, C. (1978) Effect of body position during cycling on heart rate, pulmonary ventilation, oxygen uptake and work output. *Journal of Sports Medicine and Physical Fitness*, **18**, 49–56.

Faria, I., Sjøgaard, G. and Bonde-Petersen, F. (1982) Oxygen cost during different pedalling speeds for constant power output. *Journal of Sports Medicine and Physical Fitness*, **22**, 295–299.

Faria, I.E. and Cavanagh, P.R. (1978) *The Physiology and Biomechanics of Cycling*, John Wiley, New York.

Firth, M., Nelson, H., Nuttall, A., White, J. and Collier, D. (1987) Using the 'Moser method' to improve the quality of your training. *Cycling Weekly*, 22 January, 12–13.

Firth, M.S. (1981) A sport-specific training and testing device for racing cyclists. *Ergonomics*, **24**, 565–571.

Folinsbee, L.J., Wallace, E.S., Bedi, J.F. and Horvath, S.M. (1983) Exercise respiratory pattern in elite cyclists and sedentary subjects. *Medicine and Science in Sports and Exercise*, **15**, 503–509.

Gaesser, G.A. and Brooks, G.A. (1975) Muscular efficiency during steady-rate exercise: effect of speed and work rate. *Journal of Applied Physiology*, **38**, 1132–1139.

Garry, R.C. and Wishart, G.M. (1931) On the existence of a most efficient speed in bicycle pedalling and the problem of determining human muscular efficiency. *Journal of Physiology*, **72**, 425–437.

Gollnick, P., Armstrong, R., Saltin, B., Saubert, C. and Shephard, R. (1973) Effects of training on enzyme activities and fibre composition of human skeletal muscle. *Journal of Applied Physiology*, **34**, 107–111.

Hagberg, J.M., Giese, M.D. and Mullin, J.P. (1974) Effect of different gear ratios on the metabolic response of competitive cyclists to constant load steady-state work. *Medicine and Science in Sports*, **7**, 175 (Abstract).

Hagberg, J.M., Giese, M.D. and Schneider, R.B. (1978) Comparison of three procedures for measuring $\dot{V}O_{2max}$ in competitive cyclists. *European Journal of Applied Physiology*, **39**, 47–52.

Hagberg, J.M., Mullin, J.P., Bahrke, M. and Limburg, J. (1979) Physiological profiles and selected psychological characteristics of national class American cyclists. *Journal of Sports Medicine and Physical Fitness*, **19**, 341–346.

Hagberg, J.M., Mullin, J.P., Giese, M.D. and Spitznagel, E. (1981) Effect of pedalling rate on submaximal exercise responses of competitive cyclists. *Journal of Applied Physiology; Respiratory, Environmental and Exercise Physiology*, **51**, 477–481.

Hahn, A.G., Tumilty, D. McA., Telford, R.D. and Wakefield, B.T. (1986) Effect of test duration on maximum oxygen uptake in elite road cyclists, in *Sports Science* (eds J. Watkins, T. Reilly and L. Burwitz), E. and F.N. Spon, London, pp. 36–42.

Hamley, E.J. and Thomas, V. (1967) Physiological and postural factors in the calibration of the bicycle ergometer. *Journal of Physiology*, **191**, 55–57P.

Hargreaves, M., Costill, D.L., Coggan, A., Fink, W.J. and Nishibata, I. (1984) Effect of carbohydrate feedings on muscle glycogen utilization and exercise performance. *Medicine and Science in Sports and Exercise*, **16**, 219–22.

Heck, H., Mader, A., Hess, G., Mucke, S., Muller, R. and Hollman, W. (1985) Justification of the 4 mmol lactate threshold. *International Journal of Sports Medicine*, **6**, 117–130.

Henriksson, J. and Bonde-Petersen, F. (1974) Integrated electromyography of quadriceps femoris muscle at different exercise intensities. *Journal of Applied Physiology*, **36**, 218–220.

Hermansen, L. (1973) Oxygen transport during exercise in human beings. *Acta Physiologica Scandinavica* (Suppl.), **399**, 1–104.

Hermansen, L., Hultman, E. and Saltin, B. (1969) Oxygen uptake during maximal treadmill and bicycle exercise. *Journal of Applied Physiology*, **26**, 31–37.

Hollman, W. and Venrath, H. (1962) Experimentelle untersuchungen zur bedeutung einer trainings unterhalb and uberhalb der dauerbelastungs-grenze, in *Korbs*, W.U.A., Carl Diem Festschrift, Frankfurt, AM/Wein.

Hull, M.L. and Jorge, M. (1985) A method for biomechanical analysis of bicycle pedalling. *Journal of Biomechanics*, **18**, 631–644.

Israel, S. and Weber, J. (1972) *Problems de langzeitausdauer im Sport*, Barth, Leipzig.

Ivy, J.L., Costill, D.L., Fink, W.J. and Lower, R.W. (1979) Influences of caffeine and carbohydrate feedings on endurance performance. *Medicine and Science in Sports and Exercise*, **11**, 6–11.

Jackson, A.S., Pollock, M.L. and McNabb, W. (1986) Effect of inter and intra tester error on predicting body density from skinfolds. *Kinanthropometry III* (eds T. Reilly, J. Watkins and J. Borms) E. and F.N. Spon, London, p. 34.

Jordan, L. and Merrill, E.G. (1974) Relative efficiency as a function of pedalling rate for racing cyclists. *Journal of Physiology*, **241**, 810–811.

Karlsson, J. and Jacobs, I. (1982) Onset of blood lactate accumulation during muscular exercise as a threshold concept – theoretical considerations. *International Journal of Sports Medicine*, **3**, 190–201.

Karvonen, M., Kentala, E. and Mustala, O. (1957) The effect of training on the heart. *Annales Medicine Experimentalis et Bioligiae Fenniae*, **35**, 307–315.

Knapik, J.J., Jones, B.H., Toner, M., Daniels, W.L. and Evans, W.J. (1983) Influence of caffeine on serum substrate changes during running in trained and untrained individuals. *Biochemistry of Exercise*, **13**, 514–519.

Krebs, P., Zinkgraf, S. and Virgilio, S. (1983) The effects of training variables, maximal aerobic capacities, and body composition upon cycling performance time. *Medicine and Science in Sports and Exercise*, **15**, 133 (Abstract).

Kyle, C.R. (1979) Reduction of wind resistance and power output of cyclists and runners travelling in groups. *Ergonomics*, **22**, 387–397.

LaFortune, M.A., Cavanagh, P.R., Valliant, G.A. and Burke, E.R. (1983) A study of the riding mechanics of elite cyclists. *Medicine and Science in Sports and Exercise*, **18**, S24 (Abstract).

MacLaren, D.P.M. and Morgan, G.D. (1985) Effects of sodium bicarbonate ingestion on maximal exercise. *Proceedings of the Nutrition Society*, **44**, 26A (Abstract).

Mader, A. and Heck, H. (1986) A theory of the metabolic origin of 'anaerobic threshold'. *International Journal of Sports Medicine*, **7**, 45–65, Suppl.

Manning, J.M. and Dooly-Manning, J. (1986) Anaerobic power tests which can be used interchangeably. *Medicine and Science in Sports and Exercise*, **18**, S24. (Abstract).

McArdle, W.D., Katch, F.I. and Pechar, G.S. (1973) Comparison of continuous and discontinuous treadmill and bicycle tests for maximum $\dot{V}O_2$. *Medicine and Science in Sports*, **5**, 156–160.

McGregor, M., Adin, W. and Sekeli, P. (1961) Influence of posture on cardiac output and minute ventilation during exercise. *Circulation Research*, **9**, 1089–1092.

Merrill, E.G. (1980) The B.C.C.S. physiological test program. British Cycling Coaching Scheme. *Coaching News*, Summer, 13–25.

Merrill, E.G. and White, J.A. (1984) Physiological efficiency of constant power output at varying pedal rates. *Journal of Sports Sciences*, **2**, 25–34.

Miller, F.R., Lindholm, S. and Manredi, T.G. (1985) Anaerobic threshold and 15 km time trial cycling performance. *Medicine and Science in Sports and Exercise*, **17**, 217 (Abstract).

Niinimaa, V., Dyon, M. and Shephard, R.J. (1978) Performance and efficiency of intercollegiate cross-country skiers. *Medicine and Science in Sports*, **10**, 91–93.

Nonweiler, T. (1956) The air resistance of racing cyclists. Report No. 106. The College of Aeronautics, Cranford, UK.

Nordeen-Snyder, K. (1977) The effects of bicycle seat height variation upon oxygen consumption and lower limb kinematics. *Medicine and Science in Sports*, **9**, 113–117.

Overend, T., Paterson, D.H. and Cunningham, D.A. (1986) Interval and continuous training: effects on ventilation threshold. *Medicine and Science in Sports and Exercise*, **18**, S69–S70.

Pollock, M.L., Schmidt, D.H. and Jackson, A.S. (1980) Measurement of cardiorespiratory fitness and body composition in the clinical setting. *Comprehensive Therapy*, **6**, 12–17.

Powers, S.K., Byrd, R.J., Tulley, R. and Calender, T. (1982) Effects of caffeine ingestion on metabolism and performance during graded exercise. *Medicine and Science in Sports and Exercise*, **14**, 176 (Abstract).

Protti, A., Meltzer, A. and Sucec, A. (1986) Effect of preliminary exercise on the onset of metabolic acidosis during incremental exercise. *Medicine and Science in Sports and Exercise*, **18**, S11 (Abstract).

Ribisl, P.M., Rejeski, W.J., Brodowicz, G. and King, D. (1982) Influence of training and instrumentation upon ratings of perceived exertion in cycle ergometry. *Medicine and Science in Sports and Exercise*, **14**, 158 (Abstract).

Ricci, J. and Leger, L.A. (1983) Maximal oxygen consumption of cyclists from treadmill and bicycle ergometer and velodrome tests. *European Journal of Applied Physiology and Occupational Physiology*, **50**, 283–290.

Saltin, B. and Åstrand, P.O. (1967) Maximal oxygen uptake in athletes. *Journal of Applied Physiology*, **23**, 353–358.

Saltin, B. and Karlsson, J. (1971) Muscle glycogen utilization during work of different intensities, in *Muscle Metabolism During Exercise* (eds M.B. Pernow and B. Saltin), Plenum, New York.

Sanderson, D.J. and Cavanagh, P.R. (1985) An investigation of the effectiveness of force application in cycling. *Medicine and Science in Sports and Exercise*, **17**, 224 (Abstract).

Seabury, J.J., Adams, W.C. and Ramey, M.R. (1976) Influence of pedalling rate and power output on energy expenditure during bicycle ergometry. *Medicine and Science in Sports*, **8**, 52 (Abstract).

Secher, N.H. and Nygaard, E. (1976) Glycogen depletion pattern in Types 1, 11-A and II-B muscle fibres during maximal voluntary static and dynamic exercise. *Acta Physiologica Scandinavica*, Suppl., **440**, 100.

Seifert, J.G., Langerfeld, M.F., Rudge, S.J. and Bucher, R.J. (1986) Effects of glucose polymer ingestion on ultraendurance bicycling performance. *Medicine and Science in Sports and Exercise*, **18**, S5 (Abstract).

Sharkey, J.B. and Holleman, J.P. (1967) Cardiorespiratory adaptations to training at specific intensities. *Research Quarterly*, **38**, 698–704.

Siri, W.E. (1961) Body composition from fluid spaces and density, in *Techniques for Measuring Body Composition* (eds J. Brozek and A. Henshel), National Academy of Sciences, pp. 223–244.

Sjøgaard, G. (1984) Muscle morphology and metabolic potential in elite road cyclists during a season. *International Journal of Sports Medicine*, **5**, 250–254.

Sjøgaard, G., Neilsen, B., Mikkelsen, F., Saltin, B. and Burke, E.R. (1985) *Physiology in Cycling*, Movement Publications Inc, Ithaca, New York.

Soden, P.D. and Adeyefa, B.A. (1979) Forces applied to a bicycle during normal cycling. *Journal of Biomechanics*, **12**, 527–541.

Stromme, S.B., Ingjer, F. and Meen, H.D. (1977) Assessment of maximal aerobic power in specifically trained athletes. *Journal of Applied Physiology*, **42**, 833–837.

Suzuki, Y. (1979) Mechanical efficiency of fast-and slow-twitch muscle fibres in man during cycling. *Journal of Applied Physiology*, **47**, 263–367.

Swain, D.P., Coast, J.R., Milliken, P.S., Clifford, P.S. and Stray-Gundersen, J. (1986) The effect of body size on the oxygen cost of bicycling. *Medicine and Science in Sports and Exercise*, **18**, S81 (Abstract).

Taunton, J.E., Taunton, C.A. and Banister, E.W. (1974) Alterations in 2,3-DPG and P50 with maximal and submaximal exercise. *Medicine and Science in Sports*, **6**, 238–241.

Thomson, J.A., Green, H.J. and Houston, M.E. (1978) Glycogen depletion in human muscle as a function of four fibre types, in *Biochemistry of Exercise* (eds F. Landry and W.A.R. Orban), Symposia Specialists, Miami.

Thorstensson, A. and Karlsson, J. (1976) Fatigability and fibre-composition of human skeletal muscle. *Acta Physiologica Scandinavica*, **98**, 318–322.

Wang, Y., Marshall, R.J. and Shephford, J.T. (1960) The effect of changes in posture and of graded exercise on stroke volume in man. *Journal of Clinical Investigation*, **39**, 1051–1061.

Wasserman, K., Whipp, B.J., Koyal, S.N. and Beaver, W.L. (1973) Anaerobic threshold and respiratory gas exchange during exercise. *Journal of Applied Physiology*, **35**, 236–243.

Weatherwax, R.S., Ahlberg, A., Deady, M., Otto, R.M., Perez, H.R., Cooperstein, D. and Wygand, J. (1986) Effects of phosphate loading on bicycle time trial performance. *Medicine and Science in Sports and Exercise*, **18**, S11 (Abstract).

White, J.A. and Al-Dawalibi, M. (1986) Assessment of the power performance of racing cyclists. *Journal of Sports Sciences*, **4**, 117–122.

White, J.A. and Al-Dawalibi, M. (1987) A comparison of two incremental protocols for the determination of maximal aerobic power, in *Proceedings of Sport and Science* (ed. A.E. Hardman), British Association of Sports Sciences, Birmingham University.

White, J.A. and Ford, M.A. (1983) The hydration and electrolyte maintenance properties of an experimental sports drink. *British Journal of Sports Medicine*, **17**, 51–58.

White, J.A. and Ford M.A. (1984) The carbohydrate maintenance properties of an experimental sports drink. *British Journal of Sports Medicine*, **18**, 64–69.

White, J.A., Quinn, G., Al-Dawalibi, M. and Mulhall, J. (1982a) Seasonal changes in cyclists' performance Part 1. The British Olympic road race squad. *British Journal of Sports Medicine*, **16**, 4–12.

White, J.A., Quinn, G., Al-Dawalibi, M. and Mulhall, J. (1982b) Seasonal changes in cyclists' performance Part 11. The British Olympic track squad. *British Journal of Sports Medicine*, **16**, 13–21.

White, J.A., Ward, C. and Nelson, H. (1984) Ergogenic demands of a 24 hour cycling event. *British Journal of Sports Medicine*, **18**, 165–171.

Whitt, F.R. and Wilson, D.G. (1974) *Bicycling Science*, Cambridge, MA, MIT Press.

William, W.W. (1986) Effect of intravenous caffeine on liver glycogenolysis during prolonged exercise. *Medicine and Science in Sports and Exercise*, **18**, 192–196.

Withers, R.T., Sherman, W.M., Miller, J.M. and Costill, D.L. (1981) Specificity of the anaerobic threshold in endurance trained cyclists and runners. *European Journal of Applied Physiology and Occupational Physiology*, **47**, 93–104.

Part Three
Sport on Water and Ice

8
Swimming

Thomas Reilly

8.1 BACKGROUND

Although the aquatic environment is essentially alien to the human, it affords many challenges and attractions for sport and recreation purposes. Swimming is one of the most exciting of the Olympic sports and most of the developed countries have devoted considerable financial outlay to the construction of indoor swimming facilities. It is also one of the most physiologically exacting sports: the tournament competitive schedules of top swimmers and their training programmes are arguably more severe than in any other sport. Swimming is also an attractive pastime, its cardiovascular benefits being promoted for health and general fitness. Risk of musculoskeletal injury is minimal compared to jogging and dance aerobics because body weight is buoyed up by the water: this accounts for the use of swimming in rehabilitation of track and field athletes after injury. Besides their attractions to bathers, the open waters are also the site of the swimming component of triathlon competitions and ocean waters are used for endurance and cross-channel races.

Research in swimming has a history that goes back to the beginning of this century (Clarys, 1987), yet it seems fair to state that until recent years its development has lagged behind the scientific study of running and cycling. This was largely due to difficulties in making physiological measurements of swimming subjects which tended to discourage scientists from specializing in this sport. Nowadays a considerable body of knowledge about swimming is available to sports scientists. This has resulted from ingenuities in extrapolating backwards from observations made immediately after all-out swimming efforts, design of instrumentation for obtaining good quality data during activity in the swimming pool, and development of swim simulators and swimming tanks with good fidelity to realistic conditions.

Additionally, much information about characteristics of elite swimmers can be obtained from observations on land; for example, of physique, body composition, fibre type, haematological status and so on. Similarly, effects of swim training may be measured using accepted physiological criteria either at rest or after a standard exercise stress such as swimming at a fixed velocity.

The growth of research interest in swimming is evident from the development of special interest groups and the escalation of specialized laboratory facilities. A milestone in the sharing of scientific information about swimming was the First International Symposium on Bio-mechanics and Swimming held in Brussels in 1970. This gathering reassembles every four years under the auspices of the International Society of Biomechanics, the sequence of meetings being Brussels (1974), Edmonton (1978), Amsterdam (1982), Bielefeld (1986) and Liverpool (1990). More frequent have been the meetings on Swimming Medicine held under the auspices of the Medical Committee of the Federation Internationale de Natation Amateur (FINA): both meetings cover physiological as well as medical and biomechanical aspects of the sport.

Since the swimming flume, analogous to a treadmill of moving water, was first developed (Åstrand and Englesson, 1972) at Stockholm, other specialized laboratories have utilized this type of facility. Sophisticated swimming flumes are utilized in swimming research at Buffalo in the USA; at Colorado Springs, the site of the US Olympic Committee's sports science accommodation; at the Universities of Tsukuba and Tokyo, and other sites in Japan, in Milan and Rome, Italy, and in other countries. A 200 m long basin has been built by the Dutch Ship Canal Company for studies of fluid mechanics related to shipping: it has been utilized for fundamental research in swimming by collaborative Belgian and Dutch studies (Clarys, 1985).

This chapter describes physiological aspects of stroke dynamics in swimming. The physical and physiological demands of swimming and the methods used in their assessment are then outlined. The anthropo-metric and physiological characteristics of growing and elite swimmers are then considered. Unique demands such as thermoregulation and ultra-distance swimming are examined before, finally, training for swimming is considered.

8.2 SWIMMING STROKES

The competitive swimming events comprise two symmetrical strokes (butterfly and breast-stroke) and two asymmetrical strokes (backstroke and front crawl). Freestyle swimmers invariably employ the front crawl

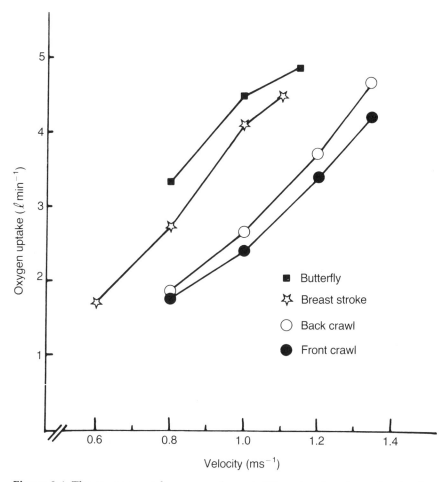

Figure 8.1 The oxygen uptake mean values at different swimming velocities for the four competitive strokes (after Holmer, 1979).

technique whereas medley races include the combination of the four competitive strokes. The crawl is the most economical of the techniques, requiring only about 71% of the energy expended in breast-stroke at a comparable speed (Holmer, 1974). The backstroke is probably close to the front crawl in physiological economy whereas the butterfly is marginally more costly than the breast-stroke (Figure 8.1).

In sprint swimming, performance is determined by reaction time at the start, technique in starting, turning and touching at the finish and, most importantly, swimming velocity. Speed off the blocks is a function of the neuromotor system and so fast innate reactions bestow a small advantage in starting. The distance the swimmer travels before contacting the water is also likely to prove advantageous. Muscle strength could be important in gaining distance in this airborne phase, as the stronger individual would produce a greater horizontal impulse from the blocks and consequently have the greater horizontal take-off velocity and so travel further through the air. Elite male swimmers tend to travel further than females through the air before hitting the water in all competitive strokes but this is largely accounted for by differences in stature (Miller, Hay and Wilson, 1984). The flight time decreases at 200 m and above, reflecting its relative unimportance as the competitive distance increases.

Elite male and female swimmers also differ in their turning techniques and these differences may be ascribed to muscle strength as well as stature. For all strokes males have a larger glide into and out of the turn. In freestyle events the speed of the approach is increased, the swimmers initiate their turns further from the wall and execute them with a faster turning motion as the distance of the race decreases. Thus the importance of muscular power in accomplishing a good turn is more pronounced in sprint swimming. Also, as the race distance increases the length of the glide out from the wall decreases, probably reflecting a corresponding decline in force of the thrust against the wall as the swimmer tries to conserve energy for the swimming action (Chow, Hay and Wilson, 1984). In breast-stroke the pattern of gliding from the turn differs between the sexes, elite men swimmers having short times and fast average speeds out compared to the longer times and distances out of female swimmers. These may be partly due to different strategies in using the complete underwater stroke allowed after each turn in this stroke.

The amount of time spent in turning can vary between 20 and 40% of the total time depending on the stroke and whether the pool is short pool length or the full Olympic size. In all strokes the swimmer is underwater during the push-off phase of the turn and this necessitates breath-holding. During this period of suspended breathing the alveolar PCO_2 increases and there is a corresponding fall in alveolar PO_2. The average breath-holding times during competition have been measured by Craig (1986) as 5 s for breast-stroke, 4.3 s for freestyle, 3.7 s in butterfly and 3.3 s in backstroke. (Berkoff, finalist in the 100 m men's backstroke at the Seoul Olympics, was exceptional in that he swam the first 30 m underwater and was underwater for 10 m on the turn.) It seems that biomechanical considerations in optimizing a turn are in most circumstances not limited by the increased PCO_2 and decreased PO_2 that occur in this time. The strong urge to breathe after about 5.5 s need not compromise the completion of a well-executed turn.

The swimmer's horizontal velocity in the water is determined by the stroke frequency (SF) and the distance travelled per stroke (d/S). The

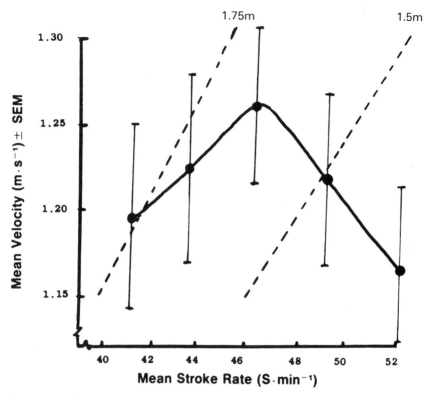

Figure 8.2 The relation between stroke rate and swimming velocity in club swimmers (Swaine and Reilly, 1983).

concerted influence of these two parameters is determined by such factors as anthropometric profile, muscular strength and endurance, and biomechanical competence. Maximum velocity is attained at a unique combination of d/S and SF, which are closely analogous to the load and frequency in contracting the arm and shoulder muscles. This inverted 'U' relationship is illustrated in Figure 8.2 from data obtained on club-level swimmers. Craig, Boomer and Gibbons (1979) found that swimmers participating in the US Olympic trials achieved higher velocities (i.e. at the shorter distances) by an increase in SF and a slight drop in d/S compared to events swum at lower velocities; this suggests that the optimum relationship is influenced by competitive distance. A study of Commonwealth Games swimmers showed that the speed of stroking (calculated from cine-film) followed a descending order from freestyle, to butterfly, to backstroke, to breast-stroke in 100 m and 200 m for both men and women: however, the men's SF values were similar for freestyle, butterfly and breast-stroke. In general the speed of the stroking action ($\dot{S}$) – rather than the actual stroke frequency – decreased as the event progressed, possibly reflecting reliance on slow-twitch fibres as fatigue occurs in the fast-twitch muscle fibres. The mean stroke length was consistently found to decrease as the event progressed, suggesting that the recovery between strokes is shortened (Pai *et al.*, 1984).

A study of the 1984 US Olympic trialists showed that those reaching the finals differed from those that did not by virtue of a greater distance per stroke in almost all the competitive events (Craig *et al.*, 1985). A greater distance per stroke is achieved by increasing the force generated by the active muscles. The velocity profiles in races of 200 m and longer indicated that as fatigue developed, the distance per stroke decreased. The inability of muscle to maintain maximal force in repeated contractions is well recognized and is a classical characteristic of muscle fatigue. The faster swimmers compensated for the reduced distance travelled per stroke by maintaining or increasing stroke frequency more

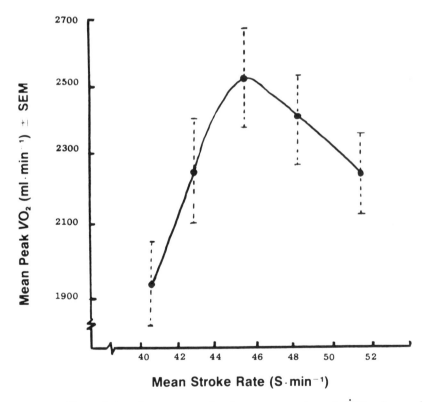

Figure 8.3 The relation between stroke frequency and peak $\dot{V}O_2$ observed during all out exercise on an isokinetic swim bench (Swaine and Reilly, 1983).

than their slower competitors. There is a possible trade-off such that oxygen cost of submaximal swimming is minimal and the highest attainable oxygen consumption ($\dot{V}O_{2peak}$) is maximized at a specific level of interaction of SF and d/S. It seems that the optimum stroke frequency (SF_{opt}) is that which is freely chosen by the individual swimmer. Swaine and Reilly (1983) determined the SF_{opt} in seven swimmers from free-style trials over 366 m (400 yards). Each subject then performed a maximal experimental test for measurement of $\dot{V}O_{2peak}$ on five separate occasions, simulating the freestyle arm action on an isokinetic swim bench. Stroke rate was manipulated according to the five frequencies used in the swim trials, corresponding to very slow, slow, optimum, fast and very fast. The mean $\dot{V}O_{2peak}$ on the isometric swim bench was also found to vary as an 'inverted U' curvilinear function of SF, the correlation between SF_{opt} and SF at the highest $\dot{V}O_{2peak}$ being 0.99 (Figure 8.3). The results confirmed that the freely chosen SF produces the top performance in swimming to attain maximum velocity and the highest peak $\dot{V}O_2$ values on the swim bench.

8.3 ANATOMICAL DEMANDS OF SWIMMING

The swimmer needs great muscular force and anaerobic power for fast propulsion through the water. In distances greater than 100 m the aerobic power and muscular endurance are emphasized. Sharp, Troup and Costill (1982) showed that the muscle power of the arms expressed as watts per pull on a 'biokinetic swim bench' was highly related to sprint swimming velocity, the correlation coefficient being 0.94. Reilly and Bayley (1986, 1988) showed high correlations between peak power over 5 s on a similar swim bench test and swimming velocity in young male and female swimmers; the correlation coefficients were lowered when differences in body size were eliminated. The strength of the correlations faded as the swim distance was increased from 30 to 90 m, and further to 360 m where aerobic factors would become the more important determinants of performance.

Swimming calls on muscle groups additional to the arms, depending on the stroke and on the leg-kick pattern. The muscles utilized and the patterns of recruitment also differ according to the proficiency of the swimmer. Examination of muscle activity during swimming using electromyography has tended to concentrate on front-crawl where it is believed that 30–44 individual skeletal muscles play an important role (Clarys, 1985). The research group at Vrije Universiteit, Brussels, headed by Clarys has systematically examined the activity of 25 muscles in the front crawl using special surface electrodes and a radio-telemetric system for transmitting the EMG signal to a recorder placed poolside.

Table 8.1 Average front crawl muscle action as percentages of the relative maximal isometric contraction

Muscle	Most frequent no. of contraction and pattern	% muscle action/ cycle competition swimmers	% muscle action/ cycle non-competition swimmers
M. extensor digitorum	2	30.23	38.35
M. flexor capri ulnaris	2	*	43.10
M. tricep caput laterali	3	38.78	28.92
M. tricep caput longum	2	39.47	35.64
M. bicep brachii	2	27.00	34.61
M. deltoideus pars ant.	2	33.12	23.43
M. deltoideus pars med.	2	37.33	31.97
M. deltoideus pars post.	3*	27.58	36.33
M. sterno cleido mast.	2	25.54	21.81
M. trapezius sinistra (respiration right)	2	29.91	22.57
M. trapezius dextra (respiration right)	1	24.51	29.54
M. lattissimus dorsi	2	92.34	23.66
M. pectoralis major (clav.)	2	36.75	26.10
M. pectoralis major (sterno)	2	43.27	39.66
M. rectis abdominis (Pars superior)	2	83.13	37.86
M. rectis abdominis (Pars inferior)	2	91.96	48.33
M. obliquus ext. sinistra	2	24.49	39.92
M. obliquus ext. dextra	2	28.64	35.84
M. glutaeus maximus (pars sup.)	2	79.52	41.40
M. glutaeus maximus (pars inf.)	2	122.41	31.18
M. rectus femoris	2*	21.61	24.57
M. semitendinosus	2*	18.53	36.57
M. tibialis anterior	..*	..*	22.70
M. glastrocnemius cap. lat.	2*	19.13	36.13
M. bicep femoris	..*	..*	32.5

* These muscles show a highly variable contraction pattern.

The relative intensity of muscle action is indicated as percentage of the maximum isometric contraction for each individual muscle (Table 8.1).

Of the 25 muscles 20 were found to exhibit two contraction peaks – generally during the gliding, pull and push phase of the action – with a relative relaxation during the recovery phase. High and wide recoveries accounted for variability in the EMG of the posterior portion of the deltoids. Irregularity in the EMG of leg muscles was explained by individual variation in the leg kick. The top swimmers showed subtle differences from good swimmers in the patterns of muscle use with each stroke, as shown in Figure 8.4 (Clarys, 1985). An important distinction was the greater exploitation of the trunkal muscles by the top swimmers, presumably in maintaining a streamlined posture for motion through the water. It is generally thought that the main propulsive force in the front crawl is obtained from the arm and shoulder muscles, with the legs playing a supportive role. Clarys (1985) concluded that trunk muscles, including gluteus maximus, have a more important activity than the arm and shoulder musculature in distinguishing between correct and faulty swimming technique – trunk, pelvic and leg muscle activity best discriminating between the top and the less-successful swimmers. Such observations lay stress on the need for proper co-ordination of all involved muscle groups for perfection of swimming strokes.

The pattern of muscle involvement in swimming is also partly reflected in the injury patterns that are incurred. Although the incidence of musculoskeletal injury is low compared to running and contact sports, chronic and arduous training regimens may induce injury. The most frequent site of injury is the shoulder joint, especially in free-style and back stroke where the joint is placed towards the limit of its range of movement. In these strokes complete rotation of the arm makes the supraspinatus muscle most vulnerable. Injury to the trapezius is found in breast-strokers while impingement injury of supraspinatus and biceps tendons is found in butterfly as well as free-style swimmers. Symptoms are apparent as pressure impingement on the rotator cuff muscle group as maximal abduction is neared in each of these styles. Strengthening the shoulder muscles and attention to flexibility training can aid prevention (Reilly and Miles, 1981).

In butterfly swimming vigorous extension of the back and the strong dolphin kick places mechanical stress on the lumbar spine. Well-trained butterfly specialists tend to have stronger spinal extensors than flexors, attributable to the special breathing action in this stroke and the dolphin kick (Mutoh, 1978). It is assumed that the butterfly stroke requires vigorous spinal extension which would cause lumbar lordosis and in turn give rise to low back pain. For specialist butterfly swimmers, strength and flexibility exercises for the lower back are recommended as is inclusion of other swimming styles in their work-outs.

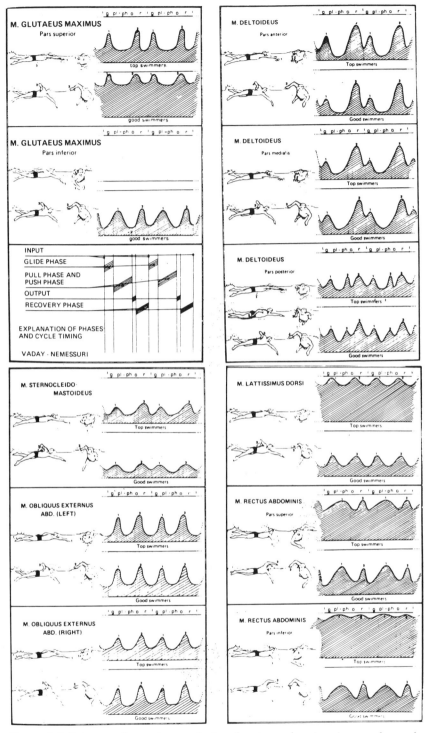

Figure 8.4 Patterns of muscle use during front crawl swimming as shown by normalized electromyographic profiles for different levels of competitive skill (from Clarys, 1985).

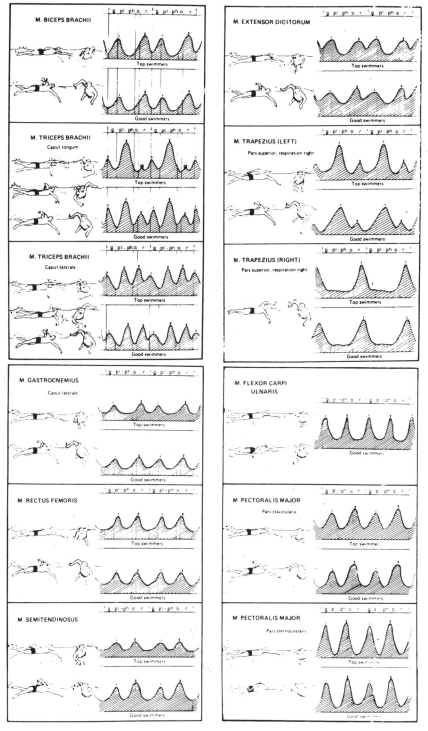

Fig. 8.4 *continued*

In the breast-stroke there is a constant build-up of tension in the collateral tibial ligament as forces in knee extension, valgus stress and terminal external rotatory stress are sequentially applied in the whip-kick of the stroke (Kennedy, 1978). The result is a chronic ligamentous irritation, and the kick may need to be modified so that there is less external rotation of the tibia. The medial meniscus may also be strained, especially in unfit breast-stroke swimmers, due to forced separation of the medial articular surface of the tibia from the medial femoral condyle. Strain in the adductor magnus is also a feature of this stroke because of the powerful adduction of both legs from a position of wide abduction, concomitant with full extension of hips, knees and ankles (Reilly and Miles, 1981).

8.4 PHYSICAL DEMANDS

In swimming, the skeletal muscles work to overcome drag, the resistance of the water on the body, as well as to move the limbs. Passive drag, determined by towing subjects in an outstretched body position, increases approximately as a squared function of velocity. Passive drag varies with the contour or shape of the body but is more highly correlated with cross-sectional area than with body surface area. Some swimmers aim to minimize drag and so shave their body hair prior to competing. In swimming, there is active participation in propulsion, energy being expended while changes in body shape take place. Generally it is assumed that the active drag force during swimming is greater than the passive drag.

The overall work-rate or mechanical power output (P) of the swimmer can be calculated, assuming that velocity fluctuations within each stroke cycle have a negligible effect on estimates. The equation is of the form:

$$P = D_a v$$

where D_a represents the active drag and v indicates velocity. The percentage of the total energy cost per unit time, $\dot{E}$, that is used to overcome the mechanical work of the drag force is expressed by the efficiency factor, e:

$$e = \frac{P}{\dot{E}} = \frac{D_a v}{\dot{E}}$$

Based on these expressions the total efficiency of front crawl has been reported to exceed 15% (Pendergast et al., 1978) while breast-stroke efficiency is only about 5–6% (Holmer, 1979, 1983). These values compare with conventional estimates of about 22% for cycle ergometry (Reilly and Brooks, 1982) and 12% for weight-lifting (Reilly, 1983): it should be recognized, however, that such comparisons are not very informative because of the different activities and methodologies used. In general, the total efficiency is found to improve with skill in swimming, and tends to be higher in women swimmers than in men. This is presumably because women have on average lower drag than men, mainly due to their smaller body size and their relatively lower body density (Pendergast et al., 1977). Increasing the efficiency would achieve a higher swimming velocity for a given oxygen uptake, or tax the oxygen transport system to a less extent for a constant velocity. (The $\dot{V}O_2$ at a given speed can be used as a measure of swimming economy to bypass the difficulty of calculating an efficiency value.) For the individual swimmer, improving the swimming stroke is likely to be the most effective means of elevating the efficiency value.

It is to be expected that the state of training influences the efficiency and that well-trained swimmers have higher efficiencies than the untrained at any given velocity. The swimmer's speed may also affect the efficiency value: for the same swimmer performing the same stroke, efficiency is reported to be lowest at low and at high speeds. The loss of efficiency at low speed has been attributed to the lack of a planing action and at high speed to the development of a bow wave (Faulkner, 1967).

The mechanical efficiency is defined by the ratio of the power output to the power input: a precise measurement of both functions has in the past proved problematic in the context of swimming. Many of the technical difficulties associated with the measurement of mechanical efficiency in swimming were overcome by a group of Dutch research workers. First, they developed a respiratory valve with negligible drag which eased the task of measuring oxygen uptake during swimming (Toussaint et al., 1987). This provided the necessary information on power input. As the magnitude of the resistance can be derived from the propulsive force, so force measurement was utilized in calculating active drag (Hollander et al., 1986) so that the power output could be calculated. The system for measuring active drag provides the swimmer with fixed push-off pads, mounted 1.35 m apart on two 23 m horizontal rods 0.8 m below the water's surface. The force of the swimmer's push-off action is measured by a transducer connected to one of the rods at the end of the pool. At a constant velocity of swimming the average propulsive force will be equal to the average drag force.

The average force in swimming front crawl at 1.55 m s^{-1} was calculated to be 66.3 N. In a group of top swimmers, gross mechanical efficiency at velocities between 1 and 1.6 m s^{-1} ranged from 5 to 9.5%. The male swimmers were found to require higher power outputs than the females for a given speed but the difference in efficiency values between them disappeared at similar power output levels (Toussaint,

1988). At high power output values the higher efficiencies are partly an artefact of the calculation procedures since gross efficiency increases in magnitude in correspondence with increases in power output.

Toussaint *et al.* (1988) further developed the concept to describe 'propelling efficiency' in swimming (the product of mechanical and propelling efficiency equals total efficiency which reflects the O_2 cost of performing 'useful work'). To do this the power output was partitioned between that used to overcome drag and that part which gives water a kinetic energy change (P_k). The latter was quantified by comparing at the same velocity the power input during swimming free with that swimming on the system for measuring active drag where the push-off is against a fixed point (i.e. $P_k = 0$). The difference between the two conditions reflects P_k during swimming and allows calculation of propelling efficiency. This was shown to be an important determinant of swimming performance. Clearly the biomechanical perfection of the swimming action plays an important part in maximizing swimming efficiency; so too does biomechanical analysis complement physiological examination to help our understanding of competitive swimming motion.

8.5 METABOLIC DEMANDS

The earliest attempt to quantify the relationship between swimming speed and energy expenditure was made by Karpovich and Millman (1944). The swimmers held their breaths during experimental swims and afterwards breathed into a Douglas bag. The researchers collected expired air for 20–40 minutes after swimming at a range of velocities and calculated the so-called 'oxygen debt'. The oxygen consumption in excess of the resting level was deemed to be the oxygen cost of swimming. Data were obtained on front crawl, backstroke, breast-stroke and butterfly. The procedure is now known to be flawed because the oxygen consumption post-exercise is elevated over and above the oxygen deficit incurred in exercise.

The oxygen consumption has also been examined during actual swimming, the Douglas bag being supported by a gantry over the lane used. Alternatively it might be carried by a research assistant along the poolside, the swimmer using the inside lane. Achievement of steady-state conditions poses a problem as the exact control of swimming speed is suspect: the swimmer may be paced by a platform whose speed is variable, or by a series of lights along the lane marker which are tripped in sequence, but the turns inevitably disrupt the rhythmic swimming actions.

In a swimming flume a large volume of water is circulated in a basin

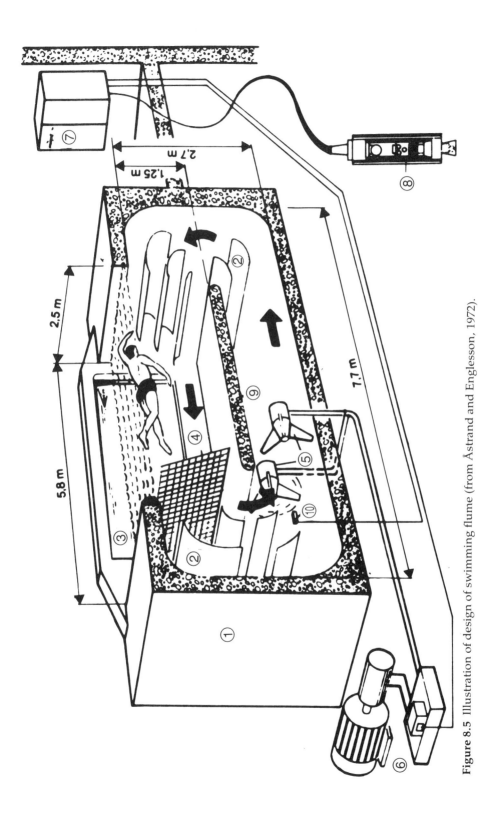

Figure 8.5 Illustration of design of swimming flume (from Åstrand and Englesson, 1972).

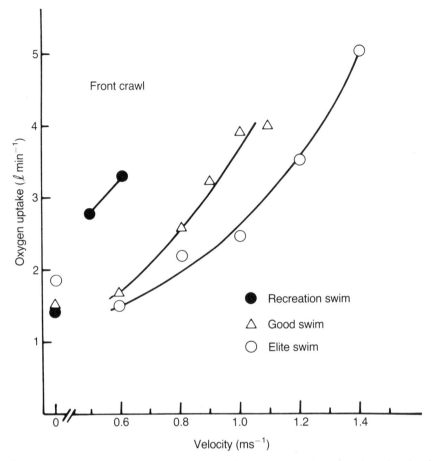

Figure 8.6 Oxygen uptake as a function of swimming velocity in three levels of front-crawl proficiency (after Holmer, 1979).

by twin propelled pumps. Guide vanes help to produce a more uniform and near-laminar flow of water in the central part of the test basin where the subject swims (Figure 8.5). The swimmer can be observed through a side window and through which cine-film pictures of the swimming actions may be taken. By controlling the rotation speed of the propellors the speed of the water can be varied from 0 to 2 m s^{-1}. While swimming the subject may be linked to on-line respiratory gas analysis systems and have transducers attached for recording force and stroke parameters.

The relationship between swimming velocity and oxygen consumption has not been entirely resolved since various reviewers have described it as linear (Lavoie and Montpetit, 1986) and non-linear (Holmer, 1979). It seems that a linear model may fit the data satisfactorily in the mid-range of swimming velocities (see Figure 8.1) for all the competitive strokes. At low velocities the oxygen cost is equivalent to that in treading water. In general the $\dot{V}O_2$ per distance travelled increases as a function of speed for all strokes but is relatively constant at lower velocities up to about 1.2 m s^{-1} for skilled swimmers (Pendergast *et al.*, 1978). The data agree with the earlier comment that front crawl is the most economical of the strokes. At high velocities the increased drag calls for an exponential rise in energy output which can only be met by increasing the demand on anaerobic metabolism.

The energy spent in accelerating the body within each swimming cycle is thought to be negligible in front and back crawl but is likely to be significant in breast-stroke (Holmer, 1979). The oxygen uptake at a given velocity – earlier referred to as swimming economy – differs not only with the stroke but also with the level of competence of the swimmer. Figure 8.6 shows that only for the recreational swimmer does the energy cost of slow swimming in front-crawl considerably exceed that of treading water. The differences between the good and the elite swimmers become more pronounced the higher the swimming velocity.

The energy cost of propulsion by the legs alone was reported to be 2–4 times greater than the energy cost of a similar propulsion force using either the arms alone or the whole stroke (Karpovich and Millman, 1944). Holmer (1974) analysed the energy cost of the leg kick, arm stroke and whole arm stroke for the four competitive styles. Although the energy at a given submaximal velocity was independent of stroke for breast-stroke and butterfly, it was higher during leg kicking but lower during arm swimming than during swimming the whole stroke in front crawl or back crawl. The data supported the belief of coaches that leg kicking is high in energy expenditure and should be reduced in distance swimming.

The shorter the competitive event the greater is the demand on anaerobic metabolism for furnishing the required energy. It appears that anaerobic metabolism via phosphagen stores and glycolysis provides a major contribution to total energy requirements in competitive events up to and including 200 m whilst from 800 m upwards aerobic metabolism plays an increasingly dominant role. High levels of blood lactate have been reported in samples taken immediately after racing by Sawka *et al.* (1979) and by Torma and Szekely (1978). The highest lactate levels followed the 100 m and 200 m swims, the peak value of 20 mM being found after a 200 yard (182 m) individual medley. In the study by Sawka *et al.*, swimmers in the 200 yard butterfly, backstroke, breast-stroke and freestyle races had similar mean blood lactate levels ranging from 16.4 to 20.6 mM. Competitors in the two longest events of the Collegiate meeting examined – 500 and 1000 yard freestyle races – had mean blood lactate concentrations of 15.6 and 10.0 mM respectively.

The relation between blood lactate and swimming velocity has been used to practical advantage in various ways. The simplest application is that of Mader, Heek and Hollman (1978) who recommended interpolating between two values to ascertain the velocity corresponding to a blood lactate concentration of 4 mM. The two trials are performed at 85% and at 100% of the swimmer's maximal speed. The velocity corresponding to this 4 mM value (V-4 mM) has been found to be a good predictor of performance in running and cycling but may have greater practical use in guiding the prescription of training for swimmers than in predicting their performance. Above a value of about 4 mM the lactate levels rise disproportionately to the increase in velocity, reflecting the increased reliance on anaerobic metabolism. A further approach is to establish for an individual the swimming velocity that corresponds to the maximal lactate level. Elliott and Haber (1983) found this was a reasonably good method of predicting 100 m and 200 m breast-stroke performance potential.

Acknowledgement of the anaerobic component of metabolism in sprint swimming has led to the use of 'controlled frequency breathing' or hypoxic training to enhance tolerance of lactate. The active muscles do not decrease their oxygen uptake with the reduction in minute ventilation ($\dot{V}_E$), indicating that pulmonary ventilation does not limit the oxygen consumption in this condition (Dicker et al., 1980). However, the fall in $\dot{V}_E$ does lead to a retention of CO_2 or hypercapnia. Since CO_2 in solution is a weak acid, this causes a fall in blood pH (increased acidity) which could be counterproductive to performance.

Ingestion of alkalinizers has been advocated as an acute method of increasing the blood pH and enhancing the buffering capacity of the blood in order to improve sprint swimming performance. There is evidence from cycling and running studies (MacLaren, 1986) that ingestion of sodium bicarbonate pre-event can improve performance. It is reasonable to expect similar results in swimming, provided the timing and concentration of the dosage are right.

8.6 CARDIORESPIRATORY DEMANDS

One of the effects of immersion in water is increased pressure on the thorax and this necessitates respiratory adjustments. The vital capacity is reduced by about 10%, the expiratory reserve volume falls and the inspiratory reserve volume is utilized. The fall in vital capacity is partly due to displacement of blood into the thorax, but more to impedance of the respiratory muscles. Adjustments in surface swimming are not as pronounced as in vertical head-up immersion in water but nevertheless they are significant. The frequency of breathing is synchronized with the stroke rate and the respiratory cycle includes a forced inspiratory phase. Lung compliance is practically unchanged during breast-stroke but is about 30% less than on land during the backstroke (Holmer, 1979).

Despite the strain on the ventilatory apparatus, most swimmers show near-normal ventilation responses rather than hyperventilation. As previously mentioned the oxygen uptake does not seem to be compromised by a fall in $\dot{V}_E$ in 'controlled frequency breathing' swimming. Alveolar ventilation per breath has been reported to be higher during maximal swimming than in maximal running. Although the alveolar-arterial O_2 pressure gradient is lower during maximal swimming, the O_2 saturation of arterial blood is similar to that found in maximal running (Holmer et al., 1974).

There are also cardiovascular adjustments to immersion that are evident in surface swimming. The water induces a reflex bradycardia but immersion or the supine body posture can increase stroke volume by elevating diastolic filling. For a given $\dot{V}O_2$ the submaximal heart rate has been found to be lower during swimming than in exercise on land, either running or cycling (Magel, 1971). On dry land the greater utilization of small muscle groups in arm exercise causes an increase in heart rate over that found in running at a comparable $\dot{V}O_2$: this will partly compensate for the bradycardia in swimming and might explain why Holmer et al. (1974) obtained no significant difference in values for heart rate at a set $\dot{V}O_2$ during swimming and running. Nevertheless, a lowered heart rate during maximal swimming is consistently found in both elite and recreational swimmers (Holmer, 1979). This is not the case with cardiac output which usually approximates maximal values as confirmed by dry-land ergometry.

Generally the central cardiovascular responses to a stepwise increment in swimming intensity are similar to observations on conventional ergometry. Nevertheless the lowered heart rate when exercising in water would invalidate the use of a heart rate–$\dot{V}O_2$ relation, determined on dry-land exercises, for prediction of energy expenditure in the water. This has prompted some researchers to use post-exercise heart rate values as an index of the relative physiological strain in swimming and for estimating the demands on the oxygen transport system.

Heart rate–swimming velocity relations have been employed for prediction of competitive performance with reasonable success. Treffene's (1983) prediction model utilizes heart rate–velocity curves determined after at least three 3-min steady-rate swims. The protocol allows calculation of the maximal constant velocity at which the swimmer's heart rate reaches its maximum and the model makes assumptions about the total anaerobic energy used. Results obtained showed good agreement between the predicted swimming velocities and actual competitive velocities for 200 m and 400 m events.

8.7 THERMOREGULATION

The thermal conductivity of water is much greater than that of air and so the body may lose heat rapidly when swimming. This has implications for performance, especially endurance swimming, and for training.

The body's core temperature is finely regulated about a value of 37°C and this is normally increased by 1.5–2.5°C by sustained exercise on dry land. Mean skin temperature is about 33°C but a stationary subject immersed in water at this temperature will feel slightly cold. An individual will feel comfortable in water at 35°C but this will cause the core temperature to rise gradually: this suggests that the human body is poorly designed for spending long spells in the water.

The skin temperature adjusts rapidly to that of the ambient water and in a matter of minutes will reach equilibrium with it. This is achieved by altering blood flow to the skin in response to sensory receptors for cold and warmth that are triggered by the water's temperature. Heat production by the body in water depends on the level of activity. Consequently swimming pool temperatures of 30°C are preferred by learners, 28–30°C by recreational swimmers whilst competitors are satisfied with water temperatures in the range 25–27°C. Open water swimmers would be suited to marginally lower temperatures but frequently have to accept water temperatures that are much colder. In circumstances where body temperature falls due to a net loss of heat, the swimmer may shiver: this is an involuntary mechanism which stimulates contraction of skeletal muscles in order to generate heat internally.

The anthropometry of the swimmer determines how quickly heat will be lost from the body in cold water. Subcutaneous fat provides a protective layer of insulation against the cold and so lean swimmers tolerate cold much less well than their fatter counterparts. Body size is also a factor, the larger the individual the lower is the body surface area relative to body mass and the greater is the amount of heat retained. The report by Pugh and Edholm (1955) showed how the protective value of these factors varied dramatically in two ultra-distance swimmers in water of 15°C. The larger and fatter individual showed no decrease in rectal temperature for 7 hours, after which his radial pulse was impalpable for 50 min. The lighter and leaner individual was taken from the water after half-an-hour when his rectal temperature had dropped from 37 to 34.5°C.

A Canadian study of competitors in a 32 km race in 18.5°C water also reported a relation between body temperature and percentage body fat. The mean rectal temperature was 35.5°C post-exercise, the mean performance time being 8 h and 32 min for 16 men. Thyroxine levels in blood were correlated with race time, indicating the attempt of the

thyroid gland to prevent hypothermia in the slower swimmers. Prolonged exercise elevates blood cortisol levels but the rise in cortisol was
most pronounced in the swimmers with the lowest body temperatures
(Dulac *et al.*, 1987). This suggests an additive effect of cold stress and
sustained exercise on the activity of the adrenal cortex.

The muscle mass may also serve to insulate the body against heat loss
when immersed in cold water. When Canadian researchers took
physique of their subjects into account, they found that those with the
greater muscularity and fat combined survived longer before core
temperature dropped to dangerous levels (Ross *et al.*, 1980). It is not
surprising that the best Channel swimmers tend to be large in body size,
well-padded with layers of fat and have the muscular make-up to
provide the strength for propulsion during long distance swims.
Besides, they tend to take the extra precaution of greasing their bodies
with lanolin to protect them against the cold.

The level of physical activity dictates net heat loss or gain in water and
so the greater the intensity of effort the lower is the water temperature
for optimal physiological efficiency. However, Nadel (1977) showed that
lean swimmers were unable to achieve their maximal oxygen uptakes at
water temperatures of 26°C, while a fatter group of subjects showed a
similar failure only when the water temperature was lowered to 18°C. At
the lower water temperatures muscle temperature also falls and the
enzyme activities associated with vigorous exercise are retarded. The
leaner swimmers could attain only 85% $\dot{V}O_{2max}$ at 18°C, 92% at 26°C but
reached maximum at 33°C, demonstrating the interactions of water
temperature and swimming intensity on body temperature and performance in the water. Nadel (1977) found that at 40% $\dot{V}O_{2max}$
oesophageal temperatures increased at 33°C while decreasing at 26°C
and more so at 18°C. When the intensity was raised to 70% $\dot{V}O_{2max}$,
oesophageal temperature increased at a water temperature of 26°C.
Similar trends were apparent in the research of Holmer and Bergh (1974)
who found that oesophageal temperature was constant at water
temperatures of 26°C, in swimmers working at 50% $\dot{V}O_{2max}$, except for a
decrease in low-fat subjects.

Muscle function is adversely affected by cold, contractile force
deteriorating when muscle temperature falls below 27°C, which is about
the normal temperature of swimming-pool water. The impairment can
be demonstrated by the progressive decline in grip strength with
increased cooling of the arm. Water temperature as low as 2°C will soon
reduce grip strength to half the normal level. Muscle fatigue curves are
adversely affected by an 8 min immersion in 10°C but complete recovery
occurs within 40 min (Horvath, 1981). Synovial fluid in the joints
increases its viscosity as temperature falls, increasing resistance to
motion which should adversely affect swimming efficiency. It is not

clear to what extent the decrements in muscle function are due to subnormal muscle temperature, circulatory changes, local metabolite activity, viscosity changes in connective tissue or subjective discomfort. Neuromuscular co-ordination may also be impaired. As muscle temperature falls below 27°C the muscle spindles respond to only 50% of normal to a standardized stimulus and this will affect co-ordination. As hand temperature drops below 23°C movements of the limbs get clumsy: the drop in finger temperatures will be more pronounced and at skin temperatures of 13–16°C manual dexterity is severely impaired. The outcome of these changes may be the breakdown in executing the swimming action and consequent fatigue: core temperature would then fall rapidly in cold water and at this stage the endurance swimmer will need to be rescued from the open water.

One condition where a slight drop in core temperature might have subsequent advantages is in the triathlon. The first of the three events is the open water swim, followed by the cycle race and then the marathon run. Hessemer *et al.* (1984) showed that pre-cooling core temperature by 0.4°C and mean skin temperature by 4.5°C before 60 min of submaximal cycling produced an overall 6.8% increase in work-rate compared to control conditions. Thus the cooling effect of the swim could be of benefit in the ensuing cycling and running events.

The effects of exercise in water on the vascular space, on renal function and related hormones differ from the responses to cycling and running. Immersion results in a shift in blood from the lower body vessels to the thorax and entry of fluid into the vascular spaces. The large increase in aldosterone and vasopressin (ADH) secretion that occurs during and after exercise on land is practically cancelled during submaximal swimming (Bôning *et al.*, 1988). There is a small increase in urine production which is more than counteracted by a usual absence of sweat production. These changes would enable the circulation to function well in prolonged swimming sessions where risk of hyperthermia is minimal.

8.8 CHARACTERISTICS OF SWIMMERS

8.8.1 Anthropometry

The typical morphology of top swimmers is apparent even to the naked eye. Swimmers at high levels of competition tend to be tall, broad shouldered and heavily muscled, particularly in the shoulder and upper trunk muscles. Body length provides an advantage in starting, turning and finishing while long segments have advantages for stroking technique. Additionally, for a given speed a taller subject needs less power than a smaller individual to progress the same distance in the water.

The average height of male Olympic finalists 1976–1980 was: freestyle 100 m, 191 cm and 1500 m 181 cm; backstroke 188 cm; breast-stroke 183 cm; butterfly 187 cm; individual 400 m medley 183 cm. Corresponding values for body weight were: freestyle 190 m, 80.6 kg and 1500 m 70.1 kg; backstroke 77.2 kg; breast-stroke 77.7 kg; butterfly 79.3 kg and individual 400 m medley 73.3. kg. Values were not only higher for height and weight than those for a reference population: finalists were both taller and heavier for their height by 2.8 kg than the non-finalists (Khosla, 1984). According to Lavoie and Montpetit (1986) there appears to have been a trend towards increasing body height without a proportionate increase in weight in Olympic swimmers since the Tokyo Olympics in 1964. This cannot be explained by variations in age as the average age of swimmers at the four Olympiads 1968–1980 was relatively constant at 20.1 ($\pm$ 1.0) for males and 17.5 ($\pm$ 0.9) years for females.

The figures from the Olympic finalists suggest that there are differences in anthropometric profiles between events, the freestyle sprinters and backstroke specialists being tallest. This separation was more pronounced in 47 of the best male USA swimmers examined by Spurgeon and Sargent (1978). A later study of outstanding world female swimmers by Spurgeon and Giese (1984) showed the freestyle and backstroke sprinters to be tallest and the sprint butterfly group to be shortest.

The characteristic skeletal features of swimmers are apparent at an early age. Good adolescent swimmers tend to be tall for their weight (Åstrand et al., 1963) and have high bi-acromial (shoulder to shoulder) breadths (Malina, 1982). The skeletal breadth cannot be accounted for by any influence that earlier training might have had on bone growth.

The physique can be described in terms of somatotype dimensions – endomorphy, mesomorphy and ectomorphy. Average ratings for top swimmers are 2:5:3 for males and 3:4:3 for females (Hebbelinck, Carter and De Garay, 1975; Carter, 1982). The high mesomorphy ratings are partly due to muscle development resulting from strength training programmes; they reflect the strong requirement for muscular power in overcoming water resistance.

Club swimmers tend to carry a little more weight as body-fat than comparable athletes in gymnastics or track athletics but Olympic swimmers are clearly ectomorphic. Average body-fat percentages reported for swimmers are about 7% for males and 19% for females (Fox, 1984). These are well below the normal values of 15% and 25% for males and females respectively: indeed top USA Collegiate female swimmers reach average values as low as 14.5% in the peak of their competitive season (Meleski and Malina, 1985).

Body-fat values are most pronounced in endurance and channel swimmers. The subcutaneous fat has insulation properties for thermo-regulatory purposes and adds buoyancy to the swimmer in the water. The higher body-fat values in females mean they have lower body densities than males: this allows them to swim higher in the water which in turn reduces drag. Strenuous training programmes tend to keep body-fat levels low because of the high total expenditure of energy in daily work-outs, so a high body-fat level and an endomorphic physique are incompatible with success in swimming, except in endurance events. The greatest advantage of the buoyancy added by fat may be in enabling the learner to keep afloat more easily while acquiring stroking skills.

8.8.2 Muscle strength and power

It has already been emphasized that muscle strength and power are important requirements for swimming. Besides, swimming coaches prescribe strength training programmes for development of muscle strength: coupled with the strength training stimulus of vigorous swimming actions, the outcome is an apparent hypertrophy of the main musculature involved. Lavoie, Taylor and Montpetit (1981a), for example, reported enlarged fibre areas in both slow twitch (ST) and fast twitch (FT) fibres of the triceps brachii muscle in swimmers.

A study of West Australian pre-adolescent male and female swimmers (Bloomfield et al., 1986) found that their grip strength and thigh flexion strength did not differ from that of specialist tennis players or non-competitive controls. The swimmers did possess greater leg and arm extension strength than the tennis players and the non-competitors. This was presumably a specific effect of their regular training as the swimmers were averaging five sessions per week compared to three sessions for the tennis players. The leg extension strength could have been developed in the leg kicking action in the water while extension strength at the shoulder joint provides the majority of the propulsive force in all the swimming strokes.

In adult swimmers the strength of a bent-arm pull has traditionally been employed for specific strength testing. Faulkner (1967) reported that a swimmer of 76 kg should be expected to average 136 kg force on a 90° bent-arm pull or 1.78 kg per kg body weight. This is almost 40% greater than the performance of the average undergraduate, 33% if corrected for differences in body weight. Bloomfield and Sigerseth

(1965) found that sprint swimmers were about 10% stronger than middle distance swimmers as measured by a test of shoulder joint strength. This is needed for sprint events where the percentage of maximal strength involved in each pull is about five times greater than in distance swimming.

In recent years the design of swim-benches with electromagnetic resistance has facilitated the measurement of muscular power in a pulling action that mimics the swimming movement. The Biokinetic Swim Bench shown in Figure 8.7 (p. 247) allows the researcher to pre-set the speed of action and has regulation speed settings numbered from 0 to 9. These correspond to mean velocities of 1.6, 2.05, 2.66 and 3.28 m s^{-1} for 0, 3, 6 and 9 settings respectively during the swimming action. Sharp, Troup and Costill (1982) found a positive correlation between power output expressed as watts per pull and sprint swimming. Reilly and Bayley (1988) applied the Wingate Anaerobic Test of Dotan and Bar-Or (1983) for testing swimmers on the swim-bench. They found that peak power output on the swim-bench was significantly related to sprint swimming performance whereas peak power output, using the arms on the standard Wingate cycle ergometer test, was more weakly related to sprint swimming whilst leg power could not be used as a performance predictor. The power output on the swim-bench tends to be much lower than the arm power in the standard Wingate test: the main factor is the long period within a simulated stroke cycle when the arm muscles are inactive, muscle force being applied mostly during only part of the swimming motion when the arms are in the pull and push phases of the stroke.

Although there have been various attempts to identify muscle fibre types of top swimmers, the results have been inconsistent. This may be due to sampling problems, application of different criteria for classifying fibre types according to ultrastructure or histochemical properties. The earliest study was that of Gollnick et al. (1972) who found 75% slow twitch (ST) fibres in the deltoids of competitive swimmers. A lower value, 62%, was reported by Houston et al. (1981) whereas Costill et al. (1985) found 68% ST fibres in the same muscle of well-trained Collegiate swimmers. Lavoie, Taylor and Montpetit (1981a) reported 50% ST fibres in the triceps brachii of elite Canadian swimmers. Prins (1981) provided data which separated sprint and endurance swimmers, but samples were from vastus lateralis. His world-ranked distance swimmer had 31% FT fibres, his sprinter 76% FT fibres whereas Olympic 100 m freestyle champion Jim Montgomery has 60% FT fibres.

More complete information about fibre types of swimmers is available where the intermediate fibre type has been measured. Nygaard and Nielsen (1978) for example measured 40% ST in their swimmers, the remainder comprising 41% FTa (Type IIa) and presumably 19% FTb.

This profile closely agrees with the 60–65% of Type II fibres in the deltoids of sprint swimmers reported by Costill (1978). Maglischo (1982) has pointed out that sprint swimmers should have less ST fibres than sprint runners because the duration of sprint swims is longer, whereas distance swimmers (e.g. 1500 m) should have more FT fibres than distance runners. The majority of the swimmers he studied with Costill had fibre compositions in the deltoid muscle ranging from 30 to 68% ST fibres. Collectively the range of values reported in the literature point to the conclusion that fibre typing of arm, shoulder or leg muscles is not necessarily a good predictor of swimming potential.

8.8.3 Aerobic power

Traditionally it has been accepted that the maximal oxygen uptake or $\dot{V}O_{2max}$ is the best physiological indicator of the oxygen transport system's capability when taxed maximally. Early investigators compared swimmers with other sports specialists by measuring $\dot{V}O_{2max}$ on a cycle ergometer or treadmill. Generally values are about 7% higher on the treadmill than on the cycle ergometer but only highly trained swimmers attain during swimming the $\dot{V}O_{2max}$ reached in cycling. Less well-trained swimmers may show reductions (while swimming) of about 15 and 25% in $\dot{V}O_{2max}$ compared to cycling and running respectively (Faulkner, 1967).

Arm cycling would be preferable to pedalling with the legs as a test for swimmers although the $\dot{V}O_{2peak}$ when using the arms is only about 70% of that obtained when the legs are employed. Comparable reductions occur in $\dot{V}_E$ and heart rate. Some authors have reported correlations between $\dot{V}O_{2peak}$ for the arms and swimming performance (e.g. Holmer, 1978) but generally arm cycling or arm cranking tasks lack the specificity needed for functional testing of the aerobic power of swimmers.

More specific testing of $\dot{V}O_{2max}$ of swimmers has utilized dry-land swim simulators, free swimming in the pool, tethered swimming and swimming flumes. Disadvantages of commercially available swim benches are the absence of leg work and the limitation of shoulder roll. These criticisms could be overcome with improved designs but in realistic swimming the body travels further forward in the water than the length of the arm stroke backwards and this cannot be duplicated. In free swimming the disruption of steady-state work by the turns and the manoeuvrability of the accessories attached to the subject may pose problems. In tethered swimming the subject stays virtually stationary but pulls a weight in a line-pulley system or electrodynamometer while employing a swimming action. As the load can be increased by altering the weight on the pulley, the system is suitable for ergometry. Water flow around the swimmer does differ a little from that in true swimming, as does the alignment of the swimmer's body, but these have more implications for biomechanical studies than for physiological assessments. A swimming flume allows control of the water velocity in a basin where the subject swims, secured in a safety harness. Although the water flow around the subject may not exactly match that experienced in the swimming pool, this is a concern that the physiologist can dismiss. Indeed Holmer (1979) concluded that the physiological responses are similar for tethered swimming, flume swimming and free swimming. The enormous cost of the swimming flume means that it is virtually inaccessible except to specialist research teams and many scientists may have to work with the other methods.

The $\dot{V}O_{2peak}$ observed during exercise on a swim bench is 73–74% of the $\dot{V}O_{2max}$ obtained pedalling a bicycle ergometer. Peak heart rates are about 85% of those attained during a $\dot{V}O_{2max}$ test. The $\dot{V}_{Emax}$ is disproportionately reduced, partly because swimmers try to emulate their aquatic breathing patterns and partly because pressure of the bench on the thorax restricts chest expansion in the inspiratory phase (Swaine and Reilly, 1983).

The $\dot{V}O_{2max}$ values from a range of Swedish internationals place the swimmers alongside the alpine skiers and 400 m for men, but the women were higher still being alongside the orienteers and 400–800 m runners (Åstrand and Rodahl, 1970). The range extended to values of 70 ml kg^{-1} min^{-1} for males and 60 ml kg^{-1} min^{-1} for females. The figures reflect the high degree of aerobic conditioning in the swimmers, although the tests were not specific to swimming. Another consideration is the absolute oxygen uptakes (l min^{-1}) that can be attained, since the body weight is supported while swimming. The importance of $\dot{V}O_{2max}$, in relative and absolute terms, as a predictor of performance potential in the various strokes is yet to be fully determined from swim-specific tests.

8.9 TRAINING

8.9.1 Training principles

The training regimens undertaken by competitive swimmers are arduous by any standards. Most top swimmers train twice a day most days of the week, and average 4–5 hours training which may approach 20 km each day, amounting to 70–90 km a week. This swim training may be supplemented by dry-land exercises for development of flexibility and muscle strength. At most a 4-week detraining or off-season rest period is taken, although some elite swimmers may have 2–3 periods each year when the training load is lightened considerably.

The physiological principles governing the general training programmes of swimmers are similar to those underlying cycling or middle-distance running: consequently there are many analogies among these sports in the training schedules adopted. Continuous steady-state swimming, with an emphasis on the number of laps, sets a broad base of endurance training: intermittent regimens of sustained low intensity swimming with short rest periods may also be used. This training is complemented by repetitions of 180 m or more. This phase is generally followed by repetitions of swims at maximal speeds at distances less than 100 m. Additionally, repeated swim bouts of 1–3 min duration are employed at a fast pace with less than full recovery between bouts. Active rather than passive recovery is recommended since this promotes clearance of lactate from the blood. The endurance base is set up in the closed season, the training being tapered towards the competitive season to emphasize qualitative aspects of the event.

The most comprehensive application of physiological principles to swim training is in the text of Maglischo (1982). He described five forms of training – speed training, $\dot{V}O_{2max}$ training, 'anaerobic threshold' training, lactate tolerance training and race pace training. Speed training describes short repetitions at maximal speeds using the competitive stroke style. Artificially increasing the resistance against the swimmer will help to improve muscular power but may alter stroke mechanics and may not have a favourable effect on speed. Alternatively sprint-assisted training using swim-fins or exploiting snap-back from a stretched length of tubing attached to the swimmer enable him to exceed race speeds: such methods have been shown to improve the speed of young swimmers (Rowe, Maglischo and Lytle, 1977).

There is a variety of training methods available to improve $\dot{V}O_{2max}$: the schedule recommended by Maglischo (1982) is repetitions of 3–5 min work bouts (300–600 yards) at 80–90% of race speed to attain a heart rate about 10 beats min^{-1} below maximum heart rate. These distances are used more frequently in the training of middle distance and distance swimmers. Swimming in intermittent activity at an intensity just above the 'anaerobic threshold' is a good method of training $\dot{V}O_{2max}$ (Rusko, 1987). However, it should be recognized that increases in $\dot{V}O_{2max}$ with training are limited to about 30%, so that further improvements in performance are more likely to result from physiological changes evident in submaximal responses to swimming.

The velocity of swimming corresponding to a blood lactate level of 4 mM (V–4 mM) is thought to represent a so-called 'anaerobic threshold': exercise at an intensity above this places stress on anaerobic metabolism, although at the level of exercise which produces a blood lactate concentration of 4 mM the anaerobic system is already making a significant contribution to metabolism. Swimming at intensities below V–4 mM can be sustained for relatively long periods and promotes increased activities of oxidative enzymes in the mitochondria of active muscles as well as improved capillarization. Adjustments such as increased myoglobin content of muscles and enhanced removal of lactate from active muscles would complement the physiological effects of this moderate intensity swimming and would have benefit in delaying lactate accumulation in 100 m and 200 m swim sprints. Data of Maglischo (1982) on collegiate swimmers led him to consider that the optimum intensity for raising the 'anaerobic threshold' was repeat efforts at 75–85% of maximum and heart rates of 140–150 beats min^{-1} early in the season. As the 'anaerobic threshold' is highly amenable to training the criteria can be raised to 85–90% maximum effort and heart rates of 150–170 beats min^{-1} later in the season. These exercise intensities are lower than that recommended for training $\dot{V}O_{2max}$ and so a greater quantity of work can be performed in this form of training.

Improvements in lactate tolerance are especially important in the shorter swim distances, 100 m and 200 m, although relevant also in the longer events where a sustained effort is needed in the final part of the race. Improvement in lactate tolerance is probably related to enhanced buffering capacity, increased activity of the muscle form of lactate dehydrogenase and a blunted sensitivity to progressively increasing metabolic acidosis. A major effect of endurance training is thought to be enhanced lactate clearance rather than alteration in its rate of production (Donovan and Brooks, 1983). For training lactate tolerance, Maglischo (1982) considered that intermittent swim bouts should produce blood lactate concentrations between 12 mM and peak values. An appropriate session would be three sets of 6–10 repetitions of 50 m (or 50 yards) with 10–30 s between repetitions and 3–5 min between sets. This form of training is highly demanding and should not be over-prescribed.

Race-pace training provides conditions where the proper co-ordination of stroke parameters, pattern of recruitment of active muscles and their fibre types can be practised. Additionally the swimmer will have oppor-tunity to sense the pace required in his or her competitive event. This form of training may be highly stressful and so caution is advocated in the frequency with which it should be used. One way of accommodating training at race pace is to employ an intermittent protocol where short periods of swimming and recovery are interchanged. Gullstrand and Lawrence (1987) showed that a 15 s:15 s swimming:rest ratio enabled swimmers to perform a large volume of swimming at race pace for short distance swimmers. They concluded that 40 repetitions of this 15 s sprint imposed a high aerobic loading while blood lactate accumulation was no greater than 3 mM on average.

Training schedules generally incorporate a combination of methods and an interspersion of easy sessions or easy days into the overall regimen. This avoids the risks of overtraining and chronic depletion of energy. Costill (1978) showed that a set of 60 100-yard (90 m) repetitions with 1 min rest intervals practically emptied both FT and ST fibres of glycogen, the former being reduced more early on in the session. The intensity of swimming determines the fibre types that are most employed: this was shown by Houston (1978) who alternated days of high intensity and low intensity training. The low intensity work entailed repeated swims of 50–400 m totalling 6.1 km with short rests between work bouts. The high intensity training followed an extended warm-up of moderate intensity and consisted of repetitions of 25–100 m at near race pace totalling 1.15 km but with longer rest periods between the hard efforts. Although both ST and FT fibres were utilized on the two days, the low intensity training induced greater partial reduction of glycogen in the ST fibres whilst ST and FTa fibres were about equally emptied of their glycogen depots during the high intensity day.

It is questionable whether the volume of training performed by elite swimmers is necessary for purposes of physiological adaptations and more benefit may be gained by emphasizing quality rather than quantity of training. It is likely that the large overall distances covered in swim training do increase the mechanical efficiency but the effect may be small and take a long time to accrue. Experimental studies that have compared different training regimens have not provided easy answers. A study of competitive University swimmers by Houston *et al.* (1981) concluded that a smaller quantity of high intensity activity totalling 1.65 km of specific training per day was as effective in inducing physiological changes in the deltoid muscles of subjects as was a larger quantity of moderate intensity training amounting to 3.2 km per session for 6.2 weeks. The different effects of these two regimens are unlikely to become apparent in such a relatively short time in swimmers already well-trained. Neither can experimental work establish conclusively the extent to which concentrating on biomechanically perfecting stroke technique is more rewarding than striving to improve the level of conditioning still further, once a sound physiological training state has been attained.

Some swimmers seem to thrive on a large amount of training whereas others have attained the highest competitive honours with relatively modest training schedules. One risk of imposing an excessive training load on a swimmer who is unsuited to it is that staleness due to overtraining rather than improvements in performance will result. Yet symptoms of overtraining are not easily induced, at least in the short term. Kirwan *et al.* (1988) showed that doubling the training load for experimental purposes from 4266 to 8970 m in 12 Collegiate swimmers over a 10 day period failed to have a significant adverse effect on swimming performance. The more rigorous regimen did elevate resting serum creatine kinase and cortisol concentrations but these changes were deemed to be related more to increased muscle soreness and reduced energy stores than to classical symptoms of overtraining. Such abrupt changes in training loads would not be imposed in practice and it is likely that adverse effects of chronic overtraining would eventually accrue if excessive training is imposed relentlessly.

8.9.2 Dry-land training

Apart from the time spent training in the water, competitive swimmers also engage in dry-land conditioning regimens as part of their all-year round programme, the most contentious of which is strength training. One major benefit of dry-land training is that it breaks up the monotony that can result from training day after day in the pool. Swimming training that includes dry-land activities has been shown to increase anaerobic power more than a control and that the improvement was

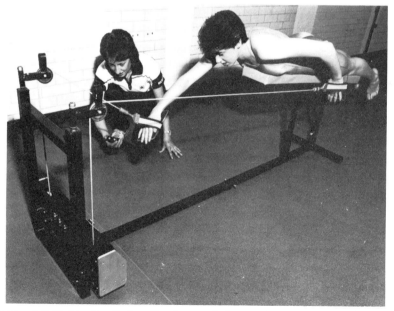

Figure 8.7 Biokinetic Swim Bench used for testing power production of swimmers and for dry-land training.

reflected in performance (Sharp, Troup and Costill, 1982). Costill (1978) reported that high intensity anaerobic training did increase muscle power but did little to improve the fatiguability of the muscle. A 7 weeks course of anaerobic power training can induce changes in muscle enzymes – creatine phosphokinase, myokinase, phosphorylase and phosphofructokinase. Strenous training programmes also increase lean body mass, but this change is most evident during the first part of the season (Meleski and Malina, 1985).

Swim coaches aim towards specificity of strength training by approximating the swimming actions in the dry-land practices. Weighted pulleys are useful in this respect. The design of swim benches has encouraged the use of swim-simulators for conditioning purposes: these are now used on a widespread basis. Models vary from isokinetic devices (Lumex Inc. Ronkonkoma) to the 'Biokinetic Swim Bench' (Isokinetics Inc, Albany, CA) shown in Figure 8.7, which is not isokinetic but rather tries to mimic the patterns of acceleration observed in pulling through water (Flavell, 1981). Similar benefits may arise from the use of kick-boards, pull-buoys, and extra costumes to provide overload of active musles by increasing drag.

The specificity of various dry-land strength training devices has been examined by Clarys *et al.* (1988). They examined the patterns of EMG activity in a variety of muscles and compared EMG profiles using the training devices with those achieved in real swimming. Supposedly specific movements on an expander device, roller board, call-craft pulley, latissimus pull and isokinetic swim bench were compared with the 'wet' EMG diagrams of the front crawl. The best results for the propulsion muscles were obtained with devices employing accommodating resistance. The pattern of muscle use in the recovery phase of the stroke was best imitated using the isokinetic machine. The authors concluded that specific training and specific learning cannot be completely accomplished with dry-land devices because of mechanical and environmental differences. The use of paddles by swimmers to increase resistance to motion in the water may also be criticized for lack of specificity. Nevertheless the grosser aspects of the training in terms of improving overall muscle power output do seem to have practical benefits (Flavell, 1981).

8.9.3 Training and young swimmers

As swimmers tend to concentrate on the sport at an early age, concern is often expressed about the wisdom of such early specialization and the adverse effects it might have on development. It has been shown that menarche in female swimmers is only marginally later than the norm compared with gymnasts in whose case it is appreciably delayed (Malina, 1982; Nomura, 1983). The most extensive study of young female swimmers was that by Åstrand *et al.* (1963). They showed there were no adverse effects of very strenuous swimming training and no chronic effects on gynaecological function when the swimmers were followed up into adult life. Female swimmers may experience amenorrhea as a result of severe training, but normal menstruation recurs with detraining or reduction of training load.

A safety feature of training in water for young swimmers is that stress on growing bones, especially in the lower limbs, is minimized by the buoyant effect of water. The respiratory muscles do have to overcome increased external resistance and the forced vital capacity seems to respond to swim training at an early age (Bloomfield *et al.*, 1986). Otherwise the physiological responses to swim training that are apparent in the adult are closely mirrored in the young swimmer.

8.9.4 Training and time of day

A majority of swimmers train twice a day and this usually entails an early morning session. At this time the level of body temperature,

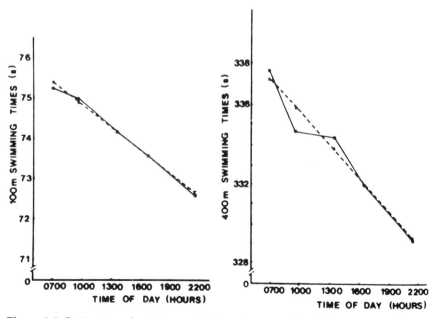

Figure 8.8 Swim times for 100 m and 400 m front crawl at different times of day (Baxter and Reilly, 1983). The dashed line represents values predicted by a linear trend.

metabolism, arousal of the nervous system and viscosity of the joints militate against performance of strenuous exercise (Reilly, 1986). Swimmers soon adapt to a regimen of morning training, provided that their waking habits do not regress on mornings off. In effect they shift the phases of their natural circadian rhythm further forward than normal by 2–3 hours.

A study by Baxter and Reilly (1983) found that all-out swimming performance, in both 100 and 400 m front crawl, improved steadily during the day with the best times being observed in the evening (Figure 8.8). Findings implied that the highest training stimulus can be presented to the organism in the evening and that low intensity efforts can be concentrated in the morning session. Attempts to attain qualifying standards for major championships would be best made if such trials were fixed for evening meetings.

8.9.5 The annual cycle

There is also a yearly cycle of training and competition to be considered. Training which progressively increases the daily swimming distance from 8 to 18 km has been found to increase $\dot{V}O_{2max}$ of elite Canadian swimmers by 6–7% over a 6 month period (Lavoie, Taylor and Montpetit, 1981b). In an elite American group, which included several members of the Olympic team, seasonal changes were noted in body composition, mainly an increase in lean body mass and a decrease in body fat in the early part of the season (Meleski and Malina, 1985). Training is tapered during the competitive season in preparation for the major contests. In the off-season the physiological effects regress once training is ceased or drastically curtailed. The swimmers gradually increase body fat deposits but changes in the metabolic characteristics of muscle are more dramatic. Costill et al. (1985) showed pronounced alterations in biopsy samples of the deltoids of Collegiate swimmers during 4 weeks of inactivity that followed 5 months of intense training. The respiratory capacity of the muscle decreased on average by 50% after only 1 week, though no further changes were noted in the remaining 3 weeks of inactivity. Detraining had little effect on the enzymes associated with anaerobic capacity. The muscle glycogen content decreased to about 65% of its level in the trained state. After a standard swim (184 m) at 90% of the swimmer's best time, blood lactate rose from 4.2 mM when highly trained to 9.7 mM after 4 weeks of detraining, indicating a disturbance in the acid-base balance of the blood. Changes in central circulatory factors and whole-body activity are likely to occur more slowly and changes in $\dot{V}O_{2max}$ after a week's detraining are negligible. The consequences of inactivity are more easily reversed in previously well-trained swimmers than in those embarking for the first time on an arduous training programme.

The rate at which fitness is lost is markedly reduced when swimmers continue to train as little as 3 days per week, 3000 yards (2.8 km per day). Neufer *et al.* (1987) showed that lowering the training to an energy requirement approximating 30% of prior training caused little or no decrement in $\dot{V}O_{2max}$ in well-trained Collegiate swimmers. The ability to apply force during swimming was decreased by the fourth week of reduced training although no loss of muscular strength was apparent at that time. Loss of fitness was much more pronounced in another group whose training was reduced to one session per week, although the frequency of activity did slow the loss of physiological adaptations to training compared to an inactive control group. Maintenance of a moderate level of training is recommended during the off-season to counter deconditioning effects that would result from a complete cessation of training.

Some coaches of elite swimmers prefer to organize the annual programme so that it comprises three recurrent cycles of about 3–4 months each. This is to avoid the two extremes of chronic overtraining referred to earlier, on the one hand, and loss of fitness associated with a complete break, on the other. Within each cycle of training there is a build-up period, a phase of heavy training tapering towards the main competitive goal and a subsequent ease-off period. There is usually one competitive goal within each major cycle, which gets priority for the year. This systematic approach towards training enables swimmers to achieve peak levels of motivation that are demanded by the major races, although its fine-tuning is still as much art as science.

8.10 OVERVIEW

This chapter has described the main physiological demands of swimming, the characteristics of specialist swimmers and the training principles that apply. Top swimmers engage in strenuous training programmes and serious swim training commences at an early age. There is no convincing evidence of adverse biological effects of such early specialization although there may well be social consequences for the physically maturing swimmer. Similarly there are no apparent physiological reasons why swimmers cannot maintain a competitive career well into their twenties and thirties: indeed 'master competition' is increasingly accepted as serious sport. Dry-land training may offer some benefit but there is no guarantee of inevitable transfer to the aquatic environment. Biomechanical considerations should not be overlooked when attempting to maximize the efficiency of the swimming stroke and some time must be devoted to instilling the correct patterns of muscle action. The optimal training programme is likely to contain a combination of methods with a personalized programme being fitted to each individual. The components of the programme will vary according to the phase of the season as well as the amount of emphasis to be placed on swimming style.

REFERENCES

Åstrand, P.O. and Englesson, S. (1972) A swimming flume. *Journal of Applied Physiology*, **33**, 514.

Åstrand, P.O., Engstrom, L., Eriksson, B.O., Karlberg, P., Nylander, I., Saltin, B. and Thoren, G. (1963) Girl swimmers – with special reference to respiratory and circulatory adaptation and gynaecological and psychiatric aspects. *Acta Paediatrica*, Suppl. 147.

Åstrand, P.O. and Rodahl, K. (1970) *Textbook of Work Physiology*. McGraw-Hill, New York.

Baxter, C. and Reilly, T. (1983) Influence of time of day on all-out swimming. *British Journal of Sports Medicine*, **17**, 122–127.

Bloomfield, J., Blanksby, B.A., Ackland, T.R. and Elliott, B.C. (1986) The mechanical and physiological characteristics of preadolescent swimmers, tennis players and non-competitors, in *Perspectives in Kinanthropometry* (ed. J.A.P. Day). Human Kinetics, Champaign, Illinois, pp. 165–170.

Bloomfield, J. and Sigerseth, P. (1965) Anatomical and physiological differences between sprint and middle distance swimmers at the University level. *Journal of Sports Medicine and Physical Fitness*, **5**, 76–81.

Bôning, D., Mrugalla, M., Maasen M., Busse, M. and Wagner, T.O.F. (1988) Exercise versus immersion: antagonistic effects on water and electrolyte metabolism during swimming. *European Journal of Applied Physiology and Occupational Physiology*, **57**, 248–253.

Carter, J.E.L. (1982) Physical structure of Olympic athletes. Part 1. The Montreal Olympic Games anthropological project. *Medicine and Sport* Vol. 16, Karger, Basel.

Chow, J.W.C., Hay, J.G. and Wilson, B.D. (1984) Turning techniques of elite swimmers. *Journal of Sports Sciences*, **2**, 241–255.

Clarys, J.P. (1985) Hydrodynamics and electromyography: ergonomic aspects in aquatics. *Applied Ergonomics*, **16**, 11–24.

Clarys, J.P. (1987) An overview of biomechanics and its role in enhancing swimming performance, in *Proceedings of the Sixth World FINA Congress on Aquatic Sports*, Orlando, Florida.

Clarys, J.P., Cabri, J., De Witte, B., Touissant, H., de Groot, G., Huying, P. and Hollander, P. (1988) Electromyography applied to sport ergonomics. *Ergonomics*, **31**, 1605–1620.

Costill, D.L. (1978) Adaptations in skeletal muscle during training for sprint and endurance swimming, in *Swimming Medicine IV* (eds B.O. Eriksson and B. Furberg). University Park Press, Baltimore, pp. 233–248.

Costill, D.L., Fink, W.J., Hargreaves, M., King, D.S., Thomas, R. and Fielding, R. (1985) Metabolic characteristics of skeletal muscle during detraining from competitive swimming. *Medicine and Science in Sports and Exercise*, **17**, 339–343.

Craig, A.B. Jr (1986) Breath holding during the turn in competitive swimming. *Medicine and Science in Sports and Exercise*, **18**, 402–407.

Craig, A.B., Boomer, W.L. and Gibbons, J.F. (1979) Use of stroke rate, distance per stroke and velocity relationships during training and competitive swimming, in *Swimming III* (eds J. Terauds and E.W. Bedingfield), University Park Press, Baltimore, pp. 265–274.

Craig, A.B., Skehan, P.L., Pawelezyk, J.A. and Boomer, W.L. (1985) Velocity, stroke rate and distance per stroke during elite swimming competition. *Medicine and Science in Sports and Exercise*, **17**, 625–634.

Dicker, S.G., Lofthus, G.K., Thornton, N.W. and Brooks, G.A. (1980) Respiratory and heart rate responses to tethered controlled frequency breathing swimming. *Medicine and Science in Sports and Exercise*, **12**, 20–23.

Donovan, C.M. and Brooks, G.A. (1983) Training affects lactate clearance, not lactate production. *American Journal of Physiology*, **244**, E83–92.

Dotan, R. and Bar-Or, O. (1983) Load optimization for the Wingate Anaerobic Power Test. *European Journal of Applied Physiology and Occupational Physiology*, **51**, 407–417.

Dulac, S., Quirion, A., De Carufel, D., Le Blanc, J., Jobin, M., Cote, J., Brisson, G.R., Lavoie, J.M. and Diamond, P. (1987) Metabolic and hormonal responses to long-distance swimming in cold water. *International Journal of Sports Medicine*, **8**, 352–356.

Elliott, M. and Haber, P. (1983) Estimation of the peak performance in the 100 meter breast stroke on the basis of serum lactate measurement during two submaximal test heats at different velocities, in *Biomechanics and Medicine in Swimming* (eds A.P. Hollander, P.A. Huijing and G. de Groot), Human Kinetics, Champaign, Illinois, pp. 335–338.

Faulkner, J.A. (1967) *What Research Tells the Coach about Swimming*. AAHPER, Washington.

Flavell, E.R. (1981) *Biokinetics Strength Training*. Isokinetics Inc., Albany, CA.

Fox, E.L. (1984) *Sports Physiology*. Saunders, New York.

Gollnick, P.D., Armstrong, R.B., Sawbert, C.W., Piehl, K. and Saltin, B. (1972) Enzyme activity and fibre composition in skeletal muscle of trained and untrained men. *Journal of Applied Physiology*, **33**, 312–319.

Gullstrand, L. and Lawrence, S. (1987) Heart rate and blood lactate response to short intermittent work at race pace in highly trained swimmers. *Australian Journal of Science and Medicine in Sport*, **19**, 10–14.

Hebbelinck, M., Carter, K. and De Garay, A. (1975) Body build and somatotype of Olympic swimmers and water polo players, in *Swimming II* (eds J.P. Clarys and L. Lewillie), University Park Press, Baltimore, pp. 285–305.

Hessemer, V., Langusch, D., Bruck, K., Bodekar, R.K. and Breidenbach, T. (1984) Effects of slightly lowered body temperatures in endurance performance in humans. *Journal of Applied Physiology: Respiratory, Environmental and Exercise Physiology*, **57**, 1731–1737.

Hollander, A.P., de Groot, G., Van Inger Schenau, G.J., Touissant, H.M., De Best, H., Peeters, W., Meulenans, A. and Schreurs, A.W. (1986) Measurement of active drag during crawl arm stroke training. *Journal of Sports Sciences*, **4**, 21–30.

Holmer, I. (1974) Energy cost of arm stroke, leg kick and the whole stroke in competitive swimming styles. *European Journal of Applied Physiology*, **33**, 105–118.

Holmer, I. (1978) Physiological adjustments to swimming. *Geneeskunde en Sport*, **11**, 22–26.

Holmer, I. (1979) Physiology of swimming man. *Exercise and Sport Sciences Reviews*, **7**, 87–121.

Holmer, I. (1983) Energetics and mechanical work in swimming, in *Biomechanics and Medicine in Swimming* (eds A.P. Hollander, P.A. Huijing and G. de Groot), Human Kinetics, Champaign, Illinois, pp. 154–164.

Holmer, I. and Bergh, U. (1974) Metabolic and thermal responses to swimming in water at varying temperatures. *Journal of Applied Physiology*, **37**, 702–705.

Holmer, I., Stein, E.E., Saltin, B., Ekblom, B. and Åstrand, P.O. (1974) Hemodynamic and respiratory responses compared in swimming and running. *Journal of Applied Physiology*, **37**, 49–54.

Horvath, S.M. (1981) Exercise in a cold environment. *Exercise and Sport Sciences Reviews*, **9**, 221–163.

Houston, M.E. (1978) Metabolism responses to exercise with special reference to training and competition in swimming, in *Swimming Medicine IV* (eds B.O. Eriksson and B. Furberg), University Park Press, Baltimore, pp. 207–232.

Houston, M.E., Wilson, D.M., Green, H.J., Thomson, J.A. and Ranney, D.A. (1981) Physiological and muscle enzyme adaptations to two different intensities of swim training. *European Journal of Applied Physiology*, **46**, 283–291.

Karpovich, P.V. and Millman, N. (1944) Energy expenditure in swimming. *American Journal of Physiology*, **142**, 140–144.

Kennedy, J.C. (1978) Orthopaedic manifestations, in *Swimming Medicine IV* (eds B. Eriksson and B. Furberg). University Park Press, Baltimore, pp. 93–100.

Khosla, T. (1984) Physique of female swimmers and divers from the 1976 Montreal Olympics. *Journal of the American Medical Association*, **252**, 536–537.

Kirwan, J.P., Costill, D.L., Flynn, M.G., Mitchell, J.B., Fink, W.J., Neufer, P.D. and Houmard, J.A. (1988) Physiological responses to successive days of intense training in competitive swimmers. *Medicine and Science in Sports and Exercise*, **20**, 255–259.

Lavoie, J.M. and Montpetit, R.R. (1986) Applied physiology of swimming. *Sports Medicine*, **3**, 165–189.

Lavoie, J.M., Taylor, A.W. and Montpetit, R.R. (1981a) Histochemical and biochemical profile of elite swimmers before and after a six month training period, in *Biochemistry of Exercise* (eds J. Poortmans and G. Nisert), University Park Press, Baltimore, pp. 259–266.

Lavoie, J.M., Taylor, A.W. and Montpetit, R.R. (1981b) Physiological effects of training as measured by a free swimming test. *Journal of Sports Medicine and Physical Fitness*, **21**, 38–42.

MacLaren, D. (1986) Alkalinizers, hydrogen ion accumulation and muscle fatigue: a brief review, in *Sports Science* (eds J. Watkins, T. Reilly and L. Burwitz), E. and F.N. Spon, London, pp. 104–109.

Mader, A., Heek, H. and Hollman, W. (1978) Evaluation of lactic and anaerobic energy contribution by determination of post-exercise lactic acid concentration of ear capillary blood in middle distance runners and swimmers, in *Proceedings of the International Congress of Physical Activity Sciences* Vol. 4 (eds F. Landry and W. Orban), Symposia Specialists, Miami, pp. 187–200.

Magel, J.R. (1971) Comparison of the physiologic response to varying intensities of submaximal work in tethered swimming and treadmill running. *Journal of Sports Medicine and Physical Fitness*, **11**, 203–212.

Maglischo, E. (1982) *Swimming Faster. A Comprehensive Guide to the Science of Swimming*. Mayfield Publishing Co. Ltd, Palo Alto, CA.

Malina, R.M. (1982) Physical growth and maturity characteristics of young athletes, in *Children in Sport* (eds R. Magill, T. Ash and F. Small). Human Kinetics, Champaign, Illinois.

Meleski, B.W. and Malina, R.M. (1985) Changes in body composition and physique of elite university-level female swimmers during a competitive season. *Journal of Sports Sciences*, **3**, 33–40.

Miller, J.A., Hay, J.G. and Wilson, B.D. (1984) Starting techniques of elite swimmers. *Journal of Sports Sciences*, **2**, 213–233.

Mutoh, Y. (1978) Low back pain in butterfliers, in *Swimming Medicine IV* (eds B. Eriksson and B. Furberg). University Park Press, Baltimore, pp. 115–23.

Nadel, E.R. (1977) *Problems with Temperature Regulation during Exercise*. Academic Press, New York.

Neufer, P.D., Costill, D.L., Fielding, R.A., Flynn, M.G. and Kirwan, J.P. (1987) Effect of reduced training on muscular strength and endurance in competitive swimmers. *Medicine and Science in Sports and Exercise*, **19**, 486–490.

Nomura, T. (1983) The influence of training and age on $\dot{V}O_{2max}$ during swimming in Japanese elite age group and Olympic swimmers, in *Biomechanics and Medicine in Swimming* (eds A.P. Hollander, P.A. Huijing and G. de Groot), Human Kinetics, Champaign, Illinois, pp. 251–257.

Nygaard, E. and Nielsen, E. (1978) Skeletal muscle fibre capillarisation with extreme endurance training in man, in *Swimming Medicine IV* (eds B.O. Eriksson and B. Furberg), University Park Press, Baltimore, pp. 282–293.

Pai, Y.C., Hay, J.G. and Wilson, B.D. (1984) Stroking techniques of elite swimmers. *Journal of Sports Sciences*, **2**, 225–239.

Pendergast, D.R., Di Prampero, P.E., Craig, A.B. Jr and Rennie, D.W. (1977) Quantitative analysis of the front crawl in men and women. *Journal of Applied Physiology: Respiratory, Environmental and Exercise Physiology*, **43**, 475–479.

Pendergast, D.R., Di Prampero, P.E., Craig, A.B. Jr and Rennie, D.W. (1978) The influence of selected biomechanical factors on the energy cost of swimming, in *Swimming Medicine IV* (eds B. Eriksson and B. Furberg). University Park Press, Baltimore, pp. 367–78.

Prins, J. (1981) Muscles and their function, in *Biokinetics Strength Training* (ed. E.R. Flavell), Isokinetics Inc., Albany, CA, pp. 72–77.

Pugh, L.G.C. and Edholm, O.G. (1955) The physiology of channel swimmers. *Lancet*, **ii**, 761–768.

Reilly, T. (1983) The energy cost and mechanical efficiency of circuit weight-training. *Journal of Human Movement Studies*, **9**, 39–45.

Reilly, T. (1986) Circadian rhythms and exercise, in *Exercise: Benefits, Limits and Adaptations* (eds D. MacLeod, R. Maughan, M. Nimmo, T. Reilly and C. Williams), E. and F.N. Spon, London, pp. 346–366.

Reilly, T. and Bayley, K. (1986) Anaerobic power in young specialist swimmers, in *Proceedings XXIII World Congress of Sports Medicine*, Brisbane, p. 20.

Reilly, T. and Bayley, K. (1988) The relation between short-term power output and sprint performance of young female swimmers. *Journal of Human Movement Studies*, **14**, 19–29.

Reilly, T. and Brooks, G.A. (1982) Investigation of circadian rhythms in metabolic responses to exercise. *Ergonomics*, **25**, 1093–1107.

Reilly, T. and Miles, S. (1981) Background to injuries in swimming and diving, in *Sports Fitness and Sports Injuries* (ed. T. Reilly), Faber and Faber, London, pp. 159–167.

Ross, W.R., Drinkwater, D.T., Bailey, D.A., Marshall, G.W. and Leahy, R.M. (1980) Kinanthropometry: traditions and new perspectives, in *Kinanthropometry II* (eds M. Ostyn, G. Beunen and J. Simons), University Park Press, Baltimore, pp. 3–27.

Rowe, E., Maglischo, E.W. and Lytle, D.E. (1977) The use of swim fins for the development of sprint swimming speed. *Swimming Technique*, **14**, 73–76.

Rusko, H. (1987) The effect of training on aerobic power characteristics of young cross-country skiers. *Journal of Sports Sciences*, **5**, 273–286.

Sawka, M.N., Knowlton, R.G., Miles, D.S. and Critz, J.B. (1979) Post-competition blood lactate concentration in Collegiate swimmers. *European Journal of Applied Physiology*, **41**, 93–99.

Sharp, R., Troup, J.P. and Costill, D.L. (1982) Relationship between power output and sprint freestyle swimming. *Medicine and Science in Sports and Exercise*, **14**, 53–56.

Spurgeon, J.H. and Giese, W.K. (1984) Physique of world class female swimmers. *Scandinavian Journal of Sports Sciences*, **6**, 11–14.

Spurgeon, J.H. and Sargent, R.G. (1978) Measures of physique and nutrition on outstanding male swimmers. *Swimming Technique*, **15**, 26–32.

Swaine, I. and Reilly, T. (1983) The freely chosen swimming stroke rate in a maximal swim and on a biokinetic swim bench. *Medicine and Science in Sports and Exercise*, **15**, 370–375.

Torma, Z.D. and Szekely, G. (1978) Parameters of acid–base equilibrium at various swimming intensities and distances, in *Swimming Medicine IV* (eds B. Eriksson and B. Furberg), University Park Press, Baltimore, pp. 274–281.

Toussaint, H.M. (1988) Mechanics and energetics of swimming. PhD thesis, Vrije Universiteit, Amsterdam.

Touissant, H.M., Beelen, A., Rodenburg, A., Sargeant, A.J., de Groot, G., Hollander, P. and van Ingen Schenau, G.J. (1988) Propelling efficiency of front crawl swimming. *Journal of Applied Physiology*, **65**, 2506–2512.

Toussaint, H.M., Meulemans, A., de Groot, G., Hollander, A.P., Schreurs, A.W. and Vervoorn, K. (1987) Respiratory value for oxygen uptake measurements during swimming. *European Journal of Applied Physiology and Occupational Physiology*, **56**, 363–366.

Treffene, R.J. (1983) Heart rate measurement technique in swimming performance prediction, in *Biomechanics and Medicine in Swimming* (eds A.P. Hollander,
P.R. Huijing and G. de Groot), Human Kinetics, Champaign, Illinois,
pp. 339–344.

9
Rowing

Niels Secher

9.1 INTRODUCTION

Rowing imposes a challenge to the human body by the involvement of nearly all muscle groups during intense dynamic exercise. Furthermore, during each stroke a considerable muscle tension is built up making training for competitive rowing a combination of strength development and endurance. The physiology of rowing has been the subject of reviews (Secher, 1983; Hagerman, 1984), and an East German textbook on rowing has been published (Körner and Schwanitz, 1985). The appearance of these texts reflects the dramatic change in the attitude towards competitive rowing which has taken place in recent years. With the introduction of rowing ergometers by O. Vaage and E. Gjessing in Norway and Hagerman and Howie (1971) in New Zealand, it is now recognized that the assessment of certain physiological variables, such as work capacity and maximal oxygen uptake, play an integral part in the planning of oarsmen's training and have become an aid for the coach in team selection (Mahler, Andrea and Andresen, 1984). It is acknowledged that although data have been published for a number of physiological variables in oarsmen, the increasing bulk of experience gained from the use of rowing ergometers by coaches has not been collected with the aim of publishing the results. This may be especially true for the East European countries, despite their large contribution to international rowing competitions. This chapter will update the literature related to rowing and add some unpublished observations. In addition some biomechanical aspects related to rowing will be included.

9.2 ROWING COMPETITIONS

Rowing competitions are divided into two distinct, yet related disciplines:

sweep rowing and sculling. In the sweep boats each oarsman rows using a single oar approximately 4 m long, while in sculling he uses two smaller (approximately 3 m) sculls on each side of the boat. Both types of boats are rowed with the back towards the direction of the course by pulling the oar (sculls) at a cadence of 34–38 strokes per minute. In contrast to traditional rowing boats as well as to the first racing boats, the stroke is made more efficient with the use of a sliding seat, thereby adding leg extension to the work performed with the upper body and arms. A boat construction in which the outriggers and stretcher were movable, and the seat fixed was constructed in England by C.E. Poynter in 1953 (Burnell, 1955). This type of boat was used for winning the FISA championship in the single scull 1981–1982. In 1983 FISA decided not to allow the construction because it was felt that it made rowing too simple a technical discipline.

In sweep rowing the boats may include two, four or as many as eight oarsmen. Furthermore, pairs and fours are rowed both with and without a coxswain, while a coxswain is always present in the eights. Sculls are rowed without a coxswain and encompass single, double and quadruple boats. The minimum weight of the coxswain is 50 kg for the male and 40 kg for the female events. As international competitions are held on a straight flat-water course it may be argued that the role of the coxswain is minimal for steering the boat. The presence of a coxswain may, however, have a significant influence on the selection of oarsmen making the advantage of large and heavy rowers even more important than for the coxless boats.

Historically, race rowing was apparently unknown in ancient Egypt (Touny and Wenig, 1969) or to the Vikings (Wahlqvist, 1978) despite the fact that they were dependent on boats which could be rowed for transport. For a discussion of ancient oared warships see the paper of Foley and Soedel (1981). The traditional rowing competition was quite different from the present race rowing (Henningsen, 1949). Two 'knights' fought with lances and shields, and the boats and teams more-or-less replaced horses. The competition was won when one of the 'knights' fell in the water. The longest row by a single person in a traditional rowing boat may be that of O. Joensen from the Faroe Islands to Copenhagen (1670 km) in 1986 (Mortensen *et al.*, 1987).

Modern race rowing started in England with the 'Doggett's Coat and Badge' race on the Thames for professional watermen (1715) and 'between gentlemen' with the Oxford and Cambridge Boat Race (1829) and the Henley Royal Regatta (1839) (Cleaver, 1957; Dodd, 1983). For an account of the match between Harvard and Yale held since 1852 see Herrick (1948). A professional World championship in single scull was arranged from 1831 to 1952 which had such scullers as H. Kelly (1865–1867) and E. Barry (1912–1920) as winners (Cleaver, 1957). Rowing championships have been arranged by the Fédération Internationale des Société d'Aviron (FISA) since 1893 with intermissions during the two World Wars 1914–1918 and 1939–1945. In 1900 rowing appeared on the Olympic programme. Until 1962 all FISA championships were called 'European' although they were open to all nations from 1927. Accordingly, they have all been named 'World' championships since 1973. Also an open North American championship was held in 1967. Women's championships were added in 1954. Unofficial light-weight (maximum weight 72.5 kg; average weight 70 kg) championships were introduced in 1974 and made 'official' in 1985. In the same year light-weight women's championships (maximum weight 59 kg; average weight 57 kg) were introduced after an unofficial regatta in 1984. Also in 1985 the distance rowed by women was increased from 1000 m to the 2000 m distance rowed by men. A distance of 1500 m has been maintained for rowers younger than 18 years of age. It will be argued that even this distance should be increased to 2000 m. Since 1973, FISA has sponsored

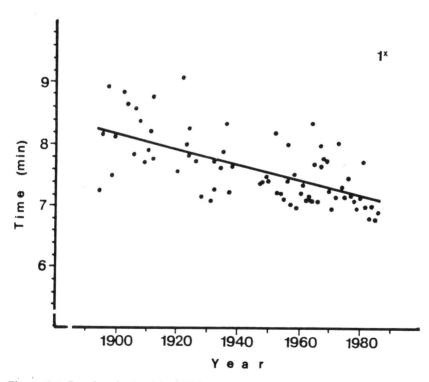

Figure 9.1 Results obtained by FISA regatta winning single scull over 2000 m 1893 to 1986. The regression line is shown.

a yearly regatta over 1000 m for master oarsmen, i.e. oarsmen older than 27 years of age. A novel has been written about competitive rowing (Kiesling, 1982). A canvas was painted in 1874 by T. Eakins representing John Biglin in a single scull (Dan, 1984).

Since the first FISA regatta took place in 1893, the mean result in the men's open class has improved by about 0.8 (range 0.6–0.9) s per year (Figure 9.1, Secher, 1973 as recalculated by N. Grujić and B. Hanel). It is possible to detect a similar 0.8 (0.2–2.1 s per year) improvement in the results obtained by the women over 1000 m in the years from 1954 to 1984. For the light-weight male rowers, the improvement of the results is only barely significant. The improvement in rowing performance represents an integrated effect of changes in training and selection of oarsmen; also the technical modifications in construction of the boats as well as the effort made by FISA to standardize the racing courses have made contributions. Currently FISA has also standardized the weight of the boats to those presented in Table 9.1.

Table 9.1 Minimum boat weight allowed in FISA championships

Boat type	4+	2×	2−	1×	2+	4−	4×	8+
Weight (kg)	51	26	27	14	32	50	52	93

Digits indicate number of oarsmen; ± the presence of a coxswain; × indicate scull boats.

The median results obtained in FISA regattae from 1974 to 1988 indicate a race duration in the men's open class of 6.5 (5.7–7.2) min and 6.6 (6.0–7.3) min for light-weights. For women's races over 2000 m 1985–1986 the times are 7.1 (6.4–8.0) min and 7.7 (7.3–8.1) min for the light-weights or 11% longer than for the men in similar events. These values indicate a difference between results obtained in the similar open and light-weight classes of 3% supporting the impression that a large body weight is an advantage.

9.3 ROWING INJURIES

Rowing is associated with few injuries. In the 1987 World championship involving 880 rowers only 40 were treated by the medical service and of these only four cases were associated with the races. They all suffered from extreme fatigue and associated hyperventilation (B. Jepsen and J. Larsen, personal communication). Thus an evaluation of the blood acid-base status of rowers after a race should have a high priority. L.M. Strayer found, by means of a questionnaire involving 931 responses from American rowers, 59 injuries (Hagerman, 1984). Of these, 26 athletes suffered from chronic low back pain, 11 from knee pain, 9 from tenosynovitis at the wrist and three from shoulder injuries. Approximately 50% of the reported injuries occurred during rowing while the other half were experienced during training on land.

9.4 THE METABOLIC COST OF ROWING

The metabolic cost and cardiac output during rowing a traditional boat were determined by Liljestrand and Lindhard (1920). They were able to demonstrate a rise in oxygen uptake with increasing speed. With the involvement of mainly the upper body and arms the maximal values reported of 1.1–2.2 l min^{-1} were small. Accordingly, the authors found maximal cardiac outputs of only 13–17 l min^{-1}.

The rowing of racing shells (and among them the sculls) is the most economical form of water locomotion (Di Prampero, 1986). The metabolic cost of rowing mainly reflects the power used to overcome the drag force of the boat in the water. Resistance to progression increases with the square of the mean speed (Balukow, 1964; Wellicome, 1967; Celentano *et al.*, 1974). It follows that power, being force times speed, should increase with speed approximately to the third power. However, from determinations of the oxygen uptake while rowing a single scull, a

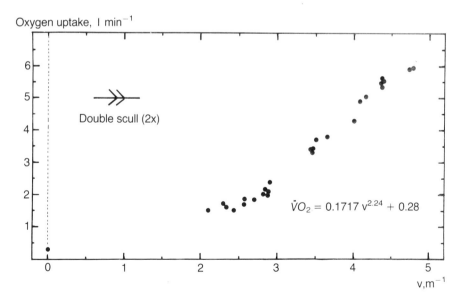

Figure 9.2 Oxygen uptake during rowing a double scull in one oarsman. Values indicated with open symbols were not included in the regression. (This figure is published with kind permission of the *Journal of Sports Sciences.*)

double scull and a pair, it has been shown that the metabolic cost of rowing increases with speed only to the 2.4 power (Figure 9.2, Jackson and Secher, 1976 as recalculated by Secher, 1983).

Determinations are complicated by the fact that the oxygen uptake is used not only for progression of the boat but also to move the body back and forth on the seat. Thus a linear relationship has been established between oxygen uptake and 'no-load' rowing at different rowing frequencies (Secher, 1983). It is of note that the oxygen uptake during 'no-load' rowing may approach as much as 4 l min^{-1}. If such determinations are taken into account and the metabolic cost of rowing is estimated as the determined oxygen uptake minus the oxygen uptake of 'no-load' rowing corresponding to the pertinent rowing frequency, the oxygen uptake used for progression increases with speed to 3.1 power (Secher, 1983). The movement of the body against the direction of the boat when the blades are out of the water may, however, contribute to boat progression as the mass of the oarsmen is much larger than that of the boat. Indeed, the maximum velocity of the boat occurs during the middle of the seat movement phase (Martin and Bernfield, 1980). Perhaps as much as half the oxygen uptake used to move the oarsman on the seat (against the direction of the boat) may play a role in boat progression.

The metabolic cost of rowing at racing speed has been calculated to increase by approximately 200 ml per decade (Secher, 1983). In 1979 the metabolic cost was calculated to 6.4 l min^{-1} suggesting a current mean value of 6.6 l min^{-1}. From measurements made on a rowing ergometer a value close to 7 l min^{-1} has been estimated (K. Jensen, personal communication).

A simultaneous determination of the metabolic cost and mechanical work of rowing has not yet been carried out although an attempt was made by Di Prampero et al. (1971). They measured the mechanical work in a coxed pair. At the same time the metabolic cost of rowing was assessed from measurement of heart rate during rowing after establishing a relationship between oxygen uptake and heart rate during rowing in a basin. From these estimates Di Prampero et al. (1971) calculated a mechanical efficiency of 18% during rowing at a cadence of less than 25 min^{-1}, and an increase to the level of 20–23% at a frequency of 35 min^{-1}.

9.5 ENDOCRINE AND METABOLIC RESPONSES TO ROWING

Circulating eosinophils have been shown to decrease from 108 to 19 mm^{-3} before the match, and even to 3 mm^{-3} after exhaustive rowing (Renold et al., 1951). This was taken to reflect mental as well as physical stress leading to increases in ACTH, adrenal cortical hormones and adrenaline. After ergometer rowing plasma adrenaline and nor-adrenaline concentrations have been shown to increase from resting values of 0.9 and 2.3 nmol l^{-1}, respectively to extremely high values of 19 and 74 nmol l^{-1} (Jensen et al., 1984; Holmqvist et al., 1986). These values are about twice as large as noted during, for example, running (Kjær et al., 1986) suggesting a role for muscle mass in the catecholamine response to maximal exercise. Also pancreatic polypeptide, a hormone under vagal control (Schwartz, 1983), increases (from 21 to 48 pmol l^{-1}) after ergometer rowing (Holmquist et al., 1986) suggesting that vagal activity may contribute to the feeling of fatigue including gastrointestinal symptoms experienced at exhaustion.

Körner and Schwanitz (1985) estimated the use of 25 000–29 000 kJ (6000–7000 kcal) per day for male and 21 000–25 000 kJ (5000–6000 kcal) for female rowers and recommended food with 56% carbohydrates, 27% fat and 17% protein. With such high energy demands it is no surprise that oarsmen tend to lose weight from off-season to in-season, i.e. from 84.5±1.5 (SEM) to 81.7±1.4 kg ($P < 0.01$) in 12 Danish oarsmen (Jackson and Secher, unpublished). Protein turnover is larger in oarsmen than in controls (Stein et al., 1983). However, the calculated protein synthesis is not increased in oarsmen, supporting the view that intense exercise does not increase basal protein turnover rate in adequately nourished individuals. The serum androgen and growth hormone responses to maximal running and submaximal rowing have been measured by Sutton et al. (1973) in 14 oarsmen. They found an increase from 690 ng ml^{-1} and 5 μU ml^{-1}, respectively at rest to 840 ng ml^{-1} and 49 μU ml^{-1} after maximal exercise, but no increases after submaximal rowing. These changes occurred despite a constant serum luteinizing hormone (62 ng ml^{-1}). It was felt that the raised level of androgen during exercise may act in association with growth hormone to increase the pubertal growth velocity. Furthermore, it may be speculated that these hormone increases may contribute to muscular development associated with exercise. Administration of testosterone, however, does not increase muscle glycogen build-up after maximal dynamic exercise (Allenberg et al., 1983).

Increases in serum concentration of myoglobin and creatinine kinase (a cellular enzyme) have been reported after 10 km rowing and still increasing values were found 1.5 h after the training bout (Hansen et al., 1982) indicating skeletal muscle cellular damage which could help explain muscle soreness after rowing.

9.6 HEART RATE DURING ROWING

The first person to record heart rate in oarsmen may have been Fraser

(1868–1869). He used a sphygmograph and noted an increase in heart rate from 68 to 90 beats min^{-1} and also in pulse pressure of the radial artery after rowing. During maximal rowing heart rates of 190–200 beats min^{-1} have been recorded (Hagerman, 1984). In well-trained oarsmen lower values are often seen, e.g. 185±3 beats min^{-1} in 14 winners of international championships (Secher et al., 1983). Furthermore, the relationship between heart rate and oxygen uptake may vary with the specific type of training applied (Secher, 1983). Droghetti et al. (1985) have used a levelling off in a heart rate–rowing velocity relationship to define an 'anaerobic threshold'.

9.7 'ANAEROBIC THRESHOLD'

At low work loads only small increases in blood lactate are seen (Bang, 1935). At high metabolic rates, the production of lactate exceeds its elimination and blood lactate increases markedly. It has been demonstrated that this increase in blood lactate takes place at a higher work load in internationally competing oarsmen than in less experienced oarsmen (Steinacker et al., 1985). The work load at which a marked increase in blood lactate is seen has been named the 'anaerobic threshold' although it has to be defined arbitrarily as, for example, the work load which elicits a blood lactate concentration of 4 mM. The exercise intensity thus defined has been found to be helpful in guidance of athletes training. Most often the work intensity is defined from the marked increase in ventilation taking place at approximately 80% of the subjects maximal oxygen uptake (Mickelson and Hagerman, 1982; Secher, 1983). A further step to indicate an appropriate training intensity has been to define the heart rate obtained at the work load giving rise to the marked increase in blood lactate or ventilation, or to define this work intensity from a relationship between heart rate and rowing velocity (Droghetti et al., 1985). With the use of heart rate to define a work intensity it should be remembered that heart rate at a given work load increases with time. Furthermore, as maximal oxygen uptake increases with training, the oxygen uptake giving rise to the 'anaerobic threshold' also increases both in terms of 1 min^{-1} and relative to the maximal oxygen uptake (from 78 to 89%, Mahler, Nelson and Hagerman, 1984).

9.8 PHYSICAL CHARACTERISTICS OF ROWERS AND THEIR INFLUENCE ON ROWING PERFORMANCE

The female winners of the 1984 Los Angeles Olympic rowing events had

Table 9.2 Height, weight, power developed during ergometer rowing, maximal oxygen uptake ($\dot{V}O_{2max}$) and ventilation ($\dot{V}_E$) in rowers of different categories

	FISA	National	Experienced	Light-weight	Women
Height (cm)	193 (18)	192 (538)	185 (14)	186 (130)	173 (40)
Weight (kg)	94 (18)	88 (545)	82 (16)	71 (130)	68 (40)
Power (W)	393 (19)	374 (515)	342 (51)	360 (147)	201 (46)
$\dot{V}O_{2max}$ (l min^{-1})	6.1 (41)	6.0 (535)	4.7 (30)	5.1 (147)	4.3 (52)
$\dot{V}_E$ (l min^{-1})	188 (28)	190 (535)	135 (60)	164 (130)	158 (46)

Averages of values from Mellerowitz and Hansen (1965), Hagerman and Lee, (1971), Carey, Stensland and Hartley (1974), Secher *et al.* (1974), Cunningham, Goode and Critz (1975), Strømme, Ingjer and Meen (1977), Hagerman *et al.* (1978, 1979), Rusko (personal communication), Larsson and Forsberg (1980), Secher *et al.* (1982a, 1983), Bouckaert, Pannier and Vrijens (1983), Mahler, Nelson and Hagerman, (1984), Tumilty, Hahn and Telford (1987) Grujić *et al.* (1987b).
Values in brackets are number of rowers included.

a median height 180 (range 172–185) cm and a weight of 79 (74–89) kg. For the men the values were 192 (182–203) cm and 92 (80–100) kg (Ziffren, 1984). These values are similar to those of rowers who have participated in physiological investigations (Table 9.2). Thus rowers are large and heavy individuals and it seems that less successful oarsmen are also lighter (Secher *et al.*, 1983; Grujić *et al.*, 1987b). It has been noted that oarsmen have long limbs and especially a long upper arm length (Stein *et al.*, 1983). Body fat has been determined to quite high values of approximately 11% in male, 9% in light-weight and 14% in female rowers (Hagerman, Hagerman and Mickelson, 1979), whereas Jackson and Secher (unpublished) found values of 7.7±0.2% during winter decreasing significantly to 6.9±0.2% during summer in 12 Danish oarsmen. It is of note that rowers are older than many other athletes with the winners in Los Angeles being 25 (19–31) years of age.

Several mathematical models of rowing have been developed (McMahon, 1971; Secher and Vaage, 1983; Sanderson and Martindale, 1986). The basis for these calculations has been that boat resistance as well as the aerobic metabolism increases to the second power of a characteristic length of the rower, e.g. with weight to two-third power (Vaage and Hermansen, 1977; Jensen *et al.*, 1984, Figure 9.3). Accordingly, small and large athletes should be able to row at a similar speed. It has also been pointed out, however, that the anaerobic metabolism should increase to the third power of a characteristic length of the rower which is more than resistance, giving the heavy oarsman an advantage. Of greater significance in making large body dimensions an advantage in rowing competitions is the constant weight of the boats (and coxswain) as

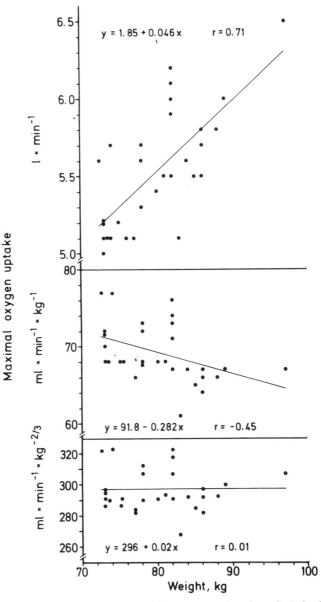

Figure 9.3 Maximal oxygen uptake of oarsmen related to their body weight. Values are expressed as l min^{-1} (top), ml kg^{-1} min^{-1} (middle) and as ml $kg^{-2/3}$ min^{-1} (bottom).

defined by FISA (Table 9.1). With a boat weight per oarsman of 41 kg as in the coxed pair, the 90 kg oarsman will have an advantage over the 70 kg oarsman of 2.0%. When the boat weight per oarsman is reduced

ROWING TIME, MIN AND S

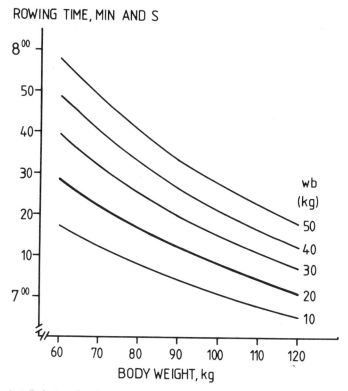

BODY WEIGHT, kg

Figure 9.4 Relationship between the calculated duration of rowing over 2000 m for men and the weight of the oarsman. The thick line represents results calculated using the approximate weight per oarsman (wb) of the coxless boats. (This figure is published with kind permission of the *Journal of Sports Sciences*.)

to 14 kg as in the coxless pair, this advantage is reduced to 1.0% (Figure 9.4). Also the distance rowed influences the advantage of the heavier oarsmen although only to a smaller extent. If the rowing distance is made shorter as has been done for the junior rowers, the importance of the anaerobic metabolism increases, thereby making large body dimensions even more important.

9.9 MUSCLE STRENGTH AND FIBRE CHARACTERISTICS

Oarsmen are large and heavy individuals (Table 9.2). Accordingly as should be expected (Asmussen and Heebøll-Nielsen, 1961), they are also strong. During rowing, the electromyogram over both arm and leg muscles has been recorded (Ishiko, 1968) and the electromyogram over the triceps muscle has been shown to decrease during the pull phase of the stroke when beginners learn to row (Gauthier, 1985). Significant correlations between rowing performance and muscle strength in a hand grip, the arms, back and legs have been demonstrated (Yamakawa and Ishiko, 1966). Bloomfield and Roberts (1972), however, saw little evidence for the importance of muscle strength for performance on a rowing ergometer (over 3 min). Furthermore, in a study of strength in nine different muscle synergies among three categories of oarsmen, Secher (1975) saw that oarsmen competing at an international level were significantly stronger only as far as strength in a simulated rowing position was concerned (2001 N *vs.* 1795 N in the oarsmen competing at a national level and 1589 N in beginners) and 'rowing strength' correlated significantly only with strength in a hand grip. Few data are available on isokinetic strength of oarsmen. Larsson and Forsberg (1980) measured isokinetic leg strength in two international competitive oarsmen and 10 oarsmen competing on a national level. Although the best oarsmen were the strongest, the differences were small and reached only a significant level when a speed of 1.05 rad s^{-1} (120 degrees s^{-1}) was applied. Isokinetic leg strength has also been reported to increase from off-season to in-season while leg flexion strength remained constant (Hagerman and Staron, 1983).

It is puzzling that while oarsmen are able to develop a strength with both their legs which equals the sum of the strength of the right and left leg (Secher, 1975), this is not the case for untrained subjects or other types of athletes (Asmussen and Hebøll-Nielsen, 1961; Secher, Rube and Elers, 1988). This difference between oarsmen and other types of athletes may reflect the fact that oarsmen are using the two legs simultaneously in the 'kick' against the stretcher although differences exist between the outer and inner leg during sweep rowing (Asami *et al.*, 1985). The difference in expression of leg strength in general noted during two and one leg extension suggests that even simple strength measurements are reflecting the central nervous system's ability to involve the muscles in the specific type of contraction demanded. Therefore, it may only be meaningful to measure strength of oarsmen in a simulated rowing position.

It may be asked what strength is needed for optimal rowing performance. During rowing at racing speed, peak forces between 700 and 900 N have been measured (Ishiko, 1968) although smaller values have also been reported in less qualified oarsmen (Asami *et al.*, 1978; Zsidegh, Apor and Bretz, 1979; Schneider, 1980). In women, a peak force of approximately 500 N was noted during ergometer rowing (Mason, Shakespear and Doherty, 1988). The force developed during dynamic contractions becomes progressively smaller with increasing shortening velocity of the muscles as expressed by the force–velocity relationship (Hill, 1938). In the force–velocity relationship the maximal power, being force times velocity, is developed at a force corresponding to about 35% of isometric strength. In order to develop a dynamic rowing strength of about 800 N (500 N in women), it may be argued that oarsmen need an isometric rowing strength of abouth 2290 N (1430 N for women). However, a force–velocity for rowing has not been established.

Oarsmens' leg muscles have a high percentage of slow twitch muscle fibres, i.e. 70–74% *vs*. 41% in controls (Larsson and Forsberg, 1980; Hagerman and Staron, 1983). Furthermore, the oarsmens' muscle fibres are large: for slow twitch (red) muscle fibres 5974 μm; for fast twitch (white) fibres 6546 μm (or expressed from the measurement of the 'lesser diameter': 3970 *vs*. 3330 μm in controls) and have many capillaries (7.3 *vs*. 3.1 capillaries around fibres in controls). For the deltoid muscle on the shoulder even a higher percentage (73–76%) of slow twitch fibres has been described (Larsson and Forsberg, 1980; Roth *et al*., 1983) while for oarswomen lower values of 55–60% have been reported for the arms and legs (Clarkson *et al*., 1983). In the deltoid muscle extremely large muscle fibres of 9000 μm have been seen (Roth *et al*., 1983) while Larsson and Forsberg (1980) reported smaller fibre sizes (3580 μm) than for the legs. The number of capillaries around fibres was also high in the deltoid muscle of oarsmen, 5.2 *vs*. 3.0 in controls (Larsson and Forsberg, 1980) while Roth *et al*. (1983) reported 2.3 capillaries per fibre. It is of interest that oarsmen's slow twitch fibres are almost as large as their fast twitch fibres and also that almost no 'untrained' fast twitch Type b fibres are seen. Together these data indicate a high adaptation to endurance as well as to strength development in a rather slow movement. An adaptation to endurance training is underlined by the finding of high activities for enzymes involved in aerobic metabolism whereas enzyme activities for anaerobic metabolism are similar to those of controls (Roth *et al*., 1983).

9.10 VENTILATION

Oarsmen show high values for ventilation during maximal exercise (Table 9.2) with a largest recorded value of 243 l min^{-1} (Secher, 1983). Also their vital capacities are large, 6.8 l with a maximal recorded value of 9.1 l, and a direct relationship between maximal oxygen uptake and vital capacity has been demonstrated (Secher, 1983). However, the best oarsmen had a larger maximal oxygen uptake for a given vital capacity than the less-experienced oarsmen. Thus the relationship between maximal oxygen uptake and vital capacity does not imply that vital capacity is limiting oarsmen's oxygen uptake. Rather the relationship between maximal oxygen uptake and vital capacity indicates that both variables increase with increasing body dimensions. Nevertheless,

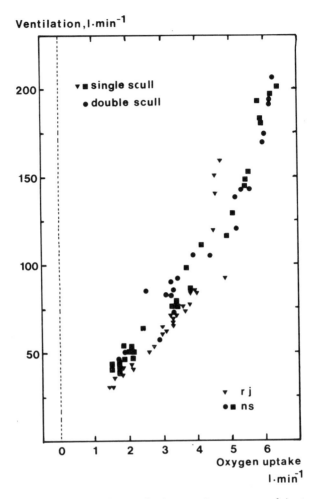

Figure 9.5 Pulmonary ventilation during rowing measured in two oarsmen. (This figure is published with kind permission of the *Journal of Sports Sciences*.)

Yamakawa and Ishiko (1966) demonstrated a positive correlation between rowing performance and the oarsmen's vital capacity.

With increasing rowing speed and oxygen uptake ventilation also increases. The increase in oarsmen's ventilation is linear up to approximately 80% of the subjects' maximal oxygen uptake and then increases markedly (Figure 9.5, Secher, 1983). The increase in oarsmen's ventilation (during running) is caused both by an increase in ventilatory frequency and tidal volume with shortening of both the inspiratory and especially expiratory time (Clark, Hagerman and Gelfand, 1983).

However, at near maximal work loads a plateau or even a decrease in tidal volume is noted.

It has been demonstrated that pulmonary diffusing capacity after maximal arm exercise decreases by approximately 7% (Rasmussen *et al.*, 1986), maybe reflecting an increase in pulmonary water content. Such an effect could also help to explain the 'regatta cough' experienced after rowing competitions. Whether pulmonary diffusion capacity decreases to a level where it may limit maximal oxygen uptake, is not known.

9.11 BLOOD AND HEART VOLUMES OF OARSMEN

Blood volume in oarsmen (average of seven oarsmen and four runners) has been determined as 95 ml kg^{-1} (7.8 l) *vs.* 76 ml kg^{-1} (5.6 l) in controls (Falch and Strømme, 1979). Also the trained individuals had a larger pulmonary blood volume of 0.7 l compared with 0.5 l in the controls. These differences reflect larger values for both erythrocyte and plasma volumes as the haematocrit (44 *vs.* 46%) did not differ significantly between groups.

It is a classical observation that training induces an increase in heart size and that the size of the heart decreases again after the end of training (Secher, 1921, 1923). Accordingly trained people have large 'sports' hearts. In oarsmen with a maximal oxygen uptake of 4.7 l min^{-1} Szögy and Cherebetiu (1974) found a heart volume of 1.1 l (13 ml kg^{-1}). Two types of large heart have been defined in athletes. In athletes involved in endurance training an increase is seen the inner diameters of the heart while the heart walls remain constant. Conversely, 'power trained' athletes show large heart walls, but normal inner diameters (Longhurst *et al.*, 1980). Howald *et al.* (1977) found normal inner diameters in oarsmen's hearts and large heart walls, whereas Keul *et al.* (1982) and Jensen *et al.* (1984) found both large inner diameters and heart walls in oarsmen. This result seems to fit to the combined adaptation to static and endurance training involved in rowing.

9.12 ANAEROBIC CAPACITY

Rowing competitions as well as 'all-out' ergometer rowing are carried out with 'an initial spurt' (Secher *et al.*, 1982a). In the first 40 s a cadence of 40–50 strokes per minute is applied. The stroke rating is then reduced and maintained at 34–38 strokes per minute until a final sprint in the last minute of the race. Thus during race rowing the second and third 500 m of the 2000 m course takes approximately 8 and 10% longer than the first 500 m (Figure 9.6). During the fourth 500 m, velocity is

500m TIMES, % OF FIRST 500m

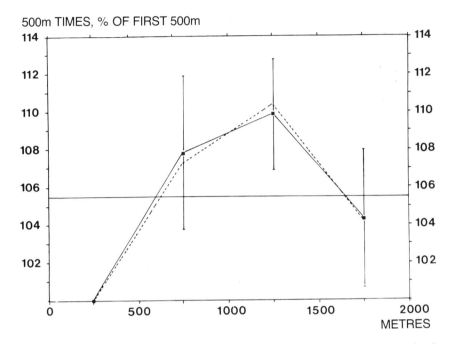

Figure 9.6 Relative 500 m racing times calculated for all participants in the finals (1st to 6th place) of the 1974 world championship FISA regatta for men. Values indicated (± SD) at the 250 m marks. Also shown are the relative 500 m times for the three first boats in each competition. Horizontal line indicates the average relative 500 m racing time. (This figure is published with kind permission of *Journal of Sports Sciences*.)

increased to the average speed of the race. During 6 min 'all-out' ergometer rowing, power decreases over the first 4–5 min to approximately 80% of the power performed in the first minute (Secher *et al.*, 1982a). Accordingly, only 14 of 22 rowers were able to perform the same total amount of work when a constant intensity was applied as when an initial spurt was allowed during 6 min ergometer rowing ($P < 0.01$; N. Grujić, personal communication). A larger power performed during all-out exercise with an initial spurt may reflect that an extremely high initial work intensity makes oxygen uptake increase faster causing the total oxygen uptake during the exertion to increase by approximately 7% compared with the constant work load exercise bout (Secher *et al.*, 1982a).

Anaerobic capacity has traditionally been indicated by the measurement of blood lactate after maximal exercise. Resting values for lactate are approximately 0.8 mM. Values for eight Norwegian oarsmen have been determined to 11 mM after treadmill running, 15 mM after a national regatta and to 17 mM after a FISA championship (Vaage, 1977). It should be noted that lactate removal increases if rowing is continued at a 40% work intensity after a 2000 m race (Koutedakis and Sharp, 1986). Blood lactate concentration increases to similar values in small and large oarsmen (Secher, 1983) arguing for the view that anaerobic capacity increases with increasing (lean) body weight. Also base excess, an indication of the metabolic acidosis, has been shown to be lower after (ergometer) rowing than after bicycling (-14 vs. -12 mM) (Haber and Ferlitsch, 1979). In female rowers venous pH has been determined as 6.9 and bicarbonate concentration as 8.1 mM (Hahn et al., 1988). However, as the distribution volumes for lactate, the hydrogen ion and base excess are not accurately known, these determinations make a quantitative assessment of anaerobic capacity difficult.

It has been suggested that maximal anaerobic capacity may be expressed quantitatively on the basis of the calculated oxygen deficit in an exertion lasting more than 2 min (Medbø et al., 1988). Oxygen deficit is the total energy expenditure (expressed in litres of oxygen) during exercise minus the accumulated oxygen uptake during exercise. During treadmill running values of 52–90 ml kg^{-1} were found (Medbø et al., 1988). For rowers including women higher values of 88–97 ml kg^{-1} have been published (Szögy and Cherebetiu, 1974; Hagerman, Hagerman and Mickelson, 1979). Thus oarsmen have a high capacity for anaerobic exercise, perhaps reflecting the contribution of adaptation to arm exercise (Koutedakis and Sharp, 1985).

The relative anaerobic contribution to a 6 min bicycle ergometer bout of exercise has been estimated in rowers to be 38% (Szögy and Cherebetiu, 1974) and a similar contribution has been reached for maximal arm exercise of 7 min duration (Roth et al., 1983). For rowing Hagerman, Hagerman and Mickelson (1979) estimated a value of 30% during a 6 min all-out exercise bout while Grujić et al. (1987a) in a similar approach reached a value of 21%. It should be noted that while all-out ergometer rowing has most often been carried out over 6 min, even FISA winning crews use approximately 6.7 min to cover the course. Thus a duration for all-out ergometer rowing of 7 min seems more appropriate.

9.13 MAXIMAL OXYGEN UPTAKE

Before the introduction of rowing ergometers, the maximal oxygen uptake of oarsmen was determined during cycling or running. The values reached have been shown to be similar to (Carey, Stensland and Hartley, 1974; Haber and Ferlitsch, 1979; Bouckaert, Pannier and Vrijens, 1983), 8% lower (Tumilty, Hahn and Telford, 1987) or 4–6%

higher (Cunningham, Goode and Critz, 1975) than during simulated rowing. Of note, Bouckaert, Pannier and Vrijens (1983) found a similar value for maximal oxygen uptake during cycling and rowing in oarsmen, but a 10% lower value during rowing in control subjects. This point was stressed further by Jackson and Secher (1976) and Strømme, Ingjer and Meen (1977) who reported values during rowing on the water that were approximately 200 ml min^{-1} higher than during cycling or uphill running. It should be noted that rowing ergometers have been constructed to simulate either sweep rowing (Hagerman and Howie, 1971) or sculling as with the use of the Gjessing or 'Concept II' ergometers. Whether maximal oxygen uptake determined on the two types of ergometers differs among 'rowers' and 'scullers' appears not to have been evaluated. The use of the Concept and Gjessing ergometers has, however, been shown to elicit similar values for maximal oxygen uptake (whereas the recorded power on the Concept ergometer was on average 9.3% higher than on the Gjessing ergometer, the results obtained on the two ergometers were mutually correlated) (Hahn et al., 1988).

The specificity of maximal oxygen uptake determinations for oarsmen is stressed by their high capacity for arm exercise. Whereas the maximal oxygen uptake during arm cranking in the general population (and leg-trained individuals) is about 70% of their maximal oxygen uptake during leg exercise, arm maximal oxygen uptake in oarsmen is approximately 90% of the value determined during leg exercise (Secher et al., 1974). For example, an arm maximal oxygen uptake as high as 5.7 l min^{-1} has been demonstrated in an oarsman, a value similar to that measured in a kayak rower (Larsson et al., 1988).

With high arm maximal oxygen uptake values for oarsmen, it may be questioned why the maximal oxygen uptake obtained during the arm and leg exercise of rowing does not far exceed the values determined during cycling or running. An explanation could be that intense exercise with one muscle group induces a vasoconstriction in an other likewise maximally engaged muscle group (Secher et al., 1977; Klausen et al., 1982).

Two different testing protocols have been developed to evaluate rowing performance. A 6 min all-out test was initially developed in order to simulate race rowing. In the other a progressive, incremental exercise to exhaustion on a variable-resistance rowing ergometer has been shown to elicit a similar maximal oxygen uptake (Mahler, Nelson and Hagerman, 1984). The values for maximal oxygen uptake in oarsmen during rowing has increased from the value of 3.4 l min^{-1} reported by Henderson and Haggard (1925) to 4.7 l min^{-1} (Hagerman and Lee, 1971) and 6.4 l min^{-1} (Hagerman et al., 1978). In the latter study a highest value of 6.6 l min^{-1} was seen, a value which has also been

measured in medal winning Danish and Yugoslavian oarsmen (Grujić
et al., 1987b). The three-times Olympic champion in the single scull,
P. Karpinen, has been reported to have a maximal oxygen uptake of
6.3 l min^{-1} (Rusko, personal communication). Some extraordinarily
high maximal oxygen uptakes of more than 7 l min^{-1} were reported in
German oarsmen by Nowacki et al. (1969, 1971). However, their
measurements may have been dominated by an overestimation of large
ventilations as oxygen uptake increased progressively with increasing
work load and were higher at altitude than at sea level.

Hagerman, Hagerman and Mickelson (1979) reported a mean value
for maximal oxygen uptake of 4.1 l min^{-1} for women and 5.1 l min^{-1} for
light-weight rowers. Values for maximal oxygen uptake in oarsmen
have also been related to success in rowing competitions and experience. Grujić et al. (1987b) reported values of 3.8 l min^{-1} for beginners,
4.3 l min^{-1} for rowers with 3–4 years of experience, 4.9 l min^{-1} for
nationally competitive oarsmen and 5.3 l min^{-1} for oarsmen who were
competing on an international level. Accordingly, Secher et al. (1983)

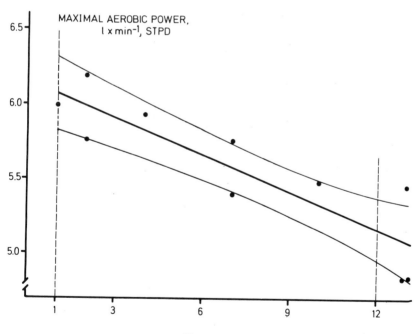

Figure 9.7 Regression line between average maximal oxygen uptake of a crew
and its placing in an international championship regatta (1971). The 95%
confidence limits of the regression line are also shown. (This figure is published
with kind permission of *Journal of Sports Sciences*.)

found internationally competitive oarsmen who had won a medal to have an average maximal oxygen uptake of 5.9 l min⁻¹ whereas less-successful oarsmen had a maximal oxygen uptake of only 5.6 l min⁻¹. Furthermore, a direct relationship has been established between results obtained in a FISA championship (1971) and the average maximal oxygen uptake of the crew (Figure 9.7, Secher *et al.*, 1982b), the winning crew having an average maximal oxygen uptake of 6.1 l min⁻¹. The literature on maximal oxygen uptake of rowers is summarized in Table 9.2. The values are dominated by the work of Hagerman *et al.* (1978, 1979) and may be too high to represent the typical rower competing on a national level. In these oarsmen a value of less than 6 l min⁻¹ seems more appropriate (Secher *et al.*, 1983; Grujić *et al.*, 1987b).

Although several studies have followed oarsmen during training for competitive rowing (Bloomfield and Roberts, 1972; Wright, Bompa and Shepard, 1976; Secher *et al.*, 1982a; Hagerman and Staron, 1983; Mahler, Nelson and Hagerman, 1984; Grujić *et al.*, 1987a) the results have not been related to the applied training programmes. An attempt to do this was made by K. Jensen and Å. Fiskestrand (Secher, 1988) who followed a group of Danish and Norwegian oarsmen. While the Danish group interrupted their aerobic training and focused on anaerobic training before each competition during the summer, the Norwegian group continued aerobic training throughout the summer. It appeared that work capacity on a rowing ergometer and maximal oxygen uptake did not increase in the Danish group while both increased markedly in the Norwegian oarsmen.

Altitude training has remained popular among some rowers even before competitions taking place at sea level. This is true despite the fact that the only controlled study on the effect of altitude training (Adams *et al.*, 1975) showed no effect of altitude training on maximal oxygen uptake beyond that obtained during training at sea level. It appears that the increase in maximal oxygen uptake which takes place after altitude training in untrained subjects is not seen in well-trained subjects (Figure 9.8). Accordingly, no effect on power during ergometer rowing or maximal oxygen uptake was found in oarsmen after altitude training. On the contrary, a control group training at sea level and following a similar training programme, did show an increase in maximal oxygen uptake (Figure 9.8, Jensen and Secher, 1986).

It seems more meaningful to express maximal oxygen uptake for oarsmen in terms of l min⁻¹ than relating the values obtained to the oarsmen's body weight (ml kg⁻¹ min⁻¹) because the rower's body weight is supported in the boat. When successful and less-successful oarsmen were compared (Secher *et al*, 1983), the two groups had a similar maximal oxygen uptake of 63–67 ml kg⁻¹ min⁻¹, but the better oarsmen had higher values in terms of l min⁻¹ reflecting their body

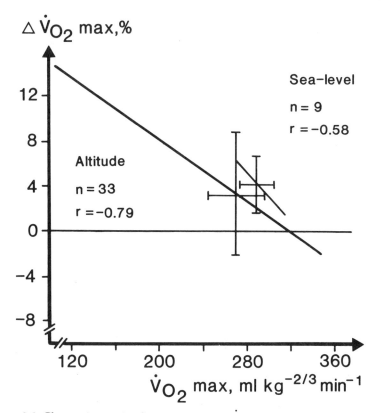

Figure 9.8 Change in maximal oxygen uptake ($\dot{V}O_{2max}$) after altitude training as indicated in the literature and in a group of oarsmen training at sea level. Changes related to the subjects' maximal oxygen uptake before the sojourn to altitude. Also shown are mean values ± SD for the groups training at altitude and sea-level.

mass of 93 kg as compared to 84 kg. Furthermore, the relationship between placing in an international competition and the team's average maximal oxygen uptake (Figure 9.7) could not be established on the basis of values expressed relative to body mass (Secher, Vaage and Jackson, 1982b).

When expressed neutral or normalized to body dimensions (Figure 9.3), oarsmen have a maximal oxygen uptake of approximately 300 ml kg$^{-2/3}$ min^{-1} (Secher *et al.*, 1983) whereas the best professional athletes may have values as high as 366 ml kg$^{-2/3}$ min^{-1} (Mikkelsen, 1980). The present winners weighing 92 kg and light-weights should, therefore, be able to attain values of 7.5 and 6.2 l min^{-1}, respectively. For female cross-country skiers Åstrand and Rodahl (1977) reported values of 3.8 l min^{-1} in 53 kg athletes. This implies that 79 kg oarswomen should be able to have maximal oxygen uptakes of 5.0 l min^{-1}. Human capability should, therefore, make a further increase in rowing performance possible.

ACKNOWLEDGEMENTS

The author's studies have mainly been supported by the Danish Sports Research Council.

REFERENCES

Adams, W.C., Bernauer, E.M., Dill, D.B. and Bomar, J.B. (1975) Effects of equivalent sea-level and altitude training on $\dot{V}O_{2max}$ and running performance. *Journal of Applied Physiology*, **39**, 262–266.

Allenberg, K., Holmquist, N., Johnsen, S.G., Bennet, E.P., Nielsen, J., Galbo, H. and Secher, N.H. (1983) Effect of exercise and testosterone on the active form of glycogen synthase in human skeletal muscle, in *Biochemistry of Exercise* (eds H.G. Knuttgen, J.A. Vogel and J. Poortsmans) Human Kinetics Publishers, Champaign, pp. 625–630.

Asami, T., Adachi, N., Yamamoto, K., Ikuta, K. and Takahashi, K. (1978) Biomechanical analysis of rowing skill, in *Biomechanics VI–B* (eds E. Asmussen and K. Jørgensen), University Park Press, Baltimore, pp. 109–114.

Asami, T., Yamamoto, K., Matsuno, A. and Fukunaga, T. (1985) Some biomechanical factors of rowing performance, in *Biomechanics IX* (eds D.A. Winter, R.W. Norman, P.P. Wells, K.C. Hayes and A.E. Patla) Human Kinetics Publishers, Champaign, pp. 477–480.

Asmussen, E. and Heebøll-Nielsen, K. (1961) Isometric strength of adult men and women. *Communication from the Danish National Association for Infantile Paralysis*, **11**.

Åstrand, P.O. and Rodahl, K. (1977) *Textbook of Work Physiology*, McGraw-Hill, New York, p. 409.

Balukow, C.N. (1964) Hydrodynamische Charakteristik der Sport-Ruderboote (German translation by E. Schatté). *Katera i Yachti*, **3**, 187–191.

Bang, O. (1935) *Mælskesyren i blodet ved muskelarbejde* (in Danish). Levin and Munksgaard, Copenhagen.

Bloomfield, J. and Roberts, A.D. (1972) A correlational and trend analysis of strength and aerobic power scores in the prediction of rowing performance. *The Australian Journal of Sports Medicine*, **4**, 25–36.

Bouckaert, J., Pannier, J.L. and Vrijens, J. (1983) Cardiorespiratory response to bicycle and rowing ergometer exercise in oarsmen. *European Journal of Applied Physiology*, **51**, 51–59.

Burnell, R.D. (1955) *Sculling with Notes on Training and Rigging*. Oxford University Press, London.

Carey, P., Stensland, M. and Hartley, L.H. (1974) Comparison of oxygen uptake during maximal work on the treadmill and rowing ergometer. *Medicine and Science in Sports*, **6**, 101–103.

Celentano, F., Cortili, G., Di Prampero, P.E. and Cerretelli, P. (1974) Mechanical aspects of rowing. *Journal of Applied Physiology*, **36**, 642–647.

Clark, J.M., Hagerman, F.C. and Gelfand, R. (1983) Breathing patterns during submaximal and maximal exercise in elite oarsmen. *Journal of Applied Physiology*, **55**, 440–446.

Clarkson, P.M., Johnson, J., Melchionda, A. and Graves, J. (1983) Isokinetic strength, fatigue, and fiber type in elite oarswomen. *Medicine and Science in Sports and Exercise*, **15**, 178 (Abstract).

Cleaver, H. (1957) *A History of Rowing.* H. Jenkins, London.

Cunningham, D.A., Goode, P.B. and Critz, J.B. (1975). Cardiorespiratory response to exercise on a rowing and bicycle ergometer. *Medicine and Science in Sports*, **7**, 37–43.

Dan, B.B. (1984) The cover. *Journal of the American Medical Association*, **252**, 452.

Di Prampero, P.E. (1986) The energy cost of human locomotion on land and in water. *International Journal of Sports Medicine*, **7**, 55–72.

Di Prampero, P.E., Cortili, G., Celentano, F. and Cerretelli, P. (1971) Physiological aspects of rowing. *Journal of Applied Physiology*, **31**, 853–857.

Dodd, C. (1983) *The Oxford & Cambridge Boat Race.* S. Paul, London.

Droghetti, P., Borsetto, C., Casoni, I., Cellini, M., Ferrari, M., Paolini, A.R., Ziglio, P.G. and Conconi, F. (1985) Noninvasive determination of the anaerobic threshold in canoeing, cross-country skiing, cycling, roller, and iceskating, rowing and walking. *European Journal of Applied Physiology*, **53**, 299–303.

Falch, D.K. and Strømme, S.B. (1979) Pulmonary blood volume and inter-ventricular circulation time in physically trained and untrained subjects. *European Journal of Applied Physiology*, **40**, 211–218.

Foley, V. and Soedel, W. (1981) Ancient oared warships. *Scientific American*, **244**, 116–128.

Fraser, T.R. (1868–1869) The effect on the circulation as shown by examination with the sphygmograph. *Journal of Anatomy and Physiology*, **3**, 127–130.

Gauthier, G.M. (1985) Visually and acoustically augmented performance feedback as an aid in motor control learning: a study of selected components of rowing action. *Journal of Sports Sciences*, **3**, 3–26.

Grujić, N., Bajic, M., Vukovic, B. and Jakovijevic, D. (1987a) Energy demand of competitive rowing. *Seventh Balkan Congress of Sports Medicine*, **112** (Abstract).

Grujić, N., Secher, N.H., Bajic, M., Turkulov, D. and Bacanovic, M. (1987b) Physiological characteristics of rowers. *Seventh Balkan Congress of Sports Medicine*, **102** (Abstract).

Haber, P. and Ferlitsch, A. (1979) Vergleichende Einschätzun des Trainings-zustandes mittels Spiroergometrischer Untersuchungen am Ruder- und Fahrraderergometer bei Rudern. *Schweiz Zeitung für Sportsmedizin*, **27**, 53–59.

Hagerman, F.C. (1984) Applied physiology of rowing. *Sports Medicine*, **1**, 303–326.

Hagerman, F.C., Connors, M.C., Gault, J.A., Hagerman, G.R. and Polinski, W.J. (1978) Energy expenditure during simulated rowing. *Journal of Applied Physiology*, **45**, 87–93.

Hagerman, F.C., Hagerman, G.R. and Mickelson, T.O. (1979) Physiological profiles of elite rowers. *The Physician and Sportsmedicine*, **7**, 74–83.

Hagerman, F.C. and Howie, G.A. (1971) Use of certain physiological variables in the selection of the 1967 New Zealand crew. *Research Quarterly*, **42**, 264–273.

Hagerman, F.C. and Lee, W.D. (1971) Measurement of oxygen consumption, heart rate, and work output during rowing. *Medicine and Science in Sports*, **3**, 155–160.

Hagerman, F.C. and Staron, R.S. (1983) Seasonal variations among physiological variables in elite oarsmen. *Canadian Journal of Applied Sports Science*, **8**, 143–8.

Hahn, A.G., Tumilty, D. McA., Shakespear, P. and Telford, R.D. (1988). Physiological testing of oarswomen on Gjessing and Concept II rowing ergometers. *Excel*, **5**, 19–22.

Hansen, K.N., Bjerre-Knudsen, J., Brodthagen, U., Jordal, R. and Paulev, P.-E. (1982) Muscle cell leakage due to long distance training. *European Journal of Applied Physiology*, **48**, 177–188.

Henderson, J.Y. and Haggard, H.W. (1925) The maximum of human power and its fuel. *American Journal of Physiology*, **72**, 264–282.

Henningsen, H. (1949) *Dystløb i danske søkøbstæder og i udlandet* (in Danish) Munksgaard, Copenhagen.

Herrick, R.F. (1948) *Red Top*. Harvard University Press, Cambridge.

Hill, A.V. (1938) The heat shortening and the dynamic constants of muscle. *Proceedings of the Royal Society B*, **126**, 136–195.

Holmqvist, N., Secher, N.H., Sander-Jensen, K., Knigge, U., Warberg, J. and Schwartz, T.W. (1986) Sympathoadrenal and parasympathetic responses to exercise. *Journal of Sports Sciences*, **4**, 123–128.

Howald, H., Maire, R., Heierli, B. and Follath, F. (1977) Echokardiographische befunde bei trainierten Sportlern. *Schweizer mediziner Wocheschrift*, **107**, 1662–1666.

Ishiko, T. (1968) Application of telemetry to sports activities, in *Biomechanics I*, Karger, Basel, pp. 138–146.

Jackson, R.C. and Secher, N.H. (1976) The aerobic demands of rowing in two Olympic oarsmen. *Medicine and Science in Sports*, **8**, 168–170.

Jensen, K. and Secher, N.H. (1986) *Højdetræning* (in Danish) (ed. L.T. Bro-Rieskov) Idrættens Forskningsråd, Copenhagen, pp. 40–43.

Jensen, K., Secher, N.H., Fiskestrand, Å., Christensen, N.J. and Lund, J.O. (1984) Influence of body weight on physiologic variables measured during maximal dynamic exercise. *Acta Physiologica Scandinavica*, **121**, 39A (Abstract).

Keul, J., Dickhuth, H.-H., Lehmann, M. and Staiger, J. (1982) The athlete's heart – haemodynamics and structure. *International Journal of Sports Medicine*, **3**, 33–43.

Kiesling, S. (1982) *The Shell Game*. W. Morrow, New York.

Kjær, M., Farrel, P.A., Christensen, N.J. and Galbo, H. (1986) Increased epinephrine response and inaccurate glucoregulation in exercising athletes. *Journal of Applied Physiology*, **61**, 1693–1700.

Klausen, K., Secher, N.H., Clausen, J.P., Hartling, O. and Trap-Jensen, J. (1982) Central and regional circulatory adaptations to one-leg training. *Journal of Applied Physiology*, **52**, 976–983.

Körner, T. and Schwanitz, P. (eds) (1985) *Rudern*, Śportverlag, Berlin.

Koutedakis, Y. and Sharp, N.C.C. (1985) Lactic acid removal and heart rate frequencies during recovery after strenuous rowing exercise. *British Journal of Sports Medicine*, **19**, 199–202.

Koutedakis, Y. and Sharp, N.C.C. (1986) A modified Wingate test for measuring anaerobic work of the upper body in junior rowers. *British Journal of Sports Medicine*, **20**, 153–156.

Larsson, B., Larsen, J., Modest, R., Serup, B. and Secher, N.H. (1988) A new kayak ergometer based on wind resistance. *Ergonomics*, **31**, 1701–1707.

Larsson, L. and Forsberg, A. (1980) Morphological muscle characteristics in rowers. *Canadian Journal of Applied Sport Science*, **5**, 239–244.

Liljestrand, G. and Lindhard, J. (1920) Zur Physiologie des Ruderns. *Skandinavishe Archiv für Physiologi*, **39**, 215–235.

Longhurst, J.C., Kelly, A.R., Gonyea, N.J. and Mitchell, J.H. (1980) Echocardiographic left ventricular masses in distance runners and weight-lifters. *Journal of Applied Physiology*, **48**, 154–162.

Mahler, D.A., Andrea, B.E. and Andresen, D.C. (1984) Comparison of six-minute 'all-out' and incremental exercise tests in elite oarsmen. *Medicine and Science in Sports and Exercise*, **16**, 567–571.

Mahler, D.A., Nelson, W.N. and Hagerman, F.C. (1984) Mechanical and physiological evaluation of exercise performance in elite national rowers. *Journal of the American Medical Association*, **252**, 496–499.

Martin, T.P. and Bernfield, J.S. (1980) Effect of stroke rate on velocity of a rowing shell. *Medicine and Science in Sports and Exercise*, **12**, 250–256.

Mason, B.R., Shakespear, P. and Doherty, P. (1988) The use of biomechanical analysis in rowing to monitor the effect of training. *Excel*, **4**, 7–11.

McMahon, T.A. (1971) Rowing: a similarity analysis. *Science*, **173**, 349–351.

Medbø, J.I., Mohn, A.-C., Tabata, I., Bahr, R., Vaage, O. and Sejersted, O.M. (1988) Anaerobic capacity determined by maximal accumulated O_2 deficit. *Journal of Applied Physiology*, **64**, 50–60.

Mellerowizt, H. von and Hansen, G. (1965) Sauerstoffkapazität und andere spiroergometrische Maksimalwerte der Ruder-Olympiasieger in Virer mit St. vom Berliner Ruderclub. *Sportssarzt und Sportsmedizin*, **16**, 188–191.

Mickelson, T.C. and Hagerman, F.C (1982) Anaerobic threshold measurements of elite oarsmen. *Medicine and Science in Sports*, **14**, 440–444.

Mikkelsen, F. (1980) *Eneren Ørsted*, Centrum, Copenhagen.

Mortensen, J., Groth, S., Lange, P., Rasmussen, B., Larsen, J. and Secher, N.H. (1987) State of physical training after rowing for 41 days in the Atlantic Ocean. *Ugeskrift for Læger*, **149**, 2851–2852.

Nowacki, P., Krause, R. and Adam, K. (1969) Maximale Sauerstoffaufnahme bei Olympiasiegern im Rudern 1968. *Pflügers Archiv*, **312**, R66–R67 (Abstract).

Nowacki, P.E., Adam, K., Krause, R. and Ritter, U. (1971) Die Spiroergometric in neuen Untersuchungssystem für den Spitzensport. *Rudersport*, **26**, I–VI.

Rasmussen, B.S., Hanel, B., Jensen, K., Serup, B. and Secher, N.H. (1986) Decrease in pulmonary diffusion capacity after maximal exercise. *Journal of Sports Sciences*, **4**, 185–188.

Renold, A.E., Quigley, T.B., Kennard, H.E. and Thorn, G.W. (1951) Reaction of the adrenal cortex to physical and emotional stress in College oarsmen. *New England Journal of Medicine*, **244**, 754–757.

Roth, W., Hasart, E., Wolf, W. and Pansold, B. (1983) Untersuchungen zur Dynamik der Energiebereitstellung während maximaler Mittelzeitausdauerbelastung. *Medicin und Sport*, **23**, 107–114.

Sanderson, B. and Martindale, W. (1986) Towards optimizing rowing technique. *Medicine and Science in Sports and Exercise*, **18**, 454–468.

Schneider, E. (1980) *Leistungsanalyse bei Rudermannschaften*. Limpert Verlag, Bad Homburg.

Schwartz, T.W. (1983) Pancreatic polypeptide: a hormone under vagal control. *Gastroenterology*, **85**, 1411–1425.

Secher, K.(1921) Experimentelle Untersuchungen über den Einfluss der Anstrengungen auf die Grösse des Herzens. *Zeitschrift für die gesamte Experimentelle Medizin*, **14**, 113–129.

Secher, K. (1923) Experimentelle Untersuchungen über die Grösse des Hertzens nach einem Aufhören des Trainierens. *Zeitschrift für die gesamte Experimentelle Medizin*, **32**, 290–295.

Secher, N.H. (1973) Results in international rowing championships 1893–1971. *Medicine and Science in Sports*, **5**, 195–199.

Secher, N.H. (1975) Isometric rowing strength of experienced and inexperienced oarsmen. *Medicine and Science in Sports*, **7**, 280–283.

Secher, N.H. (1983) The physiology of rowing. *Journal of Sports Sciences*, **1**, 23–53.

Secher, N.H. (1988) Idrætstræning (in Danish) *Månedskrift for Praktisk Lægegerning*, **66**, 167–176.

Secher, N.H., Clausen, J.P., Klausen, K., Noer, I. and Trap-Jensen, J. (1977) Central and regional circulatory effects of adding arm exercise to leg exercise. *Acta Physiological Scandinavica*, **100**, 288–297.

Secher, N.H., Espersen, M., Binkhorst, R.A., Andersen, P.A. and Rube, N. (1982a) Aerobic power at the onset of maximal exercise. *Scandinavian Journal of Sports Science*, **4**, 12–16.

Secher, N.H., Rube, N. and Elers, J. (1988) Strength of two and one leg extension in man. *Acta Physiologica Scandinavica*, in press.

Secher, N.H., Ruberg-Larsen, N., Binkhorst, R.A. and Bonde-Petersen, F. (1974) Maximal oxygen uptake during arm cranking and combined arm plus leg exercise. *Journal of Applied Physiology*, **36**, 515–518.

Secher, N.H. and Vaage, O. (1983) Rowing performance, a mathematical model based on analysis of body dimensions as exemplified by body weight. *European Journal of Applied Physiology*, **52**, 88–93.

Secher, N.H., Vaage, O. and Jackson, R.C. (1982b) Rowing performance and maximal oxygen uptake in oarsmen. *Scandinavian Journal of Sports Science*, **4**, 9–11.

Secher, N.H., Vaage, O., Jensen, K. and Jackson, R.C. (1983) Maximal oxygen uptake in oarsmen. *European Journal of Applied Physiology*, **51**, 155–162.

Stein, T.P., Settle, R.G., Howard, K.A. and Diamond, C.E. (1983) Protein turnover and physical fitness in man. *Biochemical Medicine*, **29**, 207–213.

Steinacker, J.M., Marx, U., Grünert, M., Lomert, W. and Wodick, R.E. (1985) Vergleichsuntersuchungen über den Zweistufentest und den Mehrstufentest bei der Ruderspiroergometrie. *Leistungssport*, **3**, 47–51.

Strømme, S.B., Ingjer, F. and Meen, H.D. (1977) Assessment of maximal aerobic power in specifically trained athletes. *Journal of Applied Physiology*, **42**, 833–837.

Sutton, J.R., Coleman, M.J., Casey, J. and Lazarus, L. (1973) Androgen responses during physical exercise. *British Medical Journal*, **i**, 520–522.

Szögy, A. and Cherebetiu, G. (1974) Physical work capacity testing in male performance rowers with practical conclusions for their training. *Journal of Sports Medicine and Physical Fitness*, **14**, 218–223.

Touny, A.D. and Wenig, S. (1969) *Sports in Ancient Egypt*. Edition Leipzig, Leipzig.

Tumilty, D., Hahn, A. and Telford, R. (1987) Effect of test protocol, ergometer type and state of training on peak oxygen uptake in rowers. *Excel*, **3**, 12–14.

Vaage, O. (1977) Table 16–2 in *Textbook of Work Physiology* (eds P.-O. Åstrand and K. Rodahl), McGraw-Hill, New York.

Vaage, O. and Hermansen, L. (1977) Figure 11–4 in *Textbook of Work Physiology* (eds P.-O. Åstrand and K. Rodahl), McGraw-Hill, New York.

Wahlqvist, B. (1978) *Barsk Idræt* (in Danish), Hamlet, Copenhagen.

Wellicome, J.F. (1967) Some hydrodynamic aspects of rowing, in *Rowing: A Scientific Approach* (eds A.C. Scott and J.G.P. Williams), Kaye and Ward, London, pp. 22–63.

Wright, G.R., Bompa, T. and Shepard, R.J. (1976) Physiological evaluation of winter training programme for oarsmen. *Journal of Sports Medicine and Physical Fitness*, **16**, 22–37.

Yamakawa, J. and Ishiko, T. (1966) Standardization of physical fitness test for oarsmen, in *Proceedings of the International Congress on Sports Sciences* (ed. K. Kato), Japanese University of Sports Sciences, Tokyo, pp. 435–436.

Ziffren, P. (1984) (ed.) *Olympic Record*. Los Angeles Olympic Organizing Committee, Los Angeles.

Zsidegh, M., Apor, P. and Bretz, K. (1979) Zum Einfluss des Ruderrhythmus auf motorische und kardiorespiratorische Parameter. *Leistungssport*, **9**, 448.

10
Sailing

Roy J. Shephard

10.1 INTRODUCTION

With the exception of a French symposium (Prevot and Auvinet, 1981), relatively few physiologists have studied the demands of sailing. The statement of Durnin and Passmore (1967) still seems true:

> We know of no-one who has measured the energy cost of any of the many different activities in which a yachtsman is employed . . . Most yachtsmen probably find that their recreation provides them with exercise of a light grade, but with occasional periods of moderate or heavy exercise.

The lack of interest in this activity seems due to its supposed low energy cost. However, national competitors rightly insist that sailing can be hard physical work, particularly in a high wind, and formal electromyographic studies (Vrijens, personal communication; Rogge, 1973; Beillot et al., 1979, 1981) have shown very vigorous sustained contraction of the thigh and abdominal muscles during 'hiking' (the process of counter-balancing a boat by leaning over the side of the deck). Sailing differs from most of the sports discussed in this volume, since we are dealing with a human–machine system, where the primary energy sources (winds and currents) lie outside of the body (Gabillard, 1981). Apparently advantageous characteristics of the human operator (strong arms for operating the controls, long leverage for counter-balancing the craft) may nevertheless have a negative influence on the overall performance of the human–machine system (by increasing water or wind resistance, for example). Sailing also places unusual demands on the brain. While gusts and squalls may require rapid decisions, faults in forward planning have adverse consequences for performance at a much later stage in a race. Moreover, the behaviour of opponents must be predicted far into the future. Some sailing events continue for many

Table 10.1 Categories of boat permitted in Olympic sailing competitions

Category	Length (m)	Mass (kg)	Sail area (m²)	Type of rig	Counterweight	Crew
Board sailor	(windsurfer)					
Finn	4.50	319	114	Mainsail	Keel	1
	4.77	250	277 (137+140)	Centre-attached sail	Centreboard	1
470				Mainsail+ spinnaker	Centreboard	2*
Flying Dutchman	6.04	364	390 (200+190)	Mainsail+ spinnaker	Centreboard	2*
Tornado (Catamaran)	6.10	280	235	Mainsail	Centreboard	2
Star	6.91	1460	285	Mainsail	Keel	2
Soling	8.15	2234	588 (233+355)	Mainsail+ spinnaker	Keel	3

*Trapeze seating for one crew member.

days, raising problems of circadian variations in physical and mental performance. Finally, water is a hostile medium, presenting risks of rapid death from hypothermia or drowning.

As with many other sports, it is wrong to look for a single optimal physiological profile. A solo transatlantic crossing demands very different characteristics from a dinghy race on a summer afternoon. Likewise, the classes of boat to which the sailor must be matched vary in their length, mass, sail-area, rig, type of keel and number of crew (Table 10.1). Lastly, as the wind freshens the primary task of the human operator shifts from the mental processes of complex reasoning to the physical requirements of handling ropes and counterbalancing the boat.

10.2 MECHANICS OF SAILING

The resistance to forward movement of a yacht is quite complex. Elements to be overcome include viscous resistance (motion of water of the wetted hull and of air over the sails, rigging and crew-members), induced drag (because pressure is higher on one side of a foil than the other), form drag (due to the shape of the vessel), wave resistance (Secher *et al.*, 1983; Scott and Williams, 1967), and (particularly in estuaries) tides and currents. At low speeds, friction is usually the dominant force that impedes displacement relative to the water, but as speed increases, the resistance due to wave formation rises rapidly. Thus, all boats have a maximum speed to length ratio of 1.34. Friction normally varies as the square of the velocity, although it also depends on the mass of the system, on the roughness of the hull and on the wetted area. Resistance is increased further by localized turbulence of the water around the keel and rudder and of the air around rigging and crew.

Overall resistance increases approximately as the square of the mass of boat plus crew. In heavy, fixed-keel vessels such as the Star and the Soling, the crew contribute relatively little to the total mass, but in craft such as the Finn and the 470, the crew account for up to a third of the total. More sail can be carried by a heavier crew, but this advantage is sometimes offset by a greater frictional resistance.

10.3 PHYSIOLOGICAL DEMANDS AND OPTIMUM PROFILE

10.3.1 Defining the optimum profile

The optimum profile of a sailor can be determined roughly by discussion with national and provincial coaches. More precise information can be

Table 10.2 Matrix showing correlations between competitive standings, captain's ranking of sailing ability and average rating by fellow crew-members. Correlations poorer than 0.50 have been omitted for clarity. Based on data of Niinimaa et al. (1977) for Ontario Provincial Sailing Team

	1	2	3	4	5	6	7	8	9	10	11	12
Competitive Standing												
1. International competitions with high wind	1.00	0.67	0.89	0.67	0.62	0.56	0.50	0.67	0.53	0.69		
2. with light wind		1.00	0.54	0.90			0.66	0.78			0.69	0.65
3. Regional Competitions with high wind			1.00	0.55								
4. with light wind				1.00	0.59	0.54	0.77	0.84		0.61	0.71	0.67
Captain's ranking of ability												
5. High wind conditions					1.00			0.87	0.65			
6. Resistance to mental fatigue						1.00	0.87	0.81	0.53	0.82	0.73	0.79
7. Light wind conditions							1.00	0.96		0.81	0.92	0.90
8. Overall sailing ability								1.00		0.83	0.90	0.92
Peer ranking of ability												
9. High wind conditions									1.00	0.80		
10. Resistance to mental fatigue										1.00	0.64	0.76
11. Light wind conditions											1.00	0.95
12. Overall sailing ability												1.00

obtained from regression equations relating the various physiological variables to international standings, and to ratings of sailing ability made by the team captain or individual crew members. Characteristics of winning teams can be compared with population data for the same variables (Niinimaa *et al.*, 1977; Plyley, Davis and Shephard, 1985). Finally, data for wind speed and currents can be fed into a computer, and the observed trajectory of the boat can be compared with a theoretical optimum (Gabillard, 1981).

Comparing the rankings of sailing ability made by the team captain with the averaged peer ratings of individual crew members (Table 10.2), Niinimaa *et al.* (1977) observed a satisfactory correlation for each of four criteria (ability in a high wind, $r = 0.87$; ability to resist mental fatigue, $r = 0.82$; ability in a light wind, $r = 0.92$; overall ability, $r = 0.92$). The best predictor of success in either international or regional competition was the captain's ranking of overall ability. Both captain and crew apparently took more notice of light than of high-wind performance when ranking overall sailing ability.

10.3.2 Physical characteristics

When asked to name the five best Provincial sailors, the Ontario team

Table 10.3 Profile of successful sailor, as identified by captain of Ontario sailing team. Physical and physiological characteristics relative to other members of Provincial team. Based on data of Niinimaa *et al.* (1977a)

	Five best team members	Average team member
Physical characteristics		
Competitive experience (years)	9.4	8.2
Age (years)	26.4	26.5
Height (cm)	182.0	181.5
Body mass (kg)	83.9	84.0
Body fat (%)	17.9	19.9
Physiological characteristics		
Maximum oxygen intake (l min^{-1})	4.40	4.16
Anaerobic endurance (s at 9.6 km h^{-1}, 20% slope)	109.5*	65.1
Forearm extension force (N at 90°, supine)	463	374
Forearm flexion force (N at 90°, supine)	490	452
Knee extension force (N at 135°, seated)	1064	1044
Knee extension endurance (s at 50% max force)	137.2	83.7
Stabilometer balance (s out of 180 s)	134.1	123.4

*$P < 0.001$.

captain named four of the same individuals for both low and high wind conditions. It is possible to bring out his perception of the successful competitor by comparing team averages with data for the better competitors (Table 10.3). The only distinguishing physical characteristic was a lower percentage of body fat than in some other team members. This may reflect (1) a limited difference of competitive ability among the Provincial team, (2) a focusing of perceptions on performance under light wind conditions (when mental attributes are more important than the physical or the physiological profile), and (3) lack of sufficient numbers to classify subjects by type of boat and crew position.

Comparisons with the national population as examined in the Canada Fitness Survey are more revealing (Table 10.4). Both Provincial and National teams in Canada were somewhat taller and heavier than the average person; they were also heavier than other sailors, including Japanese candidates for the Tokyo Olympic Games (62.4 kg, Ishiko, 1967), a group of 26 Czechoslovak national yachtsmen (73.9 kg, Vank, 1969), points winners in the Rome Olympics (77.2 kg, Gedda, Milani-Comparetti and Brenci, 1968) and participants in the Montreal Olympics, (Table 10.5, Hirata, 1979). Interestingly, gold medal winners in Montreal were taller, rather than heavier than the average participants. However, many sailors still deliberately add to their natural mass by soaking the upper half of a thick sweater with water, or carrying ballast bags of water around the chest (up to 10 kg is permitted under international regulations, Gouard, 1981). Much of the excess mass of the Canadian teams relative to actuarial standards was fat. The estimated percentage

Table 10.4 Physical characteristics of sailors (based on data of Niinimaa *et al.*, 1977a, Plyley, Davis and Shephard, 1985, Ishiko, 1967, and Vank, 1969)

Variable	Ontario team	Canadian team	Canada Fitness Survey	Japanese team	Czech team
Age (years)	26.5 ± 9.1	28.1 ± 6.0	20–30		
Height (cm)	181.5 ± 5.0	180.2 ± 6.4	175.4	168.6	175.6
Sitting height (cm)	94.7 ± 3.1				
Centre of gravity					
(cm from floor)	101.4 ± 4.9				
(% of stature)	55.8 ± 1.6				
Body mass (kg)	84.4 ± 6.7	79.1 ± 11.2	74.1	62.4	73.9
Excess mass (kg)	12.1 ± 6.1				
Estimated body fat (%)	19.9 ± 4.9	17.7 ± 4.3	20.6		
Shoulder width (cm)	41.2 ± 2.1				
Hip width (cm)	35.5 ± 1.2				
Quadriceps girth (cm)	47.0 ± 2.8				

Table 10.5 Physical characteristics of sailors, classified by type of boat and crew position (based on data of Plyley, Davis and Shephard, 1985 and Hirata, 1979)

Category of craft	Canadian Team				Participants in Montreal Olympics					
	Height (cm)		Body mass (kg)		Body Fat (%)		Height (cm)		Body mass (kg)	
	Skipper	Crew	Skipper	Crew	Skipper	Crew	Skipper	Crew	Skipper	Crew
Board Sailors (windsurfers)	—	172.3	—	65.7	—	14.3	—	—	—	—
Finn	—	187.7	—	85.6	—	16.5	—	182.0	—	83.0
470	177.5	178.2	70.4	69.7	13.0	14.3	175.4	174.6	68.0	68.0
Flying Dutchman	181.6	183.7	74.8	85.4	14.3	20.0	177.8	183.2	73.8	83.2
Tornado	182.1	178.5	65.9	75.5	14.0	21.7	177.8	178.2	74.0	71.0
Star	183.1	179.9	91.1	86.5	16.5	16.0				
Soling	175.5	182.6	82.9	93.0	24.0	20.9	181.0	179.5	80.5	81.0

of body fat was higher than in most classes of athlete, almost matching that reported for the general population in the Canada Fitness Survey (1983). Indeed, the thickness of eight skinfolds averaged 3 mm more than we have found in the average 25-year-old Toronto male (Shephard *et al.*, 1969).

The Canadian team coach perceived the ideal body mass to be less than 60 kg for the skipper, and more than 80 kg for the crew of 2–3 person boats. His ratings of the sailing performance of individual crews corresponded well with the adherence of teams to this pattern (Plyley, Davis and Shephard, 1985). Data for the Canadian National team and for other participants in the Montreal Olympics (Table 10.5) showed that on average the skippers were some 0.8 cm shorter, but only 5.0 kg lighter than crew members. In the lightest type of boat (470 class), both skipper and crew were lighter than the team average, whereas in the heavy Star class both crew members were heavy. In the Finn class (where a single sailor both steered and counterbalanced a short and light boat), height and body mass were much greater than for the 470 teams (where similar duties were shared between skipper and crew). In the inherently more stable twin-hulled Tornado class, both skipper and crew had a relatively light body mass. Body fat was on average 2.2% greater for the crew than for the skipper, particularly high values being observed for team members operating the Flying Dutchman, Tornado and Soling classes of boat (Table 10.5).

Normal values for many detailed anthropometric measurements are not widely available. The centre of gravity for the sailors (55.8% of the distance from the floor to the top of the cranium) was only marginally higher than for oarsmen (55.4%). A normal figure of 55.3% is cited by the Bio-Astronautics data book (Webb, 1964). University swimmers of almost identical overall height (Shephard, Godin and Campbell, 1973) showed a slightly shorter sitting height than the sailors (95.0 cm), but a greater shoulder width (43.1 cm), hip width (28.5 cm) and quadriceps girth (54.2 cm).

One might have anticipated that broad shoulders and a high centre of gravity would confer greater competitive advantage than a substantial body mass, since frictional resistance is proportional to $mass^2$ (Secher *et al.*, 1983) or $mass^{5/3}$ (Scott and Williams, 1967). However, in practice this does not seem to be the case. Data for the Ontario sailing team showed no correlations between either peer rankings or competitive success and such factors as body mass or height of the centre of gravity (Niinimaa *et al.*, 1977), while in the Montreal Olympics the gold medal winners were only 4 cm taller than the average competitors. Possibly, the very tall and thin person lacks the abdominal musculature necessary to support his or her theoretical advantage of moment during 'hiking'. Height may also be a disadvantage when changing position in a vessel.

10.3.3 Physiological demands of 'hiking'

'Hiking' demands a sustained isometric contraction of muscles on the anterior side of the body (Vrijens, personal communication; Rogge, 1973; Beillot *et al.*, 1979, 1981); the relative distribution of this demand between the quadriceps and the abdominal muscles can nevertheless be varied by attaching 'planchettes' of foam rubber to the posterior aspects of the thighs (Beillot *et al.*, 1981). The toe-strap rapidly causes ischaemia of the feet, to the point that Gouard (1981) has proposed wearing shoes with a rigid top. Blood flow is also restricted in the active muscles; the classical studies by Monod and Scherrer (1957), Royce (1958) and Rohmert (1960) have shown a progressive decrease in the perfusion of any muscle group if contraction is sustained at more than 15% of its maximum voluntary force. In an attempt to maintain perfusion there is a tachycardia, and blood pressure rises.

Niinimaa *et al.* (1977) simulated the 'hiking' manoeuvre in the laboratory. While heart rate and blood pressure rose steadily, even after five minutes the average increase of heart rate (to 137 beats min^{-1}) and blood pressure (to 198/134 mm Hg) were less than the figures observed if a quadriceps contraction was held at 40% of maximum force to the breaking point. Nevertheless, the manoeuvre induced an appreciable rise of blood glucose from 87 to 116 mg dl^{-1} (5.0 to 6.5 mM) and a decrease of serum bicarbonate (from 27.4 to 21.0 mμM).

The heart rates observed in actual sailing are quite variable (Bachemont *et al.*, 1981). On a 470 class craft, 15% of readings for the skipper, and 25% of those for the crew exceed 130 beats min^{-1}; rates drop as low as 100 beats min^{-1} while running free, but reach 140 beats min^{-1} while 'hiking'.

10.3.4 Muscle strength, endurance, flexibility and balance

The cardiovascular response to sustained isometric contraction is proportional to the percentage of maximal force which is exerted. If a sailor has strong leg and abdominal muscles, the cardiovascular penalty involved in 'hiking' should be less. Muscular development in the upper half of the body should also be helpful in counterbalancing a boat.

In keeping with these expectations, isometric strength is well developed in sailors. The average knee extension force for the Ontario team (1044 N, Niinimaa *et al.*, 1977) was much higher than that for oarsmen (741 N, Wright, Bompa and Shephard, 1975) or swimmers (720 N, Shephard, Godin and Campbell, 1973). The average handgrip force (567 N for the Canadian National Team, 610 N for the Provincial

Team) was also higher than for either the average young man (533 N, Canada Fitness Survey, 1983) or many classes of athlete (Shephard, 1978). On the other hand, values for forearm flexion (452 N) and extension (374 N) were less than in swimmers (Shephard, Godin and Campbell, 1973), oarsmen (Wright, Bompa and Shephard, 1975) and paddlers (Sidney and Shephard, 1973). Peer rankings of performance in high winds were quite closely correlated with maximal isometric force measures ($r = 0.63$ for forearm extension, $r = 0.75$ for knee extension and $r = 0.81$ for a summated muscle force index).

Dynamic force is less important to the sailor than a sustained isometric effort. It is thus understandable that isokinetic forces were not remarkable. Plyley, Davis and Shephard (1985) observed a peak isokinetic knee flexion torque of 85.7 Nm at a speed of 3.14 rad s^{-1} (180 degrees s^{-1}). This score is of the order anticipated for orienteers and alpine skiers, but is less than that found among runners and badminton players, and is much less than that for rowers. Likewise, the peak isokinetic extension torque (107.7 Nm) is comparable with that for swimmers and orienteers, less than that for badminton players, and much less than that for rowers and alpine skiers.

The muscular endurance of the sailor is well developed. Niinimaa et al. (1977) reported an ability to carry out an average of 42.6 bent-knee sit-ups in one minute, and Plyley, Davis and Shephard (1985) noted 51.7 sit-ups compared with norms of 30 for a YMCA population (Métivier and Orban, 1971) and 25 for the Canada Fitness Survey (1983). Likewise, the decrease in force for repeated contractions (isokinetic knee flexion 40.3%, isokinetic knee extension 50.0%, rhythmic arm pull 34.0%) was less than for other classes of athlete. The endurance times for isometric contractions of the knee (Niinimaa et al., 1977) conformed closely with the author's normal curve (Shephard, 1974), although the times reported by Monod and Scherrer (1957) and Rohmert (1960) were somewhat exceeded. Perhaps because it is rare to use more than 50% of quadriceps force in 'hiking', correlations with performance were greater for 50% than for 75% endurance times. The endurance at 50% of maximum force showed a correlation of 0.65 with the captain's ranking under light wind conditions, 0.67 with the ranking for high wind, and 0.55 with the ranking for mental fatigue.

Flexibility is helpful when changing positions quickly, as the boat 'goes about' at the end of a tack. Gouard (1981) suggested that the flexibility of the ankle joint was particularly important, although no figures were presented to support this contention. Plyley, Davis and Shephard (1985) measured static hip flexibility, using the 'sit and reach' test of Wells and Dillon (1952) (Table 10.6). Values were generally well-developed relative to population norms for young men, the Canada Fitness Survey finding an average of 30.7 cm for the same test.

Table 10.6 Strength and flexibility of Canadian National Sailing team, classified by crew position and type of vessel (based on data of Plyley, Davis and Shephard, 1985)

Category of craft	Handgrip force (N)		Speed set-ups (n min^{-1})		Upper body peak force (N)		Flexibility (cm)	
	Skipper	Crew	Skipper	Crew	Skipper	Crew	Skipper	Crew
Board Sailor (windsurfer)		493		49		341		31.7
Finn		611		62		334		37.0
470	579	584	57	59	325	343	42.9	44.9
Flying Dutchman	552	582	54	52	340	354	54.2	43.9
Tornado	540	540	45	47	331	350	29.0	33.9
Star	618	647			374	350	47.9	
Soling	530	601	53	46	345	363	33.5	40.7

Balance is also an important attribute, particularly when sailing the smaller craft. Scores for one simple measure of balance (the stork stand) lay at the 56th percentile of normal values for young men (Niinimaa *et al.*, 1977). A second measure of balance was obtained by means of a stabilometer; the sailors were able to keep the platform clear of the ground for 123 of 180 seconds, compared with 112 of 180 seconds for oarsmen. Scores for both the stork stand and the stabilometer were correlated with competitive success ($r = 0.66$ and 0.72 respectively).

Relating these various scores to the individual's task, (Plyley, Davis and Shephard, 1985), the skipper had a somewhat weaker handgrip than crew members (Table 10.6), particularly among those operating the two heaviest classes of vessel (Star and Soling). Muscular endurance, as shown by the number of speed sit-ups was especially well-developed in the crew of lighter vessels (Finn and 470). The upper body peak force (measured by pulling against a loaded rope, using a 'swim-bench') did not show any great differentiation between team members, although there was some tendency to greater strength among the crew of the heavier boats. Flexibility was high in the crew of the smaller craft, with particularly outstanding values for both skipper and crew of the Flying Dutchman.

10.3.5 Anaerobic and aerobic performance

The average endurance time for a 'supra-maximal' treadmill test was related to performance under high wind conditions, respective co-efficients of correlation for international and regional competition (Niinimaa *et al.*, 1977) being 0.59 and 0.69. Peak lactate concentrations 1.5–2.0 minutes after maximal and supra-maximal tests were both high normal readings (11.8 and 15.0 mE l^{-1}).

Aerobic power seems unlikely to be of great importance to the sailor, except in so far as it is associated with a greater muscle mass and thus ability to counterbalance the vessel. Probably for this reason, the absolute aerobic power (1 min^{-1}) was correlated with sailing perform-ance when there was a strong wind ($r = 0.67$ for success in international competition, 0.72 for regional competition, 0.75 for peer ranking and 0.88 for the captain's ranking). However, the directly measured maximum oxygen intake for the Ontario Provincial Team averaged only 49.5 ml kg^{-1} min^{-1} (Niinimaa *et al.*, 1977), whereas predicted values for the Canadian National Team were even lower (45.3 ml kg^{-1} min^{-1}, Plyley, Davis and Shephard, 1985). Values were marginally higher for the skipper than for the crew, with the lowest results being seen in those craft where a heavy body mass was an advantage.

10.3.6 Psychological aspects

Desirable psychological attributes (Mas, 1976; Thill, 1981) differ substantially between skipper and crew. The skipper must be capable of sustained attention (Gouard, 1981) and able to visualize a prolonged sequence of moves and counter-moves – the type of complex reasoning which is also needed in a game of chess. This particular skill can be developed through extended practice of the sport; performance under light wind conditions thus shows a strong correlation with both years of sailing experience and years of competitive experience ($r = 0.87$ and 0.93, respectively, Niinimaa *et al.*, 1977).

Although all competitors must be success oriented, the crew are more combative, and the skipper shows a great tolerance for frustration (Thill, 1981). The skipper is marked by emotional stability, (Mas, 1976), psychological endurance and dominance, but the crew are more spontaneous and impulsive. The ideal skipper is a self-directed introvert, whereas the crew are extroverts who accept orders. The close living quarters of a prolonged voyage make mutual compatibility very important. On solo voyages, the sailor must be able to sustain vigilance for long periods, and under foggy conditions, sensory isolation must be well-tolerated. Such individuals are sceptical and non-conventional (Mas, 1976). Finally, a quick eye–arm reaction time would seem desirable, enabling the skipper to respond rapidly and appropriately to sudden gusts of wind.

Whereas blood glucose concentration is increased in the early stages of 'hiking', it is probable that reserves of both muscle glycogen and blood glucose become depleted by the repeated anaerobic efforts of a long race. Given that blood glucose is essential to cerebral function, it is not surprising that measures of muscular performance are correlated with the sailor's resistance to mental fatigue (Niinimaa *et al.*, 1977), and that initial blood glucose levels are correlated with both the captain's and peer rankings of the ability to sail under light wind conditions ($r = 0.80$ for both relationships).

Eight out of nine skippers showed an increase of urinary catecholamines, dopamine and serotonin over a race (Allain *et al.*, 1981), and in view of the absence of change in plasma catecholamines and cyclic AMP, it was argued these compounds were of cerebral origin. Nine out of ten crew showed a decrease of urinary catecholamines, dopamine and serotonin over the same period.

10.3.7 Overall rating

There are several major obstacles to making an overall rating of the individual sailor's ability. We have already noted substantial differences in the optimum profile due to type of craft and crew position; this makes it difficult to obtain an adequate volume of information on the characteristics needed for any specific task. Moreover, on most craft, competitive success depends not only on the capacities of the individual, but on the way in which these attributes mesh with the characteristics of other crew members. The demands of calm weather sailing must be weighted against the features required for a high wind or a storm. Finally, many pieces of information must be combined, some having ordinal and some categoric scales.

Given these complications it is difficult to apply a traditional multiple regression analysis relating sailing performance to laboratory measurements. Niinimaa *et al.* (1977) attempted to develop independent objective scores which would describe sailing performance under light and high wind conditions. In order to avoid problems of crew interactions, they chose as their dependent measure a rating of sailing ability made by the team captain. Individual items correlated with the captain's ranking of ability were themselves ranked in non-parametric form, being given a weighting of 3 if $r > 0.9$, 2 if $r > 0.7$ and 1 if $r = 0.5$–0.7. Overall scores for a given wind condition were obtained by simple summation of the ranked and weighted non-parametric scores. Items not included in the high-wind analysis included initial serum bicarbonate, body fat, and years of competitive experience; each of these items showed a high coefficient of correlation with other variables that were included. The final scores derived in this fashion were quite closely correlated with the overall rankings by the captain ($r = 0.92$ for high wind, $r = 0.90$ for light wind) and by fellow team members ($r = 0.91$ for high wind, $r = 0.90$ for light wind).

In a high wind, the competitive value of muscle strength, balance, tolerance of anaerobic effort and resistance to mental fatigue is hardly surprising. However, the substantial correlation of rankings with absolute aerobic power was less anticipated. It cannot be attributed simply to a correlation between aerobic power and muscular strength. Possibly, the sailor who is conscientious in general training develops several aspects of fitness, including not only strength and tolerance of anaerobic effort, but also aerobic power. Possibly, the absolute aerobic power also serves as a marker of body mass and thus ability to counterbalance the boat.

Under calm weather conditions, the only physiological indicator of performance noted by Niinimaa *et al.* (1977) was the initial resting blood glucose. There have been a number of anecdotes linking blood sugar to cerebration. Thus, it would be reasonable to assume that a high initial blood glucose was an asset to the sustained mental concentration needed when sailing in a fickle wind. 'Hiking', by increasing the usage of glucose, might bring out the association between resting blood levels of this metabolite and sailing performance. An alternative hypothesis would be that a greater level of cerebral arousal improved performance, and was incidentally accompanied by a higher blood sugar. Two other items – competitive experience and the team-rating of resistance to mental fatigue – were judged of sufficient importance to include in the calm-weather assessment.

Plyley, Davis and Shephard (1985) attempted a similar type of analysis for the entire crews of various classes of craft. The only biological factor which consistently matched the performance ranking of the national coach was the differential body mass, calculated relative to 'ideal' values of 60 kg for the skipper, and 80 kg for the crew (Table 10.7).

Table 10.7 Differential mass of selected crews relative to postulated 'ideal' values of < 60 kg for skipper and > 80 kg for crew and ranking of sailing performance by Canadian National Coach (based on data of Plyley, Davis and Shephard, 1985)

| | | Differential mass (kg) | |
Coach's ranking	Soling	Flying Dutchman	Tornado
1	15.8	−5.3	−7.3
2	12.0	−9.4	−17.0
3	4.6	−13.5	−30.1

It is unlikely that physiological profiles will ever be used in formal selection of either individual team members or crews. Nevertheless, they are helpful in indicating areas of personal weakness that can be corrected by an appropriate training plan.

10.4 TRAINING DEMANDS AND REQUIREMENTS

Training for light wind conditions is largely a matter of observant practice in a boat, and with the possible exception of tactics to augment blood glucose, there seems little scope for the physiologist to contribute to such training.

Under high wind conditions, the two possible tactics are to counterbalance the boat or to lose speed by spilling wind. The counterbalancing effort depends on (1) body mass, (2) the distribution of body mass (shoulder girdle vs legs) and (3) the ability to sustain the 'hiking' position (influenced by muscle strength and the tolerance of anaerobic metabolites).

Overall body mass could be increased either by over-eating (fat) or by progressive muscle-building exercises. The increase of balancing torque is proportional to the increase of mass; if two crew members each increased their mass from 60 to 80 kg, this force would be increased by a third. At the same time, frictional resistance would rise by the square of total mass, equivalent to a 20% penalty in a 470 class vessel, but only 3% in a Soling class. The optimum regimen from the viewpoint of sailing would replace the abdominal fat of a crew member by shoulder muscle, although if there was difficulty in sustaining 'hiking', there might also be some advantage in strengthening the quadriceps and the abdominal muscles.

During the sailing season, much of the necessary exercise will be obtained from sailing itself, although if the shoulder region is weak there may be benefit from progressive isotonic activity for this region, while if body mass has been gained in the form of fat this can be corrected by an increase of general activity and a modest restriction of energy intake. In countries such as Canada, the sailing season is quite short, and an appropriate dry-land training programme is needed to conserve (and if possible, to develop) physical condition during the winter months (Wright et al., 1975, 1976). Normal circuit training (two 50-minute sessions per week) may be combined with two weekly sessions of weight-training, including (1) sit-ups from a downward sloping board with a 7 kg load behind the head (8 increasing to 15 repetitions per circuit), (2) leg presses (lying on back, elevating mass of 100–150 kg by knee extension (15 repetitions per circuit), (3) pulley work (using both arms simultaneously); 50–100 repetitions of (a) raising the arms above the head in the sagittal plane, (b) flexion of the arms towards the chest and (c) extension of the arms in the frontal plane, (4) sit-ups from a hiking position with a 7 kg load behind the head (30 increasing to 50 repetitions), (5) standard quadriceps exercises (10 repetitions for each leg at unilateral loads of 35–50 kg), and (6) standard 'clean and press' manoeuvres, starting at 45 and progressing to 60 kg (10 repetitions per circuit). On the weight-training days, each circuit of six items should be repeated three times, with a two minute rest interval between circuits. After a month of such training, one of the strength sessions can be replaced by an endurance session, where each item in the strength circuit is repeated three times before moving on to the next station. After a further month, one of the standard weekly circuit training sessions may also be replaced by an endurance session, and from the third month general condition can be maintained by running 3–6 km at the best possible speed once or twice per week.

Team members were enthusiastic about practical benefits gained from this pattern of training, commenting specifically on their greater tolerance of the 'hiking' position, and all proposed to continue or to increase their efforts in subsequent winters. The prescribed regimen decreased sub-cutaneous fat, while augmenting quadriceps girth; aerobic power was maintained, and there were gains of strength, muscular endurance and anaerobic capacity. After the dryland programme, team members were further able to reach the same heart rate and oxygen consumption with a lesser production of lactate, thus conserving precious intramuscular glycogen reserves. The lesser tendency to anaerobic work probably reflects (1) more ready perfusion of the active muscles because they are contracting at a smaller percentage of their maximal force (Royce, 1958; Lind and McNicol, 1967; Kay and Shephard, 1969), (2) a faster on-transient of blood flow to the active muscles (Linnarson, 1974), and (3) facilitation of aerobic metabolism by an increase of muscle myoglobin and enzyme concentrations (Gollnick and Hermansen, 1973; Holloszy, 1973). Conservation of glycogen and thus a higher blood glucose may have contributed to team perceptions of improved tactical ability (such as an appropriate choice of currents) after training.

The team who underwent special training made substantial gains in their competitive standings the following summer. It is difficult to be certain how far this was a direct effect of training, and how far the result of an additional year of competitive experience. However, 8 of the 10 competitors increased their quadriceps endurance, and thus presumably their ability to 'hike'. Under high wind conditions, those members of the team who improved their within-group competitive standings also showed an above average development of their anaerobic capacity.

10.5 SPECIAL CONSIDERATIONS

10.5.1 Nutrition

The main nutritional advice which emerges from the foregoing discussion is to maintain an adequate blood glucose level over a race; depending on the temperature (and thus the need for fluid), the sailor may drink 5% glucose, a polymer solution, sweetened tea or coffee, or may chew glucose-containing sweets. As in other events where major demands are placed on muscle glycogen, it is also probable that performance will be helped by a pre-race regimen designed to load the muscle with this fuel (Saltin and Hermansen, 1967). In prolonged events, body mass can decrease as much as 10 kg (Lethuillier, 1983) and account must also be taken of changes in acid–base balance and serum potassium (Mas, 1976).

Deep water sailors face the occasional hazard of shipwreck, and it is prudent to carry at least a week's supply of emergency rations (60 MJ per crew member). However, the critical factor for survival is usually the supply of fluid rather than food. If water intake is drastically reduced, urine production drops to the 'volume obligatoire' (850 ml day^{-1} on a normal mixed diet, but 550 ml day^{-1} if starving, and 150 ml day^{-1} if energy requirements can be met from sugar). As dehydration develops, water is drawn from the extracellular compartment, and the kidneys attempt to restore a normal osmotic pressure by excreting minerals. Nevertheless, osmotic pressure rises, drawing fluid from within the cells. Body mass decreases by about 1 kg day^{-1} if no water is available, and after 4 kg has been lost, both the kidneys and the circulation show signs of failure. Death usually occurs if the water loss exceeds 15 kg. Occasionally enthusiasts have suggested that survival can be prolonged by drinking seawater (Bombard, cited by Mas, 1976). The situation may be influenced by the salt content of the ocean. Nevertheless, typical sea water contains about three times as much salt as the plasma, and most authorities are now agreed that it is difficult for the ailing kidney to excrete the excess sodium ions. The mineral balance of the body is thus further distorted, and the rise in osmotic pressure of the plasma and extracellular fluid merely increases intracellular dehydration (Mas, 1976; Shephard, 1982).

10.5.2 Atherosclerosis

As with participants in some contact sports, the desire to increase body mass, if necessary by an accumulation of body fat, places the sailor at increased risk of atherosclerosis. Although there do not seem to have been any formal studies of mortality among yachtsmen, the risk that participation will provoke a 'heart attack' is augmented by (1) the relatively high age of top contestants (Mas, 1976), (2) sustained, forceful isometric contractions, with systolic blood pressures in excess of 200 mm Hg, and (3) an emphasis on muscle-building in the shoulder girdle rather than endurance training.

It is unlikely that a low-cholesterol diet will do much to protect against this risk, since the body has mechanisms for synthesizing cholesterol from other foods if there is an excessive intake of total energy. However, the danger may be less than some authors have feared, since research suggests that isometric exercise can be effective in increasing the blood levels of cholesterol-scavenging high-density lipoproteins (Kavanagh et al., 1983).

10.5.3 Hypothermia

There is some danger of hypothermia during sailing, since (1) metabolic heat production is relatively limited, (2) the speed of air movement over the clothing is increased by movement of the vessel and the substantial wind velocities encountered in an open estuary, and (3) the insulation of clothing is reduced by soaking with spray or deliberate wetting.

The danger is plainly increased if the vessel is capsized. The thermal conductivity of water is some 25 times greater than that of air, so that even if the water temperature is 20°C, the rate of resting heat loss is more than 54 kJ m^{-2} min^{-1}. For much of the year, the water temperature in many parts of the world (0–10°C) is far removed from a thermally neutral temperature (32–34°C), and core temperature quickly drops to the region (25–30°C) where ventricular fibrillation is likely.

The sudden plunge into cold water causes a sudden and intense stimulation of cutaneous cold receptors. Although there may be an initial bradycardia, this is soon replaced by an increase of heart rate and blood pressure. There is also a reflex hyperventilation, with a sensation of breathlessness and an inability to control respiration (Cabanac, 1979; Goode et al., 1975). Occasionally, the combination of such intense stimulation and the increase of cardiac work-rate may induce ventricular fibrillation, cardiac arrest ('hydrocution', Mas, 1976), or an allergic type of reaction (La Houte, 1979).

Slowing of muscular contraction, malfunction of the sensory receptors, and a progressive deterioration of cerebral function all hamper swimming as the body cools. There has been considerable discussion of the wisdom of swimming as a means of increasing body heat production; however, it is now agreed that the resultant stirring of the water immediately around the body increases the rate of heat loss (Hayward, 1975). Thus, unless the shore is close at hand, the best tactic is to minimize the exposed surface area by huddling in a 'fetal' position while awaiting rescue.

Early estimates of survival in cold water were based on the notorious 'experiments' at Dachau, where the majority of subjects were suffering from severe starvation. The survival of a well-nourished and slightly obese subject such as the average sailor is several times longer if exposed to the same water temperature (Hayward, 1975). Experiments in the US Navy (Molnar, cited by Mas, 1976) found average survival times of some 3 h at 10°C, and 1.5 h at 5°C (although consciousness was usually lost much more rapidly). A neoprene suit slowed the rate of cooling by a factor of five at a water temperature of 5°C.

10.5.4 Circadian rhythms

The influence of circadian rhythms on various aspects of human performance has been reviewed by Shephard (1984). From the viewpoint of sailing, the most important finding is that arousal and related aspects of psychological performance are at their minimum at 0300–0400 hours; the same variables reach a peak in the late afternoon. Accidents due to lack of vigilance are thus most likely during the first watch, while the skills of calm wind sailing reach their zenith in the late afternoon.

Muscle strength also shows a small diurnal variation, being greatest during waking hours and least in the early hours of the morning. However, it is not clear whether this is due to changes of core temperature and thus muscle viscosity, or whether the increase of muscle force is secondary to an increase of arousal.

Individual subjects differ in their peak hours of arousal, some people being at their best in the morning (the 'larks') and some not really waking until the evening (the 'owls'). On a long voyage, an appropriate mixture of the two types of people can improve the efficiency of watch-keeping, while if a brief race is to be held at a specific time of day, it may be possible to choose a crew whose members are at their best when the contest has been scheduled.

In solitary long distance events, it is argued that more than one hour of sleep can have an adverse effect on final placings, and some contestants wait until complete exhaustion before taking any sleep; hallucinations may result in consequence. Others endeavour to take three 2-hour or two 3-hour bouts of sleep (Lethuillier, 1982).

10.5.5 Motion sickness

The physiology of motion sickness has been reviewed by Shephard (1974b), Reason and Brand (1975) and Mas (1976). Under extreme weather conditions, even the most experienced sailors are vulnerable. While scopolamine is a fairly effective prophylactic drug, the side effects (particularly drowsiness) make it unpopular in either competition or situations where sustained vigilance is required. Difficulties can be reduced by taking light carbohydrate meals with small amounts of liquid, but avoiding cerebral stimulants such as caffeine; the degree of movement encountered can also be reduced by keeping close to the centre of rotation of the boat.

10.6 SUMMARY AND CONCLUSIONS

The physiological demands of sailing are highly specific, varying with wind-conditions, type of craft, and crew position. In a light wind, the only physiological variable yet shown to influence performance is the resting blood glucose. Under high wind conditions, the skipper should be light (<60 kg), but crew members should be heavy (>80 kg). Height does not seem a great advantage to crew, possibly because they then lack the muscular strength to exploit the added torque. Muscle strength, endurance and a tolerance of anaerobic metabolism are all desirable attributes of crew, and competitive performance can be improved by a winter training programme that develops these aspects of muscle performance in the abdominal and thigh regions. The skipper must meet intense and prolonged cerebral demands in the face of periodic isometric work; performance may thus be helped by ingestion of carbohydrate over the course of a race. The ability to sustain isometric contractions in the 'hiking' position may also be improved if the muscles are pre-loaded with glycogen. The combination of a heavy body-build, above average age for an athlete and sustained isometric contraction probably makes the yachtsman vulnerable to ischaemic heart disease. Advisors to a sailing team must further take account of the risks presented by immersion in cold water, loss of sleep, circadian variations of performance over an event, and problems of motion sickness in rough weather.

Techniques are now emerging to quantitate sailing performance, and relate this to the physiological attributes of the competitors. The next few years should see the accumulation of sufficient data to describe the ideal characteristics of human operator for the various categories of craft.

REFERENCES

Allain, H., Gouard, Ph., Robine, Ch., Kerbaol, M., Bentue-Ferrer, D., Massart, C., Aubrea, A., Nicole, M. and Van den Driessche, J. (1981) Apprôche biologique des systèmes endocrines et végetatifs du coureur de haut niveau en voile. *Cinésiologie*, **80**, 201–217.

Bachemout, F., Fouillot, J.P., Izou, M.A., Terkaia, and Drobzowski, Th. (1981) Étude de la fréquence cardiaque en deriveur et planche à voile par monitoring ambulatoire. *Cinésiologie*, **80**, 231–237.

Beillot, J., Rochcongar, P., Briend, G., Mazer, J. and LeBars, R. (1979) Apprôche biomécanique de la position de Rappel. *Lyon Mediterranée Médical*, **15**, 1283–1279.

Beillot, J., Rochcongar, P., Gouard, P., Simonet, J., Briend, G. and LeBars, R. (1981) Lc rappel sur Finn: approche biomécanique. *Cinésiologie*, **80**, 179–191.

Cabanac, M. (1979) Temperature regulation. *Annual Review of Physiology*, **37**, 415–439.

Canada Fitness Survey (1983) *Fitness and Lifestyle in Canada*. Fitness and Amateur Sport Canada, Ottawa.

Durnin, J.V.G.A. and Passmore, R. (1967) *Energy, Work and Leisure*. Heinemann Educational, London.

Gabillard, Pr. (1981) L'actualité en médecine appliquée à la voile. *Cinésiologie*, **80**, 165–178.

Gedda, L., Milani-Comparetti, M. and Brenci, G. (1968) Rapporto scientifico sugli Atleti della XVII Olimpiade Roma 1960, Instituto di Medicina dello Sport, Rome.

Gollnick, P.D. and Hermansen, L. (1973) Biochemical adaptations to exercise: anaerobic metabolism. *Exercise and Sport Sciences Reviews*, **1**, 1–43.

Goode, R.C., Duffin, J., Miller, R., Romet, T.T., Chout, W. and Ackles, K. (1975) Sudden cold water immersion. *Respiration Physiology*, **23**, 301–310.

Gouard, Ph. (1981) La préparation scientifique de haut niveau en voile, *Cinésiologie*, **80**, 157–164.

Hayward, J. (1975) Man in cold water, physiological basis for survival techniques. *Canadian Physiologist*, **6**, 89–90.

Hirata, K.I. (1979) *Selection of Olympic Champions*. Vol I, Hirata Institute of Health, Mino City, Japan, pp. 347–371.

Holloszy, J.O. (1973) Biochemical adaptations to exercise: aerobic metabolism. *Exercise and Sport Sciences Reviews*, **1**, 46–71.

Ishiko, T. (1967) Aerobic capacity and external criteria of performance. *Canadian Medical Association Journal*, **96**, 746–749.

Kavanagh, T., Shephard, R.J., Lindley, L.J. and Pieper, M. (1983) Influence of exercise and lifestyle variables upon high density lipoprotein cholesterol after myocardial infarction. *Arteriosclerosis*, **3**, 249–259.

Kay, C. and Shephard, R.J. (1969) On muscle strength and the threshold of anaerobic work. *Internationale Zeitschrift Angewandte Physiologische*, **27**, 311–328.

La Houte, L. (1979) Differents aspects prophylactiques de la pathologie de windsurfing. MD Thesis. Faculty of Medicine La Riboisière, Paris.

Lethuilier, D. (1983) Pathologie médicale et traumatique des concurrents de la 'route de Rhum' 1982. Memoire, Certificat D'étude Specialisé de Biologie et Médecine du Sport. Faculty of Medicine, Pitié Salpetrière, Paris.

Lind, A.R. and McNicol, G.W. (1967) Muscular factors which determine the cardiovascular responses to sustained and rhythmic exercise. *Canadian Medical Association Journal*, **96**, 706–712.

Linnarson, D. (1974) Dynamics of pulmonary gas exchange and heart rate changes at start and end of exercise. *Acta Physiologica Scandinavica*, Suppl. **415**, 1–68.

Mas, L. (1976) Voile. Entrainement et surveillance médicale. Editions Médicales et Universitaires, Paris.

Métivier, G. and Orban, W.A.R. (1971) The Physical Fitness performance and work capacity of Canadian adults. Aged 18 to 44 years. Canadian Association of Health, Physical Education and Recreation, Ottawa.

Monod, H. and Scherrer, J. (1957) Capacité de travail statique d'un groupe musculaire synergique chez l'homme. *C.R. Soc Biol.* (Paris), **151**, 1358–1362.

Niinimaa, V., Wright, G., Shephard, R.J. and Clarke, J. (1977) Characteristics of the successful dinghy sailor. *Journal of Sports Medicine and Physical Fitness*, **17**, 83–96.

Plyley, M.J., Davis, G.M. and Shephard, R.J. (1985) Body profile of olympic class sailors. *The Physician and Sportsmedicine*, **13**, 152–167.

Prevot, M. and Auvinet, B. (1981) L'actualité en médecine appliquée à la voile. *Cinésiologie*, **80**, 153–260.

Reason, J.T. and Brand, J.J. (1975) *Motion Sickness*, Academic Press, London, pp. 1–303.

Rogge, J. (1973) Hiking in the laboratory. *Finnfare*, February, 12–13.

Rohmert, W. (1960) Ermittung von Erholungspausen für statische Arbeit des Menschcen. *Internationale Zeitschrift Angewandte Physiolisches*, **18**, 123–164.

Royce, J. (1958) Isometric fatigue curves in human muscle with normal and occluded circulation. *Research Quarterly*, **29**, 204–212.

Saltin, B. and Hermansen, L. (1967) Glycogen stores and prolonged severe exercise, in *Nutrition and Physical Activity* (ed. G. Blix), Almqvist & Wiksell, Uppsala, p. 32.

Scott, A.C. and Williams, J.G.P. (1967) *Rowing – A Scientific Approach*. Kaye & Ward, London.

Secher, N.H., Vaage, O., Jensen, K. and Jackson, R.C. (1983) Maximal aerobic power in oarsmen. *European Journal of Applied Physiology*, **51**, 155–162.

Shephard, R.J. (1974a) Some determinants of continuous and intermittent hand-grip endurance. *Spor Hekim Derglesi*, **9**, 89–103.

Shephard, R.J. (1974b) *Men at Work. Applications of Ergonomics to Performance and Design*. C.C. Thomas, Springfield, Ill.

Shephard, R.J. (1978) *Human Physiological Work Capacity*. Cambridge University Press, London.

Shephard, R.J. (1982) *Physiology and Biochemistry of Exercise*. Praeger, New York.

Shephard, R.J. (1984) Sleep, biorhythms and human performance. *Sports Medicine*, **1**, 11–37.

Shephard, R.J., Godin, G. and Campbell, R. (1973) Characteristics of sprint, medium and long-distance swimmers. *Internationale Zeitschrift Angewandte Physiologisches*, **32**, 1–19.

Shephard, R.J., Jones, G., Ishii, K., Kaneko, M. and Olbrecht, A.J. (1969) Factors affecting body density and the thickness of sub-cutaneous fat. Data on 518 Canadian city dwellers. *American Journal of Clinical Nutrition*, **22**, 1175–1189.

Sidney, K.H. and Shephard, R.J. (1973) Physiological characteristics and performance of the whitewater paddler. *Internationale Zeitschrift Angewandte Physiologisches*, **32**, 55–70.

Thill, E. (1981) La constitution d'équipages en voile: definition des profils psychologigues des barreurs et des équipiers. *Cinésiologie*, **80**, 193–200.

Vank, L. (1969) Somatische Charakteristik der Radernfahrer in Vorbeitung an die Weltmeisterschaften 1969, in *Cycling and Health* (ed. J. Rous), Czech Amateur Cyclists Federation, Bratislava.

Webb, P. (ed.) (1964) *Bioastronautics Data Book*. US National Aeronautics and Space Administration, Washington, DC.

Wells, K. and Dillon, E. (1952) The sit and reach – a test of back and leg flexibility. *Research Quarterly*, **23**, 115–118.

Wright, G.R., Bompa, T. and Shephard, R.J. (1975) Physiological evaluation of a winter training programme for oarsmen. *Journal of Sports Medicine and Physical Fitness*, **16**, 22–37.

Wright, G.R., Clarke, J., Niinimaa, V. and Shephard, R.J. (1976) Some reactions to a dry-land training programme for dinghy sailors. *British Journal of Sports Medicine*, **10**, 4–10.

11
Sport on ice

H.A. Quinney

11.1 INTRODUCTION

This chapter focuses on three sports that each utilize ice skating as the common base for the activity. These activities are similar in that they use an ice surface and skating as the mode of locomotion, but they are extremely different and truly unique as sport activities. The three sports covered in this chapter are ice hockey, speed skating and figure skating.

From the physiological perspective, the task demands for performance of each of these activities are extremely different. Ice hockey is a 'high power', interval or intermittent type of activity which includes significant body contact, use of protective equipment and an implement called a hockey stick. The activity is very much open-skilled and demands a creative and reactive response from the athlete. Speed skating, however, is a continuous type of activity that demands as close to maximal power output as possible over periods of 37 seconds to 15 minutes. The sport demands a very high level of technical skill with the most variability being introduced by the environment. Figure skating is again quite different from both ice hockey and speed skating. This sport combines a very structured and highly technical skill (figures) with a creative free skating element which demands highly choreographed and aesthetically pleasing movement patterns. Whereas success in hockey is measured by the number of goals scored and speed skating success is measured very precisely in time to skate given distances, figure skating is judged and points awarded for each performance.

Even the skate which is most critical to skating performance, is quite different in each of these sports and factors such as ice temperature (hardness) are varied for best performance.

The chapter is organized into three sections, one for each sport, and each section deals totally independently with each topic.

11.2 ICE HOCKEY

11.2.1 Introduction

Ice hockey is a very intense, intermittent sport that requires a wide variety of motor skills as well as a high level of fitness to compete successfully at an elite level. Although there are some differences in ice surface size and rules throughout the world, the basic physiological requirements are very similar. Ice hockey places different physical and physiological demands on players depending upon position (forward, defence, goalie) and the style of play. The sport is characterized by brief periods of maximal acceleration and sprints of 5–7 s, lower intensity skating, body checking, fighting for position, shooting and passing. A game consists of three, 20 min periods of play separated by 15 min rest intervals between the periods. Most teams have four lines of forwards, three pairs of defencemen and two goalies. The lines of forwards and pairs of defence play alternate shifts on the ice resulting in an overall work to rest ratio of 1:2 or 1:3.

11.2.2 Physiological demands

Time–motion analysis of ice hockey (Green *et al.*, 1976) has revealed that the actual playing time per game ranges between 20.7 min for forwards and 28 min for defence with an average of 24.5 min for all players and a total distance of 5553 m covered. An average shift in this study included 39.75 s of uninterrupted play followed by 27.15 s of play stoppage repeated 2.3 times. Seliger *et al.* (1972) reporting on data collected on the Czechoslovakian National Team, indicated that players spend an average of 18 min on the ice made up of 18 shifts and an overall 1:3 work rest ratio. Their study also estimated that the total average distance covered in a game was 5160 m with a range of 4860–5620 m. Both of these studies also monitored heart rate throughout the games with the athletes in the study of Green *et al.* (1976) maintaining a mean on-ice heart rate (HR) of 173 beats min^{-1} compared to only 152 beats min^{-1} for the players in the study by Seliger *et al.* (1972). The mean off-ice HR was also substantially higher for the Canadian subjects, being 120 beats min^{-1} compared to 96 beats min^{-1}. Paterson (1979), reporting on younger hockey players, indicated that their mean HR on-ice was 90% or more of maximal HR with maximal HR reached during each shift on the ice. In other data reported by Green *et al.* (1978), the HR exceeded 90% of maximal and rarely went below 125 beats min^{-1} between shifts. Based on this telemetered HR data and laboratory measures of metabolic function, Green *et al.* (1976) estimated that their subjects were working at an average of 70–80% of their maximal aerobic power. Further work by Green (1979) showed that there is considerable inter-individual variability in energy expenditure in skating, emphasizing the skill level required to be an efficient skater. Based on this work, Green suggested that efficiency may be more of a factor in fatiguability than a low $\dot{V}O_{2max}$.

Green (1978) has also reported that total glycogen reduction during hockey performance amounted to 60% and this was similar for both forwards and defence even though the playing times for the defence were longer. This study showed a more marked reduction in Type I (slow) than Type II (fast) fibres which is supported by the study by Montpetit, Binette and Taylor (1979) which showed a mean overall depletion of 52%. The low glycogen depletion observed would suggest that aerobic mechanisms are predominant in ATP resynthesis. Green (1979) suggested that this notion is supported by the relatively low blood lactate levels observed.

Data on European hockey players (Wilson and Hedberg, 1975), showed substantially higher lactate levels than those reported by Green (1979) (Table 11.1) but also showed greater glycogen reduction in Type I fibres. Green (1979) argued that the low lactate levels he observed were due to the frequent stoppage of play and the changes in tempo that

Table 11.1 Blood lactate concentrations (mean ± SE) by position taken at the end of each period

Position/period	Lactate (mM)		
	1	2	3
Forwards	N = 7	N = 5	N = 1
Pre-game	1.66 + 0.15	1.42 + 0.19	
Period 1	8.62 + 1.02	6.16 + 1.90	9.9
Period 2	7.41 + 1.13	4.65 + 0.89	9.9
Period 3	5.15 + 0.30	5.63 + 0.62	8.1
Defence	N = 3	N = 3	
Pre-game	1.31 + 0.04	1.76 + 0.57	
Period 1	8.86 + 1.67	2.92 + 0.94	
Period 2	7.20 + 0.90	2.77 + 0.61	
Period 3	4.22 + 1.79	3.12 + 0.11	
Goalie	N − 1		
Pre-game	1.09		
Period 1	1.38		
Period 2	1.67		

1. Green *et al.* (1976)
2. Green *et al.* (1979)
3. Wilson and Hedberg (1975).

seldom involved more than a very few seconds of intense all-out effort followed by coasting. This pattern of play would be effective in conserving glycogen stores and optimizing the mechanisms for aerobic energy production. Wilson and Hedberg (1975) reported that their highest values for lactate were obtained following long continuous shifts of high intensity or shorter shifts involving a large component of start and stop activity.

It is quite reasonable to expect that the motor units recruited during a particular shift will vary with the type of play during that specific shift. This suggests that an all-out intense shift with little stoppage would mean that anaerobic glycolysis would provide the majority of the energy whereas in a shift composed of starts and stops and several face-offs the energy would be supplied to a greater extent through aerobic processes. In this type of shift, there would be a large contribution from the high energy phosphagens with rephosphorylation occurring during the periods of low or no activity and a resultant lower level of blood lactate.

Since this sport is associated with a seemingly cool environment there may be a misconception that ice hockey players do not encounter thermoregulatory problems, but such is not the case. All elite level hockey is played in enclosed, heated arenas and with the players clothed in protective equipment. The combination of an unfavourable microclimate created by the hockey pads and uniform, a neutral thermal environment and high metabolic activity contributes to a significant heat load. MacDougall (1979) has estimated that during a 20 min period of ice hockey a player would produce approximately 1250 kJ (298 kcal) which must be dissipated as excess heat. As a comparison, the same individual running continuously at 75% $\dot{V}O_{2max}$ for 20 min would produce only 942 kJ (225 kcal) to be dissipated. Since the primary method of heat dissipation in this situation is through sweating, significant reductions in body weight during the course of a game might be expected. MacDougall reported that 2–3 kg losses of body weight even with *ad libitum* rehydration are not uncommon. Results from Wilson and Hedberg (1975) support this observation: these authors suggested that through a careful practice of rehydration, fluid loss can be minimized. The goalies are particularly prone to problems of dehydration due to the excessive padding that they wear and the restriction on frequency of fluid replacement. In all cases, players must be taught to follow a protocol of frequent, small quantity, fluid intake throughout the game and, if the game is to be played in a particularly warm arena, pre-event hydration is advised.

Muscular strength and power are characteristics often cited as important to success in ice hockey (Wilson and Hedberg, 1975; Jette, 1977; Marcotte and Hermiston, 1975; Smith *et al.*, 1981). Strength and power are particularly important for rapid acceleration in skating, shooting, maintaining position, checking and for stopping and rapid changes in direction.

The muscle mass involved in ice hockey is consistently high with the upper body activity superimposed on intense lower limb activity. Green (1979) has suggested that this superimposition of arm exercise, if heavy enough, on heavy leg exercise can not only lead to an elevation of lactate in the exercising arms but force a reduction in blood flow as well as oxygen uptake in the exercising legs. The effect is to force a higher level of anaerobic metabolism in the legs and more rapid fatigue. Green (1983) has suggested that both acute and chronic fatigue have a major impact on hockey performance. With the frequent requirement to practise and perform at all levels of elite ice hockey, he suggested that players are in a constant state of low-frequency fatigue which causes disruption in some of the processes involved in muscle contraction as well as the tissue repair process. He further suggested that at the elite level and particularly in professional hockey the physical demands are too great due to both the number of practices and the number of games.

11.2.3 Physiological profiles

There have been several descriptive studies detailing the physiological

Table 11.2 Physical characteristics of elite ice hockey players

Team	Position	Height (cm)	Weight (kg)	Body fat (%)	Reference
Canadian Olympic Team	forwards	179.8	80.7	10.5	Smith et al. (1982)
	defence	181.8	84.9	11.1	
	goalies	173.7	72.0	10.1	
Professional	forwards	182.9	84.2	10.6	Smith et al. (1981)
	defence	182.1	88.0	12.2	
	goalies	182.7	85.8	12.1	
Czech. National Team	team	179.3	81.8	13.1	Seliger et al. (1972)
Finnish National	team	179	77.3	13.0	Rusko et al. (1978)
Swedish National Team	forwards		80.2		Wilson and Hedberg (1975)
	defence		83.7		
	goalies		73.0		
Professional	team		83.4		Green et al. (1979)
Junior and University	forwards	176.2	77.9	10.5	Houston and Green (1976)
	defence	180.8	82.2	10.1	
	goalies	173.3	72.9	9.6	

profiles of elite ice hockey players published over the past 15 years. These publications have provided a relatively sound data base for the sport.

Table 11.2 provides data on physical characteristics for elite ice hockey players from both amateur and professional teams. Smith *et al.* (1981) compared the physical characteristics of several teams and concluded that the professional players were older, heavier, and had a slightly higher percentage of body fat. The difficulties of presenting information on body fatness are well known and it is suggested that for specific

Table 11.3 Maximal aerobic power ($\dot{V}O_{2max}$) for various elite ice hockey teams

Team/position	Age	$\dot{V}O_{2max}$ ($l\ min^{-1}$)	$\dot{V}O_{2max}$ ($ml\ kg^{-1}\ min^{-1}$)	Reference (test mode)
Canadian Olympic 1980				Smith *et al.* (1982)
forwards	21.8	4.41	54.6	(cycle)
defence	22.0	4.55	53.6	
goalies	25.0	3.66	50.8	
Finnish National Team	22.0	4.75	61.5	Rusko *et al.* (1978) (treadmill)
Czech. National Team	24.0	4.47	54.6	Seliger *et al.* (1972) (cycle)
Swedish National Team				
forwards		4.21	54.0	Wilson and
defence		4.57	57.0	Hedberg (1975)
goalies		3.92	60.0	(treadmill)
Canadian Professional				Rhodes *et al.* (1985)
forwards		4.75	53.3	cycle
		4.90	57.4	treadmill
defence		4.75	51.6	cycle
		4.81	54.8	treadmill
goalies		3.48	44.1	cycle
		3.95	49.1	treadmill
Canadian University				Houston and
forwards	21.3	4.41	54.6	Green (1976)
defence	20.3	4.45	53.6	(treadmill)
goalies	17.7	4.44	54.8	
Canadian Junior				
forwards	17.9	4.32	56.3	
defence	17.8	4.54	55.6	
goalies	21.3	3.65	53.5	
Canadian University				Daub *et al.* (1983)
team	21.8	4.09	52.0	skating
		4.49	57.1	cycling

comparisons, reference will have to be made to the individual study. Lariviere, Lavalle and Shephard (1976) in their work with younger hockey players concluded that data from eight to eleven year olds were similar to data of average Canadian youth of the same age. With 14 year olds and 16 year olds, the hockey players were taller and heavier than their age-matched controls. It is likely that a selection process is already occurring at this early age in favour of taller and heavier athletes enjoying greater success in the game.

A comparison of maximal aerobic power data from the literature shows that there are no apparent differences between elite groups of ice hockey players with a normal range of 55–60 ml kg^{-1} min^{-1} being reported (Green *et al.*, 1979). There is some variability in reported data due to the mode of exercise used in the testing protocol. If some allowance was made for the cycle ergometer data in Table 11.3, the $\dot{V}O_{2max}$ data would suggest even more homogeneity. It is interesting to note that the ice skating $\dot{V}O_{2max}$ in the study by Daub *et al.* (1983) produced lower values than the cycling $\dot{V}O_{2max}$ test. The opposite might have been expected since the specificity of ice skating should utilize those muscles trained for the activity. One possible explanation would be the inability to

Table 11.4 Anaerobic power and capacity of elite ice hockey players

Team/position	Anaerobic power		Reference
1980 Canadian			
Olympic	5 s (W kg^{-1})	30 s (W kg^-)	Smith *et al.* (1982)
forwards	11.8	9.6	modified Wingate cycle
defence	11.5	9.6	test
Professional	5 s (W kg^{-1})	30 s (W kg^{-1})	Quinney *et al.* (1982)
forwards	10.6	9.1	modified Wingate cycle
defence	10.4	8.6	test
goalies	10.6	8.2	
Professional	5 s (W kg^{-1})	30 s (W kg^{-1})	Rhodes *et al.* (1985)
forwards	12.0	9.1	Modified Wingate cycle
defence	12.04	9.54	test
goalies	11.4	8.6	
University	running time(s)	lactate (mM)	Houston and Green (1976)
forwards	55.7	12.3	Cunningham–Faulkner
defence	51.7	13.3	treadmill test
goalies	51.5	12.9	
Junior			Houston and Green (1976)
forwards	63.1	12.2	Cunningham–Faulkner
defence	57.0	13.0	treadmill test
goalies	54.8	10.9	

provide sufficient resistance in free ice skating to maximally load the oxygen transport system.

There is little standardized information on anaerobic power or capacity of ice hockey players reported in the literature (Table 11.4). Houston and Green (1976) have reported anaerobic alactic power outputs (Margaria Stair climb) and anaerobic lactate capacity (Cunningham–Faulkner treadmill test) for Canadian Junior and University athletes. Smith et al. (1981), Quinney, Belcastro and Steadward (1982) and Rhodes, Cox and Quinney (1986) have reported anaerobic power data on a modified Wingate test for Canadian Olympic team and National Hockey League (NHL) professional players. It has been suggested (Blatherwick, 1983), that the anaerobic power test on the cycle ergometer is an appropriate power test for ice hockey due to the similarity of fatigue curves between this test and an anaerobic skating test.

There is relatively little muscular strength and power data in the literature. Alexander et al. (1963) and Wilson and Hedberg (1975) have reported isometric strength data for both upper and lower body. Wilson and Hedberg (1975) have also suggested (on very limited data) that there is a direct relationship between shooting velocity and percentage fast twitch fibres in the deltoid muscle. Smith et al. (1981) have reported (Table 11.5) peak isokinetic torques measured on a Cybex dynamometer, for shoulder abduction–adduction, hip flexion–extension and knee flexion–extension in Canadian Olympic and NHL ice hockey players. These authors suggested that this type of testing is important in establishing baseline data for players in the event of injury as well as in investigating left–right and cross-joint muscle balance.

Wilson and Hedberg, (1975) and Green et al. (1979) have indicated that the fibre-type distribution in elite ice hockey players is similar to untrained controls. Rusko, Haver and Karvinen (1978), however, have

Table 11.5 Isokinetic peak torque values for the shoulder, hip and knee at 0.52 and 3.14 rad s^{-1} (30 and 18° s^{-1}) for elite amateur and professional ice hockey players

| | 0.52 rad s^{-1} | | 3.14 rad s^{-1} | |
| | absolute | relative | absolute | relative |
Joint and movement	(Nm)	(Nm kg^{-1})	(Nm)	(Nm kg^{-1})
Shoulder abduction	75.7	0.91	58.7	0.71
Shoulder adduction	106.7	1.28	79.9	0.96
Hip flexion	174.4	2.10	114.2	1.37
Hip extension	277.0	3.32	203.5	2.44
Knee flexion	173.7	2.09	117.4	1.41
Knee extension	280.2	3.37	145.0	1.75

produced data that show the percentage slow twitch fibres in their National Team athletes to be considerably higher than their reference subjects; 61% slow twitch to 47% slow twitch. The studies of Green *et al.* (1979) and of Wilson and Hedberg (1975) did, however, show a large range of fibre types in their subjects; 20–71% slow twitch and 18–53% slow twitch, respectively.

Green *et al.* (1979) also showed a significant fast twitch b (Type IIb) to fast twitch a (Type IIa) shift in fibre characteristics over a season as well as increased FT fibre size. These authors suggested that these data indicate that brief, explosive type activities, if repeated often enough and for a prolonged period of time, can also induce interconversions in the FT fibre subgroups.

Green *et al.* (1979) have also suggested that practices and games do not represent sufficient endurance stress to increase $\dot{V}O_{2max}$ over the course of a season. Daub *et al.* (1983) supported this conclusion in regard to maximal aerobic power but did find positive changes in a test of submaximal skating. In subjects performing additional cycle training off-ice, there did not appear to be any greater training effect in the skating tests but a greater submaximal training effect was shown when tested on a cycle ergometer. Quinney, Belcastro and Steadward (1982) did show a significant training effect in submaximal cycle ergometer test results over the period of a season in National Hockey League players. The difference in these results is likely to have been due to the lower initial fitness level of the National Hockey League players.

11.2.4 Training for ice hockey

The competitive season for ice hockey is normally September–April with some European leagues finishing earlier and the National Hockey League finishing somewhat later. Virtually all elite players take a short post-season break from training and begin their pre-season preparation two to three months prior to the season. The majority of the pre-season training is off-ice with players beginning on-ice preparation three to four weeks prior to training camp.

The early phase of pre-season training is focused on development of an endurance base and the initial stages of a high-resistance weight training programme. Athletes are also encouraged to follow a flexibility programme throughout the training year. The mid-phase of the pre-season programme should incorporate some aerobic interval training as well as some power work in resistance training. The mode of endurance training in the pre-season is usually running or cycling. Some athletes incorporate roller skating (using a hockey skate boot and in-line rollers) into pre-season conditioning. In the late pre-season the training emphasis is on maintenance of endurance, power type resistance training, anaerobic intervals off-ice as well as ice-skating technique and high intensity skating drills. During pre-season conditioning, one or two fitness monitoring tests are usually incorporated to provide feedback to the athlete and coach.

At training camp the emphasis shifts to maintenance of the fitness levels gained in the pre-season and the majority of time is spent on-ice. Most teams do require athletes to continue off-ice conditioning during the season, particularly for endurance and strength since there is reasonable evidence to suggest there is insufficient stress on these systems during practices and games to provide a training effect.

Mini-cycles of specific high intensity interval or power training have been effectively introduced when there has been sufficient time to do so during the season. With most competitive schedules, however, this is extremely difficult.

Most coaches attempt to modify the amount of physical stress involved in games, practices and off-ice training to reduce the effects of chronic fatigue as much as possible. National Hockey League players, who have an extremely large number of performances and regular practice requirements, often operate on a delicate balance in terms of total physical stress.

11.2.5 Unique factors in ice hockey

Many ice hockey players have to cope with the combination of large numbers of performances, regular, frequent practices and a great deal of travel. The ability to adapt behaviourally to this environment is very important. Adequate rest, sound nutrition and rehydration are critical to rapid recovery.

Another major factor in ice hockey is the extensive body contact which produces additional stress on recovery between practices and performances. Abrasions, contusions, and ligamentous strains are a common hazard of the sport.

11.3 SPEED SKATING

11.3.1 Introduction

Speed skating is a continuous, high intensity activity with competitive distances of 500 m to 10 km for males and 500 m to 5 km for females. This highly technical, but relatively closed-skilled sport activity has led to the evolution of two distinct types of oval tracks for competition; the

Table 11.6 1989 World record times at all distances for short and long track speed skating

Distance (m)	Short track			Long track	
	male	*female*		*male*	*female*
500	0:44.46	0:47.77		0:36.45	0:39.01
1000	1:32.83	1:39.00		1:12.10	1:17.70
1500	2:25.25	2:34.85		1:52.06	1:59.30
3000	5:04.24	5:18.33		3:59.27	4:11.94
5000				6:44.63	7:14.30
10000				13:48.20	

Time (Min:s)

short track (111 m), and the traditional long track (400 m). Current world records at given distances are listed in Table 11.6.

In traditional long-track skating, two skaters are timed simultaneously in separate lanes. The event is normally held outdoors but indoor 400 m competition tracks are now available. At all major competitions individual event winners are recognized as well as sprint and all-round winners. The combined event winners are declared on calculation of points based on times. The sprint championship is based on 500 and 1000 m performance for both males and females and the all-round is determined from performance in the 500, 1500, 5000 and 10 000 m events for males and the 500, 1000, 1500, 3000 and 5000 m events for females.

There is sufficient emphasis on the all-round title that virtually all skaters train to be able to compete effectively at all distances. It is uncommon, however, for a skater to win both the sprint and long distance events. The skating technique and physiological adaptations required are unique to the two types of races (Åstrand and Rodahl, 1986). Unquestionably, the most remarkable series of speed skating performances occurred at the 1980 Winter Olympics with Eric Heiden of the USA winning all five of the events in Olympic record times and setting a new world record in the 10 km race.

Short track events are normally held indoors and involve a mass start. The shorter track with more cornering and moving in a group of skaters involves significantly more technical and tactical skills than 400 m track skating.

11.3.2 Physiological demands

Speed skating requires the involvement of a large muscle mass working

Figure 11.1 Aerodynamic body position for speed skating.

at high intensity over a time frame of 37 seconds to 14 minutes 37 seconds. An extremely critical component of speed skating technique is the maintenance of a body position in which wind resistance is minimized (Figure 11.1).

During speed skating the centre of gravity of the body is moving relatively parallel to the ice surface without the marked vertical component observed in running (Åstrand and Rodahl, 1986). Electromyographic studies of speed skating (Kumamoto *et al.*, 1972; Mashima *et al.*, 1972) have demonstrated significant isometric involvement of postural muscles to maintain an efficient body position and synchronous activity of all leg muscles (both flexors and extensors) during the kick movement. Significant arm movement is involved in the start and during cornering. In the normal striding position, however, the arms are placed parallel to the trunk with the hands held on the lower back to produce as aerodynamically perfect a profile as possible.

Di Prampero *et al.* (1976) have calculated the energy cost of speed skating per unit distance as the ratio of total energy expenditure to speed. They reported that it increases from 0.060 ± 0.005 ml kg^{-1} min^{-1} at ~ 5 m s^{-1} to 0.112 ± 0.006 ml kg^{-1} min^{-1} at ~ 12 m s^{-1}. These authors also partialled out the relative energy cost due to air resistance and to gravitational and inertial forces. At 10 ms^{-1} the total energy expenditure was calculated to be 0.093 ml kg^{-1} min^{-1} with 0.049 ml kg^{-1} min^{-1} spent against gravitational and inertial forces and 0.44 ml kg^{-1} min^{-1} spent against the wind. These data emphasize the importance of body position in reducing wind resistance. van Ingen Schenau (1982), in wind tunnel studies of speed skaters, supported these findings and estimated that as trunk angles increase from 20° to 25° and 30° the speed decreases from 11.71 to 11.43 and 11.17 m s^{-1} respectively based on skating a 3000 m race. He also indicated that due to anatomical factors it is not clear to what extent the trunk angle can be freely chosen. van Ingen Schenau and de Groot (1983) have developed a model in which a comparison between male and female skaters attributes one half of the difference in performance time to a higher body position in the female skaters.

Metabolically, the shorter sprint distances rely more heavily on anaerobic energy sources with the longer distances utilizing a relatively greater percentage of energy derived from oxidative sources. van Ingen Schenau, de Groot and Hollander (1983) observed that 'all-rounders' exhibit a higher aerobic capacity than sprinters but a lower anaerobic capacity both for male and female speed skaters. The high maximal aerobic power values (Table 11.8) observed in elite speed skaters clearly illustrate the importance of oxidative energy sources for this sport. Geijsel et al., (1984) concluded that the inter-individual differences in sprint skating performance at 500 and 1500 m can be attributed substantially to differences in anaerobic power among groups of well-trained skaters. High multiple correlation coefficients of $r = 0.85$ and $r = 0.90$ were observed for anaerobic power (30 s Wingate test) and stroke frequency against time for 500 m and 1500 m respectively. Even with this high degree of predictive power, the authors suggested caution in the use of the Wingate test as a predictor of sprint skating success due to the high standard error of estimate of the test. In their studies of anaerobic metabolism in speed skating over distances of 500 m to 10 km, von Kindermann and Keul (1977) and von Kindermann and Keul (1980) suggested that maximal acidosis occurs at a distance of 1000 m (16 mM). They reported values of 14.2 mM for 500 m, 15.3 mM for 1500 m, 14.8 mM for 5000 m, 13.45 mM for 10 km. Up to 5000 m, these values are significantly lower than values for maximal running of the same duration. These authors suggested that this may be due to the possible impairment of skating technique that would occur with higher levels of acidosis. Over the longer distances of 5 and 10 km the extent of lactate acidosis is very similar to running. In a correlational study of speed skating performance over 500 and 1500 m (Foster et al., 1985), the principal factors related to performance time were $\dot{V}O_{2max}$ and fat-free weight. Strength as measured by leg press was positively, but not significantly, related to performance. Rasin (1984), however, suggested that development of 'speed-strength' is extremely important in improvement of speed skating performance, particularly in younger skaters.

11.3.3 Physiological profiles

Pollock *et al.* (1982) found that speed skaters were shorter in height, lower in body weight and body fatness than average young men of similar age. The body mass index (BMI) for these skaters was 22.2 which was lower than age-matched controls and similar to data presented by Geijsel (1979) for marathon skaters. These data are also congruent with the description of speed skaters compared to other elite athletic groups by Rusko, Haver and Karvinen, (1978). The physical characteristics of elite speed skaters reported in the literature are presented in Table 11.7.

Table 11.7 Physical characteristics of elite speed skaters

Age (yrs)	Sex	Height (cm)	Weight (kg)	Body fat (%)	N	Reference
21	M	181	76.5	11.4	6	Rusko *et al.* (1978)
19.7	M	176	69.6	7.6	19	Pollock *et al.* (1982)
27.0	M	175.2	69.5	10.9	6	Geijsel (1979)
23.3	M	181	74.8	13.1	25	Geijsel *et al.* (1984)
19.7	M	179.5	72.8		15	von Schmid *et al.* (1979)
20.2	F	166.8	60.3		8	von Schmid *et al.* (1979)
20.1	M	175.5	73.9		10	Maksud *et al.* (1971)
21.5	F	164.5	60.8		13	Maksud *et al.* (1970)
	M	181.0	67.0	9.0	5	van Ingen Schenau *et al.* (1983)

Speed skaters, when considered as one athletic population, exhibit very high levels of aerobic power (Table 11.8) compared to other athletes. This applies to comparisons of $\dot{V}O_{2max}$ both in absolute and relative terms (Rusko, Haver and Karvinen, 1978).

This high aerobic power is congruent with the fibre type distribution of 69% slow twitch reported for speed skaters by Rusko, Haver and Karvinen (1978). When speed skaters are subdivided into all-rounders and sprinters, the sprinters are shown to be generally taller, heavier, and to have lower levels of aerobic power in both absolute and relative terms (von Schmid *et al*, 1979).

The anaerobic power outputs of speed skaters reported by Geisjel *et al.* (1984) (875 ± 86 W, 11.7 W kg^{-1}) are also very high when compared with ice hockey players (Table 11.4).

Table 11.8 Maximal aerobic power ($\dot{V}O_{2max}$) values for elite speed skaters

Sex	$\dot{V}O_{2max}$ (1 min^{-1})	$\dot{V}O_{2max}$ (ml kg^{-1} min^{-1})	N	Test mode	Reference
M	5.58	72.9	6	treadmill	Rusko et al. (1978)
M	4.30	61.3	18	treadmill	Maksud et al. (1980)
M	4.50	62.8	10	cycle	von Schmid et al. (1979)
F	3.71	62.5	5	cycle	von Schmid et al. (1979)
M	4.14	56.1	10	treadmill	Maksud et al. (1970)
F	2.71	46.1	13	treadmill	Maksud et al. (1970)
M	4.8	64.4	5	cycle	van Ingen Schenau et al. (1983)
M	4.4	59.4	5	skating	van Ingen Schenau et al. (1983)

A number of authors (Cumming, 1975; Holum, 1980; Rasin, 1984) indicated the importance of muscular strength and power training for speed skating. However, there are no adequate descriptive data in the literature.

Another important attribute identified for speed skating (von Schmid et al., 1979; Åstrand and Rodahl, 1986) is the ability to tolerate high levels of lactate during training and competition.

11.3.4 Training for speed skating

Training for speed skating differs significantly according to the availability of ice tracks. Holum (1980) estimated that 60% of the training by United States athletes is done off-ice due to the lack of skating facilities. European skaters also do significant dry-land training, but with better access to ice facilities than North American skaters, a greater percentage of their training is done on-ice.

As with other sports, the yearly training calendar for speed skating is developed around major competitions from December to March. The off-season is characterized by development of the endurance base with running, cycling and roller skating programmes. This training is supplemented with resistance training for strength and power with a shift in emphasis to power work as the phase of training on-ice approaches. The generalized running and cycling training off-ice is also supplemented with exercises that imitate the body position and movement patterns found in skating (Holum, 1980).

Cycling as the main off-season training mode for skating has been strongly endorsed by Geijsel (1979) and Geijsel et al. (1984) who showed a strong parallelism between skating and cycling performance. This similarity is evidenced by the number of elite skaters who also compete at a high level in track or road cycling. Eric Heiden is one excellent example of an athlete who excelled in this combination of activities.

The development of roller skates with in-line rollers mounted on speed skating boots has led to the possibility of significant training off-ice technically identical to conditions on-ice. Bedingfield and Wronko (1981) completed a biomechanical analysis of two elite skaters performing on-ice and on a 400 m running track with this type of roller skates. Their overall conclusion was that roller skating on a level surface was excellent technical training for ice speed skating. This conclusion was based on a high degree of similarity in range of joint angles, stride time, segment angular velocities and body position. The only difference noted with the roller skating, was the reduced speed (12.10 to 6.25 m s^{-1}) due to increased frictional force. This decreased speed was not seen as a disadvantage since it presented a natural overload effect.

The majority of tempo training is left to the on-ice phase with the extensive use of interval training in the pre-competition phase. The maintenance of conditioning gained in the off-season is also a priority at this time along with the extensive attention to skill work.

Coaches have found that monitoring the total amount of physical stress is extremely important in training and becomes critical in the immediate pre-competition period. Another major factor in training, particularly for the all-rounder, is the blending of the high power and endurance elements of their training programme.

11.3.5 Unique factors in speed skating

The most important factor not discussed so far is the variability of the physical environment in speed skating. With the advent of artificial tracks, some of the variability of the sport has been reduced, but until the sport is moved entirely indoors the vagaries of weather will remain a significant training and competition factor. Snow, extreme cold or warm temperatures and wind velocity all provide extreme variability. Athletes must cope with these very extreme environments and at specific times their performances do suffer. Elite athletes in this sport are also required to travel extensively for training and competition which places an additional stress on the athletes.

11.4 FIGURE SKATING

11.4.1 Introduction

Figure skating has traditionally been associated with dance and only recently has evolved into what could be considered a more athletic event. A large component of figure skating performance is still artistic expression which demands careful choreography and dance training. The sport also requires high speed and power movements which necessitates extensive physical training both off-ice and on-ice.

Figure skating competition includes three events – singles (for both males and females), pairs (one male and one female as a team) and dance (one male and one female as a team). At the elite level, performers usually specialize in only one event. In each event, performances are evaluated by a panel of judges.

The singles event requires skaters to perform compulsory figures which involve the tracing of intricate, precise patterns with the edges of the skate blades. This event also requires two freestyle skating routines – a short programme that must not exceed 2 min 15 s and a long programme that must not exceed 4 min for females and 4 min 30 s for males. The short programme must include certain elements which are common for all competitors. The long programme has greater flexibility in composition but must be well balanced with jumps, spins, steps, and other linking movements.

The pairs competition requires only the freestyle short programme (2 min 15 s maximum) and a 4 min 30 s maximum duration programme. The performance in the short programme involves a co-ordinated skating routine that requires a specific group of seven elements. These elements include jumps, lifts, spins, spirals, and step sequences. The long programme requires a well-balanced routine that meets a number of specific element requirements.

The dance competition includes compulsory dances (3), an original set pattern dance and a free dance of 4 min duration. There is strong emphasis on originality, use of the entire skating surface and artistic expression.

In all of the freestyle and dance performances, the judges mark on technical merit and artistic impression.

11.4.2 Physiological demands

Performance of the compulsory figures is a highly technical skill which places only a low physical demand on the body. Perhaps the greatest requirement for this part of the sport is a general endurance component which allows the athlete to practice for extended periods of time. A secondary component would be sufficient strength to allow the learning of the complex skills and the controlled transitions to edges as the performer moves through the figure.

The short and long programme for singles and pairs is an interval type of activity with fast and slow skating, maximal jumps, twists, spins, spirals, and lifts in pairs skating.

From a physiological perspective, the primary requirements are muscular strength, power and endurance with sufficient aerobic and anaerobic power and capacity to practise for extended periods of time and to complete the long programme without excessive fatigue. Excellent flexibility is also an essential component, as it is in dance.

Seliger (1968), monitoring the performance of a long programme calculated that the energy expenditure averaged 0.84 kJ (0.20 kcal) kg^{-1} min^{-1}. Due to the diverse nature of skating, power movements would be expected to require high energy expenditure and the glide phases only low metabolic demand. With the careful placement of high power elements in the programme some degree of replenishment can be introduced. The continuous tempo of the performance is sufficiently high, however, that this would be minimal. Niinimaa, Woch and Shephard (1979) reported that skaters exercised at 75–80% of $\dot{V}O_{2max}$ during the long programme performance and reached maximal heart rates several times. Most exercise lactate levels in this study reached 11.9 ± 3.6 mM, indicating significant anaerobic metabolic requirements. Woch, Niinimaa and Shephard (1979) reported that maximal heart rates were attained several times during a skating performance and that heart rate was elevated by anticipation of difficult movements. These authors attributed the high heart rate in part to emotional factors, breath holding and muscle tensing.

The requirement for high levels of muscular strength, power and endurance is evident in the repetitive execution of jumps, rapid acceleration, and lifts.

11.4.3 Physiological profile

Ross et al. (1976a) have characterized figure skaters as 'small, lean and muscular' and suggested that this body type has a particular advantage in singles competition. Niinimaa, Woch and Shephard (1979) supported

Table 11.9 Physical characteristics of elite male (M) and female (F) figure skaters

Age (yrs)	Sex	Height (cm)	Weight (kg)	Body fat (%)	N	Reference
18.2	M	164.4	56.5	7.5	12	Faulkner (1976)
15.7	F	156.8	48.6	13.0	18	Faulkner (1976)
22.6	M	166.9	57.7		5	Niinimaa et al. (1979)
18.0	F	160.2	55.6		4	Niinimaa et al. (1979)

this generalization with their data on elite Canadian skaters (Table 11.9). Their data also show only small standard deviations which suggest that this body type is uniform in the skating population. Ross *et al.* (1976b) have characterized the somatotype of female skaters as ectomesomorphic (2.6–3.8–3.0) and male skaters (Ross *et al.*, 1977) as mesomorphic (1.7–5.0–2.9).

It has also been demonstrated that both male and female figure skaters are late maturers (Ross, Brown and Yu, 1976a). Peak strength and stature velocities are reached approximately one year later than the general population and the age of menarche of female skaters is delayed by more than one year (Ross *et al.*, 1976b). The advantage to the female figure skaters was suggested to be in the extended period of leanness which would be helpful in the performance of advanced jumps.

Table 11.10 outlines the aerobic power values of elite male and female figure skaters reported in the literature. Niinimaa, Woch and Shephard (1979) have suggested that an aerobic power of 47–52 ml kg^{-1} min^{-1} is required for females to skate at an elite level.

Table 11.10 Aerobic power of elite male (M) and female (F) figure skaters

Sex	$\dot{V}O_{2max}$ (l min^{-1})	$\dot{V}O_{2max}$ (ml kg^{-1} min^{-1})	N	Exercise mode	Reference
M	3.38	58.5	5	treadmill	Niinimaa *et al.* (1979)
F	2.72	48.9	4	treadmill	Niinimaa *et al.* (1979)
F		47.7		cycle	Gordon *et al.* (1969)
F		52.5		treadmill	McMaster *et al.* (1979)

Niinimaa, Woch and Shephard (1979) also reported maximal lactate values of 13.0 and 13.6 mM for male and female skaters, respectively, following maximal treadmill exercise. These values reflect a relatively high level of anaerobic metabolic capacity.

Static strength measurements indicate extremely well-developed leg strength, and less-than-average upper body strength (Niinimaa, 1982). This study also reported that standard field tests of power indicated significantly higher power output than average values noted in age-matched controls.

11.4.4 Training for figure skating

Traditionally, figure skating training has involved extended on-ice practice (3–5 h per day) with off-ice emphasis on dance and flexibility training (McMaster, Liddle and Walsh, 1979; Ferstle, 1979). This approach to preparation is changing rapidly with the evolution of the sport reflecting a more 'athletic' performance requirement. Training off-ice including cycle or running training to increase aerobic and anaerobic power and resistance training to increase muscular strength, power and endurance is now common. This increased emphasis on off-ice training has had a significant impact upon both the athletes' tolerance of extended skill practice and reduced fatigue during competitive performance (McMaster, 1977; McMaster, Liddle and Walsh, 1979).

11.5 OVERVIEW AND SUMMARY

Ice hockey is a sport that involves high intensity, intermittent activity. Elite players are physically large, with moderately low body fat and high strength and power both in upper and lower extremities. There is an important endurance component in the activity but it is believed to be most critical for rapid restoration of the high energy phosphagen pool. The specific physiological attribute of player's may predetermine the type of play for which they are best suited. Significantly greater attention is now being given to the overall fitness requirements for this sport, particularly in North America.

Speed skating is a highly technical sport of a continuous nature that requires maximal performance over periods of 37 s to 14 min. The athletes have highly developed aerobic and anaerobic power systems with some differentiation between sprinters and all-rounders. Specific preparation for short track and long track events is required but the basic technique is the same. Body position is the major factor in developing an efficient skating technique and accounts for a large amount of the total energy expended. A large anaerobic component is evident even in the longest duration events.

Figure skating is a sport which combines the elements of single and partner performance in technically demanding athletic movements which must also demonstrate a high degree of artistic expression. The evolution of the sport to a greater emphasis on the athletic movements has required a change in training and preparation from the traditional on-ice and dance training to more systematic off-ice conditioning. Physically, skaters are small, lean muscular athletes with moderate levels of aerobic and anaerobic power and capacity.

ACKNOWLEDGEMENTS

The author would like to thank Mr G. Snydmiller and Ms H. Wilkin for their research assistance and Mrs J. Harris for typing the manuscript.

REFERENCES

Alexander, J., Drake, C., Reichenbach, P. and Haddow, J. (1963) Effect of strength development on speed of shooting of varsity ice hockey players. *Research Quarterly*, **35**, 101–106.

Åstrand, P.O. and Rodahl, K. (1986) *Textbook of Work Physiology*. McGraw-Hill, New York.

Bedingfield, E.W. and Wronko, C.J. (1981) Biomechanical analysis of ice versus roller skating. Unpublished research report to the Canadian Amateur Speed Skating Association.

Blatherwick, S. (1983) Hockey: optimizing performance and safety, a round table discussion. *The Physician and Sportsmedicine*, **11**, 73–83.

Cumming, G. (1975) Speedskating, in *The Scientific Aspects of Sports Training* (ed. A. Taylor), C.C. Thomas, Springfield, pp. 314–323.

Daub, W., Green, H., Houston, M., Thompson, J., Fraser, I. and Ranney, D. (1983) Specificity of physiologic adaptations resulting from ice-hockey training. *Medicine and Science in Sports and Exercise*, **15**, 290–294.

Di Prampero, P., Cortili, G., Mognoni, P. and Saibene, F. (1976) Energy cost of speed skating and efficiency of work against air resistance. *Journal of Applied Physiology*, **40**, 584–591.

Faulkner, R.A. (1976) Physique characteristics of Canadian figure skaters. Unpublished Master's thesis, Simon Fraser University, Vancouver.

Ferstle, J. (1979) Figure skating. In search of the winning edge. *The Physician and Sportsmedicine*, **7**, 129.

Foster, C., Holum, D., Lemberger, K., Pollock, M.L. and Pels, A.E. (1985) Laboratory correlates of speedskating performance. *Medicine and Science in Sports and Exercise*, **17**, 269.

Geijsel, J., Bomhoff, G., van Velzen, J., de Groot, G. and van Ingen Schenau, G.J. (1984) Bicycle ergometry and speed skating performance. *International Journal of Sports Medicine*, **5**, 241–245.

Geijsel, J.S.M. (1979) Training and testing in marathon speed skating. *Journal of Sports Medicine and Physical Fitness*, **19**, 277–285.

Gordon, T.I., Banister, E.W. and Gordon, B.P. (1969) The caloric cost of competitive figure skating. *Journal of Sports Medicine and Physical Fitness*, **9**, 98–103.

Green, H. (1978) Glycogen depletion patterns during continuous and intermittent ice skating. *Medicine and Science in Sports*, **10**, 183–187.

Green, H. (1979) Metabolic aspects of intermittent work with specific regard to ice hockey. *Canadian Journal of Applied Sport Sciences*, **4**, 29–34.

Green, H. (1983) Hockey: optimizing performance and safety. *The Physician and Sportsmedicine*, **11**, 73–83.

Green, H., Bishop, P., Houston, M., McKillop, R., Norman, R. and Stothart, P. (1976) Time–motion and physiological assessments of ice hockey performance. *Journal of Applied Physiology*, **40**, 159–163.

Green, H., Daub, B., Painter, D. and Thomson, J. (1978) Glycogen depletion pattern during ice hockey performance. *Medicine and Science in Sports*, **10**, 289–293.

Green, H.J. and Houston, M.E. (1975) Effect of a season of ice hockey on energy capacities and associated functions. *Medicine and Science in Sports*, **7**, 299–303.

Green, H.J., Thompson, J.A., Daub, W.D., Houston, M.E. and Ranney, D.A. (1979) Fiber composition, fiber size and enzyme activities in vastus lateralis of elite athletes involved in high intensity exercise. *European Journal of Applied Physiology*, **41**, 109–117.

Holum, D. (1980) Dryland drills for speed skating. *Athletic Journal*, **61**, 9–10; 24–26.

Houston, M. and Green, H. (1976) Physiological and anthropometric characteristics of elite Canadian ice hockey players. *Journal of Sports Medicine and Physical Fitness*, **16**, 123–128.

Jette, M. (1977) The physiological basis of conditioning programs for ice hockey players, in *Toward an Understanding of Human Performance in Exercise Physiology for the Coach and Athlete* (ed. E.J. Burke), Mouvement Publications, Ithaca, N.Y.

Kumamoto, K., Ito, M., Ito, K., Yamashita, N. and Nakagawa, H. (1972) Electromyographic study of the ice skating. *Proceedings of the International Congress of Winter Sports Medicine*, 130–134.

Lariviere, G., Lavalle, H., and Shephard, R. (1976) A simple skating test for ice hockey players. *Canadian Journal of Applied Sport Sciences*, **1**, 223–228.

MacDougall, J. (1979) Thermoregulatory problems encountered in ice hockey. *Canadian Journal of Applied Sport Science*, **4**, 35–38.

Maksud, M., Farrel, P., Foster, C., Pollock, M., Hare, J. and Anholm, J. (1980) Maximal physiological responses of Olympic speed skating candidates. *Medicine and Science in Sports and Exercise*, **12**, 142.

Maksud, M., Hamilton, L. and Balke, B. (1971) Physiological responses of a male Olympic speed skater – Terry McDermott. *Medicine and Science in Sports*, **3**, 107–109.

Maksud, M., Wiley, R., Hamilton, L. and Lockhart, B. (1970) Maximal $\dot{V}O_2$, ventilation, and heart rate of Olympic speed skating candidates. *Journal of Applied Physiology*, **29**, 186–190.

Marcotte, G. and Hermiston, R. (1975) Ice hockey, in *The Scientific Aspects of Sports Training*, (ed. A.W. Taylor) C.C. Thomas, Springfield, Illinois, pp. 222–229.

Mashima, H., Aoki, J., Maeshima, T., Shimizu, T. and Sato, T. (1972) Telemetric electromyography in the training of speed skaters. *Proceedings of the International Congress of Winter Sports Medicine*, pp. 124–129.

McMaster, W., Liddle, S. and Walsh, J. (1979) Conditioning program for competitive figure skating. *American Journal of Sports Medicine*, **7**, 43–47.

McMaster, W.C. (1977) Interval training in figure skating. *Medicine and Science in Sports*, **9**, 58.

Montpetit, R., Binette, P. and Taylor, A. (1979) Glycogen depletion in a game-simulated hockey task. *Canadian Journal of Applied Sport Sciences*, **4**, 43–45.

Niinimaa, V. (1982) Figure skating: what do we know about it? *The Physician and Sportsmedicine*, **10**, 5106.

Niinimaa, V., Woch, Z. and Shephard, R. (1979) Intensity of physical effort during a free figure skating program, in *Science in Skiing, Skating and Hockey*, (ed. J. Terauds and H. Gross) Academic Publishers, Del Mar, California, pp. 75–81.

Paterson, D. (1979) Respiratory and cardiovascular aspects of intermittent exercise with regard to ice hockey. *Canadian Journal of Applied Sport Sciences*, **4**, 22–28.

Pollock, M., Foster, C., Anholm, J., Hare, J., Farrel, P., Maksud, M. and Jackson, A. (1982) Body composition of Olympic speed skating candidates. *Research Quarterly for Exercise and Sport*, **53**, 150–155.

Quinney, H.A., Belcastro, A. and Steadward, R.D. (1982) Seasonal fitness variations and pre-playoff blood analysis in National Hockey League players. *Canadian Journal of Applied Sport Sciences*, **7**, 237.

Rasin, M.S. (1984) Speed-strength of young speed skaters. *Teoriya i Praktika Fizicheskoi Kultury*, **4**, 36.

Rhodes, E.C., Cox, M.H. and Quinney, H.A. (1985) Physiological monitoring of National Hockey League regulars during the 1985–86 season. *Canadian Journal of Applied Sport Sciences*, **10**, 36.

Ross, W., Brown, S., Faulkner, R., Vajda, A. and Savage, M. (1976a) Monitoring growth in young skaters. *Canadian Journal of Applied Sport Sciences*, **1**, 163–167.

Ross, W., Brown, S., Faulkner, R. and Savage, M. (1976b) Age of menarche of elite Canadian skaters and skiers. *Canadian Journal of Applied Sport Sciences*, **1**, 191–193.

Ross, W.D., Brown, S.R. and Yu, J.W. (1977) Somatotype of Canadian figure skaters. *Journal of Sports Medicine and Physical Fitness*, **17**, 195–205.

Rusko, H., Haver, M., Karvinen, E. (1978) Aerobic performance capacity in athletes. *European Journal of Applied Physiology*, **38**, 151–159.

Seliger, V. (1968) Energy metabolism in selected physical exercise. *Arbeitsphysiologie*, **25**, 104–120.

Seliger, V., Kostka, V., Grusova, D., Kovac, J., Machovcova, J., Pauer, M. Pribylova, A. and Urbankova, R. (1972) Energy expenditure and physical fitness of ice-hockey players. *Arbeitsphysiologie*, **30**, 283–291.

Shkhvatsabaya, Y. (1977) Physical working capacity of young hockey players. *Cor Vasa*, **19**, 333–339.

Smith, D., Wenger, H., Quinney, H., Sexsmith, J. and Steadward, R. (1982) Physiological profiles of the Canadian Olympic hockey team. *Canadian Journal of Applied Sport Sciences*, **7**, 142–146.

Smith, D.J., Quinney, H.A., Wenger, H.A., Steadward, R.D. and Sexsmith, J.R. (1981) Isokinetic torque outputs of professional and elite amateur ice hockey players. *Journal of Orthopedic and Sport Physical Therapy*, **3**, 42–7.

van Ingen Schenau, G. and de Groot, G. (1983) On the origin of differences in performance level between elite male and female speed skaters. *Human Movement Science*, **2**, 151–159.

van Ingen Schenau, G.J. (1982) The influence of air friction in speed skating. *Journal of Biomechanics*, **15**, 449–458.

van Ingen Schenau, G.J., de Groot, G. and Hollander, A.P. (1983) Some technical, physiological, and anthropometrical aspects of speed skating. *European Journal of Applied Physiology*, **50**, 343–354.

von Kindermann, W. and Keul, J. (1977) Lactate acidosis with different forms of sports activities. *Canadian Journal of Applied Sport Sciences*, **2**, 177–182.

von Kindermann, W. and Keul, J. (1980) Anaerobic supply of energy in high speed skating. *Deutsche Zeitschrift für Sportmedizin*, **5**, 142–147.

von Schmid, P., Kindermann, W., Huber, G. and Keul, J. (1979) Ergospirometrie und sportartspezifische leistungsfahigkeit von lisschnellaufern. *Deutsche Zeitschrift fur Sportmedizin*, **30**, 136–144.

Wilson, G. and Hedberg, A. (1975) *Physiology of Ice Hockey: A Report*. Canadian Amateur Hockey Association, Ottawa.

Woch, Z.T., Niinimaa, V. and Shephard, R.J. (1979) Heart rate responses during free figure skating manoeuvres. *Canadian Journal of Applied Sport Sciences*, **4**, 274–276.

Part Four
Games and
Exercises

12

The racquet sports

Thomas Reilly

12.1 INTRODUCTION

Racquet games tend to be played either on a divided court area (over a net) or on a shared court (against a wall). Tennis and badminton are the most popular of the former whilst squash and racquetball are examples of the latter. The games vary in terms of size of the playing area, type of racquet used and the type of missile and each has its own set of rules for competitive play. A common link between the games is that each entails intermittent exercise with vigorous involvement of both lower and upper body musculature during bouts of activity. Engagement of upper limb muscle groups is largely unilateral, except when the two-handed backhand stroke is used in tennis. All the sports call for fast reactions, quick acceleration, fast arm, leg and whole-body movements and an ability to change direction quickly.

Tennis is one of the world's most popular games and is a major professional sport. Varieties of tennis do exist, such as Real Tennis and Japanese Tennis, but the game formally known as Lawn Tennis is the one most played universally. The game is played on different surfaces, from grass, clay and concrete to wooden and synthetic surfaces, outdoors and indoors. The court dimensions for the game are 23.8 m × 12 m with the height of the net set at 1 m. Competitive singles matches may last from 50 min to 2.5 hours for women's and 2–5 hours for men's depending on the number of sets played, length of average rallies, pace of play and so on. For example, the duration of the women's singles in the Olympic Games finals in 1988 when Steffi Graf defeated Gabriella Sabatini over 2 sets (6–3, 6–3) was 80 min: at Wimbledon she defeated Martina Navratilova over 3 sets in 2 h 15 min on each occasion in 1988 and 1989. During 1989 Stefan Edberg lost to Boris Becker (6–0, 7–5, 6–4) in 2 h 12 min in the men's final at Wimbledon and to Michael Chang in the French Championship final over 5 sets in 4 h 39 min.

Figure 12.1 Typical racquet used (left to right) in lawn tennis, Japanese tennis and short tennis. Squash and badminton racquets are included for comparison.

The arm muscles are loaded by the weight of the racquet which is greater in tennis than in the other sports examined (Figure 12.1). Most top lawn tennis players currently use the mid-size rather than the so-called jumbo-sized racquet. The increase in size over conventional designs was introduced to maximize the area of the 'sweet spot' for effective contact with the ball. Materials technology has also contributed to the stringing of racquets to suit the tennis player (Reilly and Lees, 1984). The early metal racquets increased vibration on the strings and such high frequency vibrations were thought to induce injury known as 'tennis elbow' (Sanderson, 1981). Adult sized racquets also place excessive demands on the musculature of juvenile players and 'short-tennis' with specially adapted racquets, balls and even courts has evolved as a consequence. This avoids overstressing the soft-tissues and growing bones of younger players as they learn the basic skills of the game.

Badminton is played either indoors (especially in Europe) or outdoors when the air is still (notably in Asia). The missile is known as a shuttlecock which has traditionally been made of goose feathers but more recently has been predominantly of plastic. The court dimensions are smaller than for tennis, being 13.4 m × 6.1 m, whilst the net is much higher at 1.55 m. It is recognized that the striking action in badminton entails more movement at the wrist joint and less emphasis on the large muscles at the shoulder joint compared to that in tennis. Typically the duration of a badminton match is less than half that of a tennis contest but the rest pauses between bouts of play are shorter.

Racquetball and squash originated from the game of 'fives' which was itself played without a racquet. Both games are played on a court resembling that of the Spanish pelota and Gaelic or American handball alley. In fact, in many USA venues the courts are shared between handballers and racquetball players. The rules of play are very similar in these two games, but the main difference is that the handballer hits the ball with the hand whilst the racquetball player uses an implement like the traditional tennis racquet but with a shorter handle. In contrast the squash racquet has a smaller head and a longer handle than that used in racquetball.

The dimensions of the racquetball court are 12.12 m in length, 6.06 m wide, 6.06 m high, with a back wall of minimum height 3.64 m. The dimensions are altered slightly for courts with front wall only, or with front and side walls. The squash court is smaller, being 9.7 m long, 5.45 m wide, 4.85 m high and a backwall at least 1.97 m high. The ball can be played off the ceiling in racquetball, but not in squash. The ball used in racquetball has a livelier bounce than a squash ball, being variable in the latter case according to the level of play.

Racquetball originated in North America where it has attained its greatest popularity. Nevertheless it spread quickly overseas and gained recognition where squash courts and handball alleys could be adapted for use. By the time of the 1988 World Championships in Hamburg, West Germany, there were 22 nations taking part in the women's team event and 21 in the men's competition.

Until 1988 at Seoul, none of these racquet sports was on the Olympic Games calendar although badminton featured in major events such as the Commonwealth Games. Consequently, they have attracted less detailed attention from scientists than have the traditional Olympic sports. Nevertheless the racquet sports have achieved considerable respectability in national promotions of 'sport for all'. Irrespective of the sport concerned, it is usually assumed that the physiological demands of competition and the necessity for rigorous training increase with the level of participation. It is expected also that at any particular level, singles play is more physiologically demanding than doubles play and each sport makes its own unique demands.

In the sections that follow the four sports selected for discussion are considered and where appropriate comparisons are made between them. The physiological demands of match play are described as are the physical characteristics of players. Training and other considerations are also treated in some detail.

12.2 TENNIS

12.2.1 Demands of the game

Work-rate and energy expenditure

In tennis the periods of exercise are generally brief and long rallies such as occur in squash are rare. Standard rest periods are permitted during games and between sets when players change ends. There is relative inactivity also as players prepare to serve or receive the ball or await its retrieval when out of play. This period is likely to be decreased in length when play takes place on indoor courts with walled restraints compared to more open outdoor courts.

In studies of tennis matches the ball was noted to be in play from 17% (Docherty, 1982) to 23.6% (Misner *et al.*, 1980) and 26.5% (Elliott, Dawson and Pyke, 1985) of the time. In the first of these studies the average duration of rallies was $4.3(\pm 0.6)$ s, $4.2(\pm 0.9)$ s and $4(\pm 0.4)$ s for players of low, medium and high skill levels, respectively. This contrasts with the 10 s duration noted by Elliott, Dawson and Pyke (1985) whose games took place on a hard surface, a factor likely to increase opportunities for extending rally lengths. Grass courts tend to favour players with a fast service and a forceful volley rather than those who prefer ground strokes and so games on this surface are relatively short. Clay court rallies are much longer in comparison. It should be acknowledged also that professionals who like to play from the baseline (e.g. Chris Evert and Ivan Lendl) may sustain rallies for even longer than 10 s.

Seliger *et al.* (1973) conducted a motion analysis in conjunction with a physiological study of 10 min model games. The average number of strokes by each player in this time was $62(\pm 10)$. The player ran $128(\pm 46)$ m within the period of rallies and this comprised 54% of the total distance covered. A distance of $111(\pm 20)$ m was walked between rallies. There were $30(\pm 3)$ rallies and $29(\pm 3)$ intervals in the 10 min.

Players competed in these 10 min games wearing Douglas bags. The energy expenditure during play was calculated to be $43.5(\pm 8)$ kJ min^{-1} or $10.4(\pm 1.9)$ kcal min^{-1}. This was 9.2 times the resting metabolic rate. The excess oxygen consumption post-exercise was $2.64(\pm 1.46)$ l over a 26 min recovery. It was estimated that 88% of the energy during play was derived aerobically and 12% anaerobically, the oxygen uptake during the 10 min period of play being about 50% $\dot{V}O_{2max}$. Friedman, Ramo and Gray (1984) reported similar levels of energy expended among experienced tennis players. In this case subjects were middle-aged and energy expenditure was predicted from heart rate during play. The mean value was 38.5 kJ (9.2 kcal) min^{-1} corresponding to 7–8 times

Table 12.1 Reported mean energy expenditure levels for male players in singles matches for the four racquet sports

Authors	Energy expended (kcal min⁻¹)			
	Badminton	Tennis	Squash	Racquetball
Bartunkova et al. (1979)	9.0	10.4		
Brooks and Fahey (1984)	6.6	7.4	14.4	—
(expressed kcal per 68 kg)				
Coad et al. (1979)	10.6	—	—	—
(mean of 3 age groups 20–50 years)				
Conrad (1976)	—	8.3	16.7	—
Friedman et al. (1984)	—	9.2	—	—
Gordon (1958)	—	7.1	10.2	—
Montpetit et al. (1977)	—	—	12.2	12.2
Montpetit et al. (1987)	—	—	11.0	10.0
Sinclair and Goldsmith (1978)	—	—	—	13.6
van Rensburg et al. (1982)	—	—	17.6	—
Widdowson et al. (1954)	3.5	3.5	5.0	—
Yamaoka (1965)	6.6	10.9	—	—

1 kcal = 4.186 kJ.

the resting metabolic rate. It was estimated that subjects were exercising at a mean level of 62% $\dot{V}O_{2max}$, the maximal oxygen uptake being a modest 44 ml kg⁻¹ min⁻¹.

Although the general conclusion of Seliger et al. (1973) that the aerobic system is only lightly taxed is supported by other studies (Table 12.1), the contribution of anaerobic metabolism to tennis play is likely to have been underestimated. This is because the calculations averaged data over the intermissions and the periods of play to compute values for the 10 min match. Fox (1984) seemingly concentrating on the periods of activity provided the following figures: 70% for ATP-PC and lactic acid systems (anaerobic), 20% lactic acid O_2 (aerobic) and 10% O_2 (aerobic). That there is little accumulation of lactate is shown by the low levels of 'oxygen debt' (elevated oxygen consumption post-exercise) and the blood lactate levels of 3(±1) mM on average (n = 16) noted by Kindermann and Keul (1977). One would not expect to find high levels of lactate in the blood when the duration of exercise is less than 5 s.

The summary of data in Table 12.1 suggests that tennis is marginally more demanding than badminton in terms of oxygen transport but considerably less than squash and racquetball. The figures provided by Widdowson, Edholm and McCance (1954) were obtained on military cadets and probably apply only to casual recreational games rather than to serious sport. They may also reflect a now obsolete attitude towards competition in these games which even at recreational level has become intense.

Yamaoka (1965) obtained values of 45.6 kJ (10.9 kcal) min^{-1} for a singles match over 52 min and 32.2 kJ (7.7 kcal) min^{-1} for a doubles match over 54 min, each being of three sets. The mean $\dot{V}O_2$ observed by Seliger et $al.$ (1973) was 2.0 l min^{-1} for females and 2.5 l min^{-1} for males playing in singles games. These authors showed that there was a correlation between the level of competition and the oxygen consumption, the relation being evident in both men's and women's play. The Japanese and Czech studies demonstrate that the intensity of exercise is greater in singles play than in doubles, and in men's matches compared to women's.

Heart rate

The heart rate response to tennis play has been employed as an index of the strain on the cardiovascular system. The results have been expressed both in absolute terms and as a percentage of the heart rate range to assess the extent to which the game taxes the circulatory system.

The data of Seliger et $al.$ (1973) indicated a mean value of 143 beats min^{-1} (range 132–151 beats min^{-1}), corresponding to about 60% of the heart rate range. Misner et $al.$ (1980) reported a mean figure of 60% of the age-adjusted maximum heart rate in recreational tennis players aged 25–52 years. Rittell and Waterloh (1975) reported a mean heart rate of 150($\pm$10) beats min^{-1} during play. This agrees with the data of Elliott, Dawson and Pyke (1985) for male College tennis players over 60 min on a hard surface, whose values corresponded to 78% of the maximal heart rate and the observations of Friedman, Ramo and Gray (1984) on middle-aged players over 50 min.

Doherty (1982) found that the exercise heart rate expressed as a percentage of the predicted maximum heart rate did not exceed 70% during 30 min of play. The variation between skill levels was not significant (Figure 12.2). As regards its value as a mode of exercise for general prescription, it was concluded that tennis may have value in improving fitness status of individuals who have poor initial fitness levels. It was thought to have limited value for individuals above a $\dot{V}O_{2max}$ value of 35 ml kg^{-1} min^{-1} and thus inappropriate for maintaining a good standard of aerobic fitness.

Although tennis does not constitute steady-rate exercise, the fluctuations in heart rate during a match are not very great. Friedman, Ramo and Gray (1984) concluded that the heart rate during 50 min of play reached a steady-state level despite the stop-and-start nature of the game. Elliott, Dawson and Pyke (1985) observed marginally higher heart

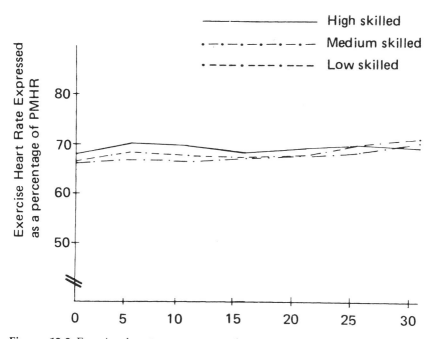

Figure 12.2 Exercise heart rate expressed as a percentage of the predicted maximal heart rate over 30 min tennis play in three different levels of skill (from Doherty, 1982).

rates in between rallies (mean 153 beats min^{-1}) compared to the exercise periods (150 beats min^{-1}), suggesting that these recovery periods are used for restoration of energy systems via oxygen transport. The rest allowed when players change ends would permit the heart rate to drop appreciably, although the fall would be temporary.

The heart rate does seem to differ between the server and the receiver, and this applies to both the exercise and subsequent recovery periods. The difference noted by Elliott, Dawson and Pyke (1985) was about 10 beats min^{-1} while the ball was in play and 8 beats min^{-1} between rallies. The difference reflects the more dominant role the server may take in dictating the game. The receiver is by no means in a passive role and can attempt to control play once the first service is returned.

Speed of movement

The foregoing sections have shown that tennis places only moderate demands on the aerobic system. The major demands are placed on the individual during the 5 s or so of highly intense activity during a rally. This entails good footwork, quick reactions and fast limb movements.

These considerations have implications for the manner in which fitness training regimens should be directed.

The serve initiates play in a rally and the server endeavours to complete the rally with the first serve. To do this, great speed of action and accuracy are called for. Ball velocities leaving the racquet reach 50 m s^{-1} in top male professionals (Cooper and Glassow, 1972) with one report of a speed of 68 m s^{-1} (Gray, 1974). Values exceeding 50 m s^{-1} have also been reported for serving velocities of women tennis players (Owens and Lee, 1969). Although the speed of the ball over the net would be reduced from that on leaving the racquet, the top speed easily exceeds that reported for other sports including golf and baseball (Gray, 1974).

Limb velocities reached in tennis, certainly among top players, exceed the contractile velocity range of human skeletal muscle, indicating that ballistic elements are involved in the movements. Groppel (1986) commented that ballistic actions in some players cause large accelerations of body segments, followed by decelerations of those segments prior to impact. In contrast other players were reported to have a smoother pattern of acceleration and deceleration.

For actions such as serving in tennis and smashing in badminton forearm angular velocities faster than 20 rad s^{-1} have been noted. Indeed Buckley and Kerwin (1988) reported a mean angular velocity of 44($\pm$4) rad s^{-1} through the elbow extension phase in tennis serving. They concluded that the powerful co-contraction of the biceps brachii and triceps muscles, observed during this movement, may be more related to joint stabilization than extension. Thus, such fast movements call for a co-ordination of activity among those muscles acting as synergists.

A detailed analysis of the major muscles used in the various tennis strokes has been presented by Kirby and Roberts (1985). These include the phases of the forehand, backhand and tennis serve. The analyses, based on EMG studies and a consideration of joint motions, review the role of muscle groups in all the major joint complexes of trunk and upper and lower limbs.

A consequence of the very fast limb movements and ball velocities in tennis is that the opponent has very little time in which to respond. In open play the normal human reaction time of about 200 ms may be inadequate to follow the tennis ball from the opponent's racquet and then take appropriate action. This problem would be accentuated in exchanges close to the net. A ball moving at 50 m s^{-1} would travel the entire length of the tennis court in less than half a second. Plagenhoef (1970) concluded from cinematographical data that a fast-reacting male player standing in one spot needed 370 ms to play the ball: a player forced to react more quickly than this would not be able to play the shot.

Anticipation is important, as is a rapid change of direction if the first prediction of ball flight is seen early to be wrong. The ability to return the ball from all parts of the court is likewise dependent on speed of movement. Good footwork to secure a position from which to return the ball, judge velocity, direction and spin of the ball accurately are called for. In his review of speed, reaction time and 'body quickness' in tennis players, Gray (1974) cited evidence that tennis players were faster than team games players in hand, leg, and combined hand and leg movements.

These considerations have given rise to the recommendation of training regimens that mimic movement patterns occurring in play. This principle of specificity is now recognized for all the racquet sports. Nevertheless players need to maintain the ability to move quickly and react rapidly throughout the match: tiring or loss of concentration towards the end of a set may lose them the match.

Nutritional considerations

Tennis as a professional activity varies almost unrecognizably from lawn tennis as a recreation. Professional players may be engaged in their sport either in training or competitions (singles and doubles) for 6 h a day, 5–6 days a week. This contrasts with the recreational player who may be satisfied with 60 min tennis once a week during the summer.

The calls on glycogen metabolism during training and match-play may almost exhaust substrate stores within the active muscles. For this reason a high carbohydrate diet has become accepted practice among top tennis players. Such a dietary regimen has been advocated by Haas (1983) and followed by Martina Navratilova, Ivan Lendl and Jimmy Connors, among others. The recommendation is to shift the usual distribution of macronutrients from 25% protein, 45% carbohydrate and 30% fat to 10–15% protein, 65–85% carbohydrate and 5–20% fat, approximately. The emphasis is placed on complex carbohydrates or starches (such as pasta, potatoes, whole grain bread, rice and so on) which contain about 90% of the total energy from carbohydrates in the diet. This energy is more readily stored in liver and in muscle prior to exercise than is the energy from simple carbohydrates (sweets and sugars) and so improves fuel supply to the active muscles during match-play.

Heat stress

Since tennis is predominantly a summer sport, many competitions take place in warm to hot environmental conditions. Match-play may place great demands on the body's thermoregulatory system if heat and high humidity are combined. Besides, the temperature of the court surface at the end of the day may be much hotter than the environment and create an additional heat load on players. Special attention is directed to avoiding dehydration due to loss of body water in sweat. Top tennis players are remarkably sensible about fluid replacement and take every opportunity to drink during respites from play, even during the first intermission. Small amounts taken in regularly in the intervals between play provide partial replacement of fluid lost in sweat. The primary need is for water, though glucose in so-called 'energy drinks' would be beneficial if blood glucose levels begin to fall in the case of a prolonged contest.

The metabolic loading during tennis play is moderate and so the main source of heat strain is likely to be environmental. Dawson *et al.* (1985) showed that 60 min of play in cool conditions (21°C WBGT) induced only a rise of 0.8°C in rectal temperature. When a similar exercise level was undertaken in hot conditions, comprising 35°C dry bulb temperature and 65% relative humidity (30.9°C WBGT) in an environmental chamber, weight loss increased from 1.3 to 2.4% of body weight and rectal temperature rose by 1.3°C. This was sufficient to induce impairment in a tennis skill test (consisting of service, ground strokes and volleys) compared to performance following match-play in cool conditions. Results illustrate that skills deteriorate in conditions of thermoregulatory strain and underline the need for adequate fluid ingestion.

12.2.2 Characteristics of players

In sports such as tennis, competence in the skills of the game seems to be the overriding requirement for success. When players of equal ability meet in competition, the one with the most favourable physical, physiological and psychological characteristics, whether acquired through endowment or training, may gain the advantage. In such circumstances a fundamental structural measure such as stature may be important for victory.

Height provides an advantage in serving, volleying, in reaching for a ball and in cutting off an opponent's drive at the net. Although there are exceptions to the general rule, a majority of top tennis players do seem to be taller than average, but the trend is more apparent in females. This is borne out in anthropometric studies of large samples of skilled players.

Medved (1966) looked at the heights of a large number of adult athletes in Yugoslavia to determine any predispositions for certain sports. The male tennis players were almost identical to the normal

Zagreb population (175±1 cm): the female tennis players were 2.8 cm taller than control subjects, their mean height being 164.8(±1.5) cm.

The height of the male Czech players in the national top 50 was found to be 181(±5) cm: body weight was 75.5(±6.2) kg (Seliger *et al.*, 1973). Figures for experienced USA male players of 179.6 cm and 77.1 kg, and for females mean values of 163.3 cm and 55.7 kg have been reported (Fox, 1984). The Western Australian Senior Women's squad had values of 163.1(±4.5) cm and 60.9(±8.0) kg (Pyke, Elliott and Pyke, 1974). The height and weight of the professionals examined by Copley (1980) were 182.8(±1.1) cm and 76.5(±1.2) kg for males and 167.3(±1.1) cm and 60.7(±1.4) for females. These figures suggest that the average tennis player is larger in body size than the average population value. Outstanding examples in the contemporary female game include Steffi Graf, Martina Navratilova and Hana Mandlikova. Male players taller than six feet (1.83 m) include Becker, Lendl and Edberg. Nevertheless, success at the top level of play has been gained by male players smaller than average in stature, most notably Ken Rosewall and Rod Laver.

Body composition data in the literature suggest that tennis players have less body fat than average for the population at large but not surprisingly have more body fat than endurance runners. Normative values for individuals in their mid-20s are 16% for males and 25% for females. The mean percentage body fat of the Czech top males was 13.9% (Seliger *et al.*, 1973). The professionals examined by Copley (1980) had mean (±SD) values of 11.8(±0.6)%. Values for USA players were 15.2% and 16.3% for a sample of veteran players aged 42 years (Fox, 1984). Reported figures for females are 20.3% (Fox, 1984), 22.1% (Copley, 1980), 23.3% (Powers and Walker, 1982) and 24.2% (Katch, Michael and Jones, 1969) but many top contemporary female players are likely to have mean values below 20%. Indeed the average for the Western Australian Senior Women's squad was 18.1(±2.3)% whereas that for the Junior Girls was 16.5(±1.7)% (Pyke, Elliott and Pyke, 1974).

The somatotype of top tennis players should tend towards ecto-mesomorphy as a lean and muscular physique would be suitable for this sport. This is confirmed by the observations of Gray (1974) on top USA players. The somatotypes of male and female professional players has been reported as 2.2:4.6:3 and 3.1:3.9:3.6 respectively. Professional players were found to be more mesomorphic than amateurs (Copley, 1980). They should, therefore, have a greater muscular strength. A higher than normal grip strength is expected because of the need for isometric strength in critical phases of guiding the racquet through competitive strokes. The muscular forces generated in serving and volleying are probably greater than in the strokes of the other racquet sports.

Copley (1980) compared muscle and bone measurements of professional and amateur players and concluded that intensive tennis play promotes muscle and bone hypertrophy in the upper limbs. Buskirk, Anderson and Brozek (1956) also concluded that playing tennis leads to muscular hypertrophy in the dominant forearm. They noted that muscle diameter at mid-ulna and grip strength both differed between the arms in tennis players. A difference between arms was also observed in the ratio of muscle diameter to bone diameter measured at mid-ulna. This denoted a unilateral muscular hypertrophy. Observations on the top 15 Louisiana female juniors, age 15.8 ± 0.4 years, disclosed significantly greater forearm circumference in the preferred hand. This hand also had a 22% higher grip strength than the non-preferred hand (Powers and Walker, 1982). It is also possible that there is an asymmetrical muscular development in shoulders of competitive tennis players.

Seven nationally ranked tennis players were studied by Buskirk, Anderson and Brozek (1956) using X-ray measurements of the forearms. The researchers concluded that vigorous tennis play may cause an increase in the length of the radius and ulna in the dominant arm. Other measures that differed between arms were hand area, hand width, third finger length, wrist width and forearm circumference. Overall, the evidence is that strenuous tennis play may stimulate bone growth as well as muscle development though it is not clear at what age this stimulus is most effective.

The heart volumes of tennis players tend to be essentially indistinguishable from normal values (Kindermann and Keul, 1977). This suggests that the circulatory strain during tennis play is insufficient to induce adaptive enlargement of cardiac dimensions. The resting heart rates (68 ± 4 beats min^{-1}) and blood pressures (128/78 mm Hg) of outstanding young female players with 6 years experience in the game and 15 h practice per week were similarly within the normal range of values (Powers and Walker, 1982).

The $\dot{V}O_{2max}$ of tennis players may also be ordinary. Docherty (1982) reported $\dot{V}O_{2max}$ values of British Columbia players, predicted from heart rate responses to a cycle ergometer test. Results were 43.4(±7.6), 43.9(±7.7) and 44.6(±7.3) ml kg^{-1} min^{-1} for low skilled, medium skilled and high skilled tournament singles players. These values are close to those expected of individuals without endurance training. The 15 young female elite players studied by Powers and Walker (1982) had $\dot{V}O_{2max}$ values averaging 48 ml kg min^{-1}: their results for VC (3.3 ± 0.2), FEV_1 (3.0 ± 0.1) and $\dot{V}_{Emax}$ (101 ± 3.2 l^{-1}) were also higher than values for untrained females of the same age. The male professionals at the South African championships had predicted $\dot{V}O_{2max}$ values of only 50 ml kg^{-1} min^{-1} (Copley, 1980). Peronnet et al. (1987) cited a value of 60 ml mg^{-1} min^{-1} for top class male tennis players, similar to that of ice-hockey internationals, but did not provide any details of measurement to support the figure. Such values may apply to those players who undertake rigorous intermittent or endurance training as part of the preparation for professional tennis.

Whereas the $\dot{V}O_{2max}$ is used as a measure of aerobic power, PWC_{170} is employed as a measure of aerobic capacity. It refers to the power output that corresponds to a heart rate of 170 beats min^{-1} in the individual under examination. Studies of physical working capacity (PWC_{170}) of tennis players have shown results close to normal values. Means for Western Australian squad players were 693($\pm$99) kg m min^{-1} (113$\pm$16 W) for junior girls, 1037($\pm$14) kg m min^{-1} (169$\pm$23 W) for junior boys and 838($\pm$175) kg m min^{-1} (137$\pm$28 W) for senior women (Pyke, Elliott and Pyke, 1974). These modest values for all the groups were in contrast to the relatively fast times on a speed test lasting 7–10 s. This in turn may reflect the emphasis on anaerobic power rather than aerobic factors that the game places on its players.

12.2.3 The professional tennis circuit

Professional tennis play entails a carousel of tournament and championship competitions. Elite players may continue to compete throughout the year with little or no off-season lull. Thus their fitness levels are maintained reasonably well throughout the year. The major championships – Australian, French, Wimbledon and USA – practically span the four seasons. Besides, all-weather surfaces and indoor facilities make it possible to continue competition all year-round. These factors mean that seasonal fluctuations in fitness levels of top tennis players are considerably less than in field games players with a recognized competitive season.

The opportunity to participate in a merry-go-round of tournaments may tempt players to compete too frequently. One risk is that muscle injuries may be induced or niggling injuries aggravated. Another is that there may be frequent disruption of the player's routine by exigencies of travel, changes of accommodation, loss of sleep and so on. Top players recognize the need to settle in quickly to an accustomed daily routine. This may be difficult if they have travelled across multiple time-zones.

Time-zone shifts disturb the body's normal circadian rhythms. An example is the rhythm in body temperature which varies during the solar day, peaking at about 1700 hours and reaching a trough at night time about mid-sleep. Many performance characteristics vary throughout the day in close concordance with the curve in body temperature. The symptoms of disorientation that accompany desynchronization of rhythms after crossing multiple time-zones are known as 'jet-lag'. It may take up to one day for every time zone crossed for the body to adjust to the new local time, although this adjustment is faster when travelling westward than when going eastward (de Looy *et al.*, 1988; Reilly, 1987). Many top tennis players participate in exhibition matches despite suffering from jet-lag but take much more care with their preparation for major events by arriving in good time.

12.3 BADMINTON

12.3.1 Demands of the game

Work rate and energy expenditure

Badminton participants are actually engaged in rallies for approximately one-third of the playing time. This is almost twice as high as the proportionate time engaged in actual play in tennis, although the average rally length is about the same in the two sports. It means that, in contrast to tennis, relatively little time is lost in retrieving the shuttle before resuming play. There are also more rallies in badminton in a given period of time than in tennis, as the duration of rallies is approximately the same in the two sports.

Docherty (1982) reported mean durations of 4.9($\pm$1.3) s, 4.2($\pm$0.5) s and 4.9($\pm$0.7) s per rally for badminton players of low, medium and high skill levels, respectively. The figures from Danish recreational badminton are in close agreement, Coad, Rasmussen and Mikkelsen (1979) finding average work periods of 5.1 s and average rest periods of 9.3 s. This work:rest ratio was independent of whether the event was mixed, singles or doubles, as was the duration of a game. A 3-game match lasted 36–45 min irrespective of the type of event.

Despite the shorter respites from activity during badminton play, the mean energy expenditure in the game is marginally lower than in tennis (Table 12.1). This is probably due to the greater distance covered in tennis play during bouts of activity, the necessity to return to position after a point, the greater forces used in tennis strokes and the larger muscle mass involved in playing the game.

Energy cost of playing badminton increases with the level of competition. The rate of 31 kJ (6.4 kcal) min^{-1} rises to 44 kJ (10.5 kcal) min^{-1} from recreational to competition matches (Coad, Rasmussen and Mikkelsen, 1979). The intensity of activity is lowered as players age; Coad, Rasmussen and Mikkelsen (1979) observed mean energy expenditures of 53 kJ (12.6 kcal) min^{-1}, 43 kJ (10.3 kcal) min^{-1} and 38 kJ (9.0 kcal) min^{-1} in males singles matches in age groups 20–29, 30–39 and 40–49 years respectively. A similar trend was noted in doubles and in mixed doubles play. Younger players do not necessarily operate at a high relative loading. Bartunkova *et al.* (1979) found oxygen uptake values of 1.9 l min^{-1} in junior representative players during a 10 min game. This corresponds to an energy expenditure of 37.7 kJ (9 kcal) min^{-1}. The proportionate loading of the oxygen transport system was 52% $\dot{V}O_{2max}$, indicating only moderate strain on aerobic mechanisms.

Compared to continuous exercise with the same relative aerobic loads, the lactate concentrations found in blood samples during badminton are low. Mean values for males are less than 3 mM, although the highest value found by Mikkelsen (1979) was 5.7 mM. This was attributed to utilization of creatine phosphate in muscle during intense brief spurts of action, and possibly to liberation of oxygen from myoglobin within muscle to supply the necessary energy aerobically.

The level of energy expenditure of international standards of play is greater than at club level. This is in agreement with the observations on oxidative capacity of muscle and the aerobic power of the top players. Players at this level would have the skills to force opponents to cover more ground by hitting the shuttle towards the boundaries of the court. This would increase the rally length, raise the work-rate of players and hence the energy expenditure.

The type of competition will also affect the energy expenditure level. In doubles play participants have less floor space to cover than in singles play and a lower rate of energy expenditure would be expected. This was confirmed by Yamaoka (1965): the mean energy expended in one set (9.5 min) of doubles play was 22.2 kJ (5.3 kcal) min^{-1} compared to a mean value of 27.6 kJ (6.6 kcal) min^{-1} for one set (11.5 min) of singles. Coad, Rasmussen and Mikkelsen (1979) reported differences of about 15%, mean values being 52.7 kJ (12.6 kcal) min^{-1} for singles and 45.6 kJ (10.9 kcal) min^{-1} for doubles in the 20–29 years age category. The energy expenditure in mixed doubles was intermediate between these events in all the age groups examined, the higher levels of energy being expended by the male partner.

Heart rate

Observations of heart rate during badminton play support the notion that this activity may be employed for promoting fitness through recreational activity. The junior players monitored during 10 min play by Bartunkova *et al.* (1979) showed mean values ranging from 142 to 162 beats min^{-1}. These constituted 70–80% of the subjects' predicted maximum heart rate. Rittell and Waterloh (1975) recorded higher values still, 175($\pm$6) beats min^{-1}, although the play monitored may have been excessively intense.

Docherty (1982) compared heart rates of badminton players of three ability levels with counterparts in squash and tennis. For all standards of

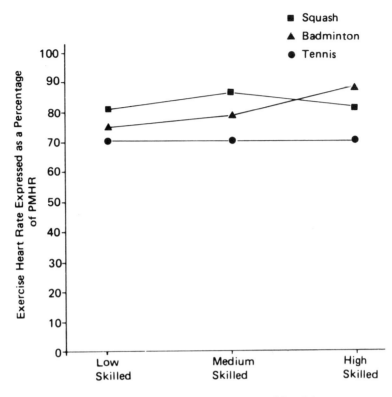

Figure 12.3 Mean heart rate during squash, badminton and tennis for three different ability groups. Values are given as a percentage of the predicted maximal heart rate (from Doherty, 1982).

play, badminton produced higher heart rates than did tennis. Values were less than observed in squash players, except at the highest skill level. The figures exceeded 70% of the predicted maximum heart rate for the low and medium skilled group and 80% for the highly skilled badminton players (Figure 12.3).

The higher heart rates in badminton compared to tennis seem to contradict the energy expenditure results where marginally higher values were observed for tennis. The short rest pauses in badminton are probably inadequate for heart rate to drop to any notable extent and this has repercussions in the period of activity that follows. The figures would also be influenced by the fact that light muscle group work and the lighter racquet (as used in badminton) entail less oxygen consumption for a given heart rate than does large muscle group work.

Additionally isometric activity with the player stationary but poised for action, and overhead actions occur more often in a rally in badminton than in tennis and may contribute to the elevated heart rates found in badminton.

12.3.2 Characteristics of players

Body size does not seem to be an essential determinant of success in badminton. Most adult players are taller than the top of the badminton net which must be 1.55 m from the floor at the posts and 1.524 m clear of the floor in the centre. A majority of top players hail from Asian countries, such as China, Korea, Indonesia and Malaysia, where natives tend to be small in stature. Players from these countries are not at a disadvantage when playing against taller opponents from Europe. The average values for height and weight for top Danish and Dutch players were 182($\pm$6) cm and 74.1($\pm$8.6) kg for males and 165($\pm$5) cm and 57.0($\pm$4.7) kg for females (Mikkelsen, 1979). Thus top European male players tend to be taller than average while females are close to normal population values.

Body composition data tend to be scarce but percentage body fat levels are likely to be similar to that of tennis players at the top level of play. A value of 9% of total body weight as fat was observed in a top British international (unpublished observations, Liverpool Polytechnic). Excess body weight as fat is disadvantageous in moving quickly across court and in leaping to strike the shuttle.

Flexibility is important in reaching the shuttlecock. Many retrievals are obtained with the spine and the shoulder joint in hyperextension and supranormal flexibility in the joints is expected of players. Top players need flexible thigh muscles – hamstrings and hip adductors particularly – to facilitate agility on court.

In the serve there is emphasis on accuracy in placing the missile rather than speed of propulsion and the serve is rarely intended to be an ace. Muscle strength would not appear to be as pronounced a requirement as in tennis since the forces generated in striking the shuttlecock are not as great as in hitting the tennis ball. Nevertheless leg muscle strength values measured on World-class players are quite impressive. Mikkelsen (1979) noted that elite badminton players had large muscle fibres compared to recreational players. Muscle hypertrophy was most pronounced in the slow twitch fibres which were 8% larger than the fast twitch (Type a) and 18% larger than the FTb Type fibres. The ST fibres constituted 56% of the total number of fibres in the vastus lateralis muscle of the male players and 61% in females. These tend towards the muscle fibre distribution of endurance athletes.

The study of the top Danish and Dutch players also showed that the muscle hypertrophy tended to be unilaterally biased (Mikkelsen, 1979). Measurements on both calves and thighs showed a significantly thicker right leg. The right leg also had a 17% higher SDH-activity, as reflected in muscle samples from vastus lateralis, indicating an aerobic adaptation in the muscle of that limb. The higher than normal SDH activity in the right leg was accounted for by the large fibres and the fibre distribution. Values for SDH activity of the top players were still well below those noted in top distance runners. The asymmetry in muscle strength was probably due to the use of the preferred leg in generating great force against the ground in the penultimate step prior to striking the shuttle. Presumably this posture has a greater physiological impact than the seemingly more symmetrical ready position.

The aerobic component of badminton is underlined by additional observations of the leg muscles of top players. These showed that the capillary supply per muscle fibre was tending towards that found in endurance athletes. As aerobic demands of badminton are close to tennis and less than squash or racquetball, exceptional values of $\dot{V}O_{2max}$ would not be expected. Nevertheless we have recorded a value of 68 ml kg^{-1} min^{-1} for a top British international player, Steve Baddeley (unpublished observations, Reilly). His $\dot{V}_{Emax}$ was 177.6 l min^{-1}, PWC$_{170}$ was 1466 kgm min^{-1} (240 W) and ventilatory threshold was 77% $\dot{V}O_{2max}$: these values indicate an excellent aerobic profile. Results for international squads have not been so high. Values for nine international males reported by Mikkelsen (1979) were 59.4($\pm$3.7) ml kg^{-1} and 52.9($\pm$4.4) ml kg^{-1} min^{-1} for nine female players. Corresponding values for top Chinese players, including Thomas Cup and All-England Champions, were 63.4($\pm$4.0) and 53.3($\pm$3.6) ml kg^{-1} min^{-1} respectively (Sukun and Wang, 1988). Such values may be due to endowment but could also be due in part to rigorous training. An advantage of a high aerobic power is that it would enable the individual to force a more intensive pace of play throughout a match against a less fit opponent, as indicated by $\dot{V}O_{2max}$.

12.4 SQUASH

12.4.1 Demands of the game

Work rate and energy expenditure

Squash imposes a non-rhythmical pattern of activity on performers, similar in principle to the other racquet games. The use of the walls helps to sustain activity for longer than in tennis or badminton and a mistimed stroke may not be so costly an error since the ball might still stay in play within the walled court. At low standards of play rallies may be short but they increase in length appreciably at high standards of competition. Docherty (1982) found mean rally durations of 4.4($\pm$0.8) s, 8.4($\pm$1.7) s and 8.8($\pm$1.0) s for low, medium and highly skilled Canadian games. Hughes (1985) compared county standard and recreational players, noting that the former had more shots per game, more rallies and longer rallies. The patterns of play differed markedly in that the recreational players attempted more outright winning shots, were less accurate in their straight play and more haphazard in their cross-court play. At international level rallies may be much longer than at county standard and a 5-game match may last for up to 3 hours.

Competitors are engaged in actual play for proportionately longer in squash than in the other racquet sports. Docherty (1982) found that in a 30 min game play was in progress for 15 min on average, compared to about 5 min for tennis and 10 min for badminton. The figure is likely to underestimate the actual playing time at the top level of play, because of the longer rallies and short respites. The highly skilled group in Docherty's (1982) study played for 17 min out of the 30 min compared to 12 min in the low-skilled game. A similar trend was noted by Mercier et al. (1987): in matches between 'high-skilled' players the ball was in play for 61% of the time, compared to 42% when games were between players described as 'average skilled'.

The figures reported by Docherty (1982) and Mercier et al. (1987) presumably referred to the American hardball game. Generally, authors fail to acknowledge in their reports a distinction between the American game and the now more popular international softball game. In the American code, a game is ended when the leader secures 15 points, each exchange being terminated by a point in favour of the player who wins the rally. In the softball code a game is won with 9 points, and a point

Table 12.2 Mean heart rates ($\pm$SD) during squash play in various studies. Mean age of subjects and duration of play are also given. Heart rates are also expressed as a percentage of the subjects' maximum

	Mean age (years)	Duration (min)	Heart rate (beats min^{-1})	%HR_{max}
Beaudin et al. (1978)	29	45	155 $\pm$ 8	84
Docherty and Howe (1978)	30	30	—	79
Mercier et al. (1987)		30	154 $\pm$ 16	83
Montpetit et al. (1987)	27	50	147 $\pm$ 18	79
Northcote et at. (1983)	33	40	149 $\pm$ 18	80
van Rensburg et al. (1982)	26	68	161 $\pm$ 12	88

may only be scored by the server. Despite these differences the two squash codes seem to induce similar levels of physiological strain (Table 12.2). Consequently the skill level of players may have more impact on physiological responses than whether the softball or hardball game is being played.

Unequal levels of skill may impose different work-rate patterns on players. The superior players may force the opponent to cover more court space by astute tactical strokes, causing the opponent to tire more quickly. Top players tend to pivot their movements from a central position on court, moving forward, backward, laterally or diagonally as individual strokes require.

Reports of energy expenditure during squash (hardball or softball) testify to its more intensive aerobic demands compared to tennis and badminton (Table 12.1). Values estimated for competitive matches are close to those reported elsewhere for top class soccer play (Reilly, 1986). These may approach a 75% fractional utilization of $\dot{V}O_{2max}$. Indeed Beaudin, Zapiec and Montgomery (1978) calculated that squash players were exercising at 77% of $\dot{V}O_{2max}$ during a match. They noted also that lactate does not rise appreciably in the blood of experienced players, finding only a twofold rise over pre-exercise levels after 45 min of play. This is close to the mean value of 2.7 mM observed by Mercier *et al.* (1987) over 30 min of play and by Garden *et al.* (1986) after 45 min play; a mean of about 3 mM was found by Potts *et al.* (1986) after 60 min play and by van Rensburg *et al.* (1982) after 68 min, whilst a value of about 2.5 mM was reported by Noakes *et al.* (1982) for a 90 min match. These are below the level at which accumulation of lactate in the blood would contribute to fatigue. In the study by van Rensburg *et al.* (1982) the exercise intensity was deemed to approach the blood lactate inflection point which in those players was found to average 79% $\dot{V}O_{2max}$.

Garden *et al.* (1986) reported increases in blood glucose, pyruvate, alanine and glycerol as well as the small increase in blood lactate during a 40 min game of squash. They noted a marked decrease in insulin levels but an increase in catecholamines, ACTH, prolactin and growth hormone. The relative rise in noradrenaline was greater than in adrenaline: interestingly both peaked after 25 min of play when competitiveness was deemed to be greatest. The authors concluded that the complex hormonal changes observed during squash make it impossible to isolate specific effects on metabolism. Levels of ketone bodies and non-esterified fatty acids increased in the post-exercise period. Since levels of non-esterified fatty acids are related to cardiac dysrhythmias in ischaemic tissue, a cool-down period was recommended. This recommendation is especially pertinent to those using squash for maintenance of cardiovascular health.

The relatively high level of energy expenditure during squash would ultimately reduce muscle glycogen stores to low levels in the event of a long drawn-out contest. As leg muscles are more active than arm and shoulder muscles – the former being active with each stride, the latter only with each stroke and differentially with the type of stroke – they are most likely to be affected first. In anticipation of prolonged matches, competitive squash players might well benefit from the type of high carbohydrate diet recommended by Haas (1983) and discussed in the context of tennis in an earlier section.

If carbohydrate is ingested shortly before match-play it might well impair performance by expediting onset of either hypoglycaemia or muscle glycogen depletion and inhibiting mobilization of free fatty acids. Noakes *et al.* (1982) gave players 67 g of carbohydrate in a 250 ml solution 25 min before a match. The players felt no benefit from the energy drink and showed significantly elevated serum insulin and growth hormone concentrations over the first half of the match compared to control conditions prior to competing. Endurance-trained individuals tend to have enhanced glucose tolerance and a diminished insulin response to ingested carbohydrate, a characteristic which would afford some protection from developing adverse metabolic responses to pre-exercise feeding. Such reactions would be more likely to occur in relatively unfit individuals who ingest high carbohydrate food or drinks shortly before going on court.

Cardiovascular responses to squash

Circulatory strain

The energetic demands of squash place a strain on the oxygen transport system: the game also places a prolonged and severe workload on the myocardium. Heart rate and stroke volume increase to provide the active muscles with oxygenated blood. As heart rate is elevated above a level which induces an adaptive response in cardiac function, recreational squash has been promoted for its beneficial effects on the heart and for reducing risks of coronary heart disease. Concern about the safety of the game for otherwise sedentary individuals was raised after reports of sudden death during or after playing squash. Northcote, Evans and Ballantyne (1984) examined a series of 30 sudden deaths associated with playing squash. The ages of individuals ranged from 22 to 66 years and only one was female. Twenty two had collapsed on court, the other eight in the hour after play. Although all individuals had been playing for at least 2 years with an average frequency of 2.3($\pm$1.3) times per week, coronary heart disease was the probable cause of death in the vast majority. Although the major cause of death was cardiovascular disease, causes were similar to those reported for sudden deaths in other sports.

In another study Northcote, MacFarlane and Ballantyne (1983) observed significant cardiac arrhythmias in a normal population during squash play. They also observed a high proportion of extra systoles in the vulnerable post-exercise period. They recognized that players who smoked after a match, with a consequent rise in blood fatty acids and release of catecholamines, would increase the risk. Exercise can precipitate arrhythmias in a coronary prone population, and individuals with behavioural predispositions towards cardiovascular disease may be tempted to drive themselves too strenuously during competitive play.

Heart rate

There is evidence of an interaction between skill level and the elevation of heart rate while playing squash. Whereas heart rate increases with the standard of play in badminton, lower heart rates are noted in highly skilled players in squash compared to less competent counterparts. (Figure 12.3). Values are highest in low-skilled players when they play more competent opponents (Mercier et al., 1987). Irrespective of the level of play, the heart rates exceed 75% of the predicted maximal heart rate, an intensity that would place unfit individuals under a high circulatory strain. This is borne out also by the data shown in Table 12.2. Docherty and Howe (1978) recorded heart rates above 80% of the predicted maximum but results were independent of skill level. A different trend has been observed in middle-aged players: Blanksby et al. (1980) found that heart rates of an otherwise sedentary group were generally lower than those noted in a habitually active group who presumably could operate at a higher level of activity. Values for both groups were in turn lower than the mean of about 160 beats min⁻¹ found in experienced players aged 26 years. When the predicted maximum heart rate was taken into account, both middle-aged groups (mean age 45 years) were exercising at a higher percentage than the 74% of maximum noted in top players.

The average heart rate of South African league players in matches between 63 and 80 min in duration was $161(\pm 12)$ beats min⁻¹ (van Rensburg et al., 1982). The heart rate response was found to be subject dependent, the variation between subjects being greater than the intra-individual variation.

Mean heart rates during play taken from different studies are listed in Table 12.2. The mean value corresponded to 72% of the heart rate range in the study by Montepetit, Beauchamp and Leger (1987), 71% in the study by Mercier et al. (1987) and 77% in that by Beaudin, Zapiec and Montgomery (1978). This should be sufficient to induce a training effect on cardiac function.

Mercier et al. (1987) showed evidence of a cardiovascular drift during 30 min of squash play. Mean heart rates for three consecutive 10 min periods were 149($\pm$15), 154($\pm$12) and 159($\pm$17) beats min^{-1}. This trend was not evident in matches exceeding 60 min (van Rensburg *et al.*, 1982) which presumably require a more precise pacing of effort.

Blood pressure

Another topic of interest is the way that blood pressure responds to playing squash. Systolic pressure has been found to rise quickly at the onset of a squash match to reach a value of 170–185 mmHg within about 6–8 min (Blanksby *et al.*, 1980). From there on there is a small decline in systolic pressure, attributable to vasodilation of the vascular bed of the exercising muscles. Diastolic pressure falls by 6–12 mmHg from the beginning to the end of a 39 min period of play. Such changes are compatible with observations of blood pressure responses to submaximal steady-rate exercise using conventional ergometers. Although Blanksby *et al.* (1980) thought that their observations on blood pressure raised no cause for concern, they warned that anyone with an already elevated blood pressure profile should seek medical advice before stepping onto a squash court, especially in summer when the weather is warm.

Heat stress

Approximately 25% of the energy consumed in strenuous exercise leads to the production of muscular work, the remainder being dissipated as heat. Body temperature rises during strenuous exercise and in general the build-up of heat is a function of the level of activity. The heat stress is accentuated in hot environmental conditions. A rise in body temperature from 37° to 41°C would constitute hyperthermia and so this heat must be lost to avoid heat injury. The major physiological mechanisms for losing heat are first, redistribution of cardiac output so that part goes to the skin for cooling; secondly, eccrine glands are stimulated to secrete sweat onto the surface of the body where heat is then lost by evaporation of this sweat. The still air within a walled squash court means that the facility for convective cooling is limited. It is aided by provision of ventilation bricks behind the tin at the base of the front wall or a fan on the ceiling which are the most common forms of ventilating the court.

During squash play lasting 39 min in a court where temperature did not exceed 22.2°C (relative humidity below 60%), Blanksby *et al.* (1980) found that rectal temperatures of competent club players rose to about 39°C. Values showed a steady rise throughout play. Although temperatures had not reached dangerous levels, they might do so in hotter conditions and after a more prolonged period of play.

Similar results were noted in the South African inter-provincial and league players studied by Noakes *et al.* (1982). Rectal temperatures after 90 min play were 39°C and the average weight loss during the match was 2.0 kg. On-court temperatures were described as normal and not excessively hot.

Rectal temperatures on average reached 39.4°C in South African league players after 68 min in dry bulb temperatures that did not exceed 25°C (van Rensburg *et al.*, 1982). The mean sweat loss in that time was 2.04 l and a fluid deficit of 1.62 l was incurred. Serum electrolyte concentrations following match-play were in general agreement with reports on athletes exercising at a similar level and duration.

As skilled performance may be affected after loss of body water amounting to 4% of body weight, it is important that squash players sweating liberally should seek re-hydration. This would attenuate further rises in core temperature. The major requirement is for water. It is important also that players do not commence a game already dehydrated. This might happen if they had large amounts of alcohol the night before, alcohol acting as a diuretic. Although players are best advised to avoid eating for 3 hours or so before a match, they could drink water up to 20 min before going on court.

12.4.2 Characteristics of players

Squash is played in an enclosed court and playing the ball off the side-walls increases the margin of error compared to tennis or badminton. Being tall would not be any particular advantage in playing the game, nor would a large body size. This is borne out by data on competitive players who tend on average to be close to population norms. Body composition would be important as excess body fat would increase the energy expended in moving around the court. At top levels of competition body fat values tend to be lower than normal but without reaching the low figures found in endurance events such as distance running. The Western Australian senior (age 25.6) male players ($n = 15$) studied by Pyke, Elliott and Pyke (1974) had 12.0(±2.0)% body weight as fat compared to about 16% in an aged-matched normal population. The mean (± SD) values for top South African league players was 10.1(±2.7)% according to van Rensburg *et al.* (1982).

Squash players tend to lack the arm strength that is found in tennis players. The Australian squash players studied by Pyke, Elliott and Pyke (1974) had poorer elbow extension strength as determined by cable ten-siometry than had junior boys tennis players, values being 28.5(±4.4) kg and 36.3(±6.1) kg respectively. The top South African players studied by van Rensburg *et al.* (1982) were intermediate in physique between sprinters and distance runners, their mean somatotype being 1.9:4.2:2.7.

Data on aerobic parameters suggest that squash players at senior levels of competition are quite well trained. The 'high level' Canadian players studied by Mercier *et al.* (1987) had a mean $\dot{V}O_{2max}$ of 56.0($\pm$6.1) ml kg^{-1} min^{-1}. The mean $\dot{V}O_{2max}$ of 13 German players studied by Steininger and Wodick (1987) was 58.5($\pm$8.1) ml kg^{-1} min^{-1}. These values were for seven male and six female players, who were not considered separately in the report. It is likely that the average value for the males was in the range 61–64 ml kg^{-1} min^{-1} and for the females about 53–56 ml kg^{-1} min^{-1}. Average $\dot{V}O_{2max}$ of 15 South African players in the country's top league was 59.5($\pm$4.8) ml kg^{-1} min^{-1}, individual results ranging from 50 to 66 ml kg^{-1} min^{-1}.

Pyke, Elliott and Pyke (1974) reported results for physical working capacity (PWC$_{170}$) of Western Australian players. The mean value of 1212 ($\pm$173) kg m min^{-1} (198$\pm$28 W) is comparable to values for good Rugby Union players reported by Rigg and Reilly (1988). The range of maximal heart rates of squash players – 195($\pm$6) beats min^{-1} found by Steininger and Wodick, (1987) and 184($\pm$9) beats min^{-1} reported by van Rensburg *et al.* (1982) – is similar to that found in the normal population.

Although VO_{2max} data provide useful descriptions of physiological fitness for activity such as squash, they lack specificity for testing fitness for the game. Various attempts have been made to devise a sport-specific test of aerobic fitness for squash, usually mimicking the activity patterns of play. Steininger and Wodick (1987) utilized a test in which the pace of an on-court running drill could be dictated by pulsed light and physiological responses (for example blood lactate) could be measured at each stage. Fitness measures derived from such tests were more highly correlated with ranked playing ability of subjects than were indices such as $\dot{V}O_{2max}$ and the running level corresponding to a blood lactate of 4 mM (referred to as the 'anaerobic threshold').

12.5 RACQUETBALL

12.5.1 Demands of the game

Work rate and energy expenditure

During a racquetball singles match the ball is in play slightly less than half the time (Faria and Lewis, 1982; Montgomery, 1981; Morgans, Scovil and Bass, 1984). Faria and Lewis (1982) reported from observations on 20 players that the average playing time was 32% of the total game time and that 90% of the rallies were shorter than 10 s. Morgans, Scovil and Bass (1984) found that the average rally time was 8.6 s and the ball was in play for 47% of the total game. The average rally time in doubles play of 8.3 s is similar but the ball is out of play for marginally longer, 10.3 s in doubles compared to 9.6 s in singles. The fact that the

Table 12.3 Length of rallies in racquetball (% of total match time) according to whether players were matched in ability or not (from Montgomery, 1981)

	Percentage of total	
Ball in play	Equal ability	Unequal ability
1 – 5 s	45	54
6 – 10 s	36	31
11 – 15 s	12	9
16 – 20 s	4	4
20 s	2	2

task is shared between partners in a team should mean that doubles play is less demanding on the cardiovascular system than is singles competition.

The patterns of play may differ when players of unequal ability meet on court. Montgomery (1981) reported that though the ball was in play for 44% of the time for equally matched and unequally matched games, in the latter case there was a reduction in the average length of rally and in the recovery period (Table 12.3). Very few rallies lasted longer than 15 s.

The average duration of a rally is similar in squash and racquetball, but the ball is in play more in squash. This implies that the recovery period is longer in racquetball. Reasons for this may be that the larger court size in racquetball means it takes longer to retrieve the ball, or that a higher intensity of activity during play is compensated for by a longer respite for players to recover. However, there are not sufficient data on blood lactate concentrations in racquetball players to permit a calculation of the contribution of anaerobic mechanisms to metabolism during play.

Energy expenditure during racquetball has been estimated from heart rate measures. The observations have been linked to relationships between heart rate and $\dot{V}O_2$ established for each individual during graded exercise in laboratory conditions. Although such a procedure is open to criticism, it provides a rough estimate of the rate of energy expenditure in the game.

Reports indicate that the energy expenditure in racquetball is very close to the rates reported for playing squash. Sinclair and Goldsmith (1978) found values of 57 kJ (13.6 kcal) min^{-1} and 60 kJ (14.3 kcal) min^{-1} in novice and intermediate players respectively. Played as part of physical education programmes, racquetball entails an energy expenditure of 43 kJ (10.3 kcal) min^{-1} (Adamson, 1977). Montpetit, Leger and Girardin (1977) reported higher levels of energy expenditure for advanced racquetball players, 50.1 kJ (12.2 kcal) min^{-1}. This was similar to observations on squash players at a similar level of performance.

Montpetit, Beauchamp and Leger (1987) monitored energy expenditure during play by direct measurement of $\dot{V}O_2$. They used the Douglas Bag method of collecting expired air, a procedure likely to slow down the pace of play. The energy expenditure in their Category C Intermediate ability players was 42($\pm$6) kJ min^{-1} (10.0($\pm$1.4) kcal min^{-1}). Although this value for energy cost is lower than the other estimates, it compared favourably with a value of 46($\pm$8) kJ min^{-1} (11($\pm$1.9) kcal min^{-1}) in squash players of a similar standard. The $\dot{V}O_2$ during the games was 57% and 51% of $\dot{V}O_{2max}$ during squash and racquetball respectively. These figures would probably be exceeded if the subjects competed unencumbered by the apparatus.

Heart rate

A few studies of the intensity of exercise during racquetball have used mean heart rate as a criterion. The motivation has primarily been to examine the suitability of racquetball as a mode of exercise for promoting cardiovascular fitness. Results are compared to the guidelines of the American College of Sports Medicine which recommends that the intensity of exercise should be within 60–90% of the heart rate range (maximum minus resting heart rate) or 50–85% of $\dot{V}O_{2max}$. This intensity should be maintained for 15–60 minutes of activity to tax the oxygen transport system: a typical racquetball match lasts 50 min when players are equally matched and 34 min when opponents are unequal in ability (Montgomery, 1981).

Research supports the use of racquetball for promoting cardiovascular fitness, although there are circumstances when the training stimulus might be too low. The mean heart rate observed in 16 racquetball players over 50 min of play was 152($\pm$14) beats min^{-1} (Montpetit, Beauchamp and Leger, 1987). This represented 76%($\pm$4) of the maximum heart rate range. Morgans, Scovil and Bass (1984) observed that mean heart rate was 161($\pm$9) beats min^{-1} in singles which represented 83($\pm$5)% of the heart rate span. These figures were lowered in doubles play to 145($\pm$9) beats min^{-1} and 67($\pm$10)% of the heart rate range. Since each player has a smaller amount of the court to cover in doubles play, the reduction in work-rate accounts for the reduced strain on the cardiovascular system.

The comparative abilities of players also affects work rate since the more competent player can tactically manipulate the pattern of play to overload his less-able opponent. Montgomery (1981) showed that highly ranked players had mean heart rates of 146 beats min^{-1} when competing against weaker opponents whose figures were as high as 181 beats min^{-1}

or 90% of the heart rate range. These results suggest that racquetball players should select individuals of equal skill for best effects, since playing stronger opposition might overload them unduly. The levelling out process within the game's structure means that highly competent players rarely encounter lowly ranked opponents.

12.5.2 Characteristics of players

Racquetball players tend to be similar in anthropometric measures to tennis and squash players, but there is considerable variability in physique. The 15 male USA tournament players studied by Morgans, Scovill and Bass (1984) were tall and heavy, mean height being 180(±6) cm and weight 80.3(±7.7) kg. The 16 Canadian players of intermediate ability studied by Montpetit, Beauchamp and Leger (1987) were smaller, their mean body weight being 71.9(±5.2) kg which was similar to squash players of a similar standard of play. The adult male players studied by Montgomery (1981) were 73 kg in weight, and aged 30 years. Values reported for USA female racquetball players – height 173 cm and weight 68 kg (Fox, 1984) – suggest that players tend on average to be taller than the general population.

The percentage body fat of the USA male tournament players was 17(±6)% (Morgans, Scovill and Bass, 1984), a figure much higher than the 8.1% reported for a professional player (Pipes, 1979). The mean value for the racquetball players studied by Montgomery (1981) was 12%. It is likely that most competitive players would fall within this range. The figure of 14% reported for USA female players (Fox, 1984) suggests that these performers are much leaner than the normal population.

Data on functional measures of the oxygen transport system indicate unexceptional values in USA tournament players. Mean $\dot{V}O_{2max}$ (46.2±8.3 ml kg^{-1} min^{-1}) and $\dot{V}_{Emax}$ (102.5±18.4 l min^{-1}) values were only slightly higher than the average of the population. Resting heart rates were 68(±11) beats min^{-1}, maximum heart rate 183(±12) beats min^{-1}, resting blood pressure 124/76 mmHg and maximum blood pressure 188/76 mmHg (Morgans, Scovill and Bass, 1984). These are within the normal range for subjects of similar age, 32(±7) years. The players exercised for 7.6(±3.1) hours per week, 77% of which was devoted to playing racquetball.

The Canadian players studied by Montpetit, Beauchamp and Leger (1987) had more impressive results. Their mean $\dot{V}O_{2max}$ was 54.1(±7) ml kg^{-1} min^{-1}, resting heart rate 58(±6) beats min^{-1} and maximum heart rate 183(±10) beats min^{-1}. These compared with figures of 55(±6) ml kg^{-1} min^{-1}, 56(±6) and 186(±8) beats min^{-1}, respectively for squash players of comparable ability level. The Canadian players studied by Montgomery (1981) had similar profiles – mean $\dot{V}O_{2max}$, 55 ml kg^{-1} min^{-1}; resting heart rate, 55 beats min^{-1}; maximum heart rate, 190 beats min^{-1}.

It seems that there is as yet insufficient research to outline a physiological profile of top racquetball players. Information on what the requirements might be can be garnered from an examination of patterns of activity during play, as described in an earlier section. Physiological responses to match-play also provide a guide to the intensity of exercise and the specific demands of the game.

12.6 OVERVIEW

The racquet sports provide a form of varied physical activity, attractive both for leisure and competitive purposes. The court games of squash and racquetball entail a higher metabolic loading than tennis or badminton. They therefore provide the higher training stimulus to the cardiovascular system, but as a corollary require a high level of aerobic fitness. Each sport incurs unique demands with largely asymmetrical muscular loading, particularly in the preferred arm.

The physiological responses to match-play differ with the level of play and whether singles or doubles competition is involved. Unlike competitors in individual sports, players are less free to choose the intensity of exercise since this may be dictated by the opponent's pattern of play. The player with tactical superiority may manipulate the pace of activity either to place his opponent under increased physiological stress or to ease his own level of exertion.

The intermittent nature of activity in the racquet sports has implications for the selection of training regimens. This has given rise to the use of intermittent training, such as sets of shuttle runs with a designated rest period between sets, for conditioning of players. Recognition of the unique demands of each game has led to the development of specific on-court drills appropriate for that sport. Drills that induce high metabolic acidosis are not essential, since high blood lactate levels have not been observed in any of the racquet sports. Nevertheless some anaerobic practices are advised so that the player can cope when a sustained burst of anaerobic activity is called for. Anaerobic power, agility and fast movements are required for each of the racquet sports. A high degree of general fitness is desirable for play at a serious competitive level: this will enable participants to practise at a high intensity for extended periods and to force a strenuous level of play on the opponent.

The general fitness programme should contain flexibility exercises, for trunk and for upper and lower limbs. Such exercises would serve to counter any impairment in flexibility associated with hypertrophy of muscle. They would also furnish a degree of safety from injury, especially in extension and rotary movements of the back and shoulder joints and adduction/abduction at the hip. Attention is also directed to maintaining muscular strength on the non-playing side of the body. These practices need to be integrated into the weekly routine of skills work and match-play so that there is an overall benefit to performance during competition.

Attention to nutrition and diet is also advocated. The diet should contain the micronutrients, minerals and vitamins compatible with healthy living. For players with a heavy regimen of training and competition, a diet high in complex carbohydrates is recommended. A light meal is advised prior to competition and should be eaten about 3 hours before match-play, according to individual preferences. Fluid replacement during a match is important in lengthy contests and in cases where players incur high sweat losses. Alcohol is not an efficient means of rehydration since it acts as a diuretic. Its hangover effects and other adverse reactions mean that players who aspire to success in their racquet sport will choose to avoid it. Such a choice must be matched to a comprehensive and systematic approach towards training and match-play for the player's true potential to be realized.

REFERENCES

Adamson, C.L. (1977) The energy cost of playing racquetball in physical education. Unpublished thesis, Eastern Kentucky University, Richmond.

Bartunkova, S., Sufarik, V., Melicharova, E., Bartunek, A., Seliger, V., Uk, F. and Bures, J. (1979) Energeticky vydaj u badminton. *Teor Praxe del Vych*, **27**, 369–372.

Beaudin, P., Zapiec, C. and Montgomery, D. (1978) Heart rate response and lactic acid concentration in squash players. *Research Quarterly*, **49**, 406–412.

Blanksby, B.A., Elliot, B.C., Davis, K.H. and Mercer, M.D. (1980) Blood pressure and rectal temperature responses of middle-aged sedentary, middle-aged active and 'A' grade competitive male squash players. *British Journal of Sports Medicine*, **14**, 133–138.

Brooks, G.A. and Fahey, T.D. (1984) *Exercise Physiology: Human Bioenergetics and its Applications*. John Wiley, New York.

Buckley, J.P. and Kerwin, D.G. (1988) The role of the biceps and triceps brachii during tennis serving. *Ergonomics*, **31**, 1621–1629.

Buskirk, E., Anderson, K.L. and Brozek, J. (1956) Unilateral activity and bone and muscle development in the forearm. *Research Quarterly*, **27**, 127–131.

Coad, D., Rasmussen, B. and Mikkelsen, F. (1979) Physical demands of recreational badminton, in *Science in Racquet Sports* (ed. J. Terauds). Academic Publishers, Del Mar, CA, pp. 45–54.

Conrad, C.C. (1976) How different sports rate in promoting physical fitness. *Medical Times*, **104**, 65–72.

Cooper, J. and Glassow, R. (1972) *Kinesiology*. C.V. Mosby, St. Louis.

Copley, B.B. (1980) A morphological and physiological study of tennis players with special reference to the effects of training. *South African Journal for Research in Sport, Physical Education and Recreation*, **3**, 33–44.

Dawson, B., Elliot, B., Pyke, F. and Rogers, R. (1985) Physiological and performance responses to playing tennis in a cool environment and similar intervalist treadmill running in a hot climate. *Journal of Human Movement Studies*, **11**, 21–34.

de Looy, A., Minors, D.S., Waterhouse, J.M., Reilly, T. and Tunstall-Pedoe, D. (1988) *The Coach's Guide to Competing Abroad*. National Coaching Foundation, Leeds.

Docherty, D. (1982) A comparison of heart rate responses in racquet games. *British Journal of Sports Medicine*, **16**, 96–100.

Docherty, D. and Howe, B. (1978) Heart rate response of squash players relative to their skill level. *Australian Journal of Sports Medicine*, **10**, 90–92.

Elliot, B., Dawson, B. and Pyke, F. (1985) The energetics of singles tennis. *Journal of Human Movement Studies*, **11**, 11–20.

Faria, I.E. and Lewis, F. (1982) Metabolic responses to playing racquetball. *Medicine and Science in Sports and Exercise*, **14**, 147 (Abstract).

Fox, E.L. (1984) *Sports Physiology*, Saunders, Philadelphia.

Friedman, D.B., Ramo, B.W. and Gray, G.J. (1984) Tennis and cardiovascular fitness in middle-aged men. *The Physician and Sportsmedicine*, **12**, 87–92.

Garden, G., Hale, P.J., Horrocks, P.M., Crase, J., Hammond, V. and Nattrass, M. (1986) Metabolic and hormonal responses during squash. *European Journal of Applied Physiology*, **55**, 445–449.

Gray, M.P. (1974) *What Research Tells the Coach about Tennis*. AAHPER, Washington.

Groppel, J.L. (1986) The biomechanics of tennis: an overview. *International Journal of Sport Biomechanics*, **2**, 144–155.

Haas, R. (1983) *Eat to Win*. Penguin, Harmondsworth.

Hughes, M. (1985) A comparison of the patterns of play of squash, in *Ergonomics International '85* (eds I.D. Brown, R. Goldsmith, K. Coombes and M.A. Sinclair), Taylor and Francis, London, pp. 139–141.

Katch, F., Michael, E.D. and Jones, E.M. (1969) Effects of physical training on the body composition and diet of female athletes. *Research Quarterly*, **40**, 99–104.

Kindermann, W. and Keul, J. (1977) Lactate acidoses with different forms of sports activities. *Canadian Journal of Applied Sport Sciences*, **2**, 177–182.

Kirby, R. and Roberts, J.A. (1985) *Introductory Biomechanics*. Mouvement Publications, Ithaca, NY.

Medved, R. (1966) Body height and predisposition for certain sports. *Journal of Sports Medicine and Physical Fitness*, **6**, 89–91.

Mercier, M., Beillot, J., Gratas, A., Rothcongar, P., Lessard, Y., Andre, A.M. and Dassonville, J. (1987) Adaptation to work load in squash players: laboratory tests and on court recordings. *Journal of Sports Medicine and Physical Fitness*, **27**, 98–104.

Mikkelsen, F. (1979) Physical demands and muscle adaptation in elite badminton players, in *Science in Racquet Sports* (ed. J. Terauds), Academic Publishers, Del Mar, CA, pp. 55–67.

Misner, T.E., Boileau, R.A., Courvoisier, D., Slaughter, M.H. and Bloomfield, D.K. (1980) Cardiovascular stress associated with the recreational tennis play of middle aged males. *American Corrective Therapy Journal*, **34**, 4–8.

Montgomery, D.L. (1981) Heart rate response to racquetball. *The Physician and Sportsmedicine*, **9**, 59–62.

Montpetit, R.R., Beauchamp, L. and Leger, L. (1987) Energy requirements of squash and racquetball. *The Physician and Sportsmedicine*, **15**, 107–112.

Montpetit, R.R., Leger, L. and Girardin, Y. (1977) Le racquetball, le squash et le condition physique. *Le Medicin du Quebec*, **12**, 119–123.

Morgans, L.F., Scovill, J.A. and Bass, K.M. (1984) Heart rate responses during singles and doubles competition in racquetball. *The Physician and Sportsmedicine*, **12**, 64–72.

Noakes, T.D., Cowling, J.R., Gevers, W. and Van Niekark, J.P. de V. (1982) The metabolic response to squash including the influence of pre-exercise carbohydrate ingestion. *South African Medical Journal*, **62**, 721–723.

Northcote, R.J., Evans, A.D.B. and Ballantyne, D. (1984) Sudden death in squash players. *Lancet*, **1**, 148–151.

Northcote, R.J., MacFarlane, P. and Ballantyne, D. (1983) Ambulatory electrocardiography in squash players. *British Heart Journal*, **50**, 372–377.

Owens, M.S. and Lee, H.Y. (1969) A determination of velocities and angles of projection for the tennis serve. *Research Quarterly*, **40**, 750–754.

Peronnet, F., Thibault, G., Ledoax, M. and Brisson, G. (1987) *Performance in Endurance Events*. Spodyn Publishers, London, Ontario.

Pipes, T.V. (1979) The racquetball pro: a physiological profile. *The Physician and Sportsmedicine*, **7**, 91–94.

Plagenhoef, S. (1970) *Fundamentals of Tennis*. Prentice-Hall, Englewood Cliffs, NJ.

Potts, A., Gamble, D., Lowery, A. and Jakeman, P. (1986) The total energy cost of simulated squash routines. Communication to Sport and Science Conference (Chichester).

Powers, S.K. and Walker, R. (1982) Physiological and anatomical characteristics of outstanding female junior tennis players. *Research Quarterly*, **53**, 172.

Pyke, S., Elliott, C. and Pyke, E. (1974) Performance testing of tennis and squash players. *British Journal of Sports Medicine*, **8**, 80–86.

Reilly, T. (1986) Fundamental studies in soccer, in *Beitrage zur Sportspielforschung* (ed. R. Andresen), Verlag Ingrid Czwalina, Hamburg, pp. 114–120.

Reilly, T. (1987) Circadian rhythms and exercise, in *Exercise: Benefits, Limits and Adaptations* (eds D. MacLeod, R.J. Maughan, M. Nimmo, T. Reilly and C. Williams), E. and F.N. Spon, London, pp. 346–366.

Reilly, T. and Lees, A. (1984) Exercise and sports equipment: some ergonomics aspects. *Applied Ergonomics*, **15**, 259–279.

Rigg, P. and Reilly, T. (1988) A fitness profile and anthropometric analysis of first and second class Rugby union players, in *Science and Football* (eds T. Reilly, A. Lees, K. Davids and W.J. Murphy), E. and F.N. Spon, London, pp. 194–200.

Rittell, H.F. and Waterloh, E. (1975) Radiotelemetrie bei Tennis, Badminton und Tischjennisspieler. *Sportarzt Sportmedizin*, **15**, 144–150.

Sanderson, F.H. (1981) Injuries in racket sports, in *Sports Fitness and Sports Injuries* (ed. T. Reilly), Faber and Faber, London, pp. 175–182.

Seliger, V., Ejem, M., Pauer, M. and Safarik, V. (1973) Energy metabolism in tennis. *Internationale Zeitschrift für Angew Physiologie*, **31**, 333–340.

Sinclair, G.D. and Goldsmith, B.C. (1978) Scientists nail down racquetball benefits. *National Racquetball*, **6**, 82–84.

Steininger, K. and Wodick, R.E. (1987) Sports-specific fitness testing in squash. *British Journal of Sports Medicine*, **21**, 23–26.

Sukun, M. and Wang, S. (1988) The measurement of aerobic, anaerobic capacity and extremital strength of Chinese top badminton players, in *Abstracts New Horizons of Human Movement*, Vol. III. SOSCOC, Seoul, p. 252.

van Rensburg, J.P., van der Linde, A., Ackerman, P.C., Kielblock and Strydom, N.B. (1982) Physiological profile of squash players. *South African Journal for Research in Sport, Physical Education and Recreation*, **5**, 25–56.

Widdowson, E.M., Edholm, O.G. and McCance, R.A. (1954) The food intake and energy expenditure of cadets in training. *British Journal of Nutrition*, **8**, 147–155.

Yamaoka, S. (1965) Studies in the energy metabolism in athletic sports. *Research Journal of Physical Education*, **9**, 28–40.

13
Football

Thomas Reilly

13.1 INTRODUCTION

Football describes a number of codes of match-play, the major one being soccer or association football which is played on a world-wide basis. The next universally popular are Rugby Union and Rugby League, both of which are physical contact sports. National variations of football exist, the best known being American Football, Australian Rules and Gaelic Football. Top players from the latter two codes have met regularly in international competition (Australia versus Ireland) in a hybrid game known as 'compromise rules'. This has shown closely the similarities between the games, despite the gross differences that appear to a naive observer unaware of the common origins of the various football codes.

A common aspect of all the games is the necessity of team work to complement individual skills. These include kicking, passing, carrying or travelling with the ball, catching or controlling the ball and tackling. Besides, all the games call for movement within the field of play, either directly contributing to the play or anticipating its direction. The activity is intermittent, regularly changing in intensity: during play it may vary from a sequence of all-out sprints to a casual recovery standing or walking. The cycles of activity and rest are largely unpredictable: they result from the spontaneity of the player or are imposed by the pattern of play. Because of the relatively large field of play, team members must be mobile, capable of covering ground quickly when necessary to support team mates in defence or attack. This has physiological consequences that are reflected in the level and type of fitness needed for match-play.

The field dimensions vary with the different codes as do the rules of play, methods of scoring, the number of players and substitutions. The duration of play also differs, being longest in American Football and shortest in Gaelic Football (70 min) and the Rugby games (80 min). There are also variations within codes, the so-called 'small-sided games' achieving increased popularity in recent years. These include 4-a-side, 5-a-side and indoor soccer, 'Rugby 7's and Gaelic Football 7-a-side tournaments. In general these raise the intensity of play, call for increased fitness of players or alternatively increase the training stimulus when such games are used for practice purposes. Participation of females in football is now widely promoted, especially in soccer and Gaelic Football while mixed teams of male and female play Rugby Union in the form of 'New-image Rugby' in which physical contact is eliminated.

The physiological fitness levels required for match-play depend on the work-rate demands of the game which vary with the level of com-petition. Each of the football codes can be expected to impose its own particular demands. Specific positional roles within each code may demand unique physiological attributes. These are reflected in the anthropometric and physiological fitness profiles of the football players. Variations in fitness profiles according to playing position are more pronounced in the physical contact games – Rugby and American Football – whereas versatility in playing roles is more feasible in Gaelic Football and soccer than in the other codes.

Historically, not many sports physiologists have been attracted to examine football in detail because of the lack of adequate experimental models to study the games in the laboratory. Nor have they been warmly welcomed by football practitioners, sceptical of the role of the physiologist and suspicious of the influence of science on the game. Nevertheless, there has been considerable interest among players and coaches in fitness for football and its development and so an impressive body of knowledge has accumulated about scientific aspects of football. The universal popularity of association football is expressed in the fact that it has gained the most research attention. Consequently, the emphasis in this chapter is devoted mainly to soccer. The demands of the game are first described before proceeding to a review of the fitness profiles of players. The information on training and habitual activities of players is then considered. The other football codes are briefly reviewed, the national football games together and the Rugby games together.

13.2 SOCCER

13.2.1 Work rate

Soccer matches last 90 min and the patterns of activity in this time can be expressed as work-rate profiles. These may be determined by methods of motion analysis which give useful pointers to the physiological stresses imposed by match-play. Although the physiological demands of soccer may vary according to the system of play or tactics employed, there are some consistencies in the movement profiles displayed during the course of a match. Each game calls for about 1000 discrete bouts of action incorporating rapid and frequent changes of pace and direction, execution of games skills and so on. In English League First Division matches players change activity every 5–6 s on average, have brief rest pauses averaging only 3 s every 2 min, although rest breaks tend to be longer and more frequent at lower levels of competition. Sprints average about 15 m and occur every 90 s or so whilst players run at a cruise or sprint once every 30 s (Reilly and Thomas, 1976).

In normal locomotion the energy expenditure is a direct function of the distance travelled and so the distance covered in a game may be a crude guide to the work rate of individual players. The methodology for measurement of distance must be reliable, objective and valid. Studies on top Australian (Withers *et al.*, 1982), Belgian (Van Gool, 1987), Canadian (Mayhew and Wenger, 1985), English League (Reilly and

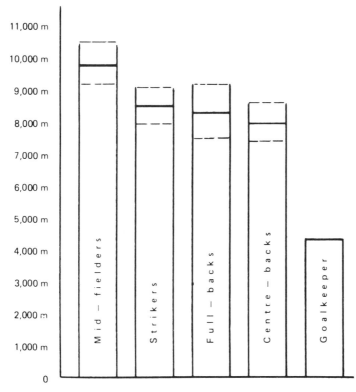

Figure 13.1 Mean (± SD) distance covered per game according to playing position in soccer (from Reilly and Thomas, 1976).

Thomas, 1976) and Swedish (Saltin, 1973) teams indicate that the distance covered by outfield players varies between 8 and 13 km approximately. The proportion of the overall distance covered in possession of the ball is low, varying between 0.25 and 4%, with defenders tending to release the ball earlier than attackers.

The overall pattern of activity is acyclical and players may sometimes be placed in circumstances where they have sole responsibility for achieving victory or saving a defeat. They need the fitness as well as the game skills to create such situations or respond successfully when they occur unexpectedly. This calls for a wide range of physical and physiological attributes. An ability to sustain runs and recover quickly to take up a position to receive the ball from a team mate in possession increases the options available to the player with the ball. The observation of a high correlation between aerobic power ($\dot{V}O_{2max}$) and distance covered per game supports the adoption of training regimens that develop the oxygen transport system (Thomas and Reilly, 1976; Smaros, 1980). This is especially the case where a high work rate is expected of players. In addition to the strong correlation ($r = 0.89$) with the total distance covered in a game, Smaros (1980) found that the $\dot{V}O_{2max}$ also influenced the number of sprints that players were able to attempt in a match.

In conventional English League soccer which employed a 4–3–3 team formation, the distance covered per game was seen to vary according to positional roles (Figure 13.1). The greatest distances are covered by midfield players, the least among the outfield players by central defenders. Full-backs and strikers have the more flexible roles whereas the centre-backs cover a relatively higher proportion of their movements going backwards or sideways. These unique elements of work rate should be mimicked in practice drills for effective training of players for positional roles.

Systems of play that demand high work rate profiles – such as 'total football' exemplified by the Dutch national team of the 1970s, the 'Reep system' employed by Wimbledon and Watford in the English League in the 1980s and the style of play used by Eire in the 1988 European Nations Championship – may reduce the differences between positions in the aerobic fitness of players. This levelling effect will be enhanced if a common training regimen is used by all members of the playing squad.

On average, the overall distance covered by outfield players during a match consists of 25% walking, 37% jogging, 20% cruising sub-maximally, 11% sprinting and 7% moving backwards (Reilly and Thomas, 1976). The frequency of sprints tends to be greater in midfielders and strikers than in full-backs and centre-backs. Midfielders act as a link between defence and attack and need to be capable of sustained running. Strikers are often required to run 'off the ball' to create space for team-mates, to divert defenders or to force them to play the ball. The ability to generate movement off the ball is influenced by fitness as well as tactical sense. Although the pace of activity tends to be slower in centre-backs compared to the other positions, these players still need to be capable of running at speed for short distances. They also require great anaerobic power in jumping to win aerial possession of the ball. Their abilities in jumping are also exploited for offensive purposes in set-plays close to the opponents' goal.

It is noteworthy that the goalkeeper covers about 4 km in the course of a match. This activity level can be partly accounted for by the necessity to maintain arousal. When involved in the play the goalkeeper needs to be able to react quickly and with agility. This work rate profile implicates anaerobic power rather than any demands on the oxygen transport system. Although the work rate profile is low, the goalkeeper is directly involved in play more frequently than any single outfield player (Reilly and Thomas, 1976).

At high standards of play a fatigue effect is noticeable in the second half as a drop in the work rate (Reilly and Thomas, 1976). This has been shown to be related to a reduction in energy stores within the active muscles. Saltin (1973) found that players with a lower glycogen content in their thigh muscle at the start of a game covered 25% less distance than the others. An even more marked difference was noted for running speed; players with low glycogen content covered half the total distance walking and 15% at maximal speed compared with 27% walking and 24% sprinting for the players with high initial glycogen levels. In players with high and low muscle glycogen stores pre-start these values were found to be reduced to 32 and 6 mM kg^{-1} respectively, when muscle biopsy samples were taken at half-time.

These findings have implications for both training and nutritional preparation of players. It is reasonable to expect that an elevation in aerobic power and capacity will help to sustain a high work rate profile throughout the game. Endurance training also promotes increased utilization of fat as an energy source, thereby sparing the muscle glycogen. It also means that muscle glycogen levels should not be lowered by strenuous training the day before or the morning of an important game. A diet rich in carbohydrate can augment muscle glycogen values and so contribute to the better maintenance of a high work rate profile throughout 90 min play.

13.2.2 Physiological demands

Heart rate

Generally it is impractical to make physiological measurements on players during serious competitions, although scientists have developed

Figure 13.2 Soccer players fitted with radio telemeter for transmission of ECG to recorder on the side of the pitch. The short-range system is shown on the left. Its signals can be played back by means of a computer post-game.

indirect methods of estimating physiological loadings. It is unrealistic to encumber players with heavy monitoring devices or to interrupt the game for invasive measurements such as blood sampling. Research strategies employed have varied from use of model games and friendly matches where measurements were allowed, to adoption of non-invasive indices of physiological strain. The data obtained may be married to observations in a laboratory context to refine the inferences that may be made from the field studies.

Heart rate is one index of the physiological strain incurred by the footballer during match-play. It is relatively unobtrusive as it can be monitored continuously by radio telemetry. The subject wears chest electrodes attached to a lightweight radio transmitter, the signal being picked up by a receiver on the sidelines (Figure 13.2). Alternatively, short-range telemetry may be used, the receiver being worn like a watch on the wrist of the player: the signal is retained in the memory of the receiver and played back for analysis after the game.

Use of heart rate in such field contexts has been defended on the grounds that it is at once an indicator of the total circulatory load imposed on the body. The heart rate accelerates with increasing exercise intensities to raise cardiac output so that the circulatory system can meet the needs of the active muscles for oxygen. Increased blood flow to the skin resulting from a heat load will be reflected in increased heart rate as will an emotional consequence of executing game skills. Because of the relatively short recovery periods in soccer the heart rate stays at an elevated level and fluctuations during play are not very large. This is reflected in observations made during simulated competitions and friendly matches.

Seliger (1968a) studied players during a 10 min model game and found mean heart rates of 160 beats min^{-1} and peak values that were 166 beats min^{-1} on average. The standard deviation for both mean and peak measures was 14 beats min^{-1}. Mean values for Czechoslovak soccer players were reported in another publication (Seliger, 1968b) to be about 165 beats min^{-1}. These values were equivalent to sports such as kayak paddling which had a mean heart rate of 166 beats min^{-1}. In these studies it should be mentioned that subjects wore a respirometer on their backs while playing, so that oxygen consumption could be measured.

Measurements of heart rate have been made on English League footballers when playing friendly matches. In order to ensure that observations could be validly extrapolated to real contests, the work rate of individuals was compared between the two conditions. The distance covered in friendly games was shown to be within 2% of the competition data (Reilly, 1986). Heart rate was found to be 157 beats min^{-1} for the outfield players and 124 beats min^{-1} for the goalkeeper. The heart rates stayed close to steady-rate values during play, the coefficient of variation being less than 5%. The mean heart rates corresponded to 80% of the maximum heart rates. When the resting (48 ± SE = 1 beats min^{-1}) and maximal (198 ± SE = 1 beats min^{-1}) heart rates of the players were taken into account, it was calculated that subjects were exercising at 68% of the heart rate range.

A study of a Danish First Division team noted that heart rate was about 77% of the heart rate range for 66% of the playing time (Rohde and Espersen, 1988). For the larger part of the remaining time the heart rate was above this level. When the higher resting heart rates (60 beats min^{-1}) of the Danish players are taken into account, the results are in broad agreement with observations on the English League players.

It is likely that a player with a high level of aerobic fitness will be able to sustain a higher exercise intensity than a colleague of poorer fitness. Agnevik (1970) reported a mean heart rate of 175 beats min^{-1} during a major match in one of the top players in the Swedish team; with the exception of some brief periods of play the heart rate was maintained below the player's maximum rate of 189 beats min^{-1}.

Mean heart rates of the players in a Belgian University team during a friendly match were 169 beats min^{-1} in the first half and 165 beats min^{-1}

in the second half. These corresponded respectively to 86.7% and 84.4% of the maximal heart rate. During the game the distance covered was 10 225 ($\pm$ SD = 580) m: the slightly lower heart rates in the second half are likely to have been due to a reduced work rate since players covered 444 m less in the second half than in the first (Van Gool, Van Gerven and Boutmans, 1988).

As work rate profiles differ between positions, it is reasonable to expect that this may be reflected in heart rate values. Van Gool, Van Gervan and Boutmans (1983) presented data on players from four outfield positions. The mean heart rate was 155($\pm$ 11) beats min^{-1} for the centre-back, 155($\pm$16) beats min^{-1} for the full-back, 170($\pm$ 9) beats min^{-1} for the midfield player and 171($\pm$ 13) beats min^{-1} for the forward. Another forward was found to have a mean heart rate of 168 beats min^{-1}. This pattern of different positional demands closely corresponds to the work rate profiles that emerged when expressed as total distance covered per game.

The results of these studies suggest that the strain on the circulatory system during soccer play is relatively high. Exercising at this intensity should provide a good training stimulus, provided such participation is frequent enough. Although there are brief respites in activity during a game, the heart rate is maintained at a fairly high level all through. Differences in relative physiological strain between positional roles are small, but do demonstrate the individual work rate profiles of the various positions. An important contribution of aerobic fitness to team performance would lie in the greater exercise intensity that could be sustained throughout play.

Metabolic demands

The energy expended in playing soccer may be calculated from the oxygen uptake and the non-protein respiratory exchange ratio. Although measurement of oxygen uptake is likely to interfere with normal play, some studies have been performed with players wearing respirometers during casual games. Durnin and Passmore (1967) quoted a range of 21–50 kJ (5–12 kcal) min^{-1} for the energy requirements in soccer and concluded that few players expend more than 2512 kJ (600 kcal) in a game. Covell, Din and Passmore (1965) reported a range of 22–44 kJ (5.2–10.6 kcal) min^{-1}. A study of Japanese players of undefined skills reported that metabolic requirements of playing soccer were 1–2 times the resting metabolic rate for goalkeepers and 5–7 times for the other players (Yamaoka, 1965). The excess cost of a 90 min game over resting metabolism was 2461 kJ (588 kcal). If a value of 5 kJ (1.2 kcal) min^{-1} is assumed for resting metabolism the rate of energy expenditure would amount to about 32.2 kJ (7.7 kcal) min^{-1}.

The subjects in these studies were undergraduates kicking a ball about a pitch and may be more representative of soccer played as a leisure activity than as a competitive game. The values are likely to under-estimate the energy demands of serious match-play.

The players studied by Seliger (1968a) were probably taking the game more seriously than the British or Japanese students. Their mean $\dot{V}O_2$ was 3.18 l min^{-1}: this corresponded to an energy expenditure of 5191 kJ (1240 kcal) over the game. In another study the energy used was 4940 kJ (1180 kcal) corresponding to a rate of 54.8 kJ (13.1 kcal) min^{-1} or a $\dot{V}O_2$ of 35.5 ml kg^{-1} min^{-1} (Seliger, 1968b). The inspired ventilation volume averaged 76 l min^{-1}: relatively hard exercise is implied when this rate is sustained for 90 min.

As apparatus for collection of expired air during play can hamper activity of the player, an alternative approach has been to use heart rate measurements for predicting the level of energy expenditure. This requires the establishment of a relation between heart rate and $\dot{V}O_2$ in laboratory conditions, where treadmill running would be the most suitable exercise mode, and estimating the $\dot{V}O_2$ during play from the average heart rate. The extrapolation from the laboratory to the field context assumes that the relation established from the treadmill test holds up under game conditions. Since the procedure averages out fluctuations in activity during play it offers a rough rather than a precise guide to estimating the metabolic load.

In First Division English League soccer it was projected from heart-rate data that the energy expenditure during competition was 69 kJ (16.4 kcal) min^{-1} (Reilly, 1979). The calculated rate for 21 outfield players was 73 $\pm$ 4 kJ (17.4 $\pm$ 0.9 kcal) min^{-1} and for two goalkeepers 19 and 22 kJ (4.5 and 5.25 kcal) min^{-1}. The outfield players were estimated to be exercising at an average close to 75% whereas the goalkeepers were below 50% of their maximal aerobic power. Using a similar approach Van Gool, Van Gerven and Boutmans calculated that Belgian players exercised at an average of approximately 75% of $\dot{V}O_{2max}$. These authors demonstrated that players with high work rates – the 'toilers' of the team – may have to tax this capacity higher still.

Marathon runners tend to race at about 75% $\dot{V}O_{2max}$ so this comparison gives some indication of the aggregate intensity of com-petitive soccer. The soccer player does not cover as much ground in a game as would a competent marathon runner in 90 min and so the energy expenditure in soccer is likely to be grossly underestimated if based solely on the distance covered. The intermittent nature of activity means that players frequently rely on anaerobic mechanisms for brief bursts of intense action which accentuate the metabolic load. The activity during the course of play includes abrupt accelerations and decelerations, changes of direction and angled runs. Skills of the game also impose physiological demands additional to the metabolic cost of running. On the other hand use of individual regression lines relating heart rate and $\dot{V}O_2$ is likely to overestimate the energy cost of playing the game. This might arise from thermal and emotional influences on the heart rate which are not reflected in $\dot{V}O_2$, or the cardiovascular drift – increase in heart rate and a fall in stroke volume – that might occur during 90 min exercise.

About 16% of the distance covered by players in a game is in moving backwards or sideways, the proportion being greater in centre-backs. The added physiological costs of unorthodox directions of movements have been examined by getting nine soccer players to run on a treadmill at three speeds (5, 7 and 9 km h^{-1}) – running normally, running backwards and running sideways (Reilly and Bowen, 1984). The extra energy cost of the unorthodox modes of running increased disproportionately with speed. Running backwards and running sideways did not differ in terms of energy expenditure or in the rating of perceived exertion (Table 13.1). Clearly, improving the efficiency in these unorthodox modes of running would be of benefit to the player.

To establish the magnitude of the additional physiological demands of a game skill, the energy cost of dribbling a soccer ball was examined in laboratory conditions (Reilly and Ball, 1984). The procedure enabled precise control over the player's activity while expired air, blood lactate and perceived exertion were measured. Dribbling the ball at 9, 10.5, 12 and 13.5 km h^{-1}, each for 5 min, was made possible by means of a rebound box in front of the treadmill which returned the ball to the player's feet. The energy cost of dribbling – one touch taken every 2–3 full stride cycles – was found to increase linearly with the speed of running and the added cost of dribbling was constant at 5.2 kJ (1.24 kcal) min^{-1} (Figure 13.3). This value may vary in field conditions

Table 13.1 Mean ($\pm$ SD) for energy expended (kJ) and ratings of exertion at three speeds and three directional modes of motion ($n = 9$). Data are taken from the study by Reilly and Bowen (1984)

Speed (km h^{-1})	Forwards	Backwards	Sideways
Energy expended (kJ)			
5	37.05 $\pm$ 2.60	44.83 $\pm$ 6.11	46.05 $\pm$ 3.18
7	42.28 $\pm$ 1.67	53.41 $\pm$ 3.52	56.30 $\pm$ 6.15
9	50.57 $\pm$ 4.94	71.41 $\pm$ 6.99	71.04 $\pm$ 7.53
Perceived exertion			
5	6.67 $\pm$ 0.05	8.56 $\pm$ 2.01	8.67 $\pm$ 2.00
7	8.00 $\pm$ 1.41	11.22 $\pm$ 2.95	11.33 $\pm$ 3.16
9	10.22 $\pm$ 2.11	14.00 $\pm$ 2.00	13.78 $\pm$ 2.54

according to the closeness of ball control the player exerts. When dribbling, the stride rate increases and the stride length shortens compared with normal running at the same speed and these changes are likely to contribute to the added energy cost. Increasing or decreasing the stride length beyond that freely chosen by the individual increases the oxygen uptake for a given speed (Cavanagh and Williams, 1982). The energy cost may be increased further in practice by the tactics of irregularly changing individual stride lengths or feigning lateral movements whilst dribbling in order to deceive an opponent. The shorter than normal length of stride when dribbling is perhaps necessary to achieve controlled contact with the ball and propel it forward with the desired amount of force by the swinging limb. Muscle activity required for kicking the ball and action of synergists and stabilizers to aid balance while the kicking movement is completed are also likely to contribute to the added energy cost.

Perceived exertion was also increased while dribbling in the study of Reilly and Ball (1984) and this reflects the elevation in metabolism. Assuming that the perception of effort is ultimately a limiting factor in

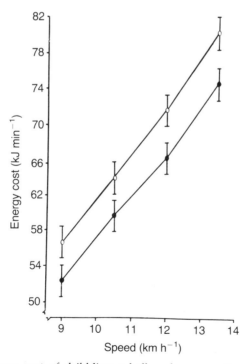

Figure 13.3 Energy cost of dribbling a ball and comparative data for normal running at four different speeds (from Reilly and Ball, 1984).

all-out efforts, an implication is that top running speeds may not be attained in dribbling practices unless the frequency of ball contact is reduced. This is exemplified in match-play when a wing player uses a kick ahead to allow himself sufficient time to accelerate past an opposing defender. This manoeuvre would reduce the energy consumption in covering a given distance dribbling the ball by cutting down the number of contacts and would attenuate the physiological strain in retaining ball possession at that speed.

Blood lactate levels are also increased as a consequence of dribbling the ball, the elevation being disproportionate at the high speeds (Figure

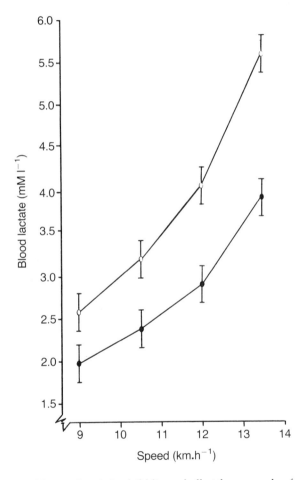

Figure 13.4 Blood lactate levels in dribbling a ball at four speeds of running on a treadmill. The lower line shows data for normal running without the ball (from Reilly and Ball, 1984).

13.4). In the study by Reilly and Ball (1984) the 'anaerobic threshold' (defined as lactate inflection point) was calculated to occur at 10.7 km h^{-1} for dribbling but not until 11.7 km h^{-1} in normal running. This result suggests that the metabolic strain of dribbling practices may be underestimated if the anaerobic components are not considered.

The added cost of dribbling does not on its own contribute substantially to the energy expenditure in a complete game because of the relatively small amount of time the individual is in possession of the ball. Nevertheless, it does have implications for training. Exercise with the ball will induce a greater physiological training stimulus at a given speed of motion than normal running. It suggests also that the myriad of other actions and alterations in activity during play that are superimposed on the requirements to cover distance may have considerable impact if these additional loads are aggregated.

Energy for brief bouts of activity can be obtained from alactic sources – the phosphagens and oxygen bound to myoglobin – but the main mechanism is anaerobic breakdown of glycogen. The reduction of muscle glycogen can be as high as 84% in active muscles at the end of a game (Agnevik, 1970) but this can occur as a result of aerobic metabolism or repetitive high-intensity bouts of exercise supported by anaerobic glycolysis. The degree of anaerobic contribution to metabolism in soccer play has been examined by various researchers by looking at the blood lactate concentrations. Generally the blood lactate levels were determined from samples obtained at half-time and at the end of play. Variability may arise as a consequence of the type of activity

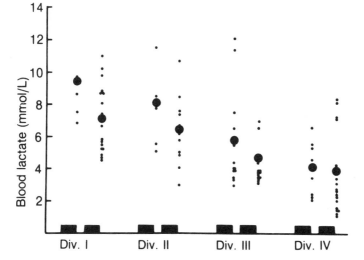

Figure 13.5 Blood lactate values during match-play for four Divisions of the Swedish League (from Ekblom, 1986).

prior to measurements being made. Values also depend on the level of competition. The reports vary enormously from low to moderate levels of lactate to rather high levels in the work of Ekblom (1986; Figure 13.5).

Average blood lactate levels of outfield players in German championship games, determined at half-time and at the end of the game, varied between 4 and 6 mM (Gerisch, Rutemoller and Weber, 1988). The mean level was slightly higher after the first half (5.58 mM) than at the end of the game (4.68 mM), possibly reflecting a decline in work-rate in the latter part of the game. The authors concluded from their measurements that there were regular occurrences of peak lactates of about 7–8 mM.

Lactate levels varied significantly between German teams differing in endurance capacities when man-to-man marking was used. In contrast lactate levels were very similar between the teams when a 'zone-coverage' strategy was employed. Presumably the players can match their activities to their endurance fitness levels by an astute choice of tactics.

The highest lactate levels during soccer have been reported by Ekblom (1986), mean values ranging from about 8 mM for Swedish Division I games to about 4 mM for Division IV games (Figure 13.5). The figures for the top league are above the level that could be sustained continuously and so reflect the intermittent high intensity runs. Indeed peak values above 12 mM were reported: however, the capability of players to respond to further demands for sustained sprints is likely to be affected. The results showed a consistently lower lactate concentration at the end of the game compared to the first half values. This ties in with the observations that the greatest rate of decline in muscle glycogen levels occurs in the first half of the game. A Finnish study showed that this decline occurs predominantly in the slow-twitch fibres (Smaros, 1980), suggesting that the aerobic metabolism may play the larger part in utilizing muscle glycogen. A greater recruitment of fast-twitch fibres might be expected in top-class matches where the intensity of soccer play is at its highest.

The average blood lactate levels in other studies are more consistent with the view that blood lactate does not rise appreciably during soccer and that very high levels are infrequently reached. Besides, the low-level activity of walking and jogging helps to remove lactate from blood after its production in the muscles during high intensity runs. Mean values noted for a Danish First Division team were 4.4 ($\pm$ SD = 1.9) mM; this figure is slightly above the level at which steady-state exercise might be sustained for 90 min or so (Rohde and Espersen, 1988). Lower values still were observed in elite young Australian players, although in this case calf venous samples were analysed (Tumilty et al., 1988). The mean values post-game were 2.4($\pm$ 2) mM, the pH levels of 7.33 ($\pm$ 0.04) indicating only mild acidosis. Bicarbonate values post-game (21.8 $\pm$ 1.1 mM) suggested that buffering mechanisms had not been taxed to the same extent as in a sequence of 20 m sprints with short recovery periods.

13.2.3 Characteristics of soccer players

Anthropometry

Top soccer teams tend to have an average age of about 25 years with a typical standard deviation of 2 years or so (Reilly, 1979). Players 20 years of age or less do feature in the top club teams but they tend to reach the pinnacle of their own playing careers some years later. The majority of professional players are in their twenties and the few who continue to play at a high level until well into their thirties are exceptions. From his study of entrants at the Tokyo Olympic Games in 1964, Hirata (1966) concluded that success in ball games such as soccer, hockey, basketball and volleyball is mainly accomplished in the period 24–27 years, soccer being the earliest of these. Goalkeepers seem to have longer playing careers than outfield players and it is not unusual to find players at international level in their late thirties in this position. This may be related to a lower incidence of chronic injuries and degenerative trauma

Table 13.2 Mean (± SE) height and weight of soccer teams in a sample of reports in the literature

	Height (cm)	Weight (kg)
English League, First Division (White et al., 1988)	180.4 ± 1.7	76.7 ± 1.5
English League, First Division (Reilly, 1975)	176.0 ± 1.1	73.2 ± 1.5
Tottenham Hotspur (Reilly, 1979)	178.5 ± 1.3	77.5 ± 1.3
Aberdeen F.C. (Williams et al., 1973)	174.6 ± 0.9	69.4 ± 2.1
Dallas Tornado (Raven et al., 1976)	176.3 ± 1.2	75.7 ± 1.9
South Australian Representatives (Withers et al., 1977)	178.1 ± 3.6	75.2 ± 2.2
Italian Professionals (Faina et al., 1988)	177.2 ± 0.9	74.4 ± 1.1
Ujpesti Dozja, Budapest (Apor, 1988)	176.5 ± 1.7	70.5 ± 1.3
Honved, Budapest (Apor, 1988)	177.6 ± 1.1	73.5 ± 1.6

in goalkeeping compared to outfield positions. A loss of motivation to continue playing or a reluctance of management to renew contracts of the older players may contribute to an earlier than necessary retirement from playing professional soccer. Active athletes can maintain fitness levels well into their thirties before physiological functions begin to show signs of deterioration.

Data on height and weight of soccer teams suggest that players vary widely in body size (Table 13.2). Principal component analysis of fitness data on English League First Division players found that 23% of the total variance among individuals could be accounted for by a component related to body size, while a further 10% was explained by a component related to body density (Reilly and Thomas, 1980). Lack of height is not in itself a bar to success in soccer, though it might determine the choice of playing position.

It should be recognized that mean values have only limited use for comparative purposes when the variability is large. A coach may modify his team configuration and style of play to accommodate individuals without the expected physical attributes of conventional positional roles but who compensate by superior skills and motivation. The average body size may also represent ethnic or racial influences: for example the North African and the Korean teams playing the World Cup final matches have tended to be smaller than their European and South American rivals. Japan's team in the 1964 Olympic Games was described as especially small and light for playing at that level (Hirata, 1966) and illustrated characteristic ethnic differences from others, Asians on the whole being smaller than non-Asians. Many top European teams contain players of different ethnic backgrounds and this can make the interpretation of anthropometric profiles more difficult.

Height does bestow an advantage to the goalkeeper, the centre-backs and to the forward used as the 'target man' for winning possession of the ball with his head. Thus a particular stature may orientate players towards specific positional or tactical roles. Among Australian National squad members it was shown that defenders tended to be the tallest and heaviest players whereas the mean height and weight of the midfield players were well below the overall squad means (Cochrane and Pyke, 1976). A study of English players at College level confirmed that the goalkeepers (mean 180 cm) were the tallest while the midfield players (mean 173 cm) were the smallest (Bell and Rhodes, 1975). This trend was supported by observations of professional English League players, the centre-backs being taller than the full-backs with midfield players being the smallest of those playing outfield (Reilly, 1979).

There appears to be a general trend in the population that the lower the level of play the greater is the body size of players. An extensive study of Yugoslav soccer players found that when the players were classified according to the level of performance those of top class ability tended to be slightly smaller and lighter than those of moderate ability (Medved, 1966). Nevertheless this trend in body size brings no guarantee of success in the game. It is possible that a particular body size will encourage acquisition of certain skills and force a gravitation towards a specific playing position: this is likely to occur before maturity so that the individual will tend to favour one positional role before playing at senior level.

Body composition is an important aspect of fitness for soccer as superfluous body fat acts as dead weight in activities where body mass must be lifted repeatedly against gravity in locomotion during play. Generally, the amount of fat in an adult male in his mid-twenties is about 16.5% of body weight. The lowest values among athletic groups are found in distance runners with mean levels 4–7%. Values as low as 8.3% have been reported for attacking and defending backs in American Football (Wilmore and Haskell, 1972). Soccer players, even at the highest level, tend to have depots of body fat that seem higher than optimal. Hirata's (1966) study of Olympic Games players led him to conclude that they were 'a little stout' as well as rather small. Observations on professional players show values between 9 and 19%, including 14.9% for Aberdeen FC players (Reid and Williams, 1974) and 9.6% for members of the Dallas Tornado FC team (Raven et al., 1976). The mean percentage body fat reported for Brazilian players was 10.7%, the national level players being just below 10% (De Rose, 1975). The average for College players in outfield roles was found to be 14.7% (Bell and Rhodes, 1975). Higher values tend to be found in goalkeepers than in outfield players, probably because of the lighter metabolic loading imposed by match-play and training on goalkeepers. Soccer players accumulate body fat in the off-season: a mean percentage body fat as high as 19.3% was noted for a top English League team starting pre-season training (White et al., 1988). Thus the habitual activity of players at the time of measurement, their diet and the stage of the competitive season should be considered when body composition is evaluated. The observations may depend on the methods of measuring or estimating percentage body fat and the scale of measurement error should be recognized when results are being compared.

Soccer players tend to be well developed in muscularity especially in the thigh and this produces a characteristic body shape or physique. Somatotyping offers a convenient method of describing the physique of players according to three dimensions – endomorphy, mesomorphy and ectomorphy. The somatotype of English College players seemed to vary around the basic 3:5:2.5 profile; professional players also tend to occupy a similar area of the somatochart when average values for the team are plotted (White et al., 1988). Mean rating of the Australian soccer squad was 3:5:3, again emphasizing a tendency towards mesomorphy (Cochrane and Pyke, 1976). Ratings for top Czech players averaged

2.5:4.6:2.5 (Chovanova and Zrubak, 1972) and 3:5.1:2.5 (Stepnicka, 1977), these players meriting the description of middle to strong mesomorphs. The somatotype of top Hungarian players was reported to be 2.1:5.1:2.3, the players with only a few exceptions belonging to the balanced mesomorphy category (Apor, 1988). The muscular make-up could be expected to be advantageous in game contexts such as tackling, turning, accelerating, kicking and so on.

A comparison of top English League players with the 1960 Olympic athletes studied by Tanner (1964) using similar procedures showed that the soccer players closely resembled the 400 m hurdlers in weight and thigh circumference, but were shorter and had higher skinfold thicknesses and endomorphy ratings (Reilly, 1979). Thigh and calf circumferences, endomorphy and skinfold thicknesses approximated the values of triple jumpers who were lighter and taller. Controlled output of anaerobic power is required in parts of these athletic events and periodically in soccer play. The English League players were on average heavier and smaller than the Olympic athletes (the 400 m hurdlers and triple jumpers) they most closely resembled in physique but were unlike any of the other track and field athletes.

Muscle function

Various tests of muscle strength and power have been employed for assessment of soccer players. These have ranged from performance tests and measurement of isometric strength to contemporary dynamic measures using computer-linked isokinetic equipment. Tests of anaerobic power have also evolved as well as short-term performances on the force platform that can have relevance to soccer play.

Since the early part of the century grip strength has been used as an indicant of gross body strength. Mean values for English League professionals was reported to be 50.4 ($\pm$ SE = 1.2) kg compared to an average of 52.9 kg for Japanese professionals (Reilly, 1979). Observations on Dallas Tornado professionals, mean 46.2 ($\pm$ SE = 0.3) kg, were similar to the general population of similar age and size. Stronger than normal grips would be expected in soccer players from the trend towards mesomorphy that is apparent in experienced players. Nevertheless the average back strength of the Japanese internationals was 148.8 kg which was equivalent to results obtained for 20 year olds in the general population. One repetition maximum bench press was used by Raven et al. (1976) as a field test of muscular fitness of the Dallas Tornado professionals, a mean value of 73($\pm$ SE = 4) kg being observed. This is not impressive when compared to values produced by weight-trainers or American Football specialists.

Strength in the lower limbs is of obvious concern in soccer: the quadriceps, hamstrings and triceps surae groups must generate high forces for jumping, kicking, tackling, turning and changing pace. The capability to sustain strong contractions is also important in maintaining balance and control. Shephard (1973) suggested that isometric strength is important in maintaining a player's balance on a slippery pitch and also contributing to ball control. For a goalkeeper almost all the body's muscle groups are important for executing his skills. For outfield players the lower part of trunk, the hip flexors and the plantar flexors and dorsiflexors of the ankle are used most exactingly. Upper body strength is employed in throw-ins and the strength of the neck flexors could be important in forcefully heading the ball.

Soccer players are generally found to be only a little above average in isometric muscle strength. This may reflect inadequate attention to resistance training in their habitual programme. Besides, isometric strength may not truly reflect the ability to exert force in dynamic conditions.

Brooke et al. (1970) found non-significant correlations between soccer kick length and static and explosive leg strength. A leg dynamometer was used to measure static strength while a short shuttle run and a vertical jump test were used as indices of explosive leg strength. The authors concluded, albeit tentatively, that a degree of learned skill in the applied task of kicking predominated over the degree of basic strength required. The interaction of strength and velocity of the moving limb may also be a relevant factor. Asami and Togari (1968) did find a relation between knee extension power and ball speed in instep kicking, both increasing with experience in the game. Cabri et al. (1988) also reported a significant relation between leg strength, measured as peak torque during an isokinetic movement, and kick performance indicated by the distance the ball travelled. The relationship was significant for both eccentric and concentric contractions of hip and knee joints in flexion and extension.

An implication of the positive relation between leg strength and kick performance is that strength training could be effective in improving the kicking performance of soccer players. It seems that, given a certain level of technique, strength training added to the normal soccer training will improve both muscular strength and kick performance (De Proft et al., 1988). Soccer players have greater fast speed capabilities than normal (Oberg et al., 1986) and this may be an important determinant of technique in kicking the ball.

The throw-in distance of soccer players has been found to be related to pull-over strength and trunk flexion strength by Togari and Asami (1972). These authors also showed that training methods using a medicine ball increased strength measures but without a corresponding increase in throw distance. This demonstrates a degree of specificity in the throwing skill and suggests that individual players should be pre-selected to take tactical long throws.

As aerobic power tends to be greatest in midfield players and least in goalkeepers and centre-backs, it is conceivable that the latter might compensate by superior muscle strength. Oberg *et al.* (1984) did show that goalkeepers and defenders have higher knee extension torque at 0.52 rad s^{-1} than midfield players and forwards. The result was due to differences in body size since correction for body surface area removed the positional effect.

The vertical and standing broad jumps have been employed as measures of 'explosive leg strength'. Mean values for the vertical jump have included 50 cm for the Australian World Cup team (Cochrane and Pyke, 1976), 53 cm for North American Soccer league profess-ionals and 58 cm for English League professionals (Thomas and Reilly, 1979). Observations on US players have been 56 cm at collegiate level, 56 cm for the national junior team, 56 cm for the national senior team and 58 cm for Olympic trialists (Kirkendall, 1985). English League players cleared 219($\pm$ SE = 3) cm in the standing broad jump. The superior performances in this and in the vertical jump were found among goalkeepers and centre-backs and in forwards operating as target men. Midfielders had relatively low scores in both tests. The perform-ances of two centre backs and one striker in the vertical jump were similar to results reported for international high jumpers (Reilly, 1979).

In exercise of short duration the splitting of high energy intramuscular phosphagens contributes together with anaerobic glycolysis to the maximal power a player can develop. These substrates (ATP, creatine phosphate and glycogen) may be used for combustion by muscle at the onset of exercise and result in a high anaerobic work production. Margaria, Aghemo and Rovelli (1966) designed a stair-run test from which the maximum power output can be calculated. Measurement is made of the time taken for the player to run between two stairs, the vertical distance between which is known. The anaerobic power of Olympic soccer players measured in this way was found to be less than pentathletes, sprinters and middle-distance runners (Di Prampero *et al.*, 1970). Another research group found higher values in representative soccer players (mean 1.65 kg m^{-1} kg^{-1} s^{-1} i.e. 16.2 W kg^{-1}) than in basketball players, walkers and runners at the same competitive level (Withers, Roberts and Davies, 1977). Caru *et al.* (1970) studied 95 young soccer players aged 14–18 years and reported mean values ranging from 1.53 kg m^{-1} kg^{-1} s^{-1} (15 W kg^{-1}) at 14 to 1.64 kg m^{-1} kg^{-1} s^{-1} (16 W kg^{-1}) at 18. These values were significantly higher than in non-athletes of similar ages but no significant differences were apparent among any of the playing positions examined. This may have been due to the number of versatile players at this stage who may not settle into a successful positional role until later in their career.

Bosco, Luhtanen and Komi (1983) described a method for measuring mechanical power output in jumping. It requires repeated jumping for a given period, usually 60 s, the flight time and jumping frequency being recorded. Kirkendall (1985) reported values of 23 W kg^{-1} for professional indoor soccer players and 21 W kg^{-1} for collegiate players, results which are consistent with observations on volleyball and basketball players. Performance at various parts of the 60 s activity can be compared, the tolerance to fatigue as the test progresses being indicative of the anaerobic glycolytic capacity.

Tests described so far involve either static contractions or dynamic contractions in the sagittal plane. The ability to turn quickly and side-step calls for motor co-ordination and is reflected in a standardized agility run test. Dallas Tornado players were found to have average times on the Illinois Agility Run above the 99.95 percentile for the test norms (Raven *et al.*, 1976). The test distinguished the soccer players as a group from the normal population better than any field test used for strength, power and flexibility.

Muscle strength and joint flexibility are important safety factors in soccer. Strength imbalance between the limbs increases the likelihood of injury: comparison of strength data between left and right legs can be of benefit in screening for injury predisposition. Factor analysis of a number of strength and muscular power tests on English professional players showed the stronger individuals were the more successful in avoiding injuries throughout the season (Reilly and Thomas, 1980).

Muscle tightness, particularly in the hamstring group, has been linked with increased risk of muscle injury in Swedish professionals (Ekstrand, 1982). Indeed two-thirds of the players had flexibility values poorer than non-players. This may be partly an adaptation, partly also a reflection of inadequate attention to flexibility practices in training. Poorer range of motion has also been noted at the ankle joint in Japanese (Haltori and Ohta, 1986) and English League (Reilly, 1979) players, although the goalkeepers were exceptions among the English professionals. This may be an adaptive response of soft tissue around the ankle which improves stability at the joint.

The oxygen transport system

Pulmonary function

Pulmonary function tests are frequently used as measures of the adequacy of the respiratory system. Vital capacity (VC), the volume of gas that can be forcibly expired after a maximum inspiration, represents the approximate useable capacity of the lungs. The residual volume (RV) represents the air remaining in the lungs after a complete exhalation. For Dallas Tornado professionals, mean values ($\pm$ SE) for VC (BTPS) were 5.3($\pm$ 0.1) l, for RV 1.385 ($\pm$ 0.117) and for total lung capacity 6.735 ($\pm$ 0.224) l (Raven *et al.*, 1976). Mean VC values for English League players were 5.8($\pm$ 0.2) l at the start of pre-season training and 5.9($\pm$ 0.16) l at the beginning of the competitive season (Reilly, 1979). These values were significantly higher than the 5.15($\pm$ 0.1) l predicted from height and age using a standard nomogram. It seems that VC represents a structural component of the body, similar to other assessments of body size and this is the basis of predicting pulmonary capacity from body surface area or body size. Several authors have reported that VC is higher in athletes than in non-athletes of similar body size and this superiority seems to be due more to genetic factors than to training.

The lung power of English League subjects as indicated by FEV_1 (forced expiratory volume in 1 s) was 4.95($\pm$ 0.2) l. This was significantly higher than the predicted value of 4.3($\pm$ 0.04) l. The forced expiratory flow rate was 10.6($\pm$ 0.32) l s^{-1} (Reilly, 1979). The FEV_1/VC(%) was 84%, being close to the normal rate of exhalation in a forced single breath. A higher proportion (90%) was reported for Hungarian footballers, although mean values ($\pm$ SD) of VC were 5.9($\pm$ 0.4) l for Honved and 5.8($\pm$ 0.4) l for Ujpesti Dozsa players (Apor, 1988).

Pulmonary function does not normally appear to be a factor limiting the maximal aerobic performance and the main use of single-breath spirometry is in screening for any impairment or lung obstruction. The oxygen transport system in strenuous exercise may be affected by pulmonary ventilation, pulmonary diffusion, the O_2-carrying capacity of the blood, the cardiac output and the arteriovenous difference in oxygen saturation. It is reasonable to expect that the maximum breathing capacity, the maximum rate at which air can be breathed in and out per minute, should be high in soccer players to furnish the oxygen transport system with the necessary supplies of air throughout 90 min of play. More information about dynamic pulmonary function in soccer players has been obtained from measurements of maximum minute ventilation ($\dot{V}_{Emax}$) during exercise tests designed for assessing $\dot{V}O_{2max}$.

Reported values of $\dot{V}_{Emax}$ of soccer players exhibit a large variation. These include 108.3($\pm$ 16.9) l min^{-1} for Aberdeen FC (Williams, Reid and Coutts, 1973), 125.2($\pm$ 17.8) l min^{-1} for Honved, Budapest and 141.2($\pm$ 7.0) l min^{-1} for Ujpesti Dozsa Budapest (Apor, 1988), and 153.6($\pm$ 4.1) l min^{-1} for Dallas Tornado professionals (Raven *et al.*, 1976). To what extent these reflect differences in the protocol used for exercise testing is uncertain. In general the figures are well below those anticipated for top-class middle-distance runners whose $\dot{V}_{Emax}$ values would typically exceed 170 l min^{-1}.

Cardiac function

The heart responds to strenuous training by becoming larger and more effective as a pump. The chambers (particularly the left ventricle) increase in volume from a repetitive overload stimulus such as endurance running whilst the walls of the heart thicken and may grow stronger as a result of a pressure stimulus. Cardiac muscle hypertrophy is reflected in a greater stroke volume and a larger ventricular size enables more blood to fill the chamber before the heart contracts. Both are manifested in a slower frequency of beating at rest and this is apparent in observations on well-trained athletes.

Heart rates of top soccer players at rest tend to be much lower than the average of 72 beats min^{-1} found in the general population. Mean values ($\pm$ SE) reported include 48($\pm$ 1) beats min^{-1} for English League players (Reilly, 1979), 50($\pm$ 1) beats min^{-1} for Dallas Tornado players (Raven et al., 1976) and 52($\pm$ 2) beats min^{-1} for the Roumanian League champions (Balanescu, Vokulescu and Bobocea, 1968). These values suggest a large degree of cardiac adaptation to training. The 'resting circulatory efficiency' in the English League players was also reflected in low diastolic blood pressures, mean blood pressure being 120/70 mmHg. The slower heart rate allows extended relaxation time during diastole for the pressure to drop below the normal level of about 80 mmHg. The pulse pressure represents the difference between systolic and diastolic pressures and the value of 50 mmHg for the English League players is superior to the normal 40 mmHg and the 42 mmHg reported for 201 Olympic Games athletes of a previous generation (Berry et al., 1949).

The 'resting circulatory efficiency' was identified by Reilly and Thomas (1977a) as a principal component of fitness for soccer using multivariate analysis of data from a battery of fitness tests: it significantly discriminated between levels of playing proficiency. This advantage is likely to be transferred to exercise and post-exercise recovery. The heart rate response to submaximal exercise is used for estimating $\dot{V}O_{2max}$ and for measuring the physical working capacity (PWC_{170}). The kinetics of heart rate recovery post-exercise is also shown to be related to the state of endurance training (Bunc, Heller and Leso, 1988) and has been utilized for fitness assessment.

Quick recovery from strenuous exercise may be important in soccer which involves intermittent efforts interspersed with short rests. The Harvard Step Test designed initially for College men and later used in testing of military conscripts provides a fitness index which is based on the recovery of pulse rates over 3.5 min after a standard work rate. The test has a long history of use in the fitness assessment of athletes. Thomas (1975) reported a Harvard Index of 117 for soccer players. This closely agrees with the figure of 119.5 reported for Olympic Games soccer players by Ishiko (1967). The highest value reported for an English League player was 127 (Reilly, 1975). According to test norms these values are classed as excellent, though they are well below the 160.2 reported for Olympic Games marathon runners (Ishiko, 1967) and the 172.4 and 174.2 reported by Cureton (1956) for two world record holders in middle-distance and distance running on the track.

Although easy to administer the Harvard Step Test has now lost favour due to the availability of alternatives that can be employed during exercise. Similarly the PWC_{170} test has limited relevance to soccer as it is usually conducted on a bicycle ergometer, an exercise mode unsuitable for soccer players. A convenient practical test for footballers is the multi-stage shuttle run (Leger et al., 1988). The speed is dictated by a rhythm on a tape recorder, the pulse rate response to each running intensity being monitored. This test is now accepted as a valid method of indirectly estimating the maximal oxygen uptake and is suitable for testing of football squads.

The maximal heart rates of soccer players are close to the rates expected for non-athletic populations of similar age and race. Neverthe-less there is a large variation in the maximal heart rates reported and this may be due in part to the exercise protocol used for testing. The mean values ($\pm$ SE) include 179($\pm$ 2) beats min^{-1} for South Australian representatives (Withers, Roberts and Davies, 1977), 176($\pm$ 8) beats min^{-1} for the 1984 West German national team (Nowacki et al., 1988), 179($\pm$ 2) beats min^{-1} for English League First Division players (White et al., 1988), 188($\pm$ 2) beats min^{-1}) for US club professionals (Raven et al., 1976) 193 beats min^{-1} for Danish semiprofessionals (Bangsbo and Mizuno, 1988) and 198($\pm$ 1) beats min^{-1} for English League soccer players (Reilly, 1975). Indications are that the maximal heart rate does not increase with training but may show a slight reduction as a result of lowered sympathetic drive at maximal effort.

Maximal oxygen uptake ($\dot{V}O_{2max}$)

The average values of $\dot{V}O_{2max}$ for top-level soccer players tend to be high, supporting the belief that there is a large contribution from aerobic power to playing the game. Nevertheless values do not reach the same levels as in specialist endurance sports such as cross-country running and skiing, distance running or orienteering where values frequently exceed 80 ml kg^{-1} min^{-1}. Values for elite players lie in the region 55–70 ml kg^{-1} min^{-1}, the higher values tending to be found at the top level of play and when players are at peak fitness.

Mean $\dot{V}O_{2max}$ reported for 11 members of the Swedish national team was 56.5 ml kg^{-1} min^{-1}: the corresponding figure for 50 top Swedish players was 58.6 ml kg^{-1} min^{-1} (Åstrand and Rodahl, 1977). The authors argued that as soccer permits brief pauses between bursts of physical effort, the same level of aerobic power is not required in the players as in events calling for long-lasting continuous effort at near maximal intensity. Another report on top Swedish players stated that maximal aerobic power of the national team has increased over the last two decades (Ekblom, 1986). The average value of 61 ml kg^{-1} min^{-1} corresponds to that reported for a group of top level Australian players (62 ml kg^{-1} min^{-1}) by Withers, Roberts and Davies (1977). The top players in the Swedish squad had values of 65–67 ml kg^{-1} min^{-1} with individual values close to 70 ml kg^{-1} min^{-1}.

Nowacki et al. (1988) reviewed 26 studies of $\dot{V}O_{2max}$ of German soccer players at various levels of play. Over half the studies were conducted using a cycle ergometer which would have underestimated the true $\dot{V}O_{2max}$ of the players. The highest values reported using a treadmill test were for a German club team, mean 69.2($\pm$ 7.8) ml kg^{-1} min^{-1}. On the treadmill the 1978 National German squad ($n = 17$) had a mean value of 62.0($\pm$ 4.5) ml kg^{-1} min^{-1} whereas the Austrian National team ($n = 9$) had poorer values at 58.3($\pm$ 4.3) ml kg^{-1} min^{-1}.

Values for professional players tend to be higher than for amateurs, though this can depend on the quality of training and the standard of competition. Ekblom (1986) cited values of 45–50 ml kg^{-1} min^{-1} for Swedish recreational players. Values for the Ethiopian players competing in the Mexico Olympic Games tournament were 43 ml kg^{-1} min^{-1} on average (Di Prampero et al., 1970). Higher standards of fitness were attained by German amateur players, mean values being 50–56 ml kg^{-1} min^{-1} in the studies reviewed by Nowacki et al. (1988). Top Italian amateurs seem to have higher standards still but this may be connected with their frequency of competition and intensity of training. Faina et al. (1988) reported values of 64.1($\pm$ 7.2) ml kg^{-1} min^{-1} for six amateur players, which were as good as those of 17 professional players measured and better than the 63.2 ml kg^{-1} min^{-1} for a national World Cup star. The mean $\dot{V}O_{2max}$ of four Danish semiprofessionals studied by Bangsbo and Mizuno (1988) was 66 ml kg^{-1} min^{-1}: the profile of mitochondrial enzyme activities in the gastrocnemius of the players was closer to that of endurance athletes than to strength-trained individuals.

It is likely that the $\dot{V}O_{2max}$ of professional soccer players does improve significantly in the pre-season period when there is an emphasis on aerobic training. It is debatable whether further emphasis on improving the $\dot{V}O_{2max}$ will add to the quality of play. Hypothetically, when two teams of equal skill meet, the one with superior aerobic fitness would have the edge, being able to play the game at a faster pace throughout. Apor (1988) provided data on Hungarian players which showed perfect rank-order correlation between mean $\dot{V}O_{2max}$ of the team and finishing position in the Hungarian First Division Championship. Mean $\dot{V}O_{2max}$ for the 1st, 2nd, 3rd and 5th teams were 66.6, 64.3, 63.3 and 58.1 ml kg^{-1} min^{-1} respectively. It is possible that common factors such as stability in the team, avoidance of injury and so on help to maintain both $\dot{V}O_{2max}$ and team performance independently.

There is some evidence that $\dot{V}O_{2max}$ will vary with positional role.

When English League players were subdivided into positions according to their 4–3–3 configuration, the midfield players had significantly higher aerobic power values than those in the other positions. The central defenders had significantly lower relative values than the other outfield players while the full-backs and strikers had intermediate values (Reilly, 1975). Indeed the significant correlation between $\dot{V}O_{2max}$ and distance covered in a game ($r = 0.67$) demonstrates the need for a high work-rate in midfield players as they act as a link between defence and attack. The goalkeepers were found to have lower values than the centre-backs. This observation has been confirmed by others. Four goal-keepers in the German National squad had values of 56.2($\pm$ 1.2) ml kg^{-1} min^{-1} compared to 62.0($\pm$ 4.5) ml kg^{-1} min^{-1} for the squad as a whole (Hollmann et al., 1981). A study of 95 young non-professional players aged 14–18 found that goalkeepers had significantly lower $\dot{V}O_{2max}$ values than outfield players (Caru et al., 1970). No differences were observed among outfield positions but players were still at developmental ages and so were unlikely to have been totally specialized in positional roles.

Although the $\dot{V}O_{2max}$ indicates the maximal ability to consume oxygen in strenuous exercise, it is not possible to sustain exercise for very long at an intensity that elicits $\dot{V}O_{2max}$. The upper level at which prolonged exercise can be maintained is thought to be indicated by the so-called 'anaerobic threshold' which is usually expressed as the work-rate corresponding to a blood lactate concentration of 4 mM. This has been measured at 77% $\dot{V}O_{2max}$ in English League First Division players (White et al., 1988), a value close to the usual race pace in a marathon. It should be noted that the intermittent nature of soccer means that frequently players operate at above this intensity although the average fractional utilization of $\dot{V}O_{2max}$ is about 75%, as explained earlier.

The maximal oxygen consumption depends to a large extent on the oxygen supplied to the tissues and so the maximal cardiac output is an important physiological parameter. There is evidence that high cardiac outputs at maximal exercise parallel high $\dot{V}O_{2max}$ values (Åstrand and Rodahl, 1977), although there is little specific information about the maximal cardiac output of soccer players. The oxygen pulse of top soccer players has been determined by calculating the oxygen consumed per heart beat at maximal exercise. Highest average values reported have been 29.1 ml beat^{-1} for a German League team, 27.9 ml beat^{-1} and 28.2 ml beat^{-1} for the 1974 and 1981 national German teams (Nowacki et al., 1988) and 25.2($\pm$ 4.7) ml beat^{-1} for Honved Budapest (Apor, 1988). Since the maximal heart rate differs little between sporting and sedentary populations, these high results are largely attributable to favourable $\dot{V}O_{2max}$ values.

13.2.4 Training

Soccer training embraces both preparation for match-play and attaining the necessary physical conditioning to last a competitive season at an optimum level of fitness. For the professional player it comprises both an occupational requirement and a rehearsal for public performances. The manifold requirements of soccer match-play dictate that a number of discrete objectives should be incorporated into soccer training. These range from strength and endurance work, flexibility and agility activities, playing skills and match drills and practice of tactical manoeuvres in mock-up and realistic match conditions. The emphasis on each aspect may vary with the stage of the competitive season, the success of the team and the discretion of the team coach. An example of the emphasis placed on the major components of training is shown in Figure 13.6.

Flexibility work is advocated both as a warm-up and in its own right for a long-term improvement of range of motion. It is usually performed at the beginning of the training session. Stretching exercises have also been recommended immediately after training (Ekblom, 1986). Ekstrand (1982) has shown that soccer players tend to be less flexible than non-athletes and that inflexibility, particularly in the hamstring muscle

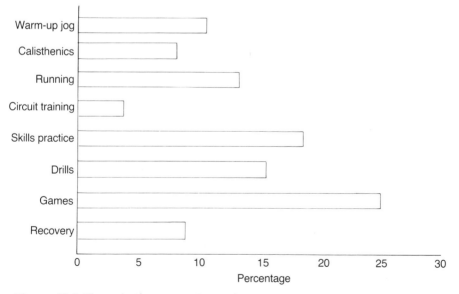

Figure 13.6 The relative proportions of training time devoted to different components of the session (from Reilly, 1979).

group, predisposes to injury. A prophylactic programme of exercises which included flexibility work, was found to reduce the incidence of injury in Swedish League players.

The physical fitness work in Figure 13.6 covers both strength and circuit weight-training as well as continuous and intermittent running. Strength training has been shown to be of benefit in that a group of Belgian club players who engaged in extra weight-training improved both their leg strength and kick performance compared to a control group of colleagues (De Proft *et al.*, 1988). Strength training has also been shown to be effective in reducing injury risk; Reilly and Thomas (1980) found that players with the greatest muscular strength, determined in a range of muscle groups, outlasted their weaker colleagues better through a season of English League soccer. The players who did extra voluntary strength training had the lowest incidence of muscle injury. Training leg extensor strength bestows stability to the knee, the joint most commonly injured in soccer but this should be balanced with training the knee flexors to maintain an appropriate flexor/extensor strength ratio. Restoration of muscle strength post-injury is especially important to avoid risk of re-injury when the player returns to full training or competition.

Agility drills have importance since the ability to move direction quickly is essential in the game. This can be incorporated into fitness drills by slalom and shuttle runs. Where possible the drills should be performed with the ball: this is more attractive to players and is more specific to the game (Reilly, 1975).

The physiological strain in the various components of soccer training are represented in Table 13.3. It is evident from the heart rate and estimated energy expenditure values that the training increases in intensity as the session progresses. The hardest efforts are retained for

Table 13.3 Mean ($\pm$ SD) heart rate and estimated energy expenditure during different categories of soccer training regimens (from Reilly, 1986)

	Heart rate (beats min^{-1})	Energy expended (kJ min^{-1})
Warm-up	120 $\pm$ 2	38.9
Flexibility/calisthenics	112 $\pm$ 3	31.4
Running	144 $\pm$ 4	58.6
Circuit and weight-training	125 $\pm$ 4	43.1
Skills practice	128 $\pm$ 5	45.2
Drills	137 $\pm$ 4	53.6
Games	157 $\pm$ 7	68.6
Recovery periods	102 $\pm$ 3	22.6

match-play and this denotes that the major physiological stimulus may come from playing the game. Running drills lack reliability when used as fitness tests to monitor progress in training, the likelihood being that players perform maximally in a game situation more readily (Reilly, 1975).

The metabolic loading during skills practices is relatively light. Periodically skills could be practised under conditions of higher loading corresponding to the physiological stress of match-play. This would apply to professionals whose skills are already well-learned and who could benefit from 'pressure-training'. Novice players on the other hand need to be fresh to improve their skills which would otherwise break down under conditions of fatigue.

The purpose of 'pressure training' is to force the execution of game manoeuvres under exacting conditions. An example might be the practice of defensive moves by confronting two centre-backs with three attackers or the use of conditioned games which limit possession of the ball to not more than two touches in order to improve passing skills. Since positional roles have to some extent their own specific requirements, some training drills should be tailored to the needs of individual players. An obvious example is the goalkeeper who does not need the aerobic capacity of the busiest outfield players.

It is noteworthy that games provide a strong training stimulus to the oxygen transport system and additionally they mimic the pattern of activity of true competition. The training stimulus is enhanced by small-sided games such as 4-a-side. Such activity induces metabolic loading which, on average, exceeds 80% $\dot{V}O_{2max}$ (MacLaren *et al.*, 1988).

Most soccer teams compete regularly on a weekly basis during the playing season and sometimes twice a week. The frequency of match-play may be increased further in the case of successful teams involved in both league and cup competitions and in outstanding players featuring in representative matches. College and University players with affiliation to extra-varsity clubs may participate twice a week in competitive matches. The main difficulty of such a routine that entails 3 games every 8 days is that there is inadequate time for a progressive build-up of training and preparation. Generally soccer fixtures are arranged for week-end competition so that there is a 7-day cycle of activity.

The usual pattern is that the energy expenditure values vary throughout the week. The training load builds up to a mid-week peak before tapering off in preparation for week-end competition. This is sensible practice as the ease-off before the week-end allows restoration of muscle glycogen levels reduced below normal by the hard training in mid-week. Players who start a game with glycogen levels already reduced are at a disadvantage, since their work rate would be impaired in the second half. Glycogen levels are markedly lowered after a full game and may not be fully restored for 24 h afterwards. A study of European Cup finalists, Malmo FC, showed that players were not aware of the importance of sufficient nutritional carbohydrate in their diet to help recovery post-match. Only 47% of the total energy was in the form of carbohydrate compared with 55–60% advised for elite athletes (Jacobs *et al.*, 1982).

The typical weekly cycle of energy expenditure in professional soccer players shows a week-end harmonic due to the energy consumed in match-play. Outside of the occupational training regimen players tend to have a rather sedentary life-style (Reilly and Thomas, 1979). An innovation used by the West German National side in the 1980s was 'regeneration training'. This consisted of light exercise which might be conducted on the morning after the game or even in the evening immediately after match-play. It was designed to alleviate muscle soreness, dampen the activity of the nervous system from an elevated level and orientate the players towards the preparation for their next match. The procedure has shown that it is not necessary to have a complete break from training after competition.

The general trend in training of English League soccer players is to concentrate fitness work into a 6-week pre-season conditioning period. The tendency has been for players to have a complete break from strenuous exercise in the off-season and so they start this period in a poor state of fitness (Reilly and Thomas, 1977b; White *et al.*, 1988). The training in the pre-season period is arduous, comprising approximately 3 h per day, which is double the time devoted to training in mid-season. An example of the distribution between game-related and fitness work is given for a first-class English League team in Table 13.4, the split being approximately equal.

Table 13.4 Pattern of pre-season training schedule of the first team squad of a First Division English League team (after White *et al.*, 1988)

Days	Game-related training (min)	Fitness/conditioning (min)
Monday	75	115
Tuesday	85	65
Wednesday	Golf (recreation)	—
Thursday	90	105
Friday	Game preparations	—
Saturday	Game day	
Sunday	Free day	
Totals (min)	250	285
Proportions (%)	46.7	53.3

The pre-season programme of fitness training is effective in improving the aerobic power and endurance capacities of players. Body composition is altered in that the percentage of body weight as fat is lowered. This is a result of the high energy expenditure in training during this period. An adverse effect of the concentration on endurance exercise is that muscle strength may be impaired. The English League players studied by Reilly and Thomas (1977b) showed pronounced improvements in cardiovascular fitness measures over 6-weeks pre-season training but strength in the lower-limb muscle groups decreased. The level of strength had returned to normal when players were re-tested later in the season (Thomas and Reilly, 1979). This ties in with experimental work which shows that a bias towards exclusive use of endurance training can impair muscle strength. The answer is to have a more circumspect approach towards pre-season conditioning and introduce a balanced programme of exercises. This would complement a light regimen of training in the off season, which inevitably is at the discretion of the individual player. This work out of season would help to compensate for the fall in oxidative enzyme activities noted by Bangsbo and Mizuno (1988) in the calf muscles of Danish soccer players during 3 weeks of detraining. Loss of mitochondrial enzyme activity is recovered during re-training but the rate at which this regain occurs is slower than the loss during detraining.

Once the competitive season gets underway there seems to be little fluctuation in physical fitness profiles of soccer players. The level of fitness is maintained as a result of the training stimulus presented by match-play, complemented by normal training. The overall fitness profile may change as a result of movement into and out of the first team according to injury patterns, changes in personnel, playing success and judgements of manager and coach (Reilly and Thomas, 1980). The ability to tolerate a heavy competitive schedule during the season will depend partly on fitness but also on astute employment of training practices, sound nutrition, sensible habitual activity and life-style and absence of injury. These factors, along with a preservation of team morale, are not exclusive to soccer but are common to the other football codes.

13.3 AMERICAN FOOTBALL

American football is the largest spectator sport in the USA and is also popular outside North America, in Australia and in Japan for instance. In recent years it has gained widespread appeal in Europe and its major spectacle, the Super Bowl, is now watched live on TV worldwide. Games consist of four quarters and although each lasts only 15 min of actual play the game itself may be spread over 3–4 hours. The frequent interchange of offensive and defensive line-ups on the field of play as possession changes hands means that players are only intermittently directly involved in play. When play is in progress the action is brisk and intense. Consequently the game makes high demands on speed, anaerobic power and muscular strength rather than on aerobic power. The game calls for an array of physical skills that vary with designated positional roles.

Each team has a 45 man squad. This includes three quarterbacks, five running backs, four wide receivers, two tight ends, eight offensive linemen, seven defensive linemen, seven linebackers, four defensive backs, one kicker and one punter, plus three others. The offence contains linemen (tackles, guards and ends) and centres: the defence has secondary lines (safety, guards), linebackers (outside, middle) and linemen (ends and tackles). A typical 3–4–4 defensive unit will have a tackle and two ends, four linebackers and four defensive backs.

The most important game manoeuvres revolve around the quarterback. His choice of move to a large extent determines the team's chances of success. He depends for his effectiveness on the protection afforded by his defence. It is important that his choice of play is 'completed': the distance gained in so doing calls for speed of motion and agility as well as catching ability on the part of the linemen and receivers.

As the game is a physical contact sport, tackling and blocking are important skills. The game is unique among the football codes in the amount of protective clothing worn by players to safeguard against injury. Although the protective equipment appears cumbersome, it is important that it does not interfere with running, or execution of any other skills of the game.

13.3.1 Demands of the game

Periods of play are generally intense before players gain respite at each 'down' or change of possession. Periods of continuous play longer than 30 s are rare. This suggests that most emphasis is on anaerobic power and speed of action. As players regularly have intervals off the field of play, they are not called on to make multiple repeated sprints as in soccer or Australian Rules football.

The main demands seem to be on alactic anaerobic power with some demands on anaerobic glycolysis. It is unlikely that blood lactate reaches very high levels or that there is pronounced hypoxia within muscles. The current use of oxygen for recovery when players reach the sideline is unnecessary and has little to recommend it (Wintee, Snell, and Steay-Gunderson, 1989). No great demands are placed on aerobic metabolism, the average expenditure of energy being 37.7 kJ (9 kcal) min^{-1} (Brooks and Fahey, 1984).

Fast limb speed is not limited to the legs: the quarterback particularly needs a fast arm action to throw the ball powerfully and accurately when opportunity presents itself. This requirement applies to all players who pass the ball.

Whole-body muscular strength is a requirement in tackling. This applies to shoulder, arm, trunk and lower limb strength. Agility is needed to manoeuvre into positions of effectiveness and also to avoid opponents.

13.3.2 Characteristics of players

American footballers on average tend to be taller and leaner than participants in the other football codes. Mean height of players in the studies reviewed by Douge (1988) was 190 (range 182–193) cm, weight 107 (81–143) kg. Wilmore and Haskell (1972) examined 44 professional players according to positional role. The offensive linemen and tight ends were the tallest (mean 193.5 cm) followed by defensive lineman (193 cm). The latter were by far the heavier group, mean weight 120.6 kg compared to the 113.2 kg of the former groups. The mean height of defensive backs (184 cm) was similar to that of offensive backs and receivers (184 cm) but they were the much lighter, being 85 kg compared to 91.8 kg. The players as a whole were appreciably taller and heavier than professionals studied 30 years earlier by Welham and Behnke (1942). It seems that the contemporary game at top level calls for large players more than in the previous generation.

The average body composition of players studied by Wilmore and Haskell (1972) consisted of 14.4% body fat. The range varied from 4 to 20%. Highest values were found in defensive linemen (18.7%) and linebackers (18.5%), lowest values in defensive backs (7.7%) and offensive backs and receivers (8.3%), with offensive linemen and tight ends possessing intermediate values (15.5%). The authors believed that two of the linebackers were overweight and went on to describe how shedding excess body fat actually improved their performance. They concluded that the lean body mass rather than total body weight was the critical factor relative to performance ability in this and probably in the other positions. Quarterbacks and kickers have values of 14.4% (Fox, 1984).

Studies on US College players confirm the trend of very high percentage body fat values in linemen and low values in backs. Burke, Winslow and Straub (1980) reported a mean value of 13% for 20 backs and 21.8% for 33 linemen. Defensive backs tend to have less body fat than offensive backs, comparative mean values being 9.6 and 13.8% (Smyth and Byrd, 1976), 7.3 and 11.5% (White, Mayhew and Piper,

1980), 11.5 and 12.4% (Wickkiser and Kelly, 1975) and 6.7 and 11% (Gettman, Storer and Ward, 1987) in four separate studies. The defensive backs rely more on agility and speed of movement whilst the extra weight helps the offensive backs in maintaining momentum when moving forward.

The studies reviewed by Douge (1988) showed that the physique of American footballers was endomesomorphic. Japanese players of the game were leaner but tended towards extreme mesomorphs (Ikai, Asahina and Yokobori, 1964). This should help in tackling and blocking positions. Carter (1968) also showed that College footballers were largely endormorphic-mesomorphs. When comparing linemen and backs, he found that the backs were significantly lower on endomorphy, higher on ectomorphy and shorter and lighter than the linemen. Carter (1970) reported mean somatotypes of 4:6:1.5, 3:6:1.5 and 3.5:5.5:2 for San Diego, Iowa and Oregon University players. These figures show the importance of a muscular physique at the top level of American College football.

The data reviewed by Douge (1988) also found American footballers to have greater flexibility and faster running speed over 40 yards (37 m) than soccer, Rugby or Australian Rules players. Their greatest advantage, however, was in muscular strength. Mean values (kg) for bench press for the various codes were 73 for soccer and 82 for Australian Rules, 86 for Rugby players compared to the 138 kg for American footballers. Part of the advantage is due to body size but it does reflect also the emphasis placed on upper body strength for purposes of tackling.

Measures of lung function have indicated that professional footballers have below average vital capacity measures, the mean being 94.3% of the value predicted from a standard nomogram. Wilmore and Haskell (1972) found no consistent relation between height or weight and vital capacity or total lung volume. The values of the defensive backs were especially poor, being 83% of the predicted vital capacity. These results contrasted with an earlier study of 16 Collegiate footballers by Novak, Hyatt and Alexander (1969) whose players were smaller but who averaged 1 l higher than the professionals.

The average maximal heart rate of the professional footballers studied by Wilmore and Haskell (1972) was 185 beats min^{-1}. This varied from 179 (offensive backs and receivers) to 198 beats min^{-1} in defensive backs. These differences reflected the wide variation between individuals and the small sample of players in these positions who were examined. The $\dot{V}_{Emax}$ values similarly varied widely from 149.3 for three linebackers to 189.6 l min^{-1} for four offensive linemen and tight ends.

The $\dot{V}O_{2max}$ values of American footballers are quite modest, the highest values being found in defensive backs (54.5 ml kg^{-1} min^{-1}), the lowest in defensive linemen (43.5 ml kg^{-1} min^{-1}). Since defensive linemen carry a greater proportion of body weight as fat than other players, correcting for this by expressing $\dot{V}O_{2max}$ per kg lean body mass brought the defensive linemen closer to the values attained by the defensive and offensive backs and wide receivers (Wilmore and Haskell, 1972). Nevertheless they were still well below the results obtained for the linebackers and offensive linemen. Although the defensive backs were comparatively the best of the players in aerobic power their values are not compatible with expectations in aerobic sports and reflect the pronounced anaerobic metabolic load in playing the game. This is corroborated in the study by Gettman, Storer and Ward (1987) whose professional players had an average $\dot{V}O_{2max}$ of 49.2 ml kg^{-1} min^{-1}. A strenuous 14-week conditioning programme improved this value by only 6%.

13.3.3 Training

Training for American football places emphasis on development of strength and muscle power, in accordance with the demands of the game. Consequently the vast majority of teams are well equipped with weight-training facilities, including isokinetic and multi-station apparatus. Free-weights are still widely used and are the first choice of many coaches. Specific dynamic practices include use of tackle dummies where skills of the game can be improved against fabricated resistance.

The three major lifts recommended by Kulund (1982) for American footballers are bench press, power cleans and full squats. These are supplemented by chin-ups, dips, sit-ups, pull-downs, upright rows and other exercises at the discretion of the coach or trainer. The off-season programme entails three high intensity work-outs per week, reduced to twice weekly sessions during the competitive season to maintain the muscle strength already acquired.

Overload is a recognized principle of training, the active muscles adapting to supra-normal loads placed on them by becoming stronger. The importance of resistance training for footballers was underlined by Loft (1981) who advocated exercises for specific playing positions. Weighted shoes were advised for punters and kickers for practising the high kick. A weighted ball was recommended for practice of passing, punting and centring. Execution of a wrestler's bridge and pivot whilst supporting a weight 9–18 kg on the chest was recommended for linemen. The linemen could also use a press bar for increased effort with shoulder shrug and leg lift. The main needs of a tackle player according to Kulund (1982) are leg strength, a strong lower back and arm; shoulder strength is used to deliver a rising blow while arm and shoulder strength are employed in absorbing blows without incurring injury. These muscle groups can be strengthened by a balanced regimen of weight-training.

Despite the recommendation to continue fitness training in the off-season many players return to pre-season practices clearly overweight. In the past the use of sweat-suits in a misguided attempt to shed unwanted weight quickly led to fatalities from hyperthermia. The footballer clad in the usual protective clothing and exercising in the heat would have impaired the facility for losing heat by evaporation of sweat. This would cause body temperature to rise to a dangerous level while the player also became slowly dehydrated. Use of a mesh jersey would allow for evaporative and convective cooling of the body. The risks of heat injury are now recognized by trainers and replacement of body fluids during practices is given a high priority.

13.4 AUSTRALIAN RULES AND GAELIC FOOTBALL

Australian Rules competition is held in a large oval field with 18 players on each team. The game consists of four quarters, each of 25 min duration. The ball is moved quickly from end to end with the purpose of scoring and this promotes a flowing style of game. A score of 6 points is awarded when the ball crosses between two central uprights and 1 point if it misses these but goes between the two side uprights. As the game is continually in motion all players need to have good running ability, agility in avoiding tackles, catching and kicking skills and sound tactical sense.

The Gaelic football field is approximately 40 m longer than a soccer pitch with 15 players on each side. Goalposts at each end have a crossbar, a goal (equal to 3 points) being scored beneath it, a point if the ball crosses above the bar and between the posts. The ball is round like a soccer ball in contrast to the oval shape of that used in the Australian Rules game. Apart from the shape of the ball and the scoring system, the two games are very similar and they have many skills in common. These include high catching, long distance kicking for accuracy, passing and moving the ball downfield. Players from the two codes quickly adapt to the laws of the 'Compromise Rules' game which has been played at international level (Ireland versus Australia) for nearly a quarter of a century.

The usual duration of Gaelic football games is 60 min, consisting of two 30 min halves. This is increased to 35 min per half in inter-county championship games. The normal energy reserves of the body should be able to sustain intense match play more easily in this than in the Australian Rules game because of its shorter duration. The extent to which the stores of glycogen are deployed in competition depends on the work-rate profiles and patterns of activity in each of the two football codes.

13.4.1 Demands of the games

The movement patterns of Australian Rules players during a game are in general similar to those observed in soccer. Players on average cover over 10 km per game, composed of 27% walking, 53% jogging and the remaining 20% striding or sprinting. Carrying the ball accounts for less than 2% of the total distance covered (Douge, 1988). Of the distance covered sprinting, 30% involves sprints of less than 5 m, 27% refers to sprints between 5 and 10 m, 21% 10–20 m, 11% 20–30 m, 6% 30–40 m and only 5% in excess of 40 m. On average players may have to sprint more than 40 m only twice or three times per game.

Pyke and Smith (1975) have suggested that the work-rate profiles differ according to positional role. The rover, ruckman and centreline players have to cope with sustained efforts whilst the half-back flanker and backpocket player have comparatively short bursts of activity. They provided data which indicated that the distance covered by a half-back flanker in a game was about 77% of that of a rover. This is roughly the difference between the work-rate of a centre-back and a midfield player in soccer.

Although there has been no systematic analysis of activity in Gaelic football, the patterns are likely to resemble those of the Australian Rules game. This generalization may be restricted to inter-county matches where there is much greater emphasis on work rate and movement off-the-ball to lose markers than at club level. As in Australian Rules, Gaelic footballers may need to accelerate quickly to receive or intercept a pass, or leap to catch a high kick. The ball is rarely out of play for long so there are few long respites for players during a match. The toe-to-hand method of carrying the ball means that many forwards are likely to cover more distance in possession of the ball than do Australian Rules or soccer players.

The work-rate of the goalkeeper in the Gaelic game is relatively light, otherwise the physiological demands tend to be well distributed among the outfield players. These consist of three full-backs, three half-backs, two midfield players, three half-forwards and three full-forwards. In the Australian Rules game the heaviest work-load is likely to fall on the 'rovers'. The percentage of the match time spent in various activities by four players in that role was reported by McKenna, Sandstrom and Chennells (1988). Walking took 44% of the time, jogging 40%, high intensity runs 5%, game-related activity 2.5% and for less than 9% of the time the players were stationary. The mean duration of a high intensity run was 2.7($\pm$ 0.7) s, the maximum being 10.4 s and one occurred every 73 s on average.

The overall physiological strain on players in these two football codes is represented by the irregular superimposition of changes of pace and anaerobic efforts on a background of light to moderate aerobic activity. The activity patterns denote a call on aerobic metabolism and on intramuscular phosphagens. Anaerobic breakdown of glycogen is implicated in the longer sprints. This is supported for Australian Rules football by the observations of Pohl, O'Halloran and Pannall (1981) that anion gap increased and blood bicarbonate levels decreased during play, changes compatible with mild metabolic acidosis.

It is thought likely that a hard game of Australian Rules football would take muscle glycogen stores to very low levels. The activity patterns and distance covered are similar to those of soccer players whose glycogen depots in thigh muscles were found to near depletion at the end of a game (Saltin, 1973). McKenna, Sandstrom and Chennells (1988) showed that on a day following a match the peak values for $\dot{V}O_2$ and $\dot{V}_E$ were below normal maximal levels, an observation compatible with reduced muscle glycogen levels. It was suggested that a diet rich in carbohydrate would facilitate recovery from the exercise-related decrements in aerobic power.

Indices of cardiorespiratory strain during Australian Rules matches confirm the relatively high load on the oxygen transport system. Mean heart rate during competition has been reported as 161 beats min^{-1}, a value comparable to observations on soccer players (Douge, 1988). The average loading on Gaelic footballers is likely to be close to this, at least at inter-county and senior club levels of play. 'Rovers' in the Australian game seem to have higher heart rates than other players. Pyke and Smith (1975) reported a mean value of 178 beats min^{-1} for a player in the roving position during a league game. The rate did not fall below 150 beats min^{-1} at any stage and fluctuated between 170 and 185 beats min^{-1} most of the time. It is unlikely that any Gaelic Football player operates at this high level.

13.4.2 Characteristics of players

Australian Rules players tend to be large in body size. Mean height and weight of players were 183 cm and 80 kg respectively, in the review by Douge (1988). The range for both measures is quite large, 176–193 cm for height and 79–93 kg for body weight. This variability was attributed to demands of specific positional roles. Tallness is an advantage in contesting aerial possession of the ball and catching the ball is an important skill in the game.

Burke, Read and Golland (1985) studied 119 Australian Rules

footballers from Victoria. They found a gradation in body size with the level of competition, the players in a top level professional team being the tallest and heaviest, with players in an amateur association club being the smallest and lightest and those in a low level professional club having intermediate values.

Gaelic footballers tend to be similar in body size to their Australian counterparts, although a small stature is not a bar to success in the game. The study by Watson (1977) found that players in successful teams were taller and heavier than their less successful opponents. Mean ($\pm$SD) values for teams in the 1989 Gaelic football final were: height, 183($\pm$5) cm and 182($\pm$5) cm; weight, 82.2($\pm$7.4) and 81.7($\pm$6.1) kg, for Mayo and Cork players respectively. Taller players tend to be distributed in the central positions, forming a line from full-back to full-forward. The smaller individuals tend to be dispersed on the wings and to be placed in attack rather than in defence.

Generally body fat values are found to be low among top Australian Rules players, with a mean of 10% (range 8–14%) being reported (Douge, 1988). Burke, Read and Golland (1985) reported mean values of 13% for a top Victorian team, average values being higher for a lower-level professional club and 15.4% for amateur players. These values were determined at the beginning of the competitive season: changes in body fat were more pronounced during the season in the lower-level players, but the magnitude of such changes was small (Burke, Golland and Read, 1986). Values of 13–14% were average for good Gaelic footballers (Watson, 1977).

The physique of Australian Rules players tends to be mesomorphic, the muscular make-up being beneficial in the physical contact associated with the game. Though there are no detailed studies of top Gaelic foot-ballers, there is clearly a tendency towards mesomorphy among players. The leg muscles are employed in drop-kicking and punting, the arm muscles are used in hand-passing the ball while whole-body musculature can be deployed in shoulder-to-shoulder charging and in tackling.

The mesomorphic physique of Australian Rules players is also reflected in their muscular strength. Players were found on average to be superior in maximal bench press (82 kg) to soccer players (73 kg) although values were not as high as the 86 kg reported for Rugby Union footballers or the 138 kg of American footballers (Douge, 1988). Mean values for the Fitzroy FC (near Melbourne) reached 91 kg after a period of strength training (Jones and Laussen, 1988).

The ability to jump and catch the ball in the air is an important skill in the Australian Rules game. This requirement applies to all outfield players to some extent. Consequently it is not surprising that reported values for vertical jump are higher among these players than in any of the other football codes: the range reported was 52–62 cm and the mean value 57 cm (Douge, 1988).

In the studies reviewed by Douge (1988) the average values for flexibility were similar for Australian Rules and soccer players but the figures were slightly inferior to those for Rugby and American footballers. This may be due to a lack of attention to flexibility exercises in the training regimens of Australian Rules players. This criticism is likely to be extended to players of the Gaelic game.

The sprinting speed of Australian Rules players compares poorly with that of top American Football players. Pyke and Smith (1975) reported average times of 5.25 s for Perth (Western Australia) players over 40 yards (36.6 m). The corresponding time for Dallas Cowboy professionals was 0.35 s faster, despite being 23 kg heavier than the Australian Rules players. This reflects the emphasis on anaerobic power in the American game compared with the more aerobic nature of the Australian code.

The inference of a moderately high aerobic demand in playing the Australian Rules game is supported by observations of $\dot{V}O_{2max}$ of players (Douge, 1988). The 64 ml kg^{-1} min^{-1} attributed as average for top level players is much higher than values for comparable standards of Rugby and American football. There are few positional roles in the game that do not demand a reasonably high aerobic capacity and those playing as 'rovers' probably have the highest work-rates of all.

Similar inferences can be made from the data on physical working capacity of Gaelic footballers. Watson (1977) found that PWC_{170} values were higher in successful teams than in the less successful county teams even when the data were corrected for the larger body size of the former. Values tended to be highest close to provincial or All-Ireland championship finals and were thought to be associated with training for such events.

13.4.3 Training

The training for Australian Rules among the top sides is much more systematic than for Gaelic football. It usually involves 4–5 sessions a week with 1–2 rest days. Besides, players typically have one match, sometimes two, per week.

The traditional conditioning programme for the game placed emphasis on aerobic exercise. Jones and Laussen (1988) described the introduction of a more comprehensive programme which incorporated a regimen of strength training. Running drills were also designed to more closely resemble activity patterns in the game. The programme which was adopted by the Fitzroy FC team also utilized a game skill combat-running circuit: this presumably would provide the agility and acceleration related to competitive play. The conditioning drills included, for example, blocks of 20 7 s sprints, repeated every 20 s with 2 min rests between sets.

The study of the Fitzroy players also demonstrated how the usual seasonal organization of fitness training could be improved. An important introduction was a 6-week period of conditioning prior to Christmas. This allowed more concentration on skills work early in the year prior to the peak of the competitive season from April to September.

During the playing season the training load seems to be distributed unevenly through the week. The most arduous session tends to be on Tuesday evening: from then on the training is tapered in preparation for Saturday's competition. Training is resumed on Sunday but tends to be light in order to recover from the effects of the strenuous activity associated with the previous day's contest. This cyclical organization of the training load is sensible as it ensures that players start their match physiologically recovered from the training sessions earlier in the week.

Gaelic football is still exclusively an amateur game and this is perhaps reflected in the training programmes. Highly organized training is mainly concentrated in the championship season, May to September, with League and friendly matches providing the main training stimulus in the remainder of the year. A consequence is that teams who do not advance from the first round of championship matches may not attain high fitness standards. This is supported by the study of Watson (1977) who found that PWC_{170} tended to be highest among players preparing for provincial and All-Ireland finals.

13.5 RUGBY FOOTBALL

Rugby Union and Rugby League are both played at international level and are major sports in Britain, France, Australia and New Zealand. Each has its own World Championships, the inaugural event for Rugby Union being held in 1987. Rugby Union players still maintain amateur status whereas Rugby League is played both as an amateur and professional sport, the majority of its top players being professionals. The two games are broadly similar and players from the amateur code do not seem to experience great difficulty when switching to the professional game.

Rugby Union has 15 players a-side, seven backs (ball carriers) and eight forwards (ball winners), the Rugby League game having two forwards less. Differences in the rules of the game are mainly reflected in the smoother flow of play in Rugby League. Rucks, mauls and line-outs are the prerogative of Rugby Union and the conduct of play after a tackle is more simply defined by the rules of Rugby League.

General application of physiological principles to these games is problematic, not only because of differences between the Rugby codes but more so because of the host of factors that determine the load on individual players. Each positional role has unique demands and there is less homogeneity among these roles – particularly in Rugby Union – than in other football codes. The type and frequency of training also varies markedly with the level of play, especially in the amateur game. Besides, performance in the game relies on tactical considerations, interplay of individuals in tactical moves, proficiency of players in the skills of catching, passing, kicking, tackling and those specific to playing positions. The game requires a mixture of fast reactions, speed, agility, muscular strength, anaerobic and aerobic power but not in a clearly definable way. These difficulties notwithstanding, an attempt can be made to assess the game of Rugby from a biological standpoint and match this assessment with descriptive observations on players and on game demands. Such observations almost exclusively refer to Rugby Union.

13.5.1 Demands of the games

Rugby League and Rugby Union matches are both set for 80 min of play. The time for which the ball is actually in play is consistently measured as less than 30 min in Rugby Union: time is spent in preparing scrums and line-outs for play to re-commence. Penalty takers also take time to prepare for kicks and time is also needed for players to re-form after rucks and mauls have broken down. According to Williams (1976) a typical Rugby Union game would be made up of about 140 sequences of actions, the average activity/rest periods being 20 s/40 s. The frequency and duration of pauses are less in the Rugby League code with the result that players are actively engaged in play more than their Rugby Union counterparts. This, together with the fact that there are fewer players on the field, suggests that Rugby League is the more strenuous of these football codes.

There is little in the way of reliable data on the work-rates of players in either game. Estimates of the distance covered in a Rugby Union game range from 4.8 to 9.6 km (Reid and Williams, 1974). Morton (1978) provided a mean value of 5.8 km per game: the figures provided by Williams (1976) were less – 5.5 km for forwards and 3.8 km for three-quarters. Since the point of play can switch quickly from one end of the pitch to the other as a result of strategic kicking of the ball, much of the distance covered in a game is likely to be caused by the need to reassume formations for play to continue. According to Morton (1978) 37% of the overall distance was covered walking, 29% jogging and 34% in striding or sprinting. Figures for Canadian players (centres and props only) showed that players spend about 85% of their time in low intensity activity. Of the remaining 15% spent in intensive activity, 6% of the time was found to be related to running and 9% to tackling, pushing and competing for the ball (Docherty, Wenger and Neary, 1988).

The activity is intermittent but movement with the ball is generally carried out at speed. This is most pronounced in the backs, although forwards are frequently called upon to run all-out. Indeed it has been estimated that Rugby Union forwards in international matches may have to cover one-third of the total distance at top speed (Williams, 1976). Nevertheless the fastest runs are expected of the wing-three-quarters, whether in attacking moves or in covering in defence.

Although emphasis is placed on anaerobic metabolism during these fast moves, there is ample time to recover during the periods of low intensity activity. Blood lactate levels do not rise appreciably, post-match measurements indicating mean values of $2.8(\pm 1.6)$ mM (Docherty, Wenger and Neary, 1988). Players need a sufficient level of aerobic fitness to be able to sustain activity to the end of the game. All players need muscular power to change speed and direction quickly when necessary, to slip tackles and to support colleagues in set plays. The need for great muscular strength is most pronounced in the forwards, on whom the team depends for winning possession in scrums, rucks and mauls. Isometric strength in leg, trunk and shoulder muscles is clearly important in scrummaging. Power in these muscle groups would be a factor in co-ordinating and controlling the shove against the opposing scrum. Power in the legs would be important in jumping to gain possession in the line-outs in the Rugby Union game.

The competitive season in the British Isles spans the winter months. Matches frequently take place in environmental temperatures that are too cold for comfort. In cold–wet conditions finger temperatures may fall to the point where handling the ball is severely impaired. In such circumstances the wearing of gloves will help to maintain hand temperatures in the comfortable zone and preserve manual dexterity. The British Lions team touring New Zealand in 1983 were thus disadvantaged by the cold in the test match at Invercargill as the opposing All-Blacks three-quarter line players were all gloved. It is salient to note that the wearing of gloves came into disrepute in the English Rugby League in winter of 1988, the gloves being employed for violent ends.

The cold weather may also be a factor in occurrence of injury in the game. A study of the time of the game in which muscle injuries were incurred found a significantly higher incidence of injury in the period after half-time (Reilly and Hardiker, 1981). The suggestion was made that players get cold while standing outdoors during the 5 min intermission and are susceptible to injury after re-starting the game without a warm-up.

Environmental temperatures during the competitive Rugby season are generally much warmer in the southern than in the northern hemisphere. Indeed Rugby matches – in Australia and South Africa, for example – may be played in conditions that precipitate heat stress. University Rugby players competing in air temperatures of 24–25°C were found to have rectal temperatures of 39.4°C at the end of a game (Cohen *et al.*, 1981). Temperatures were elevated equally in backs and forwards, but the forwards sweated more, being larger in body size. The conventional provision of oranges to players is practically useless in combatting the dehydration that occurs in such circumstances. More attention should be paid to the fabric of clothing worn by Rugby teams in conditions where hyperthermia is a risk.

13.5.2 Characteristics of players

There is a wide variety of physical characteristics among Rugby players. The diversity depends on the positional role, the level of play and the range of skills required by the game. The characteristics should not differ markedly between Rugby Union and Rugby League as players manage to switch to the professional game without too much difficulty.

The most noticeable difference between Rugby Union backs and forwards is in terms of body size, the latter being on average about 20 cm the taller. These average values disguise differences within the backs and forwards: second-row forwards (and lock and No. 8) for example, are taller than the remaining players in the unit and their height rather than their anaerobic power gives them the advantage in jumping in line-outs. Second-row and back-row players tend to be taller in first class compared to second class Rugby Union teams, again demonstrating the importance of height in top-class play (Rigg and Reilly, 1988). The hooker tends to be the smallest of the forward players with the prop-forwards being only a little taller. Most teams use the hooker to throw the ball into the line-out where he would have little chance of acquiring possession.

Body weight is an important factor in scrummaging because it is difficult for forwards to shove backwards a heavy pack of opponents. It is preferable to have this weight as lean body mass rather than fat which would constitute an extra energy demand when the forward has to move around the field of play. The heaviest of the top Rugby Union club players examined by Rigg and Reilly (1988) were the second-row forwards (101 ± 7 kg), the lightest were the half-backs with 24 kg less body weight. The mean percentage body weight as fat varied from 13.6(± 2.1)% in front-row players to 10.4(± 1.5)% in the backs. These values compared with 14.6% reported by Bell (1980) for Rugby forwards and 12.7% reported by Williams, Reid and Coutts (1973) as the average for a University Rugby Union team. The front-row players were the least mobile members of the team, suggesting that the extra body fat adversely affected their sprint times. The data reported by Bell (1979) for 56 College players showed that the forwards (19.5%) were significantly fatter than the backs (12.2%). These figures suggest that forwards may be selected at this level of play on the basis of their body weight rather than lean body mass, a criterion that would be inappropriate at a higher standard of play.

Although specific positions attract particular body shapes, e.g. the pear shape of the prop forward; forwards as a group are not easily distinguished from backs on the basis of physique. A study of the somatotype of the British Polytechnic Rugby Champions found mean profiles of forwards (4.5:5:2.5) to be similar to the backs (4:5:2.5) (Reilly and Hardiker, 1981). A study of French players reported mean somatotypes of 3:5:3 for the backs whereas the forwards clustered around a 4:5.5:2 profile (Boennec, Prevot and Ginet, 1980). All players could be described as mesomorphic, with the forwards being more endomorphic and less ectomorphic than the backs. This would agree with the lower levels of body fat found in the backs.

In contact games frailty or linearity in physique is commonly assumed to foster injury occurrence. Skeletal muscle is considered to protect underlying structures against external sources by presenting an intervening fleshy shield on impact. A study of student players failed to find evidence that subcutaneous body fat afforded any protection against injury. The players most susceptible to injury were those heavily muscled and high in endomorphy who probably lacked the ability to escape unscathed from critical incidents in the game (Reilly and Hardiker, 1981).

The muscular strength of Rugby players as measured by the maximum bench press (mean 86 kg) is higher than that of soccer players, similar to that of Australian Rules players (mean 82 kg) but much less than the average of 138 kg of American footballers (Douge, 1988). Upper body strength is particularly important for tackling in Rugby and it is possible that this function is better developed in the professional Rugby League game whose training regimens are more systematized. It is also important in scrummaging. Performance of press-ups has been found to be superior in first class compared to second class Rugby Union club players, and among the positional roles was best in front-row players and poorest in second-row forwards (Rigg and Reilly, 1988).

Jumping ability is important for catching the ball in the line-out and fielding high kicks. Comparative studies indicate that Rugby Union players are on average not as good as Australian Rules footballers in jumping (Douge, 1988). Although players at the top level of play are better jumpers than players at a lower calibre of play, the difference between playing positions is not very marked (Rigg and Reilly, 1988). It seems that forwards gain advantage from their height more than from their leg muscle power in jumping for ball possession in line-out play.

The anaerobic power of Rugby Union players has been measured using a vertical jump test (Maud, 1983), a treadmill test (Cheetham *et al.*, 1988) and the Wingate Anaerobic Power Test on a cycle ergometer (Rigg and Reilly, 1988). Maud reported higher anaerobic power output and anaerobic capacity (measured via a 40 s test on a cycle ergometer) in forwards than in backs. The differences are likely to have been due to an influence of body size.

Cheetham *et al.* (1988) measured the power output of Rugby Union forwards during a 30 s test on a non-motorized treadmill and compared results with those previously obtained on running backs. The average power output of the forwards was lower than that for the backs, mainly due to a greater fatigue in the forwards during the test. Peak power output of the forwards was higher than for the backs but was inferior when values were corrected for body weight. Those forwards with the highest peak power outputs during the test also experienced the greatest fatigue and had the largest increases in blood lactate concentration.

A similar trend was observed by Rigg and Reilly (1988) who used the Wingate Power Test for measurement of peak power and mean power over 30 s. The absolute power output was higher in forwards than in backs but this position was reversed when data were expressed per kg body weight. The exceptions were the back-row players whose values for the first class clubs were 1071 ± 108 W and 10.6 ± 1.2 W kg^{-1} for peak power, and 903 ± 39 W and 8.9 ± 0.4 W kg^{-1} for mean power. The back-row players were found to be the fastest sprinters of all the forwards tested.

The influence of body weight has also been noted in tests of aerobic fitness of Rugby Union players. The physical work capacity has been measured using heart rate responses to cycle ergometry and the power output corresponding to a heart rate of 170 beats min^{-1} (PWC_{170}) calculated. Rigg and Reilly (1988) found that this test clearly distinguished between first class and second class players, except for the front-row forwards. These had the poorest results of all players tested (210 ± 37 W), except when the absolute values uncorrected for body weight were compared to those of the half-backs. The highest values (258 ± 38 W) were found in back-row players, in keeping with their foraging role in loose play.

The mean $\dot{V}O_{2max}$ of 20 College forwards was reported to be 46.3 ml kg^{-1} min^{-1} in a University Rugby Union team (Williams, Reid and Coutts, 1973). Average values of USA club backs were 59.5 ml kg^{-1} min^{-1} compared to 54.1 ml kg^{-1} min^{-1} observed in forwards (Maud, 1983). Results for Japanese inter-college players did not differ between positional groups, mean values ($\pm$ SD) being 54.7($\pm$ 7.2) ml kg^{-1} min^{-1} for forwards, 55.8($\pm$ 6.7) ml kg^{-1} min^{-1} for half-backs and 54.5($\pm$ 6.4) ml kg^{-1} min^{-1} for three-quarters (Ueno, Watai and Ishii, 1988). The data available for forwards are insensitive to separating the individual positions: it is likely, for example, that back-row players have higher standards of aerobic fitness than front-row players because of the greater work-rate demands of that position.

The average ($\pm$ SD) maximal heart rates reported for the USA club players studied by Maud (1983) of 182($\pm$ 9) beats min^{-1} for the forwards and 189($\pm$ 8) beats min^{-1} for the backs were within the normal range of population values. The corresponding mean $\dot{V}_{Emax}$ values were 174.6($\pm$ 25.6) l min^{-1} and 176.1($\pm$ 16.0) l min^{-1}, respectively. The values of 11 University Rugby Union players studied by Williams, Reid and Coutts (1973) of 110($\pm$ 16.6) l min^{-1} were nearer the normal population values and probably reflect the smaller size of University players compared to club competitors. However, the poor performances of the players in an endurance-run test compared to professionals in soccer suggest that aerobic fitness may have been neglected in the training of these players.

13.5.3 Training for Rugby

A strategy for training for the games of Rugby Union and Rugby League can be evolved from an analysis of the demands of the games. This shows that players must be prepared for intermittent sprinting with recovery periods that vary markedly between all-out spurts. Players also need the type of endurance training that will enable them to sustain 80 min of play, leaving them capable of all-out efforts towards the end of the game.

The shorter recovery periods in Rugby League compared to Rugby Union are due to the almost immediate continuation of play that follows a tackle. It would seem, therefore, that Rugby League players would have a greater call for aerobic fitness training than their Rugby Union counterparts. The physical training regimens of Rugby League players attempt to follow as closely as possible the patterns of activity during the game. Among the professional Rugby League clubs, organized training is more frequent than among the top Rugby Union clubs and is likely to provide a more effective training stimulus to the oxygen transport system.

The distribution of labour amongst Rugby Union players in a team is quite marked, each position having its own training requirements. It can be argued that squad training sessions are best focused on practising team drills and game skills and that physiological fitness should be developed independently by team members. This places an onus on individual players: the result has been that left to their own devices amateur Rugby players do not pursue strenuous training programmes but rely on match-play for a training stimulus.

As Rugby is a contact sport there is a recognized need to develop muscle strength in both upper and lower limbs. A variety of muscle groups are used in the skills of the game such as kicking, passing, tackling and breaking tackles. Weight-training can be employed for improving muscle strength. Weight-training can also be incorporated into a circuit of exercises for aerobic fitness training. Conventionally some circuits have been employed by Rugby clubs in their pre-season training. Currently, circuit-weight training can be accommodated using multi-station equipment. The circuit can include 12 or so stations, players rotating from station to station until the circuit is complete. Each successive station varies the muscle group involved to avoid local muscular fatigue. Recovery periods are kept short so that the training stimulus for the oxygen transport system is maintained at an adequate level. The training can be designed so that muscle strength or muscle endurance are emphasized at specific stations.

Muscle strength specific to games skills of forward players can be developed on scrummaging machines. Such apparatus allows the forwards to train as a unit although it cannot adequately simulate the finer skills associated with a co-ordinated shove. Sophisticated scrummaging racks, instrumented for measuring the forces generated in a shove, are now commercially available: they can provide useful feedback on performance of scrummaging.

Power in the leg muscles needs to be developed for jumping, accelerating and decelerating and changing direction of movement rapidly. Agility running drills are best practised in field conditions. Fast actions and changes of direction are difficult if the major joint complexes are stiff. Consequently, flexibility exercises are also recommended. Rugby players do seem to attend to this aspect of training as they score favourably on flexibility measures compared to players in the other football codes (Douge, 1988).

The coach or trainer will decide which elements of training may be performed on an individual basis and which drills are best practised by the whole squad. Examples of training for individual and team purposes are contained in the coaching manuals (e.g. Williams, 1976).

13.6 OVERVIEW

Applications of physiological principles to the football games is far from straightforward. Nevertheless some progress has been made in understanding the physiological stresses entailed in playing the games and the training needed for highly competitive match-play. The establishment of comprehensive physiological profiles of top players has helped too in relating how individual strengths contribute to team successes.

Undoubtedly there are common threads between the football codes but each is in many senses unique. Aerobic fitness is a major requirement in top class soccer: anaerobic fitness and muscular power are emphasized in American Football. Between these extremes Australian Rules and Gaelic Football call for versatility among outfield players and a high degree of all-round fitness. In all the games some variability in fitness is inevitable and the problem for the coach is to weld this variability between individuals into an effective and coherent unit.

The physical contact in playing football provides a common factor among the codes. It calls for muscular strength and a robust skeletal structure. An aftermath of match-play is that training may be disrupted for 1–2 days while the player recovers from soft-tissue bruising and stiffness following hard physical contact. In this respect the footballer envies the athletes in individual sports who are less subject to such external factors.

REFERENCES

Agnevik, G. (1970) *Fotboll. Idrottsfysiologia Rapport* No. 7., Trygg-Hansa, Stockholm.

Apor, P. (1988) Successful formulae for fitness training, in *Science and Football* (eds T. Reilly, A. Lees, K. Davids and W.J. Murphy), E. and F.N. Spon, London, pp. 95–107.

Asami, T. and Togari, H. (1968) Studies on the kicking ability in soccer. *Research Journal of Physical Education*, **2**, 267–272.

Åstrand, P.O. and Rodahl, K. (1977) *Textbook of Work Physiology*. McGraw-Hill, New York.

Balanescu, F., Vokulescu, A. and Bobocea, A. (1968) The cardiovascular response during exercise in athletes. *Internationale Zeitschrift für Angewandte Physiologie*, **25**, 361–372.

Bangsbo, J. and Mizuno, M. (1988) Morphological and metabolic alterations in soccer players with detraining and retraining and their relation to performance, in *Science and Football* (eds T. Reilly, A. Lees, K. Davids and W.J. Murphy), E. and F.N. Spon, London, pp. 114–124.

Bell, W. (1979) Body composition of Rugby Union football players. *British Journal of Sports Medicine*, **13**, 19–23.

Bell, W. (1980) Body composition and maximal aerobic power of Rugby Union forwards. *Journal of Sports Medicine and Physical Fitness*, **20**, 447–451.

Bell, W. and Rhodes, G. (1975) The morphological characteristics of the association football player. *British Journal of Sports Medicine*, **9**, 196–200.

Berry, W.T.C., Beveridge, T.B., Bainsby, E.R., Chalmers, A.K., Needham, B.M., Mayer, H.E.M., Townsend, H.S. and Daubney, C.G. (1949) The diet, haemoglobin values and blood pressure of Olympic athletes. *British Medical Journal*, **1**, 300–304.

Boennec, P.M., Prevot, M. and Ginet, J. (1980) Somatotype de sportif de haut niveau, resultats dans huit disciplines differentes. *Medicine du Sport*, **54**, 45–54.

Bosco, C.P., Luhtanen, P. and Komi, P. (1983) A simple method for measurement of mechanical power in jumping. *European Journal of Applied Physiology*, **50**, 273–282.

Brooke, J.D., Clinton, N.M., Cosgrove, I.N., Dimple, D. and Knowles, J.E. (1970) The relationship between soccer kick length and static and explosive leg strength. *British Journal of Physical Education*, **1**, XVII–XVIII.

Brooks, G.A. and Fahey, T.D. (1984) *Exercise Physiology: Human Bioenergetics and its Applications*. John Wiley, New York.

Bunc, V., Heller, J. and Leso, J. (1988) Kinetics of heart rate responses to exercise. *Journal of Sports Sciences*, **6**, 39–48.

Burke, E.J., Winslow, E. and Straub, W.V. (1980) Measures of body composition and performance in major College football players. *Journal of Sports Medicine and Physical Fitness*, **20**, 173–180.

Burke, L.M., Golland, R.A. and Read, R.S.D. (1986) Seasonal changes in body composition in Australian Rules footballers. *British Journal of Sports Medicine*, **20**, 69–71.

Burke, L.M., Read, R.S.D. and Golland, R.A. (1985) Australian Rules football: an anthropometric study of participants. *British Journal of Sports Medicine*, **19**, 100–103.

Cabri, J., De Proft, E., Dufour, W. and Clarys, J.P. (1988) The relation between muscular strength and kick performance, in *Science and Football* (eds T. Reilly, A. Lees, K. Davids and W.J. Murphy), E. and F.N. Spon, London, pp. 106–153.

Carter, J.E.L. (1968) Somatotype of College football players. *Research Quarterly*, **39**, 476–481.

Carter, J.E.L. (1970) The somatotype of athletes. *Human Biology*, **45**, 535–569.

Caru, B., Le Coultre, L., Aghemo, P. and Pinera Limas, F. (1970) Maximal aerobic and anaerobic muscular power in football players. *Journal of Sports Medicine and Physical Fitness*, **10**, 100–103.

Cavanagh, P.R. and Williams, K.R. (1982) The effect of stride length variation on oxygen uptake during distance running. *Medicine and Science in Sports and Exercise*, **14**, 30–35.

Cheetham, M.E., Hazeldine, R.J., Robinson, A. and Williams, C. (1988) Power output of Rugby forwards during maximal treadmill sprinting, in *Science and Football* (eds T. Reilly, A. Lees, K. Davids and W.J. Murphy), E. and F.N. Spon, London, pp. 206–210.

Chovanova, E. and Zrubak, A. (1972) Somatotypes of prominent Czechoslovak ice-hockey and football players. *Acta Facultatis Rerum Naturalium Universitatis Comenianae Anthropologia*, **21**, 59–62.

Cochrane, C. and Pyke, F. (1976) Physiological assessment of the Australian soccer squad. *Australian Journal for Health, Physical Education and Recreation*, **75**, 21–25.

Cohen, I., Mitchell, D., Seider, R., Kahn, A. and Phillips, F. (1981) The effect of water deficit on body temperature during Rugby. *South African Medical Journal*, **60**, 11–14.

Covell, B., El Din, IV, and Passmore, R. (1965) Energy expenditure of young men during the weekend. *Lancet*, **i**, 727–728.

Cureton, T.K. (1956) Relationship of physical fitness to athletic performance and sports. *Journal of the American Medical Association*, **162**, 1139–1149.

De Proft, E., Cabri, J., Dufour, W. and Clarys, J.P. (1988) Strength training and kick performance in soccer players, in *Science and Football* (eds T. Reilly, A. Lees, K. Davids and W.J. Murphy), E. and F.N. Spon, London, pp. 108–103.

De Rose, E.H. (1975) Determination of the ideal body weight and corporal composition of 16 professional soccer players, in *Questions of Athletes Nutrition*: Abstracts of the Reports of the International Symposium. Leningrad: Leningrad Institute of Physical Culture.

Di Prampero, P.E., Pinera Limas, F. and Sassi, G. (1970) Maximal muscular power, aerobic and anaerobic, in the athletes performing at the XIXth Olympic Games in Mexico. *Ergonomics*, **13**, 665–674.

Docherty, D., Wenger, H.A. and Neary, P. (1988) Time–motion analysis related to the physiological demands of Rugby. *Journal of Human Movement Studies*, **14**, 269–277.

Douge, B. (1988) Football: the common threads between the games, in *Science and Football* (eds T. Reilly, A. Lees, K. Davids and W.J. Murphy), E. and F.N. Spon, London, pp. 3–19.

Durnin, J.V.G.A. and Passmore, R. (1967) *Energy, Work and Leisure*. Heinemann, London.

Ekblom, B. (1986) Applied physiology of soccer. *Sports Medicine*, **3**, 50–60.

Ekstrand, J. (1982) Soccer injuries and their prevention. Doctoral thesis: Linköping University.

Faina, M., Gallozzi, C., Lupo, S., Colli, R., Sassi, R. and Marini, C. (1988) Definition of the physiological profile of the soccer player, in *Science and Football* (eds T. Reilly, A. Lees, K. Davids and W.J. Murphy), E. and F.N. Spon, London, pp. 158–163.

Fox, E.L. (1984) *Sports Physiology*. Saunders College Publishing, New York.

Gerisch, G., Rutemoller, E. and Weber, K. (1988) Sports medical measurements of performance in soccer, in *Science and Football* (eds T. Reilly, A. Lees, K. Davids and W.J. Murphy), E. and F.N. Spon, London, pp. 60–67.

Gettman, L.R., Storer, T.W. and Ward, R.D. (1987) Fitness changes in professional football players. *The Physician and Sportsmedicine*, **15**, 92–101.

Haltori, K. and Ohta, S. (1986) Ankle joint flexibility in College soccer players. *Journal of Human Ergology*, **15**, 85–89.

Hirata, K. (1966) Physique and age of Tokyo Olympic champions. *Journal of Sports Medicine and Physical Fitness*, **6**, 207–222.

Hollmann, W., Liesen, H., Mader, A., Heck, H., Rost, R., Dufaux, B., Schürch, P., Lagerström, D. and Fohrenbach, R. (1981) Zur Hochstund Dauerleistungsfahigkeit der deutschen Fussball-Spitzenspieler. *Deutsch Zeitschrift für Sportmedizin*, **32**, 113–120.

Ikai, M., Asahina, K. and Yokobori, S. (1964) Research in sports medicine since 1949, in *Sports Medicine in Japan* (ed. Japanese Society of Sports Medicine), Meiji Life Foundation of Health and Welfare, Tokyo, pp. 95–177.

Ishiko, T. (1967) Aerobic capacity and external criteria of performance. *Canadian Medical Association Journal*, **96**, 746–749.

Jacobs, I., Westlin, N., Karlson, J., Rasmusson, M. and Houghton, B. (1982) Muscle glycogen and diet in elite soccer players. *European Journal of Applied Physiology*, **48**, 297–302.

Jones, C.J. and Laussen, S. (1988) A periodised conditioning programme for Australian Rules football, in *Science and Football* (eds T. Reilly, A. Lees, K. Davids and W.J. Murphy), E. and F.N. Spon, London, pp. 129–213.

Kirkendall, D.T. (1985) The applied sport science of soccer. *The Physician and Sportsmedicine*, **13**, 53–59.

Kulund, D.N. (1982) *The Injured Athlete*. Lippincott, Philadelphia.

Leger, L.A., Mercier, D., Gadoury, C. and Lambert, J. (1988) The multistage 20 metre shuttle run test for aerobic fitness. *Journal of Sports Sciences*, **6**, 93–101.

Loft, B.I. (1981) Injuries and their prevention in American football, in *Sports Fitness and Sports Injuries* (ed. T. Reilly), Faber and Faber, London, pp. 93–98.

MacLaren, D., Davids, K., Isokawa, M., Mellor, S. and Reilly, T. (1988) Physiological strain in 4-a-side soccer, in *Science and Football* (eds T. Reilly, A. Lees, K. Davids and W.J. Murphy), E. and F.N. Spon, London, pp. 76–80.

Margaria, R., Aghemo, P. and Rovelli, E. (1966) Measurement of muscular power (anaerobic) in man. *Journal of Applied Physiology*, **21**, 1661–1664.

Maud, P.J. (1983) Physiological and anthropometric parameters that describe a Rugby Union team. *British Journal of Sports Medicine*, **17**, 16–23.

Mayhew, S.R. and Wenger, H.A. (1985) Time motion analysis of professional soccer. *Journal of Human Movement Studies*, **11**, 49–52.

McKenna, M.J., Sandstrom, E.R. and Chennells, M.H.D. (1988) The effects of training and match-play upon maximal aerobic performance: a case study, in *Science and Football* (eds T. Reilly, A. Lees, K. Davids and W.J. Murphy), E. and F.N. Spon, London, pp. 87–92.

Medved, R. (1966) Body height and predisposition for certain sports. *Journal of Sports Medicine and Physical Fitness*, **6**, 89–91.

Morton, A.R. (1978) Applying physiological principles to Rugby training, *Sports Coach*, **2**, 4–9.

Novak, L.P., Hyatt, R.E. and Alexander, J.F. (1969) Body composition and physiologic function of athletes. *Journal of the American Medical Association*, **205**, 764–770.

Nowacki, P.E., Cai, D.Y., Buhl, C. and Krummelbein, U. (1988) Biological performance of German soccer players (professionals and juniors) tested by special ergometry and treadmill methods, in *Science and Football* (eds T. Reilly, A. Lees, K. Davids and W.J. Murphy), E. and F.N. Spon, London, pp. 145–157.

Oberg, B., Ekstrand, J., Moller, M. and Gillquist, J. (1984) Muscle strength and flexibility in different positions of soccer players. *International Journal of Sports Medicine*, **5**, 213–216.

Oberg, B., Moller, M., Gillquist, J. and Ekstrand, J. (1986) Isokinetic torque levels in soccer players. *International Journal of Sports Medicine*, **7**, 50–53.

Pohl, A.P., O'Halloran, M.W. and Pannall, P.R. (1981) Biochemical and physiological changes in football players. *Medical Journal of Australia*, **1**, 467–470.

Pyke, F. and Smith, R. (1975) *Football: The Scientific Way*. University of Western Australia Press, Nedlands.

Raven, P., Gettman, L., Pollock, M. and Cooper, K. (1976) A physiological evaluation of professional soccer players. *British Journal of Sports Medicine*, **109**, 209–216.

Reid, R.M. and Williams, C. (1974) A concept of fitness and its measurement in relation to Rugby football. *British Journal of Sports Medicine*, **8**, 96–99.

Reilly, T. (1975) An ergonomic evaluation of occupational stress in professional football. Unpublished PhD thesis, Liverpool Polytechnic.

Reilly, T. (1979) *What Research Tells the Coach about Soccer*. AAHPERD, Washington.

Reilly, T. (1986) Fundamental studies on soccer, in *Sportwissenschraft und Sportpraxis* (ed. R. Andresen), Verlag Ingrid Czwalina, Hamburg, pp. 114–121.

Reilly, T. and Ball, D. (1984) The net physiological cost of dribbling a soccer ball. *Research Quarterly for Exercise and Sport*, **55**, 267–271.

Reilly, T. and Bowen, T. (1984) Exertional cost of changes in directional modes of running. *Perceptual and Motor Skills*, **58**, 49–50.

Reilly, T. and Hardiker, R. (1981) Somatotype and injuries in adult student Rugby football. *Journal of Sports Medicine and Physical Fitness*, **21**, 186–191.

Reilly, T. and Thomas, V. (1976) A motion analysis of work-rate in different positional roles in professional football match-play. *Journal of Human Movement Studies*, **2**, 87–97.

Reilly, T. and Thomas, V. (1977a) Applications of multivariate analysis to the fitness assessment of soccer players. *British Journal of Sports Medicine*, **11**, 183–184.

Reilly, T. and Thomas, V. (1977b) Effect of a programme of pre-season training on the fitness of soccer players. *Journal of Sports Medicine and Physical Fitness*, **17**, 401–412.

Reilly, T. and Thomas, V. (1979) Estimated energy expenditures of professional association footballers. *Ergonomics*, **22**, 541–548.

Reilly, T. and Thomas, V. (1980) The stability of fitness factors over a season of professional soccer as indicated by serial factor analyses, in *Kinanthropometry 11* (eds M. Ostyn, G. Beunen and J. Simons), University Park Press, Baltimore, pp. 245–257.

Rigg, P. and Reilly, T. (1988) A fitness profile and anthropometric analysis of first and second class Rugby Union players, in *Science and Football* (eds T. Reilly, A. Lees, K. Davids and W.J. Murphy), E. and F.N. Spon, London, pp. 194–200.

Rohde, H.C. and Espersen, T. (1988) Work intensity during soccer training and match-play, in *Science and Football* (eds T. Reilly, A. Lees, K. Davids and W.J. Murphy), E. and F.N. Spon, London, pp. 68–75.

Saltin, B. (1973) Metabolic fundamentals in exercise. *Medicine and Science in Sports*, **5**, 137–146.

Seliger, V. (1968a) Heart rate as an index of physical load in exercise. *Scripta Medica*, Medical Faculty, Brno University, **41**, 231–240.

Seliger, V. (1968b) Energy metabolism in selected physical exercises. *Internationale Zeitschrift fur Angewandte Physiologie*, **25**, 104–120.

Shephard, R.J. (1973) The physiological demands of soccer, in *Proceedings of the International Symposium on the Medical Aspects of Soccer*. CONCACAF, Toronto.

Smaros, G. (1980) Energy usage during football match, in *Proceeding 1st International Congress on Sports Medicine Applied to Football*, Volume II (ed. L. Vecchiet), D. Guanello, Rome.

Smyth, D.P. and Byrd, R.J. (1976) Body composition, pulmonary function and $\dot{V}O_{2max}$ of College football players. *Journal of Sports Medicine and Physical Fitness*, **16**, 301–308.

Stepnicka, J. (1977) Somatotypes of Czechoslovak athletes, in *Growth and Development* (ed. O. Eiben), *Physique Symposia Biology Hungary*, **20**, 357–364.

Tanner, J.M. (1964) *The Physique of the Olympic Athlete*. Allen and Unwin, London.

Thomas, V. (1975) *Exercise Physiology*. Crosby Lockwood Staples, London.

Thomas, V. and Reilly, T. (1976) Application of motion analysis to assess performance in competitive football. *Ergonomics*, **19**, 530.

Thomas, V. and Reilly, T. (1979) Fitness assessment of English League soccer players throughout the competitive season. *British Journal of Sports Medicine*, **13**, 103–109.

Togari, H. and Asami, T. (1972) A study of throw-in training in soccer. *Proceedings of the Department of Physical Education*, College of General Education, University of Tokyo, **6**, 33–38.

Tumilty, D. McA., Hahn, A.G., Telford, R.D. and Smith, R.A. (1988) Is 'lactic acid tolerance' an important component of fitness for soccer, in *Science and Football* (eds T. Reilly, A. Lees, K. Davids and W.J. Murphy), E. and F.N. Spon, London, pp. 81–86.

Ueno, Y., Watai, E. and Ishii, K. (1988) Aerobic and anaerobic power of Rugby football players, in *Science and Football* (eds T. Reilly, A. Lees, K. Davids and W.J. Murphy), E. and F.N. Spon, London, pp. 201–205.

Van Gool, D. (1987) De fysieke belasting tijdens een voetbalwedsfrijd: Studie van afgelegde afstand, hartfrequintie, energieverbruck en lactaatbepalingen. Unpublished PhD thesis, University of Leuven.

Van Gool, D., Van Gerven, D. and Boutmans, J. (1983) Heart rate telemetry during a soccer game: a new methodology. *Journal of Sports Sciences*, **1**, 154.

Van Gool, D., Van Gerven, D. and Boutmans, J. (1988) The physiological load imposed on soccer players during real match-play, in *Science and Football* (eds T. Reilly, A. Lees, K. Davids and W.J. Murphy), E. and F.N. Spon, London, pp. 51–59.

Watson, A.W.S. (1977) A study of the physical working capacity of Gaelic footballers and hurlers. *British Journal of Sports Medicine*, **11**, 133–137.

Welham, W.C. and Behnke, A.R. (1942) The specific gravity of healthy men. *Journal of the American Medical Association*, **118**, 490–501.

White, J., Mayhew, J.L. and Piper, F.C. (1980) Prediction of body composition in College football players. *Journal of Sports Medicine and Physical Fitness*, **20**, 317–324.

White, J.E., Emergy, T.M., Kane, J.L., Groves, R. and Risman, A.B. (1988) Pre-season fitness profiles of professional soccer players, in *Science and Football* (eds T. Reilly, A. Lees, K. Davids and W.J. Murphy), E. and F.N. Spon, London, pp. 164–171.

Wickkiser, J.D. and Kelly, J.M. (1975) The body composition of a College football team. *Medicine and Science in Sports*, **7**, 199–202.

Williams, G., Reid, R.M. and Coutts, R. (1973) Observations on the aerobic power of University Rugby players and professional soccer players. *British Journal of Sports Medicine*, **7**, 390–391.

Williams, R. (1976) *Skilful Rugby*. Souvenir Press, London.

Wilmore, J.H. and Haskell, W.L. (1972) Body composition and endurance capacity of professional football players. *Journal of Applied Physiology*, **33**, 564–567.

Wintee, F.D., Snell, P.G. and Steary-Gunderson, J. (1989) Effects of 100% oxygen on performance of professional soccer players. *Journal of the American Medical Association*, **262**, 227–9.

Withers, R.T., Maricic, Z., Wasilewski, S. and Kelly, L. (1982) Match analysis of Australian professional soccer players. *Journal of Human Movement Studies*, **8**, 159–176.

Withers, R.T., Roberts, R.G.D. and Davies, G.J. (1977) The maximum aerobic power, anaerobic power and body composition of South Australian male representatives in athletics, basketball, field hockey and soccer. *Journal of Sports Medicine and Physical Fitness*, **17**, 391–400.

Yamaoka, S. (1965) Studies on energy metabolism in athletic sports. *Research Journal of Physical Education*, **9**, 28–40.

14
Court games: volleyball and basketball

Don MacLaren

14.1 INTRODUCTION

A majority of the studies describing physiological and anthropometric profiles of elite athletes have been concerned with runners, swimmers and cyclists. The bias is probably due to the comparative ease in relating such profiles to success in these sports, where individual performance can be measured precisely. The more skilful individual sports (such as racquet sports) and team games present the researcher with more complex problems, as the physiological demands of these sports and the fitness required are not so easily determined. This chapter is concerned with court games which call for a variety of individual skills that are executed in the context of competitive match-play. More specifically, the author's expertise is in the field of volleyball and hence the chapter leans heavily on aspects of this sport, although a strong emphasis is also placed on the demands and fitness requirements of basketball.

Volleyball and basketball have a similar genesis in history in so far as both were developed in the USA in the 1890s by physical educators attached to the YMCA. Basketball was invented in 1891 by James Naismith, a student at the International YMCA Training School in Springfield, Massachusetts. He had been set the task of devising a game consisting of techniques adapted from existing games and which could be played in a gymnasium. The need was for a game of vigorous activity that would be simple, interesting and could be played indoors or outdoors. The first games were played using a ball (soccer ball) and two peach baskets suspended approximately 10 feet (3 m) above the ground or railings – hence the name, basketball. The game spread rapidly throughout the USA and then to the rest of the World, so much so that it was featured in the 1904 Olympic Games before becoming an official Olympic Games sport in 1936.

Volleyball was invented in 1896 by William Morgan, a physical education director of the YMCA in Holyoke, Massachusetts. Apparently impressed with the popularity of basketball, he decided that it might be equal fun to play the bladder of a basketball over a lawn tennis net spread across an indoor court. As with basketball, the YMCA movement helped to spread the game throughout the World, although it was not until after the Second World War that the game flourished. Volleyball was only recognized as an Olympic sport from 1964 onwards.

The popularity of both volleyball and basketball can be realized on examination of the results of a survey carried out by the IOC in 1970 into the spread of Olympic sports throughout the World (Table 14.1). This popularity probably arises from the fact that both games can be played indoors or outdoors and use minimum amounts of equipment. One only has to see the number of outdoor basketball boards and rings when travelling through Europe or the USA, or to see the volleyball nets and posts along the beaches in the Mediterranean or the Copacabana to realize the recreational potential of these sports. Improvised courts for both games are evident in abundance in Asia, Africa, Oceania and South America and the games are promoted at a basic level in all the continents. Both sports can be played by all ages and both sexes, although volleyball has lent itself more for play as a mixed sport; a mixed professional league was introduced in the USA in the 1970s. Played competitively, both sports require a high level of fitness, although the emphasis on different aspects of fitness varies with the sport and the level of competition.

The various components of play in volleyball, for example, have their own physical requirements; strength of fingers and wrists for volleying,

Table 14.1 Number of registered players and Federations participating in Olympic sports (after Nichols, 1973)

Sport	Registered players (million)	Registered Federations
Basketball	65	127
Volleyball	65	110
Soccer	25.8	135
Shooting	25.5	94
Athletics	19.5	143
Swimming	10.5	98
Skiing	8	47
Judo	6	78

ability to jump high for blocking and spiking and flexibility, agility and speed for movement around the court. Furthermore, since volleyball matches have no time limit and matches can last for 2–3 hours, muscular and cardiorespiratory endurance are also needed. Similar requirements can be envisaged with respect to basketball, although cardiorespiratory endurance may not appear to be as important as in volleyball since basketball matches do not last as long (2 × 20 minute halves, plus time-outs).

This chapter will examine the temporal demands and characteristics of play in volleyball before describing the energetic and metabolic demands of the game. References will be made to basketball where appropriate, such as the heart rate and energy expenditure of playing the sport. Anthropometric and physiological characteristics of elite and College volleyball and basketball players will be considered. The literature pertaining to 'success' in these sports will be examined briefly for anthropometric and physiological markers before suggestions for training are made.

14.2 DEMANDS OF MATCH-PLAY

14.2.1 Temporal demands and characteristics of play

Sports may be classified according to the temporal nature of the matches, into those sports which have set time limits (i.e. soccer, Rugby and so on) and those sports in which a set number of matches, sets, holes or games have to be played (i.e. squash, tennis, golf). Basketball is

Table 14.2 Average duration (min:s) of volleyball matches and sets played during the Munich and Montreal Olympics and the Mexico World Championships (after Wielki, 1978)

	Men		Women	
Event	Average duration of match	Average duration of set	Average duration of match	Average duration of set
Olympic Games (Munich 1972)	94:48	25:30	83:04	23:45
World Championships (Mexico 1974)	84:58	23:45	71:59	20:47
Olympic Games (Montreal 1976)	84:00	22:34	84:18	21:20

a game of two 20 min halves and so falls into the first of these two categories, whereas a volleyball match is played until a team obtains 3 sets of 15 points per set, irrespective of how long it takes. Table 14.2 illustrates the findings from a study of elite volleyball matches (Wielki, 1978). The average duration of men's and women's matches was approximately 90 min whereas that for each set was between 20 and 25 min. These figures, however, do not reflect the fact that some matches lasted as long as 178 min for men or 149 min for women (i.e. longest matches at Munich, 1972) or as short as 36 min for men and 28 min for women (i.e. shortest matches at Mexico World Championships, 1974). Correspondingly the longest sets were between 45 and 55 min long whereas the shortest sets were between 7 and 11 min in duration (Wielki, 1978).

A basketball coach or player knows from the start of a match that there will be approximately 40 min of play with an interval between the two 20 min sessions. A volleyball coach or player can have no pre-conception of the duration of a match. In a tournament situation the result might be that the winners are either the team with the greatest stamina or indeed the team that has played fewest sets. For example, Wielki (1978) highlighted the fact that the ladies finalists at the Montreal Olympics, the USSR and Japan, had spent significantly differing amounts of time on court during their preliminary matches (USSR = 298 min; Japan = 216 min). That the Japanese ladies won the Olympic title by beating the USSR ladies team in 55 min, when the average match duration during this tournament was 84 min, may have been due to the fatigue felt by the USSR ladies from having played longer matches, rather than a testimony to the greater skill of the Japanese ladies! However, it should be pointed out that the reverse arose with regard to the men's finalists, Poland and the USSR. The Polish team had to play

Table 14.3 Temporal analyses of volleyball matches

	Lecompte and Rivet (1979)	Fiedler (1979)	Dyba (1982)	Viitasalo et al. (1987)
Mean duration of rally	9.7s	9.0s	7.0s 8.6s	6.6s
Mean duration of rest	11.7s	12.0s	13.3s 13.9s	14.2s
Rally: Rest ratio	1:1.2	1:1.3	1:1.2 1:1.6	1:2.2
Mean duration of a set (min:s)	16:48	—	18:33	24:00
Total match time (min:s)	84:00	—	93:23	108:50

for a total of 543 min before the final whereas the USSR team played for a total of 266 min, yet Poland won the gold medal in a match against the USSR that lasted 146 min. The importance of endurance training and the need for correct nutrition for maintaining sustained effort during tournament play in volleyball needs to be stressed and will be dealt with later.

Volleyball is a game of high intensity exercise interspersed with rest periods. Table 14.3 illustrates the findings from four studies whereby temporal analyses of volleyball games were undertaken. It is noticeable that the player spends more time at 'rest' than in active play. The implications are that during a match lasting 84 min, only 38 min involve actual play whereas 46 min cover 'rest'. Viitasalo *et al.* (1987) analysed matches between Finland and Hungary, and between the USA and USSR. The most frequent values for duration of rallies in the Finland–Hungary and the USA–USSR matches were 4 s and 7 s respectively and those for the 'rest' durations 12.5 s and 9.5 s respectively. Furthermore, these authors analysed individual player performances and noted the times for 'high intensity performances', i.e. movements performed with speed and using large muscle groups as in spiking, blocking, serving, retrieving and so on. The results demonstrated that the Finnish players engaged in a 'high intensity performance' approximately every 24 s whilst at front court and every 42 s at back court. If we assume that a volleyball player spends an equal proportion of time in back court as in front court, then we can calculate that a 'high intensity performance' will be encountered every 30 s approximately. This means that in an 84 min match of which 38 min actually involve play, there are 19 min of intense effort, i.e. 23% of the total match time. Similar results have been obtained by Conlee *et al.* (1982), who reported that the centre blocker/ spiker was required to perform an explosive jump on average once every 43 s.

These observations were on elite volleyball play, but variations are possible if lower standard matches are analysed or indeed if player position is taken into consideration. In Olympic and World Championships 54% of the rallies ended after the first net encounter and 77% by the second net encounter (Dyba, 1982), although this is not evident in local club or recreational games where reasonable rally lengths can be seen.

Technical demands of the game and the tactical systems employed have led to players adopting specific roles during matches. This imposes particular requirements on these players. Most volleyball teams have adopted the style of play where the setter plays at No. 2 front court, the No. 3 is a centre blocker/spiker and No. 4 is the 'power spiker'. As a consequence of analysing matches from the 1978 World Championships and the 1980 Moscow Olympic Games, Baacke (1981) demonstrated that the setters spent 15–35% of their total activity in blocking, 3–10% in spiking and 32–80% in setting, whereas the respective values for 'power hitters' and centre blocker/spikers were 20–35% and 35–45% in blocking, 20–45% and 5–25% in spiking, and 5–15% for both groups in setting. If these figures are linked with the previous suggestion that 19 min of an 84 min match entail 'high intensity performance', then the spikers and blocker/spikers will spend between 7.5 and 15 min of that time in jumping activities whereas the setters will spend between 3.5 and 8.5 min in jumping activities and up to 15 min in setting activities. The implications of these statistics for the specific training of these types of players are obvious and will be dealt with in a later section.

Although this type of information describes demands on individual players it does not give a picture of the number of jumping actions (for example) that a player in one of these positions makes. Rivet (1978) collected such data on a whole volleyball tournament of 10 matches played by an elite women's team. Out of a total of 868 jumps counted, 541 were block jumps (62%) and 327 were spike jumps (38%). When these data were further subdivided into the percentage distribution of the jumps for each position, it was discovered that 158 block jumps (27.3%) were made by the setters, 297 by the centre blocker/spikers (48.5%) and 86 by the 'power spikers' (24.3%). Furthermore, the setters made 78 spike jumps (23.7%), the centre blocker/spikers made 124 spike jumps (37.8%) and the power hitters 125 jumps (37.9%). In other words, the centre players made nearly half the number of jumps of the whole team. At international level one would expect a higher proportion of spike jumps from the power hitter than reported in Rivet's study. Indeed observations by coaches of international teams show that 60–80% of the spike attacks are likely to be made by the power spikers compared with the 38% stated by Rivet (1978). Nevertheless, the strenuous nature of volleyball appears to be mainly concerned with repeated jumping activities over a prolonged period of time interspersed with brief 'rest' phases.

The explosive nature of the spike and block jumps together with the rest periods led Fox and Mathews (1974) to classify volleyball as a sport relying 95% on the ATP-PCr system and 5% on the lactic acid system (La-O_2); no contribution from the aerobic system was denoted. This was supported by the findings of Rodionova and Plakhtienko (1977) who concluded that 63.2–79.3% of the energy for playing volleyball was anaerobic. Certainly the 7–10 s duration of rallies is too short a period to allow for substantial energy from anaerobic glycogenolysis which would lead to severe muscle glycogen reduction in the fast glycolytic (FG) muscle fibres, whereas the 25–45 s 'rest' periods between the 'high intensity performances' are sufficiently long to replenish the ATP-PCr stores in muscle (Harris *et al.*, 1976). The consequences of playing volleyball for energy sources and metabolites are discussed later.

The evidence provided so far presents an overview of the physical demands of playing volleyball. These demands should be manifested in physiological and metabolic measurements. The next two sections are concerned with such measures.

14.2.2 Energetics: oxygen consumption and heart rate

Several approaches to the indirect measurement of energy expenditure have been suggested, such as the use of movement counters (Laporte *et al.*, 1979), pedometers (Kemper and Verschuur, 1977; Washburn and Montoye, 1980), accelerometers (Montoye *et al.*, 1983), measurement of oxygen uptake (Margaria, Aghemo and Rovelli, 1966; Maron *et al.*, 1976) and heart rate (HR) monitoring (Shephard, 1967). Of these methods, the monitoring of HR is attractive because it uses a physiological parameter shown to be related to the severity of physical activity. The use of HR to estimate energy expenditure is based on the assumption of a close linear relationship between HR and oxygen uptake ($\dot{V}O_2$) or energy expenditure. The HR and $\dot{V}O_2$ are measured over a range of exercise intensities using either a treadmill or a bicycle ergometer and an individual HR-$\dot{V}O_2$ relationship is established (Bradfield, 1971). This relationship can then be used to estimate energy expenditure using telemetred heart rates during an activity. Limitations associated with using HR measures to predict energy expenditure have been highlighted by Washburn and Montoye (1986) and include factors such as emotion, heat, non-steady state situations and the mode of exercise. However, the high correlation coefficients ordinarily obtained between HR and $\dot{V}O_2$ (Christensen *et al.*, 1984; Morgan and Bennett, 1976) support the use of the HR-$\dot{V}O_2$ relation for estimating energy expenditure.

In field conditions it is not usually possible to measure $\dot{V}O_2$ directly without hindering performance. It is more practical to use telemetred heart rates during match-play after having established a linear regression equation between HR and $\dot{V}O_2$ for each player. A source of error additional to those mentioned above does accrue for volleyball and basketball players: the HR-$\dot{V}O_2$ relationship is usually established using a treadmill whereas the demands of the game necessitate actions such as jumping, diving, and backwards and sideways movements. Nonetheless, telemetred HR values related to $\dot{V}O_2$ have been used to estimate the energy expenditure during volleyball and basketball although the measurement error in doing so has not been quantified.

Table 14.4 Energy expenditure of various sports (based on a 70kg man)

Sport	*Energy expenditure* ($kJ\ min^{-1}$)
Badminton	26.8
Basketball	41.0
Cycling	50.2
Hockey	39.8
Gymnastics	19.7
Running – Jog	62.0
– 8 min $mile^{-1}$	75.0
Soccer	41.4
Squash	63.2
Swimming	48.1
Volleyball	10.5 – 40.6

Table 14.4 illustrates energy expenditure values from different literature sources for a variety of sports. It is evident that whereas basketball is deemed to be a sport of reasonably intense activity from its energy expenditure of 41 kJ min^{-1}, values computed for volleyball are generally lower. The variation in estimated energy expenditure in volleyball is appreciable as can be realized on examination of Table 14.5. These discrepancies could have resulted from the use of non-specialist volleyball players as subjects, or the use of competitive or non-competitive games situations. The higher values obtained by Fleck and Case (1981) and exceeded in a study by Gore and MacLaren (unpublished observations, 1985) could be due to the fact that both studies used competitive matches and experienced players. Furthermore, the differences between the latter two studies could

Table 14.5 Estimates of energy expenditure during volleyball play in various sources

Author	*Energy expenditure* ($kJ\ min^{-1}$)
Durnin and Passmore (1967)	10.5 – 21.0
Rodionova and Plakhtienko (1977)	30.5
Fleck and Case (1981)	40.6
Reilly (1981)	24.0 – 27.0
Brooks and Fahey (1984)	15.1

Table 14.6 Energy expenditure calculations for various sports (based on Seliger, 1968)

Sport	Energy expenditure ($kJ\ min^{-1}$)	Heart rate ($beats\ min^{-1}$)
Basketball	64.5	170
Boxing	67.4	148
Canoe-paddling	38.1	143
Kayak-paddling	131.9	176
Soccer	52.7	165
Volleyball	29.3	110 – 125
Weight-lifting	219.8	120 – 123

be because female subjects were used in the former whereas male subjects were used in the latter study in which the mean energy expenditure was estimated at 52.5 kJ min^{-1}. If body mass or fat-free mass were incorporated into the units, then the figures from the two studies may well agree. It must be pointed out that no study has yet been published which has described the estimated energy expenditure of playing international standard volleyball.

The only reported study actually measuring $\dot{V}O_2$ whilst playing volleyball or basketball was that by Seliger (1968). In this study 16 male subjects played volleyball for 14 min whilst breathing via a half mask into a collection 'gas bag' carried on their backs. The mean value of 0.42 kJ kg^{-1} min^{-1} would represent a value of 29.3 kJ min^{-1} for a 70 kg person. A value of 0.92 kJ kg^{-1} min^{-1} for playing basketball was obtained on 15 male subjects, this being equivalent to a value of 64.5 kJ min^{-1} for a 70 kg person (Table 14.6). Measured mean heart rates ranging from 110 to 125 beats min^{-1} confirm the comparatively low energy expenditure for volleyball play, whilst the mean HR of 170 beats min^{-1} for basketball reflects the greater energy demands of this game. One would expect that $\dot{V}O_2$ determined by this method would be higher than normal due to the fact that subjects had to carry a 'gas bag' during the game. That this effect was not pronounced in volleyball could have been due to the nature of the game (recreational rather than competitive) and/or of the players (recreational rather than experienced).

Volleyball therefore appears to be a game classified as a very light to light activity, whereas basketball can be classified as a heavy activity in terms of its aerobic energy demands. Certainly a $\dot{V}O_2$ of 22 ml kg^{-1} min^{-1} for playing volleyball (Seliger, 1968) would constitute an intensity of 50% $\dot{V}O_{2max}$ or less. Gore and MacLaren's unpublished data on six male volleyball players in a club game correspond to a mean value of 55.5% $\dot{V}O_{2max}$ (range 42–70% $\dot{V}O_{2max}$). The $\dot{V}O_2$ of 40 ml kg^{-1} min^{-1} for playing basketball (Seliger, 1968) on the other hand would constitute a demand in excess of 70% $\dot{V}O_{2max}$ for an elite basketball player (assuming that such a person has a $\dot{V}O_{2max}$ of 60 ml kg^{-1} min^{-1}.

Further support for these findings has come from studies in which telemetred heart rates have been obtained. Such studies have shown mean HR values of 127 beats min^{-1} (Viitasalo *et al.*, 1987), 139 beats min^{-1} (Fardy, Hritz and Hellerstein, 1976), 144 beats min^{-1} (Dyba, 1982) and 155 beats min^{-1} (Walker, 1973) for playing volleyball. The mean heart rate in the unpublished work of Gore and MacLaren was 149 beats min^{-1}. These values are lower than those found in other team sports such as for basketball (154–195 beats min^{-1}) (McArdle, Magel and Kyvallos, 1971), 11-a-side soccer (157 beats min^{-1}; Reilly, 1986), and 4-a-side soccer (172 beats min^{-1}; MacLaren *et al.*, 1988). The results appear to reflect the moderate activity level in volleyball. It must be emphasized that the results reported are mean values and therefore will mask the intermittent aspects of the game as well as the possible differences between playing positions.

Dyba (1982) closely monitored HR in his study of the Ontario junior men's provincial volleyball team, and made a number of interesting observations:

1. The greater the number of net encounters (i.e. the longer the rally), the greater the HR, i.e. average of 141 beats min^{-1} at a zero net encounter increased to 151 beats min^{-1} in rallies of 5 or more net encounters.
2. Heart rate averaged over 150 beats min^{-1} for the first set, then decreased with successive sets to 140 beats min^{-1} in the fourth set before rising to 143 beats min^{-1} in the final set.
3. Average HR values were greater when playing front court (146 beats min^{-1}) than when playing back court (141 beats min^{-1}).
4. Setters had a higher average game HR (150 beats min^{-1}) than did middle blocker/spikers (143 beats min^{-1}) and power hitters (141 beats min^{-1}). This resulted from the higher HR values of the setters when playing back court compared to the other players, i.e. the HR of a setter remains consistent throughout front court and back court play.

These findings were not supported by Walker (1973) who found no difference in the heart rates between setters and spikers. Rodionova and Plakhtienko (1977) determined the heart rates and calculated the energy costs of the various actions in volleyball (Table 14.7). Since their paper gave no indication of the number of actions performed, it is difficult to assess the value of their findings other than that the results are broadly dissimilar to Dyba's (1982).

As already stated, studies of the heart rate responses of males to playing basketball have shown higher values than observed during

Table 14.7 Energy costs and mean heart rates of various actions in volleyball (after Rodionova and Plakhtienko, 1977)

Volleyball action	Energy cost (kJ)	Heart rate (beats min^{-1})
Spike	10.5	138
Block	4.9	—
Serve	5.1	104
Receive	4.6	131
Set/dig	4.9	120 – 126

volleyball play (McArdle, Magel and Kyvallos, 1971; Ramsey *et al.*, 1970). The mean HR values for female basketball players in the study by McArdle, Magel and Kyvallos (1971) varied between 154 and 195 beats min^{-1} whilst playing, although the values ranged from 105 to 204 beats min^{-1}. The heart rate whilst playing was approximately 81–95% of the HRmax. Estimated energy expenditure for these female players was 29.82–49.56 kJ min^{-1}, which would support the contention that basketball is a moderate to heavy activity. Ramsey *et al.* (1970) studied the HR response of a male basketball player, whose values ranged from 155 to 190 beats min^{-1}. An interesting finding in this study was that even during rest periods such as time outs and foul shots, the HR did not decrease below 155 beats min^{-1}.

14.2.3 Metabolism

The consideration of volleyball as an 'aerobic' game is equivocal. If it were true, high lactic acid levels might be expected during or immediately after matches. Studies measuring the blood lactate response to playing volleyball have found values of 3.6 mM for a representative junior district team (Dyba, 1982), 9.8 mM for elite male College players (Conlee *et al.*, 1982), 2 mM for a good club team in Finland (Viitasalo *et al.*, 1987), 3.5 mM for the Finnish national team (Viitasalo *et al.*, 1987), and 2.1–3.4 mM for elite female players in the German league (Künstlinger, Lugwig and Stegmann, 1987). Notwithstanding the limitations of measuring lactate after a match in terms of timing sample collection and controlling for prior activity, these values are not high enough to imply a significant contribution of energy from anaerobic glycogenolysis. Alactate anaerobic energy use, the resynthesis of phosphagen stores, and the oxygen bound to myoglobin seem to be more important. Christensen, Hedman and Saltin (1960) have shown that high intensity work interspersed with short rest periods could result in the work regimen being continued without undue fatigue and a low blood lactic acid concentration. Such a scenario appears to obtain in volleyball. Thus the comparatively low accumulation of lactic acid suggests that even though volleyball involves intense, explosive movements, either these actions are not repeated often enough to promote 'anaerobic' fatigue, or any lactate produced during the intense periods can be metabolized during the less intense phases (Hermansen and Stensvold, 1972).

Lactate levels after basketball matches do not seem to have been seriously studied. It may be surmised that since data previously presented have indicated that basketball play results in HR values of 170 beats min^{-1} and entails an exercise intensity in excess of 70–75% $\dot{V}O_{2max}$, a high blood lactic acid concentration would probably be observed. Indeed at such work intensities, most individuals would be close to or above their 'lactate threshold'. Therefore, prolonged play at such intensities would result in lactate concentrations above 4 mM, the consequences of which could be fatigue from metabolic acidosis (Wenger and Reed, 1976). The numerous interruptions in the game could allow some removal of lactate. The fact that each half of the game lasts for 20 min, that time-outs may be called, and that players can be substituted frequently could result in lower lactate values than might be expected. Basketball play has been classified as deriving 85% of its energy expenditure from the phosphagen stores (ATP and PCr) and 15% of its energy from anaerobic glycogenolysis (La-O$_2$) by Fox and Mathews (1974). These energy systems could not provide all the energy if games lasted for a continuous period of 20 min. It has been calculated that the phosphagen stores could provide energy for between 6–8 s, whereas anaerobic glycogenolysis could provide energy for about 60 s before high levels of lactic acid in the muscle induced fatigue (Bergstrom et al., 1971). For 85% of the energy to be derived from phosphagens and 15% from La-O$_2$ during 20 min halves, there should be periods of vigorous action lasting no longer than 20 s followed by less vigorous or even rest periods to allow for phosphagen replenishment and oxidation of lactate.

Studies on muscle glycogen depletion have highlighted the importance of carbohydrate as an energy source during exercise, and further point to the use of specific muscle fibre types during such activity. Reduction of muscle glycogen stores has been correlated with fatigue in laboratory investigations (Bergstrom, Hermansen and Hultman, 1967) and with reduced performance in the field (Saltin, 1973). The latter study on soccer players showed that players with a reduced muscle glycogen store pre-match covered less distance in the game and the percentage of the total distance covered walking was greater in these players compared with those who started with normal muscle glycogen depots. Although no studies on muscle glycogen levels have been reported in basketball players, two studies have used volleyball players. Conlee *et al.* (1982) and Viitasalo *et al.* (1987) examined the glycogen depletion patterns of the vastus lateralis muscle after playing volleyball. Elite male volleyball players were used in both studies where glycogen depletion was found to occur in both slow oxidative (SO) and fast glycolytic (FG) fibres, although predominantly in the SO fibres. In the study by Conlee *et al.* (1982) biopsies were taken after four 60 min matches, whereas in the study by Viitasalo *et al.* (1987) the samples were taken after a five set match in a training camp. Table 14.8 highlights the changes shown in the two studies. These findings would confirm that volleyball is probably a sport of low to moderate intensity, and that the recruitment of SO fibres results in their significant depletion of glycogen. The lower glycogen depletion in the FG fibres reinforces the points made earlier concerning the brief, explosive actions and that they are likely to be recruited for such activities as spikes and blocks, but during the less intense activities it is most likely that mainly SO fibres are used.

Attention should also be drawn, in Table 14.8, to the partially depleted glycogen stores before the matches. Conlee *et al.* (1982) found

Table 14.8 Glycogen depletion patterns as a consequence of playing volleyball

Study	Fibre type	PAS stain (%) Before match	After match
Conlee *et al.*	Slow oxidative		
(1982)	Dark	68	4
	Medium	31	47
n = 6	Light		52
	Fast glycolytic		
	Dark	91	40
	Medium	8	56
	Light	0	4
Viitasalo *et al.*	Slow oxidative		
(1987)	Dark	8	5
	Medium	54	40
n = 3	Light	38	55
	Fast glycolytic		
	Dark	38	30
	Medium	57	65
	Light	5	5

that 32% of the SO fibres were partially or totally depleted of glycogen before the match whereas Viitasalo *et al.* (1987) reported approximately 92% of the SO fibres partially or totally depleted. It must be pointed out that in the latter study the match took place after three days of volleyball camp training, and the total muscle glycogen content had decreased by 67% before the match concerned. This highlights the need for a high carbohydrate dietary intake to replenish muscle glycogen stores when players are engaged in successive days of volleyball play.

The section on 'temporal demands' of playing volleyball showed that in a tournament such as the Olympic Games or World Championships, teams must be prepared to play for up to 700 min in order to win a medal. Since matches are likely to be played on consecutive or alternate days with training sessions in between, the reduction of muscle glycogen stores is a possibility. In order to ensure that this does not occur, it is imperative that a high carbohydrate diet is eaten. Costill and Miller (1980) have shown that three consecutive days of heavy endurance training resulted in almost total muscle glycogen depletion when the carbohydrate intake was 40% of the total energy, but that these glycogen stores were maintained when the carbohydrate intake was 70%. However, in order to consume 70% of the diet as carbohydrate, an 85 kg male volleyball player would be expected to consume 1680 g of carbohydrate if he expended 24 MJ per day. The values for a 67 kg female volleyball player would be 800 g carbohydrate if 18.5 MJ of energy were expended per day. Foods such as bread, potatoes, pasta and rice would be preferable to confectionary products from a health point of view, although supplementation with high carbohydrate drinks could be of benefit. The value of carbohydrate drinks (glucose or maltodextrins) during training and during matches is well established in terms of offsetting fatigue (Coyle and Coggan, 1984), and should be practised. Carbohydrate supplementation during exercise has been shown to preserve blood sugar levels and conserve muscle glycogen stores (Hargreaves *et al.*, 1984).

Further evidence of the 'aerobic' nature of volleyball has been provided by Künstlinger, Ludwig and Stegmann (1987) who examined selected hormonal and metabolite concentrations after competitive matches played by elite female players. The authors concluded that volleyball provokes almost the same metabolic changes as seen in endurance sports. They showed that the exercise-induced changes in lactate, glucose, free fatty acids (FFA) and cortisol corresponded to results obtained by Scheele *et al.* (1975) after 25 km running. However, the changes in catecholamines appear to be strongly influenced by the short intense exercise periods, i.e. corresponding to higher than 80% $\dot{V}O_{2max}$. Essen (1978) has demonstrated that intermittent exercise at a high intensity leads to an enhanced oxidative metabolism, and to the liberation and oxidation of fatty acids; similar results are obtained by continuous intense exercise. Since the work:rest ratio associated with volleyball is close to the 1:1 work:rest ratio in the study by Essen (1978), the findings of low lactate (2.5 mM) and high FFA (0.95–1.3 mM) by Künstlinger, Ludwig and Stegmann (1987) may have a similar explanation. In volleyball the long duration of the matches (60–180 min) and the short periods of high intensity play result in elevated catecholamine and cortisol levels. Together with the low lactate concentrations, the hormonal response will enhance lipolysis in adipose tissue and β-oxidation in muscle.

It appears therefore that the metabolic responses to playing volleyball are similar to that found in moderate intensity endurance activities, in that significant glycogen depletion in SO fibres is evident, and the plasma hormonal and metabolite changes are in concordance. Since volleyball may be classified as a sport consisting of short bouts of intense activity (extended for between 30 and 180 min), are there any specific characteristics developed by the elite player? The next sections deal with the physical and physiological characteristics of elite volleyball and basketball players.

14.3 CHARACTERISTICS OF PLAYERS

14.3.1 Height and weight

Unique types of body size and proportion may constitute important prerequisites for successful participation in particular sports. Tanner (1964)

Table 14.9 Height and weight of basketball and volleyball players at three Olympic games

	Basketball		Volleyball	
	Height (cm)	Weight (kg)	Height (cm)	Weight (kg)
Tokyo (1964)				
male	189.4	84.3	183.8	79.0
female	—	—	170.8	65.0
Munich (1972)				
male	192.0	85.5	188.8	83.2
female	—	—	173.0	69.0
Montreal (1976)				
male	195.0	88.0	189.5	85.5
female	177.0	70.0	175.0	67.0

has shown that those who were successful at the Olympic Games had definite body characteristics that were clearly specific to the competitive event. Indeed Khosla (1983) stated that although an ideal physique was not sufficient in itself for excellence in a sport, its lack (even in the presence of compensating attributes) may be a severe handicap to a potential athlete. Such statements can be suitably applied to sports such as volleyball and basketball.

Examination of the heights and weights of elite male volleyball and basketball players from the Tokyo (1964), Munich (1972) and Montreal (1976) Olympic Games (Table 14.9) highlights the fact that these players were tall and that the trend appeared to be towards an increase in height and weight. Carter (1984) reported that the average heights of male track athletes at the Montreal Olympic Games was 176 cm. This value was 13.5 cm below that for male volleyball players and 19 cm below that for male basketball players. The only groups of sportsmen to approach equivalent heights were shot putters (191 cm), discus throwers (188 cm), 100 m freestyle swimmers (191 cm) and 100 m backstroke swimmers (190 cm).

Recent research on elite male volleyball and basketball players has illustrated the development of the trend towards an increase in height, and the variation in height for positional play in basketball (Table 14.10). At the present time few top-ranked male volleyball nations have many players less than 190 cm in height in their team. The obvious advantage of possessing such an impressive height arises from the fact that volleyball is played over a net at a height of 2.43 m for men. The higher above the net a player can reach, the more likely he or she is to successfully block or spike past an opponent. The top international male players are expected to spike and block the ball in a zone approximately 3.30 m above ground level, and so this would necessitate possessing both great height and vertical jump capability. The shorter the player, the higher he has to jump in order to play successfully in this aerial zone. Indeed, if the player were too short he might then not be physically able to reach the necessary heights despite a good vertical jumping ability.

Elite male basketball players are even taller than the volleyball players, especially the centres and forwards (Table 14.10). This physical attribute is particularly important when it is realized that the game involves physical contact (i.e. no separation of the teams) with the intention of getting the ball in a 'basket' elevated 10 feet (3.05 m) above ground level. The playmakers (guards) are the more skilful players and are used to set up the attacks which are completed by the taller players. Furukawa (1974) reported that there was a very strong relation between basketball players' height and success at the Mexico Olympic Games.

Table 14.10 Height and weight of elite male basketball and volleyball players reported in research papers

Team	Height (cm)	Weight (kg)	Author(s)
Volleyball			
England	185.5 ± 6.2	78.5 ± 3.2	Black (1980)
Canadian National	188.9 ± 4.2	85.0 ± 3.8	Carter (1984)
USA National	193.0 ± 3.9	85.5 ± 4.5	Puhl *et al.* (1982)
Finland National	192.0 ± 5.8	85.7 ± 6.8	Viitasalo (1982)
USSR National	193.0 ± 5.4	90.1 ± 7.9	Viitasalo (1982)
Finland National	195.0 ± 6.2	89.5 ± 6.6	Viitasalo *et al.* (1987)
Basketball			
USA Professional			
centres	214.0 ± 5.2	109.2 ± 13.8	Parr *et al.* (1978)
forwards	200.6 ± 5.0	96.9 ± 7.3	
guards	188.0 ± 10.3	83.6 ± 6.3	
Elite University (USA)			
centres	205.7 ± 0.03	97.2 ± 7.0	Vaccaro *et al.* (1979)
forwards	197.1 ± 4.6	92.8 ± 5.4	
guards	186.4 ± 6.4	75.5 ± 4.4	
Brazil National			
centres	206.6 ± 4.1	102.1 ± 17.6	Soares *et al.* (1986)
forwards	196.9 ± 4.6	92.0 ± 6.9	
guards	185.4 ± 8.6	79.3 ± 7.3	
Argentina	195.1 ± 9.3	90.3 ± 8.5	Soares *et al.* (1986)
Canada	198.2 ± 9.2	90.8 ± 10.8	
Puerto Rico	195.6 ± 8.8	89.6 ± 12.1	
Dominican Republic	195.1 ± 12.3	79.8 ± 6.3	
Cuba	196.7 ± 8.1	—	
Mexico	197.1 ± 7.7	87.6 ± 4.1	
English Nat. League	191.0 ± 10.1	—	Bale and Scholes (1986)

Certainly in professional basketball, centres and forwards are unlikely to be selected unless they are in excess of 200 cm in height.

Elite female volleyball and basketball players are approximately 14 cm and 22 cm shorter than their male counterparts, respectively (Table 14.11). The reported mean height of female participants at the Montreal Olympic Games (162.0 ± 6.1 cm) was exceeded by 13 cm for volleyball players and 15 cm for basketball players. Table 14.11 illustrates the

Table 14.11 Height and weight of elite female basketball and volleyball players reported in research papers

	Height (cm)	Weight (kg)	Author(s)
Volleyball			
USA National	177.8 ± 8.3	67.2 ± 6.9	Spence *et al.* (1980)
USA National	178.3 ± 4.2	70.5 ± 5.5	Puhl *et al.* (1982)
USA National	179.3 ± 7.7	68.5 ± 7.6	Fleck *et al.* (1985)
USA University Squad	178.9 ± 4.7	71.6 ± 5.0	Fleck *et al.* (1985)
Basketball			
USSR National	173.0 ±	71.2	Carter (1984)
Montreal Olympic participants	177.8 ± 9.2	—	Khosla (1983)
English Nat. League	171.4 ± 7.6	—	Bale and Scholes (1986)
centres	187.3	78.2	Spurgeon *et al.* (1980)
forwards	182.4	73.0	
guards	171.0	62.8	

height and weight characteristics of elite female volleyball and basketball players reported in the literature, and these findings further highlight their tallness. This bias in height does raise some interesting questions. Since physical size is required for elite participants, how do some Asian, African and Latin populations cope with this requirement? The twelve Japanese women gold medallists at the Montreal Olympic Games ranged in height from 169 to 180 cm. Fewer than 0.3% of women from Japan would be expected to be taller than 169 cm (reference mean = 152 cm). The Japanese have been able to select players of the right physique and technical capability from a population smaller in size than in most western countries, where the reference mean is 10 cm higher than in Japan. The height of the volleyball net for female players is 224 cm above ground level, and the elite players would be expected to play in an aerial zone approximately 300 cm above ground. As with the men, tallness and good jumping ability would be essential pre-requisites for participation at elite levels.

14.3.2 Body composition and physique

Elite male volleyball and basketball players, in keeping with many other elite athletes, tend to be lean and muscular. This is reflected in the mean percentage body fat measures of male volleyball players as varying from 10.5 to 14% (Montecinos *et al.*, 1982; Puhl *et al.*, 1982; Viitasalo *et al.*, 1982, 1987) and basketball players from 7.1 to 13.5% (Parr *et al.*, 1978;

Gillam, 1985). These values are not as low as those reported for distance runners, swimmers or wrestlers, but are lower than those for Rugby, soccer and hockey players, and for the normal population (i.e. 15% body fat). Likewise, elite female volleyball and basketball players have a comparatively low percentage body fat, i.e. 11.7–18.3% for elite volleyball players (Puhl *et al.*, 1982; Fleck *et al.*, 1985) and 15.4–20.1% for elite basketball players (Spurgeon, Spurgeon and Giese, 1980). Studies on College standard female volleyball and basketball players typically report higher body fat values, i.e. 21.4–25.7% and 15.8–26.9% for volleyball and basketball respectively. Although these figures are useful in providing reasonable guidelines for percentage body fat in these sports, caution must be expressed when interpreting such data due to the methods of assessing body fat. All the above studies used skinfold thickness measures, but varied in the use of skinfold sites. Nonetheless, the results seem reasonable in view of the fact that both sports involve explosive jumping actions where any excess of body weight carried in the form of fat would lead to a lowered jumping capability.

The physique of these athletes has also been determined and expressed as to endomorphy, mesomorphy and ectomorphy ratings. Values in the literature on state and Collegiate teams in these sports have provided mean values of 2:5:3 for volleyball and 2.5:5:3.5 for basketball players. Female volleyball and basketball players have mean values of 4:4:2 and 4.3:4.5:3 respectively. These results reinforce the belief that leanness and muscularity are requisites for playing these sports at a high standard. Appropriate combinations of these features should result in better jumping ability, flexibility and speed of movement around the court.

Various studies have examined the physical characteristics of elite and successful teams at volleyball and basketball in order to determine which factors are most important. Such studies have correlated either height (Gladden and Colacino, 1978; Ongley and Hopley, 1981; Alexander, 1976) or body fat (Morrow *et al.*, 1979; Fleck *et al.*, 1985; Ongley and Hopley, 1980; Riezebos *et al.*, 1983) with success in playing either volleyball or basketball. Although height is largely genetically determined, the percentage body fat values could result from the training performed by these players. It would appear therefore that a coach of a national squad should take into consideration the height of players available to him and work on a physical conditioning programme to decrease percentage body fat.

14.3.3 Maximum oxygen uptake

Traditionally, maximum oxygen uptake ($\dot{V}O_{2max}$) is regarded as the best determinant of aerobic capacity. A high $\dot{V}O_{2max}$ indicates a good capacity for endurance activity (Bergh *et al.*, 1978). Tables 14.12 and 14.13 give the $\dot{V}O_{2max}$ values reported for elite male and female volleyball and basketball players. For elite male volleyball players the average $\dot{V}O_{2max}$ of 56 ml kg^{-1} min^{-1} is higher than the average shown for elite male basketball players (50 ml kg^{-1} min^{-1}) and for professional American Footballers (44–53 ml kg^{-1} min^{-1}; Wilmore *et al.* 1976), within the range reported for soccer players (53–67 ml kg^{-1} min^{-1}; Raven *et al.*, 1976; 57–67 ml kg^{-1} min^{-1}; Apor, 1988), but lower than middle-distance

Table 14.12 Maximum oxygen uptake of elite male volleyball and basketball players

Group	$\dot{V}O_{2max}$ (ml kg^{-1} min^{-1})	n	Mode of test	Author(s)
Volleyball				
Japan	48.6 ± 6.2	14	bicycle	Toyoda (1974)
GDR	65.2 ± 6.1	21	bicycle	Placheta *et al.* (1969)
USSR	56.4 ± 1.3	12	bicycle	Parnat *et al.* (1975)
USSR	60.2	—	—	Rodionova and Plakhtienko (1977)
Rumania	52.8 ± 1.4	10	bicycle	Cherebetu and Szogy (1976)
Czechoslovakia	43.2 ± 5.2	12	bicycle	Horak (1974)
Ontario Province	51.6 ± 2.3	11	treadmill	Dyba (1982)
USA	56.1 ± 2.2	8	treadmill	Puhl *et al.* (1982)
Brigham Young Univ.	56.4 ± 5.8	6	—	Conlee *et al.* (1982)
Australian State Team	56.4 ± 4.0	6	treadmill	Ongley and Hopley (1981)
France	52.3 ± 4.3	13	bicycle	Jousellin *et al.* (1984)
Finland	56.6 ± 3.3	10	treadmill	Viitasalo *et al.* (1987)
Basketball				
USSR	55.3 ± 1.8	14	bicycle	Parnat *et al.* (1975)
USA professionals				
centres	41.9 ± 4.9	4	treadmill	Parr *et al.* (1978)
forwards	45.9 ± 4.3	15		
guards	50.0 ± 5.4	15		
Univ. of Maryland				
centres	56.2 ± 1.1	3	treadmill	Vaccaro *et al.* (1979)
forwards	59.3 ± 8.2	5		
guards	60.6 ± 7.0	5		
Brazil National				
centres	59.7 ± 6.9	7	Estimated	Soares *et al.* (1986)
forwards	59.9 ± 5.1	9		
guards	74.4 ± 6.8	5		

runners (70 ml kg^{-1} min^{-1}; Rusko, Hara and Karvinen, 1978) or distance runners (70–78 ml kg^{-1} min^{-1}; Costill *et al.*, 1976, Rusko, Hara and Karvinen, 1978). For elite female volleyball players the average $\dot{V}O_{2max}$ of 50.8 ml kg^{-1} min^{-1} is approximately 10% lower than for their male counterparts, lower than the average for female basketball players (52.7 ml kg^{-1} min^{-1}), female distance runners (59.1 ml kg^{-1} min^{-1}; Wilmore and Brown, 1974) and female cross country skiers (59.1 ml kg^{-1} min^{-1}; Rusko, Hara and Karvinen, 1978). Values of $\dot{V}O_{2max}$ for athletes in different sports have been reported by Wilmore (1979).

The problem with making comparisons of $\dot{V}O_{2max}$ data from various literature sources can be related to the methods of testing employed and to the gas collection and analysis devices used. However, a study by Joussellin *et al.* (1984) examined the $\dot{V}O_{2max}$ of elite French athletes from a variety of sports (Table 14.14). The results highlight the comparatively low relative $\dot{V}O_{2max}$ of male and female volleyball players, yet the values for female basketball players are quite impressive.

It appears that in spite of the temporal demands of volleyball play and of the glycogen depletion patterns seen in the SO muscle fibres which point to an aerobic demand in the game, elite volleyball players do not possess $\dot{V}O_{2max}$ values as high as typical endurance trained athletes. The values reported for basketball players are likewise lower than might be

Table 14.13 Maximum oxygen uptake of selected female volleyball and basketball players

Group	$\dot{V}O_{2max}$ (ml kg^{-1} min^{-1})	n	Mode of test	Author(s)
Volleyball				
USA Univ. team	33.0 ± 2.6	6	predicted	Fardy *et al.* (1976)
USA	43.2 ± 15		treadmill	Spence *et al.* (1980)
Australian State team	46.8 ± 5.5	6	treadmill	Ongley and Hopley (1981)
USA Univ. team	50.6 ± 5.7	14	treadmill	Puhl *et al.* (1982)
France	52.7 ± 4.5	27	bicycle	Jousselin *et al.* (1984)
USA	48.8 ± 5.1	13	treadmill	Fleck *et al.* (1985)
Basketball				
USA College players	38.7 ± 4.1	7	bicycle	Sinning and Adrian (1968)
USA College players	42.9	—	treadmill	Sinning (1973)
USA College players	50.1	20	treadmill	Riezebos *et al.* (1983)
France	57.2 ± 1.3	13	bicycle	Jousselin *et al.* (1984)

Table 14.14 $\dot{V}O_{2max}$ values for male and female athletes (after Jousselin *et al.*, 1984)

Sport	$\dot{V}O_{2max}$ (ml kg^{-1} min^{-1})
Males	
Athletics	
800–1500 m	52.9 ± 3.6
3000–5000	71.8 ± 5.0
Marathon	75.9 ± 4.6
	81.3 ± 6.2
Boxing	64.7 ± 6.3
Cycling (road)	71.1 ± 6.6
Handball	57.2 ± 5.0
Modern pentathlon	73.0 ± 11.0
Soccer	63.9 ± 5.5
Table tennis	58.0 ± 5.5
Volleyball	52.3 ± 4.3
Females	
Athletics	
100–200 m	52.9 ± 4.8
800 m	59.2 ± 3.4
1500–3000 m	66.4 ± 4.8
Basketball	57.2 ± 13.0
Modern pentathlon	55.5 ± 3.5
Table tennis	53.0 ± 3.8
Volleyball	52.7 ± 4.5

expected. The fact that the game of basketball does not usually last longer than 60 min, that there are rest opportunities during stops in the game, and that the height and weight characteristics of basketball players would place them at a disadvantage in terms of relative $\dot{V}O_{2max}$ values, could account for the low $\dot{V}O_{2max}$ observations in players. If one considers the severe physiological stresses encountered during basketball games, a high $\dot{V}O_{2max}$ would be advantageous. Any increase in endurance capacity would result in fatigue being offset to a later point in the game or in lower levels of fatigue throughout the game. Since fatigue does result in impairment in skilled performance (Reilly and Smith, 1986) and also in increased possibilities of injury, enhancement of endurance would be useful for basketball players. The differences in $\dot{V}O_{2max}$ values associated with player position, as found in the studies reported in Table 14.12, show that guards have a greater aerobic power.

This is probably a consequence of the style of play undertaken by these teams whereby the guard is the play-maker and has the highest work-rate.

14.3.4 Muscular power measures

Power is most commonly assessed by tests such as the vertical jump (Sargent, 1921), stair run test (Margaria, Aghemo and Rovelli, 1966), Wingate 30 s bicycle test (Bar-Orr, Dotan and Inbar, 1977) and sprinting on a non-motorized treadmill (Lakomy, 1984). The ease of performing the vertical jump test, the fact that no expensive apparatus is necessary, that it correlates well with other power tests, and that it can be performed almost anywhere has led to its being frequently used as a measure of power. Since the test can be performed in a number of

Table 14.15 Vertical jump values for male and female volleyball and basketball players

Group	Vertical jump (cm)	Author(s)
Volleyball		
(male)	75.1 ± 7.6	Black (1980)
Australian state team	66.2 ± 5.5	Ongley and Hopley (1981)
Canada	75	CVA Bulletin (1978)
Ontario state team	66.2 ± 7.6	Dyba (1982)
USA	67.0 ± 11.5	Puhl *et al.* (1982)
Mens Open	67.4 ± 6.9	Gladden and Colacino (1978)
Mens senior (+ 40 years)	57.5 ± 5.4	
USA (females)	49.6	Gladden and Colacino (1978)
USA	49.4 ± 5.8	Spence *et al.* (1980)
Australian state team	49.5 ± 4.4	Ongley and Hopley (1981)
USA	45.9 ± 6.3	Puhl *et al.* (1982)
USA	52.4 ± 4.5	Fleck *et al.* (1985)
USA University team	45.5 ± 6.4	Fleck *et al.* (1985)
Womens Open	49.6 ± 6.0	Gladden and Colacino (1978)
Basketball		
(males)		
Brazil National		
centres	55.9 ± 8.1	Soares *et al.* (1986)
forwards	66.8 ± 8.3	
guards	61.6 ± 8.5	
(females)		
USA College team	37.0 ± 1.0	Riezobos *et al.* (1983)

different ways (i.e. from a crouching stance or using rebound from an upright position, hands free or one held immobile) and may employ force platform or cinematographic data, it is not surprising that these methods could result in variations in the reported values. For a more detailed discussion of anaerobic tests the reader should consult Vandewalle, Peres and Monod (1987).

Table 14.15 presents data on the vertical jump values of male and female volleyball and basketball players. The results reflect the high power outputs generated by such athletes. Indeed results from the Japanese men's volleyball team from 1961 (72.5 cm), 1964 (79.0 cm), 1968 (86.4 cm) and 1972 (90.9 cm) appear to have paralleled their improvement from 8th place in the 1964 to 2nd in the 1968 Olympics, to the gold medal in the 1972 Olympics (Toyoda, 1974). The ability to generate vertical height is of importance in top class volleyball. As previously mentioned, the elite male volleyball players are required to play at a height 330 cm above ground level (i.e. 87 cm above net height) whereas elite female players are required to play at a height of 300 cm above the ground (i.e. 76 cm above net height).

In a study by Viitasalo et al. (1982), the Finland and USSR men's volleyball teams had their height of rise of centre of gravity measured under laboratory conditions as well as during an international match. The results from this study (using a force platform in the laboratory and video analysis of the match) produced static jump heights of 41.1 cm and 43.3 cm, counter-movement jump heights with hands fixed of 46.0 cm and 49.4 cm and counter-movement jump heights with hands free of 55.9 cm and 55.8 cm for the Finnish and USSR teams respectively. These values are lower than those reported for vertical jump heights in Table 14.15, yet the USSR team was the Olympic and World Champion and the Finland team was ranked 9th in Europe. Analysis of the match played between these teams (which the USSR won) showed that the USSR team spiked the ball 10 cm higher than the Finnish team could, although in all other respects the teams were similar. The extra height gained by the USSR players in their spike contacts could have been a significant factor in their success. Certainly it lends support to the observations of Cox (1974) who analysed 107 games and found that the volleyball skills which most significantly related to success in order of influence were the spike, spike defence, service reception, setting, serving and finally free ball passes. In fact, the spike and spike defence produced greater contributions to predicting team success than the other four skills combined.

Basketball players do also possess good vertical jump capabilities, although not quite to the same extent as volleyball players. The greater height and weight of elite basketball players imposes a physical presence on court which is more important in the court contacts than having a smaller player who is a good vertical jumper. Examination of the findings from Soares *et al.* (1986) shows that the taller, heavier forwards do have comparatively lower vertical jump values than the shorter forwards and guards.

The average vertical jump value of approximately 50 cm for female volleyball players compares favourably with average values reported for normal males as well as male athletes cited in other studies (Gladden and Colacino, 1978). The results are approximately 15 cm lower than those for their male counterparts.

Despite the fact that volleyball players have a relatively high maximal power output, the observations by Gladden and Colacino (1978) using the Margaria stair test had mean values of 1169 W for male players, 1029 W for senior male players (i.e. over 40 years old) and 830 W for female players. The senior male players compared favourably with the mean values reported by Margaria, Aghemo and Rovelli (1966) for normal subjects aged 20–30 years old (1050 W). The male and female players' values were both significantly higher than the average values of males and females of a similar age. No findings with respect to basketball players and the stair test were located in the literature.

The only data on a Wingate-type of power test was obtained by Nakamura, Mutoh and Miyashita (1986). Table 14.16 illustrates their findings on this 10 s all-out bicycle sprint test using elite male Japanese athletes. The high power outputs generated by volleyball and basketball players are clearly evident. A study by Crielaard and Pirnay (1981) on elite Belgian runners produced similar findings, i.e. sprinters 1021 ± 139 W; short-middle distance runners 761 ± 45 W; middle-long distance runners 688 ± 46 W; marathon runners 551 ± 48 W and

Table 14.16 Power output generated during a 10 s bicycle ergometer sprint (after Nakamura, Mutoh and Miyashita, 1986)

Sport	n	Power (W)
Volleyball	27	1215 ± 129
Track-cyclists	19	1189 ± 99
Basketball	32	1188 ± 134
Ice-hockey	18	1175 ± 119
Baseball	61	1128 ± 158
Road-cyclists	15	1086 ± 120
Rugby	61	1080 ± 156
Soccer	84	1034 ± 128
Wrestling	10	983 ± 168
Male students	26	930 ± 187

students, 710 ± 58 W. Clearly, volleyball and basketball players would be expected to have values similar to the sprinters.

Research findings with respect to the power generated and vertical jump achieved by elite volleyball players highlight the type of conditioning needed. No group of athletes has been found to surpass volleyball players in vertical jumping ability. Since height reached above the net is advantageous, tall players who are good jumpers are the norm at elite levels of play. Too great a height, such as seen with the basketball centres, could be disadvantageous when playing backcourt positions. Hence a balance needs to be achieved in volleyball play between height and jumping ability when playing front court and speed of movement and flexibility when playing backcourt. Indeed, when examining characteristics relating to success in women's volleyball, Fleck et al. (1985) highlighted power (as indicated by the vertical jump) as the crucial physiological characteristic and low percentage body fat as the most important physical characteristic. Coaches and players, therefore, should be aware of the need for a physical conditioning programme to ensure good vertical jumping ability and to reduce body fat.

14.3.5 Muscle fibre characteristics

Skeletal muscle is not purely a homogenous group of muscle fibres with similar metabolic and functional properties. Based on two contractile properties (fast and slow twitch) and on two metabolic profiles (oxidative and glycolytic), three skeletal muscle fibres have been identified i.e. fast glycolytic (FG), fast oxidative glycolytic (FOG) and slow oxidative (SO) (Costill et al., 1976; Komi and Karlsson, 1978). The distribution of muscle fibre types in various athletic populations has been studied (Costill et al., 1976; Thorstensson et al., 1976; Bergh et al., 1978) and from these data a relationship between endurance activity and high percentage of SO fibres as well as sprint activity and high percentage of FG fibres has been established (Bergh et al., 1978). It should be made clear that many such studies report the muscle fibre type as being FG and SO, without recourse to the FOG fibres. It would be more correct to establish that the authors in these studies are referring to oxidative or glycolytic potential rather than to specific fibre types, since the FOG fibres may interchange between oxidative and glycolytic depending on the training or sport undertaken.

Two studies have examined the muscle fibre characteristics of elite volleyball players (Conlee et al., 1982; Viitasalo et al., 1987). Conlee et al. (1982) found that their male volleyball players possessed 56.5% FG fibres in the vastus lateralis muscle (range 45–69%) whereas Viitasalo et al. (1987) found that the Finland team possessed 56–60% FG fibres.

Both these studies appear to be in agreement, and the values are similar to those reported for sprinters and jumpers (62% FG; Thorstensson *et al.*, 1977) and professional soccer players (59.8% FG; Jacobs *et al.*, 1982). It is clear from various research publications (see Wilmore, 1979) that the fibre types (or more correctly, the oxidative/glycolytic potential of the muscles) of elite volleyball players are not predominantly of one contractile or metabolic characteristic.

14.4 TRAINING

Studies which have examined the changes resulting from training and playing volleyball or basketball can provide useful information as to the demands of the sport and the adaptations accruing from such participation. Three studies have examined the cardiovascular responses of playing these sports. The study concerned with volleyball used six members of a women's inter-collegiate team and compared selected fitness variables at the beginning and at the end of a competitive season (Fardy, Hritz and Hellerstein, 1976). The season lasted for a period of 7 weeks and involved two 2-hour practice sessions per week and a total of 14 matches (35 sets in total). Significant improvements in physical work capacity and estimated $\dot{V}O_{2max}$ were found to occur. No measure of anaerobic capacity was employed. Since the average heart rate during practice sessions (134 beats min^{-1}) corresponded to 67% of the maximum heart rate, the results are in keeping with other studies that have shown similar cardiorespiratory improvements when exercising continuously at these exercise intensities.

The two other studies examined responses to basketball play through a season in males (Cabrera, Smith and Byrd, 1977) and females (Sinning and Adrian, 1968). The former study showed that after 10 weeks of training and competition a 7.7% increase in $\dot{V}O_{2max}$ was evident. The authors concluded that 'participation in basketball is not conducive to the development of high levels of aerobic power, but does result in some favourable modifications in body structure (i.e. reduced weight and body fat) and function (i.e. reduced heart rate at submaximal work)'. The latter study showed similar findings in terms of a significant improvement in $\dot{V}O_{2max}$ (34.4 to 38.8 ml kg^{-1} min^{-1}) but the authors concluded that 'the basketball participants had not approached their potential physical condition'.

These studies have shown that some improvements in the cardiovascular and oxygen transport systems occur. However, the results must be treated with caution owing to the type of subject used (i.e. non-elite players), and the limited scope of measures employed (i.e. no anaerobic or muscular power measures undertaken).

Volleyball and basketball can be considered moderately stressful aerobic sports with elements of anaerobic energy involvement. Since the construction of a training programme should be based on accurate knowledge of the demands of the game, training for these sports should include activities promoting endurance capacity as well as those that develop vertical jump ability, agility and speed. What type of training methods can be employed to improve these fitness components?

Endurance can be improved by either continuous training methods (e.g. running for 30 min or more at an appropriate intensity) or by interval training methods (e.g. repeated bouts of jumping or running followed by rest intervals). Both methods will lead to improvements of aerobic capacity provided the overload principle is applied. The progressive overload principle implies that the training load is gradually increased as the person's fitness improves. The application of the overload principle to interval training is accomplished by manipulating the rate and distance of the exercise period, number of repetitions and number of sets during each workout, the duration of the relief interval, the type of activity during the relief interval and the frequency of training per week (Fox and Matthews, 1974). Specified training programmes must be planned for the volleyball or basketball player according to the demands of the game made on that player, i.e. player position must be accounted for. Research confirms that brief high intensity work bouts will result in improvements in all energy systems in a short period of time (Fox *et al.*, 1973). Although the specificity involved in using interval training methods such as jump training would appear to be preferable to continuous distance running, no study has been published which has examined the merits of continuous versus interval training in volleyball or basketball players. Most coaches advocate the use of continuous running for 3–9 km on at least three occasions a week as essential for a basic level of endurance. The use of small-sided games over an extended period of time could also help to enhance endurance, as would any training session in which skills are practised over periods of 60 min or more.

The capacity to jump high is of paramount importance for elite volleyball and basketball players. The usual forms of training to improve vertical jump include weight-training, jump training and plyometrics. Weight-training incorporating squats, leg press, knee extension, thigh curl and calf raises, has been used as the traditional method of improving leg strength and thereby of improving jumping ability.

The results of numerous studies using weight-training as an exercise mode for improving vertical jumping ability have not conclusively shown significant improvements. The use of subjects differing in skill and in initial fitness status, the time period for the training, the specific nature of the training, the muscle groups trained and so on, have all contributed to the disparate findings. There is no doubt that the improvements, if any, due to a set training programme employed by elite athletes will be substantially less than if a sedentary group is used. Furthermore, there may be a need to extend the training period over months rather than weeks to elicit any improvements.

Vertical jump training has long been considered useful to improve jumping ability due to the specificity of its actions. Volleyball and basketball players have always used this form of training to supplement the jumping actions involved in the normal skills training regimens. An interesting training method for developing muscle power is known as plyometric training (Verhoshanski, 1968). The training is based on the principle that a rapid stretching of a muscle just prior to its shortening will result in a much stronger contraction. The stretching of the muscle (or eccentric contraction) is produced through depth jumping, bounding, or hopping. Depth jumping requires an athlete to drop from a height and, upon landing, immediately perform a jumping movement. The height of the drop is an important consideration since too low a height (i.e. 20 cm) or too great a height (i.e. 100 cm) will not result in significant improvements (Brown, Mayhew and Boleach, 1986).

Four studies have been selected in order to appreciate the improvements in leg strength and vertical jumping ability using the various forms of training mentioned above. Thorstensson *et al.* (1976) examined the effects of an 8-week weight-training (squats), vertical jump and broad jump schedule using male physical education students. The training involved three sessions a week of squats (3 sets of 6 repetition maximum), vertical jump and broad jump (3 sets of 6 repetitions). Significant improvements were found with respect to IRM squat (+ 85 kg), vertical jump (+ 7 cm), and broad jump (+ 11 cm). It must be noted that the study used comparatively fit but not elite athletes, that the training period was over 8 weeks and that the overload principle was applied.

A study by Clutch *et al.* (1983) also examined the effects of weight-training and jump training using a group of inexperienced male undergraduates. The jump training was in the form of depth jumping as well as vertical jumps. The authors also performed a second experiment in which they used a weight-training class and elite volleyball players as their subjects. In the first experiment the undergraduates underwent a weight-training programme consisting of 3 sets of half-squats with 4–6 repetitions per set. The groups were then divided into three – Group 1, engaged in 4 sets of 10 maximum jump repetitions per session, Group 2, engaged in 4 sets of 10 repetitions of depth jumps from a height of 30 cm and Group 3 engaged in 2 sets of 10 repetitions of depth jumps from a height of 75 cm and 2 sets of 10 repetitions from a height of 110 cm. All three groups significantly improved their vertical jumping capability: Group 1 by 2.1 cm, Group 2 by 3.4 cm and Group 3 by 3.0 cm. There were no significant differences between the groups. In the second experiment, 16 members of a weight-training group and 16 players from the Brigham Young University volleyball team were randomly assigned to either a weight-training group or a weight-training group plus depth jumping. Training consisted of:

1. Weight-training – 3 sets of 6 repetitions of dead lift, bench press and parallel squat; two sessions per week.
2. Depth jumping – 4 sets of 10 jumps, two sets from 75 cm and two sets from 110 cm; two sessions per week.
3. Volleyball players also trained for 2.5 h on 5 days per week.

The training programme lasted over a period of 16 weeks. The group of weight-trainers showed a significant 3.7 cm improvement of vertical jump as a result of weight-training and depth jumping but no change as a consequence of weight-training only. The group of volleyball players showed significant improvements in vertical jump of 3.2 cm and 4.3 cm for weight-training depth jumping and weight-training respectively. It seems that depth jumping is useful in enhancing vertical jumping capability for athletes who are doing no other jumping, but adds nothing where a considerable amount of jumping occurs as a requirement for the sport (i.e. volleyball or basketball).

Bosco *et al.* (1982) performed a study over 12 months using the Finland men's volleyball players ($n = 8$) who, in addition to their normal training and weight-training, used plyometrics. The players performed 7–9 sets of 10 vertical jumps from a height of approximately 70 cm. A 4 min rest period was allowed between each set and three sessions per week were undertaken. Vertical jump was measured by the rise height of the centre of gravity. No significant improvements were found in vertical jump ability when jumping from a static position. However, in the measure of vertical jump preceded by a counter-movement, there was a significant improvement of 6 cm.

The final study to consider is that by Brown, Mayhew and Boleach (1986) who examined the effects of a 12 week period of plyometric training on performance of the vertical jump test. A group of 26 male high school basketball players were randomly assigned to a control group or to a group where in addition to basketball practice and match-play, the subjects performed 3 sets of 10 repetitions of depth jumping from a 45 cm bench. Training sessions took place on alternate days over the 12 weeks and resulted in a total of 34 sessions. Vertical jump with arm swing (VJA) and without arm swing (VJNA) were determined before and after the 12 weeks. A 2.8 cm increase in VJNA and a 3.7 cm increase in VJA were found in the control group, whereas the plyometric group had a 5.3 cm increase in VJNA, 7.3 cm increase in VJA. The authors concluded that 57% of the increase in vertical jump by the plyometric group was due to improvement in jumping skill and 43% was due to strength gain.

The four studies described have been used to highlight a number of points concerned with the effects of training regimens on leg strength and vertical jump ability. Those studies which use non-elite subjects are likely to show significant gains in strength and vertical jump irrespective of the form of training and even over a short period of time. Studies in which well-trained subjects are used need a longer training period to show significant gains, and if vertical jump gains in particular are desirable then some form of jump training is necessary. The implication for training of volleyball and basketball players is that weight-training and depth jumping would appear useful methods of promoting vertical jump ability. Depth jumping appears to train the muscles to contract faster; for vertical jumping ability to improve, the development of leg strength exclusively may not be enough. Leg muscles must be trained to react as quickly as possible; plyometric training appears to maximize the co-ordination of neuromuscular skills and muscle strength. The best heights to perform depth jumping seem to be about 40 cm. At heights greater than this, too much force is required to counteract the fall and at heights lower than this, insufficient training stimulus is applied to the muscle (Brown, Mayhew and Boleach, 1986).

Despite the advantages of plyometric training, there are problems associated with depth jumping and rebound jumping. Eccentric muscle contractions have been shown to result in muscle soreness (Newham et al., 1983b; Komi, 1984), possibly as a result of changes in muscle cell ultrastructure (Newham et al., 1983a). Furthermore, Boocock et al. (1988) have shown that bounding activities result in an increase in spinal loading (as measured by spinal shrinkage) and that this results in increased muscle soreness rating and low-back pain rating on the days following such exercise. Finally, it should be pointed out that it is likely that depth jumping from too great a height over an extended period of months may result in knee injuries due to the forces applied across the patella tendon. In order to prevent these situations arising, it is advisable to build up training slowly and to incorporate a weight-training programme before the plyometric programme in order to strengthen the muscles involved.

Training for volleyball and basketball should include components to enhance endurance capacity and the ability to jump high. Methods of achieving these have been briefly discussed in this section, and in more detail in other chapters in this book. Considerations such as the development of agility and speed are important but are beyond the scope of this chapter.

14.5 OVERVIEW

This chapter has attempted to provide an insight into the physiological, anthropometric and metabolic characteristics of volleyball players and to a lesser extent basketball players. An understanding of these characteristics coupled with an understanding of the demands of match-play could lead the coach or player to devise appropriate training methods to improve fitness for the sport. Although some research has highlighted that 'success' in volleyball or basketball is correlated with height (a genetic factor and not one that can be increased by training), other components such as low percentage body fat and the ability to jump high can be affected by training. The information provided is based on published research where elite players have been used as subjects wherever possible. Studies which have used subjects of a lower standard must be treated with caution, although they have been included for illustrative purposes. The comparative lack of good research on elite volleyball play and in particular on elite basketball players reflects the difficulties of relating laboratory-based measures to successful performances in complex team games. An understanding of the demands of the sport leading to good fitness training regimens is an essential, but not the only, consideration leading to success at elite levels. Skill, psychological make-up of the players, and team tactics are also extremely important. However, these latter three factors are not likely to lead to success if players are not fit.

REFERENCES

Alexander, M.J.L. (1976) The relationship of somatotype and selected anthropometric measures to basketball performance in highly skilled females. *Research Quarterly*, **47**, 575–585.

Apor, P. (1988) Successful formulae for fitness training, in *Science and Football* (eds T. Reilly, A. Lees, K. Davids and W.J. Murphy), E. and F.N. Spon, London, pp. 95–107.

Baacke, H. (1981) Statistical match analysis for evaluation of players and teams performances. *Volleyball Technical Journal*, **7**(2), 45–56.

Bale, P. and Scholes, S. (1986) Lateral dominance and basketball performance. *Journal of Human Movement Studies*, **12**, 145–151.

Barr-Orr, O., Dotan, R. and Inbar, O. (1977) A 30 second all-out ergometric test: its reliability and validity for anaerobic capacity. *Israel Journal of Medical Science*, **13**, 126.

Bergh, U., Thorstensson, A., Sjodin, B., Hulten, B., Piehl, K. and Karlsson, J. (1978) Maximal oxygen uptake and muscle fibre types in trained and untrained humans. *Medicine and Science in Sport and Exercise*, **10**, 151–154.

Bergstrom, J., Harris, R.C., Hultman, E. and Nordesjo, L.O. (1971) Energy rich phosphagens in dynamic and static work, in *Muscle Metabolism during Exercise* (eds B. Pernow and B. Saltin), Plenum, London, pp. 342–356.

Bergstrom, J., Hermansen, L. and Hultman, E. (1967) Diet, muscle glycogen and physical performance. *Acta Physiologica Scandinavica*, **71**, 140–150.

Black, W. (1980) Unpublished observations English Volleyball Association.

Boocock, M.G., Garbutt, G., Reilly, T., Linge, K. and Troup, J.D.G. (1988) The effects of gravity inversion on exercise-induced spinal loading. *Ergonomics*, **31**, 1631–1637.

Bosco, P.C., Komi, P.V., Pulli, M., Pittera, C. and Montonev, H. (1982) Consideration of the training of the elastic potential of the human skeletal muscle. *CVA Technical Journal*, **6**(3), 75–81.

Bradfield, R.A. (1971) A technique for determination of usual daily energy expenditure in the field. *American Journal of Clinical Nutrition*, **24**, 1148–1154.

Brooks, G.A. and Fahey, T.D. (1984) *Exercise Physiology: Human Bioenergetics and its Application*, John Wiley, New York.

Brown, M.E., Mayhew, J.L. and Boleach, L.W. (1986) Effect of plyometric training on vertical jump performance in high school basketball players. *Journal of Sports Medicine and Physical Fitness*, **26**, 1–4.

Cabrera, J.M., Smith, D.P. and Byrd, R.J. (1977) Cardiovascular adaptations in Puerto Rican basketball players during a 14-week session. *Journal of Sports Medicine and Physical Fitness*, **17**, 173–180.

Carter, J.E.L. (1982) Physical structure of Olympic athletes. Part 1. The Montreal Olympic Games Anthropological Project. *Medicine and Sport Science*, Vol. 16, Karger, Basel.

Carter, J.E.L. (1984) Physical structure of Olympic athletes. Part 2. Kinanthropometry of Olympic athletes. *Medicine and Sport Science*, Vol. 18, Karger, Basel.

Cherebetu, G. and Szogy, A. (1976) The effects of a short period of aerobic preparation of the Romanian volleyballers. *FIVB Bulletin*, **68**, 30–35.

Christensen, C.C., Frey, H.M.M., Foenstelen, E., Aadland, E. and Refsum, E.E. (1984) A critical evaluation of energy expenditure estimates based on individual O_2 consumption/heart rate curves and average daily heart rate. *American Journal of Clinical Nutrition*, **37**, 468–472.

Christensen, E.H., Hedman, R. and Saltin, B. (1960) Intermittent and continuous running. *Acta Physiologica Scandinavica*, **50**, 269–286.

Clutch, D., Wilton, M., McGown, C. and Bryce, G.R. (1983) The effect of depth jumps and weight training on leg strength and vertical jump. *Research Quarterly for Exercise and Sport*, **54**, 5–10.

Conlee, R.K., McGown, C.M., Fisher, A.G., Dalsky, G.P. and Robinson, K.C. (1982) Physiological effects of power volleyball. *The Physician and Sportsmedicine*, **10**, 93–97.

Costill, C.L. and Miller, J.M. (1980) Nutrition for endurance sport: carbohydrate and fluid balance. *International Journal of Sports Medicine*, **1**, 2–14.

Costill, D.L., Daniels, J., Evans, W., Fink, W., Krahenbuhl, G. and Saltin, B. (1976) Skeletal muscle enzymes and fibre composition in male and female athletes. *Journal of Applied Physiology*, **40**, 149–154.

Cox, R.H. (1974) Relationship between selected volleyball skills components and team performance of men's northwest 'AA' volleyball teams. *Research Quarterly*, **45**, 441–446.

Coyle, E.F. and Coggan, A.R. (1984) Effectiveness of carbohydrate feeding in delaying fatigue during prolonged exercise. *Sports Medicine*, **1**, 445–458.

Crielaard, J.M. and Pirnay, F. (1981) Anaerobic and aerobic power of top athletes. *European Journal of Applied Physiology*, **47**, 295–300.

Durnin, J.V.G.A. and Passmore, R. (1967) *Energy, Work and Leisure*, Heinemann, London.

Dyba, W. (1982) Physiological and activity characteristics of volleyball. *Volleyball Technical Journal*, **6**(3), 33–51.

Essen, B. (1978) Studies on the regulation of metabolism in human skeletal muscle using intermittent exercise as an experimental model. *Acta Physiologica Scandinavica*, **454**, 1–32.

Fardy, P.S., Hritz, M.G. and Hellerstein, H.K. (1976) Cardiac responses during women's intercollegiate volleyball and physical fitness changes from a season of competition. *Journal of Sports Medicine and Physical Fitness*, **16**, 291–300.

Fiedler, M. (1979) *Volleyball*. Ost, Berlin.

Fleck, S.J. and Case, S. (1981) Weight loss and calories expended by international calibre women volleyball players. *Volleyball Technical Journal*, **6**, 51–56.

Fleck, S.J., Case, S., Puhl, J. and VanHandle, P. (1985) Physical and physiological characteristics of elite women volleyball players. *Canadian Journal of Applied Sport Sciences*, **10**, 122–126.

Fox, E.L., Bartels, R.L., Billings, C., Mathews, D.K., Bason, R. and Webb, W.M. (1973) Intensity and distance of interval training programs and changes in aerobic power. *Medicine and Science in Sports*, **5**, 18–22.

Fox, E.L. and Mathews, D.K. (1974) *Interval Training: Conditioning for Sports and General Fitness*. W.B. Saunders, Philadelphia.

Furukawa, M. (1974) A study on the characteristics of basketball games seemed from players' heights at the Tokyo and Mexico Olympic Games. *Research Journal of Physical Education*, **18**, 351–366.

Gillam, G.M. (1985) Identification of anthropometric and physiological characteristics relative to participation in College basketball. *NSCA Journal*, **7**, 34–36.

Gladden, L.B. and Colacino, D. (1978) Characteristics of volleyball players and success in a national tournament. *Journal of Sports Medicine and Physical Fitness*, **18**, 57–64.

Hargreaves, M., Costill, D.L., Coggan, A., Fink, W.J. and Nishibata, I. (1984) Effect of carbohydrate feedings on muscle glycogen utilization and exercise performance. *Medicine and Science in Sports and Exercise*, **16**, 219–222.

Harris, R.C., Edwards, R.H.T., Hultman, E., Nordsjo, L.-O., Nylind, B. and Sahlin, K. (1976) The time course of phosphoryl creatine resynthesis during recovery of the quadriceps muscle in man. *Pflügers Archiv European Journal of Physiology*, **367**, 137–142.

Hermansen, L. and Stensvold, I. (1972) Production and removal of lactate during exercise in man. *Acta Physiologica Scandinavica*, **86**, 191–201.

Horak, J. (1974) Czechoslovakian physical fitness tests. *CVA Technical Journal*, **1**(4), 10–12.

Jacobs, I., Wrestlin, N., Karlsson, J., Rassmusson, M. and Houghton, B. (1982) Muscle glycogen and diet in elite soccer players. *European Journal of Applied Physiology*, **48**, 297–302.

Joussellin, E., Handschuh, R., Barrault, D. and Rieu, M. (1984) Maximal aerobic power of French top level competitors. *Journal of Sports Medicine and Physical Fitness*, **24**, 175–182.

Kemper, H. and Verschuur, R. (1977) Validity and reliability of pedometers in habitual activity research. *European Journal of Applied Physiology*, **37**, 71–82.

Khosla, T. (1983) Sport for tall. *British Medical Journal*, **287**, 736–738.

Komi, P.V. (1984) Fatigue and recovery of neuromuscular function, in *Medicine, and Sport Science*, Vol. 17, Karger, Basel, pp. 187–201.

Komi, P.V. and Karlsson, J. (1978) Skeletal muscle fibre types, enzyme activities and physical performance in young males and females. *Acta Physiologica Scandinavica*, **103**, 210–218.

Künstlinger, W., Ludwig, H.G. and Stegmann, J. (1987) Metabolic changes during volleyball matches. *International Journal of Sports Medicine*, **8**, 315–322.

Lakomy, H.K.A. (1984) An ergometer for measuring the power generated during sprinting. *Journal of Physiology (London)*, **354**, 33P.

Laporte, R., Kuller, L., Kupfer, D., McPartland, R., Matthews, G. and Casperson, C. (1979) An objective measure of physical activity for epidemiological research. *American Journal of Epidemiology*, **109**, 158–168.

Lecompte, J.C. and Rivet, D. (1979) Tabulated data on the duration of exchanges and stops in a volleyball game. *Volleyball Technical Journal*, **4**(3), 87–91.

MacLaren, D., Davids, K., Isokowa, M., Mellor, S. and Reilly, T. (1988) Physiological strain in competitive 4-a-side soccer: in *Science and Football* (eds T. Reilly, A. Lees, K. Davids and W.J. Murphy), E. & F.N. Spon, London, pp. 76–80.

Margaria, R., Aghemo, P. and Rovelli, E. (1966) Measurement of muscular power (anaerobic) in man. *Journal of Applied Physiology*, **21**, 1662–1664.

Maron, M.B., Horvath, S.M., Wilkerson, J.E. and Gliner, J.A. (1976) Oxygen uptake measurements during competitive marathon running. *Journal of Applied Physiology*, **40**, 836–838.

McArdle, W.D., Magel, J.R. and Kyvallos, L.C. (1971) Aerobic capacity, heart rate and estimated energy cost during women's competitive basketball. *Research Quarterly*, **42**, 178–186.

Montecinos, R.M., Guajardo, J.E., Lara, L., Jara, F. and Gatica, P. (1982) Evaluation of physical capacity in Chilean volleyball players, in *Exercise and Sport Biology* (ed. P.V. Komi), Human Kinetics, Champaign, Illinois.

Montoye, H.J., Washburn, R., Servais, S., Ertl, A., Webster, J.G. and Nagle, F.J. (1983) Estimation of energy expenditure by a portable accelerometer. *Medicine and Science in Sport and Exercise*, **15**, 403–407.

Morgan, D.B. and Bennett, T. (1976) The relation between heart rate and oxygen consumption during exercise. *Journal of Sports Medicine and Physical Fitness*, **16**, 38–44.

Morrow, J.R., Jackson, A.S., Hosler, W.W. and Kachurik, J.K. (1979) The importance of strength, speed and body size for team success in women's intercollegiate volleyball. *Research Quarterly*, **50**, 429–437.

Nakamura, Y., Mutoh, Y. and Miyashita, M. (1986) Maximal anaerobic power of Japanese elite athletes. *Medicine and Science in Sport and Exercise*, **18**, 52.

Newham, D.J., McPhail, G., Mills, K.R. and Edwards, R.H.T. (1983a) Ultrastructural changes after concentric and eccentric contractions of human muscle. *Journal of Neurological Science*, **61**, 109–122.

Newham, D.J., Mills, K.R., Quigley, B.M. and Edwards, R.H.T. (1983b) Pain and fatigue after concentric and eccentric muscle contractions. *Clinical Science*, **64**, 55–62.

Nichols, K. (1973) *Modern Volleyball For Teacher, Coach and Player*. Henry Kimpton, London.

Ongley, B. and Hopley, J. (1981) A comparison between state level and non-state level Western Australian volleyball players. *Sports Coach*, **5**, 30–35.

Parnat, J., Viru, A., Savi, T. and Nurmekuri, A. (1975) Indices of aerobic work capacity and cardio-vascular response during exercise in athletes specializing in different events. *Journal of Sports Medicine and Physical Fitness*, **15**, 100–105.

Parr, R.B., Wilmore, J.H., Hoover, R., Bachman, D. and Kerlan, R. (1978) Professional basketball players: athletic profiles. *Physician and Sportsmedicine*, **6**, 77–84.

Placheta, F., Israel, S. and Israel, G. (1969) Die bestimmung des training szustandes von volleyball spielem. *Theorie und Praxis der Korperkultur*, **4**, 354–363.

Puhl, J., Case, S., Fleck, S. and Van Handel, P. (1982) Physical and physiological characteristics of elite volleyball players. *Research Quarterly for Exercise and Sport*, **53**, 257–262.

Ramsey, J.D., Ayoub, M.M., Dudek, R.A. and Edgar, H.S. (1970) Heart rate recovery during a College basketball game. *Research Quarterly*, **41**, 528–535.

Raven, P.B., Gettman, L.R., Pollock, M.L. and K.H. Cooper (1976) AS physiological evaluation of professional football players. *British Journal of Sports Medicine*, **10**, 209–216.

Reilly, T. (1981) Considerations in endurance training, in *Sports Fitness and Sports Injuries* (ed. T. Reilly), Faber and Faber, London, pp. 79–90.

Reilly, T. and Smith, D. (1986) Effect of work intensity on performance in a psychomotor task during exercise. *Ergonomics*, **29**, 601–606.

Reilly, T.P. (1986) Fundamental studies in soccer, in *Sportwissenschaft und Sportpraxis: Beiträge zur Sportspielforschung* (ed. R. Andreson), Verlag Ingrid Czwalina, Hamberg, pp. 114–120.

Riezobos, M.L., Paterson, D.H., Hall, C.R. and Yuhasz, M.S. (1983) Relationship of selected variables to performance in women's basketball. *Canadian Journal of Applied Physiology*, **8**, 34–40.

Rivet, D. (1978) One has to jump in volleyball. *CVA Technical Journal*, **4**(3), 83–86.

Rodionova, A.F. and Plakhtienko, V.A. (1977) Energetics of volleyball. *Yessis Review*, **12**, 98–99.

Rusko, H., Hara, M. and Karvinen, E. (1978) Aerobic performance capacity in athletes. *Journal of Applied Physiology*, **38**, 151–159.

Saltin, B. (1973) Metabolic fundamentals in exercise. *Medicine and Science in Sport*, **5**, 137–146.

Sargent, D.A. (1921) Physical test of man. *American Physical Education Review*, **26**, 188–194.

Scheele, K., Herzog, W., Ritthaler, G., Wirth, A. and Weicker, H. (1975) Metabolic adaptations to prolonged exercise. *European Journal of Applied Physiology*, **41**, 101–108.

Seliger, V. (1968) Energy metabolism in selected physical exercises. *Internationale Zeitschrift für Angewphysiologie Einschl Arbeitsphysiologie*, **25**, 104–120.

Shephard, R. (1967) Pulse rate and ventilation as indices of habitual activity: theoretical aspects. *Archives of Environmental Health*, **15**, 562–567.

Sinning, W.E. (1973) Body composition, cardiorespiratory function and rule changes in women's basketball. *Research Quarterly*, **44**, 313–321.

Sinning, W.E. and Adrian, M.J. (1968) Cardiorespiratory changes in College women due to a season of competitive basketball. *Journal of Applied Physiology*, **25**, 720–724.

Soares, J., Mendes, O.C., Neto, C.B. and Matsudo, V.K.R. (1986) Physical fitness characteristics of Brazilian national basketball team as related to game functions, in *Perspectives in Kinanthropometry* (ed. J.A.P. Day), Human Kinetics, Champaign, Illinois, pp. 127–133.

Spence, D.W., Disch, J.G., Fred, H.L. and Coleman, A.E. (1980) Descriptive profiles of highly skilled women volleyball players. *Medicine and Science in Sport and Exercise*, **12**, 299–302.

Spurgeon, J.H., Spurgeon, N.L. and Giese, W.K. (1980) Physique of world-class female basketball players. *Scandinavian Journal of Sports Science*, **2**, 63–69.

Tanner, J.M. (1964) *The Physique of the Olympic Athlete*. Allen & Unwin, London.

Thorstensson, A., Karlsson, J., Viitasalo, J.T., Luhtanen, P. and Komi, P.V. (1976) Effect of strength training on EMG of human skeletal muscle. *Acta Physiologica Scandinavica*, **98**, 232–236.

Thorstensson, A., Larsson, L., Tesch, P., Karlsson, J. (1977) Muscle strength and fibre composition in athletes and sedentary men. *Medicine and Science in Sport and Exercise*, **9**, 26–30.

Toyoda, H. (1974) Lists of physical performances of volleyball players. *CVA Technical Journal*, **1**(3), 17–32.

Vaccaro, P., Clarke, D.H. and Wrenn, J.P. (1979) Physiological profiles of elite women basketball players. *Journal of Sports Medicine and Physical Fitness*, **19**, 45–54.

Vandewalle, H., Peres, G. and Monod, H. (1987) Standard anaerobic exercise tests. *Sports Medicine*, **4**, 268–289.

Verhoshanski, Y. (1968) Are depth jumps useful? *Yessis Review of Soviet Physical Education and Sport*, **3**, 75–78.

Viitasalo, J.T. (1982) Anthropometric and physical performance characteristics of male volleyball players. *Canadian Journal of Applied Sport Sciences*, **7**, 182–188.

Viitasalo, J.T., Bosco, C., Sauro, R., Montonen, H. and Pittera, C. (1982) Vertical jump height, aerobic and anaerobic performance capacity in elite male volleyball players. *Volleyball*, **5**, 18–21.

Viitasalo, J.T., Rusko, H., Pajala, O., Rahkila, P., Ahila, M. and Montonen, H. (1987) Endurance requirements in volleyball. *Canadian Journal of Applied Sports Science*, **12**, 194–201.

Walker, J. (1973) Conditioning requirements for power volleyball. *International Volleyball Review*, **3**, 39–40.

Washburn, R.A. and Montoye, H.J. (1980) Accuracy of pedometers in walking and running. *Research Quarterly for Exercise and Sport*, **51**, 695–702.

Washburn, R.A. and Montoye, H.J. (1986) Validity of heart rate as a measure of mean daily energy expenditure, in *Exercise Physiology: Current Selected Research* Vol. 2 (eds C.V. Dotson and J.H. Humphrey), AMS Press, New York.

Wenger, H.A. and Reed, A.T. (1976) Metabolic factors associated with muscular fatigue during aerobic and anaerobic work. *Canadian Journal of Applied Sports Science*, **1**, 43–48.

Wielki, C. (1978) Standardization of the duration of volleyball meets. *CVA Technical Journal*, **4**(3), 37–50.

Wilmore, J.H. (1979) The application of science to sport: Physiological profiles of male and female athletes. *Canadian Journal of Applied Sport Sciences*, **4**, 103–115.

Wilmore, J.H. and Brown, C.H. (1974) Physiological profiles of women distance runners. *Medicine and Science in Sports*, **6**, 178–181.

Wilmore, J.H., Parr, R.B., Haskell, W.L., Costill, D.L., Milburn, L.J. and Kerlaw, R.K. (1976) Athletic profile of professional football players. *Physician and Sportsmedicine*, **4**, 45–54.

15

Physiology of sports: an overview

Thomas Reilly and Niels Secher

15.1 INTRODUCTION

Competition is a fundamental feature of sport. During competition physiological functions may be taxed severely, the particular stress depending on the sport in question, the tactics employed and the type of fitness possessed by the contestants.

Previous chapters focused on a variety of sports and highlighted the specific demands each placed on participants. They also attempted to outline typical profiles of top competitors and the fitness requirements for success at a high level. It is evident that genetic and structural factors are important in many sports. In others a high standard of training is essential and inherited predispositions need to be nurtured for sporting potential to be realized. For example, individuals endowed with the possibility to obtain a high oxygen uptake need to complement this with rigorous training in order to achieve maximal performance. If they engage in endurance events they must also develop the ability to sustain a high fractional utilization of their maximal oxygen uptake ($\% \dot{V}O_{2max}$) and become physiologically efficient in performing their activity.

The aim of sports training is to improve fitness and skills. The design of training programmes on sound physiological principles requires an understanding of the acute metabolic responses to exercise and how these are modified by repeated exposures over time. Achieving a match between training stimulus and demands of the sport is far from easy, as a consideration of strength training testifies. The real world is further complicated by factors such as stage of the season, competitive programme, nutrition, injury risk, health status and team performance.

Despite these difficulties, it has been shown that scientific principles can be applied to particular sports. A systematic description of the sport's unique demands forms a basis from which training programmes can be refined. Carefully chosen fitness test batteries may then be used to assess the suitability of players to meet the demands. Results provide feedback on individual strengths and weaknesses to the coach or athlete. Ergometers designed to improve the specificity of fitness testing have also gained acceptance as training aids, thus providing a further service for the sport in question.

In this text it was impractical to take all sports in turn for individual consideration. This chapter tries to cover some of the gaps that remain by providing an overview and, where data are available, referring to sports not considered in previous chapters.

15.2 WORK-INTENSITY

Analysis of the actions, movements and work-intensity of individuals during competition provides a starting point in outlining the demands of the sport. Motion analysis can be used to highlight the frequency and level of activity cycles during games and the recovery periods typically occurring between bouts of activity. From these intensity or work rate profiles, the relative contributions of anaerobic and aerobic processes towards the total metabolism have been estimated (Fox, 1984; Sharkey, 1986).

Conventional methods of motion analysis have been applied for studying football games (see Chapter 13). These can be modified for application to other field games such as hockey, hurling and lacrosse and to indoor sports such as table tennis. Contemporary computerized notation analysis also has potential for establishing intensity profiles; hitherto this technique has been employed more for studying patterns of play than for physiological investigations (Hughes, 1988).

Tables estimating the relative contributions of aerobic and anaerobic processes towards total energy expenditure place activities like bobsled, diving, luge, ski-jumping, 100–110 m hurdling, field events (jumping and throwing) and weight-lifting towards the anaerobic end of the continuum. Sports classified as 80% anaerobic include alpine skiing, baseball, cricket, fencing, gymnastics, softball and surfing (Sharkey, 1986). Sports with 70% dependence on anaerobic processes include aikido, boxing, judo, karate, roller skating, synchronized swimming, taekwondo and wrestling. Those with mixed demands (40–60%) include canoeing, hockey, kayaking, lacrosse, motocross and mountaineering. Biathlon, cross-country skiing, equestrian events, orienteering and triathlon are placed towards the aerobic end of the continuum.

Of relevance also are types of actions and activities in the sport. The muscle groups engaged in executing sport skills may be identified and then isolated in specific training drills. To this end electromyography (EMG) has proved useful in establishing the sequencing of muscles in performing sports skills. The EMG may also be employed to establish the extent to which available training devices faithfully represent the muscle activity of the sport.

It is also relevant to consider the mode of muscular contraction when designing training drills. Though sport is usually conceived as using muscles either concentrically or eccentrically in dynamic actions, many sports engage muscles in isometric actions. Isometric activity in the back muscles is important in maintaining the desired posture of the long-jumper in flight and in countering high centrifugal forces as the thrower rotates prior to releasing the hammer. Isometric actions are also implicated where large external resistances have to be overcome before movement is initiated. This happens in sports such as tug-o-war, weight-lifting and wrestling and in Rugby scrummaging. The archer needs isometric strength in the arms to draw and hold the bow steady, usually for about 8 s for each shot whilst the sight is aligned with the target prior to 'loose'. In other sports muscle tension must be held for longer than this and muscle endurance is called for.

The muscle groups that determine performance in the sport, as well as their modes of contraction, need to be appraised in designing training programmes and fitness test batteries. In long and high jumping a complete stretch-shortening cycle of muscle action is implicated. In handball the leg muscles are important for moving quickly around the court whereas the arms are critical in handling, passing, shooting and blocking. In water-skiing the leg muscles are taxed dynamically whilst the arms and shoulders are used mainly statically. Thus the training programme and fitness test battery need to be multivariate and tailored to the sport in question.

15.3 DEMANDS OF THE SPORT

The level of energy expenditure has been used as a convenient method of comparing the aerobic intensity of various sports. In the main the values have been derived from measurements of oxygen uptake during simulated competitive contexts. Alternatively they have been estimated from measurements of heart rate during play coupled with laboratory measures of heart rate and oxygen consumption during incremental exercise tests. Direct measurement of oxygen uptake during field activities by means of telemetry is now possible and is likely to be used in future investigations.

The values in Table 15.1 are a reflection of the strain on the oxygen transport system. Accepting the limitations of ascribing averaging-out

Table 15.1 Severity of selected sports based on typical energy costs collected from various sources for male subjects. These values may underestimate the energy expenditure in top flight competition in some cases (after Reilly, 1981)

Light (kJ min⁻¹)		Moderate (kJ min⁻¹)		Heavy (kJ min⁻¹)		Very heavy (kJ min⁻¹)	
Archery	13–24	Baseball	20–27	Boxing	46–60	Cross-country running	63–67
Billiards	11	Cricket	21–33	Handball	46–50	Cross-country skiing(uphill)	78
Bowls	17	Fencing	21–42	Hockey	36–50	Orienteering	60
Croquet	13–17	Gymnastics	10–50	Judo	41–55		
Fishing	13–18	Horse riding	13–42	Wrestling	50–59		
Golf	20	Mountain-climbing	42				
Softball	17	Tobogganing	30				
Table-tennis	15–22						

procedures to competitive sports, the figures provide a rough indication of the aerobic demands of the sports. They are helpful also in establishing the relevance of 'aerobic-type' training for the sports performer.

Sports classified as 'light' place negligible demands on the oxygen transport system. Competitors in these events are better advised to use training drills specific to the sport rather than to embark on general aerobic fitness training regimens.

At the other end of the scale are sports such as cross-country running and skiing which place very heavy demands on the oxygen transport system. Top orienteers have unique demands in that they encounter rough terrain and have to make critical decisions on route selection under strenuous exercise conditions.

An important factor is the relative loading that can be tolerated without skills being adversely affected. Studies have shown that neuromuscular and cognitive performance are improved by concomitant exercise up to 40–50% $\dot{V}O_{2max}$, reflecting a warm-up effect (Reilly and Smith, 1986). The optimal performance level may be maintained in some circumstances up to about 75% $\dot{V}O_{2max}$, above which skilled performance generally deteriorates (Evans and Reilly, 1980). A hallmark of top performers is that they consistently maintain a high standard of skill under exacting conditions.

In locomotor sports, execution of game-related tasks may add substantially to the demands of the sport. The energy expenditure incurred in dribbling a hockey ball at 10 km h^{-1}, for example, was found to increase by 15 kJ min^{-1} over that observed in running at a similar speed (Reilly and Seaton, 1990). The corresponding elevation in heart rate was 23 beats min^{-1}. The extra costs were attributed to postural requirements and the combined arm and leg exercise as well as the carriage of the hockey stick. Similar considerations would apply to sports such as hurling, lacrosse and shinty, although the added load over normal running would differ between sports.

Sports with standard rest and activity periods permit the participant a choice of how the overall effort is to be deployed. Boxing, for example, is classified as 'heavy work'. A boxer, lacking confidence in his own endurance, may choose to gamble on a knock-out victory by forcing the pace in the early rounds.

Within sports the energetic demands can vary according to the class of competition. This applies particularly to sports such as canoeing and kayaking and to skiing events. The former can range from sprint races to 40 km (and longer) marathons. The latter ranges from explosive-type anaerobic events such as ski-jumping to 60 km cross-country competitions.

According to Åstrand and Rodahl (1986), sports which engage large muscle groups for 1 min or more may tax $\dot{V}O_{2max}$ and in consequence may also impose maximal loading on the circulatory system. Thus heart rates of 205 beats min^{-1} have been recorded at the end of just over 2 min downhill ski-racing. The maximal heart rates may include an emotional tachycardia due to anxiety associated with performance. This effect of a psychological component has been shown in studies of rock-climbing: mean heart rates ($\pm$ SD) for 11 subjects during a 15 min climb were 166 ($\pm$ 22) beats min^{-1}, being higher than was necessitated by the physical requirements of the task (Williams, Taggart and Carruthers, 1978).

Activities that maximally tax the circulatory system may also entail a high degree of anaerobic loading; thus post-exercise blood lactate concentrations of 12 mM have been recorded after downhill skiing whilst values after giant slalom events have reached 15 mM (Åstrand and Rodahl, 1986). Values of 8–14 mM have been reported after 1000 m canoe races (Shephard, 1987). In sports that engage small muscle groups, higher blood lactate levels are incurred at a given oxygen uptake than in activities employing large muscle groups.

As sports participants may be reluctant to perform to their utmost in simulated competitions, measurements in model contests may not truly reflect the demands of serious competition. Åstrand and Rodahl (1986) reported heart rates of 155–174 beats min^{-1} during a 5–10 min simulated moto cross race. This range compared to 180–200 beats min^{-1} in a real race over 45 min. In the simulated event blood lactate levels (2–12 mM) were more variable than observed at the end of the actual race (5–8 mM).

Indirect calorimetry or analysis of post-exercise blood lactate levels are not appropriate for studying so-called explosive or power events. These events may last only a few seconds and call for extraordinary levels of anaerobic power output and neuromuscular co-ordination. They include jumping (long, high, triple, pole vault, ski-jumping, gymnastics) and throwing (shot, discus, javelin, hammer, pitching) events. Measurements of ground reaction forces and calculations of instantaneous power output using a force platform have provided useful means of evaluating such activities. These techniques may be combined with film-analysis to match and compare training and competitive performances.

15.4 CHARACTERISTICS OF PERFORMERS

15.4.1 Anthropometry

Body size characteristics may become important in determining success in many sports. Height is an advantage in sports such as volleyball and basketball and arm reach is an asset to the boxer. Body mass is a factor

Table 15.2 Anthropometric data on top performers in a range of sports. Mean values for height, weight and percentage body fat are given, the range indicating the spread of mean values reported in the literature. Figures are based on the summary of Rusko (1976), Withers and Roberts (1981), Wilmore (1983) and various other reports

Sport	Sex	Height (cm)	Weight (kg)	% body fat
Baseball	Male	183	83.3–88	12–14
Canoeing	Male	182	79.6	12
Cross-country skiing	Male	175	66.6–73.2	8–13
	Female	161–163	53.6–59.1	13–22
Discus	Male	186–191	105–111	16
	Female	168	71	25
Gymnastics	Male	178	69.2	5–6
	Female	158–163	51.5–57.9	10–24
Hockey	Female	162–165	58.0–62.9	16–26
Jockeys	Male	158	50.3	14
Jumping and Hurdling	Female	166	59.0	21
Netball	Female	175	74.4	29
Orienteering	Male	—	72.2	16
	Female	—	58.1	19
Pentathlon	Female	175	65.4	11
Shot	Male	188–192	113–126	17–20
	Female	168	78.1	28
Skiing				
Alpine	Male	177	70.1–75.5	2–14
	Female	165	58.8	21
Nordic	Male	176–182	70.4	9–11
Ski jumping	Male	174	69.9	14
Softball	Female	168	64.0	27
Weight-lifting				
Power	Male	176	92	16
Olympic	Male	177	88.2	12
Body-builders	Male	172–179	83.1–88.1	8
Wrestling	Male	172–178	62.3–81.8	4–14

influencing performance in throwing events and hence the size of throwers at the Olympic Games has increased systematically since the post-war Games of London (1948). Body mass also imposes resistance to movement and so is an important factor in contact games.

Gross muscular strength tends to increase with size, giving the large individual an advantage in contests where absolute strength is important. As strength of an individual muscle is related to its cross-sectional area, the lean body mass may be more decisive than total body mass. In order to eliminate the influence of body size, sports such as boxing and wrestling are split into weight categories. For a given weight category the taller individual is likely to benefit from his longer reach.

In boxing and wrestling contestants often have to lose weight quickly in order to make their weight limits before competing. Often this is done by cutting down on fluids. Impaired performance results from this forced dehydration, since there may not be adequate time from weigh-in to contest to replace body fluids completely. This practice of dehydration is particularly dangerous if the contest takes place in hot conditions and has therefore been forcefully condemned by authorities such as the American College of Sports Medicine.

Body proportions differ between individuals and may result in a predisposition towards certain sports. Female rhythmic gymnasts in some countries are considered for specialist training on the basis of having long legs and arms, a short trunk and narrow hips. Weight-lifters tend to have short legs relative to their trunk; this lowers their centre of gravity and aids their lifting technique. High hurdlers generally have long legs and relatively short trunks. Discus throwers are found to have relatively long arms and this is of mechanical benefit in accelerating the discus prior to release. These trends were first observed in the studies of Olympic competitors reported by Tanner (1964).

One advantage that small individuals do possess is in heat dissipation. Loss of heat is enhanced when there is a large body surface area relative to body mass, this ratio increasing the smaller the individual. Thus, marathon runners in the main tend to be smaller than average.

The composition of the body is an important aspect of fitness. The percent body weight as fat may be calculated from measurements of body density. The usual procedure is underwater weighing. Biochemical methods include measurement of body water or measurement of total body potassium, from which the amount of body fat can be calculated. A commonly adopted method is to estimate body fat from measurement of skinfold thicknesses. More advanced techniques include ultrasound, X-ray, computer aided tomography (CAT), bioelectric impedance and infrared interactance.

Typical body fat percentages reported for elite performers, along with heights and weights, are included in Table 15.2. In activities where body weight has to be repeatedly lifted against gravity, extra mass in the form of fat is disadvantageous. Extra weight in the form of muscle mass will contribute to performance in sports events where great forces are produced. The jumper, sprint runner and gymnast will want to capitalize on strength training by improving the force generating capability of muscle.

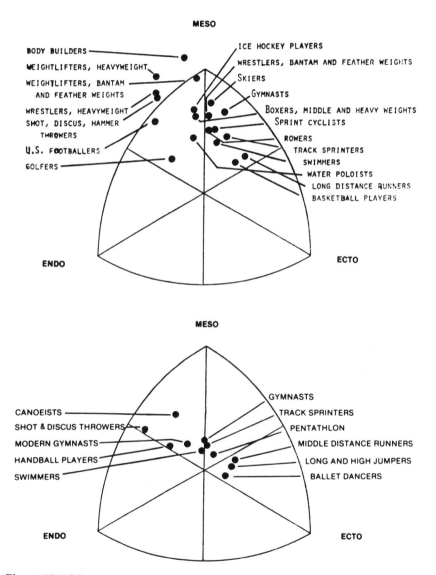

Figure 15.1 Mean somatoplots of selected groups of outstanding male (top) and female (bottom) athletes (from Carter, 1980).

Table 15.3 Reported percentage of slow twitch fibres in the thigh muscles of various sports groups. Average values are quoted which may belie large differences between individuals (after Rusko, 1976; Komi *et al.*, 1977; Bergh *et al.*, 1978; Fox, 1984)

	Females	*Males*
Orienteers	58	68–77
Cross-country skiers	60–61	63–65
Alpine skiers	—	63
Badminton	57	63
Canoeists	—	58
Ski-jumpers	—	55
Handball	—	53
Javelin throwers	43	50
Downhill skiers	—	48
Weight-lifters	—	45
Wrestling	—	45
Shot and discus	52	37
Sprinters and jumpers	37	20–35

Female endurance athletes tend to have low levels of body fat and when engaged in rigorous training are often found to be amenorrheic. Low levels of body fat are also reported for female gymnasts. Gymnasts generally start specialist training at an early age and frequently reach peak performance before attaining biological maturity. Delayed menarche is documented in gymnasts and ballet dancers but there is no evidence of any eventual effect on reproductive function.

It should be mentioned that body fat levels may show wide variations throughout the season. Female Collegiate gymnasts in USA were found to reduce body fat levels from 21% pre-season to 13% at the end of the competitive season, lean body mass increasing by only 0.2 kg in this period (Vercruyssen and Shelton, 1988). This seasonal fluctuation should be taken into consideration as it may account for the range of values reported in Table 15.2 for top performers. The different methodologies used to derive percent body fat values may also have introduced variability into the results.

The usual method of describing physique is termed somatotyping. This incorporates three dimensions – endomorphy (fatness), meso-morphy (muscularity) and ectomorphy (linearity). The tendency for athletes to gravitate towards the task they are best suited to has been extensively described (De Garay, Levine and Carter, 1974). The somatotype is mainly inherited but is to some degree affected by nutrition and training. Olympic athletes tend to appear in the northern section of the somatochart and weight-lifters and throwers beyond its northern boundaries (Figure 15.1). Anaerobic power specialists are clearly separated on the chart from endurance athletes and particular sports performers at top level tend to cluster together.

15.4.2 Muscle performance

Many sports call for the generation of high forces (Figure 15.2) and high power outputs. The principles of the Wingate Anaerobic Power Test may be applied to other ergometric modes. Thus the test has been applied to swimmers exercising on a swim-simulator (Reilly and Bayley, 1988), a device that can be adapted for canoeists by attachment of paddles to it. Anaerobic power output may also be measured on a subject running on a self-propelled treadmill, a technique that is appropriate for games players (Cheetham *et al.*, 1988). It is desirable that the mode of exercise should replicate as closely as possible the conditions of the sport when anaerobic power is being assessed.

Mean power outputs over 30 s are compared for different specialists in Table 15.4. These values refer to leg exercise but show wide variations. Comparison of different laboratory reports is imprudent because of differences in instrumenting the cycle ergometer and in implementing the test. It has been shown, for example, that if the work done in overcoming the inertia of the flywheel is ignored in the calculations, the peak power output is underestimated (Lakomy, 1986).

A different approach is to measure 'oxygen deficit' i.e., the oxygen demand of exercise not covered during the exercise. By this means it has been shown that maximal anaerobic capacity can be defined (Medbø *et al.*, 1988). Typical values are in the range 60–90 ml kg^{-1} during running and the oxygen deficit does not exceed the value obtained after 2 min of maximal exercise.

15.4.3 Maximal oxygen uptake

The maximal oxygen uptake ($\dot{V}O_{2max}$) is the best overall measure of aerobic power. When used to express the 'fitness' of the individual units neutral to body dimensions (e.g., ml kg$^{-2/3}$) should be used (Secher *et al.*, 1983). In sports without weight categories where the body mass is not repeatedly lifted against gravity, the absolute value expressed in l min^{-1} is important. In sports that do entail repetitive or sustained running, the relative value in ml kg^{-1} min^{-1} is more crucial. Both absolute and relative values may be relevant: in cross-country skiing, for

Table 15.4 Anaerobic power output on the stair run test (Margaria, Aghemo and Rovelli, 1966) and on the Wingate Test. Data are from Di Prampero, Pinera-Limas and Sassi (1970); Komi et al. (1977); Withers and Roberts (1981); MacDougall, Wenger and Green (1983); Ready and van der Merwe (1986), and other sources

| | Stair Test | | | | Wingate Test (30 s) | | | |
	Female (W)	$W\,kg^{-1}$	Male (W)	$W\,kg^{-1}$	Male MP(W)	$W\,kg^{-1}$	Female MP(W)	$W\,kg^{-1}$
Baseball	—	—	—	—	1128	—	—	—
Boxing	—	—	878	15	—	—	—	—
Canoeing	—	—	1097	15	—	—	—	—
Fencing	—	—	1046	15	—	—	—	—
Field hockey	955	16.5	859	11.5	—	—	—	—
Hurdling	—	—	—	—	—	—	—	9.4
Ice-hockey								
forwards	—	—	1367	17.7	—	—	—	—
backs	—	—	1403	17.3	—	—	—	—
goalkeeper	—	—	1049	14.3	—	—	—	—
Netball	953	12.8	—	—	—	—	—	—
Skiing								
Alpine	—	—	985	—	—	—	—	—
Cross-country	679	—	869	—	—	—	—	—
Jumping	—	—	977	—	—	—	—	—
Nordic	—	—	907	—	—	—	—	—
Orienteering	751	—	1006	13.9	—	—	—	—
Pentathlon	—	—	1270	18.9	—	—	—	—
Shooting	—	—	—	14.1	—	—	—	—
Softball	801	12.5	1145	—	—	—	—	—
Speed skating	—	—	—	—	—	—	—	—
Synchronized swimming	—	—	—	—	—	—	356	6.3
Wrestling	—	—	1139	17.2	639–983	8.2	—	—

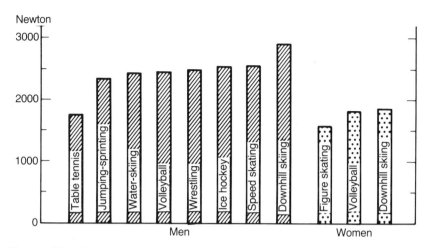

Figure 15.2 Maximal isometric strength in different groups of top sports performers (from Karlsson *et al.*, 1978).

Table 15.5 The $\dot{V}O_{2max}$ (ml kg^{-1} min^{-1}) of elite athletes as reported in the literature (Saltin and Åstrand, 1967; Rusko, 1976; Bergh *et al.*, 1978; Withers, 1978; Withers and Roberts, 1981; MacDougall, Wenger and Green, 1983; Åstrand and Rodahl, 1986)

	Female	*Male*
Cross-country skiing	59–68	78–85
Orienteering	59–61	77
Biathlon	—	73
Modern pentathlon	56	73
Canoeing	—	67–70
Boxing	—	65
Lacrosse	53	—
Alpine skiing	51	63–70
Ski jumping	—	61–62
Hockey	45–59	48–65
Softball	45	—
Netball	45	—
Gymnastics	38–48	60
Handball	—	57
Fencing	43	59
Baseball	—	40–60
Wrestling	—	57
Weight-lifting	—	48–56
Table-tennis	43	58
Archery	40	59

example, the total mass acting on the skis may be important in going downhill whilst the relative value is more significant in level or uphill work.

Values for $\dot{V}O_{2max}$ reported in the literature for a range of sports at top level are given in Table 15.5. It is clear that elite performers in cross-country skiing, orienteering and biathlon have high values: in contrast performers in sports with low aerobic demands tend to have $\dot{V}O_{2max}$ values close to general population norms. Indeed there is a close correlation between the $\dot{V}O_{2max}$ of top performers and the average rate of energy expenditure in the sport, as shown in Table 15.1. In field games, such as hockey and lacrosse, there may be some variation according to positional role, though this depends on the style of play adopted.

Measurement of $\dot{V}O_{2max}$ requires laboratory facilities for collecting expired air and analysing its volume, O_2 and CO_2 content. The type of ergometer used is important and where possible should be suited to the sport in question. The oxygen uptake values obtained on a cycle ergometer tend to be about 7% lower than those obtained on a running treadmill, although cyclists may attain equal values on the 2 ergometers. The need to match the ergometer to the sport when measuring oxygen uptake in the laboratory has led to the use of sport-specific ergometers such as used for testing canoeists, rowers and skiers.

The muscle mass employed in exercise affects the highest oxygen uptake value that can be attained. Normal individuals attain $\dot{V}O_2$ values when using the arms that are only about 70% of the values they can realize in leg exercise such as pedalling a cycle ergometer. Individuals highly-trained in arm exercise can reach a higher percentage (Secher et al., 1974). It has been found that some canoeists could get close to 100% of their $\dot{V}O_{2max}$ (developed during leg exercise) whilst exercising on an arm ergometer and in a canoe: for most highly trained paddlers the ratio will be about 90%. Experienced paddlers using their arms can reach the same heart rates as on a treadmill but oxygen consumption is limited by a lower respiratory minute volume, stroke volume and arteriovenous O_2 difference (Tesch, 1983).

15.4.4 Heart volume

The $\dot{V}O_{2max}$ presents an overall picture of the functional integration of the lungs, heart, blood and muscles in maximal aerobic work. The ability of the circulation to cope with the needs of active muscles for oxygenated blood is thought to be a major factor limiting aerobic exercise. Thus in sports with high aerobic demands, a large cardiac output will be of benefit to the performer. The cardiac output is a function of stroke volume and heart rate and its maximal value increases in response to endurance training.

Endurance training causes an increase in the maximal cardiac output by increasing the chamber size of the left ventricle. The result, evident at rest, is a greater stroke volume and a lowered heart rate. Heart volumes, corrected for body weight, are closely related to $\dot{V}O_{2max}$ values. The data in Table 15.6 and Figure 15.3 indicate that highest values are noted in cross-country skiers and cyclists, who tend also to have high levels of aerobic power. Weight-lifters tend to have ordinary values for heart volume. They may, however, have increased wall thickness, particularly for the left ventricle. This is due to thickening of the myocardium in response to a pressure stimulus.

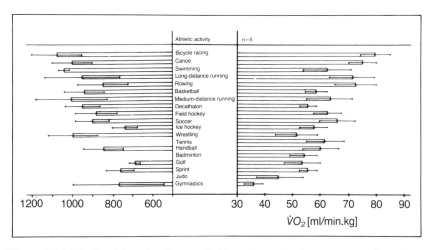

Figure 15.3 Maximal heart volumes (left) and maximal oxygen uptake values (right) for top athletes tested at the Cologne Institute for Circulatory Research and Sports Medicine. Mean values for the five best in each sport discipline are shown (after Rost, 1987).

15.5 PREPARATION FOR COMPETITION

Sports require combinations of strength, speed, endurance, agility and flexibility, to varying degrees. Paramount in importance is how these factors are integrated to enhance the skills of the sport. Thus training programmes are designed to develop desirable fitness levels, ally them to sports skills so that the individual or team can achieve the aims set. This entails both a far-sighted preparation to reach major goals for the season and short-term build up to the next impending competition.

Principles of training are now well established. Training theory refers

Table 15.6 Heart volume (ml kg^{-1}) for male members of national teams of West Germany (Roskamm, 1967)

Weight-lifters	10.8
Gymnasts	11.7
Wrestlers	12.2
Handball	12.4
Boxers	12.7
Pentathlon	12.8
Cross-country skiers	13.2

firstly to the principle of overload – physiological systems improve in function when challenged to work at supra-normal levels. The training stimulus threshold represents the exercise intensity below which no biological adaptation accrues. As the training programme proceeds, the load must be progressively increased to elicit further adaptive reactions. This gradual rise in the training stimulus is referred to as progressive resistance when related to strength training (see Chapter 2). Thus the training programme is regularly revised in 3–4 week cycles. It is recognized that gains become increasingly more difficult to attain.

The second principle is known as specificity. This stipulates that training practices should reflect the activity of the sport. This applies to the pattern of muscle involvement and to the speed of action. Thus sports simulators should be designed so that they duplicate as closely as possible the important motions of the sport in question. The most widespread use of simulators is in dry-land training for water sports: these include swimming, surfing (sailboard), canoeing and rowing. Larsson et al. (1988) provided data supporting the use of a canoe and rowing ergometer as a training aid for top Danish internationals. The question of specificity is also pertinent to the use of ski-simulators and artificial ski slopes. Although there is no perfect substitute for the true environmental conditions, dry-land equipment which is useful for training purposes can be designed.

The third principle is referred to as reversibility. It denotes that once training is discontinued, the physiological adaptations regress. Saltin et al. (1968) reported that $\dot{V}O_{2max}$ was decreased by about 25% in response to 3 weeks of bed rest. There are also changes in the oxidative capacity of muscle if training is terminated. It is advisable to avoid complete breaks in activity and to operate a maintenance fitness programme in the off-season. Runners or games players forced into inactivity by lower limb injuries may at least maintain physiological adaptations in central mechanisms by cycling or swimming. This helps retain cardiovascular fitness whilst avoiding risks of re-injury associated with repetitive weight-bearing.

Since each individual is biologically unique, training principles are best expressed in programmes tailored to individual needs. This is especially difficult to do in sports with combined events. These include decathlon, heptathlon, pentathlon – where all-round abilities are required – and biathlon and triathlon – where a combination of skills and aerobic fitness is demanded. In such sports individuals must identify their weaknesses and the components of fitness training that may help to remedy them.

The severity of the training programmes of Olympic and professional athletes is reflected in their extraordinarily high daily energy expenditure values. This emphasises the need for an adequate energy intake. The energy intakes of cyclists, distance runners and weight-throwers may approach 7000 kcal(29.3 MJ) day^{-1}. Grafe (1971) considered that an intake of 6000 kcal(25.1 MJ) day^{-1} was desirable for top cross-country skiers, canoeists and swimmers. Field hockey players, handball and basketball players had a need of about 5600 kcal(23.4 MJ) daily. A figure of 5000 kcal(20.9 MJ) day^{-1} was cited for specialists in sailing, fencing and table-tennis, presumably because of the long-duration of their practices. A rounded off value of 4600 kcal(19.3 MJ) day^{-1} was advised for pole-vaulters, divers and middle-to-welter weight boxers.

Attention to diet and activity is especially important in the days immediately prior to competitions. The benefit of a high carbohydrate diet is recognized for sports such as cycling, road-running, football and tennis. Adequate hydration pre-start and fluid replacement during or after exercise are important when competition takes place in hot conditions. Also recognized is the necessity to taper training so that the athlete feels fresh for competition. A reduction in training load allows restoration of normal muscle glycogen stores. With the appropriate dietary manipulations (see Chapter 5) these stores will be elevated to supranormal levels. The athlete can then approach the competition in a positive frame of mind and freely recovered from the fatigue of previous hard training.

Practically all sports competitions induce stress reactions in participants. Indeed the thoughts of pushing themselves to their limits, incurring defeat, getting injured and facing crises of confidence may cause anxiety. Physiological responses include increased plasma catecholamines, electrodermal activity, palmar sweating and tachycardia. Heart rates monitored under resting conditions pre-start indicate that high-risk sports such as motor-racing and ski-jumping induce high levels of emotional tension (Figure 15.4). Some competitors may need to be counselled to cope with this level of stress.

Anxiety is also associated with limb tremor. This needs to be

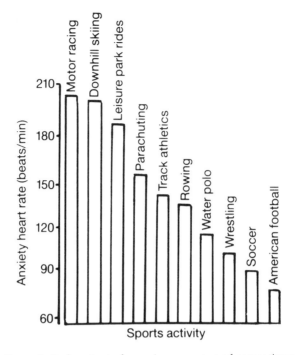

Figure 15.4 Pre-activity heart rate for various sports and recreations (after Reilly, 1988).

minimized in target sports such as archery, darts, shooting and in billiards and snooker. Pharmacological agents used to minimize tremor have included alcohol, benzodiazepines, barbiturates and beta blockers. Use of the latter as ergogenic aids has been a point of contention in recent years. The International Olympic Committee's Medical Commission decided to test for use of beta blockers in the biathlon, bobsled, figure skating, luge and ski-jump competitions at the 1988 Winter Olympic Games. At the 1988 Summer Games in Seoul tests for beta blockers were performed in the archery, diving, equestrian, fencing, gymnastics, modern pentathlon, sailing, shooting and synchronized swimming events.

The warm-up procedure prior to competition may provide an opportunity for the athlete to implement self-coping strategies. This supplements the physical effects of a warm-up in raising muscle temperature towards an optimum level for performance, increasing joint flexibility and eliminating stiffness. These are also thought to be important in reducing the risk of subsequent injury. The warm-up is also the last physical rehearsal of skills prior to their execution in a full-blown competitive context.

15.6 CONCLUSION

This chapter has attempted to fill in some gaps remaining after the systematic coverage of the major sports and games. It is hoped that specialists whose sports have not been examined in any detail will also be helped by the form of analysis used for sports in previous chapters.

It is recognized that there is no universal formula for training and success in any given sport. Each sport regularly produces champions whose approach to competition differs from his, her or their contemporaries and predecessors. A deeper understanding of the physiological basis of the sport will help to determine the extent to which the champions' practices should be generally adopted. Too many athletes blindly follow the whims of their mentors. It is hoped that this text will promote a more critical approach to training and competition by outlining the physiological base that underpins these events.

REFERENCES

Åstrand, P.O. and Rodahl, K. (1986) *Textbook of Work Physiology*. McGraw-Hill, New York.

Bergh, U., Thorstensson, A., Sjodin, B., Hultén, B., Piehl, K. and Karlsson, J. (1978) Maximal oxygen uptake and muscle fibre types in trained and untrained humans. *Medicine and Science in Sports and Exercise*, **10**, 151–154.

Carter, J.E.L. (1980) The contribution of somatotyping to kinanthropometry, in *Kinanthropometry III* (eds M. Ostyn, G. Beunen and J. Simons), University Park Press, Baltimore, pp. 409–422.

Cheetham, M.E., Hazeldine, R.J., Robinson, A. and Williams, C. (1988) Power output of Rugby forwards during maximal treadmill sprinting, in *Science and Football* (eds T. Reilly, A. Lees, K. Davids and W. Murphy), E. and F.N. Spon, London, pp. 206–210.

De Garay, A.L., Levine, L. and Carter, J.E.L. (1974) Genetic and anthropological studies of Olympic athletes. Academic Press, New York.

Di Prampero, P.E., Pinera-Limas, F. and Sassi, G. (1970) Maximal muscular power, aerobic and anaerobic, in 116 athletes performing at the XIXth Olympic Games in Mexico. *Ergonomics*, **13**, 665–674.

Dotan, R. and Bar-Or, O. (1983) Load optimization of the Wingate Anaerobic Power Test. *European Journal of Applied Physiology*, **51**, 409–417.

Evans, A.D.B. and Reilly, T. (1980) The relation between performance in a throwing task and work-induced activation. *Ergonomics*, **23**, 1147–1149.

Fox, E.L. (1984) *Sports Physiology*. Saunders College Publishing, New York.

Grafe, H.K. (1971) Nutrition, in *Encyclopedia of Sports Sciences and Medicine* (ed. L.A. Larson), Collier-MacMillan, London, pp. 1126–1130.

Hale, T., Armstrong, N., Hardman, A., Jakeman, P., Sharp, C. and Winter, E. (1988) Position statement on the physiological assessment of the elite competitor. British Association of Sports Sciences, Leeds.

Hughes, M. (1988) Computerised notation analysis in field games. *Ergonomics*, **31**, 1585–1592.

Karlsson, J., Eriksson, A., Forsberg, A., Kallberg, L. and Tesch, P. (1978) *The Physiology of Alpine Skiing*. United States Ski Coaches Association, Utah.

Komi, P.V., Rusko, H., Vos, J. and Vihko, V. (1977) Anaerobic performance capacity in athletes. *Acta Physiologica Scandinavica*, **100**, 107–114.

Lakomy, H.K.A. (1986) Measurement of work and power output using friction-loaded cycle ergometers. *Ergonomics*, **29**, 509–517.

Larsson, B., Larsen, J., Modest, R., Serup, B. and Secher, N.H. (1988) A new kayak ergometer based on wind resistance. *Ergonomics*, **31**, 1701–1707.

MacDougall, J.D., Wenger, H.A. and Green, H.J. (1983) *Physiological Testing of Elite Athletes*. Canadian Association of Sports Sciences, Ottawa.

Margaria, R., Aghemo, P. and Rovelli, E. (1966) Measurement of muscular power (anaerobic) in man. *Journal of Applied Physiology*, **21**, 1662–1664.

Medbø, J.I., Mohm, A.-C., Tabata, I., Bahr, R., Vaage, O. and Sejersted, O.M. (1988) Anaerobic capacity determined by maximal accumulated O_2 deficit. *Journal of Applied Physiology*, **64**, 50–60.

Ready, A.E. and van der Merwe, M. (1986) Physiological monitoring of the 1984 Canadian Women's Olympic field hockey team. *Australian Journal of Science and Medicine in Sport*, **18**, 13–18.

Reilly, T. (1981) *Sports Fitness and Sports Injuries*. Faber and Faber, London.

Reilly, T. (1988) Alcohol, anti-anxiety drugs and exercise, in *Drugs in Sport* (ed. D.R. Mottram), E. & F.N. Spon, London, pp. 127–156.

Reilly, T. and Bayley, K. (1988) The relation between short-term power output and sprint performance of young female swimmers. *Journal of Human Movement Studies*, **14**, 19–29.

Reilly, T. and Seaton, A. (1990) Physiological strain unique to field hockey. *Journal of Sport Medicine and Physical Fitness*, (in press).

Reilly, T. and Smith, D. (1986) Effect of work intensity on performance in a psychomotor task during exercise. *Ergonomics*, **29**, 601–606.

Roskamm, H. (1967) Optimum patterns of exercise for healthy adults. *Canadian Medical Association Journal*, **22**, 895–900.

Rost, R. (1987) *Athletics and The Heart*. Year Book Medical Publishers, Chicago.

Rusko, H. (1976) *Physical Performance Characteristics in Finnish Athletes. Studies in Sport, Physical Education and Health, 8*. University of Jyvaskyla, Jyvaskyla.

Saltin, B. and Åstrand, P.O. (1967) Maximal oxygen uptakes in athletes. *Journal of Applied Physiology*, **23**, 353–358.

Saltin, B., Blomqvist, G., Mitchell, J.H., Johnson, R.L., Wildenthal, K. and Chapman, C.B. (1968). Response to submaximal and maximal exercise after bedrest and training. *Circulation*, **38**, Suppl. 7.

Secher, N.H., Ruberg-Larsen, N., Binkhorst, R.A. and Bonde-Petersen, F. (1974) Maximal oxygen uptake during arm cranking and combined arm plus leg exercise. *Journal of Applied Physiology*, **36**, 515–518.

Secher, N.H., Vaage, O., Jensen, K. and Jackson, R.C. (1983). Maximal aerobic power in oarsmen. *European Journal of Applied Physiology*, **51**, 155–162.

Sharkey, B.J. (1986) *Coaches Guide to Sport Physiology*. Human Kinetics, Champaign, Illinois.

Shephard, R.J. (1987) Science and medicine of canoeing and kayaking. *Sports Medicine*, **4**, 19–33.

Tanner, J.M. (1964) The physique of the Olympic athlete. Allen and Unwin, London.

Tesch, P.A. (1983) Physiological characteristics of elite kayak paddlers. *Canadian Journal of Applied Sport Sciences*, **8**, 87–91.

Vandervalle, H., Peres, G. and Monod, H. (1983) Relation force-vitesse lors d'exercise cycliques realises avec les membres superieurs. *Motricite Humaine*, **2**, 22–25.

Vercruyssen, M. and Skelton, L. (1988) Intraseason changes in the body composition of Collegiate female gymnasts. *Journal of Sports Sciences*, **6**, 205–217.

Williams, E.S., Taggart, P. and Carruthers, M. (1978). Rock climbing: observations on heart rate and plasma catecholamine concentrations and the influence of oxprenolol. *British Journal of Sports Medicine*, **12**, 125–128.

Wilmore, J.H. (1983) Body composition in sport and exercise: directions for future research. *Medicine and Science in Sports and Exercise*, **15**, 21–31.

Withers, R.T. (1978) Physiological responses of international female lacrosse players to pre-season conditioning. *Medicine and Science in Sports*, **10**, 238–242.

Withers, R.T. and Roberts, R.G.D. (1981) Physiological profiles of representative women softball, hockey and netball players. *Ergonomics*, 24, 583–591.

Index

Abdominal strength 307
Acceleration 84–6
ACTH 356
Active muscle mass 315
Adipose tissue 11
ADP 14–16, 26–7
Adrenaline 21, 27, 116, 265, 356
Adrenal medulla 11
Aerobic capacity 105–6, 113, 303
  see also % $\dot{V}O_{2max}$
Aerobic metabolism 102–4, 108, 133, 138
Aerobic power 105–6
  of sailors 303
  see also $\dot{V}O_{2max}$
Age
  marathon runners 131
  race walkers 160
Agility 391, 398, 418
Aikido 466
Air pollution 122
Air resistance 105, 125, 323
Alactic anaerobic energy 26, 127–8, 437
Alanine 356
Alcohol 7, 366, 482
Alkalinizers 234
Alpine skiing 486, 470, 474
Altitude 108, 128, 278
Amenorrhea 133–4, 474
American football 401–6
American handball 339
Ammonium 28
Anabolic steroids 94
Anaemia 127, 133, 145–6
Anaerobic capacity 106, 113, 273–5, 475

Anaerobic endurance
  sailors 291, 298
Anaerobic glycogenolysis 102, 106, 139, 186, 314
  in football 383, 390, 408
Anaerobic metabolism 102–4
  in swimming 122
Anaerobic power 29, 106, 195–6, 390, 402, 416, 475
Anaerobic tests 450
Anaerobic threshold 20–6, 103, 111, 138–9, 178, 185–6, 189, 193, 197–8, 244–5, 266, 361, 383
  see also Lactate threshold
Androgens 114
Annual training cycle 250–1
Anthropometry
  American football 403–5
  Australian Rules 408–10
  badminton 353–4
  basketball 441–4
  figure skaters 328
  Gaelic football 408–10
  ice-hockey 315
  marathon runners 130
  middle distance runners 105
  race walkers 158
  racquetball 364–5
  rowers 266–7
  Rugby football 414–17
  sailors 291–4
  speed skaters 323–5
  sprinters 72–3
  squash 360–1
  swimmers 238–40
  tennis 346

Anthropometry *cont.*
  various sports 470–5
  volleyball 441–4
Anxiety 481
Archery 58, 467–8, 477, 482
Arm exercise 478
Assymetrical limb development 348
Assymetrical muscle strength 354
Atherosclerosis 304
ATP 11–13, 26–7, 29, 88–9, 92, 102,
  116, 174, 186, 195, 202–3, 390
ATPase 14, 74
ATP–CP system 199, 202–3, 341, 432,
  438
a-v O_2 difference 126

Backhand 337
Backstroke 218–20, 233
Backwards motion 380
Badminton 337–8, 350–4, 434, 474, 481
Balance (in sailors) 298
Ballet dancers 473
Barbiturates 482
Basal metabolic rate 5
Baseball 159, 451
Basketball 58, 159, 427–63, 470, 473,
  480
Bent arm pull 240
Benzodiazepines 482
Beta blockers 482
Biathlon 466
Bicarbonate 28–9, 187, 295
Bicarbonate loading 115–16, 234
Bicycle design 190
Billiards 468
Biokinetic swim bench 223, 241, 247–8
Biomechanical analysis 176
Biomechanics
  running 131
  walking 156
Blood doping 115, 127
Blood glucose 156, 295, 299–300
Blood lactate 21–6, 109, 113, 122,
  138–9, 175, 186, 193, 197–200, 274–5,
  470
  court games 437–8, 440
  ice hockey 383–4

Rugby football 413
sailing 298
soccer 381–4
speed skating 323–5
squash 356
swimming 233–4, 244–6, 250
Blood lactate accumulation 139–40
  see also OBLA
Blood pH 234
Blood pressure 116, 162, 295, 304, 348,
  393
Blood viscosity 127
Blood volume 132, 273
Boat categories 288
Bobsled 466, 482
Body building 49, 160, 473
Body composition 5–6, 387, 403,
  414–15
Body fat 108, 130, 471
Body fat assessment 108, 130, 472
Body fat percent
  badminton 353
  court games 444–5, 452
  cycling 177
  football 387, 403, 409, 414–15
  ice hockey 315
  marathon running 130
  race walking 158, 161
  racquetball 364–5
  sailing 291
  speed skating 324
  squash 360
  swimming 239, 250
  various sports 471
Body surface area 158, 160
Bone growth 134, 249, 348
Bowls 468
Boxing 434, 466, 469–70, 472, 476, 480
Bradycardia 167
Braking 87
Breath holding 220
Breast-stroke 218–20, 225, 228, 233
Broad jump 390
Buffering capacity 28, 110, 113, 116,
  187
Butterfly 218–20, 225, 233

Caffeine 19, 116, 147, 192–3

Calcium 134
Calorimetry 470
Canoeing 434, 466, 469–71, 473–4,
    476–9, 481
Capillarization 109–10, 126, 129–30,
    133, 137, 139
Carbohydrate intake 146–7, 345, 365,
    440
Carbohydrate loading 18, 146–7
Cardiac arrhythmia 358
Cardiac muscle 393
Cardiac output 126, 132, 137, 305, 396
Cardiovascular disease 116, 357
Cardiovascular drift 358, 380
Cardiovascular responses
    swimming 235
Catecholamines 11–13, 299, 356–8,
    440–1, 482
Centre of gravity 82, 294, 456
Channel swimming 237
Cholesterol 116, 304
Circadian rhythms 249–50, 289, 305–6
Circuit training 302, 398
Circulatory strain
    racquet sports 357
    soccer 378
    see also Cardiovascular responses
Clay courts 340
Clothing 414
Cold 236–7, 304–5, 314, 326, 413–14
Compromise Rules football 371, 406
Concentric actions 45, 90, 467
Continuous running 110–12, 138
Controlled frequency breathing 234
Coronary heart disease, see
    Cardiovascular disease
Cortisol 114, 440–1
Coxswain 260
Cramp 144
Creatine kinate 53
Creatine phosphate 16, 102, 390
    see also Phosphocreatine
Creatine phosphokinase 108
Cricket 466, 468
Croquet 468
Cross-country running 468
Cross-country skiing 466, 469–71, 474,
    476–7, 480

Cybex 50–1, 196, 198
Cyclic AMP 299
Cycling 173–213

Dance 326
Darts 482
Decathlon 481
Dehydration 143, 193–4, 304, 346, 360,
    472
Delayed menarche 329, 474
Depth jumping 455–7
Detraining 251
Diastole 110
Diastolic pressure 359
Diet 145, 345, 365
Dietary supplements 145
2,3-Diphosphoglycerate 127–8, 133,
    201
Discus 442, 471–4
Diving 466, 480
Dolphin kick 225
Diuresis 147
Dopamine 259
Douglas bag 230
Downhill skiing 470
Drag 176, 180, 190, 228–33, 263, 289
Dribbling 380–3
Drugs 93–4, 482
Dry land training 247–8, 302–3

Eccentric actions 45, 52–3, 90, 455–7,
    467
Eccentric training 52–3, 90–1
Efficiency 122, 155–7, 180–2, 313
Elasticity of muscle 156
Electrical stimulation 54
Electrodermal activity 482
Electrogoniometry 154–5
Electrolyte balance 143–4
Electromyography 60, 154, 176, 182–3,
    228–30, 237, 344, 467
Embden–Meyerhof pathway 10
Energy balance 4–7
Energy crises 3
Energy expenditure
    badminton 350–1
    court games 433–7
    figure skating 328

Energy expenditure *cont.*
  ice hockey 314
  racquetball 361–3
  rowing 263
  running 103, 121–5, 131
  sailing 287
  soccer 378–9, 398–9
  speed skating 322
  swimming 233
  tennis 340–2
  walking 154–7
Energy intake 413, 480
Energy stores 7–13
Eosinophils 264
Equestrian events 466, 482
Ergogenic aids 114–15
Ergometer rowing 259, 264, 275–6
Ergometry 175, 177, 478
  see also Ergometer rowing

Fasting 147
Fatigue 46, 58, 89, 147, 177–8, 266, 330,
    375, 430, 438, 448
  low frequency 315
  onset 3, 15–18
Fatty acids 11–12, 18, 103, 116, 147,
    192, 440
Female–male differences 132–4, 323
Fencing 159–60, 466–8, 476, 480–2
FEV_1 162, 392
Fibre recruitment 111, 182–3, 203, 313
Fibre types 13–15, 56–7, 73–5, 89, 92,
    107–8, 111, 129–30, 133, 177–8,
    183–5, 241–2, 246, 271, 313, 318–19,
    439, 452–3, 474
Field hockey 159–60
Figure skating 311, 326–30
Fishing 468
Fitness
  racquet sports 365
  soccer 386
  testing 466
Flexibility 225, 296–7, 353, 365–6, 391,
    397, 404, 410, 452, 482
Fluid intake 144, 314
Force (maximum) 41, 45
Force platform 450, 470
Force-velocity 45, 50–1

Fractional utilization of $\dot{V}O_{2max}$ 122–4,
    134
Frictional resistance 289, 302
Front crawl 218, 232
Fuel utilization 128–9, 133, 138–9,
    191–3

Gaelic football 372, 406–11
Gaelic handball 339
Gait analysis 154–5
Genetic factors 105, 129, 134, 137, 458,
    465
Glide 220
Glucagon 10
Glucose 18, 144, 191–2, 357, 440
Glycerol 13, 356
Glycogen 27, 103, 146, 246, 375,
    399–400, 408, 440, 481
Glycogen loading, *see* Carbohydrate
    loading
Glycogenolysis 8, 21, 27, 116
Glycogen reduction 191, 313, 432,
    438–40, 447
Glycogen resynthesis 20, 146, 191
Glycogen sparing 116, 133, 139, 191,
    193, 203
Glycolysis 8, 102, 233
Glycolytic capacity 133, 138, 175
Glycolytic enzymes 8–9, 108–10, 133
Glycolytic pathway 106, 139
Goalkeepers
  Gaelic football 407
  ice hockey 315
  soccer 375, 377, 385, 396
Golf 469, 473
Golgi tendon organs 60
Grass tennis courts 340–3
Grip strength 249, 347–8
Growth hormone 356
Gymnastics 434, 466, 470–3, 480–1

Horse riding 468, 470
  see also Equestrian events
Hurdling 471–2, 476
Hurling 466, 469
Hydrogen ions 28
Hyperplasia 56

Hyperthermia 141
Hypertrophy 129, 133, 547
Hypnosis 59
Hypoglycaemia 10
Hypothermia 141, 304–5
Hypoxia 21

Ice hockey 312–20, 451, 473, 476, 481
  see also Hockey
Ice skating 311, 314, 320–30
Immersion 234–5, 305
Individual medley swim 253
Injuries
  rowing 262
  rugby 413
  soccer 391, 401
  supraspinatus 225
Insulin 13, 191, 356
Interval training 111–12, 200–3, 454
Intracellular buffers 109
Ischaemia 109
Isokinetic strength 270, 296, 318, 388–90
Isokinetic training 50–1, 196, 198, 270
Isometric activity 322, 467, 477
Isometric strength 43–5, 84, 295–6, 389, 413
Isometric training 43, 47–8, 51–2

Jet lag 349–50
Judo 466, 481
Jumping 432, 456–7, 466, 470–1, 473–4, 477

Karate 466
Kayak 434, 466, 469
Ketones 13, 138, 356
Kick performance 389
KIN-COM 50–1
Kinetic energy 230
Knee angle 82
Knee extension strength 43–4, 84

Lacrosse 466, 477
Lactate 16, 20, 341
Lactate dehydrogenase 184
Lactate removal 104

Lactate threshold 21–6, 102–3, 107, 111, 115, 165, 185, 197, 438
  see also Anaerobic threshold
Lactate tolerance 28, 244–7
Lactate tolerance training 244–7
Lactic acid 102–3, 106–7, 109, 113, 139, 432
  see also Lactate
Leg strength 42–6
  see also Knee extension strength
Length-tension relation 43
Lipolysis 441
Low back pain 225, 457
Luge 466
Lung compliance 235
Lung function, see Pulmonary function; FEV_1; Pulmonary diffusion capacity

Malate dehydrogenase 128, 183–4
Manual dexterity 238
Marathon running 24, 121–52
Margaria stair test 390, 449
Maximal heart rate 110, 126, 137, 365, 470
  see also Heart rate
Maximal oxygen uptake, see $\dot{V}O_{2max}$
Maximal velocity 86–8
Maximal voluntary contraction (MVC) 45, 47–8, 58–61
Mechanics (of skating) 289
Medical miniscus strain 228
Menarche 329, 474
Mental performance 289
Mesomorphy 105, 289
  see also Somatotype
Metabolic load, see Energy expenditure
Middle distance running 101–20
Mitochondria 108, 110, 114, 138, 401
Motion analysis 175–6, 373, 466
Motion sickness 306
Motocross 466
Motor unit 49, 76
Motor pool 41
Mountaineering 466
Multiple regression analysis 300
Muscle biopsy 110

Muscle blood flow 110, 127, 143, 295, 303
Muscle cross-sectional area 41, 55–8, 75
Muscle endurance 114, 295–8
Muscle fatigue 222
Muscle fibre type, *see* Fibre types
Muscle hypertrophy 114, 348, 353
    see also Hypertrophy
Muscle length 42–6
Muscle mass 30, 270
Muscle soreness 53, 91, 457
Muscle spindles 60
Muscle strength 41–67, 240–42, 270, 291, 295–8, 318, 328, 347, 388–91, 398, 406, 454, 472–7
    see also Isokinetic strength; Isometric strength; Knee extension strength
Muscle tightness 391
Myofibrils 57–8
Myoglobin 303, 383, 437

NEFA 356
Netball 471, 476
Neural factors 58
Neuromuscular control 59, 77, 83–4
New image Rugby 372
Noradrenaline 11, 356
    see also Catecholamines
Notation analysis 466
    see also Motion analysis
Nutrition 144–7, 190–4, 303–4, 345, 365, 375, 408
    see also Diet; Carbohydrate loading

OBLA 24–6, 138–40, 185–7, 197–202
    see also Anaerobic threshold; Lactate; Lactate threshold
Oestrogen 134
Oligomenorrhea 133–4
Olympic Games, *see* History
Omnikinetic training 51–2
Optimal stroke frequency 222
Orienteering 160, 466, 468, 471, 474, 476–7
Overhead throw 389
Overload 200, 203, 405, 454–5, 479
Overtraining 108, 112, 114, 204–5

Oxidative capacity of muscle 108, 128, 133, 138, 354
Oxygen consumption
    swimming 232–3
    tennis 340–2
Oxygen debt 16, 103
Oxygen deficit 16, 107, 275, 475
Oxygen extraction 126
Oxygen pulse 396
Oxygen transport 392, 467
Oxyhaemoglobin 109

Pancreas 10–11
Parachuting 482
P_{CO_2} 220
Peak $\dot{V}O_2$ 222–3, 243, 408
Pedalling rate 180–1
Pelota 339
Pentathlon 448, 471–3, 476–7, 480
Perceived exertion 155, 382
pH 27–9, 109, 113, 116, 187, 195
Phosphagens 233, 437–8
    see also ATP–CP system
Phosphate loading 187
Phosphocreatine 16, 26–7, 174
    see also Creatine phosphate; ATP–CP system
Phosphofructokinase 9, 92, 113
Phosphorylation 9–11, 26
Physical contact 419
Physical working capacity, *see* PWC$_{170}$
Physique, *see* Somatotype
Plasma volume 143
    see also Blood volume
Plyometrics 53–4, 90–1, 454–7
Positional role
    American football 402, 405
    Australian Rules 407
    Gaelic football 407
    ice hockey 313–15
    Rugby football 412
    soccer 374, 395–6
Power output
    court games 451
    cycling 181
    jumping 391
    Rugby 416
    swimming 228–30, 475

Preferred limb 83
Pre-season training 400–1
Progressive resistance exercise (PRE)
   46–9, 61
Prolactin 356
Psychology 299, 306
Pulmonary diffusion capacity 109, 273
Pulmonary function
   American football 404
   oarsmen 271–3
   race-walking 162
   soccer 391–2
   swimming 234–5
   tennis 348
PWC_{170}
   badminton 354
   Gaelic football 410–11
   squash 361
   soccer 393
   tennis 349
Pyramid training 49
Pyruvate 8–11, 356

Quadriceps, *see* Knee extension
   strength; Leg strength

Race-walking 153–72
Racquets 338
Racquetball 337–9, 361–5
Racquet sports 337–70
Radio telemetry 376
   see also Telemetry
Reaction forces in walking 155
Reaction time 77–81, 299, 344–5
Recovery 417
Real tennis 344–5
Rectal temperature 140–2
Red blood cells 115, 127
Reep system 374
Regeneration training 400
Rehydration 144, 314
Repetition maximum (RM) 48, 50, 56
Reversibility 480
Resistance training 51
Respiratory exchange ratio 5, 13
Rhythmic gymnastics 472
Rock climbing 470
Roller skating 326, 466

Rowing 259–86
Rugby League 411–19
Rugby scrummaging 467
Rugby Union 411–19
Running economy 103–5, 108, 110, 131
Running style 131

Sailing 287–309, 480
   ability 290–1
   crew position 293
Scopolamine 306
Scrummaging racks 418
Seasonal variations 180, 401
Series elastic component (of muscle)
   86
Serotonin 299
Serve
   badminton 353
   tennis 344
Shinty 469
Shooting 476, 482
Simulator
   rowing 475
   swimming 217, 243, 475
Skating 182, 477
Ski-jumping 466, 469, 471, 476–7, 482
Skiing 469, 471, 474, 476–7
Sleep loss 306
Softball 466, 471, 476–7
Somatotype
   American football 387–8
   Australian Rules 409
   court games 445
   middle distance runners 105
   Rugby football 415
   soccer 387–8
   speed skating 329
   swimming 239
   tennis 347
   various sports 473–4
SPARK 51
Specificity 90, 199, 242, 248, 479
Speed 86–8, 93, 113–14
Speed-endurance 91
Speed skating 311, 320–6, 330
Spinal loading 457
Spirometry 392
   see also Pulmonary function

Sprint start 80–4
Sprinting 72–99
Squash 337–9
Staleness 114
Steady state 103, 106
Stereophotogrammetry 156
Steroids 114
Strain gauges 176
Stock car drivers 160
Strength-endurance 91
Strength training 41–67, 113, 137,
    203–4, 248
Stress 465, 481–2
Stress fractures 134
Stride length 72–3, 85–7, 132, 381
Stride rate 73, 87, 132
String tension 338
Stroke frequency (swimming) 220–1
Stroke volume 109–10, 126, 132, 137,
    357
Stroking (swimming) 218–221
Succinate dehydrogenase 113, 128,
    183–4
Sudden death 337–9
Surfing 466, 479
Sweating 140–1, 143, 314, 406
Swimming 217–57
Swimming flume 218, 230–2
Swimming pool temperature 237
Synchronized swimming 466, 476

Table tennis 448, 468, 477
Tactics 116
Taekwondo 466
Telemetry 376, 436, 467
Temperature, effects on performance
    140–1
Tennis 337
Tennis elbow 338
Testosterone 114
Tethered swimming 242
Thermoregulation 140–4, 236
Throwing 466, 470–1, 473–4
Time–motion analysis 312
    see also Motion Analysis; Notation
    analysis
Tobogganing 468
Tour de France 6–7, 173

Training
    adaptations 40, 110–14, 134,
    137–40, 302–3
    pre-season 319, 326
    principles 243
    tempo training 321
    training volume 135–6
        American football 405–6
        Australian Rules 410–11
        cycling 199–206
        ice hockey 312
        ice skating 326
        Rugby football 417
        sailing 301–3
        soccer 397–401
        sprinting 89–93
        swimming 243–51
    see also Dry land training; Strength
    training; Interval training; Weight
    training
Travel 345
Triacylglycerol 12
Triathlon 217, 466, 480
Tug-of-war 467
Turning (in swimming) 219–20

Uphill walking 163

Variable resistance 51
Vasopressin 238
Vertical jump 392, 449–52, 456–7
Vital capacity 162, 392
    see also Pulmonary function
Vitamins 115, 145
Vitamin C deficiency 7
Volleyball 160, 427–64, 470, 477
$\dot{V}O_{2max}$ 102–8, 111–15, 122–8, 130–7,
    139, 147, 179–80, 196–7, 204
    specificity of 276
        American football 404–5
        Australian Rules 420
        badminton 354
        court games 445–9
        cycling 179
        figure skating 329
        ice hockey 316
        marathon runners 122–6

$\dot{V}O_{2max}$ *cont.*
 middle distance runners 105
 race-walking 159–63
 rowing 275–80
 Rugby 416
 sailors 191
 soccer 324, 394–5
 speed skating 324
 swimmers 242–3
 squash 361
 various sports 475–8
 see also Aerobic power
% $\dot{V}O_{2max}$ 122–4, 134, 186
 court games 435–6
 marathon running 124
 race walking 162
 racquetball 356
 soccer 375, 399
 squash 363
 see also Aerobic capacity

Warm-up 186, 469, 482

Water-polo 473, 482
Water skiing 467, 477
Weight-lifting 58, 61, 434, 466, 471–2,
 474, 480
Weight training 41–67, 203–4, 302,
 454–6
Wind resistance 105, 125, 323
Wingate Test 195, 241, 323, 416, 449,
 475
Work rate, in
 Australian Rules 407
 badminton 350–1
 Gaelic football 407
 racquetball 361–3
 Rugby League 412
 Rugby Union 412
 soccer 373–4
 squash 354–7
 swimming 228
Wrestling 451, 466–7, 471–2, 476–7

Young swimmers 248–9